Frommer's

Iceland

1st Edition

by Evan Spring & Zoë Preston

Here's what the critics say about Frommer's:

"Amazingly easy to use. Very portable, very complete."

—*Booklist*

"Detailed, accurate, and easy-to-read information for all price ranges."

—*Glamour Magazine*

"Hotel information is close to encyclopedic."

—*Des Moines Sunday Register*

"Frommer's Guides have a way of giving you a real feel for a place."

—*Knight Ridder Newspapers*

WILEY

Wiley Publishing, Inc.

Published by:

Wiley Publishing, Inc.

111 River St.

Hoboken, NJ 07030-5774

ISBN: 978-0-470-17841-6

Editor: Alexia Travaglini
Production Editor: M. Faunette Johnston
Cartographer: Andrew Murphy
Photo Editor: Richard Fox
Production by Wiley Indianapolis Composition Services

Front cover photo: Near Akureyri: Goðafoss, or "Waterfall of the Gods"
Back cover photo: South of Reykjavík: Man standing by the Blue Lagoon

For information on our other products and services or to obtain technical support, please contact our Customer Care Department within the U.S. at 800/762-2974, outside the U.S. at 317/572-3993 or fax 317/572-4002.

Wiley also publishes its books in a variety of electronic formats. Some content that appears in print may not be available in electronic formats.

Manufactured in the United States of America

5   4   3   2   1

Contents

List of Maps   vi

1 The Best of Iceland   1

1 The Best Natural Wonders 1

2 The Best Towns & Villages 4

3 The Best Big-Name Hikes 5

4 The Best Hikes Off
the Beaten Track 6

5 Iceland's Best Museums 7

6 The Best Accommodations
for Local Flavor 8

7 The Best Icelandic Restaurants 9

8 The Best of Iceland Online 10

2 Planning Your Trip to Iceland   12

1 The Regions in Brief 12

2 Visitor Information & Maps 13

3 Entry Requirements 13

4 When to Go 14

   Calendar of Events 15

   The Big Round-Up 18

5 Iceland in the Off Season 19

6 Getting There 20

7 Money & Costs 23

8 Travel Insurance 24

9 Health & Safety 25

10 Specialized Travel Resources 27

11 Sustainable Tourism/Ecotourism 31

12 Staying Connected 31

   Frommers.com: The Complete
Travel Resource 32

13 General-Interest Tours &
Packages 35

14 Special-Interest Trips 36

15 Getting Around Iceland 37

16 Tips on Accommodations 43

   The Case for Hostels 44

   Packing Suggestions for Iceland 47

17 Tips on Dining 48

18 Recommended Books 50

   Fast Facts: Iceland 51

3 Active Iceland   56

1 Aerial Tours 56

2 Biking 57

3 Bird-Watching 58

4 Caving 59

5 Dog Sledding 59

6 Fishing 60

7 Glacier Tours 61

8 Golf 62

9 Hiking 63

10 Horseback Riding 65

11 Hunting 66

12 Jeep Tours 66

13 Kayaking 67

14 Photography 67

15 Pools & Spas 68

16 Rafting 69

17 Rock Climbing 69

18 Scuba Diving & Snorkeling 69

19 Skiing & Ski Touring 70

20 Whale-Watching 71

4 Suggested Iceland Itineraries   72

1 Iceland in 4 Days 72
2 Around the Ring Road 74
3 Iceland in 1 Week 77

4 Iceland in 2 Weeks 79
5 Hiking Iceland 81

5 Reykjavík   83

1 Orientation .83
2 Getting Around 84
3 Organized Tours 85
  Fast Facts: Reykjavík 86
4 Where to Stay 88
5 Where to Dine 98
  Waiter, There's a Fly in My Pickled
  Ram Testicles 100

6 What to See & Do 107
7 Pools, Spas, Outdoor Activities &
  Spectator Sports 119
  Reykjavík Thermal Pool Guide 121
8 Shopping .123
9 Reykjavík Nightlife 127

6 Near Reykjavík   133

1 Hafnarfjörður 133
  Notes on Entering
  the Countryside 134
  "Hidden People" Lesson #1:
  Origins 136
2 Mosfellsbær 136
  Halldór Kiljan Laxness
  (1902–1998) 137
3 Esja, Hvalfjörður & Akranes 138

4 Golden Circle: Þingvellir, Geysir
  & Gullfoss 140
  Why Does Þingvellir Church Have
  Two Altarpieces? 144
5 The Blue Lagoon (Bláa Lónið) 150
6 Keflavík 152
  The U.S. Pull-Out 154
7 Reykjanes Peninsula 156
8 Hveragerði, Selfoss & Nearby 160
  A Day Hike in Hengill 162

7 West Iceland   166

1 Borgarnes, Reykholt & Farther
  Inland 166
2 Snæfellsnes 172
  Horseback Riding on the
  Southern Coast 176
  "Hidden People" Lesson #2:
  Elves 177
  Whale-Watching & Horseback
  Riding on the North Coast 180

3 Stykkishólmur & Breiðafjörður 184
4 Westfjords: The Southwest
  Coast 188
  Cliff-Scaling Icelanders
  to the Rescue 192
5 Central Westfjords 195
6 Ísafjörður & Ísafjarðardjúp 198
7 The Strandir Coast 206
8 Hornstrandir Nature Reserve 210

8 North Iceland   214

1 Húnaflói .214
    The Cowboy of Skagaströnd 220
2 Skagafjörður 221
    Why Build a House with Turf? 222
3 Akureyri .230
    Fast Facts: Akureyri 233
4 Near Akureyri 244

5 Mývatn & Krafla 250
6 Húsavík & Nearby 259
    Was Iceland's First Settler
    Not a Viking? 261
    The Saga of Icelandic Whaling 262
7 Jökulsárgljúfur National Park 266
8 The Northeast Corner 271

9 South Iceland   277

1 Westman Islands
    (Vestmannaeyjar) 277
    The Great Puffling Rescue 283
2 Þjórsárdalur & Hekla 286
    Ascending Hekla 289
3 Landmannalaugar, Fjallabak &
    Surroundings 289
    The Laugavegurinn 292
4 Hella, Hvolsvöllur & Markarfljót
    Valley 293
    Njáls Saga & Its Sites 295
5 Þórsmörk .298

    The Fimmvörðuháls Trek 300
6 Skógar, Vík & Mýrdalsjökull 301
    "Hidden People" Lesson #3:
    Troll Tales 304
    Katla: The Next Big One? 305
7 Kirkjubæjarklaustur &
    Laki Craters 308
8 Vatnajökull, Skeiðarársandur &
    Skaftafell National Park 311
    The Glacier Mystique 312
9 Between Skaftafell & Höfn 315

10 East Iceland   319

1 Höfn 319
2 Lónsöræfi .324
3 Lower Eastfjords: Djúpivogur
    to Fáskrúðsfjörður 326
4 Middle Eastfjords: Reyðarfjörður,
    Eskifjörður & Neskaupstaður 331
5 Egilsstaðir 332
6 Inland From Egilsstaðir: Lögurinn,
    Snæfell & Kárahnjúkar 336

    Kárahnjúkar: Iceland's Most
    Divisive Buzzword 338
7 Seyðisfjörður 340
    A Day Hike in Seyðisfjörður 343
8 Borgarfjörður Eystri 345
    "Hidden People" Lesson #4:
    Elves & Modern Iceland 348
9 Fljótsdalshérað Valley 350
10 Egilsstaðir to Mývatn 351

11 The Interior   352

1 Kjölur Route 352
    The Kjölurvegur Trek 355
2 Sprengisandur Route 356

3 Askja, Kverkfjöll & Eastern
    Interior Routes 359

Icelandic Pronunciation & Useful Vocabulary   364

1 Pronunciation Guide 364
Icelanders: On a First-Name Basis 365

2 Basic Vocabulary & Phrases 365
3 Glossary of Geographical Terms 367

Index   368

List of Maps

Iceland   2
Iceland in 4 Days   73
Around the Ring Road   75
Iceland in 1 Week   78
Iceland in 2 Weeks   81
Hiking Iceland   82
Where to Stay & Dine in Reykjavík   90
What to See & Do in Reykjavík   108
Near Reykjavík   135
Þingvellir   143
Keflavík   153
West Iceland   167
Snæfellsnes   173

Westfjords   189
Ísafjörður   199
North Iceland   215
Akureyri   231
Mývatn   251
Húsavik   260
Jökulsárgljúfur National Park   267
South Iceland   279
Heimaey Island   281
East Iceland   321
Höfn   323
Egilsstaðir   333
Seyðisfjörður   341
The Interior   353

An Invitation to the Reader

In researching this book, we discovered many wonderful places—hotels, restaurants, shops, and more. We're sure you'll find others. Please tell us about them, so we can share the information with your fellow travelers in upcoming editions. If you were disappointed with a recommendation, we'd love to know that, too. Please write to:

Frommer's Iceland, 1st Edition
Wiley Publishing, Inc. • 111 River St. • Hoboken, NJ 07030-5774

An Additional Note

Please be advised that travel information is subject to change at any time—and this is especially true of prices. We therefore suggest that you write or call ahead for confirmation when making your travel plans. The authors, editors, and publisher cannot be held responsible for the experiences of readers while traveling. Your safety is important to us, however, so we encourage you to stay alert and be aware of your surroundings. Keep a close eye on cameras, purses, and wallets, all favorite targets of thieves and pickpockets.

About the Authors

Evan Spring has traveled to fifty countries or so, but only Iceland has merited four return trips and made him consider repatriation. His freelance writing is widely published.

Zoë Preston has traveled widely, and finds Iceland's landscape peerless in its composition of beauty and bizarro. She studied comparative literature and art at New York University.

Acknowledgments

The authors would like to thank the following for their generous help: Einar Gustavsson at the Iceland Tourist Board; Jón Trausti Sigurðarsson at the Grapevine; "Nightlife Friend" Jón Kári Hilmarsson; Siggi Hall; Magnea Guðmundsdóttir at the Blue Lagoon; Gylfi Ólafsson at West Tours; Helgi M. Arngrímsson in Borgarfjörður Eystri; Lisa Tharpe; our wonderful editor Alexia Travaglini; our cartographer Andrew "the Falcon" Murphy; and the following tourist information center staff: Jón Páll Hreinsson in Ísafjörður, Erna in Varmahlíð, Cosima Zewe and Inga Björk in Akureyri, Kristin Jóhannsdóttir in the Westman Islands, and Sigurdís Guðjónsdóttir in Hveragerði. Evan would also like to thank his mother Marjorie Johnson for her help with *Njáls Saga*, and his father Michael Spring for taking him to Iceland for the first time.

Other Great Guides for Your Trip:

Frommer's Scandinavia
Frommer's London Day by Day

Frommer's Star Ratings, Icons & Abbreviations

Every hotel, restaurant, and attraction listing in this guide has been ranked for quality, value, service, amenities, and special features using a **star-rating system.** In country, state, and regional guides, we also rate towns and regions to help you narrow down your choices and budget your time accordingly. Hotels and restaurants are rated on a scale of zero (recommended) to three stars (exceptional). Attractions, shopping, nightlife, towns, and regions are rated according to the following scale: zero stars (recommended), one star (highly recommended), two stars (very highly recommended), and three stars (must-see).

In addition to the star-rating system, we also use **seven feature icons** that point you to the great deals, in-the-know advice, and unique experiences that separate travelers from tourists. Throughout the book, look for:

Finds	Special finds—those places only insiders know about
Fun Fact	Fun facts—details that make travelers more informed and their trips more fun
Kids	Best bets for kids and advice for the whole family
Moments	Special moments—those experiences that memories are made of
Overrated	Places or experiences not worth your time or money
Tips	Insider tips—great ways to save time and money
Value	Great values—where to get the best deals

The following **abbreviations** are used for credit cards:

AE	American Express	DISC	Discover	V	Visa
DC	Diners Club	MC	MasterCard		

Frommers.com

Now that you have this guidebook to help you plan a great trip, visit our website at **www. frommers.com** for additional travel information on more than 4,000 destinations. We update features regularly to give you instant access to the most current trip-planning information available. At Frommers.com, you'll find scoops on the best airfares, lodging rates, and car rental bargains. You can even book your travel online through our reliable travel booking partners. Other popular features include:

- Online updates of our most popular guidebooks
- Vacation sweepstakes and contest giveaways
- Newsletters highlighting the hottest travel trends
- Podcasts, interactive maps, and up-to-the-minute events listings
- Opinionated blog entries by Arthur Frommer himself
- Online travel message boards with featured travel discussions

The Best of Iceland

On each trip to Iceland, we are always struck by how often other travelers are—or intend to be—repeat visitors. Many come year after year, never exhausting Iceland's endless variations of magnificent scenery and adventure. Returning travelers immediately recognize the crisp, invigorating polar air, and what W. H. Auden called "the most magical light of anywhere on earth."

Iceland's astonishing beauty often has an austere, primitive, or surreal cast that arouses reverence, wonderment, mystery, and awe. Lasting impressions could include a lone tuft of wildflowers amid a bleak desert moonscape or a fantastical promenade of icebergs calved into a lake from a magisterial glacier.

The Icelandic people—freedom-loving, egalitarian, self-reliant, and worldly—are equally exceptional. They established a parliamentary democracy over a millennium ago, and today write, publish, purchase, and read more books per capita than any people on earth. Reykjavík, their capital, has become one of the world's most fashionable urban hot spots. In November 2007, the U.N. named Iceland the world's best country to live in, based on life expectancy, education levels, medical care, income, and other criteria.

1 The Best Natural Wonders

- **Glymur:** Iceland's tallest waterfall is nimble and graceful: Streamlets descend like ribbons of a maypole into a fathomless canyon mantled in bird nests and lush mosses. The hike there is somewhat treacherous, but those who brave it are rewarded with enchanting scenery—and possibly total solitude—all within easy range of Reykjavík. See p. 138.
- **Gullfoss:** This astounding waterfall crowns and climaxes the "Golden Circle," Iceland's most popular day tour from the capital. Gullfoss looks almost too perfectly landscaped to be real: The Hvítá river hurtles over a low tier, turns 90 degrees, plunges into a cloud of spray, and shimmies offstage through a picturesque gorge. Clear skies guarantee a rainbow. See p. 146.
- **Blue Lagoon:** The central activity at this spa—Iceland's top tourist attraction—is bathing in a shallow, opaque, blue-green lagoon amid a jet-black lava field and smearing white silica mud all over yourself. The lagoon was artificially created from pumped-in seawater and runoff from a geothermal power plant—not exactly a *natural* wonder, but it could make you feel like one. See p. 150.
- **Raufarhólshellir:** With the right preparations and precautions, anyone can just saunter right into this lava-tube cave and wander more than a kilometer (¾ mile) to its darkest depths, past eerie ice candles and tortured lava formations. See p. 161.
- **Látrabjarg:** These colossal sea cliffs at Iceland's westernmost point prove

Iceland

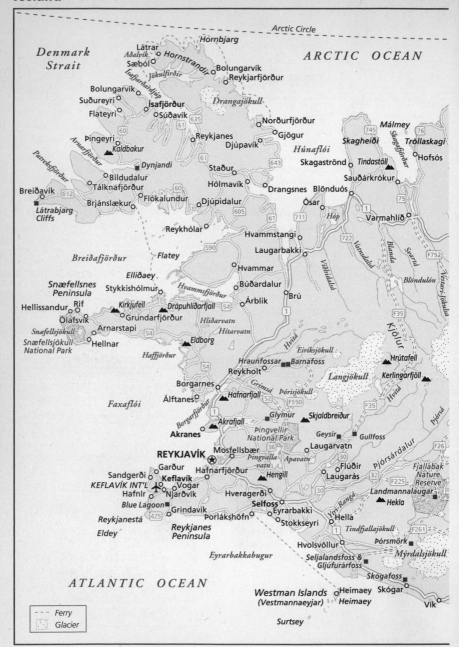

Arctic Circle

Denmark Strait

ARCTIC OCEAN

Látrar
Aðalvík
Sæból
Hornbjarg
Hornstrandir
Jökulfirðir
Bolungarvík
Reykjarfjörður
Ísafjarðardjúp

Bolungarvík
Suðureyri
Flateyri
Ísafjörður
Súðavík
635
Drangajökull
Norðurfjörður
Málmey
Þingeyri
Kaldbakur
Reykjanes
Djúpavík
Gjögur
Skagheiði
Tröllaskagi
Húnaflói
Hofsós
Arnarfjörður
Dynjandi
Staður
643
Skagaströnd
Tindastöll
Bildudalur
Hólmavík
Sauðárkrókur
Breiðavík
612
Tálknafjörður
Drangsnes
Blönduós
Brjánslækur
Flókalundur
Djúpidalur
Ósar
Látrabjarg Cliffs
605
Hóp
Varmahlíð
Reykhólar
Hvammstangi
722
Breiðafjörður
Flatey
590
Laugarbakki
Blanda
F752
Snæfellsnes Peninsula
Elliðaey
Stykkishólmur
Hvammsfjörður
Hvammar
Búðardalur
Brú
Blöndulón
Hellissandur
Rif
Kirkjufell
Drápuhlíðarfjall
54
Árblik
F35
Ólafsvík
Grundarfjörður
Hlíðarvatn
Snæfellsjökull
Arnarstapi
54
Hítarvatn
Snæfellsjökull National Park
Hellnar
Eldborg
Eiríksjökull
Hrútafell
Hafffjörður
Hraunfossar
Barnafoss
54
Reykholt
Langjökull
Kerlingarfjöll
Borgarnes
Grímsá
Þórisjökull
Faxaflói
Álftanes
Hafnarfjall
52
F550
F35
Borgarfjörður
Glymur
Skjaldbreiður
Akrafjall
Þingvellir National Park
Geysir
Gullfoss
Akranes
Mosfellsbær
Þingvalla-vatn
Apavatn
Laugarvatn
F26
REYKJAVÍK
36
30
Þjórsárdalur
Garður
Hafnarfjörður
Flúðir
Fjallabak Nature Reserve
Sandgerði
Keflavík
Hengill
Laugarás
32
F225
KEFLAVÍK INT'L
Vogar
30
Landmannalaugar
Hafnir
Njarðvík
Hveragerði
Hekla
Blue Lagoon
Selfoss
Reykjanestá
425
Grindavík
Eyrarbakki
Hella
Eldey
Þorlákshöfn
Stokkseyri
Reykjanes Peninsula
Tindfjallajökull
F261
Hvolsvöllur
Þórsmörk
Eyrarbakkabugur
Seljalandsfoss & Gljúfurárfoss
Mýrdalsjökull
Skógafoss

ATLANTIC OCEAN

Westman Islands (Vestmannaeyjar)
Heimaey
Skógar
Heimaey
Vík
Surtsey

- - - Ferry
Glacier

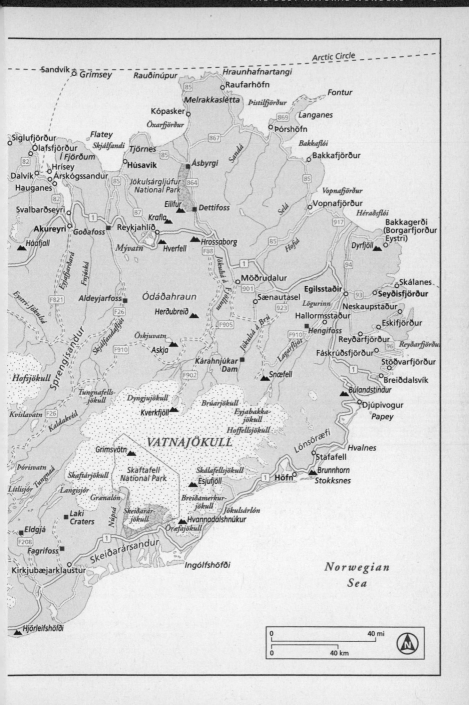

that the "ends of the earth" come with a bang, not a whimper. The sheer volume of birds is unbelievable, and the puffins are particularly willing to have their picture taken. See p. 191.

• **Hornbjarg:** These sea cliffs in Iceland's far northwest aren't easy to reach, but pilgrims are treated to the most arresting sight on the country's entire coastline. An undulating, razor-backed ridge is etched against the sky: On its inland side, a steep slope scoops down to a meadowed plateau; on its opposite side is a sheer 534m (1,752-ft.) drop to the sea. See p. 212.

• **Aldeyjarfoss:** In northwest Iceland, at the doorstep of the desolate highlands, these pummeling falls crash into a bizarre theater of columnar basalt. If you saw it in a science fiction movie, you might think they were overdoing it. See p. 250.

• **Hverfell:** Of all the monuments to Iceland's volcanism, this tephra explosion crater near Mývatn is the most monolithic: a jet-black bowl of humbling proportions, with a stark, elemental authority. See p. 253.

• **Leirhnjúkur:** In a country with no shortage of primordial, surreal landscapes, this lava field in the Krafla caldera of northeast Iceland outweirds them all. An easy trail wends its way among steaming clefts, each revealing a prismatic netherworld of mosses and minerals. See p. 254.

• **Dettifoss:** Europe's mightiest waterfall, located in northeast Iceland's Jökulsárgljúfur National Park, is a massive curtain of milky-gray glacial water thundering over a 44m (144-ft.) precipice. To stand next to it is as mesmerizing as it is bone rattling. See p. 270.

• **Fjaðrárgljúfur:** Iceland has several dramatic gorges, but this one's spiky crags and vertiginous ledges virtually summon the mystics and landscape painters. Fjaðrárgljúfur is close to the Ring Road, near the village of Kirkjubæjarklaustur in south Iceland, and the trail along the rim is a breeze. See p. 309.

• **Laki Craters:** This monstrous row of over a hundred craters, lined up along a 25km (16-mile) fissure, is scar tissue from the most catastrophic volcanic eruption in Iceland's history. Velvety coatings of grey-green moss soften Laki's terrible, bleak beauty. See p. 309.

• **Jökulsárlón:** Hundreds of sediment-streaked, blue-tinted icebergs, seemingly the work of some mad sculptor, waltz around this surreal glacial lagoon in the southeast, while seals join in the carnival procession. See p. 316.

• **Askja:** This staggering whorl of volcanic mountains, circling an 8km-wide (5 mile) bowl formed by collapsed magma chambers, is one of Earth's grandest pockmarks and the most sought-out destination in Iceland's desolate highland interior. Visitors can swim in a warm, opaque blue-green pond at the bottom of a steep crater: a real "if my friends could see me now" moment. See p. 359.

2 The Best Towns & Villages

• **Suðureyri:** This traditional yet eco-conscious fishing village in the Westfjords is pioneering a tourism model that welcomes visitors into the daily work rituals of Icelandic life. Touring a fish-processing factory or joining a fishing boat crew may not be your idea of a fun vacation—but these are authentic cross-cultural experiences you're unlikely to forget. See p. 196.

• **Ísafjörður:** The Westfjords region is almost a country unto itself, and its honorary capital has real vibrancy despite its remoteness and small population. Credit the phenomenal setting, thriving harbor, first-rate dining, hip cafes, and festivals ranging from alternative music to solo theater performance—and even "swamp soccer." See p. 198.

- **Siglufjörður:** With a single road leading in, this isolated, untouristy fjord town has a picture-perfect setting and an endearing nostalgia for its herring-boom glory days—case in point, the ambitious Herring Era Museum—and fabulous hiking. See p. 225.

- **Akureyri:** With a university, several museums, fine dining, a distinguished summer arts festival, lively downtown pedestrian streets, and active nightlife, this northern capital's 17,000 inhabitants think they have everything Reykjavík has—minus the rainy weather. See p. 230.

- **Heimaey:** As the only town in the gorgeous Westman Islands, Heimaey—surrounded by magnificent sea cliffs and two ominous volcanic cones—

would have made this list for its setting (and cute puffin population) alone. Its distinctive local identity and heroic resilience in the aftermath of a devastating 1973 eruption only add to its luster. See p. 245.

- **Vík:** This southernmost village in Iceland wears its fine setting lightly, but its landscape stays vividly etched in the mind: the lovely beaches of black volcanic sand, the spiky sea stacks offshore, and on the neighboring Reynisfjall cliffs, the most scenic walk on Iceland's south coast. See p. 303.

- **Seyðisfjörður:** The arrival point for European ferry passengers, and a fashionable summer retreat for Icelandic artists, this dramatically situated Eastfjords village has a cosmopolitan pulse that squares perfectly well with its tiny scale and pristine surroundings. Chalet-style wooden kit homes from the 19th and early-20th centuries provide a rare architectural historicity, and the country's first telegraph station is now an interesting technology museum. See p. 340.

3 The Best Big-Name Hikes

- **Hornstrandir Nature Reserve:** This saw-toothed peninsula, the northernmost extremity of the Westfjords, is for travelers whose eyes instinctually roam to the farthest corners of the map. Protected since 1975, Hornstrandir has no roads, no airstrips, no year-round residents—only the beguiling coastline, flowering meadows, and cavorting birds and foxes the Vikings first encountered over a millennium ago. See p. 210.

- **Jökulsárgljúfur National Park:** This elongated canyon park formed by Iceland's second-longest river is bookended by Dettifoss, Europe's mightiest waterfall, and Ásbyrgi, a U-shaped ravine reputed to be the hoof print of

the Norse god Óðinn's eight-legged steed. Each bend of the river brings a succession of delights on a more human scale: honeycombed basalt, woolly willows, cascading springs. See p. 266.

- **Landmannalaugar:** Your friends may refuse to believe that your photos of Landmannalaugar's astonishing rhyolite mountains—with marbled streaks of yellow, red, green, white, and purple scree—weren't "digitally enhanced." It's not only the most celebrated hiking area in Iceland, but also the ideal launch point for the Laugavegurinn, a world-renowned 4-day trek to Þórsmörk through a cavalcade of inland scenery. See p. 289 and 292.

- **Þórsmörk:** This verdant alpine oasis, encircled by monumental glaciers and river-braided valleys of silt, has the aura of an enchanted refuge—a nice counterpoint to the distinctly Martian appeal of most interior regions. The Fimmvörðuháls, an equally charmed 2-day trek threading a high mountain pass between two glaciers, connects Þórsmörk to Skógar near the south coast. See p. 298 and 300.

- **Skaftafell National Park:** Close to the "Ring Road" (Rte. 1) on the southern edge of Vatnajökull, Skaftafell is the most accessible of Iceland's major hiking destinations, with startling panoramas of serrated peaks, shimmering icecaps, and barren flood plains stretching toward the sea. At your feet is pleasant scrubland resplendent with wildflowers and butterflies. See p. 313.

4 The Best Hikes Off the Beaten Track

- **Sveinstindur–Skælingar:** Landmannalaugar unjustly steals the limelight from many nearby interior regions, most notably this amazing stretch of mountains and sediment-filled river valleys between Landmannalaugar and Vatnajökull. Views from the peak of Sveinstindur over the glacier-gouged Lake Langisjór are among the most otherworldly and sublime in all of Iceland. See p. 292.

- **Þakgil:** This idyllic campsite and its mountainous setting near the southeast edge of Mýrdalsjökull are sure to become better known. Þakgil itself is in a perfectly sheltered, stream-fed gully. The surrounding tuff mountains, formed from compacted volcanic ash, have been elaborately sculpted by wind and water erosion; trails lead right to the moraines of the receding glacier. And with a brand-new crop of snug cabins, you don't even have to rough it. See p. 304.

- **Núpsstaðarskógar:** Accessible only to rugged 4WD vehicles and committed hikers, this magical enclave of scrubby birch, sculpted gorges, and luxuriant waterfalls along the Núpsá river is virtually untouched by tourists. If you can't get there on the ground, consider an exhilarating aerial tour from the Skaftafell airfield. See p. 311 and 314.

- **Lónsöræfi:** Wonderfully removed from civilization, this private nature reserve in the mountains east of Vatnajökull is paradise for hikers who enjoy lingering over each unfolding nuance along the trail: the subtle spectra of a rhyolite rockslide; the ubiquitous waterfalls and river chasms; the fine textures of moss and lichen and tiny wildflowers. Reindeer could make a cameo. See p. 324.

- **Borgarfjörður Eystri:** This well-rounded coastal region combines many geological marvels found in the interior—particularly rhyolite mountainsides and their marbled color patterns—with an abundance of flowering plants and the romantic melancholy of its formerly inhabited fjords and inlets. Locals have put great effort into designing maps, marking trails, and organizing Jeep tours of the area. See p. 345.

- **Kerlingarfjöll:** A short detour from the relatively accessible Kjölur Route through the interior, this mountain cluster in the shadow of Hofsjökull has an astonishing range of scenery: lofty mountains, chiseled ravines, exotic geothermal fields, glimmering icecaps. . . . The clinchers are the hot springs that form enormous natural Jacuzzis and the pleasant, private lodgings at Ásgarður. See p. 355.

• **Kverkfjöll:** Deep within Iceland's highland desert interior, this geothermally restless mountain spur protrudes from Vatnajökull amid charred expanses of red, brown, and black rock dusted with lichen and moss. Though best-known for a mesmerizing glacial ice cave, Kverkfjöll is anything but a one-hit natural wonder and merits 2 or 3 days to appreciate its austere gravitas. See p. 362.

5 Iceland's Best Museums

• **Harbor House Museum** (Reykjavík; ℂ 590-1200; www.artmuseum.is): Born Guðmundur Guðmundsson in 1932, Erró—the most prominent Icelandic artist of the late 20th century—has donated most of his life's work to this contemporary art branch of the Reykjavík Art Museum. The exhibit spaces are inside a 1930s-era warehouse perfectly suited to the vast, cartoon-styled montages for which he is best known. See p. 113.

• **National Museum of Iceland** (Reykjavík; ℂ 530-2200; www.natmus.is): This museum's permanent but ever-evolving exhibit, "The Making of a Nation," covers the entire span of Icelandic history and culture. You might anticipate a numbing encyclopedic survey, but the curators' selective restraint manages to say more with less. Look out for impromptu appearances by a youth choir singing haunting scores from the past. See p. 115.

• **Einar Jónsson Museum** (Reykjavík; ℂ 551-3797; www.skulptur.is): The work of Iceland's most revered sculptor draws heavily on classical mythology and traditional folklore, with a virtuosic command of gesture and ingenious meshings of human and beastly forms. His romantic symbolism is sometimes difficult to interpret, but never fails to carry deep emotional and spiritual resonance. Einar spent as long as 10 years perfecting his works, many of which are displayed exclusively here. See p. 115.

• **Settlement Center** (Borgarnes; ℂ 437-1600; www.landnam.is): With state-of-the-art multimedia exhibits dedicated to *Egils Saga* and the first 60 years of Icelandic settlement, this engaging new museum tries almost too hard to turn learning into a kind of amusement park fun house—but we're not complaining. See p. 168.

• **Glaumbær** (Skagafjörður; ℂ 453-6173; www.glaumbaer.is): Iceland has several museums inside preserved 19th- and early-20th-century turf-roofed farm buildings; but, if you see just one, make it Glaumbær in the northwest. Fish-skin shoes and other fascinating artifacts are on view, but the most affecting moments are when you imagine the smell of burning peat and the sounds of the family clan puttering about these dark, damp, and snug rooms through the long winters. See p. 222.

• **Museum of Small Exhibits** (Near Akureyri; ℂ 463-1261; www.smamunasafnid.is): "I collect old things," explains Sverrir Hermannsson, the eccentric carpenter behind this strange and unique museum. Sverrir has meticulously culled, categorized, arranged, and mounted all sorts of things—hammers, kettles, record-player needles, belt buckles—in an art of pattern, repetition, and variation. The objects themselves may be ordinary and worthless, but as he cryptically notes, "The thought alone can be of aesthetic value." See p. 248.

• **Safnasafnið** (Near Akureyri; ⓒ 461-4066; www.safnasafnid.is): The curators of this inspiring art museum comb the country for what they call "honesty," ignoring conventional distinctions between contemporary art, folk art, and "naïve" art. The museum is not anti-elitist so much as immune to all aesthetic dogma. Whatever the grounding principles, the results are compelling: Exhibits could spotlight anything from women's needleworking tools and wooden figurines whittled by a farmer to fine photography and sculpture. See p. 249.

• **Húsavík Museum** (Húsavík; ⓒ 464-1860; www.husmus.is): Guðni Halldórsson, the intense and tireless curator of this prolific folk museum in northeast Iceland, is used to seeing most visitors to Húsavík take a whale-watching tour, giggle at the jarred penises in the Phallological Museum, and depart. Nothing wrong with that, but you might take some time to enjoy the fascinating range of regional artifacts on display here, from a stuffed polar bear to necklaces made from human hair. See p. 261.

• **Skógar Folk Museum** (Skógar; ⓒ 487-8845; www.skogasafn.is): This is without a doubt the greatest of Iceland's many folk museums, with an enormous artifact collection ranging from fishing boats to carved headboards and makeshift mousetraps. Let the staff lead you around; otherwise, you won't know what the hollow fishbone was used for. See p. 302.

6 The Best Accommodations for Local Flavor

• **Hotel Glymur** (Hvalfjörður; ⓒ 430-3100; www.hotelglymur.is): This stylish retreat is just 45 minutes from Reykjavík and 90 minutes from the international airport—but feels worlds away, especially when surveying the fjord from the vantage point of the hot tub. The rooms, all duplexes, were smartly remodeled in 2006. See p. 140.

• **Hótel Búðir** (Snæfellsnes Peninsula; ⓒ 435-6700; www.budir.is): This country-contemporary boutique hotel with an estimable restaurant is surrounded by nothing but ocean, broad sandbanks, sprawling lava, stone ruins of fishermen's huts, and a restored 19th-century church, with Snæfellsjökull loftily presiding over the scene. See p. 182.

• **Guesthouse Breiðavík** (Látrabjarg peninsula; ⓒ 456-1575; www.breidavik.net): Around the corner from Iceland's largest sea cliff, this warm and welcoming farmstay is in a breathtakingly picturesque bay with Mediterranean-hued waters. Wind down with an evening stroll on the beach, followed by a drink at Europe's westernmost bar. See p. 194.

• **Faktorshúsið í Hæstikaupstað** (Ísafjörður; 456-3868; gistias@snerpa.is): In the heart of the Westfjords' happening capital, this painstakingly restored 1788 house—with just one top-floor guest room—is as steeped in Icelandic history as anyplace you're likely to encounter outside a museum. See p. 202.

• **Heydalur Country Hotel** (Ísafjarðardjúp; ⓒ 456-4824; www.heydalur.is): With a majestic fjord and friendly seal colony, this rustic farm retreat in the Westfjords has everything you need to craft a perfect day: horseback riding, fishing, sea kayaking, homecooking, and a blissful outdoor hot pool. See p. 206.

• **Hótel Djúpavík** (Strandir Coast; ⓒ 451-4037; www.djupavik.com): Beautifully situated along the wild and remote Strandir Coast, this former boarding house for seasonal herring workers is so warmly and authentically connected to its past that any luxury deficits are irrelevant. Original driftwood boards creak underfoot, and the decaying herring factory looms wistfully nearby. See p. 209.

- **Hótel Tindastóll** (Sauðárkrókur; ℂ 453-5002; www.hoteltindastoll.com): Each large, handsome room in this lovingly restored 1884 Norwegian kit home is an ideal synthesis of luxury and provincial charm. The natural-stone hot pool in back is the finishing touch. See p. 228.

- **Hótel Reykjahlíð** (Mývatn; ℂ 464-4142; www.reykjahlid.is): Perched right on Iceland's most celebrated and scenic lake, this stately country hotel has an understated elegance complemented by a first-rate restaurant. See p. 256.

- **Country Hotel Anna** (west of Skógar; ℂ 487-8950; www.hotelanna.is): An appealing interlude for road trips along the south coast, this intimate hotel is an ideal blend of an upscale B&B and a rural farmstay, though prices reflect the former. See p. 305.

- **Fljótsdalur Youth Hostel** (Markarfljót valley; ℂ 487-8498; www.hostel.is): This charmed, turf-roofed hideaway is nestled deep within the Markarfljót valley, on the cusp of Iceland's interior. All beds are in bunk rooms and the amenities are few—but, with civilization left safely behind, things couldn't be cozier. See p. 296.

- **Guesthouse Egilsstaðir** (Egilsstaðir; ℂ 471-1114; www.egilsstadir.com): Few travelers linger in Egilsstaðir, the transit hub of east Iceland, but for the many who pass through, this lovely manorial farmhouse offers sumptuous rooms, a fine restaurant, lake views, and—that rarity of rarities—a shady grove of tall trees. See p. 334.

- **Hótel Aldan** (Seyðisfjörður; ℂ 472-1277; www.hotelaldan.com): Recent refurbishment of this 19th-century Norwegian kit building struck an exquisite balance of period restoration and sleek modern design. Aldan is easily the Eastfjords' most captivating hotel, in the region's most captivating village. See p. 344.

7 The Best Icelandic Restaurants

- **Sjávarkjallarinn (Seafood Cellar)** (Reykjavík; ℂ 511-1212): Culinary conservatives may distrust this restaurant's radical experimentation and splashy presentation—lobster with truffles served in a Mason jar? But the Seafood Cellar would be Iceland's best restaurant even if the food came in Styrofoam containers at a drive-thru window. See p. 99.

- **Fjalakötturinn** (Reykjavík; ℂ 514-6000): Traditional yet worldly (for an appetizer, think smoked lamb carpaccio with chutney and celery root salad), this stellar restaurant has a plain white dining room with a few photos of old Reykjavík on the wall. No glam appeal, but the cooking—and the country's

most refined wine list—speak for themselves. See p. 102.

- **Salt** (Reykjavík; ℂ 599-1020): Housed in the minimalist-chic Radisson SAS 1919 Hotel, this recent entry has a prize-winning celebrity chef, but the menu—emphasizing natural flavors and traditional crowd-pleasers like trout with lemon and capers, or tenderloin with crispy potatoes and béarnaise sauce—is anything but an ego trip. See p. 102.

- **Við Tjörnina** (Reykjavík; ℂ 551-8666): If smoked lamb's heart, fermented shark, and salt-cod mousse can be made palatable, leave it to the maverick chefs at this offbeat Reykjavík institution. (Don't worry: The lamb fillet in port wine sauce is just as exceptional.) Check the wall for the chefs' "band photo," and ask for a bag of leftover bread to feed the ducks in the pond outside. See p. 103.

- **Þrír Frakkar** (Reykjavík; © 552-3939): The hallmarks of a "real Icelandic restaurant" are all here: nautical decor; a wide selection of fresh seafood and seabirds, always complemented by potatoes, familiar vegetables, and rich sauces; and there's nothing dainty about the portions or presentation. See p. 103.

- **Fjöruborðið** (Stokkseyri; © 483-1550): Icelanders drive long distances—and sometimes even drop in by helicopter from Reykjavík—to butter their bibs at this famed lobster house on Iceland's southwestern coast. See p. 165.

- **Tjöruhúsið** (Ísafjörður; © 456-4419): Tucked away in an 18th-century fish warehouse, this no-nonsense Westfjords restaurant serves up amazingly fresh and tasty pan-fried fish without the slightest fuss or pretense. Ask the cook if the fish is ever frozen and you'll get a look of utter horror. See p. 204.

- **Friðrik V** (Akureyri; © 461-5775): This family-run affair, offering an impressive variety of modern European preparations, is the best restaurant outside the capital—and it's written all over the faces of the waitstaff, who deliver lectures on each dish with well-earned, unconcealed pride. See p. 238.

8 The Best of Iceland Online

- **www.icelandreview.com**: Iceland Review is an online magazine that strikes a fine balance between serious journalism and touristic concerns; the travel articles are great for scouting destinations. All previous issues are archived and searchable, and a free print version can be found in cafes and hotel rooms across the country. The site links to **What's On Iceland** (**www.whatson.is**), excellent for catching wind of scheduled events.

- **www.samkoma.com**: **Samkoma,** which means "meeting place," was set up to foster interchange between Icelanders and Canadians of Icelandic descent, but it also contains the Internet's best collection of Iceland-related links.

- **www.grapevine.is**: The Grapevine, a free left-wing magazine found all over Iceland, is a terrific resource for reviews of art, music, dining, shopping, and trips within Iceland. All issues are archived and searchable online.

- **www.nat.is**: The homepage of **Nordic Adventure Travel** delivers on its cheery promise: "We cover everything you are coming to enjoy! The whole island is air conditioned!" The endless links are particularly helpful for those planning a fishing, hunting, or hiking adventure. Click the trail icons on a national map, and detailed trail maps and descriptions appear.

- **http://blog.icelandexpress.com/iceland**: This blog, run by budget airline Iceland Express, is titled **"How Do You Like Iceland?"**—a question visitors are asked continuously. Entries are much more informed, candid, and amusing than you'd expect from an airline website.

- **http://kort.bok.hi.is**: **Antique Maps of Iceland** has high-resolution digital files of vintage, pre-1900 maps of Iceland. Some 16th- and 17th-century maps include great captions for sea monsters popping their heads out of the ocean. One reads, "He hath been seene to stand a whole day together upright upon his taile . . . and greedily seeketh after mans flesh."

- **www.edjackson.ca/19thcentury iceland**: Ed Jackson is a connoisseur of rare and long-forgotten Iceland travelogues, and his website **Travels in 19th Century Iceland** presents absorbing extracts with period photographs and illustrations. Entries are cross-indexed by location (Reykjavík, Þingvellir, and so on) and themes such as dress, customs and manners, and children.

- **www.icelandicmusic.is**: This new government-sponsored site, titled **Icelandic Music Export (IMX),** is a great way to sample the country's music scene. Features include news, events, downloadable videos, podcasts, and links to homepages of Icelandic artists. **The Icelandic Music Page (www.musik.is)** is another excellent site with links for musical events throughout the country.

- **www.halfdan.is/vestur/vestur.htm**: **The Emigration from Iceland to North America** is the best site for non-Icelanders of Icelandic descent to trace their ancestry and find living relatives.

2

Planning Your Trip to Iceland

This chapter is designed to help you with practical matters in planning your trip to Iceland: when to go, how to get there, how to get around, how to prepare. Advance planning is especially important in high season (mid-June to Aug), since tourism is booming and services have trouble meeting demand.

1 The Regions in Brief

Iceland is by far the most sparsely populated country in Europe: The size of Ireland or Kentucky, it has only 300,000 inhabitants. Two-thirds of the population live in the greater Reykjavík area, and the next largest town—Akureyri, on the north coast—has only 17,000 people. Most Icelanders live close to the coast, as the interior is largely an uninhabitable desert, impassable in winter.

Iceland's topography and unified culture do not lend themselves easily to geographic subdivisions. Route 1, known as the "Ring Road," circles the entire island but does not reach the Westfjords or many coastal towns. Chapters 7 through 10 are organized directionally; chapters 7 (West) and 8 (North) "lead" you from Reykjavík to Egilsstaðir (the transportation hub of East Iceland) clockwise, and chapters 9 (South) and 10 (East) do the same counterclockwise.

REYKJAVÍK & NEARBY Most Icelanders live in the southwest corner of the island. Reykjavík, Iceland's appealing capital, has zoomed to international prominence in the last 25 years, even becoming a trendsetter in music and nightlife. The center of town can be crossed in 30 minutes on foot, but a few miles of urban sprawl have absorbed neighboring towns such as Kópavogur and Hafnarfjörður.

From Reykjavík, many visitors take the "Golden Circle" day tour to **Gullfoss** waterfall, **Geysir** (for which all geysers are named), and **Þingvellir** National Park, where the first Icelandic parliament convened in the year 930.

Keflavík International Airport, the gateway for most international travelers, is on the **Reykjanes Peninsula,** southwest of Reykjavík. The peninsula's barren, lava-strewn landscape has several interesting sites, including Iceland's most popular tourist attraction, the **Blue Lagoon** spa.

WEST North of Reykjavík, the **Snaefellsnes Peninsula** is known for whale-watching, glacier tours, and stunning stretches of coastline. The sparsely populated **Westfjords,** with sea cliffs full of nesting birds and isolated, picturesque villages, are unjustly neglected by tourists.

NORTH The north is anchored by **Akureyri,** Iceland's "second city." The town of **Húsavík,** an hour to the east, is Iceland's best whale-watching port. The region around **Lake Mývatn** features wild geological formations, bubbling mud pools, and great bird-watching. The canyon park of **Jökulsárgljúfur** is a prime hiking destination.

SOUTH South Iceland is packed with attractions and makes for one of the greatest driving trips in the world. **Landmannalaugar, Þórsmörk,** and **Skaftafell National Park** are supreme hiking areas. The dramatic sea cliffs of the **Westman Islands** are perfect for puffin-spotting, and Heimaey, the main town, is half-buried in lava from a devastating 1973 eruption. The coastal town of **Vík** features wonderful cliff walks and black sand beaches. Further east is Iceland's best-known roadside attraction: **Jökulsárlón,** a surreal lake of icebergs calved from a glacier.

EAST Europe's largest glacier, **Vatnajökull,** anchors Iceland's southeast corner.

Glacier trips often leave from the nearby town of **Höfn.** Further north, **Egilsstaðir** is the main business and transportation hub for the region. Ferries to the rest of Europe leave from the port of **Seyðisfjörður,** the prettiest town in the **Eastfjords.** In the Eastfjords north of Seyðisfjörður, **Borgarfjörður Eystri** is one of Iceland's best but least-known hiking areas.

INTERIOR Desolate and otherworldly, the interior makes for an unforgettable adventure. In the **Askja** crater range you can swim in a lukewarm volcanic lake, and **Kverkfjöll** features bizarre ice formations formed by hot springs emerging from Vatnajökull.

2 Visitor Information & Maps

In the United States, **Iceland Tourist Board** (P. O. Box 4649) 655 3rd Ave., New York, NY, 10017 (© **212/885-9710;** www.icelandtouristboard.com), can get you started in planning your trip. Iceland does not maintain tourist offices in Canada, the United Kingdom, Ireland, Australia, or New Zealand.

A particularly useful reference is the free 240-page booklet *Around Iceland,* with practical, concise listings for virtually all accommodations, dining, attractions, and tourist services throughout the country. The booklet is easily found in hotels and tourist information centers, and can be downloaded from **www.heimur.is/world**.

For more information, see "Visitor Information" for each destination.

The most readily available large-scale, medium-scale, and thematic maps are published by **Mál og Menning,** and can be purchased overseas through **www.nordic store.net**.

Other companies are producing excellent small-scale **hiking maps** for particular areas; consult each regional chapter of this book for further information. For **road maps,** see "Getting Around Iceland," p. 37.

A fun way to prepare for a walking trip in Iceland is to visit **Google Earth** (www.googleearth.com) and print out aerial photographs of your route.

3 Entry Requirements

PASSPORTS

All visitors to Iceland must carry a passport, valid at least 3 months beyond the return date. For information on how to get a passport, see "Fast Facts," at the end of this chapter. All U.S. citizens regardless of age (even newborns) must have a passport to travel abroad. For an up-to-date, country-by-country listing of passport requirements around the world, go to the U.S. State Department website at **http:// travel.state.gov** and click the link for "Country Specific Information."

VISAS

If your trip to Iceland is under 90 days, no visa is required for passport holders in the U.S., Canada, Great Britain, Ireland, Australia, New Zealand, and many other countries. Iceland is a signatory to the Schengen Agreement, which includes Austria,

Belgium, Denmark, Finland, France, Greece, Holland, Italy, Luxembourg, Norway, Portugal, Spain, Sweden, and Germany. Citizens of these countries do not need a visa. If you are from a country not listed here, check with the **Icelandic Directorate of Immigration** (www.utl.is) to see if you need a visa and what the requirements are. In most instances, other Scandinavian embassies will handle visa applications on behalf of Iceland. If you need a visa, it must be secured in advance of your trip.

If you travel to Iceland without a visa and are not from the Schengen Area, the total stay within the Schengen Area must not exceed 3 months in any period of 6 months. If you do need a visa, it will normally apply to the entire Schengen Area.

WORK

A visa does not grant the right to work in Iceland. If you are from a European Economic Area (EEA) country, you can apply for Icelandic jobs without first securing a work permit. For more information, check with the **Directorate of Labour** (© 515-4800; www.vinnumalastofnun.is/english).

MEDICAL REQUIREMENTS

No inoculations are compulsory for travel to Iceland. For more information, see "Health & Safety," later in this chapter.

CUSTOMS

For information on what you can bring into and take out of Iceland, see "Fast Facts," p. 51.

4 When to Go

Iceland has a concentrated tourist season, peaking from mid-June through August. Many Icelanders think the summer tourists don't know what they're missing. Iceland offers plenty to do in spring, fall, even winter, and prices are dramatically lower for airfares, car rentals, and accommodations. Icelanders are avid Christmas celebrators, and the Aurora Borealis is remarkably vivid in winter. Most off-season visitors use Reykjavík as a home base, and combine city culture and nightlife with activities such as horseback riding, snowmobiling, and visiting spas (see "Iceland in the Off Season," p. 19).

On the other hand, high season is high season for good reason. Most tours and adventure trips to Iceland's most renowned natural attractions end after September. Roads in the hinterlands are generally closed from October to mid-May, and some don't open until early July. Precipitation increases in September, peaking from October through February, and frequent storms and driving rain are enough to dissuade many would-be winter adventurers.

The tourist high season corresponds with vacation time for Icelanders, but things don't shut down the way they do in, say, France. Icelanders work longer hours than most Europeans, and vacationing students fill seasonal service jobs. Some cultural institutions (theater, symphony, opera) take the summer off, while most museums outside Reykjavík are *only* open in summer. Arts and cultural festivals are also clustered in summer, except in Reykjavík, where they gravitate to the "shoulder" seasons (Apr–May and Sept–Oct). For annual holidays and events, see the "Calendar of Events," below.

In timing your visit, consider also that the number of daylight hours can have unanticipated physical and emotional effects (see "Health & Safety," later in this chapter). In early summer there is never complete darkness and the sun stays low to the horizon, creating an

Daylight Hours for Reykjavík and Ísafjörður

	Jan	Feb	Mar	Apr
Reykjavík	11:19am–3:44pm	10:09am–5:15pm	8:36am–6:45pm	6:47am–8:18pm
Ísafjörður	12:02pm–3:11pm	10:30am–5:03pm	8:47am–6:46pm	6:48am–8:27pm
	May	June	July	Aug
Reykjavík	5:01am–9:51pm	3:23am–11:30pm	3:04am–11:57pm	4:33am–10:33pm
Ísafjörður	4:50am–10:12pm	2:43am–12:02am	24 hours	4:15am–11pm
	Sept	Oct	Nov	Dec
Reykjavík	6:08am–8:45pm	7:35am–6:58pm	9:09am–5:12pm	10:44am–3:49pm
Ísafjörður	6:06am–8:57pm	7:42am–7:01pm	9:26am–5:05pm	11:19am–3:23pm

ongoing play of color and shadow. Spring and fall daylight hours are roughly the same as in North America or Europe. Days in mid-winter have only 4 or 5 hours of sunlight. These fluctuations are even more extreme in the northern part of the country.

WEATHER

Iceland is located just south of the Arctic Circle, but thanks to the Gulf Stream, temperatures are cool in summer and remarkably mild in winter. (New York's winter lows are normally lower than Reykjavík's.) Icelandic weather is unusually volatile, however. The Gulf Stream brings mild Atlantic air in contact with colder Arctic air, resulting in frequently overcast skies, fog, driving wind and rain, and abrupt weather shifts. You could well encounter four seasons in one day.

Iceland's precipitation peaks in October to February, and is lowest in May and June. Southern and western parts of the island receive the most rainfall. For English-language forecasts or further information on regional weather, contact the **Icelandic Meteorological Office** (© 902-0600; www.vedur.is).

CALENDAR OF EVENTS

For public holidays, see "Holidays" in "Fast Facts," at the end of this chapter.

January

New Year's Day. This is really a 2-day holiday, as nothing reopens until January 3. January 1.

Þrettándinn. This day marks the end of the Christmas season. Icelanders celebrate with a kind of New Year's Eve reprise, including bonfires, fireworks, and traditional songs, while kids throw snowballs at cars. January 6.

Þorrablót. This ancient Viking mid-winter tradition—named for Þorri, a month in the old Icelandic calendar—was originally a feast of sacrifice involving the blood of oxen and goats. Contemporary celebrations involve dancing, singing, drinking, and eating traditional Norse specialties, including singed sheep's head, pickled rams' testicles, and putrefied shark. Þorrablót dinners can be found in some Reykjavík restaurants; in smaller towns, visitors are often invited to join the locals. From the Friday that falls within January 19 to January 25 through most of February.

Average Monthly Temperatures in Reykjavík

	Jan	Feb	Mar	Apr	May	June	July	Aug	Sept	Oct	Nov	Dec
Temp (°F)	31	33	33	38	44	49	52	51	46	40	34	33
Temp (°C)	-1	1	1	3	7	10	11	11	8	5	1	0

February

Food and Fun (www.foodandfun.is). For 4 days Reykjavík's best restaurants create discounted set menus. In a televised competition, top international chefs are challenged to create dishes on the spot from purely Icelandic ingredients. Late February.

Winter Lights Festival (www.visit reykjavik.is). Reykjavík is dramatically lit up for this cornucopia of cultural events: anything from fashion shows to figure skating to outdoor choral performances to belly-dancing troupes. Late February.

Bolludagur. "Bun Day" is celebrated by eating cream puffs *(bollur)* in multiple varieties. In the morning children aim to catch their parents still in bed, and then beat them with colorfully decorated "bun wands" *(bolluvondur)*. Parents are then obligated to give their children one cream puff for each blow received. Monday before Ash Wednesday.

Sprengidagur. The name of this holiday translates to "bursting day" and is celebrated by eating salted meat and peas to the point of popping. Many restaurants participate. Day before Ash Wednesday.

Ash Wednesday (Öskudagur). Children dress in costume and traipse around town singing for candy. It's much like Halloween, and also a day for pranks. Seventh Wednesday before Easter.

March/April

Beer Day. This unofficial holiday marks the anniversary of Iceland's 1989 legalization of beer with an alcohol content above 2.2%. Guess how it's celebrated. March 1.

Easter Sunday. Easter holds special meaning in Iceland, as it marks the end of the long, dark winter. Most workers get a full 5 days off, from Holy Thursday to Easter Monday, and closures cause difficulties for tourists. Families gather and celebrate with smoked lamb and huge chocolate eggs. Easter weekend is especially lively in Ísafjörður, the cultural center of the Westfjords, with skiing competitions and the "I Never Went South" rock music festival (p. 201). March or April.

First Day of Summer. Summer starts early in the old Icelandic calendar. The end of long winter nights is celebrated with gift-giving, parades, street entertainment, and sporting events. The Thursday that falls within April 19 to April 25.

May

Reykjavík Arts Festival (www.artfest.is). For 16 days Reykjavík is swept up in this government-sponsored event. Many international artists and performers are included. Mid-May.

Rite of Spring Festival (www.riteof spring.is). Premiering in 2006 and sometimes overlapping with the Reykjavík Arts Festival, this privately run event focuses more exclusively on cutting-edge folk, jazz, and world music. Mid-May.

June

Seafarer's Day & Festival of the Sea. This holiday honors those who make their living by the sea, and is celebrated across the country with parades, cultural events, great seafood, and rowdy parties. Fishermen partake in rescue demonstrations, swimming and rowing races, and various strongman competitions. "Festival of the Sea" is the local celebration in Reykjavík, which may take place the following weekend. First weekend of June.

National Day. This public holiday marks Iceland's full independence from Denmark in 1944. The day starts off on a solemn and patriotic note, but by afternoon crowds have flocked to the streets to watch parades, traditional dancing, street performers, and theatrical entertainment. (One of the most meaningful gatherings is at Þingvellir National Park, where the Icelandic parliament first assembled in A.D. 930.) Each town celebrates in its own way, so check locally for details. June 17.

Summer Solstice (www.fi.is). On the longest day of the year, many Icelanders gather late at night to watch the sun dip below the horizon and scoop back up again shortly afterward. Formally organized events are rare, but visitors are usually welcome to join local celebrations. Each year Ferðafélag Íslands organizes an all-night climb up the volcano Hekla. June 21.

Viking Festival (www.fjorukrain.is). For 10 days, modern-day Viking hordes descend on Hafnarfjörður, a town neighboring Reykjavík, for traditional crafts, merrymaking in period costume, and staged battles with Christian forces. While some participants are Scandinavians, more are Britons and Germans: the Vikings' historic victims. The festival began in 1995 and is run by Hafnarfjörður's Viking Village hotel and restaurant. Between weekends it moves to Sauðárkrókur on the north coast. Mid-June.

Arctic Open (www.arcticopen.is). This 4-day championship golfing tournament in Akureyri, open to professionals and amateurs, continues into the morning hours under the midnight sun. Late June.

Akureyri Summer Arts Festival (www.akureyri.is). For 10 weeks in summer, Iceland's "northern capital" hosts an assortment of concerts and exhibitions in venues across town. Late June to August.

August

Verslunarmannahelgi (August Long Weekend or Bank Holiday Weekend). On this party weekend, Icelanders often leave town and camp out en masse. The most well-known destination is the Westman Islands, where locals join thousands of visitors at the campgrounds to hear live bands and gather round the bonfire into the morning hours. Plenty of events also take place in towns. First weekend in August.

Gay Pride (www.gaypride.is). The biggest Pride event in Iceland includes a parade, concerts, theater, and all-night parties. Second weekend in August.

Reykjavík Marathon and Culture Night (www.marathon.is). Surely the 3,500 participants in Reykjavík's annual marathon appreciate the purity of the air. Runners can choose between the full marathon, a half-marathon, a 10km (6 mile) run, or 7km (4 mile) and 3km (2 mile) "fun runs." The rest of the day and night are loaded with free concerts and cultural events, and once it's reasonably dark, a fireworks display kicks off. Third weekend in August.

Reykjavík Jazz Festival (www.jazz.is). Icelandic and international groups in a variety of styles play clubs and theaters across town. End of August/early September.

Reykjavík Dance Festival (www.dancefestival.is). Contemporary choreographers from around the world are invited to participate in this 4-day event. End of August/early September.

September

Annual Sheep and Horse Roundup (Réttir). See "The Big Round-Up," below. Early and late September.

Reykjavík International Film Festival (www.filmfest.is). This 10-day event includes film classics, premieres, retrospectives, seminars, and workshops. Late September or early October.

The Big Round-Up

Visitors in early September—especially experienced horseback riders—can discover beautiful and remote backcountry while participating in an age-old Icelandic farming ritual: the fall sheep round-up, or *réttir*. Hundreds of thousands of Icelandic sheep spend the summer grazing in highland pastures. Before winter sets in, local groups of farmers spend up to a week herding them home. Historically, this was a man's job, but women have increasingly joined in. Once the flocks are penned and sorted by their ear-marks, the farming communities let their hair down for singing, dancing, and drinking into the night. Traditionally many isolated villagers met their spouses during these events.

Most participants are experienced riders, but some accompany in 4WD vehicles or on foot; others just watch and join the party. Visitors are welcome to take part in some local round-ups, though don't expect nonstop excitement: The process could involve holding your position alone for hours in a cold rain.

Round-ups for free-roaming horses are in late September or early October, primarily in the north. Figure out which parts of the backcountry you'd like to visit, then contact local tourist information offices, travel agencies, and farm accommodations (www.farmholidays.is) for advice. Regional websites posting réttir information include www.northwest.is and www.north iceland.is. A lengthy but incomplete list of locations and dates is posted in August on www.bondi.is, website of the Farmers Association of Iceland (e-mail questions to Dr. Ólafur R. Dýrmundsson at ord@bondi.is).

October

Iceland Airwaves (www.icelandair waves.com). This 3-day showcase of Iceland's alternative/indie musical talent (with a few international bands thrown in) attracts more visitors to Iceland than any other event. Crowds are thick with notepad-wielding journalists and talent scouts; when the bands are through, top DJs spin until dawn. Icelandair sponsors Airwaves and arranges special packages from Europe and America. Mid-October.

December

Christmas season. In late December, Icelanders only get 4 or 5 hours of daylight, which could explain their enthusiasm for Christmas and its lights. Icelandic children count the 13 days leading up to the holiday with a group of "yuletide lads," all offspring of a grotesque troll named Grýla. (In traditional lore Grýla ate naughty children, but, in the 18th century, threatening them with Grýla was outlawed.) Each day from December 12 to December 24, a different lad descends from the mountains into human homes. Each lad is named for the mischief he gets into: Sausage Snatcher, Door Slammer, Bowl Licker, and so on. At bedtime children leave a shoe in the window, and wake up to find a small present from the nighttime visitor. From Christmas Day through January 6 they come in succession all over again.

New Year's Eve. Private use of fireworks is legal this one night only, and the entire citizenry sets the skies ablaze in celebration. (Reykjavík is a particularly chaotic sight.) Oceanside bonfires are another New Year's ritual. For a more refined experience in Reykjavík, try the trumpet and organ recital in Hallgrímskirkja.

5 Iceland in the Off Season

Tourists arrive en masse in June and disappear just as abruptly in early September, so Icelanders compare them to flocks of migrating birds. However, more and more visitors are coming in the off season, particularly for short vacations centered on Reykjavík. Nightlife and spas are major draws, and winter adventure travel—particularly backcountry skiing, glacier snowmobiling, and Jeep touring—is also catching on. With fewer tourists around, locals can be especially hospitable and welcoming. Prices are dramatically lower for airfares, accommodations, and car rentals, but don't expect price breaks from mid-December to mid-January.

Most museums outside Reykjavík shut down off season, while some Reykjavík cultural institutions—notably the Icelandic Opera, headquartered at the world's northernmost opera house—are only open off season. With fewer organized tours to choose from, visitors usually depend on rental cars to get around. Most major roads are plowed all year, including all of the Ring Road (Rte. 1). Winter driving conditions can be hazardous, however, and in the dead of winter, some villages can be completely cut off for days at a time. Most mountain roads and interior routes are impassable in the off season, except in specially adapted "Super Jeeps."

Icelandic winters are surprisingly moderate but have just 4 to 6 hours of daylight. Remember that late winter has more sunlight than early winter, with a corresponding increase in organized tours. From September through March, the night is dark enough to see the Aurora Borealis (aka "Northern Lights"), the startling electromagnetic phenomenon in which shafts and swirls of green (or sometimes orange or blue) light spread across the sky. Of course, depending on the weather, some off-season visitors may see only clouds. (See p. 14 for more on daylight hours and weather.)

The shoulder seasons—April to May and September to October—can be wonderful times to visit, though some destinations are inaccessible. A good general strategy is to shoot for the outlying weeks of the high season for each destination.

For a calendar of festivals and other annual events, see p. 15.

OFF-SEASON OUTDOOR ACTIVITIES

See chapter 3 for a thorough outline of outdoor activities, many of which can be enjoyed in the off season. Of particular interest are aerial tours, dog sledding, fishing, glacier tours, hiking, horseback riding, jeep tours, pools and spas, and skiing and ski touring. Icelanders even like to golf on snow-covered courses, using bright orange balls.

OFF-SEASON DESTINATIONS
REYKJAVÍK & NEARBY

Reykjavík remains equally vibrant year-round—after all, the weather has little bearing on its appeal. Cultural activities and nightlife show no signs of winter weariness, and Reykjavíkians still throng to their outdoor geothermal pools even if snow gathers in their hair. See the Calendar of Events (p. 15) for Reykjavík's many off-season festivals.

The capital is particularly lively and heartwarming during the Christmas season. Each weekend, starting in late November, the neighboring town of **Hafnarfjörður** hosts an elaborate **Christmas Village** with caroling choirs, trinket stalls, and costumed elves. On New Year's Eve, many visitors shuttle to Reykjavík just to take part in the Bacchanalian celebrations.

Outside of summer, day tours from the capital are less varied but hardly in short supply. The popular **Golden Circle** tour runs year-round, and two of its principal highlights—the **Strokkur geyser** and **Gullfoss waterfall**—are even more captivating in winter. Various companies also lead nightly **Northern Lights tours** in search of the Aurora Borealis. The **Blue Lagoon spa** in Reykjanes Peninsula is strange and magical in wintertime, with far fewer crowds.

OUTSIDE THE CAPITAL AREA

Compelling winter destinations outside Iceland's southwest corner are too numerous to list, but two regions deserve special mention: **West Iceland** and **Lake Mývatn–Krafla Caldera** in the north.

In the west, the wondrously varied scenery of **Snæfellsnes Peninsula** makes for a great road trip year-round, and **Hótel Búðir,** an idyllic getaway on the peninsula's south coast, is always open. **Ísafjörður,** the appealing **Westfjords** capital, is especially buzzing during its Easter Week music and ski festivals. Two marvelous country retreats in the Westfjords remain open all year: the **Heydalur Country Hotel,** along Ísafjarðardjúp Bay, and **Hótel Djúpavík** on the entrancing **Strandir Coast.**

Akureyri, Iceland's northern capital, is alive and kicking in the off season, with the country's best ski slope **Hlíðarfjall** close by. Many winter visitors fly to Akureyri, rent a car, and spend a couple of days surveying the myriad volcanic spectacles of **Mývatn** and **Krafla.** The geothermally heated lagoon of **Mývatn Nature Baths** remains open, and **Sel-Hótel Mývatn** arranges Jeep and snowmobile excursions, horseback riding, and go-cart joyrides on the lake. The cross-country skiing is fabulous from February onward, and, in April and May, the lake twitches with bird-watchers ushering in the tourist season.

6 Getting There

BY PLANE

Virtually all international arrivals come through **Keflavík International Airport** (KEF), about 50km (31 miles) from Reykjavík. Until recently only Icelandair and Iceland Express flew to Iceland, but additional airlines have opened up routes. Typical flight times are 3 hours from London or 5 hours from Boston. Peak season, with correspondingly higher fares, is June to August, plus the 2 weeks before Christmas and the 2 weeks after the New Year.

Icelandair (© **800/223-5500** U.S. and Canada; **0870/787-4020** in London; **0207/387-5711** in Glasgow; www.icelandair.com) flies to Keflavík from Boston, New York, Minneapolis, Orlando, Toronto, Halifax (Nova Scotia), London, Manchester, Glasgow, and several other European cities. Flights from North America are usually overnight, though from May to October daytime flights are available from New York and Boston a few times per week.

Icelandair does not have codeshare agreements with North American airlines, so you'll need other means of getting to an Icelandair gateway airport. However, Icelandair does "interline" with major U.S. and Canadian domestic air carriers, allowing passengers to travel from non-Icelandair gateways on "through-fare" tickets. With through-fare tickets, passengers are protected in case of delays or re-routings, and can check luggage to their final destinations.

Icelandair offers a good range of discount packages, combining airfare, hotels, and sometimes tours. Midweek flights are often significantly cheaper. Icelandair fares between the U.S. and Europe can include a free stopover for up to 7 days in

Iceland, pending availability. Icelandair's price schemes sometimes make a flight from the U.S. to London (with a free stopover in Reykjavík for up to 7 days) cheaper than a simple flight to Reykjavík.

If you have any flexibility with your travel dates, sign up for Icelandair's free "Lucky Fares" e-mail newsletter, which alerts you to special online-only fares. All fares, except for some special offers, are discounted for children under 12.

Join Icelandair's **frequent flier program,** called "Saga Club." Members earn extra miles by flying Air Iceland (Iceland's main domestic airline), upgrading to "Saga" class, or patronizing a few partner companies. U.S. Diners Club cardholders can exchange their award points for Saga Club miles, and Visa and MasterCard issue credit cards co-branded with Icelandair for earning Saga Club miles.

With average prices that are considerably lower than Icelandair's, **Iceland Express** (© 0870/240-5600 in the U.K.; 550-0600 in Iceland; www.icelandexpress.com) connects Reykjavík with London Stansted as well as 13 European countries in summer and six in winter. Iceland Express also has e-mail alerts for special offers; sign up at the website. Kids under 12 get 50% off Iceland Express flights.

Currently the cheapest flights from London to Iceland are on **British Airways** (© 800/247-9297 from North America; 0870-850-9850 from the U.K.; 1300-767-177 from Australia; 09-966-9777 from New Zealand; www.ba.com), which flies to Reykjavík from London

Gatwick. Prices, however, vary significantly by day.

SAS Scandinavian Airlines (© 0208/990-7159 from the U.K.; www.flysas.com) flies to Reykjavík from Oslo and Stockholm; prices from Stockholm consistently beat Icelandair.

Atlantic Airways (© 298/341010; www.atlanticairways.com) connects the Faeroe Islands to Europe and Iceland, and is useful to those visiting the Faeroes on their way to or from Iceland.

ARRIVING AT KEFLAVIK INTERNATIONAL AIRPORT

Keflavík International Airport (airport code KEF; © 425-0680; www.airport.is) is sometimes called "Leifur Eiríksson Air Terminal" or "Reykjavik Airport," even though Reykjavík has a small, domestic airport in the city proper. Extensive renovations to Keflavík International were completed in 2007, and the airport sees over two million passengers each year. Arriving passengers must go through another **security** check before clearing customs. For a list of what you can import to Iceland, see "Customs," p. 52.

For information on **ATMs** and money exchange, see "Money & Costs," p, 23. The airport has a **tourist information** desk with brochures galore, but the staffperson cannot make hotel or tour reservations for you. (If you're staying in Reykjavík, see "Visitor Information" in chapter 5 for booking agencies.) The airport has several **car rental** desks; see "Getting Around Iceland," p. 37.

Iceland *and* Greenland?

If you've ever wanted to explore Greenland, your trip to Iceland could be an ideal opportunity. Iceland is Greenland's closest access point by plane, and you can even visit on a day tour. **Air Iceland (570-3030;** www.airiceland.is) flies year-round from Reykjavík to Greenland's east coast, and twice a week in summer to south Greenland. Air Iceland and **Eagle Air (562-4200;** www.eagleair.is) both offer Greenland day tours. Two-night packages from Reykjavík are available through **Icelandair.**

Tip: Alcohol prices in the airport may seem high, but they're far lower than elsewhere in Iceland; so consider buying duty-free before you leave the airport. Icelandair prohibits alcohol from being transported in carry-on luggage, so if you're taking this airline and want to buy duty-free, wait until Keflavík. Customs limits you to 1 liter of wine or 6 liters of beer, plus 1 liter of spirits. If you're not carrying spirits or beer, then you can bring in 2.5 liters of wine.

Note: For tips on traveling between the airport and Reykjavík, see "Orientation," in chapter 5.

BY BOAT

The *Norröna,* a Faeroese **car ferry** operated by **Smyril Line** (℃ 570-8600; www.smyril-line.com), connects Iceland to the U.K., Norway, Denmark, and the Faeroe Islands. The ferry sails between April and early September from either Bergen (Norway) or Hanstholm (Denmark) to Seyðisfjörður in east Iceland. Along the way it stops at Lerwick (Shetland Islands) and Tórshavn (Faeroe Islands). From mid-June through August, the ferry also stops at Scrabster (Scotland). In April, May, early June, or September, car travelers coming from the U.K. can still connect to the *Norröna* by taking a different car ferry to Lerwick or Tórshavn and connecting there. **P&O Scottish Ferry** (℃ 0129/525-3455; www.poscottishferries.com) or **North Link** (℃ 0845/600-0449; www.northlinkferries.co.uk) sail from Aberdeen or Kirkwall (both Scotland) to Lerwick.

The *Norröna* arrives in Iceland once per week. The ferry makes a 2- or 3-night stopover in the Faeroe Islands in both directions. Passengers have three sleeping options: their cars, sleeping-bag accommodation in rather primitive rooms for nine persons with one bathroom, and cabins. In summer, round-trip tickets from Scotland to Iceland for two passengers with one car

in sleeping-bag accommodation could be anywhere from $500/£250 to $3,040/£1,520. Package deals are advised, especially in summer, though you usually get a windowless room. Some packages also cover tours and accommodation on land in the Faeroes and Iceland. The ferry is best for travelers who want to bring their own vehicle; otherwise, it does not generally present any savings over flying.

From February to September, the cargo carrier **Eimskip** takes up to three passengers on its *Dettifoss* and *Goðafoss* ships, which travel a weekly "northern route" between Reykjavík, Tórshavn, Rotterdam, Hamburg, Gothenburg, Fredriksstad, and Aarhus. Each carrier has one double cabin and two singles, and passengers receive full board. Depending on your point of origin and cabin type, prices range from 97,125kr–144,000kr ($1,554–$2,304/£777–£1,152) for a double cabin one way. Bringing a car costs around $700/£350 extra. Book though **Iceland Total** (℃ 585-4300 in Iceland; www.icelandtotal.com).

Anyone bringing a vehicle to Iceland must bring registration, proof of insurance, and a valid drivers' license. A temporary import permit for the car, valid for 1 month, is issued at the port of entry and can be extended. See "Getting Around Iceland," later in this chapter, for information on driving in Iceland.

CRUISES

Iceland is fast becoming a major cruise ship destination; the number of cruise ship visitors has expanded four-fold in the last 10 years. Iceland is often a featured stopover on transatlantic routes. **Hurtigruten** (from the U.K. ℃ 020/8846-2666; from the U.S. ℃ 800/323-7436; www.hurtigruten.com) is one place to check, and **Princess Cruises** (℃ 800/774-6237 in North America; www.princess.com) runs two cruises from London's Southampton port with stops in Iceland. **Voyages of Discovery** (from the U.S. $\textcircled{C}$ **866/ 623-2689;** from the U.K. $\textcircled{C}$ **0144/ 446-2150;** from Australia $\textcircled{C}$ **02/ 9955-8599;** www.voyagesofdiscovery. com) includes Iceland in several cruises. **Iceland Experience** ($\textcircled{C}$ **800/661-3830** in North America; www.iceland-experience. com) lists three North Atlantic cruises that

include Iceland. **Elderhostel** ($\textcircled{C}$ **800/ 454-5768;** www.elderhostel.org), a nonprofit company organizing trips for travelers age 55 and up, has an excellent Arctic cruise. See "Special-Interest Trips," p. 36, for an educational cruise within Icelandic waters. The website **www.cruiseiceland. com** has a useful page of links to most cruise companies that make Iceland stops.

7 Money & Costs

Iceland is a wealthy nation that relies heavily on imports; but at $180/£90 a night for "budget hotels," $15/£7.50 for burgers, and $12/£6 for a beer, Iceland's prices may come as a shock. High prices affect locals as well: special charter flights to Europe and the U.S. are arranged just for shopping expeditions. Remember that visitors are entitled to a refund on the value-added tax (VAT, or sales tax) for purchases of eligible goods—see p. 123 for more information. See "Tips on Accommodations," later in this chapter, for more money-saving advice.

CURRENCY

Iceland's monetary unit is the **krona** (sometimes abbreviated as "ISK," but written as "kr" in this book), plural **kronur.** Coins come in 1, 10, 50, and 100 kronur denominations; bank notes are in denominations of 500kr ($8/£4), 1,000kr ($16/£8), 2,000kr ($32/£16), and 5,000kr ($80/£40). Prices listed in this book reflect **exchange rates** at press time: 62.5kr to the dollar and 125kr to the British pound. Dollars, pounds, and euros are easily exchanged for kronur. For current conversion rates, try **www.xe.com/ucc.**

ATMS/CURRENCY EXCHANGE

You could spend a lot of time and effort obtaining Icelandic currency in advance of arrival, but ATMs are the most practical and reliable way to get cash at fair exchange rates. Upon arrival at Keflavík International Airport, you'll easily find ATMs and the currency exchange desk, both run by **Landsbanki Íslands,** which has fair exchange rates. *Tip:* Avoid exchanging money at hotels, which tend to have high transaction fees.

ATMs are found in most villages around Iceland, though not all ATMs are accessible 24 hours. Icelandic ATMs generally accept all major debit, credit, and cash-only cards. **Cirrus** ($\textcircled{C}$ **800/424-7787;** www.master card.com) and **PLUS** ($\textcircled{C}$ **800/843-7587;** www.visa.com) cards are almost universally accepted in Icelandic ATMs .

CREDIT & DEBIT CARDS

Credit cards are safe, convenient, and generally offer good exchange rates. Note, however, that many banks now assess a 1% to 3% "foreign transaction fee" on all charges you incur abroad.

In Iceland you'll need a PIN to withdraw cash advances on your credit card. You will *not* need a PIN for most credit card purchases, but occasions may arise (particularly at automated gas pumps). If you've forgotten your PIN, call the number on the back of your card and ask that it be provided to you.

Icelanders love credit and debit cards, and will commonly whip one out just to buy an ice cream cone. Most shops and tourist establishments accept credit cards; you can even charge a taxi ride. Visa and MasterCard are the most widely accepted, though American Express and Diner's Club are useful as well. Electron, Maestro, and EDC debit cards are increasingly accepted at retail stores.

TRAVELER'S CHECKS

These days, traveler's checks are less necessary because most cities have 24-hour ATMs. However, traveler's checks are still widely accepted in Iceland.

8 Travel Insurance

The cost of travel insurance varies, but expect to pay between 5% and 8% of the vacation itself. You can get quotes from more than a dozen companies through **InsureMyTrip.com**.

U.K. citizens may find an annual travel insurance policy is cheaper. **www.moneysupermarket.com** compares prices across a wide range of providers for single- and multi-trip policies.

Most big travel agents offer their own insurance and will probably try to sell you their package when you book a holiday. Britain's **Consumers' Association** recommends that you insist on seeing the policy and reading the fine print before buying travel insurance. **The Association of British Insurers** (© 020/7600-3333; www.abi.org.uk) gives advice by phone and publishes *Holiday Insurance*, a free guide to policy provisions and prices. You might also shop around for better deals: Try **Columbus Direct** (© 0870/033-9988; www.columbusdirect.net).

TRIP-CANCELLATION INSURANCE

Trip-cancellation insurance will help retrieve your money if you have to back out of a trip or depart early, or if your travel supplier goes bankrupt. Trip cancellation traditionally covers such events as sickness, natural disasters, and State Department advisories. With **expanded hurricane coverage** and **"any-reason"** cancellation coverage, you'll be refunded a substantial portion of your prepaid trip cost. **Travel-Safe** (© 888/885-7233; www.travelsafe.com) offers both types of coverage. **Expedia.com** also offers any-reason cancellation coverage for some packages.

For details, contact one of the following recommended insurers: **Access America** (© 866/807-3982; www.accessamerica.com); **Travel Guard International** (© 800/826-4919; www.travelguard.com); **Travel Insured International** (© 800/243-3174; www.travelinsured.com); and **Travelex Insurance Services** (© 888/457-4602; www.travelex-insurance.com).

MEDICAL INSURANCE

For travel overseas, most U.S. health plans do not provide coverage, and the ones that do often reimburse you only after you return home.

Check the fine print to make sure coverage extends to any adventure activities you have planned for Iceland, such as whitewater rafting, horseback riding, or winter sports. If you require additional medical insurance, try **MEDEX Assistance** (© 410/453-6300; www.medexassist.com) or **Travel Assistance International** (© 800/821-2828; www.travelassistance.com).

Canadians should check with their provincial health plan offices or call **Health Canada** (© 866/225-0709; www.hc-sc.gc.ca).

LOST-LUGGAGE INSURANCE

On international flights (including U.S. legs of them), baggage coverage is limited to approximately $9.07 per pound, up to about $635 per checked bag. If you plan to check items more valuable than what's covered by the standard liability, see if your homeowner's policy covers your valuables, get baggage insurance as part of your comprehensive travel-insurance package, or buy Travel Guard's "BagTrak" product.

9 Health & Safety

STAYING HEALTHY

Icelanders are blessed with a very healthy environment. The use of geothermal and hydroelectric power has made pollution almost negligible. Some say Iceland has the purest tap water in the world, and even surface water is generally potable. The incidence of insect, water, or food-borne infection is extremely low. In 2007, a smoking ban went into effect in bars, restaurants, accommodations, and cafes.

Iceland's extreme variations in daylight hours may wreak havoc with your body clock, so bring an eye mask to help you sleep in summer. In the short days of winter, Icelanders combat depression through the traditional practice of downing a shot of cod liver oil each morning; the oil is rich in Vitamin D, generated by sunlight on the skin.

The sun can be stronger than many visitors suspect at such a northerly latitude. Bring sunblock and lip balm to protect your skin, and sunglasses to protect your eyes from the glare.

In spring and summer you may want to bring insect repellent with DEET to fend off the midges that can be an annoyance in certain interior regions. Iceland has a few bees and wasps, so anyone with an Apoidea allergy should bring a portable remedy. Bring seasick pills if you plan on any boating activities, long ferry rides, or bumpy road trips.

OUTDOOR SAFETY

Icelanders visiting the U.S. are amused by all the warning signs and guardrails. If Iceland tried to match these precautions, it would be quickly bankrupted. Always use care in Iceland's untamed outdoors. Thoroughly research the potential hazards of any journey, and talk to someone with local knowledge before setting out. Bring a first-aid kit to any remote destination.

Be prepared for Iceland's notoriously abrupt shifts in weather. For forecasts,

check with the **Icelandic Meteorological Office** (© **902-0600;** www.vedur.is). Keep in mind that the temperature usually drops about 1° for every 100m (328 ft.) of elevation. Even near the coastline in summer, night temperatures can drop below freezing. Always carry warm and waterproof clothing and footwear, even in summer.

Bring a map and compass for longer walks, or ideally, a GPS unit. A cell phone is also useful for emergencies, though coverage is unlikely in remote areas (see "Staying Connected," below).

ROCKS & FOOTING

Rocks and rock faces in Iceland are often loose and crumbly. Hiking shoes with good ankle support are advised. Be careful not to loosen rocks that could tumble onto someone below you, and be aware of potential rockfalls or avalanches. Take special care to have solid footing on mountaintops and clifftops, where winds are strongest.

GEOTHERMAL AREAS & VOLCANOES

In geothermal hotspots, most tourists know better than to stick their fingers in boiling mud pots, but other dangers are not so obvious. Sometimes unwary visitors step right through a thin crust of earth into boiling mud below. Lighter colored soil is usually the most dangerous. Stick to paths and boardwalks when provided, and always seek advice before approaching active volcanoes.

GLACIERS

Even road-trippers who seldom stray from their cars are likely to encounter a glacier face-to-face. Do not set off on a glacier without some experience or advice from a local expert. Organized trips with professional guides are the safest route. Glaciers can collapse without warning, and even a smooth surface can disguise hidden, deadly crevasses. If you walk onto a glacier despite the danger, follow other footprints or snowmobile tracks. Generally, the best time for glacier traverses is from mid-February to mid-July, with optimal conditions between March and May.

Do not venture into ice caves; even experienced guides seldom lead groups there. Also beware of quicksand that can form from meltoff at the glacier's edge.

EMERGENCY SHELTERS

The **Icelandic Association for Search and Rescue** (© 570-5900; www.icesar.com) maintains several bright orange emergency shelters in remote interior and coastline locations, and along some roads, often in high mountain passes. The shelters are identified on most maps and are stocked with food, fuel, and blankets. These are to be used *in emergencies only*. If you are forced to use something, make sure to sign for it so it can be replaced.

SEARCH & RESCUE

Locals constantly encourage visitors to inform someone before venturing into risky areas alone. For most trips you can simply leave your name and itinerary with a local tourist information office or park warden. For more risky ventures, you should register at the Reykjavík office of the **Icelandic Association for Search and Rescue,** Skógarhlíð 14, Reykjavík (© 570-5900; www.icesar.com); local and online registration is in the works.

GENERAL AVAILABILITY OF HEALTH CARE

Iceland has very high-quality medical care and more doctors per capita than any other country on earth. Virtually all doctors speak English reasonably well. Reykjavík and larger towns have hospitals. Most smaller towns have at least one doctor and one pharmacy *(apótek);* if you need a doctor, ask at any local pharmacy or business. Most pharmacies are open

9am to 6pm, and over-the-counter medicines are accessible, if expensive. Iceland's barren interior is another story entirely: you could be hours from even the most rudimentary form of care.

WHAT TO DO IF YOU GET SICK AWAY FROM HOME

For emergencies in Iceland, dial © **112.**

If you get sick in Iceland, you can usually just call or show up at the nearest hospital or health center. For medical assistance in the Reykjavík area, see "Fast Facts" in chapter 5.

Even insured U.S. citizens may have to pay all medical costs upfront and be reimbursed later. Before leaving home, find out what medical services your health insurance covers. To protect yourself, consider buying medical travel insurance (see "Medical Insurance," under "Travel Insurance," above).

U.K. and E.U. citizens will need a **European Health Insurance Card (EHIC)** available at www.ehic.org.uk to receive free or reduced-costs health benefits during a visit to Iceland. The European Health Insurance Card replaces the E111 form, which is no longer valid. For advice, ask at your local post office or see www.dh.gov.uk/travellers.

CRIME

Crime isn't nonexistent, but it's not much of a problem in Iceland. Outside Reykjavík, Icelanders rarely lock their doors. The country has fewer than 1,000 police officers, most of them unarmed, and the total prison population is under 200.

Simply use the same precautions you would anyplace in the world. Don't carry a purse that doesn't close. Don't openly rifle through wads of cash in the middle of a busy street. Carry your wallet in a front pocket to prevent pickpocketing. Don't carry all your money and credit cards in the same place. Keep car doors locked, and do not leave valuables exposed (use a hotel safe when possible).

10 Specialized Travel Resources

TRAVELERS WITH DISABILITIES

Iceland has more options and resources for travelers with disabilities than ever before, but you must call well in advance to secure your plans. Reykjavík and Akureyri are fairly accommodating, and new public buildings have to meet a strict code for wheelchair access. But, in the countryside, accessible facilities are few and far between, and tours often involve traversing long distances over rough ground or unpaved paths. (One bright spot is Iceland's top tourist attraction, **The Blue Lagoon** (p. 150), which has good wheelchair access.)

Always make specific inquiries at hotels before booking. The website **www.whenwetravel.com** lists wheelchair-accessible hotels in Reykjavík. All farms in the **Icelandic Farm Holidays** network (p. 29) have been evaluated for accessibility; click the "Facilities for Disabled" link at www.farmholidays.is, or call ✆ **570-2700**.

Most museums and other tourist attractions offer reduced admission prices for travelers with disabilities. Air Iceland offers reduced rates, as does Smyril Line, the ferry connecting Iceland to Europe.

TRANSPORTATION

All **airlines** flying to and from Iceland can accommodate travelers with disabilities, and Air Iceland, the main domestic airline, generally has no trouble with wheelchairs.

Buses in Reykjavík are all wheelchair-accessible, but buses elsewhere usually don't have lifts or ramps. The largest tour operators each have a few wheelchair-accessible buses.

The **car ferries** *Baldur* (which connects Snæfellsnes Peninsula to the Westfjords), *Herjólfur* (which connects the Westman Islands to the mainland), and *Norröna* (which connects Europe to

Seyðisfjörður in east Iceland) are all wheelchair accessible.

Hertz Car Rental (✆ **522-4400; www.hertz.is**) offers a specially fitted car for wheelchair users, but does not have cars with hand controls.

ORGANIZED TOURS

The tour company **Hópferðatþjónusta Reykjavíkur** (Brunastaðir 3; ✆ **587-8030;** hrtravel@simnet.is) organizes trips for the travelers with disabilities in specially designed coaches.

Nordic Visitor (Austurstræti 17, Reykjavík; ✆ **511-2442;** www.icelandvisitor.com) is a travel agency with experience customizing tours for travelers with disabilities.

Some travel agencies outside Iceland can customize Iceland tours and itineraries for travelers with disabilities. Among them are **Flying Wheels Travel** (✆ **507/451-5005;** www.flyingwheelstravel.com) and **Accessible Journeys** (✆ **800/846-4537** or 610/521-0339; www.disabilitytravel.com).

HELPFUL ORGANIZATIONS

Sjálfsbjörg, Hátun 12, Reykjavík (✆ **550-0300;** www.sjalfsbjorg.is; Mon–Fri 8am–4:15pm), which literally means "self-help," is Iceland's association for travelers with disabilities, with 17 chapters throughout the country. This organization can answer questions or offer advice on your itinerary. If you call and the recorded message comes on, press "2" to reach an agent. While several hotels have wheelchair-accessible rooms, Sjálfsbjörg also rents out two fully accessible apartments and three guest rooms in their own building.

Organizations that offer a vast range of resources and assistance to travelers with disabilities include **MossRehab** (✆ **800/CALL-MOSS;** www.mossresourcenet.org); the **American Foundation for the Blind (AFB)** (✆ **800/232-5463;**

www.afb.org); and **SATH (Society for Accessible Travel & Hospitality)** (*©* 212/447-7284; www.sath.org). **AirAmbulanceCard.com** is now partnered with SATH and allows you to preselect top-notch hospitals in case of an emergency.

Access-Able Travel Source (*©* 303/232-2979; www.access-able.com) offers a worldwide database of travel agents with experience in accessible travel, plus links to resources.

British travelers should contact **Holiday Care** (*©* 0845-124-9971 in the U.K.; www.holidaycare.org.uk) to access a wide range of travel information and resources for travelers with disabilities and elderly people.

GAY & LESBIAN TRAVELERS

Iceland was much more homophobic in 1978, when the country's first gay organization was founded in Reykjavík. The small population and close-knit family networks made it difficult for gays and lesbians to escape the disapproval of older generations. Today gay marriages are legal, several prominent cultural figures are openly gay, and gay and lesbian couples walk freely through the streets of Reykjavík. Outside the capital there isn't any gay scene to speak of, but the worst any gay couple is likely to encounter is a frown.

The main gay and lesbian organization in Iceland is **Samtökin '78,** Laugavegur 3, 4th floor, Reykjavík (*©* 552-7878; www.samtokin78.is), which is open Monday to Friday from 1 to 5pm and holds open-house social gatherings at their **Rainbow Cafe** Mondays and Thursdays 8 to 11:30pm and Saturdays 9pm to 1am. Iceland's main lesbian organization is **Konur með Konum** (www.kmk.is), which means "Women with Women." The website posts events and other useful information.

Félag STK Stúdenta (FSS), Pósthússtræti 3-5, Reykjavík (*©* 411-5590; http://gay.mis.is), the gay and lesbian student organization at the University of Iceland, welcomes e-mails from young visitors.

www.gayice.is has the best online schedule of gay events. The **Reykjavík Gay Pride Festival** (www.gaypride.is) usually takes place the first week of August. For the gay and lesbian scene in Reykjavík, see "Nightlife," in chapter 5.

In the award-winning **documentary film** *Hrein og Bein* (Straight Out), nine gay Icelandic youths tell their coming-out stories.

The following travel guide is also available: *GetawayGay Iceland* (Queer & There Publishing).

ORGANIZED TOURS

Alyson Adventures (*©* 800/825-9766; www.alysonadventures.com), an adventure travel agency based in Key West, FL, has two Iceland trips, one with mountain biking and one with multiple outdoor activities.

Zoom Vacations (*©* 866/966-6822; www.zoomvacations.com) has a 6-night tour based in Reykjavík, with daytime bike excursions.

Great Canadian Travel Company (*©* 800/661-3830; www.iceland-experience.com) has a "gay party weekend tour" from Toronto only.

SENIOR TRAVEL

Iceland is often thought of as a travel destination for rugged outdoorsy types. Seniors who fit this description and those who don't will have no trouble finding plenty of adventure in the great outdoors. Age simply shouldn't factor into whether Iceland is the right destination, and senior tourists are anything but a rare sight throughout the country. Chapter 3 lays out a wide range of outdoor activities for all tastes and ability levels.

When deciding whether to rent a car, though, consider that driving in Iceland is hazardous and requires very good reflexes, coordination, and vigilance (see

"Getting Around (By Car)," below). Unless you are fully confident in your driving abilities, an organized tour is the safer bet.

Senior discounts are usually available at museums and other tourist attractions. Note that the retirement age for Icelanders is 67. Travelers age 65 or 66 are not normally entitled to discounts, though gatekeepers at various attractions may not be inclined to argue.

Many reliable agencies and organizations target the 50-plus market. **Elderhostel** (℗ **800/454-5768;** www. elderhostel.org), a not-for-profit company, arranges worldwide study and adventure programs for those age 55 and over, with a few "intergenerational" trips. Elderhostel has eight first-rate tours to Iceland, from 9 to 35 days long. **ElderTreks** (℗ **800/741-7956** or 416/558-5000 outside North America; www.eldertreks.com) offers an 11-day small-group Iceland tour, restricted to travelers 50 and older, for around $5,000/£2,500.

Members of **AARP,** 601 E St. NW, Washington, DC 20049 (℗ **888/ 687-2277;** www.aarp.org), get discounts on hotels, airfares, and car rentals. AARP and Travelocity have teamed up to create **AARP Passport** (www.travelocity.com/ AARP/home), which can find discounted air/hotel packages in Iceland online for AARP members.

TRAVELING WITH CHILDREN

Iceland is a wondrous and magical place no child will ever forget. Most tour companies welcome children (with the exception of the most rigorous trips, of course) and charge 50% less for children under 12. Discounts are usually available for transportation and tourist attractions, and sometimes for accommodations as well. **Air Iceland,** the main domestic airline, offers 50% off for children ages 2 to 11 when tickets are booked over the phone; even greater discounts may be available online.

A widespread Icelandic custom is for hotels, guesthouses, and farm accommodations to offer **"family rooms"** sleeping three to five people, sometimes with cooking facilities. Even youth hostels commonly have family rooms. Often an accommodation has only one or two such rooms; the only way to be sure is to ask. In the **Fosshótel** chain (℗ **562-4000;** www.fosshotel.is), one child under 12 stays free per room (Fosshótel's prices generally aren't cheap, however). The recommended **Icelandic Farm Holidays** network of farm accommodations (℗ **570-2700;** www.farmholidays.is) is usually cheaper than hotels and offers children a glimpse of Icelandic country life.

See chapter 3 for a full array of outdoor activities and adventures your children can enjoy. Whale-watching is an obvious choice. Horseback riding is great even for totally inexperienced children, since Icelandic horses are small, even-tempered, and manageable. Horse farms are spread all over the country, so a hired ride is usually within easy reach. Bird-watching may seem like the last thing your child would be interested in, but sidling up to a remote cliff edge and gazing down at the crashing surf, while puffins perch close by and other birds glide upward in the wind currents, is quite a thrill for anyone. Virtually every village in Iceland has a geothermally heated swimming pool, many with water slides, toys, and games for children. *Remember:* Iceland cannot possibly install guard ropes and warning signs at every location that poses danger to children, so mind them at all times.

For activities in or near Reykjavík, see "Reykjavík with Kids," p. 114.

Iceland is a safe and personal enough country that parents may feel comfortable leaving their children with local babysitters. You can always ask the staff at your accommodation to recommend someone.

Family Travel Forum (www.family travelforum.com), a comprehensive site, offers customized trip planning and has plentiful information on Iceland. The recommended book *Frommer's 500 Places to Take Your Kids Before They Grow Up* includes a few Iceland locales. To locate accommodations, restaurants, and attractions that are particularly kid friendly, look for the **Kids** icon throughout this guide.

STUDENT TRAVEL

Iceland is tough for students on a tight budget. Youth hostels and "sleeping-bag accommodation" at guesthouses and farms can be lifesavers; see "Tips on Accommodations," later in this chapter. The backpackers' website **travellers-point.com** offers a number of private rooms in Iceland for as little as $50/£25 per night.

For travelers age 12 to 26, the **"Youth Restricted Fare" on Air Iceland** offers big savings if you're willing to fly standby and take your chances on availability. Multi-trip **bus passes** from **TREX** (© 587-6000; www.trex.is) also have student discounts.

The **International Student Travel Confederation (ISTC)** website (www. istc.org) offers the **International Student Identity Card (ISIC)** and lists companies, attractions, and accommodations in Iceland that offer student discounts. The card, which also provides students with basic health and life insurance and a 24-hour helpline, is valid for a maximum of 18 months. You can apply for the card online or in person at **STA Travel** (© 800/781-4040 in North America; www.statravel.com); check the web to locate STA Travel offices worldwide. If you're no longer a student but still under 26, STA's **International Youth Travel Card (IYTC)** entitles you to some discounts. Travel CUTS (© 800/592-2887; www.travelcuts.com) offers similar services for both Canadians and U.S.

residents. Irish students may prefer to turn to **USIT** (© 01/602-1904; www. usit.ie), an Ireland-based specialist in student, youth, and independent travel.

SOLO TRAVELERS

With so many excellent group adventure tours to choose from, Iceland is a great place to fly solo. Even those normally allergic to organized tours find the Icelandic experience far more personal and less tame than the usual. (See chapter 3 for a full range of outdoor activities and tours.)

Single travelers can avoid paying a "single supplement" by rooming with other solo travelers or finding a roommate before they go. **Travel Buddies Singles Travel Club** (© 800/998-9099; www. travelbuddiesworldwide.com), based in Canada, runs small, intimate, single-friendly group trips and will match you with a roommate free of charge; an Iceland trip is usually offered. **TravelChums** (© 212/787-2621; www.travelchums. com) is a respected Internet-only travel-companion matching service.

Rental cars give you unmatched freedom and flexibility as a traveler in Iceland, and solo travelers may want to find car mates to share the costs. One place to start is the bulletin board at the Reykjavík City Hostel (p. 97). **Samferða** (www. samferda.net), a useful Icelandic **carpooling website.**

VEGETARIAN TRAVEL

Icelandic diets are meat-heavy, but fresh vegetables have become more widely available in recent years, partly because of local production in geothermally heated greenhouses. Pasta dishes are common on menus. The few vegetarian restaurants and health-food stores in the country are concentrated in Reykjavík and Akureyri.

VegDining.com and **Happy Cow's Vegetarian Guide** (www.happycow.net) are good resources for Iceland's vegetarian dining options.

11 Sustainable Tourism/Ecotourism

Each time you take a flight or drive a car, CO_2 is released into the atmosphere. You can help neutralize the damage by purchasing "carbon offsets," from **Carbonfund.org** (www.carbonfund.org) and **TerraPass** (www.terrapass.org) in the U.S., and from **Climate Care** (www.climatecare.org) in the U.K. Iceland has its reputable **Iceland Carbon Fund** (Kolviður; www.kolvidur.is); the website helps calculate your damages and choose a tree-planting project or other remedy.

Once in Iceland you can base your activities on hiking, biking, horseback riding, or other activities that do not consume fossil fuels. Several Icelandic companies have earned certification from **Blue Flag** (www.blueflag.org), a Danish organization that certifies beaches, marinas, whale-watching tours, and other businesses for sustainable oceanside development.

Nordic Swan, located in Stockholm (© **08/5555-2400;** www.svanen.nu/eng/), certifies accommodations for adhering to strict environmental practices. The only certified Icelandic accommodations are the Reykjavík City Hostel (p. 97) and Eldhestar (p. 164).

Green Globe (www.greenglobe21.com) is another important eco-certification label. Icelandic recipients include **Íshestar,** a horseback riding tour company (p. 122); **Whale Watching Reykjavík** (p. 120); and *every* community on the Snæfellsnes Peninsula (p. 172). The only Icelandic accommodations to receive full Green Globe certifications are **Hotel Hellnar** (p. 182) on the Snæfellsnes Peninsula, and the **Country Hotel Anna** (p. 305) in south Iceland.

The village of **Suðureyri** in the Westfjords has set an intriguing precedent by basing their entire economy on environmentally sustainable principles. Visitors can participate in local fishing life; see p. 196 for details.

The **Association of Independent Tour Operators (AITO)** (www.aito.co.uk) is a group of specialist operators leading the field in making holidays sustainable; plenty of Icelandic tour operators are listed.

Environmental issues often come up in conversation with Icelanders, so you may want to read up on the hot-button topics. Iceland has resumed whaling and the subject often provokes emotional responses (p. 262). For information about the ethics of whaling, visit the **Whale and Dolphin Conservation Society** (www.wdcs.org). The most heated political debate in Iceland's recent past concerned Kárahnjúkar (p. 338), a dam built in the eastern highlands to provide power for an aluminum smelter in the Eastfjords.

The website **www.savingiceland.org** has a pronounced radical slant but contains links to informative articles on environmental issues facing Iceland.

12 Staying Connected

TELEPHONES

Calls to Iceland from overseas require the **country code prefix,** which is **354.** All phone numbers within Iceland are seven digits. Numbers beginning with 6 and 8 are reserved for mobile phones. No calls are "long distance" within Iceland, and you don't need to dial the prefix.

To call Iceland: Dial the international access code (011 from the U.S.; 00 from the U.K., Ireland, or New Zealand; or 0011 from Australia), then 354 and the seven-digit number.

To make international calls from Iceland: Dial 00, then the country code (U.S. or Canada 1, U.K. 44, Ireland 353, Australia 61, New Zealand 64), then the

Frommers.com: The Complete Travel Resource

It should go without saying, but we highly recommend **Frommers.com,** voted Best Travel Site by *PC Magazine.* We think you'll find our expert advice and tips; independent reviews of hotels, restaurants, attractions, and preferred shopping and nightlife venues; vacation giveaways; and an online booking tool indispensable before, during, and after your travels. We publish the complete contents of over 128 travel guides in our **Destinations** section covering nearly 4,000 places worldwide to help you plan your trip. Each weekday, we publish original articles reporting on **Deals and News** via our free **Frommers.com Newsletter** to help you save time and money and travel smarter. We're betting you'll find our new **Events** listings (http://events. frommers.com) an invaluable resource; it's an up-to-the-minute roster of what's happening in cities everywhere—including concerts, festivals, lectures, and more. We've also added weekly **podcasts, interactive maps,** and hundreds of new images across the site. Check out our **Travel Talk** area featuring **Message Boards** where you can join in conversations with thousands of fellow Frommer's travelers and post your trip report once you return.

area code and number. Rates do not vary by time of day.

For directory assistance from within Iceland: For numbers inside Iceland, dial ℂ **118;** to find numbers in all other countries, **dial ℂ 114. For operator assistance within Iceland:** Dial ℂ **115. Icelandic phone books** are found beside public phones and list residents by their first name and profession.

An **online Icelandic telephone directory** can be found at **www.simaskra.is.** The site is only in Icelandic, but is still easy to use. Simply enter the name of the person or business in the search box and hit *leita* (find). If your keyboard isn't equipped for Icelandic letters, click *"Íslenskir stafir"* to access a row of special characters.

Toll-free numbers: Icelandic numbers beginning with 800 are toll free, but calling a 1-800 number in the U.S. counts as an overseas call.

Collect calls: For calls to the **United States,** call ℂ **533-5010.** For **Canada,** dial ℂ **800-9010.**

Long-distance Access Numbers: AT&T/Cingular: ℂ **800/2225-5288; MCI:** ℂ **800-9002; Sprint:** ℂ **800-9003.**

Public phones: Coin- and card-operated public phones can be hard to find, but post offices are a good bet. Using a public phone for local calls is usually cheaper than calling from a hotel. Charges for calls within Iceland vary according to time of day. Phone cards are easily found at post offices, gas stations, and markets. The smallest denomination is 500kr ($8/£4). Increasingly, public phones also accept credit cards.

International calling cards are widely available at gas stations and convenience stores across Iceland. These cards usually provide better rates than calls made from hotels or directly from public phones.

Rechargeable online phone cards: Ekit (www.ekit.com) offers rechargeable phone cards with good rates and a toll-free access number in Iceland (ℂ **800-8700**). Rates to the U.S. are currently 20¢ per minute, plus a 59¢ service charge per successful call. Rates to the U.K. are 9p to

45p per minute depending where you call, or 67p to a cellphone, plus a 29p service fee per successful call.

CELLPHONES (MOBILE PHONES)

Iceland has the world's highest per capita number of mobile phones, and coverage is reliable in most populated areas. The "Ring Road" circling Iceland is entirely covered.

The three letters that define much of the world's wireless capabilities are **GSM.** In the U.S., T-Mobile, AT&T Wireless, and Cingular use this quasi-universal system; in Canada, Microcell and some Rogers customers are GSM, and all Europeans and most Australians use GSM.

GSM phones function with a removable plastic **SIM card.** Many phones, especially in the U.S., are not "multiband" (synonymous with "tri-band" or "quad-band") and will not work in Iceland. Even if your cellphone uses GSM, and you have a multiband phone (such as many Sony Ericsson, Motorola, or Samsung models), the company you're contracted to has probably "locked" your phone. In this case, you cannot simply buy an Icelandic SIM card, insert it into your phone, and start making calls. Those with multiband phones can call their wireless operator and ask for "international roaming" to be activated on their existing account. This option is usually expensive, however: Per-minute charges are often $1 to $1.50. If you plan on using a cellphone in Iceland, you may well want to buy a prepaid GSM plan after you arrive, and either buy a phone—new phones in Iceland start around 5,000kr ($80/£40)—or bring a rented one from home.

North Americans can **rent a phone** before leaving home from **InTouch USA** (🕾 **800/872-7626;** www.intouchglobal. com) or **RoadPost** (🕾 **888/290-1606** or 905/272-5665; www.roadpost.com). InTouch will also, for free, advise you on whether your existing phone will work in Iceland; simply call 🕾 **703/222-7161** between 9am and 4pm EST, or go to **http://intouchglobal.com/travel.htm**.

Pre-paid GSM phone cards are available from Iceland's two main phone companies, **Síminn** (🕾 **800-7000;** www. siminn.is) and **Vodafone** (🕾 **1414** or 1800; outside Iceland 🕾 **599-9009;** www.vodafone.is). Both also offer GPRS services for Internet access through your phone; almost all areas in Iceland with GSM also have GPRS (a notable exception is the Westman Islands).

Síminn branches in Reykjavik include Armúli 25, east of the city center, near the Nordica Hotel (🕾 **550-7809**); Kringlan Mall (🕾 **550-6694**); and Smáralind Mall (🕾 **550-6506**). **Vodafone branches** (all locations, 🕾 **599-9009**) in Reykjavik are at Kringlan Mall, Smáralind Mall, and Skútuvogur 2, which is a little closer to downtown but harder to get to by bus. Síminn also has branches in **Akureyri** at Hafnarstræti 102 (🕾 **460-6709**); **Egilsstaðir,** at Miðvangur 1 (🕾 **470-1009**); and **Ísafjörður,** at Hafnarstræti 1 (🕾 **450-6009**). Vodafone has another branch in Akureyri (on Glerártorg).

When you sign up for a pre-paid GSM plan in Iceland, the SIM card is typically free, and the lowest starting credit is 2,000kr ($32/£16). Typical rates within Iceland are 23kr per minute or 10kr for a text message, no matter what time of the day or week. For both Síminn and Vodafone plans, the price of a call drops as much as 50% within Iceland if you are calling another cellphone operated by the same company. GPRS costs are typically 600kr ($9.60/£4.80) per megabyte, which encompasses about 400 short e-mails or 500 Web page views.

Tip: Be sure to ask for your voicemail and other prompts to be in English.

In Iceland only the caller pays for the call, even for calls from overseas. This makes cellphones a great way for people from home to keep in touch with you. Both Síminn and Vodafone will give you a four-digit prefix (1100 for Síminn, 1010 for Vodafone) for making international calls from Iceland—the Síminn rate at press time is 25kr (38¢/19p) per minute to the U.S., hardly more than a domestic call within Iceland; Vodafone rates are higher.

Your cellphone account can be continually restocked by buying pre-paid cards called *Frelsi* (Freedom) at gas stations and convenience stores around the country. To make sure you buy the right card, specify whether your cellphone uses Síminn or Vodafone.

SATELLITE PHONES

"Satphones" can be helpful in more remote parts of Iceland. Two providers serve the country: Iridium satellite phones get the best coverage, whereas GlobalStar phones get only marginal coverage with a weaker signal. Iceland has no satellite phone agency, but products can be rented or purchased from two companies.

You can rent satphones from **RoadPost** (℗ **888/290-1606;** www.roadpost.com). Iridium phone rental costs $8.99 per day, and the rate is $1.79 per minute. **InTouch USA** (℗ **800/872-7626;** www.intouch global.com) offers a wider range of phones, but phone rental costs $99 per week with a per-minute rate of $2.40. As of this writing, satphones were amazingly expensive to buy: An Iridium handset costs between $1,300 and $1,600, though if you own one the per-minute rate goes down to about 95¢.

VOICE-OVER INTERNET PROTOCOL (VOIP)

If you have Web access while traveling, you might consider a broadband-based telephone service (in technical terms, **Voice over Internet Protocol,** or **VoIP**) such as Skype (www.skype.com) or Vonage (www.vonage.com), which allows you to make free international calls from your laptop or in a cybercafe. The people you're calling may also need to be signed up. Check the sites for details.

WITH YOUR OWN COMPUTER

Several factors make Iceland a good place to bring your own computer: the widespread availability of free Wi-Fi; the difficulty of finding public Internet access terminals; the high cost of those public terminals; and the low crime rate. In Reykjavík and Akureyri you won't have trouble finding a cafe with free Wi-Fi, but in the rest of the country you'll have to ask around. Creative solutions can usually be found, from sitting in hotel lobbies (you're unlikely to be thrown out) to loitering outside library doors after closing hours. Reykjavík's international airport has a free hotspot at the Kaffitár cafe in the departure lounge.

Tip: If you want to stay in an accommodation with Wi-Fi, consult the "Amenities" listings at the bottom of accommodation listings in this book. Wi-Fi is spreading so quickly that you might ask even when we have not listed it.

If Wi-Fi is not available in your hotel, most business-class hotels throughout Iceland offer high-speed Internet cables for laptops. Call your hotel in advance to see what your options are, and call your ISP to see if they have a local Icelandic number you can dial into. For **AOL,** the local Iceland number is **511-0914;** you'll pay $6/hour on top of the call cost.

If you're traveling outside the reach of your ISP, the **iPass** network has dial-up Internet access in Iceland (℗ **599-3300** or 530-0500). An iPass provider will help you set up your computer; for a list of providers, go to www.ipass.com and click on "Individual Purchase." One solid provider is **i2roam** (℗ **866/811-6209;** www.i2roam.com).

Remember to bring a power adapter, and perhaps an Ethernet cable and phone cord as well. As in other European countries, Icelandic electricity runs at 220 volts, 50 Hz AC, and electric sockets have two round plugs; you may need an "international" power adapter that properly regulates the current to prevent computer damage. Icelandic phone jacks are the same as in North America, so Europeans will need an adapter.

WITHOUT YOUR OWN COMPUTER

Most accommodations do not provide Internet terminals for guests, so your best and least expensive resource is often the public library, which usually charges around 200kr ($3.20/£1.60) per hour. Some tourist information offices and cafes have Internet terminals for about 500kr ($8/£4) per hour.

13 General-Interest Tours & Packages

Many travelers reflexively dismiss organized tours and packages, but Iceland is a good place for even the most independent-minded traveler to reconsider. Many of the most fascinating parts of the country are difficult to access on your own, and tour companies can save you tons of time in research and planning. Icelanders themselves often sign up with the same tour companies used by tourists.

For more specialized tours, see the following section, "Special-Interest Trips." For outdoor activity tours, see chapter 3, "Active Iceland." See also the organized tours listed in each regional chapter; often the best Icelandic tour companies operate locally.

MAJOR ICELANDIC OPERATORS

Icelandair (© 570-3039; www.iceland air.com) has all kinds of tours and packages, while its domestic counterpart **Air Iceland** (www.airiceland.is) offers day tours to Lake Mývatn, the Westman Islands, and several other locations. Icelandair offers not only the usual air/hotel packages but also a good selection of outdoor adventure tours and special-interest tours, including "Ghosts, Elves, and Trolls."

Reykjavík Excursions (© 562-1011; www.re.is), Iceland's largest tour company, has an enormous selection of tours to choose from; most but not all rely primarily on bus travel. **Iceland Excursions** (© 540-1313; www.icelandexcursions.is),

Iceland's second largest tour company, is equally prolific and reputable. **Iceland Total** (© 585-4300; www.icelandtotal. com), one of Iceland's biggest travel agencies, rounds out the big three.

Nordic Adventure Travel (© 898-0355; www.nat.is) is an excellent resource for outdoor adventure tours, often with online booking discounts. **Guðmundur Jónasson Travel** (© 511-1515; www. gjtravel.is), a long-established company, has an interesting range of cross-country adventures, and is especially good for tours that involve light hiking.

Nonni Travel (© 461-1841; www. nonnitravel.is) is the leading tour operator in Akureyri, Iceland's "second city." Offerings include rafting, whale-watching, and other adventures, as well as the usual bus tours.

West Tours (© 456-5111; www.west tours.is), a recommended company with a creative range of tours, is the leading operator in the Westfjords.

NORTH AMERICAN OPERATORS

Adventures Abroad (© 800/227-8747; www.adventures-abroad.com) has a well-designed 10-day cultural tour of Iceland in August.

Borton Overseas (© 800/843-0602; www.bortonoverseas.com), a Minneapolis-based specialist in Africa and Scandinavia, has a good range of Iceland offerings.

Butterfield & Robinson (© 866/ 551-9090; www.butterfield.com), a prestigious upscale company, has a very well-designed 8-day moderate-activity walking tour, and a trip for families with children 8 and up.

Continental Journeys (© 800/ 601-4343; www.continentaljourneys.com) is a good clearinghouse for a wide variety of Iceland tours, both escorted and independent, summer and winter. **Five Stars of Scandinavia** (© 800/722-4126; www. 5stars-of-scandinavia.com), based in Olympia, WA, is a similar outfit.

The affiliated **Great Canadian Travel Company** in Winnipeg (© 800/661-3830) and **Travel 333 Chicago** (© 800/771-4833; both www.iceland-experience.com) have a good range of tours, including cruises and a 10-day "Iceland on a Budget" self-drive tour for under $2,000, with airfare from NYC.

Iceland America (© 866/892-1045; www.icelandamerica.com) is particularly good for air/hotel self-drive packages and weekend romps in Reykjavík. **Iceland Saga Travel** (© 866/423-7242; www.iceland sagatravel.com), based in Nantucket, MA, is similarly useful. **Nordic Saga Tours** (© 800-848-6449; www.nordicsaga.com), based in Edmonds, WA, has a carefully selected list of Iceland tours.

Odysseys Unlimited (© 888-370-6765; www.odysseys-unlimited.com), a well-regarded company based in Watertown, MA, has an excellent 11-day escorted tour crisscrossing the country for $3,200 and up, including airfare.

Scanam World Tours (© 800-545-2204; www.scanamtours.com) is a prominent Scandinavian specialist based in Cranbury, NJ, with a good range of Iceland options.

Scantours (© 800-223-7226; www. scantours.com), based in Los Angeles, has an enormous range of Iceland tours impressively laid out by type and departure date. The site is especially useful for scoping out off-season trips, spa trips, and cruise options.

U.K. OPERATORS

Arctic Experience Holidays (© 01737/ 218-800; www.arctic-experience.co.uk) has basic city break and self-drive tours, plus more singular options, such as horseback riding or diving tours.

Explore Worldwide (© 0870/ 333-4001; www.explore.co.uk) serves up general small-group tours of Iceland, plus "super Jeep" and volcano specialties.

Scantours (© 020/7554-3530; www. scantours.co.uk) has something for every taste, from basic fly/drive packages to multi-day horseback riding tours.

Taber Holidays (© 01274/875-199; www.taberhols.co.uk), a Scandinavian specialist, has a well-rounded list of 10 regional tours, and can also customize your itinerary. **Regent Holidays** (© 0845/ 277-3301; www.regent-iceland.com) specializes in Iceland and Greenland, and offers basic, foolproof, escorted and self-drive tours to popular sites. **Yes Travel** (© 0845/300-4845; www.yes-travel. com), an Iceland specialist, has an excellent website with a wealth of independent and escorted tour options.

14 Special-Interest Trips

For a thorough list of outdoor activity tours, see chapter 3, "Active Iceland."

EDUCATIONAL TOURS

Smithsonian Journeys (© 877/338-8687; www.smithsonianjourneys.com), affiliated with the Smithsonian Institution,

hosts several educational trips focusing on geology, hydro power, and Icelandic culture.

Astronomy Magazine leads a 6-day "Northern Lights & Lava Fields of Iceland" in October and January, hosted by an astronomy professor and focusing on Iceland's natural wonders. Bookings are through **MWT Associates** (© 877/707-7827; www.melitatrips.com).

Natural Habitat Adventures (© 800/543-8917; www.nathab.com) has "Iceland: Fjords & Glaciers," a late-May tour where naturalists give lectures aboard a Russian oceanographic vessel in a 9-day circumnavigation of the island. Prices start at $5,000 (£2,500) per person, not including airfare.

Ísafold Travel (© 544-8866; www.isafoldtravel.is) has educational tours in geology and energy technology.

Cross-Culture Journeys (© 800/491-1148 or 413/256-6303; www.ccjourneys.com) based in Amherst, MA, leads 9-day tours focusing on arts, museums, and saga history, with plenty of nature thrown in. Prices are $3,400–$3,700 (£1,700–£1,850) per person, including airfare.

Storyfest Journeys (© 301/791-9133; www.storyfest.com) leads a saga and folklore tour in May, though dates may change.

LANGUAGE COURSES

If you want to learn Icelandic, start with this online list of study programs around the country: **www.nordals.hi.is/page/other_courses**.

ICELANDIC ANCESTRY

The Snorri Program (© 551-0165; www.snorri.is) provides an opportunity for young North Americans of Icelandic descent to explore their heritage. The main 6-week program (mid-June through July) is for ages 18 to 28, but older visitors can

join a modified 2-week program in late August.

J.R.J. Super Jeeps (© 453-8219; http://frontpage.simnet.is/jeppaferdir) customizes tours for those tracing their Icelandic ancestry.

VOLUNTEER VACATIONS

Seeds of Iceland (© 845-6178; www.seedsiceland.org), a non-profit group founded in 2005, sets up volunteer 2-week "work camps" for projects ranging from environmental cleanups and trail marking to preparation for local cultural festivals.

Iceland's **Environment and Food Agency** (© 591-2000; http://english.ust.is/of-interest/conservationvolunteers) recruits around 130 volunteers each summer for conservation projects lasting 2 to 11 weeks, and ranging from trail work to wilderness management.

The **Earthwatch Institute** (© in North America 800/776-0188; in the U.K. 01865/318-831; www.earthwatch.org) leads a week-long volunteer trip in August to study glaciers.

Volunteer Abroad (© 720/570-1702; www.volunteerabroad.com) maintains an excellent database of volunteer vacation opportunities, with several options in Iceland.

TOURS FOR WOMEN

Canyon Calling (© 928/282-0916; www.canyoncalling.com), based in Sedona, AZ, leads a cost-conscious 8-day multi-activity trip for women in early July. Activities include dog sledding, rafting, whale-watching, and horseback riding.

15 Getting Around Iceland

Due to the challenges of Icelandic topography, distances are often approximations. Whether by car or by foot, always confirm your exact route before setting out, particularly if you will be traveling in more rural regions.

BY CAR

Icelanders love their cars for good reason: Iceland has **no train transport,** and many of Iceland's most beautiful sights are far from populated areas. A private vehicle can be even more necessary in the "shoulder season" (Apr–May and Sept–Oct), when most buses and tours are not operating. Renting a car is costly, but it often stacks up well against air and bus travel, especially if you have three or four passengers. Reykjavík is easy to get around in without a car, and parking there can be a nuisance, so many visitors rent a car upon leaving the city.

Route 1, usually referred to as "The Ring Road," is 1,328km (825 miles) long and circles the entire island. Almost all of it is paved, and it's plowed all winter. Only about a third of Iceland's total road network is paved, however.

BRINGING YOUR OWN CAR

Though many prefer to rent simply because of the beating administered to cars by Iceland's rough roads, Europeans have the option of bringing their vehicles to Iceland on the car ferry (p. 22). This may seem impractical at first glance, but transporting the car costs roughly the same as a regular passenger. Visitors bringing their own cars must carry registration, proof of insurance, and a driving license. Permits are issued on the ferry for 1 month, and can be extended. For more information, contact the Directorate of Customs (© 560-0300; www.tollur.is). Make sure to bring a spare tire, jack, jumper cables, and perhaps other repair tools and supplies.

RENTALS

It's generally cheaper to rent a car before you arrive at the airport. If you rent in Reykjavík (as opposed to at the airport, which is over 48km/30 miles away), most agencies will deliver the car to your hotel (or deliver you to the car) and then pick up the car (or deliver you to your hotel) when you're done.

Most agencies offer a choice between limited and unlimited mileage plans. Expect to pay at least 5,000kr ($80/£40) per day for a small car with an allowance of 75km or 100km (47 miles or 62 miles)

per day, or 7,500kr ($120/£60) per day for unlimited mileage. For a four-wheel-drive vehicle, prices start around 10,000kr ($160/£80) but are usually higher. If you pick up the vehicle in one location and drop it off in another, the drop-off fee is usually at least 5,000kr ($80/£40). Renting a car usually requires a credit card as a form of deposit.

CAR RENTAL AGENCIES Rental agencies **at the international airport** include **ALP Bílaleiga** (© 562-6060; www.alp.is), with 11 locations nationwide; **Avis** (© 591-4000; www.avis.is) with nine locations, mostly at airports; **Budget** (© 567-8300; www.budget.is) with four locations; **Hertz** (© 522-4400; www.hertz.is), with seven locations; and **National/Bílaleiga Akureyrar** (© 586-6915; www.nationalcar.is) with 11 locations.

Offices **in Reykjavík** include **Avis,** Knarrarvogur 2 and Reykjavík City Airport (© 591-4000; www.avis.is); **Bílaleiga Akureyrar/National,** Skeifan 9 and Reykjavík City Airport (© 568-6915; www.nationalcar.is); **Budget,** BSÍ bus terminal (© 562-6060) and Reykjavík City Airport (© 551-7570; www.budget.is); **Europcar,** Hjallahraun 9, Hafnarfjörður (© 565-3800; www.europcar.is); and **Hertz,** Flugvallarvegur, by Reykjavík City Airport (© 522-4420; www.hertz.is).

Local agencies are usually reliable and slightly cheaper, and you're usually getting the same product. Consider taking the Flybus from the airport to Reykjavík, then renting from a local agency once you're ready to leave the city. Agencies in the Keflavík area can also meet you at the airport. Remember that the majors will have more pickup and drop-off locations, and often better resources for dealing with breakdowns and mishaps.

Recommended local agencies that can meet you at Keflavík international airport include **Geysir,** Holtsgata 56, Njarðvík

(☎ 893-4455; www.geysir.is) and **SS Bílaleiga,** Iðjustígur 1, Njarðvík (☎ 421-2220; www.carrentalss.com).

Recommended local agencies that will deliver a car to your accommodation in Reykjavík include **A-Bílar,** Laufbrekka 4, Kópavogur (☎ 564-3300; www.abilar.is); **ÁTAK Car Rental,** Smiðjuvegur 1, Kópavogur (☎ 554-6040; www.atak.is), which carries automatics; **Berg,** Bíldshöfði 10, Reykjavík (☎ 577-6050; www.carrental-berg.com); and **Óðinn Car Rental,** Óðinsgata 9, Reykjavík (☎ 861-5160; www.odinncar.com).

The travel agency **Touris** (Frostaskjól 105, Reykjavík; ☎ 517-8290; www.tour.is) has good deals on packages combining 4WD rentals with lodging.

AGE LIMITS & LICENSES Generally you must be 21 to rent a regular car in Iceland and 23 to rent a 4WD vehicle, but company policies vary. No maximum age limit is in effect. All national driver's licenses are recognized, so you do not need an international one.

INSURANCE Basic third-party liability insurance is included in car-rental rates. Cars usually come with a standard collision damage waiver but a high deductible; in other words, if you get into a scrape you are liable for, say, the first 62,500kr ($1,000/£500) or 93,750kr ($1,500/£750) in damages, beyond which the insurance pays. For an extra cost—say, 750kr ($12/£6) per day—you could bring the deductible down to 12,500kr ($200/£100) on a standard car. This is often a good idea in Iceland, where cars face hazardous conditions.

Driving on **prohibited mountain roads** will void your insurance on regular cars. The letter "F" precedes the numbers of mountain roads on maps and road signs. Even with 4WD vehicles, insurance is often voided by attempting to cross rivers. Standard insurance does not cover damage to the car from a collision with an animal, and you may have to

compensate its owner. Even for minor accidents, be sure to get a police report so your insurance will cover it.

AUTOMATIC vs. MANUAL TRANSMISSION Even the major Icelandic car-rental companies have very few cars with automatic transmissions. They must be reserved in advance, and usually cost about 10% more.

2WD vs. 4WD Many of Iceland's most beautiful landscapes are accessible only to 4WD vehicles, so if you're in a regular car, be prepared for serious envy as you watch the 4WD vehicles turn off the Ring Road into the great unknown. All the major agencies rent 4WD vehicles and can provide you with tow ropes, shovels, extra fuel cans, and GPS navigational systems. On the other hand, the vast majority of roads are accessible to regular cars, and for the more difficult traverses, you can take buses or sign up for Jeep tours. This can save money on gas, and the environment will thank you.

CAMPERS Icelanders often travel in campers, and the concept of a "portable hotel" holds great appeal in a country with so much open space and so many accessible campgrounds.

Camper Iceland, Grófin 14C, Reykjanesbær (☎ 868-8829; www.camper.is), near the international airport, has a large selection. Four-person campers start at 85,188kr ($1,363/£682) per week with a 200km (124 miles) per day limit or 90,875kr ($1,454/£727) per week with unlimited mileage.

Other companies near the airport to try are **Geysir,** Holtsgata 56, Njarðvík (☎ 893-4455; www.geysir.is) and **J&S Car-Rental,** Bolafotur 9, Reykjanesbær (☎ 564-6000; www.js.is).

DRIVING LAWS
Icelanders drive on the right side of the road. Unless otherwise marked, speed limits are 30kmph in residential areas, 50kmph in towns, 80kmph on unpaved

roads, and 90kmph on paved roads. No right turns are allowed at red lights. In rotaries (aka roundabouts), right-of-way goes to the driver in the inside lane. Headlights must always be on.

Seat belts are mandatory in both front and back seats, and children under 6 must be secured in a car seat designed for their size and weight; these are usually available for rent, but you may want to bring your own. No one less than 140cm (4 ft. 7 in.) tall, or weighing less than 40kg (88 lb.), or under the age of 12 is allowed to ride in a front seat equipped with an airbag. Talking on cellphones is prohibited unless you have a hands-free system. Many intersections in the capital have automatic cameras to catch traffic violators.

The blood alcohol limit is extremely strict at .05%, so getting behind the wheel after just one drink could make you guilty of a serious offense. Drivers stopped under suspicion for drunk driving are usually given a "balloon" or Breathalyzer test, which cannot be refused.

To protect the fragile sub-Arctic vegetation, all off-road driving is strictly prohibited, except on some beaches.

DRIVING SAFETY

Iceland is not for Sunday drivers. Weather conditions are erratic; roads are winding and narrow, with no guardrails and many blind spots; and most routes are unpaved. We cannot emphasize enough how important it is not to speed; a majority of fatal car accidents in Iceland involve foreigners unfamiliar with the country's driving hazards.

Before you set out, ask your car rental agency about potentially difficult road and weather conditions, especially in the off season. For road conditions, Icelanders rely heavily on information continually updated by the **Public Roads Administration** at © **354-1777** (May–Oct 8am–4pm; Nov–Apr 8am–5pm) or www.vegag.is. For weather, contact the

Icelandic Meteorological Office (© 902-0600, press "1" for English; www.vedur.is).

Most roads are steeply sided and do not have shoulders—two seconds of inattention and you could topple off the road into great danger. Many road signs indicate dangers ahead, but few specify how much to reduce your speed, so always be on the safe side. Slow down whenever pavement transitions to gravel; tourists often skid off **gravel roads,** unaware of how poor traction can be on loose dirt and stones. Flying stones launched by oncoming traffic are another hazard on gravel roads, often cracking car windows; slow down and move to the side, especially if a larger vehicle is approaching. For traction, it's often safer to slow down by lowering the gears instead of using the brakes.

Most **bridges** in Iceland are single lane—signposted *Einbreið brú*—and the first car to reach it has right-of-way.

Always bring sunglasses into the car. **Glare** is a common hazard, and the sub-Arctic sun is usually low to the horizon.

Be on the lookout for **sheep** on the road, particularly when a lamb is on one side and its mother is on the other.

MOUNTAIN ROADS & FORDING RIVERS

Do *not* attempt highland interior routes in a two-wheel drive car. Roads that require 4WD vehicles are indicated by the letter "F" on road signs and maps. The safest procedure on these roads is to travel with other cars. Always carry car-repair kits and emergency supplies, and on particularly remote routes, inform someone of your travel plans before setting out. If you don't have a GPS navigational system, at least bring a compass.

Unbridged river crossings for 4WD vehicles are marked on maps with the letter "V." Water flow at these crossings can change dramatically and unpredictably from hour to hour. A sudden increase in flow can be caused not only by rain, but also by the sun melting glacial ice. Water levels are usually lower earlier in the day. Several drivers have drowned in river crossings; always seek advice if you have any doubts. Many drivers wait and watch other vehicles cross before making their own attempt. Sometimes it's necessary to check the water depth by walking into the current; bring sturdy rubber sandals, a life jacket, and a lifeline for this purpose. Before crossing, make sure the 4WD is engaged. Drive in first gear and use "low" drive if you have it. It sometimes helps to cross diagonally in the direction of the current.

OFF SEASON   In winter the weather is particularly volatile and daylight hours are limited. Most roads are open by April or May, but some interior routes are impassable as late as early July. Make sure your vehicle has snow tires or chains, and always pack blankets, food, and water in case you get stranded.

GAS STATIONS
Iceland has many long gaps between gas stations, so keep your vehicle well-fueled and know the distance to your next required fill-up. Many gas pumps are automated and remain open 24 hours. Machines for swiping your credit or debit card usually expect you to know the card's PIN (see "Money & Costs," p. 23). The machines also ask you to input the maximum amount you want to spend, but you are only charged for what is pumped. **N1** and **Olís,** the companies with the most gas stations in Iceland, both sell prepaid gas cards. Some small-town gas stations indicated on maps are tiny operations, and you may want to call ahead to make sure they're open.

ROAD MAPS
The **Iceland Road Atlas** (Stöng Publishers), updated every 2 years, is a phenomenal 585-page compendium of maps and information, and a must-have for any serious road trip. It's near impossible to find online or abroad, but available at most car-rental agencies and many gas stations and bookstores. Each map is focused narrowly on short stretches of individual roads, so you may prefer a simpler road atlas that gives you the big picture; these are easy to find.

CARPOOLING
Samferða (www.samferda.net) effectively connects people looking to carpool on specific routes at specific times. Anyone receiving a ride is expected to share the costs of gas or car rental. The bulletin board at **Reykjavík City Hostel** (p. 97) is also popular with visitors looking to split car costs.

BY BUS
Iceland's bus system is reliable and punctual. Public buses link all major towns, and even some barren interior routes are covered in summer. (Icelandic buses are impressive machines, chugging right through rocky terrain and raging rivers.) Buses are up to European standards of comfort.

Several bus companies operate in Iceland, but all scheduled routes are coordinated by Iceland's main bus company, **BSÍ** (✆ **562-1011** daily 4:30am–midnight; www.bsi.is). Bus schedules are available online or at bus stations and tourist information offices across the country. The website **www.nat.is** is also great for bus timetables and bookings; click "Travel Guide," then "Transportation," then "Bus Schedules and Rental." Most long-distance bus routes run only in summer.

Buses on the Ring Road do not require reservations, and you can pay on board with cash or credit card. In small towns the bus stop is usually the main gas station. Coverage of the Ring Road is complete from June through August, but from September through May, it extends only from Reykjavík to Akureyri in the north and to Höfn in the southeast.

Bus travel is not as inexpensive as you might think compared to car and air travel, especially for longer distances. Reykjavík to Egilsstaðir by bus costs around 15,000kr ($240/£120), more than the cost of a flight.

Bus passes can make bus travel more economical. An enjoyable way to see Iceland if you don't have a car, is on the **Full Circle Pass** sold by **TREX** (© 587-6000; www.trex.is) online or at tourist information centers. The pass is good for one trip around Iceland on the Ring Road, hopping on and off wherever you like, for 23,800kr ($381/£190). A modified pass includes the Westfjords and costs 35,300kr ($565/£282). **Reykjavík Excursions** (© 580-5400; www.re.is) offers more particular bus passports, available online or at the BSÍ terminal in Reykjavík. For example, the **Highland Circle Passport** includes the interior routes through Landmannalaugar, Sprengisandur, and Kjölur for 25,100kr ($402/£201).

An **Omnibus Passport** sold at tourist information centers covers unlimited trips on virtually all scheduled bus routes *except* through the interior. Time spans for these passes range from 1 week 29,938kr ($479/£240) to 1 month 59,938kr ($959/£480).

BY PLANE

Air travel in Iceland is common, easy, cost-efficient, and often necessary, especially in winter. Booking online and in advance is likely to save you money. Some routes are highly trafficked (like Reykjavík to Akureyri, 10 flights per day in summer) and some far less so (Reykjavík to Gjögur, twice per week).

Air Iceland (© 570-3030; www.airiceland.is) handles most domestic air travel, serving eight destinations inside Iceland (Reykjavík, Akureyri, Egilsstaðir, Ísafjörður, the Westman Islands, Grímsey, Þórshöfn, and Vopnafjörður) as well as the Faeroe Islands and Greenland. The simplest way to buy tickets is online, since they have no direct U.S. or U.K. line, and you can't book directly through Icelandair. Children under 12 get 50% off on Air Iceland.

Eagle Air (© 562-4200; www.ernir.is) connects Reykjavík to Sauðárkrókur, Hornafjörður (Höfn), Bíldudalur, and Gjögur, and also offers sightseeing tours. **Westman Islands Air** (© 481-3255; www.eyjaflug.is) flies mostly between the Westman Islands and Bakki, but also connects the Westmans to Selfoss and Hella.

Average one-way prices from Reykjavík are 5,750kr ($92/£46) to the Westman Islands (25 min.), 8,000kr ($128/£64) to Akureyri (45 min.), and 9,060kr ($145/£72) to Egilsstaðir (1 hr.).

Note: Because of Iceland's high winds and unpredictable weather, air travelers should always be prepared for delays and cancellations, especially in winter.

BY BOAT

For cruises, see "Cruises" in "Getting There," earlier in this chapter.

Iceland's **ferry system** is often used by tourists; see the map on the inside back cover for routes. The only ferries that take cars are the *Baldur,* which connects Stykkishólmur on the Snæfellsnes peninsula to Brjánslækur in the Westfjords, and the *Herjólfur,* which connects Þorlákshöfn to the Westman Islands. For information on particular ferry routes, see the regional chapters of this book.

BY BIKE

For information on biking in Iceland, see p. 57 in chapter 3.

16 Tips on Accommodations

Iceland's tourist season is concentrated from mid-June through August, and tourism is growing by about 10% each year; so booking ahead is often essential. Prices fall as much as 40% in the off season, but many accommodations close in winter, especially guesthouses.

Iceland is not the poor and provincial country it once was, and virtually all accommodations meet good basic standards of comfort and cleanliness. Mattress standards are particularly high.

Anti-smoking legislation that took effect in 2007 forbids smoking *anywhere* inside Icelandic accommodations.

ACCOMMODATION OPTIONS
HOTELS
The word "hotel" generally signifies the most luxurious choice in town, but not all hotels are superior to or more expensive than guesthouses (see below), and not all "hotel" rooms even have private bathrooms. Expect to pay at least 12,000kr ($198/£96) for the most basic hotel double with a private bathroom, 7,000kr ($112/£56) for one without a private bathroom, or 17,000kr ($272/£136) for an average business-style room.

ICELANDIC HOTEL CHAINS
International chains have few footholds in Iceland. Icelandic chains are more common. **Icelandair Hotels** (© 444-4000; www.icehotel.is) has eight three- and four-star hotels around the country. **Edda Hotels** (© 444-4000; www.hoteledda.is), in partnership with Icelandair, has 13 summer-only hotels, most of which utilize student housing; **Fosshótel** (© 562-4000; www.fosshotel.is) has 11 hotels and two guesthouses ranging from one to three stars; and **Kea Hotels** (© 460-2000; www.hotelkea.is) has six two- to four-star hotels.

GUESTHOUSES
Gistiheimilið (guesthouses) are a time-honored Scandinavian institution that is closely related to the "bed-and-breakfast." Rooms, which are usually in private houses, are most often cheaper than hotels and range in quality from the equivalent of a two-star hotel to a hostel. While private bathrooms are rare, most guesthouses are likely to have cooking facilities, sleeping-bag accommodation (see below), or a family-size apartment fitting four to six people. Because Icelanders have a highly developed sense of personal privacy, the proprietors often live in a separate house. Standards of cleanliness are usually very high.

Guesthouse prices vary greatly, but a double with a shared bathroom ranges from 5,000kr to 12,000kr ($80–$192/£40–£96). About half of Icelandic guesthouses include breakfast in the room price, and the rest usually offer breakfast for an extra 900kr ($14/£7.20) or so per person.

CABINS
Small timber cabins for travelers are sprouting up all over Iceland, usually in conjunction with an existing hotel or guesthouse. Some travelers seek them out for their comparative privacy, quiet, and convenience. The cabins are often designed for family groups of around four, with private bathrooms and cooking facilities. Prices are comparable to regular doubles.

FARM HOLIDAYS
Staying at farmhouses is the classic Icelandic way to travel, and helps visitors feel more in tune with Iceland's cultural traditions. Every farm in Iceland has its own road sign, and farm names are often unchanged from the Age of Settlement. Towns and villages did not exist for most of Icelandic history, so farmsteads have traditionally been the organizational basis of Icelandic society.

The Case for Hostels

Iceland's 25 youth hostels are hardly the exclusive domain of young back-packers. All hostels have good basic standards of service and cleanliness. Some are almost indistinguishable from guesthouses or farm stays. Most offer doubles, though the majority of rooms sleep three to six; and private bathrooms are an extreme rarity. All hostels give you the option of sleep-ing-bag accommodation or sheet rental. All have guest kitchens, and some offer meals and self-service laundry. In some remote destinations in Iceland, hostels may be your only option for lodging and dining, as well as an excel-lent source of tourist information.

All youth hostels in Iceland can be booked through one convenient **central office** (© 553-8110; www.hostel.is). The website includes good deals on adventure tours and a popular car rental package with hostel vouchers. Hostels tend to fill up even faster than hotels and guesthouses in high sea-son, so plan ahead. Many hostels close in winter. Children 5 to 12 usually stay half price.

A **Youth Hostelling International membership** (www.hihostels.com), which gives you a 20% discount on rates, can be purchased before you leave home.

A farm stay is simply a guesthouse in farm surroundings; expect comforts to be on par with those of a European bed-and-breakfast. **Icelandic Farm Holidays (IFH)** (© 570-2700; www.farmholi-days.is) classifies its 150 accommodations as "farmhouses" (where you stay in the family's home); "farmer's guesthouses" (where you stay in a separate building); "country hotels" (with hotel-like facilities, though not always private bathrooms); and "cottages" (see "Cabins," above). All accommodations are rated from the most basic, Category I, through Category IV, which guarantees well-equipped rooms with private bathrooms. Many farms offer sleeping-bag accommodation (see below) or camping. Most provide meals on request and allow use of a guest kitchen. Many have hot tubs.

Many farms offer horseback riding or other activities. Most do not offer visitors a chance to participate in the rituals of farm life, but you can always ask—they might be pleasantly surprised.

SLEEPING-BAG ACCOMMODATION

For hardy visitors on a budget, the Ice-landic custom of *svefnpoka gisting,* or "sleeping-bag accommodation," can feel like a gift from the travel gods. In many guesthouses, farm stays, and even some hotels, travelers with their own sleeping bags can get around 35% to 50% off on room rates. (You *can* bring other linens, but sleeping bags are preferred for their warmth and portability.) For the most part the beds, rooms, and amenities are the same; you're simply sparing the man-agement the trouble of washing sheets. You won't find sleeping-bag rooms with private bathrooms, however, except in rare instances. We list sleeping-bag accommodation availability and pricing in our accommodation listings, but you should always ask, nonetheless. Some accommodations offer sleeping-bag accommodation only in the off season. In Reykjavík sleeping-bag accommodation has been almost entirely phased out.

CAMPING

Iceland's many campsites make the country far more accessible to travelers of limited means. Camping typically costs only 500kr to 800kr ($8–$13/£4–£6.40) per person per night, and a few municipal campsites are free.

Icelandic campsites are safe, conveniently located, and plentiful: virtually every village has one. (Even in Reykjavík the campground is right next to the city's biggest geothermal pool, and near buses to the airport and city center.) Many campsites are adjoined to farm accommodations, even to guesthouses or hotels, not to mention all the hiking trails. Because Icelanders themselves love to camp, campsites can also be great places to meet natives.

Camping and car rental are a perfect duo in Iceland. The money you save on accommodations can go toward the car, and the car grants you the flexibility, mobility, and secure luggage storage camping doesn't normally afford. Many visitors on a budget try to do without a rental car, only to wish they had brought a tent and sleeping bag instead.

The **Camping Card** (www.camping card.is) instituted in 2006 is an unbeatable deal. It grants you (plus your spouse and up to four children under the age of 16) unlimited access to 27 campsites across the country for the entire summer at a cost of only 9,900kr ($158/£79). See their website for a list and map of participating sites; many desirable campgrounds, such as those in Þingvellir National Park, are not included. The card can be purchased online or in Iceland at N1 gas stations.

Facilities at campsites vary greatly. Some have washing machines, electricity, hot showers, and kitchens; others have only a cold-water tap and toilets. In parks and nature reserves, camping is permitted only in designated areas.

Most campsites are open June through mid-September. Camping is usually not feasible in winter, though some campsites remain open, and you can always shower at the local pool.

Iceland's heavy winds and rains present a serious challenge for campers. You'll need a very strong, waterproof tent, with the maximum number of pegs, a good sleeping mat, and a waterproof sheet for under the tent. Wood can rarely be found for campfires even when they're allowed, so bring a good stove, too. Canisters for common stove fuels are easily found in gas stations.

Campsites are not listed in this book, but as you can see, we hardly mean to discourage their use. A comprehensive list of campsites can be found at **www.camping. is**. **Nordic Adventure Travel** (**www. nat.is**) also has a helpful map of the sites. The free **camping directory** *Útilega Tjaldsvæði Íslands* is available at any tourist information center.

MOUNTAIN HUTS

Hiking organizations maintain about 70 "mountain huts" in remote interior and coastal locations, many accessible only to hikers (see "Hiking," in chapter 3). Mountain huts can be anything from multi-story structures with kitchens and wardens to bare-bones shacks. Be prepared for a lack of privacy in these accommodations: As many as 30 people can be sleeping in sardine formation on narrow foam mattresses on the floor. Sleeping space can be reserved in most huts, and many are fully booked weeks or months in advance in high season. Costs in the most popular huts are typically around 2,500kr ($40/£20) per person per night. For specific mountain huts, see the regional chapters of this book.

RENTALS

Renting a house or apartment can be a wonderful and economical option. **RENT** (✆ **555-7017;** www.rent.is) is

Iceland's best resource for rentals, from individual rooms to fully furnished apartments to a cabin near Þórsmörk, short-term or long-term.

Viatour (© 425-0300; www.viatour.is) is another good agency for summer house rentals, with a minimum stay of 3 or 4 nights.

Also see the box, "House- & Couch-Swapping," below.

THE STAR-RATING SYSTEM

Icelandic hotels are rated on a voluntary basis by the government on a one- to five-star scale. One star means breakfast is available and your room has a sink, among other minimum standards. Two stars means more options for meals and refreshments. Three stars means all rooms have private bathrooms, phones, TVs, radios, and desks. Four stars means easy chairs, satellite channels, room service, and laundry service. Five stars means room safes, secretarial services, exercise facilities, and shops—but not a single Icelandic hotel has earned this designation.

Many fine hotels and guesthouses opt out of the rating system, however, because the standardized criteria do not serve them well. A hotel in an old house, for instance, could be demoted a star if just one of its rooms lacks the requisite square footage. Accommodations with individualized room designs are particularly ill-served by the system.

SEARCHING FOR ACCOMMODATIONS IN ICELAND

This guidebook lists and describes the best accommodations Iceland has to offer. The options listed here could all be full, however, or you may need to find accommodations better suited to your itinerary.

The free 240-page booklet *Around Iceland* lists every accommodation option in the entire country, along with all restaurants; museums; gas stations; notable sites, hikes, and events; as well as services. It's available wherever tourists roam in Iceland, or you can download each chapter free at www.heimur.is/world. *Áning,* another useful publication from the same source, focuses exclusively on accommodations—and features photographs and more service details—but is less complete.

USEFUL WEBSITES

Icelanders' embrace of the Internet has made finding accommodations radically easier. The websites of regional tourist offices, listed in the respective chapters of this book, have good accommodations listings. Most Icelandic villages also have their own websites detailing lodging and other services; the website is usually the name of the village (disregard the accents, and substitute "d" for "ð" and "th" for "Þ") with "www." before and ".is" after. Note, however, that many Icelandic villages have the same name.

House- & Couch-Swapping

House-swapping (along with its humble cousin, couch-swapping) is becoming a more popular and viable means of travel; you stay in their place, they stay in yours, and you both get a more authentic and personal view of a destination. **HomeLink International** (homelink.org; $75 [£150] yearly membership) is the largest and oldest home-swapping organization, founded in 1952, with more than 11,000 listings worldwide. **InterVac.com** ($69 [£138] yearly membership) with over 10,000 listings is also reliable. Both sites have plenty of Icelandic offerings. **www.couchsurfing.com** is a free online forum for finding (and offering) a free bed, and hundreds of Reykjavíkians are signed up.

Packing Suggestions for Iceland

The items below are hardly a complete packing list, just a series of suggestions and reminders. See also "Weather" in "When to Go," p. 14.

Bathing Suit Yes, even in winter. Icelanders love their geothermal pools and hot tubs year-round, and so should you.

Binoculars These aren't just for bird nerds; you'll be glad to have them when whales, seals, dolphins, and foxes appear in the distance.

Compass/GPS Locational Device The latter is preferred, especially because compasses can be thrown off by Iceland's magnetic minerals.

Driver's License & Passport You wouldn't forget these, now would you?

Earplugs Icelanders can get pretty noisy late Friday and Saturday nights.

Electricity & Phone Adaptors See "Staying Connected," p. 31.

First Aid It's easy to scrape yourself on Iceland's endless lava rocks, so at the very least bring bandaging materials and antibacterial ointment.

Flashlight There's a good chance you'll visit a cave; bring a strong one.

Hair Conditioner The mineral content of Iceland's geothermal water can be pretty rough on hair.

Hiking Shoes Even the most sedate tours often involve walking over rough terrain. Water-resistant shoes with ankle support are advised.

Insect Repellent You'll need this if you plan on visiting the interior or the Mývatn area, especially in spring or early summer. A *head net* is even better.

Motion Sickness Pills Longer ferry rides, as well as whale-watching and sea-angling trips, traverse stretches of open sea. Iceland's winding, bumpy roads can also cause motion sickness.

Multiband Cellphone See "Staying Connected," p. 31.

Raingear Icelanders prefer **raincoats** over umbrellas, since the wind blows rain (and umbrellas) in all directions. Though it's not *always* windy, and if you visit any bird cliffs in nesting season, an **umbrella** is an ideal defense against attacks by arctic terns. Bring **rainpants** since Iceland is pretty darn rainy.

Sleeping Bag This could save you lots of money; see "Sleeping-Bag Accommodation" in "Tips on Accommodations," above.

Sleeping Mask The midnight sun can make sleeping difficult.

Sunglasses The Icelandic terrain can produce lots of glare, and with the sun so low to the horizon, sunglasses are essential for driving.

Sunscreen The sub-Arctic sun can cause sunburn even when the weather's cool, and the landscape offers few places to hide.

Towel Renting one every time you go to a geothermal pool adds up.

Tupperware Travelers in Iceland often have to carry food in tow.

Windbreaker or Windproof Shell Iceland is windy . . . penetratingly windy.

The site **www.accommodation.is** has a user-friendly search engine that lists accommodations (and contact info) by location. Hotels in Iceland (**www. hotels.is**) and Reykjavik Center (**www. reykjavikcenter.is**) take it up a notch by indicating availability of rooms or sleeping spaces within a specified time frame. The latter site, despite its name, covers the whole country.

MORE MONEY-SAVING TIPS

* **Book rooms with access to a kitchen.** Restaurants are particularly expensive in Iceland, and you can save money by cooking for yourself.
* **Ask about apartments and "family rooms" if you are traveling in a group of three or more.** These types of rooms are very common in Iceland, but are not always well-advertised.
* **Act noncommittal.** Many Icelandic guesthouses quote different prices to different people. Always ask for a price before committing, even if the guesthouse has a published rate. They could quote something lower to snag your business.
* **Be wary of packages and group tour rates.** Icelandic guesthouses often quote a *higher* rate to a travel agent than to an individual calling directly, especially outside of Reykjavík.
* **Ask about special rates or other discounts.** You may qualify for corporate, student, military, senior, frequent flier, trade union, or other

discounts. Children's discounts are very common in Iceland.
* **Book online.** Internet-only discounts are very common in Iceland; many accommodations have a standard discount *every* time you book online. Some supply rooms to Priceline, Hotwire, or Expedia at rates lower than the ones you can get through the hotel itself.
* **Remember the law of supply and demand.** You can save big on hotel rooms by traveling in Iceland's off season or shoulder seasons, when rates typically drop, even at luxury properties.

LANDING THE BEST ROOM

Travelers often assume they want a room with lots of natural light. In the nonstop daylight of Iceland's early summer, however, you might want to request a room with less sun exposure and/or good blackout curtains.

If you're a light sleeper, ask for a quieter room away from vending or ice machines, elevators, restaurants, bars, and nightclubs. Icelanders have a well-earned reputation for late-night partying on Friday and Saturday nights.

Note: Top sheets are generally not even an option in Icelandic accommodations. Also, filtered coffeemakers are rare: When we list "coffee/tea" in this book among the hotel amenities, it usually refers to an electric hot water kettle, instant coffee, and teabags.

17 Tips on Dining

Icelandic cuisine is much improved from 20 years ago, when leaden Scandinavian comfort food was the near-universal standard. Several imaginative and exciting restaurants are leading the charge in Reykjavík. The enthusiasm is palpable— sometimes waitstaff can hardly wait to explain everything happening on your plate.

Outside the capital and major towns, however, good food can be difficult to find. Village restaurants usually conform to a basic model: one menu page for burgers, another for pizzas, and, for double the price, a lamb filet or catch of the day.

Icelanders like their food saucy, salty, and well-seasoned. In good restaurants, this only complements the natural flavors of the base ingredients. Otherwise, you'll become adept at scraping sauce to the side of your plate.

Icelandic ingredients are remarkably free of contaminants. Antibiotics, added hormones, and pesticides are rare. The meat could even be described as aromatic, reflecting the healthy outdoor lifestyle of the poultry and livestock.

Restaurant service is almost always friendly and helpful, if not ingratiating. In general, waitstaff like being asked for advice when ordering. As in much of Europe, you may have to tackle someone to get your bill.

Typical dining hours are a little on the late side. On weekends it can be difficult to find anyplace open before 10am, except in hotels. Icelanders usually eat dinner around 8pm or later.

FOOD CATEGORIES
FISH & LAMB
Menu advice can be crudely edited down to two words: *fish* and *lamb*.

Sheep imports are banned, and the lamb stock is exactly what the Vikings brought over. Icelandic lambs roam so freely that they can almost be described as game meat. Many Icelanders claim they can taste the wild berries, moss, and herbs that the lambs feed on. Slaughtering starts in mid-August, peaks in September, and continues into November, so late-season visitors may get the freshest filets.

Most of Iceland's export income comes from fish. Simply put: Iceland arguably serves up the freshest fish in the world. The most common local species are cod, haddock, catfish, monkfish, halibut, trout, arctic char, and salmon.

Of course, fish and lamb are hardly the whole story. Icelandic beef is raised in equally healthy circumstances. Delicious wild reindeer from eastern Iceland appear on some menus. Icelanders also have centuries of experience cooking seabirds, especially puffins and guillemots.

PRODUCE
Iceland's freshest produce comes from geothermally heated greenhouses. Locally grown vegetables are specially marked in supermarkets; top products are tomatoes, cucumbers, and bell peppers. Icelandic salads still have some catching up to do; they're often just iceberg lettuce with a few vegetable shavings.

DAIRY
Iceland's dairy products are just as wholesome and exceptional as the fish and lamb, but far less recognized. Icelanders consume lots of whole milk; reduced fat milk is available in markets but is slow to catch on. Iceland's greatest food invention, a yogurt-like product called *skýr*, is gaining popularity abroad. Iceland also produces great cheese, especially camembert and bleu cheese.

TRADITIONAL FOODS
For more on Iceland's often terrifying traditional foods, see the box on p. 100.

SAVING MONEY
Food costs are severe in Iceland, and one decent restaurant meal will often exceed the price of a night's accommodation.

Of course, the best way to save money on food is to **cook for yourself.** Icelandic hoteliers are well aware of high food prices, and many accommodations offer access to guest kitchens

One way to save money is to focus on lunch as your main meal, since dinner prices are often much higher. On the other hand, many Icelanders get by on just soup, bread, and salad for lunch. Many convenience stores have relatively inexpensive salad bars.

Fast food is often necessary to stay solvent, or in the countryside when nothing else is available. Thankfully Iceland has the world's best hot dogs (see "Hot-Dog Utopia," p. 105), available at almost every gas station. Burgers are everywhere, and are often served with a kind of cocktail sauce reminiscent of Russian dressing.

18 Recommended Books

SAGAS

Among the great literary works of medieval Europe, the Icelandic sagas retain the most importance and immediacy to the nation that produced them. The Icelandic language has changed relatively little in the last thousand years, and today's Icelanders quite clearly comprehend the original texts. Sagas are still bestsellers in Iceland, and all students must read them.

Most sagas originate from the 12th to 14th centuries, but recount events of the 10th and 11th centuries, when Icelanders were experimenting with self-government and transitioning to Christianity. The sagas do not neatly correspond to any modern literary genre, but might be called historical novels. The storylines follow a general pattern, in which conflicts escalate into multi-generational blood feuds, and personal codes of honor must be reconciled with the maintenance of the social fabric. (Readers expecting stories of handsome knights rescuing fair-haired maidens locked in castles tend to be disappointed.) The narrative style is terse and action-oriented, with infrequent dialogue and not much of the introspective probing expected in modern novels. Yet the sagas seem remarkably contemporary in their depth of characterization, intimacy of domestic scenes, well-developed sense of irony and humor, and profound grasp of psychological motivation.

About 40 Icelandic sagas have survived, most written anonymously. The two most widely available collections are *The Sagas of Icelanders* (Penguin, 2001) and *Eirik the Red and Other Icelandic Sagas* (Oxford, 1999). As wonderful as these collections are, readers should know that both are highly selective. Of the six most canonized sagas—*Egils Saga, Eyrbyggja Saga, Grettis Saga, Hrafnkels Saga, Laxdæla Saga,* and *Njáls Saga*—the Penguin collection includes *Egils Saga, Hrafnkels Saga,* and *Laxdæla Saga,* while the Oxford collection has only *Hrafnkels Saga.*

All the major sagas are in print as individual volumes. Which one you choose could depend on which region you plan to visit: *Egils Saga, Eyrbyggja Saga,* and *Laxdæla Saga* are set in the west; *Njáls Saga* in the south; and *Hrafnkels Saga* in the east. Grettir the Strong, the hero of *Grettis Saga,* spends his final years on Drangey (p. 223) in the northwest. *Egils Saga* is the subject of a fine exhibit at the new Settlement Centre (p. 168) in Borgarnes. *Njáls Saga* is often considered the greatest literary achievement of all the sagas; see "Njáls Saga & Its Sites," p. 295.

MODERN FICTION

The dominant figure of modern Icelandic literature is Halldór Laxness (p. 137), winner of the 1955 Nobel Prize for Literature. His most renowned work is the 1946 novel *Independent People,* a compassionate and often comic story of a poor sheep farmer determined to live unbeholden to anyone. English translations of several other Laxness novels remain in print. *World Light,* from 1937, is the life tale of a marginal, starry-eyed poet, a kind of foil for Laxness to work out the conflicting imperatives of art and political engagement. *Iceland's Bell,* from 1943, explores Danish colonial oppression of Iceland in the late 17th century, with most characters based on actual historic figures. *The Atom Station,* from 1948, is a more outright political satire dealing with issues stirred up by the American-run NATO base in Iceland. *The Fish Can Sing,* from 1957, is a particularly gentle coming-of-age story about a boy's pursuit of a mysterious male operatic star. *Paradise Reclaimed,* from 1960, concerns a late 19th-century farmer who abandons his family, emigrates to Mormon Utah, and later returns to Iceland as a Mormon missionary.

Iceland produces more novels per capita than any other country, but English translations are few and far between. A notable exception is *Devils' Island,* by Einar Kárason, first published in 1983. The story is set in the 1950s, amid an endearing working-class Reykjavík community with more than its share of eccentrics and troublemakers.

Currently Iceland's most popular writer—both at home and abroad—is Arnaldur Indriðason, whose crime novels feature inspector Erlendur Sveinsson, a rather gloomy divorcee who spends his evenings reading Icelandic sagas. Seven of Arnaldur's works have been translated into English, and in 2005 his *Silence of the Grave* took Britain's coveted Golden Dagger Award.

NONFICTION

Iceland was widely venerated in Victorian England, and William Morris's translations of sagas were household reading. Several Victorians wrote Icelandic studies and travelogues, some of which have been reprinted. *Letters From High Latitudes* (Hard Press), by the prominent statesman and diplomat Lord Dufferin (1826–1902), is an often raucous account of his 1856 travels in Iceland, Norway, and Spitzbergen. (Tim Moore's *Frost on My Moustache: the Arctic Exploits of a Lord and a Loafer,* published in 2000 by Abacus, is a hilarious account of Moore's misadventures while retracing Dufferin's route.) *Iceland: Its Scenes and Sagas* (Signal Books, 2007), by the eclectic scholar, novelist, and folk-song collector Sabine Baring-Gould (1834–1924), is a magnificent

account of his 1862 journey across Iceland on horseback, interlaced with learned musings on the sagas. *Ultima Thule; Or, A Summer in Iceland* (Kessinger Publishing), written in 1875 by explorer and ethnologist Richard Francis Burton (1821–1890), is an equally penetrating and erudite portrait of Icelandic society.

Ring of Seasons: Iceland, Its Culture and History (University of Michigan Press, 2000)—by Terry G. Lacy, an American sociologist who has lived in Iceland since the 1970s—is highly engaging and insightful.

History of Iceland: From the Settlement to the Present Day, by Jón R. Hjálmarsson (Iceland Review Press, 1993), is a tidy, 200-page primer on Icelandic history. *Iceland's 1100 Years: History of a Marginal Society,* by Gunnar Karlsson (Hurst & Company, 2000; reprinted in the U.S. as *The History of Iceland,* by University of Minnesota Press), is twice as long and has a bit more intellectual heft. Readers particularly interested in the historical context of the Icelandic sagas should pick up Jesse Byock's authoritative study *Viking Age Iceland* (Penguin, 2001).

Iceland: Land of the Sagas (Villard, 1990) is a coffee-table paperback, with 150 pages split evenly between Jon Krakauer's evocative photographs and David Roberts' essayistic reflections on Iceland's landscape and literary heritage. *Iceland Saga* (The Bodley Head, 1987) also takes the reader on a kind of literary tour, but from a more informed perspective; author Magnús Magnússon translated many sagas himself.

FAST FACTS: Iceland

American Express There is no American Express office in Iceland. To wire money, use Western Union (© **800/325-6000;** www.westernunion.com). The money shows up at branches of Iceland's largest bank, Landsbankinn.

ATM Networks See "Money & Costs," p. 23.

Business Hours **Banks** are generally open Monday through Friday 9:15am to 4pm. **Shopping hours** are generally Monday through Friday from 9 or 10am to 6pm, and Saturday from 10am to early afternoon. Supermarkets and gas station convenience stores are open longer. Reykjavík and Akureyri have 24-hour markets. Hours for **museums and sights** are highly irregular.

Car Rentals See "Getting Around Iceland," p. 37.

Cashpoints See "Money & Costs," p. 23.

Country Code The country code for phone calls to Iceland is **354.**

Currency See "Money & Costs," p. 23.

Customs For complete listings of permitted items, visit the Directorate of Customs website at www.tollur.is, or call ℂ **560-0300** (daily 8am–3:30pm).

What You Can Bring into Iceland:

• *All riding and angling gear must be disinfected,* including gloves, boots, and waders. You'll need proof of disinfection from an authorized vet, or the gear will be disinfected upon arrival at your expense. For more information, contact the **Agricultural Authority** (ℂ **530-4800;** www.lbs.is).

• **Alcohol:** Travelers at least 20 years of age may bring 1 liter of wine or 6 liters of beer, plus 1 liter of spirits. If you're not carrying spirits or beer, you can bring in 2.5 liters of wine.

• **Currency:** There are no limits on foreign currency.

• **Food:** You may bring up to 3kg of food into Iceland, but no raw eggs, raw meat, or milk.

• **Pets:** All animals require a permit from the Agricultural Authority (above). Permits are hard to get, and the animal must undergo 4 weeks of quarantine, so traveling with pets is usually not an option.

• **Tobacco:** Travelers 18 or older may bring up to 200 cigarettes or 250g of tobacco, but no "moist snuff."

What You Can Take Home from Iceland:

Icelandic law forbids the export of birds, bird eggs, bird nests, eggshells, many rare minerals, all stalactites and stalagmites in caves, and 31 protected plant species. In other words, leave nature where you found it. Objects of historical or archaeological interest may not be taken out of the country without special permission.

• **U.S. Citizens:** For specifics on what you can bring back, download *Know Before You Go* online at **www.cbp.gov** or contact the **U.S. Customs & Border Protection** (ℂ **877/287-8667**) to request the pamphlet.

• **Canadian Citizens:** For a clear summary of Canadian rules, pick up the booklet *I Declare,* issued by the **Canada Border Services Agency** (ℂ **800/461-9999** in Canada, or 204/983-3500; **www.cbsa-asfc.gc.ca**).

• **U.K. Citizens:** For information, contact **HM Customs & Excise** at ℂ **0845/ 010-9000** (from outside the U.K., 020/8929-0152), or consult their website at **www.hmce.gov.uk**.

• **Australian Citizens:** A helpful brochure available from Australian consulates or Customs offices is *Know Before You Go.* For more information, contact the **Australian Customs Service** (ℂ **1300/363-263; www.customs.gov.au**).

- **New Zealand Citizens:** Most questions are answered in a free pamphlet available at New Zealand consulates and Customs offices: *New Zealand Customs Guide for Travellers, Notice no. 4.* For more information, contact **New Zealand Customs** (© 04/473-6099 or 0800/428-786; **www.customs.govt.nz**).

Driving Rules See "Getting Around Iceland (By Car)," p. 37.

Electricity Iceland uses 220 Volts, 50 Hz AC, the European standard, and plugs have two round prongs.

Embassies & Consulates

U.S. Embassy, Laufásvegur 21, Reykjavík (© **562-9100**; www.usa.is; Mon–Fri 8am–5pm).

Canadian Embassy, Túngata 14, Reykjavík (© **575-6500**; www.canada.is; Mon–Fri 9am–noon).

British Embassy, Laufásvegur 31, Reykjavík (© **550-5100**; www.british embassy.is; Mon–Fri 9am–noon).

Republic of Ireland Honorary Consulate, Ásbuð 106, Garðabær, near Reykjavík (© **554-2355**).

Australia does not have an embassy or consulate in Iceland. Services for Australian citizens in Iceland are handled through Sweden's Australian consulate, Sergels Torg 12, Stockholm (© **46/8-613-2900**; www.sweden.embassy.gov.au).

New Zealand does not have an embassy in Iceland; the nearest is in the Hague in the Netherlands at Carnegielaan 10, 2517 KH (© **31/70-346-9324**; nzemb@xs4all.nl).

South Africa Honorary Consul, Borgartún 35, Reykjavík (© **591-0355**).

Emergencies For fire, police, ambulance, or medical emergency, dial **112** from any phone.

Holidays Businesses are closed on New Year's Day, Maundy Thursday (Thurs before Easter), Good Friday, Easter Sunday, Easter Monday, First Day of Summer (third Thurs in Apr), Labor Day (May 1), Ascension Day (mid–late May), Whitsunday and Whitmonday (mid-May to early June), National Day (June 17), Bank Holiday (first Mon in Aug), Christmas Eve (from noon on), Christmas, Boxing Day (Dec 26), and New Year's Eve. For more on Icelandic holidays, see "Calendar of Events," p. 15.

Internet Access See "Staying Connected," p. 31.

Language The national language is Icelandic. English is commonly spoken, especially among younger generations. For useful Icelandic terms and phrases, and a guide to pronunciation, see the appendix.

Liquor Laws The legal drinking age in Iceland is 20. Grocery stores have only low-alcohol beer; all other alcohol is sold in state-controlled stores called *Vinbuð*, with limited opening hours. Drunk-driving laws are extremely strict; just one drink could put you over the blood alcohol limit (0.05%).

Lost & Found In Reykjavík the Lost & Found is in the police station at Borgartún 7b (© **444-1400**; Mon–Fri 10am–noon and 2–4pm). Elsewhere simply contact the local police.

Mail Iceland's Postal Service (© **580-1200**; www.postur.is/english) is reliable and efficient. General post office hours in Reykjavík are 9am to 6pm weekdays, but post offices close earlier elsewhere. Mailboxes are bright red and marked *Pósturinn.* At press time, a postcard or letter up to 20g sent within Europe is 80kr ($1.30/65p) by "A-post" or 70kr ($1.10/55p) by "B-post." A postcard or letter sent outside Europe is 105kr ($1.70/85p) by A-post, 80kr ($1.30/65p) by B-post. Heavy packages can be expensive; a 5kg (11 lb.) package via surface mail, for example, is about 3,500kr ($56/£28) to the U.S. or 3,875kr ($62/£31) to the U.K. Stamps are sold at many locations, including Nóatún supermarkets; N1, Olís, and Shell gas stations; and some bookstores. Mail typically takes 3 to 5 business days to reach Europe or the United States.

To receive mail in Iceland, you can have letters and packages sent "Poste Restante" to any Icelandic post office. The recipient's family name should be written in capital letters—otherwise, the mail could be filed by first name, as it is for Icelanders. Mail should be addressed to the recipient at "Poste Restante/[name of town] Post Office" (check the website for addresses). When collecting the mail, bring your passport for identification.

Maps See "Visitor Information & Maps," p. 13.

Passports Allow plenty of time before your trip to apply for a passport; processing normally takes at least 4 to 6 weeks but can take up to 12 during busy periods (especially spring).

For Residents of Australia: You can pick up an application from your local post office or any branch of Passports Australia, but you must schedule an interview at the passport office to present your application materials. Call the **Australian Passport Information Service** at ⓒ 131-232, or visit the government website at www.passports.gov.au.

For Residents of Canada: Passport applications are available at travel agencies throughout Canada or from the central **Passport Office,** Department of Foreign Affairs and International Trade, Ottawa, ON K1A 0G3 (ⓒ 800/567-6868; www.ppt.gc.ca).

For Residents of Ireland: You can apply for a 10-year passport at the **Passport Office,** Setanta Centre, Molesworth Street, Dublin 2 (ⓒ 01/671-1633; www.irl gov.ie/iveagh). Those under age 18 and over 65 must apply for a 3-year passport. You can also apply at 1A South Mall, Cork (ⓒ 021/272-525) or at most main post offices.

For Residents of New Zealand: You can pick up a passport application at any New Zealand Passports Office (ⓒ 0800/225-050 or ⓒ 04/474-8100) or download it from their website (www.passports.govt.nz).

For Residents of the United Kingdom: To pick up an application for a standard 10-year passport (5-year. passport for children under 16), visit your nearest passport office, major post office, or travel agency; or contact the **United Kingdom Passport Service** at ⓒ 0870/521-0410 or www.ukpa.gov.uk.

For Residents of the United States: Whether applying in person or by mail, you can download passport applications and check current processing fees at the State Department website **http://travel.state.gov.** To find a regional passport office, either check the above website or call the **National Passport Information Center** (ⓒ 877/487-2778) for automated information.

Police In an emergency dial **112.**

Safety See "Health & Safety," p. 25.

Smoking As of 2007, smoking is prohibited by law in all restaurants, cafes, bars, and accommodations.

Taxes Iceland's 24.5% VAT (sales tax) is included in prices, but tourists can get most of that back on qualified purchases; see p. 123.

Telephones See "Staying Connected," p. 31.

Time Zone Iceland is always on Greenwich Mean Time, with no daylight saving time. Thus during the winter, Iceland is 5 hours ahead of the eastern U.S. and in the same time zone as the U.K. In summer, Iceland is 4 hours ahead of the eastern U.S. and 1 hour behind the U.K.

Tipping Icelanders don't tip, not even in restaurants or taxis. Tipping is never expected from foreigners, but if you do tip, you are unlikely to offend anyone; it would be graciously accepted or politely refused. The practice is becoming a little more common in Reykjavík bars and nightclubs.

Water Iceland has some of the world's best drinking water, and all tap water is safe to drink. Even surface water is generally potable, and *Giardia,* a water-born intestinal parasite, is very rare. Avoid drinking from streams that have flowed through areas with livestock or birds. When in doubt, boil water for 10 minutes or use purifying treatments founds at camping stores.

3

Active Iceland

This chapter is not just for athletes and adrenaline addicts, but for any traveler seeking recreation and adventure in Iceland's great outdoors.

Some Reykjavík companies, all of which blur the line between tour operator and travel agency, offer a wide range of tours across Iceland. **The Activity Group,** Tunguháls 8 (© **580-9900;** www.activity.is), and **Mountaineers of Iceland,** Skútuvogur 12E (© **580-9900;** www.mountaineers.is), are oriented toward private tours and tend to be pricier. **Arctic Adventures,** Laugavegur 11 (© **562-7000;** www.adventures.is), specializes in more robust sporting activities and has very reasonable prices. **Nordic Adventure Travel,** Svarthamrar 17 (© **898-0355;** www.nat.is), and **Touris,** Frostaskjól 105 (© **517-8290;** www.tour.is), serve mostly as travel agencies but are also licensed to lead tours. The two regional companies with the most creative roster of outdoor adventures are **Nonni Travel,** Brekkugata 5, Akureyri (© **461-1841;** www.nonnitravel.is), in north Iceland,

and **West Tours,** Aðalstræti 7, Ísafjörður (© **456-5111;** www.westtours.is), in the Westfjords.

Iceland's two preeminent hiking organizations, **Ferðafélag Íslands,** Mörkin 6, Reykjavík (© **568-2533;** www.fi.is), and **Útivist,** Laugavegur 178, Reykjavík (© **562-1000;** www.utivist.is), lead small groups in down-to-earth expeditions that usually include Icelanders and revolve around hiking; others delve into anything from skiing to yoga under the midnight sun.

Keep in mind that the regional sections of this book may include local tour operators not mentioned in this chapter. Agencies offering outdoor activity tours are also listed in chapter 2, under the headings of "General-Interest Tours & Packages" (p. 35) and "Special-Interest Trips" (p. 36).

Unless otherwise indicated, tour prices quoted below include transportation (within Iceland only), meals (except for day tours), accommodation, and a guide.

1 Aerial Tours

Aerial sightseeing is mushrooming these days, and it's easy to see why. Pilots can fly almost anywhere, and many remote areas are difficult to reach by other means.

Prices may be less prohibitive than you think. Airplane tours run anywhere from 5,000kr ($80/£40) for 20 minutes aloft to 20,000kr ($320/£160) for 1½ to 2 hours. Helicopter tours are far more expensive, but maneuvers are more thrilling.

Aerial tours are scheduled by arrangement, and flight paths are usually negotiable. The minimum number of passengers ranges from two to six. If your head count is fewer, ask to team up with another group. Flights are frequently cancelled because of weather and wind conditions, so leave wiggle room in your itinerary. And prepare yourself for buffeting in the wind—all the planes are 4- to 10-seaters.

TOUR OPERATORS

Reykjavík has three similarly priced tour operators, all based at the city's domestic airport. **Eagle Air** (© **562-4200**; www.eagleair.is) has a 30-minute tour of the capital area (7,500kr/$120/£60 per person); a 4-hour midnight sun tour to Grímsey Island (30,000kr/$480/£240); and package tours combining aerial sightseeing with boat trips, white-water rafting, and snowmobiling on Vatnajökull. **Fjarðaflug** (© **562-6500**; www.fjardaflug.is) and **Odin Air** (© **551-0880**; www.odinair.is) also have tempting flight menus. Fjarðaflug's 1¾-hour "South Iceland" tour—which costs 17,900kr ($286/£143) and takes in Þingvellir, Geysir, Gullfoss, Mt. Hekla, Landmannalaugar, and Þórsmörk—is particularly grand.

Mountaineers of Iceland, Skútuvogur 12E, Reykjavík (© **580-9900**; www.mountaineers.is), and **Mountain Taxi,** Trönuhrauni 7, Hafnarfjörður (© **544-5252**; www.mountaintaxi.is), tie helicopter rides into Super Jeep romps on glaciers. Mountain Taxi also customizes helicopter excursions; the price for up to six people averages 150,000kr ($2,400/£1,200) for each hour of flying time.

Outside the capital, **Mýflug Air** (© **464-4400**; www.myflug.is), based at **Mývatn**'s Reykjahlíð airfield, is conveniently close to Krafla, Jökulsárgljúfur National Park, Askja, Kverkfjöll, and other striking landmarks (p. 242). Eagle Air, Fjarðaflug, and Mýflug Air all arrange tours from **Akureyri** (p. 230). **Atlantsflug** (© **486-2406**; www.atf.is) is based at **Skaftafell National Park,** close to Núpsstaðarskógar, the Laki craters, and Landmannalaugar (p. 314).

2 Biking

Iceland is a rewarding but also demanding locale for a long-distance bike trip. The major hazards are volatile weather, harsh winds, sandstorms, rough roads, and stones flung by passing vehicles. Any bike brought to Iceland should be very high-quality. Bring along a repair kit and be prepared for several flats since supplies are difficult to find outside Reykjavík. Make sure you are easily visible to motorists, and always wear a helmet—legally required for all children under 15. To protect Iceland's vegetation, all off-road driving—of bikes as well as cars—is absolutely forbidden.

Bicyclists along the Ring Road can use the bus as a backup in bad weather. Bikes are stored in the luggage compartment, so you might bring padding to prevent damage.

The **Icelandic Mountainbike Club,** Brekkustígur 2, Reykjavík (© **562-0099**; www.mmedia.is/~ifhk/tourist.htm), does not arrange trips or rentals for tourists but the website has suggested itineraries, a packing checklist, a message board, and tips on where to store your bike box.

See regional chapters for more information on biking by destination.

TOUR OPERATORS

On Friday evenings from June 10 through August, **Arctic Adventures,** Laugavegur 11 (© **562-7000**; www.adventures.is), leads 4-hour bike tours of Reykjavík for 4,590kr ($73/£37), with only a two-person minimum. The **Icelandic Mountainbike Club** (see above) organizes informal weekend trips for its members, and visitors are often welcome to tag along.

Blue Biking, Stekkjarhvammi 60, Hafnarfjörður (© **565-2089**; www.simnet.is/bluebiking), offers a few cycling trips in southwest Iceland, from a day-long Reykjavík tour to a 5-day excursion through Þjórsárdalur and Landmannalaugar, with luggage transport. Trips are scheduled by arrangement and usually have a four- or five-person minimum.

West Tours, Aðalstræti 7, Ísafjörður (© **456-5111;** www.westtours.is), rents mountain bikes and can help with basic logistical support, such as plotting out wonderful routes in that region; though they do not lead guided tours.

Freewheeling Adventures (from North America © **800/672-0775;** outside North America © **902/857-3600;** www.freewheeling.ca), based in Nova Scotia, Canada, schedules two guided 8-day trips each year, both with fantastic itineraries. The 305,937kr ($4,895/£2,448) rate includes luggage transport. Self-guided versions of the same tours cost 31,250kr ($500/£250) less and leave anytime.

3 Bird-Watching

In Iceland, even non-birders are at some point drawn to bird-watching. Iceland lies at a major junction of migratory routes, and hosts at least 278 species. Puffins (p. 283), universally beloved for their clownish looks and slapstick antics, are pictured on every other tourist brochure. Other common types are guillemots, arctic terns, gannets, fulmars, cormorants, kittiwakes, and razorbills. Especially coveted sightings include the barrow's goldeneye, found all summer at Mývatn; harlequin ducks, seen on several Icelandic rivers; the white-tailed eagle, occasionally spotted in Breiðafjörður bay; and the gyrfalcon, Iceland's national bird.

Hard-core birders initiate the tourist season in April and May, when nesting season reaches full swing. May and June have the optimal convergence of species variety, fine plumage, and decent weather, though a few nature reserves—notably Dyrhólaey in the south, and the northern end of Hrísey island in the north—are closed to visitors at precisely this time to protect the birds and their young. By August, bird numbers are down dramatically, but enthusiasts can find ways to keep busy all year.

Prime coastal sites include **Hafnaberg** (p. 158) and **Valahnúkur** (p. 158) on Reykjanes peninsula; **Arnarstapi** (p. 176) on Snæfellsnes peninsula; **Breiðafjörður** (p. 187), the bay between Snæfellsnes and the Westfjords; **Látrabjarg** (p. 189) and **Hornbjarg** (p. 212) in the Westfjords; **Hrísey island** (p. 245) near Akureyri; **Langanes peninsula** (p. 273) in the northeast; the **Westman Islands** (p. 277), Dyrhólaey (p. 303) and **Ingólfshöfði** (p. 315) in the south; and **Papey island** (p. 327) in the east. Inland, the foremost locale is **Mývatn** (p. 250), Europe's most diverse waterfowl habitat. The birding map *Fuglakort Íslands,* with English text and handy illustrations, is commonly available in Iceland, or order at **www.nordicstore.net** before you go.

The best online informational resource, **www.birdingiceland.com** has fantastic photography, extensive diaries, and a gripping "Rare Bird News" feature.

TOUR OPERATORS

Gavia Travel, Álfaheiði 44, Kópavogur (© **863-3939;** www.gaviatravel.com), is the only Icelandic company devoted exclusively to birding tours. Day tours of the Reykjanes (10,800kr/$173/£86) or Snæfellsnes (13,800kr/$221/£110) peninsulas are by arrangement, while 4-, 6-, and 12-day regional trips have set departure dates from March through October. Four-day, all-inclusive tours from Reykjavík cost 85,700kr to 107,700kr ($1,371–$1,723/£685–£862), and 6-day trips are 185,000kr to 210,000kr ($2,960–$3,360/£1,480–£1,680).

Icelander Tours/Highlander Adventures, Guðrúnargata 9, Reykjavík (© **892-5509;** www.icelandertours.com), schedules 10-day bird-watching tours in May and June for 233,750kr ($3,740/£1,870). The itinerary, which circles the country, includes a dip at Mývatn Nature Baths, a boat trip through the glacial lagoon Jökulsárlón, and other fun extras.

Valtours (© 557-1735; www.valtours.is), a small and cost-effective eco-tour operator, offers scheduled and custom birding tours from April to October. One-week trips with half-board at guesthouses typically cost 156,250kr ($2,500/£1,250).

Field Guides (from North America © 800/728-4953; outside North America © 512/263-7295; www.fieldguides.com), a bird tour specialist based in Austin, TX, leads a 10-day trip in July for around 298,438kr ($4,775/£2,388), not including airfare.

4 Caving

Iceland has some of the world's longest **lava-tube caves,** formed after volcanic eruptions when conduits of molten rock drain downhill. Lava pillars, mineral stalactites, ice candles, and snaking side passageways are among the intriguing formations within. Walking through these caves generally requires agility and sure-footedness but no specialized training or equipment, so virtuoso spelunkers tend to devote their energies elsewhere. **Ice caves** are also common in Iceland, but they're too dangerous to enter.

Among the many lava-tube caves worth seeking out are **Raufarhólshellir** (p. 161), near Hveragerði in southwest Iceland; **Surtshellir** and **Víðgelmir** (p. 170) in west Iceland; and **Lofthellir** (p. 255) near Lake Mývatn.

If you plan to explore any caves on your own, bring a strong flashlight, warm clothing, and sturdy shoes. Helmets, knee pads, gloves, and headlamps are also advised, and caves with icy floors may require studded boots. The smartest procedure is always to seek out expert local advice beforehand.

TOUR OPERATORS

Several Reykjavík companies offer caving tours, with all equipment provided. **Arctic Adventures,** Laugavegur 11 (© 562-7000; www.adventures.is), and **Iceland Excursions,** Höfðatún 12 (© 540-1313; www.icelandexcursions.is), offer 3- to 4-hour tours to Gjábakkahellir between Laugarvatn and Þingvellir; Arctic Adventures leaves Fridays from June to August for 5,990kr ($96/£48), while Iceland Excursions leaves Saturdays and Sundays year-round for 6,400kr ($102/£51). **Mountaineers of Iceland,** Skútuvogur 12E (© 580-9900; www.mountaineers.is), leads 5-hour private caving tours by arrangement for 13,500kr ($216/£108), with a four-person minimum. **Iceland Rovers** (© 567-1720; www.icelandrovers.is) has a 6-hour tour that begins with caving and ends with a hike to the swimmable hot springs in Reykjadalur (p. 162). The cost is rather high at 17,900kr ($286/£143). Set departures are on Sundays, and private trips are on request with a four-person minimum.

5 Dog Sledding

Dog sledding on glaciers is not an authentic Icelandic tradition; but it's a quiet and graceful alternative to roaring around on snowmobiles, ATVs, or Super Jeeps, and the sled dogs—all Greenlandic huskies—are awfully cute. Tours are possible all year, but conditions may be too unfavorable in fall and early winter. Forget about epic dog-sledding treks; all that's usually offered are short jaunts of 45 minutes to 2 hours on Langjökull or Mýrdalsjökull. Snowsuits and gloves are included in tour prices, but make sure to bring sunglasses for snow glare.

From Reykjavík, **Eskimos,** Tunguháls 19 (© 414-1500; www.eskimos.is), runs scheduled day trips to Mýrdalsjökull in summer and Langjökull in winter, starting at a whopping 31,000kr ($496/£258) per person. **The Activity Group,** Tunguháls 8 (② **580-9900;** www.activity.is), has similarly priced half-day and full-day tours on Langjökull from February to August. If you have your own transport, the best option is to drive to the base camp of **Dog Steam Tours** (② **487-7747;** www.dogsledding.is), by Mýrdalsjökull, where 50-minute tours run for 10,900kr ($174/£87); see p. 303 for more information.

6 Fishing

FRESHWATER FISHING

Many Iceland visitors are needlessly put off from the idea of freshwater fishing once they learn Eric Clapton and Prince Charles pay upward of £1,500 ($3,000) per day to cast for salmon. However, cheaper salmon permits are as low as $150 per rod per day, and lake fishing for trout and arctic char is inexpensive and sometimes free. Virtually every village has reasonably priced fishing locales nearby, and permits, when necessary, are easily purchased at the local gas station. The *Veiðikortið* **fishing card** (② **517-4515;** www.veidikortid.is), available at all N1 gas stations, gives you unlimited access to 31 lakes around the country for 5,000kr ($80/£40).

Iceland has over a hundred self-sustaining **salmon rivers,** of which 20 fall into the elite class. Most elite rivers are leased to private clubs, and fishing these rivers usually means booking through the club, staying at the club lodge, and using club equipment and guides. Less expensive permits tend to be a simpler and more straightforward matter. Most rivers have a strict fly-fishing-only policy.

Fishing season for many lakes, including most lakes in the *Veiðikortið* network, is restricted to May through September. Some lakes remain open all year, even for ice fishing. Salmon season cannot exceed 90 days per river, and the dates are usually set from the first half of June to the first half of September.

The best all-around informational resource for freshwater fishing in Iceland—including lake fishing—is the **Federation of Icelandic River Owners,** Hagatorg Square, Reykjavík (② **553-1510;** www.angling.is). The website lists all the best fishing waters and how to get there, contacts for tours and permits, regulations on fishing tackle, and the ins and outs of ice fishing. For equipment, the best store in Iceland is **Veiðihornið,** with two Reykjavík locations: Hafnarstræti 5 (② **551-6760**) and Síðumúli 8 (② **568-8410;** both locations Jun–Aug Mon–Fri 8am–7pm, Sat–Sun 9am–6pm; Sept–May Mon–Fri 10am–6pm, Sat 10am–4pm, Sun noon–4pm). The Veiðihornið website, **www.rifflehitch.com**, posts ongoing "catch reports" for all of Iceland's salmon rivers.

Note: All fishing equipment—including rods, reels, waders, and tackle boxes—must be disinfected before entering Iceland, except for brand-new items. (The disinfection facility at Keflavík International Airport recently closed.) Customs officials will need to see a veterinarian's certificate for proof. Importing any organic bait is out of the question, unless it's thoroughly cooked.

TOUR OPERATORS   For many elite rivers and some lakes, the tour operators are the fishing clubs that control the leases. The two most prestigious clubs are **Angling Club Lax-á,** Akurhvarf 16, Kópavogur (② **557-6100;** www.lax-a.is), and **Angling Club of Reykjavík,** Háaleitisbraut 68, Reykjavík (② **568-6050;** www.svfr.is), with 29 rivers and several lakes between them. Packages range from full-service pampering in luxury lodges to basic accommodation in self-catering cabins. Rivers tend to book up in advance, but it's always worth checking for cancellations. Other clubs worth scouring for package

deals are **Angling Service Strengir,** Smárarima 30, Reykjavík (© **567-5204;** www.
strengir.is), **G & P,** Þingholtsstræti 16, Reykjavík (© **551-2112;** www.vatnsdalsa.is),
and **Sporður,** Lágmúli 7, Reykjavík (© **587-0860;** www.spordur.is).

The tour company **Fly Fishing In Iceland,** Freyjugata 38, Reykjavík (© **551-2016;** www.gofishing.is), does not control any leases on rivers or lakes, but can organize all sorts of fishing itineraries in Iceland, with or without a guide, while taking care of the permit headaches. Day trips from Reykjavík are also offered.

Outside Iceland, **Angler Adventures** (from North America © **800/628-1447,** outside North America **860/434-9624;** www.angleradventures.com), based in Old Lyme, CT, is affiliated with Angling Club Lax-á and designs custom packages. **Frontiers International** (from North America © **800/245-1950;** from the U.K. © **0128/574-1340;** www.frontierstravel.com) offers two week-long fishing packages, each focusing on a specific salmon river. **Sportfishing Worldwide** (from North America © **800/638-7405;** outside North America © **513/984-8611;** www.sfww.com) based in Cincinnati, OH, organizes 4- to 12-day guided trips and works directly with property owners, bypassing the fishing clubs.

SEA ANGLING

Sea fishing is so integral to Icelandic life that someone can take you out in virtually every coastal village; if no tours are advertised, just ask around. Success is near guaranteed, at least for cod, and most tours make arrangements for you to eat your catch for dinner. Unlike freshwater fishing, permits aren't required, as long as you don't return to port knee-deep in fish. A 2- to 3-hour jaunt is around 4,500kr to 7,000kr ($72–$112/£36–£56)per person. The regional sections of this book list specific seaangling **tour operators** based in Reykjavík (chapter 5); Stykkishólmur, Látrabjarg Peninsula, Suðureyri, and Djúpavík in the west (chapter 7); Hvammstangi, Sauðárkrókur, Akureyri, Hauganes, Dalvík, Grímsey Island, and Húsavík in the north (chapter 8); the Westman Islands in the south (chapter 9); and Djúpivogur, Fáskrúðsfjörður, Stöðvarfjörður, and Seyðisfjörður in the east (chapter 10).

As with freshwater fishing, all equipment must be disinfected before entering Iceland, and a veterinarian's certificate must be supplied for proof.

7 Glacier Tours

Glaciers, which cover about 10% of Iceland's surface, are enduring objects of fascination to Icelanders (see "The Glacier Mystique" box, p. 312). Traversing glaciers is generally done on snowmobiles, Super Jeeps (see also "Jeep Tours," below), skis (see "Skiing & Ski Touring," later in this chapter), dog sleds (see "Dog Sledding," above), or by foot. In hiking tours, participants often wear crampons and walk a set distance apart in single file, fastened to each other with ropes and safety harnesses; some tours also involve wielding ice axes or rappelling (aka abseiling) into crevasses. Snowmobile tours can be tamer than expected, proceeding single-file with the slowest driver setting the pace. Expect to pay 8,000kr to 11,500kr ($128–$184/£64–£92) for an hour in a snowmobile seat. Advertised prices assume two persons per snowmobile, and riding solo costs extra.

Glaciers can be mortally dangerous; for more on glacier safety, see p. 25.

TOUR OPERATORS

Several companies offer glacier tours that start in Reykjavík and often tie in sightseeing and other outdoor activities. Langjökull, Iceland's second-largest glacier—and the glacier closest to the capital—is a popular and convenient destination. **The Activity**

Group, Tunguháls 8, Reykjavík (© 580-9900; www.activity.is), slips snowmobile rides on Langjökull into some day-long Super Jeep sightseeing tours in the 23,000kr ($368/£184) range. The year-round "Express Activity Tour" is for unadulterated snowmobiling; the 18,000kr ($288/£144) price tag includes transportation from Reykjavík, with only a two-person minimum.

Iceland Rovers (© 567-1720; www.icelandrovers.is) offers 11-hour Super Jeep trips, with a four-person minimum, from Reykjavík to Mýrdalsjökull, where you can choose between a glacier hike for 26,900kr ($430/£215) and an hour on a snow-mobile for 32,700kr ($523/£262). A very similar tour led by **Mountain Taxi,** Trönuhrauni 7, Hafnarfjörður (© 544-5252; www.mountaintaxi.is), takes 9 hours and costs 30,800kr ($493/£246), with a stop at the bird sanctuary of Dyrhólaey.

The Super Jeeps reach some beautiful, remote spots inaccessible to regular cars, but you can save lots of money by renting a car for the day and driving to Mýrdalsjökull (p. 302), where local tour operators charge 3,900kr ($62/£31) for 90-minute glacial hikes, 6,300kr ($101/£50) for 4½-hour glacial hikes, and 10,900kr ($174/£87) for an hour-long snowmobile ride. If you'd rather not drive, **Arctic Adventures,** Laugavegur 11, Reykjavík (© 562-7000; www.adventures.is), offers a well-priced tour that com-bines transport from Reykjavík with an adventurous glacial hike on Mýrdalsjökull—including a stab at ice climbing. The 9-hour round-trip costs 11,900kr ($190/£95), with guaranteed departures twice a week from mid-June through August, plus depar-tures by arrangement, with a four-person minimum.

If you would like to get married on a glacier, **Scantours** (© 020/7554-3530; www.scantours.co.uk), based in London, can craft an itinerary and make all the legal and logistical arrangements. Just don't get cold feet.

Several tour operators are listed in this book's regional chapters. For snowmobile and snow cat tours of Snæfellsjökull—the glacier visible from Reykjavík on a clear day—see p. 178. For snowmobile, Super Jeep, hiking, and ice-climbing expeditions on Mýrdalsjökull, Iceland's southernmost glacier, see p. 302. Vatnajökull, the largest glacier between the Arctic and Antarctic circles, can be approached from several direc-tions. For hiking, mountaineering, and ice-climbing tours from Skaftafell National Park, see p. 314. For snowmobile and Super Jeep tours from Jöklasel, near Höfn, see p. 317. For an unforgettable day hike from Kverkfjöll, deep in the interior, see p. 363.

8 Golf

Despite its high winds and changeable weather, Iceland is a golf-loving nation with over 50 courses. Most courses are open from May through September, and a few try to stay open all year. Course fees range anywhere from 1,500kr to 6,500kr ($24–$104/ £12–£52). Settings are spectacular, of course, and teeing off under the midnight sun is especially memorable.

For golfing in the Reykjavík vicinity, see p. 122. Other golf courses singled out in regional chapters of this book include **Hamarsvöllur** in Borgarnes (p. 170), **Vestman-naeyjavöllur** in the Westman Islands (p. 284), and Akureyri's **Jaðarsvöllur,** the site of Iceland's best-known tournament, the **Arctic Open** (p. 242).

The best online resource, with basic descriptions and contact information for every Icelandic course, is **www.nat.is;** click the "Golf Guide" link.

Britannia Golf (from North America © 877/249-7354; outside North America © 1804/346-8716; www.britanniagolf.com), a golf tour company based in Glen Allen, VA, customizes Iceland golfing itineraries lasting 2 days to a week.

9 Hiking

Of all the outdoor activities outlined here, hiking is the most fundamental to an Iceland vacation. With its stunning landscapes, fresh air, and wide open spaces, Iceland is a hiking utopia. Over 70 mountain huts across the country (p. 45) provide the infrastructure for an extensive network of backcountry routes; though hiking in Iceland hardly has to mean donning a heavy backpack and eating freeze-dried food. The country is equally blessed with short, easy hikes, not to mention tour operators who will transport luggage from hut to hut.

Independent-minded hikers who shy away from organized tours should at least reconsider the issue. Icelandic hiking tours are often just a practical means to have luggage transported and logistical hassles eased. Organized hiking groups tend to be small, laid-back, and fun, and you can keep to yourself when you want to. Moreover, Icelanders often travel with the groups—especially with the "Big Two," below.

Prime hiking season lasts from early June through mid-September, though some routes at higher altitudes are inaccessible until July. (Occasionally visitors plan their entire vacation around a specific trek, and arrive in mid-June only to find snow obstructing the trail and the mountain huts still closed.) For hiking preparations and precautions, see "Staying Healthy"—particularly the "Outdoor Safety" subheading (p. 25)—in chapter 2.

For a summary of top hikes, flip to "The Best Big-Name Hikes" (p. 5) and "The Best Hikes Off the Beaten Track" (p. 6) in chapter 1.

TOUR OPERATORS

Several additional tour operators are recommended for specific destinations in the regional chapters of this book.

THE "BIG TWO" HIKING ORGANIZATIONS

When Icelanders sign up for hiking tours, they usually go with **Ferðafélag Íslands,** Mörkin 6, Reykjavík (© 568-2533; www.fi.is) or **Útivist,** Laugavegur 178, Reykjavík (© 562-1000; www.utivist.is). Neither organization hankers too much for your business—Útivist's website doesn't even post its trip schedule in English—but foreigners are always welcome. (To skim Útivist's trips in Icelandic, find the "Ferðaáætlun" link at the website.) Trips range from a few hours to several days, with set departure dates. No frills are added, so prices remain relatively low. Generally all that's provided is transportation from Reykjavík and a guide, plus sleeping-bag accommodation in mountain huts for overnight trips, and, occasionally, luggage transport. Participants are expected to bring and cook their own food.

As far as visitors are concerned, not much distinguishes the two organizations. Útivist has slightly lower prices and schedules more trips per year: about 150, as opposed to 70 for Ferðafélag Íslands. However, Ferðafélag Íslands has a few local affiliates, some of which lead trips of their own. The key affiliates are **Ferðafélag Akureyrar** (© 462-2720; www.ffa.is; ffa@ffa.is) in Akureyri and **Ferðafélag Fljótsdalshéraðs** (© 863-5813; www.fljotsdalsherad.is/ferdafelag; ferdafelag@egilsstadir.is) in Egilsstaðir. Their trips focus on north and east Iceland respectively, but range all over the country. Neither affiliate has a website or brochure in English, but tour schedules can be gleaned from the websites; for Ferðafélag Akureyrar, find the "Ferðaáætlun" link, and for Ferðafélag Fljótsdalshéraðs, find the "Ferðir" link. (Or just call or e-mail.) This is your best chance to hike with an all-Icelandic group.

OTHER ICELANDIC COMPANIES

Arinbjörn Jóhannsson, Brekkulækur Farm, Hvammstangi (© **451-2938;** www.
geysir.com/brekkulaekur), leads fabulous 8- to 13-day hiking excursions across the
country from June through early September, with set departure dates and a maximum
group size of 14. Accommodation is in simple guesthouses, hostels, and mountain
huts, keeping the price down to a reasonable 116,375kr to 192,500kr ($1,862–$3080/
£931–£1,540). Priorities include bird-watching at seacliffs, finding rare ferns, and
socializing with the neighbors.

Fjallabak (© **511-3070;** www.fjallabak.is) offers an impressive variety of well-
designed hiking tours for day-trippers and serious backpackers alike, with set departure dates as early as April. Trips last 6 to 11 days and cost 105,000kr to 201,250kr
($1,680–$3,220/£840–£1,610)—a decent price, considering the maximum group
size is only 9 to 12.

Icelandic Mountain Guides, Vagnhöfði 7b, Reykjavík (© **587-9996;** www.
mountainguide.is), has staked out some extremely interesting and remote backpacking routes well off the tourist radar. Tours last 4 to 30 days, with set departure dates,
small group sizes (6–12), and good prices—a 9-day trek from Laki Craters to Skaftafell National Park, for instance, is 99,900kr ($1,598/£799).

INTERNATIONAL COMPANIES

Dick Phillips Icelandic Travel Service (from the U.K. **0143/438-1440;** outside the
U.K. © **44143/438-1440;** www.icelandic-travel.com) leads a series of 1- to 2-week
backpacking adventures well off the beaten path from mid-May to early September,
with group sizes of 4 to 16, and prices ranging from 369£ to 659£ ($738–$1,318).
Dick Phillips has traveled extensively in Iceland since 1960, and can also serve as a
consultant for self-guided wilderness treks.

REI Adventures (from North America © **800/622-2236;** outside North America
© **1253-437-1100;** www.rei.com/adventures) offers an exciting 8-day "Fire & Ice
Adventure" tour of south Iceland, with six departure dates in summer. Most days are
spent hiking 3 to 6 hours, and most nights are spent in small hotels. The $4,000
(£2,000) price is higher than average, though part of your fee goes toward keeping the
tour carbon neutral.

Southern Treks (© **706/291-2471;** www.southerntreks.com), based in the U.S.
state of Georgia, has a wonderful 11-day trip for $5,025 (£2,513), led by a PhD of
Old Icelandic Law, with easy to moderate day hikes all across the country. The trip
may not run every year, unfortunately.

Wilderness Travel (from North America © **800/368-2794;** outside North America © **1510-558-2488;** www.wildernesstravel.com) is a respected high-end tour company, whose 9-day hiking circuit of south Iceland—with three summer departures—costs
around $5,500 (£2,750). Hikes are moderate, consuming 4 to 6 hours per day, and
accommodation is in Iceland's nicer hotels.

World Expeditions (from the U.S. © **415/989-2212;** from Canada © **613/
241-2700;** from the U.K. © **0208/545-9030;** from Australia **6128/270-8400;** from
New Zealand **6409/368-4161;** www.worldexpeditions.com), based in Australia, leads
an exciting and well-conceived 15-day trip through south Iceland, with moderate
hikes each day and most nights spent camping or in mountain huts. The cost is
243,125kr ($3,890/£1,945), with five departure dates each summer.

10 Horseback Riding

Beginners and seasoned riders alike are enraptured by the Icelandic horse, a small breed with a gentle temperament and remarkable stamina, agility, and intelligence. One of their best-known talents is *tölting*, a kind of running trot with one foot always touching the ground. (In a popular stunt during Icelandic horse demonstrations, the rider breaks into a tölt while holding a tray of drinks in one hand.)

In summer, many young horses are released into the wilds to adapt them to Iceland's rugged terrain. In September and October, free-roaming horses and sheep are rounded up and brought home for the winter. Visitors are often welcome to participate in these important cultural rituals; see "The Big Round-Up," p. 18.

Riding tack (bridles, saddles, and such) may not be brought into Iceland. Other riding equipment (such as boots, clothing, helmets, and saddlebags) must be sterilized prior to arrival, and a veterinarian's certificate of disinfection must be presented at customs. (The disinfection facility at Keflavík International Airport recently closed.)

TOUR OPERATORS

The best tour operators are listed below, but virtually any populated area in Iceland will have riding opportunities nearby—just ask around. Several additional tour operators are recommended throughout the regional chapters of this book, specifically for Snæfellsnes peninsula and Hornstrandir Nature Reserve in the west (chapter 7); Húnaflói, Skagafjörður, Dalvík, and Mývatn in the north (chapter 8); Landmannalaugar, Hella, Hvolsvöllur, and the Markarfljót valley in the south (chapter 9); and Breiðdalsvík and Borgarfjörður Eystri in the east (chapter 10).

Booking horse trips directly through Icelandic tour companies brings the price down in almost every case. Plus, no international companies lead tours themselves; the best they can do is recommend specific routes and arrange packages that save you the trouble of finding flights and lodging in Reykjavík.

Arinbjörn Jóhannsson Touring Service, Brekkulækur Farm, Hvammstangi (© 451-2938; www.geysir.com/brekkulaekur), based at a horse farm in the northwest, has been leading wonderful 1- to 2-week pack trips for 100,625kr to 236,000kr ($1,610–$3,776/£805–£1,883) since the 1970s. Some tours tie in with the Landsmót Horse Festival (p. 293) in Hella; others join the September round-ups for horse and sheep.

Eldhestar, Vellir Farm, Hveragerði (© 480-4800; www.eldhestar.is), has a fabulous tour menu with tons of trips and departure dates: 6 days around Þórsmörk is 82,500kr ($1,320/£660), while 9 days around Landmannalaugar goes for 167,500kr ($2,680/£1,340). Day tours explore neighboring lava fields and the Mt. Hengill hiking area. The farm and its eco-hotel (p. 164) are just 40 minutes from Reykjavík.

Hestasport, Vegamót, Varmahlíð (© 453-8383; www.riding.is), based in the Skagafjörður area, offers anything from 2-hour local rides for 4,000kr ($64/£32) to 7-day history tours for 128,438kr ($2,055/£1,028) to an epic 11-day trek through the interior for 131,063kr ($2,097/£1,049). Group sizes remain small, with 4 to 12 participants.

Íshestar, Sörlaskeið 26, Hafnarfjörður (© 555-7000; www.ishestar.is), is based in the Reykjavík metropolitan area but offers a staggering range of trips in all corners of Iceland. The 12-day traverse of the Sprengisandur Route in Iceland's desert interior highlands for 226,500kr ($3,624/£1,812) is a particularly valiant route.

Laxnes Horse Farm, Laxnes Farm, Mosfellsbær (© 566-6179; www.laxnes.is), located 15 minutes outside Reykjavík in Mosfellsdalur valley, is an excellent choice for day tours from the capital. (It's also something of a rock-star haunt, judging by recent visitors Lou Reed, Nick Cave, and Metallica.) A quick 3-hour tour goes for a reasonable 4,500kr ($72/£36), including pickup and dropoff in Reykjavík.

Polar Hestar, Grýtubakki II Farm, Akureyri (✆ **463-3179;** www.polarhestar.is), based in Eyjafjörður Valley near Akureyri, has crafted two memorable 8-day itineraries through Iceland's northeastern regions; prices are 96,250kr to 131,250kr ($1,540–$2,100/£770–£1,050), with 13 departure dates.

11 Hunting

Game animals in Iceland are reindeer, seals, foxes, geese, ducks, ptarmigan, and a variety of seabirds, particularly shags, guillemots, cormorants, and razorbills. Reindeer season is from August 1 to September 15, but only around 300 licenses are auctioned each year, with a cap on the number of foreign buyers. Ptarmigan—by far the most popular target for wing shooting—can be hunted from October 15 through December 20. Most seabirds are fair game from September through early May.

Most visiting hunters bring their own guns and ammunition. To do this, you must be sponsored by one of the operators below; customs will require a police permit, which only a sponsor can secure for you. Guns can also be rented from the tour operators. *Note:* Bringing dogs of any kind to Iceland is prohibited.

Organized tours are especially convenient because the tour company takes care of the paperwork for securing licenses and exporting trophies. Group sizes remain small, usually two to five hunters. **Angling Club Lax-á,** Akurhvarf 16, Kópavogur (✆ **557-6100;** www.lax-a.is), offers hunting expeditions lasting 4 to 8 days, with everything arranged from the moment you step off the plane. **Angling Service Strengir,** Smárarima 30, Reykjavík (✆ **567-5204;** www.strengir.is), specializes in hunting trips for ptarmigan, geese, and ducks. The **Icelandic Hunting Club** (✆ **894-3905;** www.hunting iceland.com) can arrange just about any private or group tour.

12 Jeep Tours

Most organized Jeep tours are in "Super Jeeps," which are not your average 4WD vehicles. These swaggering behemoths can cost upward of $300,000 apiece, with meter-high tires, souped-up engines, and state-of-the-art GPS navigational systems that could guide drivers through a complete whiteout. Super Jeeps are especially gifted at fording rivers and driving on snow. Super Jeep tours offer unmatched privacy, comfort, flexibility, and back-road access, but you'll pay handsomely for the privilege. (If you're on a budget, be consoled that Iceland's customized buses are pretty tricked-out themselves.)

Note: Super Jeep tour brochures all brag about driving "off-road," but this only means the tours venture to remote locations on difficult roads. Off-road driving is strictly forbidden in Iceland (except on some beaches).

TOUR OPERATORS

Most Super Jeep tours are day-long excursions from Reykjavík. Popular destinations include the Golden Circle, Þjórsárdalur, Mt. Hekla, Þórsmörk, Landmannalaugar, and Langjökull. Hiking, snowmobiling, sightseeing, and other activities are usually worked into itineraries. Since the tour group is often just you and the driver, routes can be highly flexible. Prices are typically 18,000kr to 24,000kr ($288–$384/£144–£192) per person for a 9- to 12-hour tour, including Reykjavík pickup and dropoff, but not lunch. For extended tours, count on roughly 36,000kr ($576/£288) per person per day, including meals and accommodation.

The top Jeep tour operators near Reykjavík are **Iceland On Track,** Grófarsmári 18, Kópavogur (© 899-5438; www.icelandontrack.com), **Iceland Rovers** (© 567-1720; www.icelandrovers.is), **Mountain Taxi,** Trönuhrauni 7c, Hafnarfjörður (© 544-5252; www.mountaintaxi.is), **Mountaineers of Iceland,** Tunguháls 8; Reykjavík (© 580-9900; www.mountaineers.is), **Safaris,** Vallarás 2, Reykjavík (© 822-0022; www.safaris.is), and **Touris,** Frostaskjól 105, Reykjavík (© 517-8290; www.tour.is). **JRJ Super Jeep Tours,** MánaÞúfa, Varmahlíð (© 453-8219; www.simnet.is/jeppaferdir) is based near Skagafjörður in northwest Iceland, but can also launch tours from the capital. Safaris is ideal for travelers who want to drive Super Jeeps themselves in guided convoys. Otherwise, very little distinguishes the offerings of these companies.

13 Kayaking

Iceland's fjords, inlets, and sheltered coastlines are ideal for sea kayaking, which can bring you up-close to seal colonies, bird cliffs, and sea caves that are inaccessible from land. All tours recommended below are guided, and none require prior experience.

From Reykjavík, the best tour operator is **Seakayak Iceland** (© 690-3877; www.seakayakiceland.com), which leads excursions to nearby islands. The company is headquartered in Stykkishólmur, on Snæfellsnes peninsula, and day tours from there among Breiðafjörður's countless islets are highly recommended. From either point of departure, 3-hour trips cost 6,000kr ($96/£48) and 6-hour trips are 10,000kr ($160/£80), with a three-person minimum. (If you're fewer than three, see if others are signed up.) Seakayak Iceland also leads multi-day adventures—some scheduled and others by arrangement—through Breiðafjörður, with camping on uninhabited islands. **West Tours** (© 456-5111; www.westtours.is), the leading Westfjords tour operator, offers 2- to 6-hour tours for 5,000kr to 11,000kr ($80–$176/£40–£88) around Ísafjörður and Ísafjarðardjúp, with a two-person minimum; the tour in Mjóifjörður is particularly idyllic, with friendly seals en route. The best tour operator in the Eastfjords is **Kayakklúbburinn Kaj** (© 863-9939; www.123.is/kaj), offering splendid 2-hour tours for 4,500kr ($72/£36) from their base in Neskaupstaður.

14 Photography

Iceland's phenomenal scenery and magical light have long enticed professional nature photographers—and even amateur snapshooters are almost guaranteed impressive results. From experience we offer two small bits of advice. First, don't neglect the close-ups. Iceland's broad vistas always command attention, but the landscape's finer textures and patterns create fascinating worlds unto themselves. Second, have prints made by a quality developer. Iceland's subtleties of light and detail—always so enthralling in person—often don't come across in inferior prints.

In late July or early August, **Borea Adventures** (© 899-3817; www.boreaadventures.com) leads a 5-day excursion around Hornstrandir Nature Reserve, with instruction by photographer Thorsten Henn. The cost is 157,500 kr ($2520/£1260), and participants are whisked from fjord to fjord on an 18m (60-ft.) racing yacht. Nature photographer **Daniel Bergmann** (© 697-9515; www.danielbergmann.com), who lives in Stykkishólmur, conducts 1- to 11-day workshop tours around the country in June and July. The cost is $3,250 to $4,500 (£1,625–£2,250) and slots fill up months in advance. **Strabo Tours** (from North America © 866/218-9215; outside North

America **607/756-8676;** www.phototc.com), a U.S.–based photography tour company, puts together an annual 10-day Iceland trip led by a professional photographer for $4,995 (£2,498).

15 Pools & Spas

Three things are reliably found in every Icelandic village: a Lutheran church, a gas station selling hot dogs, and a public pool heated by the country's plentiful hot springs. (To put this in perspective, consider that New York City has 25 times the population of Iceland, but half as many public pools.) Geothermal pools are so important to Icelanders that the Icelandic word for "Saturday" *(laugardagur)* means "pool day" or "hot springs day." During work hours it's not unusual to see business meetings conducted in the hot tubs. Icelanders visit the pools year-round, even in rain and freezing weather, and credit them for their long lifespans (81 years-old for men and 86 for women) and low stress levels.

The regional chapters of this book do not mention all the village pools, only because they're so ubiquitous and easy to locate: just look for street signs depicting a bather. Obscure villages may only have a small pool, hot tub, shower, and changing room, while larger towns could also have lockers, lifeguards, fitness equipment, water slides, kiddie pools, an indoor pool, saunas, and a row of hot tubs, each set at a different temperature. Some farms also have pools that are open to the public, and nature has fashioned a few nice baths as well. For pools in Reykjavík, see p. 119.

Health spas take things to the next level, with massages, beauty treatments, fitness classes, and so on. For spas in **Reykjavík,** see p. 119. The best spas outside Reykjavík are the **Blue Lagoon** (p. 150) in Reykjanes Peninsula, the **NLFÍ Rehabilitation and Health Clinic** (p. 161) in Hveragerði, and **Mývatn Nature Baths** (p. 255).

Pool Etiquette

Icelanders are especially strict about pool rules, especially when they pertain to hygiene. (Remember that Icelandic pools are far less chlorinated than pools abroad, so the concern over spreading germs is not paranoia.) To avoid stern looks of disapproval—or even lectures by pool monitors—follow the simple procedures below:

- Leave shoes and socks outside the locker room, unless a sign specifically authorizes you to take them in.
- Undress completely at your locker and then walk to the showers carrying your towel and swimsuit. Stash your towel by the showers.
- Shower first, and then put your suit on. Rarely will you find a shower curtain or stall to hide behind; if you feel shy, be assured that Icelanders are both respectful of privacy and very nonchalant about this everyday routine. (Also be prepared for voluntary nudity in steam rooms, which are sex-segregated.)
- When showering, use soap, which is usually provided. Most shower rooms post a notorious sign—often photographed by visitors—depicting a human body, with red blotches over the "trouble areas" requiring particular attention.
- Don't go down water slides headfirst.
- After your swim, shower again and dry off before entering the locker room. Dripping on the locker room floor is frowned upon.

---

16 Rafting

Iceland has four glacier-fed rivers that are ideal for white-water rafting while the glorious scenery rolls by. For trips on the **Hvitá**—in the Golden Circle area, about an hour from Reykjavík—see p. 148. For trips on the **Eystri-Jökulsá** and **Vestari-Jökulsá**—both near Skagafjörður in northwest Iceland—see p. 227. Tours on these three rivers cater to most temperaments and ability levels, but the most experienced (and adrenaline-addicted) rafters head to the **Hólmsá** in south Iceland, 230km (143 miles) from Reykjavík. Hólmsá tours are run by **Arctic Adventures,** Laugavegur 11, Reykjavík (© **562-7000;** www.adventures.is) once per week from mid-June to late August, with a minimum age of 18 for rafters; an 11-hour day tour from Reykjavík, with 5 hours on the river, goes for 10,990kr ($176/£88).

17 Rock Climbing

Iceland is not a major rock-climbing destination, because its rock faces tend to be crumbly and insecure. You'll still find plenty of established routes, all detailed at **www.outdoors.is/rock-climbing-areas**. Further inquiries or requests for private guides should be directed by email to the **Icelandic Alpine Club** (info@isalp.is); their website, **www.isalp.is**, is scheduled to have extensive information posted in English. The Alpine Club plans some expeditions for members, and visitors who are serious climbers can often schmooze their way into being invited. The club also sponsors a rock-climbing festival in May or June; email info@isalp.is for details. **Klifurhúsið,** Skútuvogur 1G, at Holtavegur (© **553-9455;** www.klifurhusid.is; Mon and Wed 5–10pm, Tues and Thurs 3–10pm, Fri 4–9pm), is Iceland's only indoor climbing center. Climbs cost 700kr ($11/£5.60) plus 200kr ($3.20/£1.60) for shoe rental.

Arctic Adventures, Laugavegur 11, Reykjavík (© **562-7000;** www.adventures.is), leads a 4-hour climbing tour to a vertical rock face in Hvalfjörður, an hour north of Reykjavík. Tours cost 5,900kr ($94/£47) and run from April to November—when the weather cooperates—with a four-person minimum—if you're less than four, see if you can combine groups with others who are signed up. No experience is necessary, and the minimum age is twelve. More challenging trips can be arranged on request.

18 Scuba Diving & Snorkeling

Iceland's top two diving sites feature some fish sightings, but the main attractions are geological formations quite unlike the scenery typically found in warmer waters. The most popular site is **Silfra,** a deep, dramatic fissure at the bottom of Lake Þingvallavatn, next to Þingvellir National Park. Þingvallavatn's waters are so clear that divers experience a heady flying sensation as they plunge through the waters. The other main site, in the ocean near Akureyri, is **Strýtan,** a 55m-high (180 ft.) limestone pillar formed by a geothermal spring 70m (246 ft.) beneath the surface. Another diving highlight is *El Grillo,* an English oil tanker sunk by a German air raid on Seyðisfjörður during World War II.

The only diving-tour operator in Iceland is **PADI Dive Center,** Skipasund 85, Reykjavík (© **663-2858;** www.dive.is). All participants must be certified for diving in a dry suit; if you want to learn in Iceland, PADI offers a 4-day certification course for 54,900kr ($878/£439). Eight-hour tours from Reykjavík—either to Silfra or the ocean off Reykjanes Peninsula—are 24,900kr ($398/£199). Five-day tours of Iceland's best diving sites, with some sightseeing thrown in, are 129,900kr ($2,078/£1,039), not including lunches and dinners.

For non-divers, PADI offers a 5-hour **snorkeling** tour of Silfra from Reykjavík, for 14,900kr ($238/£119).

19 Skiing & Ski Touring

No one comes to Iceland solely for downhill skiing; the slopes just aren't good enough. On the other hand, the various forms of ski touring—cross-country skiing, Telemark skiing, backcountry skiing, ski mountaineering, and so on—are increasingly catching on.

Downhill skiers can find some perfectly nice diversions, and the scenery often compensates for deficiencies in slope lengths and vertical drops. (More cautious skiers may even appreciate Icelandic slopes' lack of trees to crash into.) The season runs from November through April, though conditions are most reliable from February to early April. Because of limited winter daylight, the major slopes are lighted and have extended evening hours.

Many smaller towns have a single ski lift on a local mountain, but few visitors would care to specifically seek these out. The best ski center in southwest Iceland is **Bláfjöll** (© 530-3000; www.skidasvaedi.is; day pass 1,700kr [$27/£14] adults, 500kr [$8/£4] children 6–16; Mon–Fri 2–9pm, Sat–Sun 10am–6pm), located 33km (21 miles) southeast of Reykjavík, off Rte. 417. Bláfjöll is the country's largest ski center, with 15 lifts, a snowboarding course, cross-country tracks, equipment rental, a snack bar, and a ski school on weekends. When Bláfjöll is open, one daily bus leaves for the slopes from the Mjódd bus terminal at Þönglabakka 1 in southeast Reykjavík (Mon–Fri 5:20pm, returning from Bláfjöll at 9:05pm; Sat–Sun 12:40pm, returning from Bláfjöll at 6pm), and several buses connect Mjódd to downtown.

The two other notable ski centers—both with equipment rental and cafes—are **Tungudalur/Seljalandsdalur** (© 456-3793; www.isafjordur.is/ski), near Ísafjörður in the Westfjords, and **Hlíðarfjall** (© 462-2280; www.hlidarfjall.is), near Akureyri in the north (for more on Hlíðarfjall, see p. 243). Tungudalur/Seljalandsdalur hosts Iceland's biggest skiing event, **Ski Week (Skíðavikan);** see p. 201.

The ski touring season generally runs from January through June, with glacier traverses more prevalent later in the season. Touring skis now come in a bewildering variety of forms, from traditional cross-country (aka Nordic) skis to heavier, wider Telemark skis and stubby mountaineering skis that convert into a kind of snowshoe.

The **Icelandic Alpine Club,** Skútuvogur 1G, Reykjavík (no phone; www.isalp.is; info@isalp.is), posts ski touring information at its website, and can answer questions if you're planning an expedition on your own. The club also sponsors a Telemark skiing festival in March.

TOUR OPERATORS

Borea Adventures, Hlíðarvegur 38, Ísafjörður (© 899-3817; www.boreaadventures. com), offers two backcountry skiing tours in the Westfjords. The first is a seven-day training course in winter mountaineering, starting each week in February, for 109,375kr ($1,750/£875); some nights are spent in guesthouses, and others are spent in snow caves or igloos that you construct yourself. The second, with six departures from March to May, is a 5-day trip into Hornstrandir Nature Reserve aboard a 18m (60-ft.) yacht, with daily excursions on cross-country skis, Telemark skis, snowshoes, snowboards—whatever you like—and the yacht stashes for exploring the fjords, inlets and sea cliffs. The cost is 144,375kr ($2310/£1155).

Ferðafélag Íslands, Mörkin 6, Reykjavík (© **568-2533;** www.fi.is), leads several cross-country skiing trips on glaciers in spring. Eyjafjallajökull is a likely destination for a day tour costing 6,000kr ($96/£48), while Drangajökull is a likely destination for a 3-day excursion costing 20,000kr ($320/£160), not including transportation from Reykjavík).

From April to early June, **From Coast to Mountains,** Hofsnes Farm, Öræfi (© **894-0894;** www.hofsnes.com), offers 6- to 8-hour cross-country ski tours across a dramatic stretch of Vatnajökull. From October to April, they lead extra-challenging 10-hour ascents of Hvannadalshnúkur, Iceland's highest peak, on Vatnajökull east of Skaftafell National Park. If conditions are right, participants can ski all the way down from the summit almost to sea level—a total distance of 11km (7 miles), with a vertical drop of over 2,000m (6,562 ft.). For either tour, departures are by arrangement, and the cost is 30,000kr ($480/£240) for one person, 40,000kr ($640/£320) for two, 45,000kr ($720/£360) for three, and 12,500kr ($200/£100) per person for groups of four to eight, including ski equipment.

Icelandic Mountain Guides, Vagnhöfði 7b, Reykjavík (© **587-9996;** www.mountain guide.is), escorts the most epic cross-country skiing and Telemarking tours, with set departures in March and April. Possibilities include a 10-day expedition through Sprengisandur for 145,000kr ($2,320/£1,160), a 9-day traverse of Vatnajökull for 136,000kr ($2,176/£1,088), and a comparatively easy 7-day alpine tour of the north, with Akureyri as a base for 119,000kr ($1,904/£952).

Útivist, Laugavegur 178, Reykjavík (© **562-1000;** www.utivist.is), offers the best selection of well-priced cross-country skiing tours. Day trips from Reykjavík leave every Sunday from mid-January to mid-March, for only 2,900kr ($46/£23). Longer excursions—scheduled from January to July—head to Þórsmörk, Landmannalaugar, Mýrdalsjökull, Drangajökull, Vatnajökull, and other popular destinations. The website does not list trips in English, but you can skim the Icelandic listings by clicking the "Ferðaáætlun" link.

20 Whale-Watching

Whale-watching tours have taken off in recent years, partly in response to all the publicity raised by Iceland's return to whale hunting (see "The Saga of Icelandic Whaling" box, p. 262). The season runs from late April to early October, and 3-hour tours cost between 3,700kr and 5,000kr ($59–$80/£30–£40) for adults. The most common sightings are minke whales—which are not particularly huge or entertaining—but lucky tour-goers also spot humpback whales, blue whales, orcas, sei whales, fin whales, white-beaked dolphins, and harbor porpoises.

The regional chapters of this book provide tour information for all the major whale-watching launch points: Reykjavík (p. 120); Keflavík, on Reykjanes peninsula (p. 154); Ólafsvík, on Snæfellsnes peninsula (p. 180); Hauganes and Dalvík near Akureyri (p. 243); Húsavík (p. 264); and the Westman Islands (p. 277). Of the above, Húsavík is the most popular launch point, with a slight edge in dramatic sightings.

4

Suggested Iceland Itineraries

Iceland vacations are often planned around a specific multi-day adventure, arranged either through a tour company or on your own. Knowing if and when you'll have a rental car—and whether it will have four-wheel drive—will affect your itinerary. Rental cars are convenient, as public transportation does not reach many parts of the country.

Some travelers are inclined to wing it and improvise their itinerary as they go, but advance planning can save you a lot of grief, particularly in mid-June through August, when accommodations and tours often fill up. All itineraries should include some slack time. In Iceland, the factors most likely to derail an overbooked itinerary are the weather and weather-based cancellations of domestic flights.

To jumpstart your planning, a few of our favorite Iceland itineraries are suggested below.

1 Iceland in 4 Days

Word is getting around that Iceland is great for casual 3- or 4-day escapes. The basic components of an Iceland long weekend are Reykjavík, and excursions from Reykjavík; and more often than not, the Blue Lagoon spa. Every night of this itinerary is spent in Reykjavík. In high season, make sure to call a few days ahead for dinner reservations (and for in-water massages at the Blue Lagoon).

Day ❶: Reykjavík

If you're out and about before 9am, head to **Grái Kötturinn** (p. 106) for pancakes, bacon, and strong Icelandic coffee. Begin the sightseeing stage at the **Tourist Information Center** (p. 84), where you can pick up maps and brochures, and arrange tours and car rentals if necessary. Nearby are three compelling sites—the **871±2 Settlement Museum** (p. 112), the **City Cathedral (Dómkirkjan)** (p. 111) in **Austurvöllur Square,** and the **Harbor House Museum (Hafnarhús)** (p. 113), dedicated to contemporary art. All three open at 10am; if you need to kill time until then, stroll over to **Tjörnin Pond** (p. 114) and gaze at the enormous 3-D map of Iceland inside **City Hall (Ráðhús)** (p. 114).

On weekends, most of Reykjavík's finest restaurants are closed for lunch; two notable exceptions, both close to Austurvöllur Square, are **Fjalakötturinn** (p. 102) and **Við Tjörnina** (p. 103). For a casual lunch, visit **Sægreifinn** (p. 106) for lobster soup and a seafood kabob. After lunch, head to the eastern half of the city center and survey Reykjavík's two main shopping streets, **Laugavegur** and **Skólavörðustígur.** Nearby is **Culture House** (p. 112), with a wonderful exhibit of medieval manuscripts. To recharge, drop into the city's oldest cafe, **Mokka Kaffi** (p. 107).

Skólavörðustígur leads uphill to Reykjavík's most iconic landmark, **Hallgrímskirkja** (p. 115), where you can ascend the elevator for a panoramic view. Don't miss

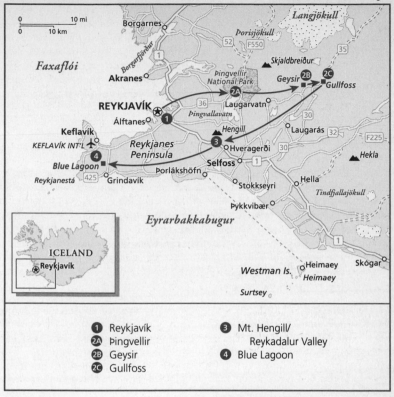

0 10 mi
0 10 km

Langjökull

Borgarnes

Þórisjökull
F550
52

35

Faxaflói

Borgarfjörður

Skjaldbreiður

Þingvellir
National Park

Geysir **2B** **2C**
Gullfoss

Akranes

REYKJAVÍK

36

2A

Laugarvatn

30

Álftanes Þingvallavatn

Keflavík

Hengill

Laugarás 32

F225

KEFLAVÍK INT'L

3 Hveragerði

Reykjanes
Peninsula

30

Hekla

Blue Lagoon

Selfoss 1

Reykjanestá 425 Grindavík

Þorlákshöfn

Hella

4

Stokkseyri

Tindfjallajökull

Þykkvibær

Eyrarbakkabugur

ICELAND

Reykjavík

Westman Is. Heimaey Skógar
Heimaey

Surtsey

1 Reykjavík	**3** Mt. Hengill/
2A Þingvellir	Reykadalur Valley
2B Geysir	**4** Blue Lagoon
2C Gullfoss	

the **Einar Jónsson Museum** (p. 115) next door, dedicated to Iceland's most renowned sculptor; weekend hours are 2 to 5pm. From here it's a half-hour walk to the **National Museum** (p. 115) south of Tjörnin Pond. If you're too pooped, catch bus 14 to **Laugardalslaug** (p. 121) for a rejuvenating taste of Iceland's geothermal bathing culture, and ply your hot tub companions for travel advice. (Be prepared for the ubiquitous question "How do you like Iceland?")

Enjoy an unforgettable dinner at **Sjá-varkjallarinn (Seafood Cellar)** (p. 99), followed by nightclub-hopping into the wee hours, and—last but not least—a 2am hot dog at **Bæjarins Bestu** (p. 105) with "everything on it."

Day **2**: The Golden Circle

An enormous wealth of day excursions depart from Reykjavík, but the most popular is the **"Golden Circle" tour** (p. 140) to **Þingvellir** (p. 142), the historic rift valley where the Icelandic parliament first convened in A.D. 930; **Geysir** (p. 146), the geothermal hot spot that lent its name to all geysers; and the majestic **Gullfoss waterfall** (p. 146). Sign up for an 8-hour bus tour (p. 140), or for more flexibility, rent a car.

Day **3**: Hot Springs Tour

The bathable geothermal hot springs of **Reykjadalur Valley** (p. 162) are tucked inside the scenic **Mt. Hengill hiking area,** near Hveragerði. The most memorable way to reach Reykjadalur is on horseback; **Eldhestar** (p. 161) offers a 9-hour tour from Reykjavík, with 5 or 6 hours in the saddle. (The small, manageable, good-natured Icelandic horse is great for beginners.) Alternatively, rent a car for the day and hike the route. The drive is less than an hour one-way, and the hike can be accomplished in as little as 2½ hours round-trip. Don't forget your swimsuit.

Day ④: The Blue Lagoon

The **Blue Lagoon spa** (p. 150)—built around a blue-green geothermal lake within a jet-black expanse of black lava—is Iceland's most popular visitor destination. Sign up with tour company **Þingvallaleið** (p. 151) for transportation to the lagoon on the way to the airport. Allow 2 hours at the lagoon, more if you plan on spa treatments or eating at the restaurant.

2 Around the Ring Road

Technically the Ring Road could be "done" in 3 days, but a week is a sensible minimum. The following whirlwind itinerary circles the country clockwise, with Reykjavík as the start and finish point. A conventional rental car can easily handle the route, though a 4WD vehicle expands your options considerably, particularly for excursions into the interior. *Note:* Some museums and other sightseeing stops may be closed outside of summer.

Day ❶: Reykjavík

The first day and night is spent in Iceland's thriving capital; see p. 72 for our recommended full-day itinerary.

Day ❷: Reykjavík to Sauðárkrókur

Depart early in the morning and head 73km (45 miles) north of Reykjavík, where the Ring Road reaches the town of **Borgarnes** (p. 168): The **Settlement Center** museum offers a surprisingly entertaining and macabre introduction to Iceland's historic and literary roots. Around 125km (78 miles) from Borgarnes, on the north coast, an optional side trip leads around the periphery of **Vatnsnes peninsula** (p. 216) on Route 711; highlights include the **Hindisvík** seal colony and the bizarre rock formation **Hvítserkur.** The unique stone church at **Þingeyrar** (p. 217), just east of Vatnsnes, is another worthwhile detour.

At **Varmahlíð** (p. 222), in the **Skagafjörður region,** turn left on Route 75 toward Sauðárkrókur. Shortly ahead is **Glaumbær,** the best of Iceland's many museums inside preserved, turf-roofed farm buildings (closing time is 6pm). After dinner in the likeable town of Sauðárkrókur—if there's still any sunlight—drive north to **Grettislaug** (p. 223) for an evening bath in a stone-lined geothermal pool overlooking the fjord.

Day ❸: Sauðárkrókur to Akureyri

Today's short drive (120km/74½ miles) allows half a day to get acquainted with Iceland's northern capital, **Akureyri** (p. 230). Leaving the Skagafjörður region, the Ring Road ascends through a gorgeous mountain pass surrounded by spiky, serrated ridges. Stop at **Halastjarna** (p. 230), a restaurant high in the hills, and build up a lunch appetite with an idyllic, 2-hour round-trip walk to **Hraunsvatn** (p. 230)

In Akureyri, visit the **Akureyri Art Museum,** the grandiose **Akureyri Church,** and Einar Jónsson's poignant 1901 sculpture **The Outlaw (Útlaginn).** Wind down with the massaging water jets at the **Akureyri Swimming Pool,** and write postcards at the **Bláa Kannan** cafe on the pedestrian shopping street

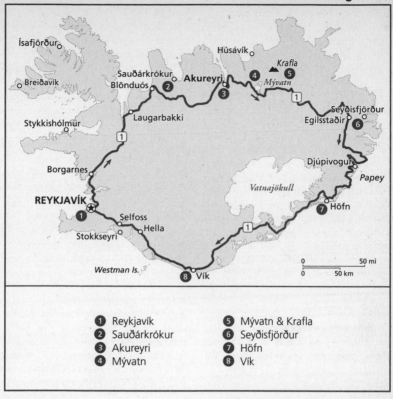

① Reykjavík
② Sauðárkrókur
③ Akureyri
④ Mývatn

⑤ Mývatn & Krafla
⑥ Seyðisfjörður
⑦ Höfn
⑧ Vík

Hafnarstræti. If your wallet can stand it, dine at **Friðrik V,** the best restaurant outside Reykjavík.

Day ④: Akureyri to Mývatn

On your way out of Akureyri, stop at the interdisciplinary **Safnasafnið Museum,** which opens at 10am. Fifty kilometers (31 miles) from Akureyri, the Ring Road meets the exquisite **Goðafoss waterfall** (p. 249). Backtrack 4km (2¼ miles), and turn right on Route 85 north to **Húsavík** (p. 259), Iceland's **whale-watching** mecca. (Call ahead if the weather is iffy.) Buy your boat tickets, then bone up before the tour at the **Whale Museum.** After the 3-hour excursion, choose between the **Húsavík Museum** (a collection of regional folk artifacts) or the **Phallological Museum**

(a collection of animal penises). For dinner, choose between Húsavík's two best restaurants, **Gamli Baukur** and **Salka.** Head back south on Route 85, then take Route 87 to **Reykjahlíð village** (p. 251) on **Lake Mývatn,** where you'll spend 2 nights.

Day ⑤: Mývatn & Krafla

The entire day is devoted to sampling the geological marvels of **Mývatn** and **Krafla** (p. 250). Drive first to **Grjótagjá,** an eerie fissure and geothermal vent, then take an hour to climb to the rim of **Hverfell,** a tephra explosion crater. Continue circling Mývatn, stopping at **Kalfarströnd Farm** for a half-hour loop trail overlooking submerged lava columns. Proceed to the **Skútustaðagígar** pseudocraters for another

30-minute ramble. Tireless travelers can add the 2-hour round-trip hike up **Vindbelgjarfjall** to survey the day's triumphs thus far.

Drive east of Mývatn to the **Hverir** (p. 254), a hellish geothermal hotspot, then head into Krafla and spend an hour exploring the surreal **Leirhnjúkur lava field** (p. 254). On your way back to Mývatn, enjoy a luxuriant, rejuvenating swim at **Mývatn Nature Baths** (p. 255). At 6pm, drop into **Vogafjós Cowshed Cafe** (p. 258) and enjoy a homemade smoked trout appetizer, while cows are milked on the other side of a plate glass window. For dinner, reserve at **Hótel Reykjahlíð** or the more casual **Gamli Bærinn** (p. 258).

Day ❻: Mývatn to Seyðisfjörður
The next gas station is far ahead; fill the tank before setting out. About 36km (22 miles) east of Reykjahlíð, exit the Ring Road onto Route 864 and proceed 32km (20 miles) to **Dettifoss** (p. 270), Europe's mightiest waterfall. Four kilometers (2½ miles) after the turnoff from the Ring Road, stop at Grímsstaðir Farm and cafe and confirm that road conditions are suitable, and be prepared for a bumpy ride. From Dettifoss, hike 1.5km (1 miles) to the more understated **Selfoss falls** (p. 270).

Return to the Ring Road and continue east. In clear weather you should have fantastic views south to **Herðubreið,** voted Iceland's favorite mountain in a national poll. Sixteen kilometers (10 miles) east of the Route 864 junction, turn right on Route 901 and proceed 8km (5 miles) to **Möðrudalur** for lunch at the **Fjalladýrð cafe** (p. 351). Ask about road conditions further ahead on Route 901, to help choose the best route to **Sænautasel** (p. 351), a reconstructed turf farm serving coffee and pancakes in the middle of Nowheresville.

From Sænautasel, return to the Ring Road and continue to **Egilsstaðir** (p. 332),

the commercial hub of east Iceland. From here it's a 28km (17 miles) detour to the lovely coastal village of **Seyðisfjörður** (p. 340), with a breathtaking descent into the fjord. Dinner is at **Skaftfell** cafe/gallery, followed by a stroll along the harbor.

Day ❼: Seyðisfjörður to Höfn
Linger in Seyðisfjörður, walking among the 19th- and early 20th-century chalet-style kit homes. Devotees of outmoded technology should visit the old telegraph station at the **Technical Museum of East Iceland** (p. 342). After returning to Egilsstaðir, decide on a route to **Höfn** (p. 319), the regional center of southeast Iceland. The Ring Road is the most direct. The longer route—which affords more Eastfjords coastal scenery—follows Route 92 to Reyðarfjörður, then Route 96 through a tunnel to Fáskrúðsfjörður and along the coast before it rejoins the Ring Road. Stops along Route 96 include **Steinasafn Petru** (p. 328), a local granny's magnificent rock collection, in **Stöðvarfjörður** (p. 340). Both routes pass **Djúpivogur** (p. 326), a charming fishing village and the launch point for 4-hour boat trips to **Papey island** (p. 327). Before dinner at Höfn's inviting **Kaffi Hornið** (p. 323), visit the supermarket on Vesturbraut to pack lunch for tomorrow.

Day ❽: Höfn to Vík
The 272km (169-mile) stretch of Ring Road from Höfn to Vík is a nonstop procession of stunning scenery. The first requisite stop is **Jökulsárlón** (p. 316), an otherworldly lake full of icebergs calved from **Vatnajökull,** Europe's largest glacier. After another 55km (34 miles), turn into **Skaftafell National Park** (p. 311) and bring your pack lunch along for a 2- to 3-hour hike to **Svartifoss waterfall,** the turf-roofed **Sel farmhouse,** and **Sjónarsker viewpoint** overlooking an incredible panorama of majestic peaks, looming glaciers, and barren flood plains.

In the tiny, isolated village of **Kirkju-bæjarklaustur** (p. 308), recharge with coffee, bagels, and lox at **Systrakaffi.** Shortly west of Kirkjubæjarklaustur, exit on Route 206 and proceed 3km (2 miles) to the lovely, contemplative **Fjaðrárgljúfur gorge** (p. 309) for an hour-long walk along the rim. For dinner in Vík, set out for the casual **Halldórskaffi** (p. 308).

Day ❾: Vík to Reykjavík
The morning is devoted to Vík's magnificent coastal environs. Allow 3 hours for the round-trip walk along the **Reynis-fjall sea cliffs** (p. 304) to the viewpoint looking west toward **Mýrdalsjökull** and the **Dyrhólaey promontory** (p. 303), identified by its enormous, natural arch of rock. (If this is too much hiking, just stroll on Vík's black sand beach and gaze at the iconic **Reynisdrangar** sea stacks.) Back behind the wheel, take Route 215 from the Ring Road to the pebbly **Reyn-isfjara beach** (p. 304) on the western side of Reynisfjall, and peer into the spellbinding sea cave **Hálsanefshellir.** If you have time, Dyrhólaey is another enticing side trip, especially for birders. Thirty-three kilometers (21 miles) west of Vík is the **Skógar Folk Museum** (p. 302), Iceland's most glorious and affecting collection of folk artifacts. One kilometer (¾ mile) away is the mesmerizing **Skógafoss** (p. 302). Now you can hightail it back to Reykjavík, with a detour to the **Fjöruborðið** (p. 165) lobster house in **Stokkseyri** for a valedictory feast.

3 Iceland in 1 Week

A driving tour through south Iceland's natural splendor—capped off by a journey to the magnificent Westman Islands—is hard to beat. This itinerary is designed for summer; for off-season travel, see "Iceland in the Off Season," in chapter 2.

Day ❶: Reykjavík
See p. 72 for our recommended Reykjavík itinerary, which includes a full day's worth of activity and an overnight stay.

Day ❷: Höfn & Vatnajökull
Take the morning flight (possible any day but Tues or Sat) to Iceland's southeast hub, **Höfn** (p. 319). Rent a car and drive to the intersection of Route F985 and the Ring Road to catch the 2pm **snowmobiling** tour (p. 317) on Europe's largest glacier, **Vatnajökull** (p. 311). (Alternatively, try cross-country skiing on Vatnajökull with outfitter **From Coast to Mountains;** p. 314.) Spend the night in Höfn or any farmstay close by.

Day ❸: Höfn to Vík
Drive west along the southern coast from Höfn to **Vík** (p. 301), along what is probably the most mind-boggling stretch of the Ring Road. The first stop is the bizarre **Jökulsárlón glacial lagoon,** full of parading icebergs. The next stop is **Skaftafell National Park,** for a 2-hour hike to the striking basalt formations of **Svartifoss** (p. 313). After a coffee break at **Systrakaffi** in the hamlet of **Kirkjubæjarklaustur** (p. 308), take an hour to peruse the rim of the contemplative **Fjaðrárgljúfur gorge** (p. 309). Spend the night in Iceland's southernmost village, Vík.

Day ❹: Vík to Hella-Hvolsvöllur
The day starts with the best walk on Iceland's south coastline: a 3-hour jaunt along the **Reynisfjall sea cliffs** (p. 304). (If this is too much hiking, take a casual stroll on the black-sand beach next to Vík.) After resuming your trip westward on the Ring Road, detour on Route 215 south to the **Reynisfjara beach** (p. 304), just west of Reynisfjall, and witness the

Iceland in 1 Week

① Reykjavík
②A Höfn
②B Vatnajökull
③ Vík
④ Hella
⑤A Hekla
⑤B Gullfoss
⑤C Geysir
⑤D Þorlákshöfn
⑥ Westman Islands
⑦ Reykjavík

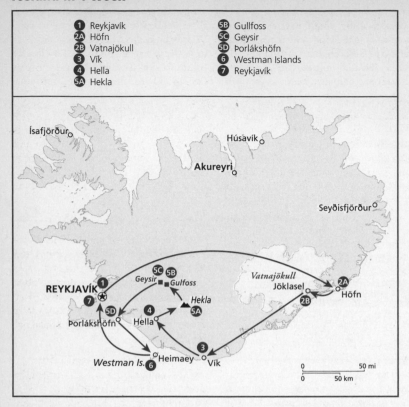

awe-inspiring sea cave **Hálsanefshellir.** The next stop is **Dyrhólaey** (p. 303), a promontory and nature reserve with bustling bird cliffs and an iconic rock archway over the sea. In the village of **Skógar,** investigate the towering **Skógafoss waterfall** (p. 302) and Iceland's best **folk museum.** Stay overnight anywhere in or near Hella or Hvolsvöllur (p. 293).

Day ⑤: Þjórsárdalur, Gullfoss & Geysir

From the Ring Road west of Hella, take Route 26 northeast into **Þjórsárdalur valley** (p. 286) for views of Iceland's most notorious volcano, **Hekla** (p. 288). Stop at the **Hekla Center** and check on the volcano's seismometer readings. Turn onto Route 32, then walk or drive to the lithe and beautiful **Háifoss** (p. 287), Iceland's second tallest waterfall. After visiting **Þjóðveldisbærinn** (p. 287), a reconstruction of a Viking longhouse from the settlement era, drive to **Stöng** (p. 287) to see the ruins that Þjóðveldisbærinn was based on. From Stöng, a short walk extends to **Gjáin gorge** (p. 287), a lush and bewitching enclave. Turn right on Route 30 and proceed north to the majestic **Gullfoss** (p. 146). Ten minutes away is **Geysir** (p. 146), where you can witness eruptions of the **Strokkur** geyser. Now head south to reach the port of **Þorlákshöfn** (p. 278) for the 7:30pm ferry (all days except Sat) to the spectacular **Westman Islands** (p. 277), where you'll spend 2 nights in the village of **Heimaey** (p. 278).

Day ❻: Westman Islands
Take a boat trip into the sea caves, play a round of golf inside a volcano crater, investigate the aftereffects of a devastating 1973 volcanic eruption, and troll the coastlines spotting puffins.

Day ❼: Westman Islands to Reykjavík
After another walk along the Westmans' dramatic coastline, take the 4pm ferry (all days except Sat) back to Þorlákshöfn and return to Reykjavík for a final evening in the capital.

4 Iceland in 2 Weeks

With 2 weeks at your disposal, consider this epic driving tour covering the highlights of west and north Iceland, with plenty of opportunities to leave the car behind and experience Iceland's great outdoors directly underfoot. Some roads are long, bumpy, and grueling—particularly in the Westfjords region. As with most driving tours of Iceland, this itinerary is doable in spring or fall, but is best experienced from early June through mid-September.

Day ❶: Reykjavík
See p. 72 for our recommended day-long Reykjavík itinerary.

Day ❷: Snæfellsnes Peninsula
Settle behind the wheel and leave Reykjavík around 9am, stopping at the **Settlement Center museum** (p. 168) in **Borgarnes** for an entertaining multimedia primer on early Icelandic history (the museum opens at 10am). The remains of the day are spent touring the circumference of **Snæfellsnes peninsula.** From the village of **Arnarstapi** (p. 176), on the peninsula's south coast, enlist for a snowmobile or snow cat tour of **Snæfellsjökull** (p. 178), then take a 2-hour walk along the sculpted lava coastline between Arnarstapi and **Hellnar.** Stroll through **Djúpalónssandur,** a picturesque beach tucked inside a rocky cove, and drive through the gnarled, surreal lava field **Berserkjahraun** (p. 180). Spend the night in Stykkishólmur.

Day ❸: Stykkishólmur to Breiðavík
Witness the uncountable islands and shallow marine habitat of **Breiðafjörður**— chowing raw shellfish straight from the shell—on the 11am **"Unique Adventure" boat tour** (p. 187) from Stykkishólmur. Then board the 3:30pm car ferry to **Brjánslækur** on the Westfjords' south

coast. Forming the convoluted clawshape in Iceland's northwest corner, the **Westfjords** (p. 188) have been criminally overlooked by the tourist industry. Drive to **Látrabjarg peninsula** and stay overnight at **Breiðavík** (p. 194), winding down with a stroll on the white sands of the idyllic bay.

Day ❹: Látrabjarg to Ísafjörður
Today's main event is a 2- to 3-hour hike along the rim of **Látrabjarg** (p. 191), Europe's largest sea cliff; sidle up to the ledges for mesmerizing views of the crashing surf and countless multitudes of puffins and other nesting birds. Stop at **Dynjandi** (p. 196)—an entrancing waterfall shaped like a wedding cake—en route to **Ísafjörður** (p. 198), the Westfjords' appealing capital, where you'll spend the next 2 nights. Get a feel for this charmed and worldly enclave by circulating among its cafes after dinner.

Day ❺: Ísafjörður & Environs
Having spent the last 3 days driving quite intensely, change pace with a day excursion to **Hornstrandir** (p. 210), Iceland's most wild and pristine coastal nature reserve. (For the most part, day tours of Hornstrandir are practical only in July and Aug.) Walk through diversely vegetated meadows and tundra, observe

native arctic foxes, and inspect the eerie remnants of abandoned settlements.

Day ❻: Ísafjörður to Djúpavík

Drive along the winding coastline of Ísafjarðardjúp Bay to the **Heydalur Country Hotel** (p. 206), and chat up the resident parrot over lunch in a converted barn. Choose among Heydalur's recreational activities—sea kayaking, horseback riding, fishing, and hiking—relaxing afterward in the natural geothermal pool. Proceed to the rugged and entrancing **Strandir Coast** (p. 206), arriving at the characterful **Hótel Djúpavík** by dinnertime. Your next 2 nights are spent here.

Day ❼: Djúpavík & Environs

After breakfast, take the 5km (3 miles) loop hike behind the hotel to a plateau with fabulous views overlooking the fjord. Tour Djúpavík's abandoned herring factory after lunch. After dinner, drive to the sublime **Krossneslaug geothermal pool** (p. 208) for an "only in Iceland" twilight swim overlooking a black pebble beach.

Day ❽: Strandir Coast to Akureyri

The lengthy drive to Akureyri—Iceland's northern capital—consumes most of the day, but there's time for a short detour to the **Glaumbær folk museum** (p. 222). Glaumbær is the best of Iceland's many museums dedicated to preserving 19th-century turf-roofed farmhouses, which are vital repositories of Icelandic cultural memory. Reach **Akureyri** (p. 230) by dinnertime.

Day ❾: Akureyri to Mývatn–Krafla

After breakfast, visit the **Akureyri Church,** with its distinctive and appealingly grandiose Art Deco twin spires. Relax at a cafe along the main pedestrian strip, then continue east on the Ring Road. Look in at **Safnasafnið,** a compelling and innovative art museum seeking to transcend the divide between contemporary and folk art. The next road

stop is the elegant **Goðafoss waterfall** (p. 249). Shortly farther is the region of **Mývatn–Krafla** (p. 250), with its astonishing concentration and variety of volcanic marvels. For your first sampling, drive just east of lake Mývatn to the geothermal field **Hverir,** and to **Leirhnjúkur** (p. 254), a menacingly strange and beautiful expanse of still-smoldering lava. Plan to spend 2 nights here.

Day ❿: Mývatn–Krafla

Today is devoted to a circuit of **Mývatn** (p. 250), taking in the steaming **Grjótagjá** fissure, the tephra explosion crater **Hverfell,** the **Kalfarströnd lava columns,** the **Skútustaðagígar pseudocraters,** and Europe's most diverse waterfowl habitat. Finish off the day at **Mývatn Nature Baths** (p. 255) with a swim in a bath-temperature, mineral-rich lake fed by underground hot springs.

Day ⓫: Húsavík & Whale-Watching

Drive to **Húsavík** (p. 259) and bone up at the **Whale Museum** before embarking on a 3-hour **whale-watching** tour (pray for humpbacks, the star performers of the whale world, to make an appearance). Afterward, choose between the **Húsavík Museum,** crammed with regional folk artifacts, and the **Phallological Museum,** crammed with mammalian members. Stock up on groceries, and, after dinner in Húsavík, drive east on Route 85 and spend the next 2 nights near the north end of **Jökulsárgljúfur National Park.**

Day ⓬: Jökulsárgljúfur National Park

Today boils down to two hikes—both as easy or as strenuous as you choose to make them—amid the wondrous scenery of Iceland's most renowned glacial river canyon. The first hike explores **Ásbyrgi** (p. 269), a lushly forested, horseshoe-shaped gorge. The second explores the lovely honeycombed basalt formations of **Hljóðaklettar,** and the red-tinted **Rauðhólar** crater row (p. 269).

Iceland in 2 Weeks

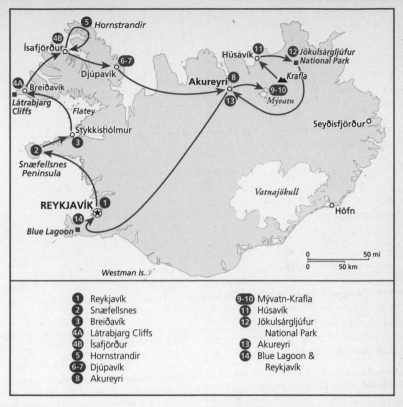

①	Reykjavík	⑨-⑩	Mývatn-Krafla
②	Snæfellsnes	⑪	Húsavík
③	Breiðavík	⑫	Jökulsárgljúfur
④A	Látrabjarg Cliffs		National Park
④B	Ísafjörður	⑬	Akureyri
⑤	Hornstrandir	⑭	Blue Lagoon &
⑥-⑦	Djúpavík		Reykjavík
⑧	Akureyri		

Day ⑬: Dettifoss & Selfoss

Drive down the canyon's eastern side to **Dettifoss** (p. 270), Europe's most powerful and awe-inspiring waterfall. From Dettifoss, take the short hike to **Selfoss** (p. 270), a more demure but equally interesting cascade along a broad arc. Return to Akureyri for a final night on the town.

Day ⑭: The Blue Lagoon

Drop off the car and fly to Reykjavík (or directly to Keflavík International Airport) first thing in the morning. Take a **Þingvallaleið** bus (p. 151) from Reykjavík or Keflavík to the **Blue Lagoon spa** (p. 150)—Iceland's number one tourist attraction—then bathe and exfoliate to your heart's content until it's time to catch your flight home.

5 Hiking Iceland

Iceland's most world-renowned trek—a four-day route blessed with astonishing scenery—is the 4-day trek known as **Laugavegurinn** (p. 292), connecting the interior wonderland of **Landmannalaugar** (p. 289) to the alpine oasis of **Þórsmörk** (p. 298). Facilities along the route are hardly luxurious, but you can hire a tour company to carry your bags from mountain hut to mountain hut. The Laugavegurinn is passable from roughly the beginning of July to early September. Book the mountain huts well in advance.

Hiking Iceland

Itinerary legend:
- ① Reykjavík
- ②-③ Landmannalaugar
- ④-⑥ The Laugavegurinn
- ⑦ Þórsmörk
- ⑧ Reykjavík

Day ①: Reykjavík

See p. 72 for our full-day Reykjavík itinerary. You'll also need this day to stock up on **groceries** (and perhaps some last-minute supplies) since provisions are generally unavailable on the trail—if you are going with a tour group, check with the operator to see if they provide food.

Days ② & ③: Landmannalaugar

Board the morning bus from Reykjavík to **Landmannalaugar,** whose rhyolite landscape is a photographer's dream. This wondrous hiking zone within **Fjallabak Nature Reserve** (p. 289) is one of the best in the country. Plan to spend 2 nights at the mountain hut run by Ferðafélag Íslands to allow yourself a leisurely day-and-a-half for exploring the region. Bathing in the natural hot springs near the accommodation is a perfect nightcap.

Days ④ to ⑦: The Laugavegurinn

Four days is the ideal amount of time to hike through this fabulous procession of interior scenery. The entire route is 55km (34 miles), with **mountain huts** spaced at roughly 14km (9-mile) intervals. You may be hankering for privacy by the time you reach Þórsmörk, so consider booking a private room at the **Húsadalur** (p. 299) for your last night in the region.

Day ⑧: Back to Reykjavík

Enjoy another day hike (p. 301) in Þórsmörk before catching the 3:30pm bus back to Reykjavík for your final evening in the capital. Round out the evening with a meal at **Salt** (p. 102)—welcome back to civilization indeed—and prepare for your next-day departure back home.

5

Reykjavík

The world's northernmost capital, Reykjavík is a captivating mix of the parochial and the worldly. It's Iceland's main entry portal; its political, economic, and cultural center; and home to most of its population. Reykjavík's ambience is simultaneously that of a city-like town and a town-like city. As Iceland's all-around nerve center, Reykjavík is the logical starting point for visitors.

For most of its history, Reykjavík suffered a backward reputation among European capitals, but this has only intensified its heady sensation of newfound wealth and authority. Thirty years ago, no one even dreamed Reykjavík would become an international arbiter of hipness, especially in music and nightlife.

Despite its reputation for wild nights, Reykjavík by day is the most subdued of European capitals. Its cosmopolitan edge seems at odds with its squat, boxy architecture. It almost feels wrong to leave the world's problems so far behind: Iceland's urban life is virtually free of crime, homelessness, and pollution. Reykjavík is committed to sustainable development, with aggressive tree planting, home heating and electrical systems powered by underground hot springs—that faint eggy smell in bathrooms is a natural by-product—and a few buses running on hydrogen fuel (look for steam emissions from the roof). One night in September 2006, the entire city agreed to turn off all lights for 30 minutes simultaneously. The stars weren't out that night, but the point was still made: Reykjavíkians honor the romance of their town's original, natural state.

Reykjavík hosts a multitude of festivals. Most events take place outside of summer, belying the widespread perception of Iceland as a one-season destination. See "When to Go," on page 14, for a schedule of annual events.

1 Orientation

ARRIVING

BY PLANE　International flights arrive at Keflavík International Airport, about 50km (31 miles) from town. (For Keflavík arrival information, see "Getting There," in chapter 2.) Taxis to Reykjavík cost around 9,000kr ($144/£72) for up to four people, so most travelers come to town on the Flybus (© 562-1011; www.flybus.is). Tickets are 1,200kr ($19/£9.60) adults, 600kr ($9.60/£4.80) children 12 to 15, and free for children 11 and under. Taxis and the Flybus are clearly positioned outside the arrival hall; both accept credit cards, but Flybus tickets must be purchased before exiting the terminal. The Flybus stops at the BSÍ bus terminal, various hotels and guesthouses, and the City Hostel. Call or check the Flybus website for a complete list of stops. Check with your accommodation if it doesn't appear on the list; they might offer a free transfer from the BSÍ terminal, or there might be a stop within easy walking distance. If that fails, you could still save money by taking the Flybus to the BSÍ terminal and catching a taxi from there. Flybus departures from Reykjavík to the airport are timed to coincide with departing international flights.

Domestic flights (and flights from Greenland and the Faeroe Islands) arrive at Reykjavík Airport, just south of the city center. For more information on domestic air travel, see "Getting Around," in chapter 2.

BY FERRY   No scheduled international ferries arrive in Reykjavík; ferries from Europe arrive at Seyðisfjörður on the east coast. For information on cruise ships, see "Getting There," in chapter 2.

VISITOR INFORMATION
INFORMATION CENTERS
The main **Tourist Information Center** (Aðalstræti 2; ℂ **590-1550;** www.visit reykjavik.is; June–Sept 15 daily 8:30am–7pm; Sept 16–May Mon–Fri 9am–6pm; Sat–Sun 10am–2pm) is in the northwestern sector of the city center, near the old harbor. On the premises is the fee-free **City Center Booking Service,** which can book accommodations, car rentals, and tours.

A smaller branch of the tourist information office is inside **City Hall (Ráðhús)** at Tjarnargata 11 (ℂ **411-1000;** year-round Mon–Fri 8:20am–4:30pm, Sat noon–4pm; May 10–Sept 15 also Sun noon–4pm).

The **Iceland Visitor Center,** Austurstræti 17 (ℂ **511-2442;** fax 511-2443; www.icelandvisitor.com; June–Aug daily 9am–10pm, Sept–May daily 10am–6pm), is a privately run, brochure-packed travel agency that's very helpful with tours, car rentals, and other service, but they can't help with accommodations.

ONLINE
Run by the city's tourist office, **www.visitreykjavik.is** has thorough, well-mapped listings of accommodations, restaurants, museums, and sights, as well as a schedule of events. *What's On* (**www.whatson.is**) covers dining, accommodation, and city activities and events. *The Grapevine* (**www.grapevine.is**), a free English-language circular, is an extremely useful guide to current happenings. *GetRvk* (**www.getrvk.com**; click "See the latest issue") is a selective and opinionated guide to Reykjavík's culture and events, with an emphasis on the cutting edge.

2 Getting Around

BY BICYCLE   Reykjavík is easily explored by bicycle and has a good network of bike paths. Riding on sidewalks and footpaths is widely tolerated, and some trails are illuminated by streetlights in fall and winter. A free biking map is available at the Tourist Information Center (see above), or downloadable from www.reykjavik.is/ paths. We recommend the popular route that takes you around the coastline and into the peaceful Elliðaár Valley.

The only major **bike rental** business in town is **Borgarhjól,** Hverfisgata 50 (ℂ **551-5653;** www.borgarhjol.net; Mon–Fri 8am–6pm, Sat 10am–2pm). They carry high-quality Trek bicycles and provide studded tires in winter. Rates are 2,000kr ($32/£16) per day with discounts for half days or longer rentals. They run an outpost at the City Hostel at Laugardalur (p. 97), and some other accommodations also arrange bike rentals.

BY BUS   Reykjavík's bus service **Strætó** (ℂ **540-2700;** www.bus.is) is very reliable. The major bus hubs are Lækjartorg (in the city center, at the north end of Lækjargata),

Hlemmur (on the eastern end of Laugavegur), and the **BSÍ bus terminal** (Vatnsmýrar-vegur 10; www.bsi.is) south of the city center. Free bus maps are available at www.bus.is (check out the impressive "Journey Planner" feature), the Tourist Information Center, and bus hubs. Most travelers use buses only to reach outlying hotels or sights such as The Pearl, Laugardalur Park, and the Árbær Museum. Local routes venture as far as the suburbs of Hafnarfjörður, Mosfellsbær, and Akranes (see chapter 6). Most long-distance routes leave from the BSÍ terminal.

Buses operate Monday to Saturday from 7am to midnight, and Sunday from 10am to midnight, with set departure times every 20 minutes, or every 30 minutes evenings and weekends. Buses S1 to S6 run until 2am on Friday and Saturday night. The flat fare of 280kr ($4.50/£2.25) adults or 100kr ($1.60/80p) children 6 to 18 is collected on the bus. No change is given, so make sure you have the exact amount. Discounted books of 11 tickets for 2,500kr ($40/£20) and 2-week passes *(gula kortið)* for 3,500kr ($56/£28) are available at the bus hubs, Kringlan Mall, and the Tourist Information Center. Transfers *(skiptimiði)* are free within a certain time frame (normally 45 min.) and must be requested from your first driver. The **Reykjavík Tourist Card** (p. 110) includes free unlimited bus travel for 1, 2, or 3 days.

BY CAR   Reykjavík's narrow one-way streets and parking regulations discourage many drivers, but by international standards the city is quite negotiable. Public parking lots in the city center—marked on most tourist maps—usually require buying a ticket at a kiosk and placing it on the front dashboard. Meters vary in cost but are usually around 80kr ($1.30/65p) per hour; fees must be paid from 10am to 6pm weekdays and from 10am to 2pm Saturday. Parking is free Sundays and evenings. One parking strategy is to simply drive out of the center where there are no meters. For information on car rentals and driving in Iceland, see "Getting Around," in chapter 2.

BY FOOT   Reykjavík is a good walking town, easily navigable on foot, with most of the tourist sites, restaurants, and shops concentrated along the central streets.

BY TAXI   Taxis are expensive: Meters start at 520kr ($8.30/£4.15), and a short ride across town is routinely 1,000kr ($16/£8). Sharing helps, as taxis charge per ride, not per passenger. The best taxi companies are **BSR Taxis** (© 561-0000) and **Hreyfill** (© 588-5522). Both accept credit cards inside the taxi. There is no need to tip (see chapter 2, p. 55, for more on tipping).

3 Organized Tours

Reykjavík Excursions   A 2½-hour **"Reykjavík Grand Excursion"** bus tour daily at 9am lets you "do" the harbor, Hallgrímskirkja, the Pearl, and the National Museum all before lunch. The price is 3,400kr ($54/£27) adults, half-price for children 12 to 15, and free for kids under 12, including museum admission and pickup/dropoff service. To go at your own pace, choose their **"Hop On–Hop Off"** tour, which runs daily June to August on open-topped double-deckers for 2,000kr ($32/£16) adults, half-price for children 12 to 15, and free for children under 12. Sights include Hallgríms-kirkja, the Pearl, the National Museum, the old harbor, Kringlan Mall, and Laugardalur Park. The bus completes the loop once each hour, so you can stop wherever you like and catch another bus an hour or two later. Your ticket is valid for 24 hours from the first use, so you can continue hopping the next morning. No advance purchase is necessary, though only cash is accepted onboard.

BSÍ bus terminal and Hilton Reykjavík Nordica. © 562-1011. www.re.is.

Iceland Excursions   The 2½-hour **"Greater Area Reykjavík Sightseeing"** bus tour, which leaves daily at 9am in summer, runs at a near-manic pace through sights farther from the city center, such as Hafnarfjörður (see chapter 6), Laugardalur Park, and the Ásmundur Sveinsson museum. The price, including hotel pickup and dropoff, is 3,100kr ($50/£25), half-price for children 12 to 18, and free for kids under 12.

Höfðatún 12, just east of Hlemmur bus station. ℭ 540-1313. www.icelandexcursions.is.

Literary Walking Tours *(Finds* Thursdays at 5pm in July and August, the City Library sponsors free, under-publicized tours of Reykjavík, led by a literary critic or an actor. Tours, which last around 1½ hours, leave from the main branch and could include anything from the Settlement Museum (for a saga reading) to the cafe/nightclub Kaffibarinn (site of debauched scenes from the cult novel *Reykjavík 101*). Call ahead to make sure the time hasn't changed.

Tryggvagata 15. ℭ 563-1717.

Haunted Iceland   This upstart offers three reasonably priced walking tours daily from June to mid-September. **"Hidden World Reykjavík,"** at 3pm, relates folklore pertaining to elves, trolls, and the like, with visits to their alleged rocky abodes. Guides for the 6pm **"Reykjavík Welcome Walk"** (soon to be renamed "Rent a Friend in Reykjavík") present a personal, opinionated outlook on city history and culture. The popular **"Haunted Walk of Iceland,"** kicking off at 8pm, focuses on ghost stories and lingers over the macabre, such as the grave of a 6-year-old accused of being the devil's child. What steers these tours clear of potential corniness is the guides' healthy infusion of modern skepticism. Each tour lasts 1½ to 2 hours, covers about 2km (1¼ mile) on foot, and leaves from the Tourist Information Center at Aðalstræti 2. Reservations are recommended, but you can just show up and pay in cash.

ℭ 843-6666. www.hauntediceland.com. "Hidden World" and "Haunted Reykjavík" 2,000kr ($32/£16) adults; 1,500kr ($24/£12) seniors/students; children under 12 free. "Welcome Walk" 1,500kr ($24/£12) adults; 1,000kr ($16/£8) seniors/students; children under 12 free.

FAST FACTS: Reykjavík

Airport   See "Arriving," earlier in this chapter.

American Express   American Express has no offices in Iceland.

Banks/Currency Exchange   Banks are usually open Monday through Friday 9:15am to 4pm, or until 6:30pm in Kringlan Mall (p. 126). All banks change foreign currency and many have 24-hour ATMs.

Bike Rentals   See "Getting Around," earlier in this chapter.

Car Rentals   See "Getting Around," earlier in this chapter and "Getting Around Iceland," in chapter 2.

Cellphones   See "Staying Connected," in chapter 2.

Doctors & Dentists   See "Medical Help," below.

Drugstores   Drugstores *(Apótek)* are usually open Monday through Friday 9am to 6 or 7pm, and Saturday to 4pm. Drugstores that stay open late include **Lyf og heilsa** (Háaleitisbraut 68 at Austurver, close to Kringlan Mall; ℭ **581-2101;**

daily 8am–midnight) and **Lyfja Apótek** (Lágmúli 5, near Laugardalur Park; © **533-2300;** daily 8am–midnight).

Embassies **U.S.:** Laufásvegur 21; © **562-9100;** consularreykja@state.gov. **Canada:** Túngata 14; © **575-6500;** rkjvk@international.gc.ca. **U.K.:** Laufásvegur 31; © **550-5100;** britem@centrum.is. Australia and New Zealand have no embassies in Iceland.

Emergencies Dial © **112** for ambulance, fire, or police. See also "Medical Help," below.

Hospitals See "Medical Help," below.

Internet Access Many accommodations offer Wi-Fi or guest terminals, and most cafes have free Wi-Fi. Otherwise, the cheapest Internet outlets are libraries (see below), usually 200kr ($3.20/£1.60) per hour. The Tourist Information Center (p. 84) has an Internet cafe upstairs; 30 minutes cost 350kr ($5.60/£2.80) and 1 hour is 500kr ($8/£4).

Laundromat Reykjavík has no self-service laundromats. If you're near Laugardalur Park, you can use the machines in the City Hostel (p. 97). One centrally located laundry service is **Uðafoss** (Vitastígur 13, north of Laugavegur; © **551-2301;** Mon–Thurs 8am–6pm; Fri 8am–6:30pm). The minimum charge is 1,600kr ($26/£13) for up to 2kg (4.4 lb.) and goes up to 2,400kr ($38/£19) for 5kg (11 lb.); they also do dry cleaning.

Libraries **The City Library** (Tryggvagata 15; © **563-1717;** www.borgar bokasafn.is; Mon 10am–9pm; Tues–Thurs 10am–7pm; Fri 11am–7pm; Sat–Sun 1–5pm) has a large selection of books in English, but non-Icelanders can't sign them out. Internet access is also available.

Lost & Found This service is located in the **police station** at Borgartún 7b (© **444-1400;** Mon–Fri 10am–noon and 2–4pm). Bus: 12, 14, or 16.

Luggage Storage Hotels can usually store luggage; otherwise, use **BSÍ bus terminal** (Vatnsmýrarvegur 10; © **591-1000;** daily 4:30am–midnight). The charge is 400kr ($6.40/£3.20) per item for the first 24 hours, 200kr ($3.20/£1.60) each additional 24 hours.

Mail See "Post Offices," below.

Markets See "Supermarkets," below.

Medical Help For emergencies, dial © **112.** The main 24-hour emergency room is at **National University Hospital,** Fossvogur (© **543-2000;** Bus: 11, 13, or 18). For non-emergencies, **Standard business hours** are 9am to 5pm Monday to Friday; doctors are on duty 24 hours at the National University Hospital (© **525-1000**) and during non-working hours at the **Kópavogur Medical Center,** Smáratorg 1 (© **1770;** Mon–Fri 5–11:30pm, Sat–Sun 9am–11:30pm; Bus: S1, S2, 12, 13, 17, 24, or 28). After 11:30pm, or on weekends and holidays, you can call the Medical Center for a telephone consultation, or possibly a "home visit." Standard appointment fees are around 3,500kr ($56/£28), but phone consultations are free. For **dental emergencies,** call © **575-0505.**

Pharmacies See "Drugstores," above.

Police   For emergencies call ✆ **112.** The main station (✆ **444-1000**) is at Hverfisgata 113-115, opposite the Hlemmur bus station. A more central station is at
Tryggvagata 19 (✆ **569-9025**).

Post Offices   Post offices are open 9am to 6pm weekdays. The central branch
(Pósthússtræti 5, at the corner of Austursræti; ✆ **580-1200**) is also open Satur-
days (June–Aug only) from 10am to 2pm. Stamps are also sold at the Mál og
Menning bookstore (p. 124).

Restrooms   Public coin-operated restrooms (50kr/80¢/40p) are in a few downtown locations, indicated by "WC" icons on tourist maps. City Hall (p. 84) has
free restrooms, and most cafes are tolerant of walk-ins.

Supermarkets   **Bónus** (Laugavegur 59; ✆ **562-8200**; Mon–Thurs 11am–6:30; Fri
10am–7:30pm; Sat 10am–6pm) is the best market in the city center. **10-11** markets are open 24 hours; a small branch is on Austurstræti 17 (✆ **552-1011**) and
a much larger one is at Barónsstígur 4 (corner of Hverfisgata; ✆ **511-5311**). At
Kringlan Mall is **Hagkaup** (✆ **568-9300**; Mon–Wed 10am–6:30pm; Thurs 10am–
9pm; Fri 10am–7pm; Sat 10am–6pm; Sun 1–5pm).

Taxis   See "Getting Around," above.

Telephone   Public phones are sparse in Reykjavík, but you can find them at
post offices, on the southwest corner of Austurvöllur Square, and on Lækjargata. They accept coins or phone cards, which are available at post offices,
gas stations, kiosks, and convenience stores. Reasonably priced overseas calls
can be made from the second floor of the main Tourist Information Center
(p. 84).

Tipping   See p. 55, chapter 2.

4 Where to Stay

With seemingly every accommodation in Reykjavík's booming hotel industry either
renovating or expanding, nightly rates are swelling as well; in exchange, you can expect
high standards of service and cleanliness, and big discounts in the off season. High season is longer in Reykjavík than in the rest of Iceland, so you are likely to encounter
peak prices and limited availability in May, June, and September as well as during the
country's peak months of July and August. Sadly, the budget-friendly practice of
"sleeping-bag accommodation"—bringing your own bedding and paying half-price—
is almost entirely phased out in the capital.

Accommodations are generally classed as either a hotel or a "guesthouse," which is
an Icelandic rendition of the B&B. (For more on accommodation types, see "Tips on
Accommodations," in chapter 2.) As offerings are similar at both, price and location
are more likely to influence your choice. Be aware that many tour packages automat-
ically place unsuspecting visitors outside the city center. Conversely, light sleepers in
downtown hotels may wonder why they paid more for the privilege of being amidst
the late-night revelry.

In the amenities section following each review below, "Flybus" (see "Arriving," earlier) indicates airport pickup and dropoff service is offered at that accommodation.

CENTRAL REYKJAVÍK
VERY EXPENSIVE

101 Hotel   Opened in 2003, this dauntingly trendy "design hotel" is for the fashionable jet-setter. The exterior is nondescript, the entrance hardly noticeable, as if to emphasize it's for folks in the know. Room decor is undeniably chic, but a bit overdone; the glossy black and white surfaces alone are enough to cause eye strain, and the sink, set at oblique angle to the rest of the room, looks like a mistake. All beds are queens or kings; bathrooms have no doors; and showers are walled with clear glass and mirrored on the inside. All rooms are spacious, so the main advantage of the double deluxes are the tubs and the quiet, as they face a (designer) inside wall.

Hverfisgata 10. ℭ 580-0101. www.101hotel.is. 38 units, 1 apt. Standard double and double balcony rooms have walk-in shower only; all others have walk-in shower and bathtub. 32,900kr–37,900kr ($526–$606/£263–£303) double; 41,900kr ($670/£335) and way up for balcony rooms, suites, and apt. Limited street parking. **Amenities:** Restaurant; bar; small exercise room; small spa with steam room; business center; room service; same-day laundry/dry cleaning; Flybus. *In room:* TV/DVD, free Wi-Fi, CD player, minibar, hair dryer, iron (on request), safe.

Hótel Borg ✦✦✦   Designed by the same architect responsible for Hallgrímskirkja, and built in 1930, the Borg was Iceland's first luxury hotel. Major 2007 renovations affirm the hotel's Art Deco roots—call it a streamlined, modern Scandinavian update on the style's bold outlines and geometric shapes. Renovated fifth-floor standard rooms have snazzy new mattresses and TVs without the extra cost. If these aren't available, ask for a room in the back; Austurvöllur Square can be a zoo on weekend nights. The stupendously luxurious "tower suite" in the spire, complete with living room and a 360-degree view of the city, is usually booked a year in advance.

Pósthússtræti 11, on Austurvöllur Square. ℭ 551-1440. Fax 551-1420. www.hotelborg.is. 56 units. May–Sept and Dec 28–Jan 2, 29,100kr–33,400kr ($466–$534/£233–£267) double; 71,000kr ($1,136/£568) for tower suite. Rates 25% lower Oct 1–Dec 27 and Jan 3–Apr 30 except suites. Children under 12 stay free in parent's room. AE, DC, MC, V. Limited street parking. **Amenities:** 4-star restaurant; bar; concierge; car rentals; business center; same-day laundry/dry cleaning; Flybus. *In room:* TV/DVD, CD player, DVD/CD library at reception, free Wi-Fi, minibar, coffee/tea, hair dryer, trouser press, safe.

Hótel Centrum ✦✦   This unaffected and relaxed hotel, focused on service and devoid of snob appeal, is a relief from the über-slick luxury accommodations that dominate the city center. Rooms are well equipped and rather old fashioned, complete with rubber matting in the shower. Triple-paned windows eliminate most street noise, and the blackout curtains are a real sleep-saver in early summer. The hotel spans three buildings: a 1764 house and two new structures that wrap around it, with coordinated design. Rooms in the old house have a bit more character, but no exceptional antiques or original fixtures or floorboards. Guests in standard rooms are nickel-and-dimed for Wi-Fi and extra TV channels. "Triples" are deluxe doubles with a pull-out bed. The most coveted dwelling is the "Hunchback of Notre Dame" suite in the tower.

Aðalstræti 16. ℭ 514-6025. Fax 514-6030. www.hotelcentrum.is. 89 units. 25,900kr–29,400kr ($414–$470/£207–£235) double; 31,100kr ($498/£249) triple; 39,900kr ($638/£319) junior suite. Rates 36%–45% lower Oct–Apr. In deluxe rooms, children under 12 stay free in parent's room. MC, V. Limited street parking. **Amenities:** Fjalakötturinn Restaurant (p. 102); bar; cafe; concierge; conference center; room service; same-day laundry/dry cleaning service; Flybus. *In room:* TV, Wi-Fi, minibar, coffee/tea, hair dryer, iron, safe.

Hótel Holt ✦✦   The reputation of this intimate four-star hotel, situated on a central but quiet residential street, rests on its Icelandic art collection and first-rate French restaurant. Original owner Þorvaldur Guðmundsson died in 1998, but rooms and

Where to Stay & Dine in Reykjavík

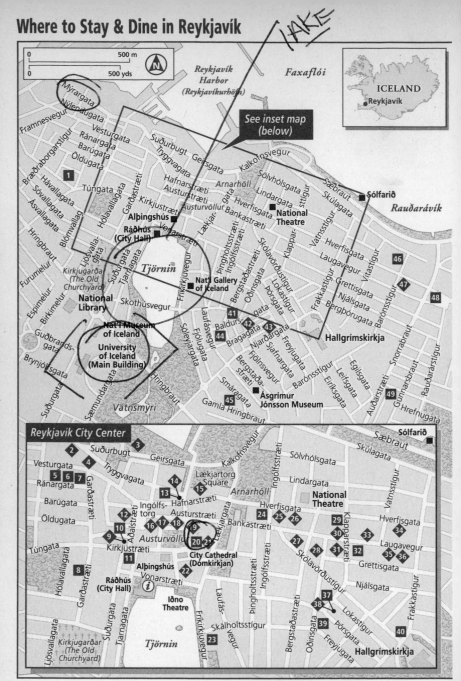

JAKE

MYVOQOTTA
MI/RARYATA

ACCOMMODATIONS ■

Álfhóll Guesthouse **6**
Anna's Guesthouse **45**
Baldursbrá Guesthouse **44**
Butterfly Guesthouse **5**
Castle House
  Luxury Apartments **23**
CenterHotel Klöpp **29**
Embassy Luxury Apartments **8**
Fosshótel Baron **46**
Grand Hotel Reykjavík **51**

Guesthouse Óðinn **39**
Guesthouse 101 **48**
Hilton Reykjavík Nordica **53**
Hotel Björk **50**
Hótel Borg **20**
Hótel Centrum **10**
Hótel Frón **32**
Hotel Holt **41**
Hotel Leifur Eiríksson **40**
Hotel Óðinsvé **37**

Hótel Vík **54**
Icelandica **1**
Kríunes Guesthouse **55**
Metropolitan Hotel **7**
101 Hotel **24**
Radisson SAS 1919 Hotel **13**
Reykjavík City Hostel **52**
Salvation Army
  Guesthouse **11**
Snorri's Guesthouse **49**

DINING ◆

Á Næstu Grösum **31**
Apótek **19**
Argentina **47**
Austur India
  Fjélagið **34**
Bæjarins Bestu **15**
Cafe Cultura **26**
Cafe Paris **18**
Einar Ben **16**
Eldsmiðjan **43**

Fjallakötturinn **9**
Grái Kötturinn **25**
Icelandic
  Fish & Chips **2**
Jómfrúin **21**
Kaffi Hjómalind **30**
Krúa Thai **4**
Mokka Kaffi **27**
Rossopomodoro **36**
Sægreifinn **3**

Salt **14**
Sandholt Bakarí **35**
Siggi Hall **38**
Sjávarkjallarinn
  (Seafood Cellar) **12**
Thorvaldsen **17**
Tíu Dropar **33**
Þrír Frakkar **42**
Vegamót **28**
Við Tjörnina **22**

common spaces are adorned with his prodigious stockpile of paintings and drawings, including several by Jóhannes S. Kjarval (p. 116). Rooms are all tastefully decorated with dark wood furniture, and the library, sitting room, and lounge are especially appealing. The rooms themselves are a bit small and not all that luxurious, but art expands and enriches the mind, right? The restaurant, appropriately called "The Gallery," has the most impressive art display of all, and a dress code is enforced. Hotel staff is accommodating, and downtown is just a 5-minute walk away.

Bergstaðastræti 37. ⓒ 552-5700. Fax 562-3025. www.holt.is. 40 units. June–Aug 23,100kr ($370/£185) doubles; 28,900kr ($462/£)231) and up junior suites and suites. Rates 11%–12% lower Sept–May. AE, DC, MC, V. Free parking. **Amenities:** Restaurant; bar; small health club/massage room, free access to nearby fitness studio; concierge; business center; room service; same-day laundry/dry cleaning service; Flybus. *In room:* TV, free Wi-Fi, minibar, hair dryer, trouser press and coffee machine (suites only), safe.

Hótel Óðinsvé ⟨⟨⟨ Like the Hótel Holt nearby, the Óðinsvé is an ideally situated mid-size luxury hotel—close to the center, but mercifully quiet on weekends. Also like the Holt, it's known for its excellent restaurant, Siggi Hall (p. 102). The Óðinsvé, however, has undergone extensive renovations for a sleeker, more contemporary look. (All the taxidermied seabirds are on their way out, to appease sentimental foreigners.) Aside from a few transitional kinks, the results are impressive. Rooms vary considerably in size, though almost all are full of light. Standard rooms on the first three floors have common balconies and a patio. Double deluxe rooms on the third and fourth floors have private balconies, and the fourth floor, added in 2004, has especially good views of Mt. Esja and Hallgrímskirkja. All double deluxe rooms have bathtubs, though not all junior suites do.

Óðinstorg Square (at the intersection of Þórsgata and Týsgi). ⓒ 511-6200. Fax 511-6201. www.hotelodinsve.is. 43 units. May–Sept 22,900kr–30,900kr ($366–$494/£183–£247) double. Rates 26%–29% lower Oct–Apr. Rates include breakfast. Children under 12 stay free in parent's room. AE, DC, MC, V. Limited street parking. **Amenities:** Restaurant; concierge; car rental; same-day laundry/dry cleaning; Flybus. *In room:* TV, free Wi-Fi, minibar, coffee/tea, hair dryer, trouser press, iron (on request), safe.

Radisson SAS 1919 Hotel ⟨⟨⟨ Of all the four-star hotels in the city center, this SAS takes top honors for stylishness, value, and service. The historic 1919 building is the former headquarters of Eimskip, the first major shipping line in Iceland, and almost matches the Borg in grandeur. Much has been made of the avant-garde sculptures of silver-coated human bodies embedded in the walls of the lobby, and the original grand marble staircase. Modern Scandinavian design—with wood lending the only "color" to the cold minimalism—rarely feels so sumptuous. Bathrooms are large, and bedroom ceilings rise to 4m (13 ft.). The added value of a deluxe room is simply more space, but rooms with harbor views book fast. Downstairs is the prestigious restaurant, **Salt** (p. 102), and a wonderful lounge with a grownup and subdued vibe.

Pósthússtræti 2. ⓒ 599-1000. 800/333-3333 from U.S.; 800/3333-3333 from U.K. Fax 599-1001. www.1919.reykjavik. radissonsas.com. 88 units. June–Aug and Dec 28–Jan 2 19,650kr–25,950kr ($314–$415/£157–£208) double; 33,200kr ($531/£266) and up for suites. Rates 18% lower Feb–Mar and Sept–Oct; 30% lower Nov–Jan, except Dec 28–Jan 2. AE, DC, MC, V. Limited street parking. **Amenities:** Restaurant; bar and lounge; small exercise room; concierge; business center; room service; same-day laundry/dry cleaning; Flybus. *In room:* TV, free Wi-Fi, minibar, coffee/tea, hair dryer, iron (on request), safe.

EXPENSIVE

CenterHotel Klöpp ⟨⟨ The newly renovated Klöpp, 1 block from Laugavegur and right smack in the action, belongs to a small Icelandic chain but has the feel of a boutique hotel. Rooms are modern, sleek, and understated, distinguished by medium-dark wood floors, granite-dominated bathrooms, and majestic red walls set off against otherwise neutral colors. Mattresses are softer than the extra-firm Scandinavian standard. The fourth floor has partial views of Mt. Esja, and the fifth floor is in the clear. Rooms 507 and 508, the "superior" doubles, are definitely worth the expense but are often booked far in advance. The corner singles, with their rounded walls, are very appealing. Interior rooms are quieter, but you can't really escape the late-night revelry in this neighborhood.

Klapparstígur 26. ℂ 595-8520. Fax 595-8521. www.centerhotels.com. 46 units. July–Aug 21,500kr–26,000kr ($344–$416/£172–£208) double. Rates 11% lower May–June and Sept; 47% lower Oct–Apr. Closed Dec 17–Dec 26. 50% off for children 7–12; free for those 6 and under. Rates include breakfast. AE, DC, MC, V. Free parking nearby. **Amenities:** Same-day laundry/dry cleaning service; room service; Flybus. *In room:* TV, free Wi-Fi, minibar, coffeemaker, hair dryer, iron (on request), safe.

Hótel Leifur Eiríksson
The rooms of this family-run hotel are small and uninspired, with narrow beds, small bathrooms, and generic furniture—but the location and friendly, relaxed atmosphere are key. The building itself is quite respectable, at the head of Skólavörðustígur, the most appealing commercial street in Reykjavík. All the action is close by, but not too close. Hallgrímskirkja and its statue of Leifur are virtually next door. Half the rooms have church views, and a few have balconies. Free coffee and juice in the lobby are always appreciated. And if you're out late and can't remember the route home, just look for the church steeple.

Skólavörðustígur 45. ℂ 562-0800. Fax 562-0804. www.hotelleifur.is. 47 units. May–Sept 17,400kr ($278/£139) double; 20,500kr ($328/£164) triple. Rates 31%–33% lower Oct–Apr. Rates include breakfast. Free for 1 child under 12 in parent's room. Special offers available online. AE, MC, V. Free parking. **Amenities:** Free Wi-Fi (in lobby); room service; same-day dry cleaning; Flybus. *In room:* TV.

Icelandica ⟨★★★
Iceland has quite an array of alternative lodging, and the Icelandica presents a particularly convincing case for escaping the hotel racket. It's the same basic arrangement: suites are cleaned each day. But a simple breakfast is delivered the previous evening, and your stay here is more private. Staff is on-hand until 6:30pm, and you can always buzz the manager's cellphone. The house, on a peaceful street a 5-minute walk from the city center, is what's known in Reykjavík as a "captain's mansion." (It's not quite a mansion, but a fishing captain did once live here.) Most suites have kitchens, but the only cooking you can do is in the microwave. Suite 204 is wonderful in winter, with its august leather-topped desk and bay window. Suite 305 is ideal in summer; it's the smallest of the deluxe suites, but has a wonderful balcony for your morning coffee.

Tungata 34. ℂ 534-0444. Fax 534-0430. www.icelandica.com. 6 units. May–Sept 18,900kr ($302/£151) junior suites; 21,900kr ($350/£175) deluxe suites. Rates up to 30% lower Oct–Apr. Rates include breakfast. AE, DC, MC, V. Easy street parking. *In room:* TV/DVD, free Wi-Fi, kitchenette, fridge, coffeemaker, hair dryer.

Metropolitan Hotel
Extensive renovations in 2004 haven't spiffed up the place so much as solidified its reputation for basic three-star comfort, convenience, and friendly service. The location is ideal: in the center, on a pretty residential street. The main drawback is the small and rather spartan rooms and bathrooms. Views are nothing to speak of, and curtains should be thicker to defend against the late-night sun. In sum, a practical if nontranscendent choice, with excellent discounts in the off season.

Ránargata 4a. ℂ 511-1155. Fax 552-9040. www.metropolitan.is. 31 units w/bathroom and shower. May–Sept 15,900kr ($254/£127) double; 19,100kr ($306/£153) triple. Rates 32%–38% lower Oct–Apr. Rates include breakfast. Discount for children ages 7–12 in parent's room; free for children 6 and under. AE, DC, MC, V. Limited street parking. **Amenities:** Concierge; laundry/dry cleaning; Flybus. *In room:* TV, Wi-Fi, fridge.

MODERATE

Anna's Guesthouse 🏛 Housed in the former Czechoslovakian embassy, this cheerful and cozily decorated haven feels more "B&B" than most Reykjavík guesthouses. Rooms are large and personalized, and guests share breakfast space around a single table in a living room with a piano. The location is good if not ideal, close to the BSÍ bus terminal and a 15-minute walk from the center. Anna, the genial proprietor, lived in Atlanta for 30 years, which could explain all the cushions and carpeting, a noticeable contrast to the expected Scandinavian sparseness. If you don't get one of the seven rooms with a private bath, you won't have to share with many others. We hope she has succeeded in adding her outdoor hot tub, planned at press time.

Smáragata 16. ☎ 562-1618. Fax 562-1656. www.guesthouseanna.is. 11 units, 7 w/bathroom. May–Sept 11,500kr ($184/£92) double without bathroom; 13,000kr ($208/£104) double w/bathroom; 13,500kr ($216/£108) triple without bathroom; 16,200kr ($259/£130) triple w/bathroom. Rates 30%–45% lower off season. Children ages 7–12 pay 1,200kr ($19/£9.60) when sharing bed with parent; free for children 6 and under. Rates include breakfast. MC, V. Easy street parking. **Amenities:** Flybus. *In room:* Free Wi-Fi.

Baldursbrá Guesthouse 🏛 *Value* Close to Tjörnin pond and a short walk north of the BSÍ bus terminal, this guesthouse is surrounded by foreign embassies. Rooms are large, comfortable, and clean; the street is quiet and reasonably close to town; and the sitting room and TV lounge are appealing—but the clinchers here are the hot tub, sauna, and grill in the back yard. Evelyne, the French manager, is very friendly and on the ball.

Laufásvegur 41. ☎ 552-6646. Fax 562-6647. http://notendur.centrum.is/~heijfis. 8 units without bathroom. July–Aug 9,750kr ($156/£78) double; June 9,313kr ($149/£75) double. Rates 17% lower in May and Dec 19–Jan 8; 28% lower Oct and Mar–Apr; and 40% lower Nov–Dec 18 and Jan 9–Feb. Rates include breakfast. Discounts on payments with cash/traveler's checks. MC, V. Free parking. **Amenities:** Outdoor Jacuzzi; sauna; free Wi-Fi (in lobby); Flybus. *In room:* No phone.

Butterfly Guesthouse 🏛 Originally designed as therapists' offices, the rooms at this good-value, centrally located guesthouse are furnished simply and painted in soothing fall colors with good soundproofing. Rooms are small but spotless, and no more than two or three rooms share each bathroom. Families and groups of three or four should look into the two appealing, sky-lighted apartments on the top floor; one apartment is smaller but has a balcony. Breakfast is free but minimal—cereal, biscuits, and coffee—but you can cook in the shared kitchen, an increasingly rare amenity. This guesthouse is one of the few to still observe the Icelandic custom of removing one's shoes upon entering. Even rarer is the accessible washer and dryer.

Ránargata 8a. ☎ 894-1864. www.kvasir.is/butterfly. 8 units, 4 without bathroom. Late May through early Sept 9,500kr–9,900kr ($152–$158/£76–£79) double without bathroom; 10,500kr–10,900kr ($168–$174/£84–£87) double w/bathroom; 14,900kr–15,900kr ($238–$254/£119–£127) family room w/ bathroom/two-person apt; 17,900kr–18,900kr ($286–$302/£143–£151) family apt. Closed early Sept to late May. AE, DC, MC, V. Limited street parking. **Amenities:** Car rental; washer/dryer (small fee). *In room:* Free Wi-Fi. Apts have TV and kitchen.

Castle House & Embassy Luxury Apartments (Kastallin Hotel) 🏛 Don't shy away from these condolike accommodations, which are increasingly common throughout Iceland. Apartments offer kitchens and more space for the money, and rooms are cleaned daily. They even wash your dishes, and will run to the store and stock your fridge, for 950kr ($15/£7.60) plus the grocery bill. No desk staff is available, but a buzzer can summon the manager by cellphone 24/7. Walls may be thin and bathrooms small, but beds are comfortable and service reliable. The units are in two separate properties, both equally central. Castle House is right on Tjörnin Pond and

has the edge in scenery, while Embassy is west of the pond and offers more seclusion. If the apartment is ready, you can check in early without paying extra.

Skálholtsstígur 2a. ℂ **511-2166.** Fax 562-9165. www.mmedia.is/apartment. 12 units. Summer 12,900kr–49,000kr ($206–$784/£103–£392) apts for 1–6 people. Rates vary with size of apt, number of occupants, and length of stay. With Internet discount, most apts for 2 cost 11,000kr–19,271kr ($176–$308/£88–£154). Rates 40% lower in winter. AE, MC, V. Easy street parking. **Amenities:** Laundry/dry cleaning service. *In room:* TV, free high-speed Internet, kitchen, fridge, coffeemaker.

Fosshótel Baron ★ *(Kids)*

The Fosshótel chain isn't known for style, sophistication, or classy furnishings, but this solid choice is in the center of town and has a range of family-friendly rooming options. Rooms and bathrooms are bright, modern, clean, and large; although most are in the dowdier section of the hotel. Studio apartments have fully equipped kitchens and comfortably sleep two adults and two children, all for the same price as the doubles. The two-bedroom apartments sleep four adults and two children, which means even bigger savings. Fosshótel's family policy is especially beneficial to parents with two young children: Two doubles for the price of two singles saves you 10,400kr ($166/£83). Children like the kiddie-themed duvets, games, and coloring books. *Tip:* Light sleepers should bring earplugs to contend with late-night street noise from nearby Laugavegur.

Barónsstígur 2–4. ℂ **562-4000.** Fax 552-4425. www.fosshotel.is. 121 units. May–Sept 20,900kr ($334/£167) doubles and studio apts; 23,900kr–27,900kr ($382–$446/£191–£223) apts. Rates 32%–40% lower Mar–Apr and Oct–Dec. Children 11 and under stay free in parent's room. Rates include breakfast. AE, DC, MC, V. Free parking. **Amenities:** Bar; tour desk; car rentals; laundry/dry cleaning; Flybus. *In room:* TV, free Wi-Fi, hair dryer. All apts have kitchen, fridge, coffee/tea.

Guesthouse 101

Not to be confused with Hotel 101—Jude Law and Leonardo DiCaprio will not be seen in the lobby—this well-run, friendly hotel is about functionality, value, and basic comforts. The spare, decent-size rooms (all with twin beds) in this converted concrete office building have a generic modern look, but the free breakfast sees you to your next meal without complaint. At the far eastern end of Laugavegur, bordering on a business district, the 101 is a short walk from the action, and the Hlemmur bus station is right around the corner.

Laugavegur 101. ℂ **562-6101.** www.iceland101.com. 18 units, 4 w/bathroom. May–Sept 9,600kr ($154/£77) double; 11,900kr ($190/£95) triple; 13,900kr ($222/£111) family room with 4 beds. Rates 25%–39% lower Oct–Apr. Rates include breakfast (May–Sept only). MC, V. Free parking. **Amenities:** Car rental; laundry service. *In room:* Sink, no phone.

Guesthouse Óðinn ★

With two adjoining houses in an ideal residential location close to downtown, this summer-only guesthouse immediately registers adept and conscientious management, value, and comfort. Some rooms still look a bit like (nice) college dorms, but renovations are proceeding quickly. The small house in back has five double rooms, whose guests share one small bathroom and a huge kitchen—larger groups can rent the whole thing. The main house has apartments and family rooms on the lower floors and renovated doubles on the top; the best double has a balcony.

Óðinsgata 9. ℂ **561-3400.** www.odinnreykjavik.com. 10 units, 1 w/bathroom. June–Aug 9,800kr ($157/£78) double without bathroom; 12,200kr ($195/£98) triple/double w/bathroom; 15,000kr–32,500kr ($240–$520/£120–£260) apts for 2, 4, or 8 people. Rates include breakfast. Closed Sept–May. No credit cards. Limited street parking. **Amenities:** Car rental; apts come with either private or shared kitchen, fridge, coffeemaker.

Hótel Frón ★ *(Value)*

This government-rated three-star hotel spanning three buildings is at the epicenter of Reykjavík shopping and nightlife. What the rooms lack in character they make up in spaciousness, price, and location. The 15 rooms facing Laugavegur—especially those with balconies—are for those who want to breathe in the chaos on weekends. "Zip-and-link" beds easily transform twins to doubles. The 20 "studio" apartments with kitchenettes are big enough to pass for suites. Most rooms on the fourth and fifth floors have good views. The Frón makes a sincere effort to accommodate early arrivals on the red-eye from North America, with free entry to your room as early as 8am.

Laugavegur 22a. (C) **511-4666.** Fax 511-4665. www.hotelfron.is. 89 units. May–Sept 13,500kr ($216/£108) doubles; 16,900kr–17,900kr ($270–$286/£135–£143) studio apts; 18,900kr–23,500kr ($302–$376/£151–£188) apts, both with Jacuzzis and 1 with a sauna. Rates 23%–33% lower Mar–Apr and Oct, and 37%–44% lower Nov–Feb. Rates include breakfast. AE, DC, MC, V. Free parking. **Amenities:** Restaurant; bar; Flybus. *In room:* TV, Wi-Fi, minibar, safe. All apts have kitchenette, fridge, microwave, and coffeemaker.

INEXPENSIVE

Álfhóll Guesthouse (★) (Value) Rooms in this summer-only 1928 guesthouse are tasteful, airy, and uncluttered. The location, residential but close to the center and old harbor, is ideal. Furnishings are a nice break from the mass-produced Scandinavian variety; the antiques aren't fine but make you feel at home, and the lack of TVs feels intentional, not cheap. Rooms facing the street are larger but potentially louder on weekend nights. The top-floor studio apartments, which have kitchens and sleep up to four, have wonderfully odd multi-gabled roof contours.

Ránargata 8. (C) **898-1838.** Fax 552-3838. www.islandia.is/alf. 11 units; only the 3 apts have private bath. May 15–Sept 1 9,000kr ($144/£72) doubles; 11,500kr ($184/£92) triples; 14,000kr–21,000kr ($224–$336/£112–£168) studio apts for 2–4 persons. Rates include breakfast, except studios. No credit cards. Closed Sept 2–May 14. *In room:* Free Wi-Fi. Apts have fridge and coffeemaker.

Salvation Army Guesthouse (Value) In case you're wondering, this place is not for charity cases (though you may feel like one after battling Reykjavík's prices). No one will try to save your soul, and the location and value are unbeatable. Sure, the furniture is aging and threadbare, the rooms are charmless and cell-like, and you'll find only one bathroom per gender on each floor. But the place is perfectly clean, and cooking for yourself in the communal kitchens makes it even more of a deal. Drinking is forbidden on the premises, but unlike the old days, the management doesn't prohibit card games.

Kirkjustraeti 2. (C) **561-3203.** Fax 561-3315. www.guesthouse.is. 50 units. 8,000kr ($128/£64) double; 10,500kr ($168/£84) triple; 13,000kr ($208/£104) room with 4 beds; 1,900kr ($30/£15) sleeping-bag accommodation and 400kr ($6.40/£3.20) to rent quilt. Breakfast available for 700kr ($11/£5.60). Limited street parking. AE, DC, MC, V. *In room:* No phone.

Snorri's Guesthouse (★) (Value) If you're on a budget, don't need your own bathroom, would like to do your own cooking, and don't mind walking 10 minutes to the city center, it's hard to find more pleasant lodging. The simple, modern rooms are decent-size; those in the original house have sinks and shared TV, while rooms in the adjacent house have TVs but no sink. Each house has a large, well-equipped kitchen, and both share a leafy patio and very agreeable breakfast area. The guesthouse is on a wide avenue with some traffic noise, so you might request a room off the street. The friendly staff is especially helpful with tours and other travel arrangements, though they take afternoons off in the low season.

Snorrabraut 61. (C) **552-0598.** Fax 551-8945. www.guesthousereykjavik.com. 23 units, 1 w/bathroom. May–Sept 9,200kr ($147/£74) double without bathroom; 12,200kr ($195/£98) double w/bathroom; 10,500kr–15,800kr ($168–$253/£84–£126) family room for 2–4 persons without bathroom; 2,500kr ($40/£20) sleeping-bag accommodation (Oct–Apr only) in doubles. Made-up bed rates 22%–27% lower Oct–Apr. Made-up bed rates include breakfast. DC, MC, V. Free parking. **Amenities:** Free Wi-Fi in lobby; car rental; Flybus (ask driver for Flóki Inn across the street). *In room:* Family rooms have TV/DVD, fridge, coffee/tea.

OUTSIDE THE CITY CENTER

Perhaps you think of hostels as the exclusive domain of scruffy young backpackers, but Iceland's prices have driven you to despair. The **Reykjavík City Hostel**/⚘, Sundlauga-vegur 34 (© **553-8110;** fax 588-9201; www.hostel.is; 40 units without bathroom; May–Sept 7,000kr [$112/£56] double; bed linens 700kr [$11/£5.60] for entire stay; discounts Oct–Apr), is really not all that different than other accommodations. You can get your own room and rent sheets. You don't need a membership card. You'll see plenty of families and seniors and people from all walks of life. The hostel even has more amenities than most hotels: guest kitchens, sauna, free parking, cafe/bar, game room, playground, free Wi-Fi (in common area), and laundry rooms, plus fun events like film showings and "pub crawls." Many tour operators offer their lowest prices through the helpful front desk. Admittedly, the ambience is sterile and the location is remote; but Flybus and airport connections are easy, and you're right next door to the Laugardalslaug pool (p. 121). Book way in advance, particularly for doubles; summer rooms sell out as early as January.

VERY EXPENSIVE

Grand Hótel Reykjavík ⚘⚘ The Grand was the talk of the hotel trade in 2007, when it added two new 13-story towers connected via a glass-enclosed atrium, making it the largest hotel in the country. Of all Reykjavík's luxury hotels, this is the most business-oriented, with primo facilities and amenities, but considerably less aesthete appeal than rivals like the Nordica or Borg. The old wing is dowdier, but until it's renovated you can save money by staying there. The new rooms are snazzy, though they won't be featured in design magazine spreads. Bathrooms all have heated tile floors and separate bathtubs and shower stalls. Though the new towers were designed to be free of electromagnetic pollution, beware of rooms on the fifth floor or below facing the atrium, as lobby noise filters in. The fitness center and Wi-Fi aren't included in the room price, which seems stingy.

Sigtún 38, 105 Reykjavík. © **514-8000.** Fax 514-8030. www.grand.is. 314 units. May–Sept 22,400kr–28,300kr ($358–$453/£179–£226) doubles; 31,200kr ($499/£250) triples; 31,900kr ($510/£255) and up for deluxe rooms and suites. Rates 34%–45% lower Oct–Apr (may exclude apt suites). Rates include breakfast. Children under 12 stay free in parent's room. MC, V. Free parking. **Amenities:** Restaurant; bar; exercise room 2,750kr ($44/£22); spa; Jacuzzi and salt-water hot tub; salon; room service; same-day laundry/dry cleaning; executive rooms; shuttle to city center (10am, 1pm, and 5pm); bike rental; Flybus. *In room:* TV, Wi-Fi 1,500kr ($24/£12), minibar, coffee/tea, hair dryer, trouser press, safe. Tower rooms have irons.

Hilton Reykjavík Nordica ⚘⚘⚘ The Nordica represents the pinnacle of sleek Scandinavian chrome-glass and natural-wood interior design. (Yoko Ono told the management she was reminded of Japan.) All rooms are "deluxe" with bathtubs, ample light, and a fine sensibility for texture, harmony, and luxury; some have mountain views. Business and executive rooms are on the eighth and ninth floors and include free access to the exceptional **NordicaSpa** (p. 120) and the panorama lounge, which has a fireplace and free wine, beer, and soda. You can upgrade for 5,000kr ($80/£40) a night pending availability: a good deal if you make use of the spa for 2,500kr ($40/£20) and free drinks. The well-known restaurant **Vox** has a fantastic lunch buffet.

Suðurlandsbraut 2. © **444-5000.** Fax 444-5001. www.reykjavik.nordica.hilton.com. 252 units. June–Oct 27,500kr ($440/£220) doubles; 32,500kr ($520/£260) and up for business/executive/deluxe rooms and suites. Rates 25%–40% lower off season. Free valet/self parking. **Amenities:** Restaurant; bar; lounge; NordicaSpa; business center; room service; same-day laundry/dry cleaning service; travel agency; shuttle bus to city center; Flybus. *In room:* TV, free high-speed Internet, minibar, coffee/tea, hair dryer, trouser press/iron, safe.

EXPENSIVE

Hótel Björk   No, this modest three-star hotel has nothing to do with Iceland's foremost international star; *björk* simply means "birch." The staff is friendly and competent, rooms are spacious, beds are comfy and new, the breakfast buffet is ample, and customer satisfaction is consistently high. Beyond that, not much distinguishes the Björk from any chain hotel. (The elegant and historic Hótel Borg is also owned by Keahotels but you'd never know.) In a quiet and rather anonymous business district, the Björk is a 15-minute walk from the city center, close to Laugardalur Park and its delightful pool. Be sure to ask if you want a queen-size bed or view of Mt. Esja.

Brautarholt 22-24. Ⓒ **460-2000** or 511-3777. www.bjorkhotelreykjavik.com. 55 units. May–Sept 17,700kr ($283/£142) double; 23,300kr ($373/£186) triple. Online discounts available. Rates 37%–38% lower Oct–Apr. Free parking. **Amenities:** Restaurant; concierge; business center; dry cleaning service; Flybus. *In room:* TV, free Wi-Fi, coffee/tea, hair dryer.

MODERATE

Hótel Vík   The Vík expanded into a neighboring building in 2007 and is in a flurry of renovation for 2008. The old wing's weathered furniture will be methodically replaced by standard Scandinavian design. The lower-than-average prices reflect the dull surroundings, as if to compensate customers for being a 20-minute walk from the city center. At least the Vík offers peace, quiet, and easy parking. Families will appreciate proximity to the Laugardalur pool, zoo, and family park and can save big in the studio apartments with kitchenettes. Second-floor rooms have mountain views. The new wing gets the nod for its nice breakfast room.

Síðumúla 19. Ⓒ **588-5588.** Fax 588-5582. www.hotelvik.is. 33 units. May 1–Sept 16 14,700kr ($235/£118) doubles; 17,800kr ($285/£142) triples; 15,800kr ($253/£126) studio apts. Rates 35%–40% lower Sept 17–Apr 30. Rates include continental breakfast. 10% discount for booking online. Free parking. **Amenities:** Bar; lounge; car rentals; Flybus. *In room:* TV, free Wi-Fi (on request), fridge.

Kríunes Guesthouse ⚓   If you want to stay in an idyllic country setting, this lakeshore retreat is a great option. The guesthouse operates a shuttle to the city center and airport, but it's really best reached by car (15 min.). The ranch-style building is Mexican-themed, but all this amounts to is a few ornate headboards. The restaurant—which has probably never seen a tortilla—specializes in local trout, which you can cast for in the lake without a permit. Canoes and foot-pedal boats are available for a fee, and horse rentals are nearby. Rooms are spacious and inviting, and the "bridal suites" (more space, a bathtub for two, and, in the larger suite, an open fireplace) won't make non-honeymooners feel out of place.

Við Vatnsenda. Ⓒ **567-2245.** www.kriunes.is. 12 units. Early May–late Sept 14,900kr ($238/£119) double; Oct to late Apr 9,900kr ($158/£79) double. 28,000kr–35,000kr ($448–$560/£224–£280) suites year-round. Rates include breakfast. MC, V. Free parking. **Amenities:** Restaurant. *In room:* TV.

5 Where to Dine

Reykjavík was mostly a culinary wasteland 25 years ago. Now it might qualify as a culinary destination, if only Iceland's landscape didn't steal so much attention. Iceland now has more wine stewards per capita than any other country in the world. With no venerated food traditions to uphold, innovative young chefs have been free to create Icelandic food in their own image, drawing inspiration wherever they find it. The quality and diversity of ingredients is astounding for such a remote outpost of the world. Unfortunately the rest of Iceland is having trouble getting up to speed.

You'll be jolted by the prices: Entrees in a typical mid-level restaurant are 3,125kr ($50/£25), and a bottle of wine is rarely below that. There's a peculiar dynamic to be aware of, however. Ingredients and labor are so costly that all meals have a high base cost, but you're still getting good value at the margin: Spend 4,688kr ($75/£38) per person and you'll likely have a good meal, spend 6,250kr ($100/£50) and you'll likely have a fantastic one. We recommend visiting the grocery store (and the hot-dog stand) a few times, sneaking some of that breakfast buffet into your bag, and then splurging on a few meals to remember. For more on Icelandic restaurants, see "Tips on Dining," in chapter 2.

VERY EXPENSIVE

Argentina ★★ STEAKHOUSE   It's easy to picture a gaucho smoking a cigar in this windowless cavern of meat consumption, and hard to find a better steak in Iceland. The meat is sold by weight, not carved from a spit at your table, as you might find in Buenos Aires—but an Argentinian chef does visit every 3 years to check up on things. Whenever possible they use the Icelandic cattle breed, which grazes widely, eats healthily, and develops slowly and naturally. The menu includes seafood, but you can't go wrong with the beef or lamb tenderloin and the good house red wine. Portions are large, and the menu doesn't even mention the accompanying baked potato and grilled vegetables. The four-course menu is well below a la carte prices, and the two-for-one "pre-theater" deal (Fri and Sat only) offers dramatic savings before 8pm.

Barónsstígur 11a. © 551-9555. Reservations recommended. Main courses 3,050kr–5,600kr ($49–$90/£24–£45); 4-course menu 6,900kr ($110/£55). AE, DC, MC, V. Sun–Thurs 6pm–midnight; Fri–Sat 5:30pm–1am; kitchen closes 90 min. before restaurant.

Einar Ben ★★ CONTINENTAL   If you want nouveau or fusion cuisine, look elsewhere. This old-guard restaurant is on the second floor of a century-old gentry townhouse, and the velvety curtains and brass chandeliers are a welcome relief from all the hip, minimalist interiors elsewhere in the fine-dining register. The menu's subtitle of "pure Icelandic" refers to native ingredients, not the dishes, which are honest French peasant fare with decent portions and hearty sauces. Lamb is always a safe choice in Iceland: Locals tend to order the filet of lamb Dijon with mountain thyme crust, lamb shank confit, and dill glaze; while foreigners tend to order the fall-off-the-bone tender lamb shank with creamed vegetables and red wine jus. The wine list is exceptional, and the spacious bar on the third floor is a wonderful spot for an after-dinner cognac.

Veltusundi 1, on Ingolfstorg Square. © 511-5090. Reservations recommended. Main courses 2,800–4,900kr ($45–$78/£22–£39); early-bird special before 7:30pm 2,750–3,250kr ($44–$52/£22–£26). AE, DC, MC, V. Mon–Fri 6–10pm; Sat–Sun 6–11pm; bar open until 2 or 3am.

Sjávarkjallarinn (Seafood Cellar) ★★★ SEAFOOD FUSION   If you distrust "concept food," just give this wildly popular restaurant a chance. The decor may be silly (you expect mermaids to appear in the fish tanks), the menu may be alienating (filet of salted cod "yellow brick": limequat, shiitake, beet root), and the presentation may be melodramatic (even the sorbet arrives in bamboo and a plume of dry steam). But no one is trying to distract you from the food, which will likely be the best you'll eat in Iceland. The menu changes every 3 months, though one consistent item is the lobster pick-me-up: the most delicate steamed langoustine in a foie-gras sauce with cauliflower, truffles, and black pepper. Plenty of non-seafood choices are also on-hand. If you have the money and 2 hours to spare, by all means get the chef's tasting menu and sample several dishes, with a few surprises thrown in. The head chef is 26-year-old Hrefna

Waiter, There's a Fly in My Pickled Ram Testicles . . .

Icelanders have faced severe hardship and learned not to let any digestible species or spare parts go to waste—hence the following guide to some of the more peculiar Icelandic specialties on your menu.

- **Horse (hestur)** The pagan practice of eating horsemeat was banned by Christian authorities in the 11th century, but they relented in the 18th century during a famine. Whatever your personal feelings for these magisterial animals, they're perfectly healthy to eat and don't taste bad, either. Traditionally the meat is eaten in stews, but you're more likely to find it served very rare, even raw.

- **Cod chins (gellur)** These walnut-size delicacies, extracted from Iceland's most bounteous fish species, are surrounded by a thick, fatty membrane that doesn't lift cleanly from the tender, savory meat inside. You'll just have to get it all down. They're best ordered in spring or fall when the cod are leaner, though some say that's missing the point.

- **Harðfiskur** Dried haddock, a staple Icelandic food for centuries, is available in every convenience store. As W. H. Auden wrote, "The tougher kind tastes like toe-nails, and the softer kind like the skin off the soles of one's feet."

- **Whale (hvalur)** The only species served up is minke whale, not an endangered species, though Iceland's recent decision to hunt them again is hardly uncontroversial. Consumption has risen thanks to tourists using the "I'll just try it once and see what its all about" rationalization. As sashimi it looks more disturbing than it tastes; the raw meat is a deep red, even purplish color. Even cooked whale steaks are served very red in the middle. And the taste? A sort of cross between tuna and beef, quite delicious when prepared properly, tough and rank otherwise.

- **Dolphin (höfrungur)** Eat these and you'll probably get mercury poisoning. Environmentalists may also pelt you with organic tomatoes.

- **Svið** This is half of a singed sheep's head, cut down the middle and laid on its side, all the better for eye contact with your meal. If you're sharing, go for the cheeks and lips and let your companions deal with the skin, tongue, brains, and eyeball. Svið is also served cold if you like, and can be found at Kjamminn restaurant in Reykjavík's BSÍ bus terminal—even at the drive-thru window!

- **Slátur** Leftover lamb parts, including the liver and blood, are minced, mixed, then sewn up and cooked inside the lamb's stomach lining.

- **Hrútspungar** These are ram's testicles pickled in whey, often mixed with garlic and pressed into a kind of cake or spread, which tastes like pâté way past the due date. Some Americans call these "Rocky Mountain oysters."

Jóhannsdóttir, the youngest member of the team and the only woman—we'd give her 10 stars if we could.

Aðalstræti 2. © **511-1212**. Reservations recommended. Main courses 3,200kr–5,900kr ($51–$94/£26–£47); tasting menu 7,200kr ($115/£58). AE, DC, MC, V. Mon–Fri 11:30am–11:30pm; Sat–Sun 5–11:30pm.

- **Puffin** *(lundi)* From May to mid-August you'll likely have an opportunity to eat Iceland's unbearably cute unofficial mascot. Puffin can be smoked, pickled, or eaten raw. Traditionally it's overcooked, but in restaurants it's almost always served rare. The crossed taste of bird and fish takes getting used to, and on a bad day the meat is reminiscent of burnt rubber marinated in fish oil.
- **Cormorant** *(skarfur)* This seabird tastes similar to puffin, only greasier and less fishy.
- **Guillemot** *(langvía)* This coastal bird's meat looks and feels like beef, but tastes like duck, with odd overtones of liver and seaweed.
- **Fulmar eggs** *(fillsegg)* These oily seabird eggs can be good appetizers. If you buy them at the market, watch out for half-hatched chicks inside.
- **Reindeer** *(hreindýr)* Santa introduced reindeer to eastern Iceland from Norway in the 18th century. All are wild, and only about 300 are culled each year; so prices are high. Hunting season is late fall, so most tourists eat vacuum-packed meat. If you can tell the difference, your taste buds are superior to ours.
- **Skýr** This is Iceland's most popular and delicious culinary invention: a kind of whipped whey. Health food crowds abroad are starting to catch on. Skýr tastes like a cross between sour yogurt, crème fraîche, cream cheese, and soft-serve ice cream, yet somehow it's nonfat. It's traditionally made with rennet, derived from calf stomach, but now it's vegetarian-friendly. You'll find all sorts of berry varieties in markets and convenience stores, a shake form at the gym, and a more liquid variety to pour on your granola at breakfast buffets.
- **Hákarl** This is Iceland's most notorious gross-out food: Greenlandic shark, uncooked and putrefied. Sharks have no kidneys, so urea collects in their blood and the meat has high concentrates of acid and ammonia. If you eat it raw, you might die. So, it's cut up and placed in an outdoor kiln for 3 months while the toxins drain out. Then it's hung to dry and cure for another 3 months. As an appetizer, the shark is served in small cubes that have the look and texture of mozzarella cheese. The taste is indescribable, but might be compared to motor oil—nothing can prepare you for its vileness. According to Icelanders, it gives you stamina. Traditionally it's washed down with *brennivín* (wine that burns), an 80-proof clear liquor flavored with angelica root or caraway seeds, and known affectionately as "Black Death" *(svartidauði)*.

EXPENSIVE

Apótek ⟨**★**⟩ FUSION Named "the pharmacy" after the business that previously inhabited the space, Apótek is one of Reykjavík's trendiest dining spots. The interior is a pretentious, postmodern pastiche of marble columns, Asian umbrella light fixtures, sheep horns "growing" out of large ceramic vases, and a mounted plywood moose head. But the food usually achieves something the design doesn't: a satisfying, creative fusion of styles, forms, and variable ingredients. Delicious examples are the seared scallops with warm asparagus salad, tomato comfit, and nut emulsion (mayo, basically), or pan-fried arctic char with cauliflower, chorizo, and beet-root sauce. Only the sushi is a sure thing, however. If the prices are too steep, consider lunch or the "pre-theatre" two-course menu from 5:30 to 7:30pm.

Austurstræti 16. ℂ 575-7900. Reservations recommended. Main courses 2,900kr–4,600kr ($46–$74/£23–£37). Pre-theater menu 2,590kr ($41/£21). AE, MC, V. Mon–Sat 11:30am–11:30pm; Sun 4–10:30pm.

Austur Indía Fjélagið ★★★ INDIAN

Run by an Indian woman married to an Ice-lander, this is hands-down the best non-European restaurant in Iceland. The chefs hail from all over India, as reflected in the menu, which describes each regional specialty in detail. Freshness is not compromised at this latitude: Meat and fish are all locally pro-duced, and imported herbs and spices are ground and mixed on-site. Indians know lamb, and Iceland has the world's best lamb meat, so put two and two together. Half the dishes are made in the tandoor oven, and the mixed lamb and chicken grill is stupen-dous. Ambience is casual but classy, with Indian antiques on display.

Hverfisgata 56. ℂ 552-1630. Reservations recommended. Main courses 2,095kr–3,595kr ($34–$58/£17–£29). AE, MC, V, MC. Sun–Thurs 6–10pm; Fri–Sat 6–11pm.

Fjalakötturinn ★★★ (Value) INTERNATIONAL

This unpretentious restaurant in the Hótel Centrum doesn't seem to consider itself upmarket, yet the food quality matches almost anything in Iceland's highest price range. It's also the *only* restaurant in Iceland with a Wine Spectator award of excellence (for 2 years running), yet wine prices are marked up much less than elsewhere. Asian touches are superbly integrated with European preparations, and the Thai marinated catfish (served in a sort of upside-down glass sombrero) is one of many sure winners.

Aðalstræti 16, in Hótel Centrum. ℂ 514-6000. Reservations recommended. Main courses 2,500kr–4,600kr ($40–$74/£20–£37). V, MC. Daily 7–10am, noon–3pm, and 6–10pm.

Salt ★★★ ICELANDIC/INTERNATIONAL

In 2005, head chef Ragnar Ómars-son took fifth place in the Bocuse d'Or competition, the culinary equivalent of the Olympics. Twenty chefs selected from around the world are given a pile of previously undisclosed ingredients, which they cook on the spot in front of a live audience and panel of judges. That kind of performance requires both profound schooling and improvisational genius, and Salt's cuisine embodies both. Each month brings a new theme (salad, the pomegranate, Oktoberfest), and each day brings a four-course spe-cial menu, designed at the chef's whim. Yet the menu is more traditional than you might expect; exquisiteness comes well before novelty. Service can be slow.

Pósthússtræti 2, in the Radisson SAS 1919 Hotel. ℂ 599-1020. Reservations recommended. Main courses 1,850kr–4,950kr ($30–$79/£15–£40); 4–5 course special menu 6,400kr ($102/£51). AE, DC, MC, V. Sun–Thurs noon–2pm and 6–10pm; Fri–Sat 6–11pm.

Siggi Hall ★★ ICELANDIC/FRENCH

Celebrity TV chef Siggi Hall doesn't do much of the actual cooking, but he conceptualizes the seasonal menu, actively over-sees operations, and often hangs around chatting up customers amid the simple, laid-back decor. Dishes are highly refined but not too complicated: most are subtle improvements on classics, with an emphasis on local ingredients. Siggi's main inspira-tions are French and Spanish, and the excellent shellfish soufflé and bacalao (salt cod) probably won't ever vanish from the menu. If you see lamb with fried shank sausage, potatoes, vegetables, and rosemary-garlic jus, you're in for a treat. Siggi is rightfully proud of the wine menu.

Óðinstorg Square (at the intersection of Þórsgata and Týsgi), in the Hótel Óðinsvé. © 511-6677. Reservations recommended. Main courses 3,200kr–4,400kr ($51–$70/£26–£35); seasonal menu 6,500kr ($104/£52). AE, MC, V. Tues–Thurs and Sun 3–10:30pm; Fri–Sat 3–11:30pm. Closed Mon.

Við Tjörnina ★★★ ICELANDIC
None of the experienced chefs at this long-running Reykjavík institution went to cooking school. If they had, they would have been told never to mix fish, fruit, and cheese, and the world would never have known their delicious plaice with banana and bleu cheese. The menu has scarcely changed over the years, as they merely refine their unique trial-and-error creations. As outsiders, perhaps they feel a certain sympathy for unpopular fish and meat—this is a great place to try something new, whether it be shark;, trout sushi; cod chins; or perhaps guillemot in an expertly balanced sauce of berries, honey, and lamb stock. If this sounds like a horror show to you, you'll delight in the more conventional offerings. The ambience matches the food's blend of tradition and eccentricity: The two intimate rooms have a great folksy-kooky aesthetic, with floral wallpaper, embroidered tablecloths, display cabinets full of tchotchkes, and an enormous, wall-mounted wax halibut.

Templarasund 3. © 551-8666. Reservations recommended. Mains 1,880kr–5,320kr ($30–$85/£15–£43). AE, MC, V. Daily noon–11pm.

Þrír Frakkar ★★★ ICELANDIC
You've come all this way and want to try "real Icelandic food"—a rather fleeting concept, but odds are this is your place. Tables are packed cozily together, and nautical miscellany clutters the walls. The menu closely follows the seasons, so the selections of fish and seabirds are there for good reason. This may be the time to sample puffin, cormorant, or whale (sushi or steak), if your conscience allows. The hashed fish with traditional, cakey Icelandic brown bread is a popular favorite, though we preferred the fantastic butter-fried halibut with lobster and lobster sauce. Presentation and the wine list are afterthoughts, but service is fast.

Baldursgata 14, at Nönnugata. © 552-3939. Reservations recommended. Mains 2,450kr–3,320kr ($39–$53/£20–£27). AE, DC, MC, V. Mon–Thurs 11am–11pm; Sat–Sun 6–11:30pm.

MODERATE

Á Næstu Grösum VEGETARIAN
Pleasantly perched above Laugavegur, this casual, cafeteria-style eatery is a long-running vegetarian standby. Ordering is simple: You point, they scoop, and all dishes and combo plates come with unlimited hummus, date chutney, and yeast- and sugar-free bread. Most ingredients are organic, and about half the dishes are vegan. The most consistent offerings are vegetable gratin with soy cheese; lasagna with spinach, basil, cottage cheese, and whole wheat; Thai curry; and chickpeas with peanuts and pineapple sauce. The dishes can be a bit gloppy and oddly indistinct from each other, but it's hearty comfort food all the same. Try an organic beer or the impressive sugar-free banana cake.

Laugavegur 20b. © 552-8410. Reservations recommended weekends. Main courses 1,250kr–1,500kr ($20–$24/£10–£12). MC, V. Mon–Sat 11:30am–10pm; Sun 5–10pm.

Icelandic Fish & Chips ★ FISH
This new, harborside organic bistro is an implicit scolding of the traditional English grease-fest. The fish—cod, spotted catfish, monkfish, and the catch of the day—is tossed in barley batter (free of white flour and refined sugar) and fried in all-natural canola oil for a remarkably light, crispy finish

that doesn't obstruct the fish's delicate flavor. Pair your fish with malt vinegar or "skýr-onnaise," the skýr-based house sauce in eight flavors, including coriander-lime, ginger-wasabi, and mango chutney. For "chips," choose between green salad, mango salad, tomato/potato salad, home fries, or onion rings.

Tryggvagata 8, at Geirsgata. © 511-1118. Main courses 1,330kr–1,580kr ($21–$25/£11–£13). MC, V. Daily 11:30am–9pm.

Jómfrúin DANISH   "Open-faced sandwich" is an oxymoron, but connoisseurs of Danish *smørrebrød* see it differently. Copenhagen even has a *smørrebrød* school, and in 1995 Jómfrúin's head chef was the first male ever to graduate. You can't go wrong with anything based on the smoked salmon, and the rye bread (heavy and dense, with whole grains and nuts) is preferable to the bland French bread. The most famous sandwich is the H. C. Andersen: rye bread with butter, crisp bacon, liver pâté, port aspic, horseradish, and parsley—"open-heart surgery sandwich" might be a better description. The most frequently ordered item, for good reason, is the fried plaice on rye with butter, tartar sauce, shrimp, asparagus, and lemon. Service is quick, though mind the odd closing time.

Lækjargata 4. © 551-0100. Sandwiches 920kr–2,175kr ($15–$35/£7.40–£17). MC, V. Daily 11am–6pm.

Rossopomodoro ✿ ITALIAN   This deservedly popular Italian restaurant is actually a franchise, with other branches in Italy, Spain, and Rio. Appetizers are dependable standards, and the main courses center on pasta and pizza with a sprinkling of fish and meat dishes. The tomato, buffalo mozzarella, and basil pizza tastes as it would in Naples, with delectable tomato sauce and a thin, thin crust. Porcini ravioli with butter and sage is one of several delicious and authentic main courses. The "garlic bread," however, is a strictly Icelandic phenomenon. Service is quick, if not exactly ingratiating, and the atmosphere is bright and casual.

Laugavegur 40a. © 561-0500. Reservations recommended for dinner. Main courses 1,400kr–3,050kr ($22–$49/£11–£24). AE, DC, MC, V. Sun–Thurs 11:30am–10pm; Fri–Sat 11:30am–11pm. Lunch (selected pizzas and pastas only) served until 2pm.

Thorvaldsen ✿ FUSION   One team runs both Sjávarkjallarinn (aka the Seafood Cellar, our favorite Reykjavík restaurant) and this restaurant-bar. The food is similarly playful and inventive, and both menus are equally enigmatic: One dessert option is "Strawberry 'lollipop': basil, pop rocks, vanilla." Start with a succulent soft-shell crab "Japanese style" (chile, BBQ, spring onion) and follow up with tuna tandoori (mashed potatoes, red chile, rocket lettuce, sansho pepper sauce). Sushi is the most reliable choice. Of course it's not quite up to Cellar level, but patrons are too distracted by that beautiful person at the next table to pay close attention to the food anyway—after 10pm Thorvaldsen becomes a suave nightspot for snappy dressers.

Austurstræti 8–10. © 511-1413. Reservations recommended on weekends. Main courses 1,890kr–3,690kr ($30–$59/£15–£30); party menu 4,290kr ($69/£34) per person. Sun–Thurs 11am–1am; Fri 11am–3am; Sat 11am–3:30am. Kitchen closes at 10pm.

Vegamót INTERNATIONAL   This is a good consensus choice. The location is central, the prices affordable. The food is eclectic (with an emphasis on Tex-Mex, Italian, and Indian) but very approachable, almost too homogenized by Nordic tastes. Surroundings are elegant and bustling, signaling the beginning of an evening rather than the end of one. Portions are generous, but the menu offers plenty of light meal

Hot-Dog Utopia

Icelanders are well aware that their *pylsur* (hot dogs) are the best on the planet, and they consume them in enormous quantities—usually *ein með öllu,* or "one with everything." A familiar and welcoming sight inside every gas station is the undulating metal rack that holds your hot dog as you dispense mayo, ketchup, and a tangy rémoulade (with finely chopped pickle) from enormous squeeze tubes. Toppings also include raw and crispy onions. But the key ingredient is the hot dog itself: The addition of lamb to the usual pork and beef mellows and deepens the flavor. You probably don't want to know any more about how they're made, however.

options. Good choices are the Mexican soft taco; the garlic fried beef strips with onion, mushrooms, and béarnaise sauce on a baguette; or any of the reliable burgers, pizza, and panini sandwiches. Late at night Vegamót transforms into one of the hippest bars in the capital. The popular "American-style" brunch (weekends until 4:30pm) includes pancakes, maple syrup, eggs, bacon, and smoothies.

Vegamótastígur 4, just below Laugavegur. ℂ 511-3040. www.vegamot.is. Reservations recommended. Main courses 1,090kr–2,790kr ($17–$45/£8.50–£23). AE, MC, V. Mon–Thurs 11am–1am; Fri–Sat 11am–5am; Sun noon–1am. Minimum age 22 after 10pm (when kitchen closes).

INEXPENSIVE

Bæjarins Bestu ⊛ HOT DOGS   This drab little shack facing a parking lot near the harbor is nothing short of a national landmark: Since 1935 it has served the country's best hot dog in the world's best hot-dog country (see "Hot-Dog Utopia," above). Any other business would add a second employee and sell T-shirts, but the only change in recent times is the addition of a framed photo of Bill Clinton, posing with the proprietor and holding a hot dog. (He ordered it with mustard only, which isn't advised, but if that's what you want, ask for a "Clinton.") Seating is limited to one outdoor picnic table. Britain's *Guardian,* voting this place "Best Hot-Dog Stand in Europe," credited the rémoulade sauce, but locals believe it's the secret cooking fluid (most think beer is involved).

Tryggvagata 101, corner of Pósthússtræti. No phone. Hot dogs 210kr ($3.35/£1.70). Daily 10am–3am.

Eldsmiðjan ⊛ PIZZA   Tucked away from the tourist byways, this first-rate pizzeria is great for a casual meal and can also deliver to your hotel. Pizzas are thin crusted but hearty, with no fewer than 46 toppings to choose from (perhaps you've always wanted a pizza combining alfalfa and snails). They tell us the most popular combo is the "pepperoni special" with jalapeños, cream cheese, pineapple, olives, garlic, mushrooms, and spices—but we couldn't bring ourselves to try it.

Bragagata 38A, at Freyjugata. ℂ 562-3838. Reservation recommended only for groups of 6 or more. Main courses 835kr–2,315kr ($13–$37/£6.70–£19). AE, DC, MC, V. Daily 11:30am–11pm.

Krúa Thai ⊛ *Value* THAI   Students on a budget have long relied on this authentic hole-in-the-wall run by a Thai family in the old harbor neighborhood. Service is fast and perfunctory, and the food is hearty, flavorful, and richly seasoned if not exactly delicate. You might expect the spiciness to be toned down for Nordic taste buds, but they do it their way unless you specify otherwise. The pad Thai is particularly spicy and delicious—though overloaded with chunky peanuts. You can ask for a free rice refill. Lunches are even cheaper.

Tryggvagata 14. ① **561-0039.** Main courses 1,000kr–1,500kr ($16–$24/£8–£12). MC, V. Mon–Fri 11:30am–9:30pm; Sat 2–9:30pm; Sun 5–9:30pm.

Sægreifinn 🍴 *Value* SEAFOOD Run by three local fisherman and crammed inside a small warehouse by the old harbor, "The Sea Baron" has the city's best seafood value and its best ramshackle ambience. You order at the counter, then sit on a fish-packing container until the food arrives in a foam container with plastic utensils. Many tourists sample whale here, as suggested by the restaurant's hilariously shameless logo, "Moby Dick on a Stick." Cod, scallops, and seasonal fish and seabirds also appear in kabob form, but the restaurant's most famous concoction is the *humarsupa* (lobster soup): a little sweet and creamy, with suggestions of celery, red pepper, tomato, cinnamon, clove, and coriander—and a decent portion of lobster.

Geirsgata 8 between Ægisgata and Tryggvagata. ① **553-1500.** Main courses 750kr–2,000kr ($12–$32/£6–£16) MC, V. Summer (usually May 15–Sept 15) daily noon–10pm; off season Mon–Thurs noon–8pm, Fri–Sun noon–10pm.

CAFES & A BAKERY

Various explanations are given for why Iceland runs on coffee: the former prohibition of beer, the high cost of alcohol, the long and dark winters, all the short spells of rain, the need to digest heavy diets. Whatever the cause, Icelandic coffee is fine and strong, and coffeehouse culture thrives in Reykjavík. (The international chains have yet to gain a foothold.) Cafes are a great place to meet locals, second only to the pools. Magazines are usually lying around, refills are often free, and you can linger for hours without being glared at. Most cafes serve food by day but function as bars and clubs at night. They generally don't open until 11am, and close at 1am, or later on weekends.

Cafe Cultura 🍴 Downstairs from the International Center, where immigrants come for assistance, the Cultura serves up respectable quesadillas, falafel, tapas, and wraps in an atmosphere not straining particularly hard for multicultural ambience. Actors from the National Theater across the street stop in, plus the usual lone laptoppers using the free Wi-Fi. This is one of the few places you'll find international music at night; check for salsa nights or free tango lessons.

Hverfisgata 18. ① **530-9314.** Main courses 390kr–1,890kr ($6.25–$30/£3.15–£15). MC, V. Mon–Fri 11:30am–1am; Sat–Sun 11:30am–4am. Kitchen closes 9pm.

Cafe Paris Spilling onto Austurvöllur Square, this cafe is Reykjavík's closest approximation of a Parisian brasserie, complete with good streetside people-watching. The menu is too long for the chefs to get every dish just right, but good standbys are the lasagna Bolognese; shrimp, mussel, and artichoke pizza; the ham and brie panini; and the French chocolate cake. Avoid the "Paris burger" and be warned that "nachos" mean plain tortilla chips.

Austurstræti 14, on Austurvöllur Square. ① **551-1020.** Reservations recommended for dinner. Main courses 390kr–2,950kr ($6.25–$47/£3.10–£24). MC, V. Mon–Thurs 8am–1am; Fri 8am–3am; Sat 9am–3am; Sun 9am–1am.

Grái Kötturinn 🍴 The Icelandic artists running this bohemian, book-lined, basement-level hideout returned from a stint in New York and grieved to find no Reykjavík cafes serving pancakes and bacon at a nice early hour. The result is "The Grey Cat," which prepares terrific coffee, sandwiches, and light meals. Taxi drivers often deliver North Americans here straight off the red-eye.

Hverfisgata 16a. ℭ 551-1544. Main courses 550kr–1,450kr ($8.80–$23/£4.40–£12). AE, MC, V. Mon–Fri 7am–3pm (only sandwiches are available from 2–3pm); Sat–Sun 8am–2pm.

Kaffi Hljómalind   Though alternative to the point of caricature—free anarchist newspapers, Tibetan prayer flags, rainbow colors, the works—you can't really argue with their policies of promoting fair trade and donating all profits to charity. The mostly organic, vegetarian food isn't bad, particularly the burritos, lasagna, pies, and soups of the day. In the evening, it often hosts live music and poetry readings.

Laugavegur 21, corner of Klapparstígur. ℭ 517-1980. Main courses 550kr–750kr ($8.80–$12/£4.40–£6). MC, V. Mon–Fri 9am–11pm; Sat–Sun 11am–11pm.

Mokka Kaffi ⍟   Nothing splashy here, not a place to be seen, just great coffee and good prices at the oldest cafe in town (since 1958). The interior is a bit dark, cramped, and worn, but it might appeal to you for those reasons. You may wonder why your book or conversation is so absorbing, and then realize no music is playing, the enlightened house policy. The small menu is most famous for its fabulous waffles with jam and whipped cream, but the panini are excellent, too.

Skólavörðustígur 3a. ℭ 552-1174. Sandwiches and waffles 300kr–580kr ($4.80–$9.30/£2.40–£4.65). MC, V. Daily 9am–6:30pm.

Sandholt Bakarí   Head baker Ásegir Sandholt studied painting before turning his artistic skills to baked goods, eventually earning the title of "Nordic Champion of Cake Decorating." One of his brilliant creations is a cake in the form of an aging, hardbound Icelandic saga, opened in the middle, with yellowed frosting "pages" curling at the edges. In the pleasant coffeehouse in back, you can order soups, salads, and sandwiches to accompany those marvelously creamy pastries.

Laugavegur 36. ℭ 551-3524. Sandwiches 350kr–780kr ($5.60–$12/£2.80–£6.25); slice of cake 460kr–525kr ($7.40–$8.40/£3.70–£4.20). MC, V. Mon–Fri 7am–6:15pm; Sat 7:30am–4pm; Sun 8:30am–4pm.

Tíu Dropar ⟨Value⟩   Loungers and caffeine addicts come for the quiet atmosphere and free coffee refills at this pleasant retreat from the commotion on Laugavegur. This is one of the few cafes to offer hearty breakfasts of eggs, bacon, and waffles. The grilled sandwiches, based mostly on ham, bacon, and gouda, are reliable. A good deal is the smoked salmon on a bagel with cream cheese and greens. And the Belgian waffles with rhubarb jam, syrup, whipped cream, Nutella, and bananas—mmm.

Laugavegur 27. ℭ 551-9380. Breakfast items 750kr–1,100kr ($12–$18/£6–£8.80); sandwiches and waffles 450kr–750kr ($7.20–$12/£3.60–£6). MC, V. Mon–Fri 9am–6pm; Sat 10am–5pm.

6 What to See & Do

In many ways, comparisons between Reykjavík and other European capitals are best left alone. The city boasts no castles, skyscrapers, grand squares, or monuments; the oldest house dates from 1764. Reykjavík's grandeur resides in its people, landscape, and culture: the museums, the music, the burgeoning restaurant and bistro culture, the geothermal pools, the style and attitude, the bustle and nightlife, and the cultivation of civic space.

As you survey the sights, keep some architectural notes in mind. Many Reykjavík buildings, largely from 1910 to 1930 but extending to the present, have corrugated iron siding, a distinctly Icelandic architectural trademark. Whatever its aesthetic merit, it was born of necessity: wood is scarce and rots in the driving wind and rain,

What to See & Do in Reykjavík

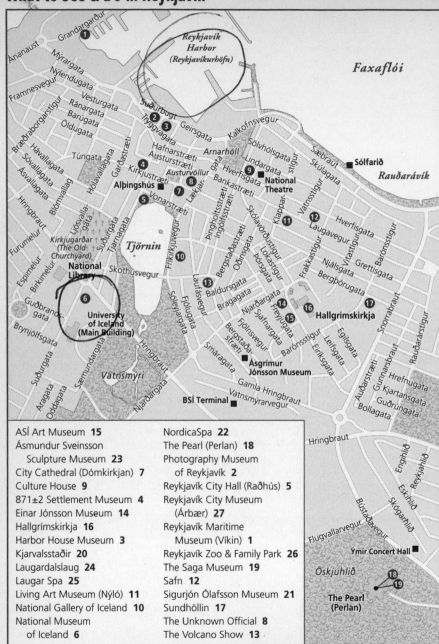

ASÍ Art Museum **15**

Ásmundur Sveinsson
  Sculpture Museum **23**

City Cathedral (Dómkirkjan) **7**

Culture House **9**

871±2 Settlement Museum **4**

Einar Jónsson Museum **14**

Hallgrímskirkja **16**

Harbor House Museum **3**

Kjarvalsstaðir **20**

Laugardalslaug **24**

Laugar Spa **25**

Living Art Museum (Nýló) **11**

National Gallery of Iceland **10**

National Museum
  of Iceland **6**

NordicaSpa **22**

The Pearl (Perlan) **18**

Photography Museum
  of Reykjavík **2**

Reykjavík City Hall (Raðhús) **5**

Reykjavík City Museum
  (Árbær) **27**

Reykjavík Maritime
  Museum (Víkin) **1**

Reykjavík Zoo & Family Park **26**

The Saga Museum **19**

Safn **12**

Sigurjón Ólafsson Museum **21**

Sundhöllin **17**

The Unknown Official **8**

The Volcano Show **13**

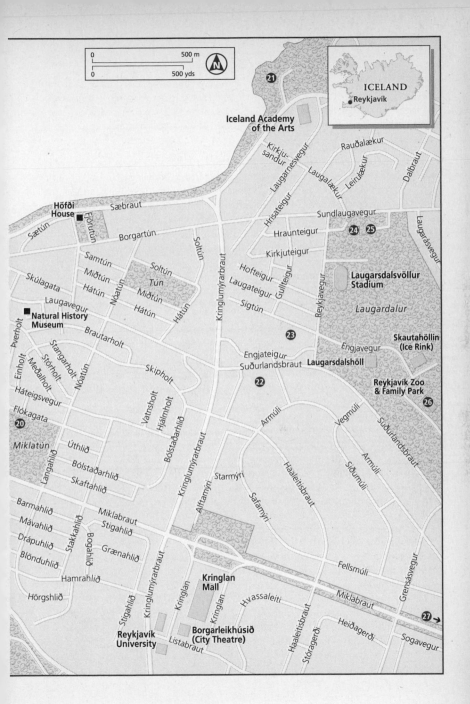

and iron is more stable in earthquakes. Since WWII, residents have brightened the cityscape with sidings and trims in cheerful reds, blues, and greens. Almost no traditional turf structures (see box, p. 222) survive within city limits.

Other Icelandic style innovations date from the Nationalist Period of architecture, roughly 1920 to 1950, and often have to do with utilizing native materials and invoking native landscapes. Look for interior and exterior walls made from solid or crushed Icelandic rock varieties, such as gabbro, rhyolite, basalt, and sometimes lava.

OLD CITY CENTER

The **tourist information center** at Aðalstræti 2 (p. 84) is a good starting point. **Aðalstræti** is the oldest street in Reykjavík, and the point from which all street numbers begin: the higher the number, the farther from Aðalstræti. Ingólfur Arnarson, traditionally regarded as Iceland's first permanent settler, is thought to have settled here around 870—though Reykjavík didn't have a proper street until the 18th century. For most of its history, Reykjavík was just one of many hereditary coastal estates. In 1613 the Danish monarch, who had imposed an oppressive trade monopoly on its Iceland colony, purchased the settlement under threat of force. Reykjavík then grew into a kind of shanty town for seasonal labor assisting Danish merchants, mostly associated with the fishing trade. The **oldest house** in Reykjavík, from 1764, is at Aðalstræti 10; plans are afoot to open the house for tours. (The **871±2 Settlement Museum,** at Aðalstræti 16, is listed below.)

A block east of Aðalstræti is **Austurvöllur Square** (aka "The Square"), an important outdoor gathering place and potent national symbol to every Icelander. In December a Christmas tree arrives here, a gift from the people of Oslo, as Iceland produces no adequate specimens. By European standards the square has little architectural distinction, but Austurvöllur has only been a public green since 1930. At the center is a **statue of Jón Sigurðsson** (1811–1879), the leading hero of Iceland's independence movement from Denmark. His birthday, June 17, was designated "National Day" after Icelandic independence in 1944. On the pedestal is a relief called "The Pioneer," depicting an early settler, amid cliffs and basalt columns, forging a trail for later generations, who are lined up waiting to follow. Both the statue and relief are by Iceland's best known sculptor Einar Jónsson (p. 115).

Jón Sigurðsson looks approvingly at **Alþingishús (Parliament House),** an 1880 stone building with a glass and stone annex added in 2002. From October to May you

---

The Reykjavík Tourist Card

This little gem can save you a bundle. The card includes admission to most major museums and galleries, along with access to public transportation and the city's pools (p. 119). Cards come in three varieties: 24-hour (1,200kr/$19/£9.60), 48-hour (1,700kr/$27/£14), and 72-hour (2,200kr/$35/£18). To calculate how soon you'll break even, consider that museums are routinely 500kr ($8/£4), pools 350kr ($5.60/£2.80), and buses 280kr ($4.50/£2.25). Most museums are free 1 day of the week, so patient and flexible schedulers can do without the card. It is active from the first time you use it until your 24-, 48-, or 72-hour period expires. Cards are available at the Tourist Information Center (p. 84), bus terminals (p. 84), the City Hostel (p. 97), and the three branches of the Reykjavík Art Museum (p. 113, 116, and 117), but not online.

can watch parliamentary proceedings from the visitors' gallery (Mon 3pm; Tues–Wed 1:30pm; Thurs 10:30am). The Alþingishús (or Alþingi) and adjacent City Cathedral represent Icelandic independence and Reykjavík's coming of age in the late 18th century. In 1797, the Danish king consolidated Iceland's northern and southern bishoprics into a single diocese in Reykjavík, just as the cathedral was being completed. The following year, the Icelandic parliament (Alþing) was moved here from Þingvellir, only to be abolished 2 years later. It was reinstated in 1845 in an advisory role to the Danish authorities. Behind the Alþingi is the **Parliament House Garden,** the country's oldest park maintaining its original design: a traditional, formal layout with paths emanating from a circular center lawn.

The elegant, understated **City Cathedral (Dómkirkjan)** ✿ (© **520-9700;** Mon–Fri 10am–4:30pm unless in use for services; Sat–Sun often busy for weddings, but open before or after; high mass Sun 11am; various masses Sun evenings; prayer mass Wed 12:10pm followed by light lunch for 500kr [$8/£4] at 12:30pm is a good counterweight to the grandiosity of Hallgrímskirkja. National independence received its first religious blessing here, and annual sessions of parliament start here with a prayer service. Completed in 1796 and enlarged in 1848, the cathedral was designed by Copenhagen's royal architect A. Winstrup, with a conventional blend of neoclassical and baroque features. The loft was the original site of the National Museum and Archives, and still has an interesting photo exhibit. Check the information box outside the church for scheduled concerts and events, listed in Icelandic but often discernable anyway.

Also in Austurvöllur Square is the **Hótel Borg,** Iceland's first luxury hotel, built in 1930 to accommodate foreign guests for the millennial celebration of Iceland's first parliamentary assembly at Þingvellir. It's been an important cultural landmark ever since: Public dances for Allied soldiers were held here during World War II; foreign visitors suffering under prohibition laws have found refuge at the bar; and Iceland's punk rockers performed here in the 1980s. Come in the morning to breakfast among parliament members, or visit for a drink in the small, wildly decorated lounge tucked between the lobby and the Borg's restaurant, **Silfur.**

One long block east of Austurvöllur is **Lækjargata,** a broad avenue dividing the western and eastern halves of the city center. Originally there was a brook here, and Tjörnin pond still drains to sea underneath the pavement.

In the courtyard behind Lækjargata 6 is **The Unknown Official** ✿. Several countries have monuments to the Unknown Soldier, but perhaps only Iceland has a sculpture honoring—and lightly satirizing—the thankless, anonymous job of the bureaucrat. The 1994 sculpture by Magnús Tómasson depicts a man in a suit holding a briefcase, with his head and shoulders subsumed in a slab of unsculpted stone.

Reykjavík's geographical center, the nondescript **Lækjartorg Square,** has an important history of public meetings. From the square, look northeast to the **statue of Ingólfur Arnarson** holding his spear aloft and the grassy slope of **Arnarhóll,** which was named for him. According to national myth, Ingólfur became Iceland's first permanent settler in 874. After his exile from Norway on murder charges, he wintered for 3 years on the south coast of Iceland. Arnarson decided on Reykjavík after following a pagan ritual that involved throwing his high-seat pillars (carved wooden columns set at the corner of a chieftain's chair) into the sea and trusting the gods to guide him to the right spot. Ingólfur's slaves, so the story goes, found the pillars 3 years later right at Arnarhóll. The statue by Einar Jónsson (p. 115) was unveiled in 1924.

Bankastræti proceeds east from Lækjartorg Square, and after 3 blocks divides into two busy commercial streets, **Laugavegur** and **Skólavörðustígur.** A block north of Laugavegur is **Hverfisgata,** another good street for strolling and people-watching.

Laugavegur (Hot Spring Path), Iceland's busiest and most prestigious commercial street, was originally built as a trail for maids walking to Laugardalur to wash laundry in the natural springs. The street's odd jumble of buildings reflects the emergent needs of commerce and benign neglect of architectural planners.

Two important centers of experimental and contemporary art, both free for visitors, are located close to each other on Laugavegur. The **Living Art Museum (Nýlistasafnið,** or Nýló), Laugavegur 26 (© **551-4350;** www.nylo.is), focuses on young, emerging artists and holds temporary exhibitions (Wed and Fri–Sun noon–7pm; Thurs noon–9pm) while **Safn,** Laugavegur 37 (© **561-8777;** www.safn.is), rotates works from a large private collection in addition to hosting short-term installations (Wed–Fri 2–6pm, Sat–Sun 2–5pm; guided tour Sat 2pm).

871±2 Settlement Museum ⊛

In 2001, on the southern end of Aðalstræti, workers excavating an underground parking garage stumbled upon the remains of a Viking longhouse. It turned out to be the oldest known evidence of human habitation in Reykjavík, dating from 871 plus or minus 2 years—thus the name of this engaging new museum. The excavated ruin lies amid a large room, surrounded by high-tech panoramic displays that tackle the larger questions of why the Vikings came to Reykjavík, how they adapted to the conditions, and what the landscape originally looked like. The ruin itself is basically just a wall foundation, and the museum's greatest feat is to bring the longhouse back to life using digital projectors.

Aðalstræti 16. © 411-6370. www.reykjavikmuseum.is. Daily 10am–5pm. Adults 600kr ($9.60/£4.80); seniors/children ages 13–17 300kr ($4.80/£2.40); children 12 and under free.

Culture House (Þjóðmenningarhúsið) ⊛

An old Icelandic proverb states, "It's better to be barefoot than without books," and Icelanders are indeed the most avid book readers and publishers in the world. The main attraction at this museum is the ground-floor exhibition of bound medieval books, where Iceland has its formative history embodied in literature on calfskin paper.

Most of the books were transcribed and bound in the 14th and 15th centuries, and are stored behind glass in low light to preserve the fragile materials. Famous treasures include several saga manuscripts, the *Book of Settlement* (an early census from the 12th century), and the earliest-known edition of the *Codex Regius of the Elder Edda,* a scholarly work largely responsible for our modern-day understanding of Norse cosmology and poetic traditions. The illustrations and design of these medieval manuscripts are below the standards of Europe's best, but some of the most captivating objects are the most primitive and obscure, for example a booklet of magic spells written in runic symbols. The exhibit explains the context and value of these books effectively, and a re-created scriptorium relates the bookmaker's craft and unenviable life of medieval scribes. Culture House displays a temporary exhibit as well.

Hverfisgata 15, east of Ingólfsstræti ("Landsbókasafn" is etched over the door). © 545-1400. www.thjodmenning. is. Admission 300kr ($4.80/£2.40) adults; 200kr ($3.20/£1.60) seniors/students; children under 18 free. Free admission Wed. Daily 11am–5pm. Free guided tours in English June–Aug Mon–Tues, Thurs–Fri 3:30pm; Sept–May Mon and Fri 3:30pm.

OLD HARBOR (HAFN)

The harbor north and west of the old city, built from 1913 to 1917, was the largest construction project to that point in Icelandic history. (Before then most ships had to drop anchor well out to sea and transport goods in by rowboat.) Dredged rocks were hauled away by a locomotive, which is still on display along the shoreline east of the harbor. Today, most boat traffic has moved east to Sundahöfn port, but the old harbor isn't a museum yet. It's great for an evening stroll when the breeze isn't too chilly.

The area most visited by tourists is the eastern pier, where Reykjavík's four remaining whale-hunting ships are absurdly lined up right across from the whale-watching tours (p. 120). The irony is not lost on the Icelanders, since the whale-watching industry has been leading the campaign against commercial whaling. The whalers are painted black on the hull and white above, with "Hvalur" written across the bow and stern. You can actually climb aboard and poke around.

The western piers harbor most fishing vessels, as well as the Óðinn, a grey Coast Guard vessel with a vertical stripe in blue, white, and red. These ships are the closest thing Iceland has to a military, and they defend the country's territorial fishing waters. They were sent out to slice British fishing nets in the so-called "Cod Wars," which date back to 1432 but culminated in the 1970s, when Britain broke off diplomatic relations. (Icelanders like to say this was the only war the British Navy ever lost.)

Harbor House Museum (Hafnarhús) ★★ This renovated 1930s warehouse, one of three branches of the Reykjavík Art Museum, houses two or three temporary exhibitions of Icelandic and international contemporary art along with the permanent collection—dominated by the works of Erró, an Icelandic-born artist who was based in Paris and best known for his large-scale comic-book–styled dreamscapes and montages. The second floor has a cafe and a wonderful reading room with hundreds of art books, children's toys, and a view over the harbor.

Tryggvagata 17. ⓒ 590-1200. www.artmuseum.is. Admission adults 500kr ($8/£4); seniors 250kr ($4/£2); children under 18 free. Free admission Thurs. Tickets good for all 3 branches of Reykjavík Art Museum and valid for 3 days. Daily 10am–5pm.

Photography Museum of Reykjavík ★ (Finds) This free museum and archive above the City Library surpasses most photographic collections in two respects. First, it has meticulously collected photographs of the Reykjavík area from every viewpoint: professional and amateur, public and personal, journalistic and aesthetic. Second, you can leaf through thousands of contact sheets in a side room full of binders; the shots are print-size, not negative-size, and the staff can even process your favorites in their own lab, priced from 1,200kr ($19/£9.60). A new exhibit is hung every 4 months.

Tryggvagata 15, 6th floor. ⓒ 563-1790. www.photomuseum.is. Free admission. Mon–Fri 10am–4pm; Sat–Sun 1–5pm.

Reykjavík Maritime Museum (Víkin) Iceland still derives most of its export income from fish, and this museum, opened in 2005 in a converted fish-freezing plant, takes an in-depth look at the country's 20th-century seafaring heritage. The permanent exhibit shares many features with local maritime museums across the country, such as well-crafted ship models and dummies in very uncomfortable-looking raincoats. The exhibit shows real curatorial professionalism but is best for those with a pre-existing fascination for objects like buoy lights and engine controls. However, the re-created captain's room and claustrophobic sleeping quarters are standouts.

Grandagarður 8. ⓒ 517-9400. www.sjominjasafn.is. June–Sept 11am–5pm. Admission adults 500kr ($8/£4); seniors 250kr ($4/£2); 18 and younger free. Bus 14.

Reykjavík with Kids

Children are well-integrated into the adult life of Iceland, and you'll feel welcome bringing them just about anywhere. Kids are often seen feeding the voracious waterfowl in **Tjörnin pond** (p. 114) by City Hall, and the opposite end of the pond has a climbing apparatus. The **Volcano Show** (p. 131) has enough geological violence and destruction to be entertaining, even if the film quality is quite outdated. **Whale-watching** (p. 120), **puffin watching** (p. 121), and the **Reykjavík Park and Zoo** (p. 117) are all pretty foolproof. **Horseback riding** and other activities are outlined in "Pools, Spas, Outdoor Activities & Spectator Sports" (p. 119). The most engaging museums for children are the **Árbæjarsafn (Reykjavík City Museum)** (p. 119), the **National Museum** (p. 115), and the **Saga Museum** (p. 118). Perhaps best of all are the **outdoor thermal pools,** a family institution throughout the country (see "Pool Guide," p. 121). The deluxe **Laugar Spa** (p. 120) can entertain your children while you pamper yourself.

AROUND THE POND

Tjörnin, the city's central pond, makes for a great circumambulatory walk. Several early-20th-century timber houses, built for the newly emergent middle class, are clustered along Tjarnargata on the western shore. It's worth strolling by to appreciate their gingerbread-house flourishes.

National Gallery of Iceland (Listasafn Íslands) 🍴 Iceland's endless variations of color, light, and natural formation have always been a boon to painters, and many of the greatest results are on display at this museum, the largest and probably the most important repository of 19th- and 20th-century Icelandic art. The gallery has no permanent exhibit, only revolving exhibits from the permanent collection. International exhibits are usually slated for the off season. The basement level has a nice area for keeping children occupied, and the top floor has a pleasant cafe.

Fríkirkjuvegur 7. ⓒ 515-9600. www.listasafn.is. Tues–Sun 11am–5pm. Free admission. Free guided tours Sun 3pm and Tues 12:40pm.

The Old Churchyard (Suðurgata or Hólavallagarður Cemetery) This cemetery 1 block west of the pond, between Ljosvallagata and Suðurgata, is full of informational panels and makes for an interesting stroll. The grave of Jón Sigurðsson, the most important leader of Iceland's independence movement, is found here: Walk from the main entrance on Ljosvallagata straight down the center, past the old chapel bell, and it's the beige obelisk on the left, a few plots before you reach the outer wall. Its lack of ostentation speaks volumes about Iceland's egalitarian ideals.

ⓒ 562-2510. www.kirkjugardar.is/kgrpensk/index.html. Cemetery open 24 hr.; office weekdays 10am–1pm.

Reykjavík City Hall (Ráðhús) This modern grey structure inaugurated in 1992 has many detractors, but its strengths are under-recognized. Design elements such as dripping, moss-covered walls nicely organicize the concrete, metal, and glass. The building seems to float at water level, humbly absorbing the lapping waves. The usual pomposity and self-importance of city halls is absent, replaced by democratic symbolism: The ground floor looks almost like a natural extension of the public street. Inside is a wonderful, enormous 3-D relief map of Iceland, which took four men 4 years to construct. City Hall has a tourist information desk, an exhibition area, and a pleasant cafe with free Internet and huge windows overlooking the pond.

North end of Tjörnin pond. © 411-1111. Free admission. Mon–Fri 8am–7pm; Sat–Sun noon–6pm. Cafe daily week-days 11am–6pm; Sat–Sun noon–6pm.

SOUTH OF THE POND

National Museum of Iceland ⊛⊛   Iceland's museums are all manageably sized; even this relatively large exhibition condensing Iceland's entire history and culture won't wear out your legs or attention. "The Making of a Nation" selects specific fig-ures, objects, and vignettes to represent stages and themes of Icelandic history: A charming, old instant-photo booth, for example, signals the onset of modernity. Inter-active elements are cutesy but effective: You can pick up a phone and have a one-way conversation with a medieval chieftain from 1117, or Guðríður the nun in her con-vent in 1323. The exhibit begins with a pagan burial site and ends with a traditional Icelandic dress refashioned by contemporary artist Ásdís Elva Pétursdóttir in transpar-ent plastic. Everything in between is worth seeing for yourself.

The ground floor houses the free **National Gallery of Photography** ⊛, which, in keeping with the exhibit upstairs, emphasizes the Iceland of yore.

Suðurgata 41. © 530-2200. www.natmus.is. National Museum admission adults 600kr ($9.60/£4.80); senior/stu-dents 300kr ($4.80/£2.40); children under 18 free. Free admission Wed. Museum and Gallery May–Sept 15 daily 10am–5pm; Sept 16–Apr Tues–Sun 11am–5pm; first Thurs of month until 9pm. Bus: S1, S3, S4, S5, S6, 11, 12, or 14.

EAST OF THE OLD CITY CENTER

ASÍ Art Museum (Ásmundarsalur)   This small selective contemporary art museum, run by the Icelandic labor union, fits several Icelandic artists into each monthly exhibition. Selections from the permanent collection are featured in July and August, usually including Jóhannes S. Kjarval's lovely painting *Fjallamjölk* (Mountain Milk) inspired by the landscape of Þingvellir.

Freyjugata 41. © 511-5353. Free admission. Tues–Sun 1–5pm.

Einar Jónsson Museum ⊛⊛   The former home and studio of Iceland's best-known sculptor, Einar Jónsson (1874–1954), holds most of his life's work. Einar was often inspired by Icelandic folklore, and his sculptures depict classical human and mythological figures in wildly imaginative and unorthodox poses. He identified with the romantic symbolists, and his sculptures speak in allegories, personifications, and ciphers. In the 1930s, W. H. Auden mockingly summarized his work as "Time pulling off the boots of Eternity with one hand while keeping the wolf from the door with the other." But these remarkable creations have become only more mystical and revelatory over time—even people not typically drawn to art will find themselves gawking in admiration and wonder. Outside is a small park with 26 bronze castings of his work, well worth a look even if the rest of the museum is closed.

Eiríksgata. © 551-3797. www.skulptur.is. Admission 400kr ($6.40/£3.20) adults; 200kr ($3.20/£1.60) senior/ students; children 15 and younger free. Free admission to sculpture park. June–Sept 15 Tues–Sun 2–5pm; Sept 16–Nov and Feb–May Sat–Sun 2–5pm. Closed Dec–Jan.

Hallgrímskirkja (Hallgríms Church) ⊛   Hallgrímskirkja, the tallest and largest church in Iceland, is Reykjavík's most photographed emblem by far, visible from everywhere in the capital. It was designed by state architect Guðjón Samúelsson (1887–1950), who never saw it completed: Work began in 1945 and continued

49 years. The church is named for Reverend Hallgrímur Pétursson (1614–1674), Iceland's foremost hymn writer, and also an ecclesiastical scholar and poet. His best-known work, *Hymns of the Passion,* is still sung and recited as verse in homes throughout Iceland (an English translation is available in the gift shop). For a fee you can ascend the 75m (246-ft.) steeple by elevator for great views over the city. At the top are three bells representing Hallgrímur, his wife, and his daughter who died young.

The distinctive exterior, with its prominent steeple, is often described in terms both primordial and futuristic—as if the church were some kind of volcano or glacier transformed into a rocket ship. Guðjón was indeed inspired by the Icelandic landscape, and the frontal columns are meant to resemble the hexagonal basalt formed by cooling lava. The interior is quite traditional in contrast, with its Gothic high-pointed vaults and tall, narrow windows. The uniform, textured-concrete surfaces can seem pedestrian, even to those accustomed to Lutheran principles of simplicity, and the altar is so ordinary as to resemble a hotel lobby. It could have been very different: a photograph hung in the entry hall depicts Einar Jónsson's proposed alternative design, a fantastical creation to rival Gaudí's cathedral in Barcelona. An Art Deco spire supports human figures in relief trudging upward amidst Middle Eastern–inspired domes.

Concerts here often involve the church's most popular interior feature: a gigantic organ built in Germany in 1992. It's about 50 feet tall, with 72 stops, 5,275 pipes, and remarkable sound projection. The church also hosts drama, art exhibitions, even public debates. Especially recommended are choral performances, a form in which Icelanders have always excelled.

A **statue of Leifur (Leif) Eiríksson** is aligned directly in front of the church, as if he's about to lead it down the hill. The statue was a gift from the U.S. to commemorate the 1,000th anniversary of the founding of Iceland's parliament. It was also a tacit acknowledgment that Leifur beat Christopher Columbus to North America by almost 500 years. (Excavations in Newfoundland have settled this question beyond a doubt.) He certainly strikes a heroic pose, but looks rather like a comic-book figure once you've seen the Viking statues in the Einar Jónsson museum next door.

Skólavörðuholt, at southeastern end of Skólavörðustígur. ⓒ 510-1000. www.hallgrimskirkja.is. Daily 9am–5pm. Suggested donation 50kr (80¢/40p). Elevator to tower 350kr ($5.60/£2.80) adults; 50kr (80¢/40p) children. Holy Communion sung Sun 11am and Wed 8am. Prayers Tues 10:30am. Meditation with organ music Thurs at noon. Anglican service in English usually last Sun of each month at 2pm. Organ concerts mid-June to mid-Aug noon on Thurs and Sat; longer performances Sun 8pm.

Kjarvalsstaðir ⓡ Jóhannes Sveinsson Kjarval (1885–1972) is the most highly regarded painter in Icelandic history, and this branch of the Reykjavík Art Museum is named in his honor. The sixties-era modernist building holds three galleries: two with temporary exhibits, and one drawing from the museum's large collection of Kjarval's paintings. Deeply inspired by native landscapes and folklore, his work is too varied to pigeonhole stylistically, but "expressionist" approximates the thick, paint-laden brushstrokes and abstract arrangements of color and shape.

Flókagata. ⓒ 517-1290. www.artmuseum.is. Admission 500kr ($8/£4) adults; 250kr ($4/£2) seniors; children under 18 free. Free admission Thurs. Tickets valid for 3 days and good for all 3 branches of Reykjavík Art Museum. Daily 10am–5pm. Bus: S1, S3, S4, S5, S6, or 13.

LAUGARDALUR

According to legend, Ingólfur Arnarson chose the name Reykjavík, or "Smoky Bay," when he saw distant steam rising from what is now Laugardalur (Hot Spring Valley). Those hot springs still heat the Laugardalslaug pool, and Icelandic families are also drawn by the zoo, family park, botanical garden, sports stadiums, and luxury Laugar Spa (see also "Pools, Spas, Outdoor Activities & Spectator Sports," below).

Ásmundur Sveinsson Sculpture Museum (Ásmundarsafn)   In the 1940s, modernist sculptor Ásmundur Sveinsson (1893–1982) designed and built this futuristic home and studio, now a branch of the Reykjavík Art Museum. The sphinx-like design was inspired by Turkish and Egyptian models, which he thought fitting for Iceland's treeless environment. The museum focuses almost entirely on his work, influenced by Henry Moore and the cubists. Often drawing from Icelandic folklore, his pieces range from recognizable human forms to pure abstract shapes. The small outdoor sculpture park, which is free and accessible at all times, features more of Ásmundur's work.

Sigtún, near the sports complex in Laugardalur Park. ✆ 553-2155. www.artmuseum.is. Single ticket 300kr ($4.80/£2.40) adults; 200kr ($3.20/£1.60) seniors/students; children under 16 free. Free admission on Thurs. Ticket for all 3 branches of Reykjavík Art Museum (good for 3 days) 500kr ($8/£4) adults; 250kr ($4/£2) seniors; children under 18 free. May–Sept daily 10am–4pm; Oct–Apr 1–4pm. Bus: S2, 14, 15, 17, or 19.

Reykjavík Zoo & Family Park *Kids*   No attempt was made here to import exotic species; this zoo is just for families to have fun and interact with the animals Icelanders know and love: sheep, horses, cattle, pigs, goats, reindeer, mink, and the arctic fox, the only indigenous land mammal. An animal petting schedule is posted each day—crabs at 3:15pm—and pony rides begin at 2pm. The aquarium, opened in 2004, holds seals and fish native to the North Atlantic. The Family Park is surefire kid entertainment, with a trampoline, bumper boats, a go-cart driving school complete with traffic lights, and a "science world," where little ones can measure their screams in big decibels. Next door is a botanical garden with a pleasant greenhouse cafe in summer.

Hafrafell (at Engjaveg, center of Laugardalur Park, behind sports complex). ✆ 575-7800. www.mu.is. May 15 to mid-Aug daily 10am–6pm; mid-Aug to May 14 daily 10am–5pm. Admission Mon–Fri 450kr ($7.20/£3.60) adults; 350kr ($5.60/£2.80) children 5–12; 4 and under free. Sat–Sun add 100kr ($1.60/80p) to ticket prices. Rides cost extra. Bus: S2, 14, 15, 17, or 19.

Sigurjón Ólafsson Museum   The sculptures of Sigurjón Ólafsson (1908–1982) span multiple developments in 20th-century art and range from formal busts to primitivist metal totems to wood pieces haphazardly stuck together. This museum inside his former oceanside studio is devoted exclusively to his work, and has a pleasant cafe with homemade pies and cakes and peaceful harbor views.

Laugarnestangi 70. ✆ 553-2906. www.lso.is. June–Aug Tues–Sun 2–5pm; Feb–May and Sept–Nov Sat–Sun 2–4pm. Closed Dec–Jan. Admission 300kr ($4.80/£2.40) adults; free for ages 12 and under. Bus: 12 or 15.

ÖSKJUHLÍÐ HILL

This wooded area well south of the city center is a perfectly nice walking, jogging, or biking retreat, but, aside from the **Pearl (Perlan),** holds little to entice visitors.

Nauthólsvík Beach   It's often said Iceland has everything the world has . . . but only one of them. Nowhere is this more true than Nauthólsvík, where runoff hot water from the city's geothermal heating system is pumped into the ocean through a beach of imported yellow sand. The ocean is still cold but swimmable, and Icelandic families flock here on warm days to sunbathe and splash around in the almost-hot tubs. The novelty can wear off quickly, and the view isn't much to speak of. **Kaffi (Cafe) Nauthóll** is close by, and you can rent towels or store valuables for 200kr ($3.20/£1.60); coffee, soda, ice cream, and hot dogs are on offer all day.

Nauthólsvegur, directly south of the Pearl. ✆ 511-6630. May 15–Aug 15 daily 10am–8pm. Bus: 16.

The Pearl (Perlan)   Rivaling Hallgrímskirkja for domination of the Reykjavík sky-line, this futuristic glass dome, built in 1991, sits atop five enormous cylindrical tanks storing 24,000 tons of the city's geothermally heated water. The first floor "Winter Garden" is leased for various expos, and features a fountain mimicking a geyser—an idea doomed never to inspire a flattering comparison. On the grass outside is a far more impressive spectacle: Another artificial geyser, but one designed to replicate the actual geyser mechanism (p. 146); eruptions are every 15 minutes or so between 1 and 5pm. The fourth floor is ringed by a free viewing deck with fabulous views over the city and beyond; inside is a cafe whose main strength is its ice cream. The top floor, which makes a complete circular revolution every 2 hours, contains a so-so, pricey restaurant (dinner only), and is accessible only to diners.

Öskjuhlíð. © 562-0200. www.perlan.is. Free admission. Daily June–Aug 10am–11:30pm; Sept–May 10am–9pm. Free admission. Cafe daily 10am–9pm. Restaurant daily 6:30–10:30pm. Bus: 18.

Saga Museum 🔆 (Kids   This privately run museum is expensive and smells like a barn, but does manage to convey Icelandic history and saga lore with an expert blend of entertainment and educational value. Listening to mini-lectures on iPods, visitors move among installations enlivened by eerily lifelike silica human figures and gore aplenty: feuding Vikings, witches burned at the stake, the beheading of Iceland's last Catholic bishop. If the kids get fidgety, send them to watch the creepy video showing the designer crafting the heads from face casts of his friends and family, and then stitching the hair on. (Ingólfur Arnarson has the face of the museum's owner.)

Inside the Pearl, Öskjuhlíð. © 511-1517. www.sagamuseum.is. Admission 1,000kr ($16/£8) adults; seniors/students 800kr ($13/£6.40); children 5–15 500kr ($8/£4). June–Aug daily 10am–6pm; Sept–May daily noon–5pm. Bus: 18.

OUTSKIRTS & NEARBY
VIÐEY ISLAND 🔆
Viðey is hardly the most dramatically situated island off the Icelandic coast, but it provides a very nice afternoon escape from Reykjavík. The island has a surprisingly grand history, and is now a showcase for environmental art.

Viðey was inhabited as early as 900. From 1225 to 1539 it was the site of a prestigious Augustine monastery, which at one point owned 116 Reykjavík estates. In 1539 the Danish king appropriated the land in the name of the Protestant Reformation. Eleven years later, Iceland's last Catholic bishop, Jón Arason, took the island by force, but he was beheaded a few months later. At the beginning of the 20th century, the country's first harbor for ocean-going vessels was built on Viðey's eastern coast, but it was soon outmoded by Reykjavík harbor. Viðey's population peaked in 1930 with 138 people, but by the 1950s the only inhabitants were birds enjoying the tranquillity. In 1983 Viðey became city property.

Viðey has no cars and is only 1 square mile in area. It consists of **Heimæy (Home island)** and **Vesturey (West island),** linked by a narrow isthmus. You can bring a bike, but several free bikes are left out for any takers; some have baby seats and all have helmets. Visitors spend most of their time strolling along the easy trails. (Pick up the free trail map in the ferry ticket office.) Thirty bird species have been counted here. The most populous is the *eider,* the seafaring duck harvested on farms all over Iceland for down feathers. Many birds nest in the grasses, so it's best to stick to the paths.

Visitors disembarking the **Viðeyjarferju ferry** (© 533-5055) won't miss **Viðey-jarstofa (Viðey House)** (© 660-7886; June–Aug daily 1–5pm), the country's first stone-and-cement structure, dating from 1755. It was originally home to Skúli

Magnússon (1711–1794), who was appointed Royal Superintendent of Iceland by the Danish crown; now it's a cafe serving coffee and waffles in summer. Close by is **Viðeyjarkirkja,** the second-oldest church in Iceland, consecrated in 1774, with Skúli's tomb beneath the altar.

Vesturey's only man-made feature is *Áfangar (Stages)* 🔑, a vast yet understated work, erected in 1990, by American minimalist sculptor Richard Serra (b.1959). Nine pairs of vertical basalt columns are spread across the land, their proportions determined by strict mathematical criteria. If you climb to the high point you can see all nine pairs, as well as a grand view of the surrounding mountains. Viðey also has a new **"Imagine Peace Tower"** designed by Yoko Ono, featuring peace prayers in 24 languages, and—during late fall—a shaft of light visible from the mainland.

The 7-minute ferry from the port of Sundahöfn, east of the city center has seven departures per day (mid-May to Sept; 11:15am–7:15pm; last ferry back at 8:30pm). Buses depart Reykjavík's old harbor 15 minutes before each ferry departure. Sundahöfn can be also reached by Bus 16. In July and August, a noon ferry goes directly from the old harbor to Viðey, returning at 3:30pm. Round-trip tickets, which include the bus, are 800kr ($13/£6.40) adults; 600kr ($9.60/£4.80) seniors/students; 400kr ($6.40/£3.20) children 6 to 18; and under 6 free.

ELLIÐAÁR VALLEY

Reykjavík City Museum (Árbær Museum or Árbæjarsafn) 🔑
This open-air folk museum, a 15-minutes drive east of the city center, is a re-created historic village built around a traditional farm. Many buildings slated for demolition in Reykjavík found refuge here; an 1842 church was transported from the north coast. Árbær was a working farm until 1948, and interior decorations are meant to represent a typical 1920s farmhouse. (Look for a marvelous piece of homegrown artwork on the wall: a bird and bouquet constructed entirely from human hair.) From June to August, staff in period costume milk cows, weave wool, and cook chewy pancakes *(lummur)* on the farmhouse stove for visitors. What really makes a visit worthwhile is a guided tour (free with paid admission) of the original turf-roofed farmhouses, so time your visit accordingly. Without a guide you won't learn how to spin yarn, how meat was smoked (with sheep manure), and how everyone washed their hair (in urine).

Kistuhylur, in Artunsholt. 🕿 411-6300. www.arbaejarsafn.is. Admission 600kr ($9.60/£4.80) adults; seniors/children under 18 free. Ticket valid for 2 visits. Free admission Fri, but guided tour requires full ticket price. June–Aug daily 10am–5pm; 90-min. guided tours at 11am and 2pm; Sept–May Mon, Wed, and Fri open only for guided tour at 1pm. Bus: S5 (to Strengur, a few minutes' walk from museum).

7 Pools, Spas, Outdoor Activities & Spectator Sports

For a thorough exploration of outdoor activities in Iceland, see chapter 3.

THERMAL POOLS

The city operates seven **thermal pools** (**www.spacity.is**), all with changing rooms, lockers, showers, wading pools for small children, and "hot pots" (hot tubs), usually organized in a row with successively higher water temperatures. All but one have water slides and other delights for children. Entrance fees are typically 350kr ($5.60/£2.80) for adults and 150kr ($2.40/£1.20) for children ages 6 to 15. Swimsuit and towel rental are typically 350kr ($5.60/£2.80) apiece.

Don't be dissuaded by poor weather. Icelanders still show up in the rain, and believe the combination of cold air and hot water greatly beneficial to health. (They have very long life spans to show for it.) For a side of the city few tourists witness, show up at 7:30am, when Icelanders have a dip before work. For more on **pool etiquette,** see "Pools & Spas," in chapter 3.

SPAS

A few Reykjavík hotels offer fitness centers, saunas, massages, and health and beauty treatments, but only at Hilton Reykjavík Nordica's **NordicaSpa,** Suðurlandsbraut 2 (© **444-5090;** www.nordicaspa.is; Mon–Thurs 6am–9pm, Fri 6am–8pm, Sat 9am–6pm, Sun 10am–4pm), do these combined services truly amount to "spa" status. NordicaSpa is especially adept at treatments utilizing Iceland's natural resources, from geothermal mud massages to seaweed wraps. Non-guests of the hotel are welcome.

Laugar Spa   This mammoth complex, opened in 2004, has spared no expense to wow patrons with the latest in super-deluxe spa and fitness technology. Features include indoor and outdoor pools, exhaustive beauty and massage treatments, and a health food restaurant. The six steam rooms are set at different temperatures, and each has a thematic fragrance. Among the Jacuzzis, choose freshwater or seawater. One pool is designed exclusively for foot-soaking. To visit the "relaxation cave," you must have your retina scanned at reception; then at the cave entrance, your eye-print is recognized and the doors snap open. (Is that really necessary?) Kids can be left in their own playrooms and movie theater while you attend to yourself.

Sundlaugavegur 30a, at the north end of Laugardalur park, next to Laugardalslaug pool. © **553-0000.** www.laugar spa.com. Gym and Spa Mon–Fri 6am–11:30pm; Sat 8am–10pm; Sun 8am–8pm. Beauty salon Mon–Fri 9am–7pm; Sat 11am–6pm. Massage salon Mon–Fri 9am–9pm; Sat 11am–6pm. Bus: 14.

WHALE-WATCHING

Reykjavík's **Faxaflói Bay** is a prime whale-watching area (though visitors headed to Húsavík on the north coast should probably wait and head out from there). The smaller and less dramatic minke whales are the most common sightings, but you stand a good chance of spying humpback whales, harbor porpoise, white-beaked dolphins, and orcas as well. From May to mid-August, whale tours also stop at **Lundey Island,** a puffin nesting site (see below). Trips last 2½ to 3 hours and leave from Ægisgarður, the easternmost pier of the old harbor.

All the tour companies are reputable, but a solid choice is **Whale Watching Reykjavík** (© **533-2660;** www.whalewatching.is), the largest operator, boasting a 98% whale-sighting success rate. Tickets are 4,100kr ($66/£33) adults, 1,800kr ($29/£14) children 7 to 15, and free for children 6 and under. Boats depart June through August at 9am, 1pm, and 5pm; April, May, and September at 9am and 1pm; and October at 1pm. The price includes warm overalls and raincoats, plus admission to an underwhelming "Nature Center" with an exhibition on marine life in Faxaflói. Most boats have a play area for kids. If you want to throw in some sea angling with your whale- and puffin watching, **Hvalalíf** (© **862-2300;** www.hvalalif.is) combines all three

---

⌒ Moments When in Iceland . . .

Visiting a genuine Icelandic thermal pool is the best antidote for culture shock. Lounging in a hot tub with Icelanders, who are quite blasé about this everyday ritual, is for many of us a far better way to interact with locals than Reykjavík's famed wild nightlife.

CLOSED
due to
accidental demolition

WEGEN BISSIGEN
EICHHÖRNCHEN GESCHLOSSEN

CERRADO

CABRAS

Κλειστό
Μετεωρίτες

POOL CLOSED
プールも
ELECTRIC EELS
閉鎖中

Hotel
closed for
facelifting

FERMÉ POUR
RAISON
DE GRÈVE
DES BONNES

FECHADO!
POR CAUSA DE
ATAQUES DOS CROCODILOS

I don't speak
sign language.

A hotel can close for all kinds of reasons.

Our Guarantee ensures that if your hotel's undergoing construction, we'll
let you know in advance. In fact, we cover your entire travel experience.
See www.travelocity.com/guarantee for details.

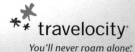

travelocity
You'll never roam alone.

©2007 Travelocity.com LP. CST # 2056372-50.

Reykjavík Thermal Pool Guide

- **Árbæjarlaug,** Fylkisvegur 9, Árbær, near Elliðaár River (© **510-7600;** Mon–Fri 6:50am–10:30pm; Sat–Sun 8am–10pm summer, 8am–8:30pm winter. Bus: 19), is a kiddie wonderland full of water toys, but has plenty for adults, too. (It's even known as a meeting place for single moms and dads.) A 15-minute bus ride from the center, this pool is one of the less touristed. Reykjavík's largest public Jacuzzi is here, but you won't find anywhere to do laps.

- **Laugardalslaug,** Sundlaugavegur 30, at the north end of Laugardalur Park (© **553-4039;** Mon–Fri 6:50am–9:30pm; Sat–Sun 8am–10pm. Bus: 14), in the eastern part of the city, is the biggest and most populated pool, with several outdoor swimming areas, an Olympic-size indoor pool, a steam room reminiscent of a whale's belly, and a massage room.

- **Sundhöllin,** Barónsstígur 16, at Bergþórugata, behind Hallgrímskirkja (© **551-4059;** Mon–Fri 6:30am–9:30pm; Sat–Sun 8am–7pm. Bus: S1, S6, or 13), is mostly indoors, so you may feel you're missing out on a true Icelandic experience (plus the kids will lament the lack of water slide). The hot pots are outside, however, with views of the city. The historic pool building was designed by the architect of Hallgrímskirkja, and each locker in the labyrinthine facilities has a fold-out dresser with mirror and stool.

- **Seltjarnarneslaug,** Suðurströnd 8, Seltjarnarnes (© **561-1551;** Mon–Fri 7am–10:30pm; Sat–Sun 8am–6:30pm summer, 8am–5:30pm winter. Bus: 11), is the least touristed pool listed here (no signs in English), and the only one featuring saltwater. You may find yourself sharing the big Jacuzzi with brave souls just in from a cold swim in the ocean. In Seltjarnarnes, Reykjavík's suburb to the west, it's not far by car or bike.

- **Vesturbæjarlaug,** Hofsvallagata, at Melhagi (© **561-5004;** Mon–Fri 6:30am–10pm; Sat–Sun 8am–10pm. Bus: 11 or 15), is a 15-minute walk from Tjörnin Pond, on the southwestern edge of the city center, near the university and just a short distance from good shoreline strolling on Ægisiða. Nauthólsvík Beach is nearby, and you can pay extra to sit under sun lamps, a nice splurge on a gloomy day.

activities for just about the same prices as above, with departures April through October at 8:55am, 12:55pm, and 4:55pm.

PUFFIN WATCHING

West of Reykjavík, the small islands of **Lundey** and **Akurey** are home to 50,000 puffins during breeding season. Many whale-watching tours include a puffin stop; but **Puffin Express** (© **892-0099**) offers a shorter, less costly tour for puffin exclusivists (for more on puffins, see p. 283), and their boats are better designed for drawing close to the bird cliffs. Tours, which last 1 hour, leave from Ægisgarður pier at the old harbor. Tickets run 2,500kr ($40/£20) adults or 1,000kr ($16/£8) for children under 12. Boats sail May to mid-August, daily at 10:30am and 4:30pm.

FISHING

Not many world capitals have good salmon fishing within city limits. The season for Reykjavík's **Elliðaár River** extends from June 1 to August 31, and opens with the mayor throwing the first cast. Contact the **Angling Club of Reykjavík** (© 568-6050; www.svfr.is) for information on permits and procedures. Also ask about trout and arctic char fishing in nearby lakes. For tackle and equipment, try **Veiðihornið,** Hafnarstræti 5 (© 551-6760), or **Útivist og Veiði,** Síðmúli 11 (© 588-6500).

For **sea angling, Hvalalíf** (see "Whale-Watching," above) has a 3-hour evening tour that leaves at 8pm, April through October, and culminates with their chef serving up your catch at their Lobstership Restaurant. Tickets for the trip are 7,000kr ($112/£56). **Whale Watching Reykjavík** (© 533-2660; www.whalewatching.is) has a 3-hour sea-angling tour for 5,900kr ($94/£47) from June to August, leaving daily at 11am, with grills on-board.

OTHER OUTDOOR ACTIVITIES

Many local farms offer 2- to 4-hour **horseback-riding tours,** which may include lunch and hotel pickup. Two excellent companies near Reykjavík are **Íshestar,** in Hafnarfjörður (© 555-7000; www.ishestar.is), and **Laxnes Horse Farm,** in Mosfellsdalur (© 566-6197; www.laxnes.is).

Reykjavík has three **golf courses.** The **Reykjavík Golf Club** (© 585-0200; www.grgolf.is) runs two 18-hole courses: the oceanside **Korpúlfsstaðir** to the northeast (Thorsvegur, off of Korpúlfsstaðavegur; Bus: 24) and the difficult **Grafarholt,** Iceland's premier championship course, to the east (Grafarholtsvegur, off Rte. 1; Bus: 15 or 18). Both are about a 15-minute drive from the city center and stay open summer evenings. Course fees are 6,400kr ($102/£51), club rental is 3,000kr ($48/£24), cart rental is 3,750kr ($60/£30), and trolley rental is 400kr ($6.40/£3.20). Closer to the center, in Seltjarnarnes, west of Reykjavík, is the casual 9-hole **Golfklúbbur Ness,** at the end of Suðurströnd (© 561-1930), with good ocean views (Bus: 11).

See chapter 3 for information on scuba diving, glacier tours, hiking, Jeep tours, aerial tours, and rafting.

SPECTATOR SPORTS

The unique Icelandic form of wrestling known as *glíma* dates back to the Viking era. The main season for competitions is from September to April. For more information, contact the **Icelandic Glíma Association** (© 514-4064). Also keep an eye out for historical reenactments at museums or special events like the **Viking Festival** in Hafnarfjörður (p. 17).

Icelanders are fanatical about the unusual and exciting sport of **handball,** once described as "water polo without the water." Iceland finished fourth in the 1992 Barcelona Olympics, and eighth in the 2007 World Cup. The height of the season is September through April. For more information, contact the **Icelandic Handball Federation** (© 514-4200; www.hsi.is).

The Icelandic national **soccer** team ranked 37th in the world in 1994, but has since declined to the 109th position, just below Armenia, Benin, and the Cape Verde Islands. If you'd like to attend a game anyway, you can check out a match at **Laugardalsvöllur Stadium,** Laugardalur Park (© 510-2914).

8 Shopping

Reykjavík is not the shopping mecca that is Paris or London, but a new wave of boldly conceptual storeowners is gaining almost as much attention as the restaurateurs. Most shops are concentrated on **Laugavegur** and **Skólavörðustígur**—so don't hold out much hope for the thrill of a back-alley discovery—but Laugavegur's offshoots and side streets are quickly building up. Other good shopping streets are **Austurstræti** (especially for souvenirs), **Hafnarstræti,** and **Bankastræti.**

Reykjavík is a good place to buy supplies before hitting the rest of the country, where goods are even more expensive. General shopping hours are 9am to 6pm weekdays and 10am to 4pm Saturdays. Almost everything is closed Sunday except for a few shops, particularly those selling woolens and puffin snow globes. *Note:* Store listings below do not indicate opening hours unless they deviate from the norm.

ARTS, CRAFTS & PHOTOGRAPHY

Fótógrafí   This new gallery sells work by over 40 Icelandic photographers, from newspaper staff reporters to landscape specialists. You can buy fine-art prints, posters, and photo books, or just admire the art. Skólavörðustígur 4a. ℭ 551-6800.

Gallery KSK   Kolbrún S. Kjarval's shop and studio offers graceful ceramic wares in all shapes and sizes, often decorated with bird themes. Locals particularly covet her tiny bowls designed to hold toothpicks or coins, a unique souvenir or gift. Skólavörðustígur 22. ℭ 511-1197.

Kirsuberjatréð   Ten Icelandic women artists run the collective known as the "Cherry Tree," where you'll find fish-skin wallets, pig-bladder boxes, mugs for left-handers, "paper" bowls made of sliced radish and zucchini, clothes embroidered with mini pom-poms, and much more. Vesturgata 4. ℭ 562-8990. www.kirs.is.

Tips Save up to 15% with a VAT Refund

Iceland Refund (ℭ 564-6400; www.icelandrefund.com) reimburses you the **Value-Added Tax** you pay (about 15% of purchase price) under the following four conditions: 1) purchases must be taken out of the country; 2) each sales receipt must total at least 4,000kr ($64/£32)—for less expensive items you can consolidate purchases at a single store; 3) purchases must be from an accredited store; and 4) you must leave the country within 3 months of purchase. When you make a purchase, request a **Global Refund Cheque,** which must be signed by the salesperson. Your refund can be claimed from the following places: Keflavík Airport, at the Landsbanki Íslands Bank at the far end of the departure hall; the Seyðisfjörður ferry to Europe, onboard prior to departure; and Reykjavík's Tourist Information Center (p. 84). If the total value of your *refund* is less than 5,000kr ($80/£40) (that is, if your total purchases amount to about 33,000kr/ $528/£264 or less), you can receive the refund directly in cash or have it applied to your credit card at the airport or the ferry; at the Tourist Information Center, you can only have it applied to your credit card. If the refund is more than 5,000kr ($80/£40), your only option is to have the refund applied to your credit card no matter where you claim it—and all goods (except woolens) need to be shown at customs before check-in for your departing flight.

BOOKS & MUSIC

English-language books are not hard to come by, as most Icelanders prefer them to translated editions. (See p. 50 in chapter 2 for book recommendations.)

Bad Taste (Smekkleysa)   After many relocations, this legendary music store/label/ gallery has settled next to companion vintage clothing stores **Elvis** and **Rokk og Rósir.** Inspired by the maxim, "Good taste is the enemy of art," the label boasts Icelandic supernovae Björk, Sigur Rós, and Múm along with lesser-known home-grown acts. An entertaining "Lobster or Fame" exhibit documents the label's history. 28 Laugavegur. © 557-3730. www.smekkleysa.net.

Bókavarðan   This antiquarian bookseller has some English-language items (for example, out-of-print travel accounts) among the dusty Icelandic tomes. You can browse old prints, maps, and postcards; and saga lovers are sure to find some precious treasure—at a price, of course. Klapparstígur 25–27 (at Hverfisgata). © 552-1710. www.bokin.is.

Mál og Menning   This respected Icelandic bookstore chain has late hours and plenty of books in English. This branch is right in the heart of things, and you can take books, newspapers, and magazines to the upstairs cafe until 10pm. Laugavegur 18. © 552-3740. Bankastræti 2. www.malogmenning.is.

12 Tónar   This store, boasting its own rock/alternative label, stocks eclectic, inter-national, home-grown—whatever music the connoisseur owners like. You'll probably be offered coffee, and you can sample CDs while hanging out on the couch. Live per-formances are usually held every other Friday. Skólavörðustígur 15. © 511-5656. www. 12tonar.is. Also open Sun 1–4pm in summer.

CLOTHING

ELM   Three women with respective backgrounds in art, textile design, and drama therapy started this wildly popular store. (Oprah often wears ELM clothing on her show.) The high-grade cotton and wool garments hug in only the right places, exud-ing comfort and flexibility. The designs, mostly black and white with the odd color burst, feature tasteful frills amid linear simplicity. Laugavegur 1. © 511-0991. www.elm.is.

Illgresi   For lovers of old Levis and retro dresses, this spunky second-hand shop sells new and used clothing, shoes, purses, CDs, and all sorts of knowingly kitsch acces-sories. No phone. Laugavegur 17 in the alley.

KronKron   This large boutique has a flair for combining the cream of the upstart designer crop with established names like Vivienne Westwood and Fred Perry. Think candy stores, cabarets, and circuses; anything from vintage Nikes to party dresses to embroidered long johns (with plenty of gear for the fellas, too). Sister shoe store **Kron** is down the street at Laugavegur 48. Laugavegur 63b (around the corner on Vitastígur). © 562-8388. www.kron.is. Additional opening hours the first Sun of the month 10am–6pm.

Liborius   Co-owner Jóhann Meunier, a real fashion scholar, is usually on hand offer-ing well-considered advice at this discerning boutique of international designers. For women he favors Ann Demeulemeester's minimalist/deconstructionist clothing. For men, he says, enough with the "post-rave-era-late-80s street culture," let's subtly bring back the dandy (first English silk socks, then Borsalino hats), then add a dash of ninja, like the Pocket Protector, a limited-edition bulletproof handkerchief. Laugavegur 7. © 551-6811. www.liborius.is.

The Naked Ape   This collective-run clothing/art/music store puts its own stamp on street-culture wear. The house line takes American Apparel clothing (mainly cotton T-shirts and hoodies) and hand-decorates it. Day-glo? Check. Snakeskin-patterned metallic tights? Check. Silkscreen everything? Check. Bankastræti 14, 2nd floor (at the corner of Skólavörðustígur). ℭ 551-1415. www.dontbenaked.com. Also open Sun 10am–4pm.

Spaksmannsspjarir   This high-end women's boutique, with grown-up styles for all ages, has a gift for striking, sexy, and original combos: feminine skirts with masculine vests, or classic cuts in modern materials. Unlike most Reykjavík fashion, the clothes actually bear Icelandic weather in mind. Bankastræti 11 (at Laugavegur). ℭ 551-2090. www.spaksmannsspjarir.is.

STEiNUNN   Steinunn Sigurðardóttir takes inspiration from Iceland's wilderness (think endless twilights, cloud vaults, and sub-Arctic flora) and specializes in pure, unmixed soft materials like silk and lambswool. The cuts are minimalist yet very feminine and textural with ruffles, bunches, and unexpected uses of fur or tulle. Laugavegur 59 2nd floor. ℭ 588-6649. www.steinunn.com.

Trilogía   The name refers to the integrated parts of this threesome: a contemporary art gallery, women's high-end fashion boutique, and production center for local designer talent and the house line. Selections are one-of-a-kind yet eminently tasteful and wearable. Laugavegur 7. ℭ 551-1733. www.trilogia.is.

CONCEPT STORES

Kisan   This store is about sensory comfort, charm, and nostalgia, like walking through Amelie's imagination. Toy livestock bones, art books, fake moustache variety sets, children's clothes from Petit Bateau—everyone is bound to find something they want but don't need. Laugavegur 7. ℭ 561-6262. www.kisan.is.

3 Floors   This recent addition was conceived with London's Dover Street Market in mind: The result is a happy chaos of design merchandise, ignoring all rules of retail organization. Floor one is about lifestyle, with music, textiles, housewares, and accessories; floor two is clothing (Alberta Feretti, Comme des Garçons, Nice Collective); and floor three is a cafe. Laugavegur 60. ℭ 511-3123.

JEWELRY

Jewelry is relatively less expensive in Iceland, especially gold and silver. You'll find countless items inspired by the country's natural features and pagan history, often made from lava stones and native minerals. Most jewelers eagerly customize designs, a good way to bring home a little piece of Iceland (especially since it's illegal to collect minerals yourself). For classic jewelry, try the well-stocked **Gull & Silfur,** Laugavegur 52 (ℭ **552-0620**) or flashier **Jón & Óskar,** Laugavegur 61 (ℭ **552-4910**).

Hansina Jensdottir   This find is great for bold, primitivist, geometric jewelry with rough edges and visible seams. Her necklaces are made of foil-thin metallic squares with visible hammer marks, and her rings are rough-hewn semi-circles of silver with stones welded onto the metal. Laugavegur 42. ℭ 551-8448.

Mariella   Each piece at the very-offbeat Mariella deals with the question, "What is Icelandic?" "The Icelandic interior is like this one," says owner Maria, pointing to a string of lava beads interrupted by glass jewels. "Very boring and rough, but then maybe you find a flower." Skólavörðustigur 12. ℭ 561-4500.

MARKETS & MALLS

Kolaportið Reykjavík's enormous flea market takes you back to the "old days"—say, 25 years ago—when Reykjavík was far less wealthy. Stalls are crammed with books, antiques, crafts, and clothes, with hardly any tourist schlock, though you'll have to really hunt for treasures. In the back is a well-priced fish market, where you can snack on pickled salmon, fulmar eggs, and shark. An ATM is on the premises. Tryggvagata 19. © 562-5030. Sat–Sun 11am–5pm. Bus S1, S3, S4, S5, S6, 11, 12, or 13.

Kringlan This 150-store mall is usually too far away to reach on foot, but features free parking, Wi-Fi, a taxi stand, and a play area where you can leave your 3- to 9-year-olds while you shop. Most stores are European chain fashion and housewares, but there are some nice quirky places, too, plus a liquor store, food court, cinema, and supermarket. 112–150 Kringlumýrarbraut. © 588-7788. www.kringlan.is. Mon–Wed 10am–6:30pm; Thurs 10am–9pm; Fri 10am–7pm; Sat 10am–6pm; Sun 1–5pm. Bus S1, S3, S4, or S6.

Smáralind Farther from the city center, this is the newer of the two malls and the biggest mall in Iceland. The stores are mostly prohibitively expensive major chains, and the restaurants and cinema stay open after hours. Hagasmáril, 201 Kópavogur. © 528-8000. www.smaralind.is. Mon–Wed and Fri 11am–7pm; Thurs 11am–9pm; Sat 11am–6pm; Sun 1–6pm. Bus S2.

OUTDOOR GEAR

Cintamani, Laugavegur 11 (© 533-3800; www.cintamani.is), the upstart competitor of fashionable 66° North (see below), has slightly lower prices, more camping gear (tents, boots, maps, and so on), and a travel agency for adventure tours. Útilíf (www.utilif.is) is the best place for technical outdoor equipment, especially for camping, climbing, cycling, and fishing—or if you just forgot your swimsuit. Reykjavík boasts two locations: Kringlan (© 545-1580) and Smáralind (© 545-1550).

66° North This Icelandic outerwear line, which began by serving fishermen, unites fashion and outdoor readiness so well as to make brands like Patagonia and REI look dowdy and utilitarian. Iceland has eight branches—Reykjavík has its second branch in **Kringlan Mall** (© 533-6066)—and they've recently reached a few North American retailers. Pricey, but a great place to pick up waterproofs, fleeces, and ski gear for men, women, and children. Bankastræti 5. © 517-6020. www.66north.com.

WOOLENS

Over centuries of harsh weather, Icelandic sheep evolved a dual-layered wool: Inner fibers are soft and insulating; outer fibers are water and dirt repellent. These qualities combine for knitwear that is surprisingly light, resilient, and wearable in all kinds of weather. Sweaters in traditional Icelandic patterns are well-known, and you'll also find wonderful hats, mittens, socks, and blankets. Don't wait until your return to Keflavík Airport to buy your sweaters; the selection isn't near what it used to be.

A miniature branch of the discount outlet in suburban Mosfellsbær (see p. 137), **Álafoss,** Laugavegur 1 (© 562-6303; www.alafoss.is), offers marginal savings over its competitors, and has a decent selection of sweaters and handicrafts. Clothing line **Farmer's Market** (www.farmersmarket.is) doesn't have its own shop, but the brand is worth seeking out for its sexier, lighter, less bulky take on traditional Icelandic sweater patterns. The sweaters are made from Icelandic wool, but don't wear one into the Handknitting Association store—they're manufactured abroad. They're available at Kisan (see above), the Keflavík airport, the Blue Lagoon (p. 150), and Geysir (p. 140).

Handknitting Association of Iceland (Handprjónasamband Íslands) This well-stocked store, with four branches across the city, is owned, run, and supplied by a cooperative of about 200 Icelandic women handknitters. The main branch is on Skólavörðustígur, but you'll find longer hours at the Lækjargata 2a branch (daily 9am–10pm) and the Saga Hotel branch (daily 8am–2pm and 4–10pm). The branch at Laugavegur 64 keeps normal hours. Skólavörðustígur 19. ✆ 552-1890. www.handknit.is.

Start Art This shop/gallery/studio space is owned by a designer and six contemporary artists, whose works rotate. Even if it's not in the front display room, don't miss GAGA Skorrdal's fab yet functional knitware—vests, dresses, miniskirts, and hats with amoebic tufts and projectiles. Laugavegur 12b. ✆ 551-2306. www.startart.is.

9 Reykjavik Nightlife

The fastest-growing tourist demographic in Iceland are long-weekenders who don't come *just* to party . . . but if there were no party they wouldn't come. Reykjavík rocks like a city 10 times its size, with more than 50 bars and clubs in the city center. Thankfully there's much more to Reykjavík's famous nightlife than bar-hopping, and any evening in the capital is full of cultural activity. For a current schedule of events, see "Visitor Information," at the beginning of this chapter.

BARS & NIGHTCLUBS

Until 1989, beer with an alcohol content above 2.2% was illegal, and other forms of booze were tightly restricted. Alcohol consumption in Iceland is actually lower than in most European countries, but when Icelanders do drink, they tend to make up for lost time. Late Friday or Saturday night, you'll likely witness dancing on every available surface, public urination, the occasional brawl, licentious sexual behavior, and so on. At least the 2007 smoking ban has made the air more hospitable.

The legal drinking age is 20, but it's not heavily policed. Some bars and clubs have a 22-and-over policy. Drinking on the street is prohibited, but the law isn't enforced—some bars will even give you a to-go cup. Drug laws are stricter, but recent years have seen a troubling surge in cocaine and amphetamine use. Reykjavík is a safe place, but as always, women should beware of accepting drinks which may have been tampered with. Many foreigners, usually men, come in search of reputedly loose Icelandic women and are disappointed.

Fashion in the club scene is surprisingly dressy for laid-back Iceland. Sneakers are usually frowned upon, and—though jeans are "in"—they'd better be hot. A certain divide has opened up between spiffier joints (b5, Thorvaldsen, Oliver) and hangouts with too many hipsters, rockers, and bohemians for any sort of dress code (Sirkus, Kaffibarinn, Boston).

On weekends, not much gets started before midnight, and clubs stay open as late as 8am. (Until a few years ago all bars had to close at 3am on weekends, but this created such mayhem in the streets that the authorities thought better of it.) Weeknights, when bars are required to close at 1am, are far more relaxed. On Thursday nights, DJs and live music often take it up a notch. Most of the clubs are cafes by day and serve food until 10pm. No bars or clubs have cover charges, unless there's live music.

Many locals save money by drinking at home and then heading out around 1am, when the lines start forming. (Icelanders don't like waiting in line and will push and shove to cut ahead.) At the end of the evening, many partiers wind down in Austurvöllur Square, near the biggest late-night taxi stand at Tjörnin Pond.

Joining the Party

- **Freaky Friday** The first Friday of every month, all day and into the evening, the trendy and adventurous line up and surrender their hair to the creative whims of the talented stylists of **Gallerí Gel**, Hverfisgata 37 (℃ 551-7733), while regulars socialize and onlookers line the walls and couches drinking beer and wine. Book ahead; beauticians take only two victims at a time (5,500kr/$88/£44 a head).

- **Night Circle Tour** Nightlife comes in a package tour, starting Friday and Saturday nights at 10pm at **Bar 11**, Laugavegur 11 (℃ 847-5337). For 3,000kr ($48/£24) you get an hour of free drinks at Bar 11, shots at two different bars, a cocktail at a nightclub, and—to complete the ritual—a hot dog. Around 40 others are along for the ride, Icelanders and tourists alike.

- **Professional Partier** Jón Kari Hilmarsson of **Nightlife Friend** (℃ 822-6600; www.nightlifefriend.is) has a lot of friends in Reykjavík, and (for a fee) you can be one of them. For around 25,000kr ($400/£200), he'll design a customized nightlife tour for up to four people, and then take you around to the hotspots, introduce you to locals, and help you cut some lines. When he started the business, he envisioned his clients as timid nerdy types, but the majority are 30-plus American males working in business/finance who see no stigma in getting professional assistance for social events.

Reykjavík bars change constantly, and listings are quickly outdated. If you're not sure where to go, trust your instincts, keep on the move, and ask locals for advice. Icelanders are very accessible, especially when they're in party mode, and the nightlife scene is nowhere near as snobby as it is trendy.

For some American-style sports bar action, complete with large-screen TVs, **Glaumbar,** Tryggvagata 20 (℃ 552-6868), is known for its loud music and late-night partying on weekends. Then there's **Sportbar.is,** Hverfisgata 46 (℃ 552-5300). Self-explanatory: bar, TV, sports, pool tables. For a bit more sophistication, try the only dedicated wine bar in Iceland: **Vinbarinn,** Kirkjutorg 4 (℃ 552-4120), is a tasteful spot behind the City Cathedral. Many locals consider it the primo place for over-30s to meet after 11pm.

Barinn Formerly "Bar 22," this no-dress-code cafe and nightspot is rapidly gaining a reputation for scenesters and wild partying. It's one of the few bars hosting DJs 5 nights a week, but they leave the top floor free for conversation. Laugavegur 22 (at Klapparstígur). ℃ 578-7800. www.barinn.is.

b5 Housed in a former bank, this cafe-bar is popular among natty young professionals savoring their mango mojitos. (You'll feel out of place in frumpy travel clothes.) The basement bank vaults have been converted into private lounges with expensive bottle service. Bankastræti 5. ℃ 552-9600. www.myspace.com/b5_bar.

Boston This recent addition is owned by Sigga Boston, the proprietor of Sirkus (see below), granting automatic hipster cachet. It's a notch more laid back, roomy, and loungy than its peers, with comfortable seating and music played at a less intrusive volume. Laugavegur 28b. ℃ 517-7816.

Cafe Oliver Dress well for this trendy and slick nightspot, jam-packed on weekends with 25 and ups. By day Oliver is a cafe/bistro, and when they make way for the

DJ and dance floor, they leave some tables out for patrons who want bottle service. Laugavegur 20a. © 552-2300. www.cafeoliver.is.

Dillon The buzzwords for this dark English-style pub are rock, students, tattoos, and beer. It's busy weeknights, with occasional live music. The DJ on Saturday is white-haired local fave Andrea Jóns, the so-called "grandmother of Icelandic rock." Laugavegur 30. © 511-2400. www.dillon.is.

Hressingarskálinn Known locally as "Hresso," this long-established Austurstræti landmark is a good consensus choice: not too glamorous, a nicely mixed crowd, plenty of space and outdoor seating, good bistro food to 10pm, live music Thursdays, and plenty of '80s and '90s hits from the DJs. Austurstræti 20. © 561-2240. www.hresso.is.

Kaffi Reykjavík This cafe, restaurant, and endearingly unhip live music venue (mostly cover bands) is best known for its **Ice Bar,** where the walls, tables, bar, and glasses are all made from glacier ice and the room is kept at 21°F (–6°C). Visitors are charged a hefty 1,500kr ($24/£12) toward the overhead, and receive gloves, a parka, and a welcome cocktail. Colored tube lighting and vodka bottles frozen into the walls set the tone. Some love it; for others it's an overpriced, touristy walk-in freezer. Vesturgata 2. © 552-3030. www.kaffireykjavik.is.

Kaffibarinn A bit of celebrity cachet here—Björk stops in, scenes from the cult film *101 Reykjavík* were shot here, and Britpop entrepreneur Damon Albarn owned a share—but celebrity cachet doesn't go far in Reykjavík. Artists, musicians, filmmakers, and, of course, tourists are the core clientele. DJs spin Wednesday to Saturday, but you can converse upstairs. Bergstaðstræti 1. © 551-1588. www.kaffibarinn.is.

Rex This weekend-only nightclub, with its velvet couches and chandeliers, walks a compelling line between seediness and glamour, so dress stylishly if not properly. The crowd tends toward well-groomed 30-somethings, but you wouldn't be surprised to come across an aged movie star in furs. Austurstræti 9. © 552-5599. www.rex.is.

Sirkus Everyone seems to have some pretense of being an artist in this hipster oasis, complete with palm-tree murals in the courtyard and a knowingly kitsch, retro interior. DJs 3 nights a week play an eclectic mix of pop, indie, salsa, techno, and metal, and you can expect a line after 1am. Look out for their annual Tom Selleck moustache competition. Klapparstígur 31, just off Laugavegur. No phone.

GAY & LESBIAN NIGHTLIFE

The perception among Reykjavík's gays and lesbians is that the city's wild nightlife doesn't extend as much to them. The population is just too small to support a major "scene." On the upside, gay and lesbian visitors feel personally welcomed, not lost in the crowd. Reykjavík is also more integrated than you might expect; there's no "gay neighborhood," and only two bars—both quiet cafes by day—have any sort of officially gay identity. **Cafe Cozy,** Austurstræti 3 (© **511-1033**), is a mixed gay-straight bar that's jam-packed on weekends. **Q Bar,** Ingólfsstræti 3 (© **551-9660**), also welcomes straights but is more officially designated a gay bar. Q has plenty of loungey seating, the music isn't too overbearing, and DJs play Wednesday to Saturday.

For more info and activities, the website **www.gayice.is** posts a schedule of events. The **Reykjavík Gay Pride Festival** (www.gaypride.is) usually takes place the first week of August. The gay and lesbian community center, **Samtökin '78,** Laugavegur 3, 4th floor (© **552-7878;** www.samtokin78.is), holds open-house social gatherings at their **Rainbow Cafe** Mondays and Thursdays 8 to 11:30pm and Saturdays 9pm to

1am (Thurs nights are especially popular among lesbians). Their library is open during these gatherings and on weekdays from 1 to 5pm. The Icelandic lesbian organization **Konur Með Konum** (www.kmk.is) posts events and useful information, like where to join the KMK gals for a game of volleyball. Gay and lesbian student visitors are usually welcome at parties sponsored by the University of Iceland's GLB organization every other week or so; email gay@hi.is for the lowdown.

LIVE MUSIC

Since the late 1980s, especially since Björk's solo career took off, Iceland has enjoyed an outsized reputation as an incubator of alternative popular music. The **Iceland Airwaves Festival** (p. 18) attracts more visitors to Iceland than any other single event. Good music can be heard virtually every night, often in galleries, stores, and other unpredictable venues, so check listings in the free circular *The Grapevine* (www.grapevine.is). Reykjavík's two alternative music store/labels *12 Tonar* and *Smekkleysa* (p. 124) are also prime places to tap into local happenings.

Why Iceland? Many look no further than Iceland's strong singing traditions. Others point to Reykjavík's ideal size: Big enough to constitute a "scene," yet small enough that—with no real record industry or celebrity culture—the scene stays down to earth. Everyone is influenced by everyone else, styles easily cross-fertilize, and no one raises an eyebrow at the most outlandishly clashing double bills. Every record is reviewed in the press, though ironically many bands have risen only after gaining foreign attention.

The alternative scene roughly divides into three camps: hard rock, indie rock, and electronica. But don't mistake the hippest, edgiest alternative bands like Sigur Rós, Múm, and Gus Gus for the entire popular music scene. Iceland's version of *American Idol*, Idol Stjörnuleit (Idol Starsearch) is watched by half the country and is as unabashedly "pop" as its American forebear.

Nasa, Austurvöllur Square (② 511-1313; www.nasa.is; daily 10pm–5:30am), Reykjavík's largest club venue, hosts every style imaginable. Another prestigious and diverse club venue, where you can usually catch two bands for less than the price of a movie ticket is **Gaukur á Stöng (aka Gaukurinn),** Tryggvagata 22, (② 551-1556; www.gaukurinn.is; Sun–Thurs 11:30am–1am, Fri–Sat 11:30am–5:30am).

A more intimate club than NASA, **Grand Rokk,** Smiðjustígur 6 (② 551-5522; www.grandrokk.is), feels very local and has "rokk" in the title for a reason. By contrast, the arena-size **Laugardalshöll,** Engjavegi 8 (② 553-8990; www.laugardalsholl.is), on a soccer ground in Laugardalur Park, hosts the biggest international acts. **Cafe Amsterdam,** Hafnarstræti 5 (② 551-3800), is a good place to catch up-and-coming bands each weekend.

THE PERFORMING ARTS
CLASSICAL MUSIC

Though overshadowed by Reykjavík's popular music scene, classical music thrives here and even has its own celebrities: Vladimir Ashkenazy has been an Icelandic citizen since 1972, and best-selling operatic tenor Garðar Thór Cortes is regularly voted sexiest man in Iceland. As with popular music, concerts have unpredictable schedules and play in unpredictable venues, so check daily listings. A highly recommended experience is to see an organ recital or choral music in **Hallgrímskirkja** (p. 115) or the more intimate **Fríkirkjan (Free Church),** Laufásvegur 13 (② 552-7270; www.frikirkjan.is), on the east side of Tjörnin Pond.

In July and August the **Sigurjón Ólafsson Museum** (p. 117) moves aside the sculptures in its main hall for a discriminating series of classical and jazz concerts Tuesday evenings at 8:30pm. Each concert is 1 hour with no interval. **Salurinn,** Hamraborg 6 (© 570-0400; www.salurinn.is), is a recently built state-of-the-art classical venue in the nearby suburb of Kópavogur. The hall is made from Icelandic materials (driftwood, spruce, crushed stone) and has fabulous acoustics.

The **Iceland Symphony Orchestra** (© 545-2500; www.sinfonia.is), founded in 1950, is quite accomplished despite its short history. Sixty performances run each season from September to June. The most regular performance time is Thursday at 7:30pm. Currently they perform at **Háskólabíó,** aka the University Cinema, on Hagatorg Square at the university complex, but in 2009 they move into **Tónlistarhús,** a flashy new performance complex by the old harbor.

The **Icelandic Opera,** Ingólfsstræti 101, between Laugavegur and Hverfisgata (© 511-4200; www.opera.is), was founded in 1978 and stages international and Icelandic operas. Unfortunately for summer tourists, the northernmost opera house in the world only opens its doors in the spring and fall.

JAZZ

Reykjavík has no full-time jazz club—the closest approximation, Cafe Rósenberg, burned down in 2007—so devotees will just have to scour the listings. The **Reykjavík Jazz Festival** (© 862-1402; www.reykjavikjazz.com) usually runs from late September to early October.

DANCE & THEATER

The **Icelandic Dance Company,** Listabraut 3 (© 568-8000; www.id.is), focuses exclusively on contemporary dance and performs at the City Theatre (see below). The **Reykjavík Dance Festival** (www.dancefestival.is) includes choreographers from around the world and runs 4 days in early September.

The **National Theater,** Hverfisgata 19 (© 551-1200; www.leikhusid.is), hosts everything from Shakespeare and Chekhov to Rodgers and Hammerstein; but most productions are in Icelandic and the whole place shuts down in July and August.

The **Reykjavík City Theatre,** Listabraut 3, behind Kringlan shopping center (© 568-8000; www.borgarleikhus.is), is also unseen by most tourists, since most plays are in Icelandic and the season lasts from late September to May.

The **Travelling Theatre Company,** Vonarstræti 3, Iðnó Theatre, near City Hall (© 551-9181; www.lightnights.com), performs "Light Nights" for most of July and August, Monday and Tuesday nights at 8:30pm. The 90-minute mélange of Icelandic folk dancing, saga scenes, ghost stories, wrestling, and so on is aimed at tourists, and is a bit amateurish but genuine. Admission is 2,500kr ($40/£20) adults, 1,800kr ($29/£14) students, but attendance is deemed unsuitable for children under 7.

CINEMA

Surprisingly Reykjavík has no full-time arty theater; offerings are generally American blockbusters (though at least movies aren't dubbed into Icelandic). Tickets are generally 800kr ($13/£6.40). The daily newspaper *Morgunbalðið* has film listings in English, or go to www.kvikmyndir.is and click the "Í Bíó" tab.

Volcano Show Since the 1950s, quasi-suicidal filmmakers Ósvaldur and Villi Knudsen have set out by copter, car, and foot to capture all of Iceland's volcanic eruptions. The presentation is disappointingly low-tech (this is no IMAX theater) and the sequencing difficult to follow. But some footage is unforgettable, notably the copter view of a glacial waterburst after the 1996 Grímsvotn eruption. A second 1-hour film, which focuses on two major eruptions in the Westman Islands, is optional. The amiable Villi will likely be there to welcome you and ask where you're from.

The Red Rock Cinema. Hellusund 6A. Ⓒ 845-9548. Tickets available at box office 30 min. before showtime, or at Tourist Information Center (p. 84). For 1-hr. program: 900kr ($14/£7.20) adults; 750kr ($12/£6) students; 250kr ($4/£2) children 10–16. For 2-hr. program: 1,150kr ($18/£9.20) adults; 950kr ($15/£7.60) students; 300kr ($4.80/£2.40) children. Showtimes in English July–Aug 11am, 3, and 8pm; Apr–June and Sept, 3 and 8pm; Oct–Mar 8pm. AE, MC, V.

6

Near Reykjavík

More and more visitors have been using Reykjavík as a home base for their entire Iceland vacation, taking day trips from the capital. Perhaps they have limited vacation time, or they're taking advantage of Icelandair's free up-to-7-day stopover on flights between North America and Europe. In any case, the area within 1 or 2 hours' drive of Reykjavík boasts an incredible wealth of scenery and activities. While it isn't quite the whole country in microcosm, it comes pretty close.

Renting a car (even just for the day) is fast becoming the most popular means of travel for this region because many sights are otherwise inaccessible. Regular bus routes have slacked off a bit in turn, but bus tours are still plentiful.

1 Hafnarfjörður

10km (6 miles) S of Reykjavík.

From the main road, it's easy not to notice Hafnarfjörður, even though it's Iceland's third-largest town (pop. 23,000) and second-busiest port. Once you've reached the harbor, however, it's clear Hafnarfjörður has a distinct identity. It was a major trading center as far back as the early 15th century, first with the British, then the Germans, before the Danish king imposed a trade monopoly on Iceland in 1602. Unlike Reykjavík, the town is carved out of the surrounding lava field.

Icelanders are often subjected to two stereotypes: 1) that they are modern-day Vikings, and 2) that they still believe in elves. Icelanders hardly disown these stereotypes, but may cringe when confronted with them in crude forms. Two of Hafnarfjörður's biggest tourist draws—the **Viking Village** and **Hidden Worlds elf tours**—play up these stereotypes outrageously. If you're visiting in June and want kitsch overload, come to Hafnarfjörður for the **Viking Festival** (p. 17).

ESSENTIALS

GETTING THERE   The drive from the center of Reykjavík is only 15 minutes; take Route 40 south to the Hafnarfjörður turnoff. Bus S1 runs every 20 or 30 minutes from Hlemmur and Lækjartorg stations in Reykjavík to Hafnarfjörður's shopping center, near the tourist information office (and a 10-min. walk from the Viking Village). The trip takes about 25 minutes. Buses connecting Reykjavík and Keflavík often stop in Hafnarfjörður. For a taxi, call **BSH** (© **555-0888**).

VISITOR INFORMATION   The **tourist office,** Strandgata 6, inside the Town Hall (© **585-5500;** www.hafnarfjordur.is), is open weekdays from 8am to 5pm; from June to August it's also open weekends, from 10am to 3pm.

Notes on Entering the Countryside

Leaving Reykjavík can be a shock to the system. Suddenly you're walking on lava rocks; or driving astride a long, dramatic fjord; or peering at thousands of squawking seabirds. The land feels strangely unformed, caught in geological transition. Without trees or thick vegetation, the earth looms in all its power and bulk. Iceland's original settlers found no natives to subdue, and never had to group their homes on hilltops in defensive clusters. Farmsteads, evenly spread throughout the land, have been the organizational basis of Icelandic society until relatively recent history. Every farm has a name—often the same name it had 1,000 years ago—and its own road sign. The name is usually derived from its surrounding geography. Still today, each farm and its natural environs merge personalities.

WHAT TO SEE & DO

Viking Village (Fjörukráin) *Kids*   Hafnarfjörður's biggest tourist draw is this over-the-top, Viking-themed restaurant and hotel. The dining hall is modeled on an old Norwegian church, with dragon heads carved on the roof, and the interior is festooned with shields, tapestries, horse hides, and runic symbols. Dinner is the main event, as actors in Viking and Valkyrie costumes sing, dance, and tell stories. Friday and Saturday nights are especially raucous. The secret of Fjörukráin's success is the combination of shameless kitsch (Viking employees storm arriving tour buses to "kidnap" visitors, who are later presented with "honorary Viking" certificates) with earnest historicism (they'll have you know *real* Vikings never had tusks sticking out of their helmets). Keep an eye on the tour groups. They've probably paid extra for combat demonstrations and the like, and you can eavesdrop. The popular "Viking menu" includes fish soup, dried haddock, lamb shank, and skýr for dessert—plus a cube of putrefied sharkmeat speared with an Icelandic flag (get your napkin ready). Plenty of conventional dishes are offered, too, and no one will make you consume raw horsemeat. For the Viking Hotel, see below.

Strandgata 55 (at Viking Village). © 565-1213. www.fjorukrain.is. Reservations recommended. Main courses 1,650kr–4,450kr ($26–$71/£13–£36); Viking menu 6,000kr ($96/£48). MC, V. Lunch Thurs–Sat noon–3pm; dinner daily 6pm–10pm; bar open late Fri–Sat.

Hidden Worlds *Kids*   Hafnarfjörður is famous for its large population of "hidden people" (see box, below), particularly elves, and local medium Sigurbjörg "Sibba" Karlsdóttir can help you find them. Hidden people pop up along the tour route, which should intrigue young kids, even if the costumes aren't terribly convincing. Afternoon tours leave twice per week in summer and last 1½ to 2 hours.

© 694-2785. www.alfar.is. Tickets 2,500kr ($40/£20).

WHERE TO STAY & DINE

Hafnarfjörður has plenty of accommodations (all listed at www.hafnarfjordur.is)—the town's sales pitch is that it's nice to be close to but outside of the "big city"—but peaceful lodgings can be found just as easily in Reykjavík. Hafnarfjörður has some decent food, but most dinnertime visitors are here to experience the Viking Village.

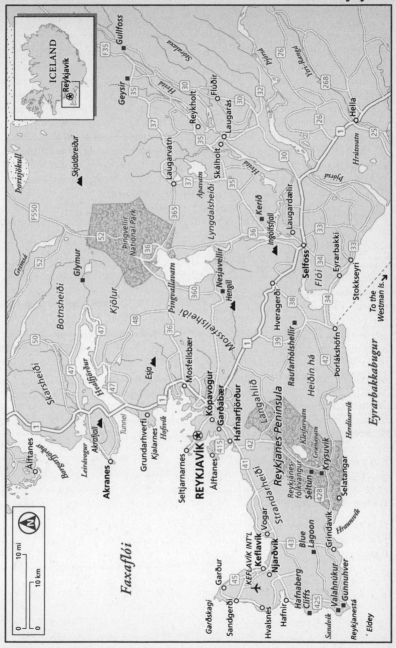

"Hidden People" Lesson #1: Origins

The term "Hidden People" *(huldufólk)* applies collectively to various human-oid creatures living in Iceland, including elves, dwarves, gnomes, trolls, and so on.

When Viking ships first arrived in Iceland, dragon heads were removed from the prows so as not to disturb the guardian spirits of the land. These spirits are ancestral to the hidden people, who have always been strongly identified with features of the landscape. Hidden people are widely mentioned in sagas written during the first centuries of settlement. For the most part they've remained a folkloric phenomenon parallel to Christian belief, but sometimes they were incorporated into Christian frameworks. In one accounting, Eve was washing her children to prepare them to meet God. God arrived sooner than expected, so she kept the unwashed children hidden, and God saw fit to keep them hidden forever.

Viking Village Hotel   While the adjoining restaurant is crammed with Viking paraphernalia, the hotel's pleasant, modern rooms are sparingly adorned with a few Viking motifs—tree stump tables, Stonehenge-inspired wall hangings, and some beds with chariot wheels. The deck is perfect for a sunset cocktail.

Strandgata 55. (C) 565-1213. Fax 565-1891. www.fjorukrain.is. 42 units. Apr–Sept 14,500kr ($232/£116) double; 16,500kr ($264/£132) for mini suite. Rates around 37% lower Oct–Mar. Rates include breakfast. MC, V. **Amenities:** Hot tub; sauna. *In room:* TV, coffee/tea, Wi-Fi.

Súfistinn   This friendly, local hangout is a good place to relax and recharge among real Hafnies. The café menu offers salads, sandwiches, quiche, and the house favorite, a hearty Indian vegetable pie.

Strandgata 9. (C) 565-3740. Small dishes 460kr–1,100kr ($7.40–$18/£3.70–£8.80). DC, MC, V. Mon–Thurs 8:15am–11:30pm; Fri 8:15am–midnight; Sat 10am–midnight; Sun noon–11:30pm.

2 Mosfellsbær

15km (9¼ miles) NE of Reykjavík.

This town hasn't been swallowed up by the overflowing capital, but its day may soon come. The outskirts of town yield to beautiful pastureland, where you'll find Mosfells-bær's main attraction: the former home of Halldór Laxness, Iceland's greatest modern writer.

The **tourist office** ((C) **566-6822;** www.mosfellsbaer.is) is at the library in the Kjarni shopping center (Þverholt 2).

Halldór Laxness Museum (Gljúfrasteinn)   Gljúfrasteinn, which became a museum in 2004, should interest most fans of the Nobel Prize–winning author. Halldór spent most of his adult life in this mid-20th-century country home, full of original furniture and artwork by close friends Jóhannes Kjarval, Svavar Guðnason, and Nina Tryggvadóttir. Halldór's well-polished 1968 Jaguar still sits in the driveway. The recommended 25-minute audio tour includes interview clips with Halldór and his wife, voiced over in English. Halldór was a fine pianist, and concerts are still held on his grand piano every Sunday at 4pm from June through August; tickets are only 400kr ($6.40/£3.20). Guests are encouraged to bring picnics and walk along the river.

Bus 15 takes you from Reykjavík to central Mosfellsbær; from there bus 27 makes four trips daily to Laxnes Farm, which is a 10-minute walk from Gljúfrasteinn—but you'll probably have to wait a few hours for the next bus back. (A horseback ride at Laxnes farm, below, could round out your itinerary.) Another alternative, if you don't have a car, is the "Wonders of Þingvellir" tour with **Iceland Excursions** (⟨ 540-1313; www.icelandexcursions.is), which combines Gljúfrasteinn with Þingvellir.

⟨ 586-8066. www.gljufrasteinn.is. Admission 500kr ($8/£4) adults, 250kr ($4/£2) ages 6–16 and 67 and over. June–Aug daily 9am–5pm; Sept–May Tues–Sun 10am–5pm. From Reykjavík by car, take Rte. 1 through Mosfellsbær, then turn right on Rte. 36; the museum is marked a few km ahead.

HORSEBACK RIDING   Across the road from the Laxness Museum (above)—but no longer connected with Halldór Laxness' family—is **Laxnes Horse Farm** (⟨ 566-6197; www.laxnes.is). A visit to the farm is recommended for those who would like a short ride near the premises or a longer tour of the area.

SHOPPING   Prices on the large selection of woolens and handicrafts at **Álafoss Factory Outlet,** Álafossvegur 23 (⟨ 566-6303; www.alafoss.is), are 15%–20% below Reykjavík levels. Coming by bus isn't worth the effort—the nearest stop is a 15-minute walk away. By car, follow Route 1 north through three traffic circles in Mosfellsbær, then turn right off the fourth traffic circle onto Álafossvegur. The store is 800m (2,625 ft.) ahead on the left. Hours are Monday through Friday 9am to 6pm and Saturday 9am to 4pm.

Halldór Kiljan Laxness (1902–1998)

Halldór Laxness, author of 62 books in a span of 68 years, is the undisputed giant of modern Icelandic literature. (For suggested titles, see p. 50.) Born Halldór Guðjónsson in Reykjavík, he left Iceland after WWI to travel. In France he converted to Catholicism, adopting the last name Laxness and middle name Kiljan, after the Irish saint. In 1927 he published *The Great Weaver from Kashmir,* his first major novel. Three years later, after an ill-fated attempt to break into the Hollywood film industry, he returned to Iceland and became immersed in socialism, which greatly informed his novels: Lead characters are typically impoverished and exploited by a corrupt establishment. But his most overriding, lifelong subject was simply the common man; and Catholicism, socialism, absurdism, and Taoism all framed this concern at different stages in his life. After winning the Nobel Prize for Literature in 1955, he was overjoyed that among his many congratulatory notes was one from a local Icelandic society of pipe layers; it was the only card to which he responded.

3 Esja, Hvalfjörður & Akranes

Esja is 22km (14 miles) N of Reykjavík; Hvalfjörður is 25km (16 miles) N of Reykjavík; Akranes is 48km (30 miles) N of Reykjavík.

This coastal area north of Reykjavík is often bypassed by visitors, but the scenery is up to Iceland's high standard, particularly Iceland's tallest waterfall, **Glymur.**

ESSENTIALS

GETTING THERE   Route 1 leads north from Reykjavík, passing Esja before reaching the tunnel across Hvalfjörður to Akranes. For Akranes, turn left after the tunnel on Route 51, then left again on Route 509. Nine buses make the trip from Reykjavík to Akranes on weekdays (six on weekends); the route—bus 15 from BSÍ or Hlemmur stations, connecting with bus 27 in Mosfellsbær—goes right past the Esja trailhead (tell the driver if that's your destination) but bypasses the coastline of Hvalfjörður by taking the tunnel.

VISITOR INFORMATION   Questions about Esja should be directed to the tourist information office in Reykjavík (p. 84). Hvalfjörður is in Akranes township. The **Akranes Tourist Information Center,** Kirkjubraut 8 (𝄏 **431-1780;** www.visit akranes.is), is open daily mid-May to mid-September from 10am to 5pm, and daily 1pm to 5pm the rest of the year; another **branch** (𝄏 **431-1780**) is at the Akranes Museum Center, below. The **Borgarnes tourist information office** (𝄏 **437-2214;** www.west.is) is also helpful.

EXPLORING THE AREA

Climbing **Esja** 𝄐 is formidable but rewarding, and the mountain's main trails are well-marked and negotiable. Several routes lead up Esja, which is more of a volcanic range than a single peak. The recommended and most popular trail starts at a parking area along Route 1. (Heading north from Reykjavík, it's at the base of the mountain; look for the sign "Gönguleiðir á Esju" just after a driveway marked "Mógilsá.") From there it's a 780m (2,559-ft.), 4km (2½-mile) ascent to the marvelous Þverfellshorn lookout. Allow at least 5 hours for the return trip. The tallest peak (914m/2,999 ft.) is 3km (2 miles) farther along, but only tempts very devoted hikers. The excellent Myndkort "photomap," compiled from aerial satellite photographs, details all of Esja's trail routes.

North of Esja, drivers on Route 1 pass through a very deep, 6km (3¾-mile) **tunnel beneath Hvalfjörður,** completed in 1998. (*Beware:* It's a speed trap.) On the far side are Iceland's only toll booths, which collect 900kr ($14/£7.20; Visa/MasterCard accepted) per car. The tunnel shortened the thru-route by 47km (29 miles), but the old route around the fjord is a scenic drive and the only way to reach Glymur.

Hvalfjörður means "whale fjord," and, if you keep your eyes fastened on it, you might see why. At 30km (19 miles) it's the longest fjord in southwest Iceland, and was an important naval base for the Allies in WWII.

Translating to "clamor," **Glymur** 𝄐𝄐 is the tallest waterfall in Iceland (200m/656 ft). What Glymur lacks in raw power, it makes up for in lithe beauty. Getting there is half the fun, with great views out to the fjord and surrounding countryside, and into a dramatic gorge filled with nesting birds in late spring and early summer. When the flow is substantial, Glymur is as breathtaking as Gullfoss (p. 146), but with 99% fewer tourists, thanks to its inaccessibility to cars. Glymur is also relatively unknown because the path is somewhat dangerous: the trail requires real caution, good balance, and agility. Also, the waterfall is less spectacular when the flow tapers off; ask around at local hotels and information centers to get an educated guess based on rain and meltoff.

To reach the trail to Glymur, turn off the main road at the head of Hvalfjörður. The parking area is a few minutes ahead. From the car park, a fenced-off dirt road bears toward the right, but the trail bears slightly left, marked with yellow-painted stones. In 2 to 3 minutes the trail divides, again without posted signs, though both routes are still marked with yellow rocks. The trail bearing left takes you up the west side of the gorge. This trail is shorter and easier but you don't get a good view of the waterfall. The right-hand path takes you across the river and up the east side of the gorge and is fully worth the extra effort. It reaches the river in 20 minutes or so; you have to wind through a cavity in the cliff to reach the shore, and then cross the river on a round wooden beam, while holding on to a steel suspension cable. Allow 2½ hours round-trip for the hike up the east side of the river.

Continuing west on Route 47 along the north shore of Hvalfjörður, you'll soon pass a deserted **whaling station.** At the tip of the peninsula is **Akranes,** a fishing and cement-factory town of around 6,000. The first settlers, who came as early as 880, are believed to have been Irish hermits. Akranes commemorates its founding each second weekend in July with the **Irish Days festival;** events include a sandcastle competition, a beach barbecue, and a contest to see who has the reddest hair. Just east of town is **Akrafjall,** the town's twin-peaked patron mountain. At 555m (1,804 ft.), Akrafjall's southern peak **Háihnúkur** 🐾 is a less exhausting climb than Esja. A well-marked trail to the top runs along the edge of a cliff full of great black-backed gulls and other birds. The parking area is along Route 51, at the Akranes hot water utility.

Akranes Museum Center   Iceland has many small-town folk museums. While this is one of the better and larger ones, it's typically hit or miss. In the **Icelandic Sport Museum,** one of several installations in the museum complex, you'll find entertaining artifacts such as a bike hand-twisted by Jón Páll Sigmarsson, Iceland's three-time winner of the "World's Strongest Man" competition. You'll also find some track star's stinky old sneakers, exhibited in all earnestness. Even better than the extensive **rock and mineral collection** is the **cartography exhibit,** which has good English captions explaining the old surveying equipment and the personalities of all the sea monsters on 17th-century maps. Several old fishing vessels lie outside on the lawn.

Garðar. 🔔 **431-5566.** www.museum.is. Admission 500kr ($8/£4) adults; 300kr ($4.80/£2.40) seniors; children ages 15 and under free. May 15–Sept 14 daily 10am–5pm; Sept 15–May 14 daily 1–6pm. Entering Akranes on Rte. 509, turn left at first roundabout onto Esjubraut; at next roundabout turn left onto Garðagrund; then take second left on Safnasvæði, and the Museum Center is ahead on the left.

WHERE TO STAY

Most day trippers from Reykjavík won't find reason to stay overnight, but Hvalfjörður offers a few beautifully situated accommodations.

Guesthouse Kiðafell   This pleasant, down-home accommodation near the south shore of Hvalfjörður, 38km (24 miles) from Reykjavík, consists of four tidy, wood-paneled guest rooms on the upper floor of the farmer's house. Dinner is served on request, access to an Internet terminal is free, and short horseback riding tours are available.

🔔 **566-6096.** www.dagfinnur.is/kidafell. 4 units w/shared bathroom. 4,400kr ($70/£35) single; 8,800kr ($141/£70) double. Rates include breakfast. Sleeping-bag accommodation 2,500kr ($40/£20) per person, not including breakfast (700kr/$11/£5.60). MC, V. From the southern junction of Rte. 1 and Rte. 47 (the junction south of the tunnel), take Rte. 47 east for about 4km (2½ miles), then turn right on Rte. 460 and the farm is 200m (656 ft.) ahead. *In room:* No phone.

Hótel Glymur ✹✹   Perhaps instead of staying in the capital for your first or last night in Iceland, you'd prefer communing peacefully with coastal fjord scenery—and getting some luxury and style, too. This place more than fits the bill, even if, in your views out to the fjord, a factory just clouds your peripheral vision.

Rte. 47. ✆ 430-3100. Fax 430-3101. www.hotelglymur.is. 22 units. May–Sept 22,300kr ($357/£178) double; 34,900kr ($558/£279) and up for suites. Rates around 25% lower Oct–Apr. Rates include breakfast. Special offers available online. MC, V. From the northern junction of Rte. 1 and Rte. 47 (the junction north of the tunnel), take Rte. 47 east for 12km (7½ miles). **Amenities:** Restaurant, bar; outdoor hot tub; same-day laundry service. *In room:* TV, coffee/tea, hair dryer, minibar, Wi-Fi.

WHERE TO DINE

For an excellent "country chic" dinner in Hvalfjörður, make a reservation at **Hótel Glymur** (above). The menu is stripped down to four entrees (catch of the day, lamb, chicken, and vegetarian) ranging from 3,470kr to 4,490kr ($56–$72/£28–£36). From noon to five it's a less expensive cafe, serving Turkish lamb soup, fresh salad, hot waffles, and "Grandmother's fish balls."

In **Akranes,** the **Galito Restaurant,** Stillholt 16–18 (✆ 430-6767; main courses 1,000kr–5,000kr ($16–$80/£8–£40); DC, MC, V; Sun–Thurs 11:30am–9pm, Fri–Sat 11:30am–10pm), has a typical small-town menu—burgers, pizza, fish, lamb, and perhaps a reindeer special—with a touch more pizzazz. For a casual meal at the town's best hangout, try **Café Mörk,** Skólabraut 14 (✆ 431-5030).

---

4 Golden Circle: Þingvellir, Geysir & Gullfoss

Þingvellir is 49km (30 miles) NE of Reykjavík; Geysir is 118km (73 miles) NE of Reykjavík; Gullfoss is 125km (78 miles) NE of Reykjavík.

The "Golden Circle" route isn't notably golden or circular, but whatever the marketing term, it still would have become the most popular day tour in Iceland. Each Golden Circle tour has its minor variations, but all include three major sights: **Þingvellir** ✹✹, meaning "Parliament Fields," where the Icelandic parliament first convened in 930; **Geysir** ✹, a geothermal hotspot for which all geysers are named; and **Gullfoss** ✹✹, a majestic waterfall. Nearby sights are often incorporated into the route, particularly the **Nesjavellir power plant, Kerið crater,** and **Skálholt,** once the most dominant settlement in south Iceland. The Golden Circle is often called "requisite," a "must-see," or "*the* day tour."

ESSENTIALS

GETTING THERE   Bus tours are popular and convenient, but many visitors prefer the flexibility of a rental car. The cost of a single Golden Circle bus ticket is only slightly less than renting a cheap car for 1 day, and the stop at Þingvellir, for instance, is never long enough for a hike into the valley. With a car you might also work in **Hveragerði** (p. 161) or the **Þjórsárdalur valley** (p. 286). The roads are open all year but can be very slippery and dangerous in winter. *Note:* If you plan on taking the interior Kjölur Route (p. 352) to Akureyri, you can see Geysir and Gullfoss then.

By car, Þingvellir is less than an hour from Reykjavík; take Route 1 north of Mosfellsbær, then turn right on Route 36. From Þingvellir, continue east on Route 36, turn left on Route 365, and turn left again on Route 37 in Laugarvatn; when Route 37 ends, turn left on Route 35. From there it's a short way to Geysir, and another 10 minutes to Gullfoss.

Regular service from **Reykjavík Excursions** (© 562-1011; www.re.is) costs a bit less than a formal tour and is an economical way to spend all day at Þingvellir. Bus 6 leaves from BSÍ terminal in Reykjavík daily mid-June through August at 8:30am, stopping at Þingvellir (9:15am–10:15am), Laugarvatn (10:45am), Geysir (11:15am–1pm), and Gullfoss (1:15–2pm). Bus 6a does the reverse route without extended stops, arriving back at Reykjavík at 4:45pm. A one-way ticket to/from Þingvellir costs 1,000kr ($16/£8); to/from Geysir 2,300kr ($37/£18); to/from Gullfoss 2,550kr ($41/£20). Children ages 4 to 11 get 50% off.

Bus 2 on **Þingvallaleið** (© 511-2600; www.bustravel.is) leaving Reykjavík's BSÍ terminal daily at 12:30pm from June through August, stops at Hveragerði, Selfoss, Laugarvatn, Geysir, and Gullfoss—and on the return trip, Reykholt, Laugarás, Selfoss, and Hveragerði—but does not allow time for sightseeing.

Bus 2 leaves BSÍ terminal at 12:30pm daily June through August, reaching Gullfoss at 3:15pm and Geysir at 4:25pm.

Organized bus tours leave from Reykjavík's BSÍ terminal, and prices include free hotel pickup and dropoff. Standard tours generally last 8 hours and leave at 8:30 or 9am. **Reykjavík Excursions** (© 562-1011; www.re.is) charges 7,000kr ($112/£56) for the standard Golden Circle tour, which includes Kerið Crater and Hveragerði. For Gullfoss and Geysir only, the "Gullfoss Geysir Direct" tour costs 5,700kr ($91/£46) and lasts 5½ hours. Children ages 12 to 15 get 50% off; ages 11 and under ride free. The Golden Circle tour from **Iceland Excursions** (© 540-1313; www.iceland excursions.is) costs 6,600kr ($106/£53) and includes Nesjavellir geothermal power plant, Skálholt, Kerið Crater, and Hveragerði. "Gullfoss & Geysir Express" costs 5,200kr ($83/£42) and lasts 6 hours. For the more culturally inclined, the 5-hour "Wonders of Þingvellir" tour, focusing exclusively on Þingvellir and the Halldór Laxness Museum (p. 136), costs 4,800kr ($77/£38), with departures June to August 20 weekdays at 1pm. Ages 13 to 17 get 50% off; ages 11 and under ride free. **Iceland Total** (© 585-4300; www.icelandtotal.is) has a Golden Circle tour focusing exclusively on the big three destinations for 6,813kr ($109/£55).

VISITOR INFORMATION   Þingvellir has two **visitor centers** (www.thingvellir.is). Approaching from Reykjavík, the first you come to is the **interpretive center,** at the top of the Almannagjá fault; the turnoff from Route 36 is marked "Fræðslumiðstöð" (June–Aug daily 9am–7pm; Apr–May and Sept–Oct daily 9am–5pm; Nov–Mar Sat–Sun 9am–5pm). The center has fun and informative video displays explaining the area's natural and cultural history. Farther along Route 36 is the **information center** (© 482-2660; May–Sept daily 8:30am–8pm; the cafe is also open Apr and Oct 8:30am–8pm and Nov–Mar Sat–Sun 9am–5pm) with cafe and bookshop. The plan is to expand services at the interpretive center; so, by the time you are reading this, you may be able to find maps or park rangers there. Many visitors skip the information center anyway, since from the interpretive center it's a short and agreeable approach on foot down to the historical sites.

The **Geysir Center** (© 480-6800; www.geysircenter.com; June–Aug daily 9am–10pm, May and Sept daily 9am–8pm, Oct and Apr daily 10am–4pm), across the street from the geothermal area, has an information desk, cafe, and extensive souvenir shop.

The unstaffed **Gullfoss visitor center** (Mon–Fri 9am–6pm; Sat–Sun 9–7pm) is right next to a **cafe and gift shop** (© 486-6500; Oct–Apr daily 8am–6pm; May–Sept 8am to as late as 10pm), where questions can be directed.

ÞINGVELLIR 𝄐𝄐

Þingvellir, a rift valley bounded by cliffs to the east and west, about 6km (3¾ miles) apart, is the symbolic heart of the Icelandic nation, though it's hardly clear why at first glance. The first Icelandic parliament (or *Alþing*) convened here in 930, and remained here off and on through 1798. (The Alþing, now in Reykjavík, is widely considered the oldest continuously-operating parliamentary institution in the world; it was actually disbanded for many years by Iceland's colonial rulers, so the Isle of Man has its own claim to this streak.) Þingvellir's annual parliamentary meetings were hardly limited to legislative sessions and court proceedings, however. They were also a news conference, trade fair, singles event, poetry reading, and circus ring all rolled into one. To Icelanders, Þingvellir is not only where their political independence originated, but also where their oral and literary traditions were passed on, and where their very sense of peoplehood formed. In the 19th and early-20th centuries, Þingvellir became a potent symbol and meeting place for the growing nationalist movement for independence from Denmark. In 1930, marking the millennium of the first Alþing, Þingvellir became Iceland's first national park. When Iceland gained formal independence in 1944, 20,000 people—one-sixth of the country's population—gathered at Þingvellir. The proclamation of independence was read in the pouring rain, followed by 2 minutes of silence, and then the peal of church bells. In 2004 Þingvellir became a UNESCO World Heritage site. It's still used for national commemorations. *Note:* The tourist industry will tell you that the land to the west is "North America," tectonically speaking, and the land to the east is "Europe" or "Eurasia;" but the land to the east can't really be called Eurasia, because there's another major rift line farther east, running from Hella and Hvolsvöllur in the south to Mývatn in the north.

Þingvallavatn, the largest natural lake in Iceland, forms Þingvellir's southern boundary; 90% of its water comes from underground springs and fissures. Þingvellir sits directly on the continental rift: Land west of the **Almannagjá (Everyman's Gorge)** is moving west, and land east of the **Hrafnagjá (Raven Gorge)** is moving east. These borders have moved about 70m (230 ft.) apart in the last 10,000 years and continue to separate at about 8mm (⅓ in.) per year. The broad, lava-covered plain in the middle has fallen about 40m (131 ft.) in the same time span, forming the cliffs on either side. (In other words, 10,000 years ago the top of Almannagjá was level with what is now the valley floor.) In 1789, after an earthquake, the valley floor fell 5 feet in 10 days. The entire plain is riven with small crevices from all this geological stretching.

EXPLORING ÞINGVELLIR

Þingvellir is no Versailles; the only visible remnants of the old parliamentary gatherings are hardly more than lumps in the ground. All the main historical sites are clustered in the southwest corner of the park, and the vast majority of visitors never venture farther. This area was a good assembly site because the cliffs served as a natural amphitheater, the river provided fish and drinking water, and the plains held plenty of room for encampments. The rest of the park is undeveloped except for walking trails.

The parking areas closest to the sights are at the interpretive center and down in the valley off Route 362, about 150m (492 ft.) from the church. From the interpretive center there's a nice view of the valley, and a broad, well-tended path leads a short distance down through the **Almannagjá (Everyman's Fault)** to the designated **Lögberg (Law Rock),** marked by a flagpole. (No one knows for certain where the original rock

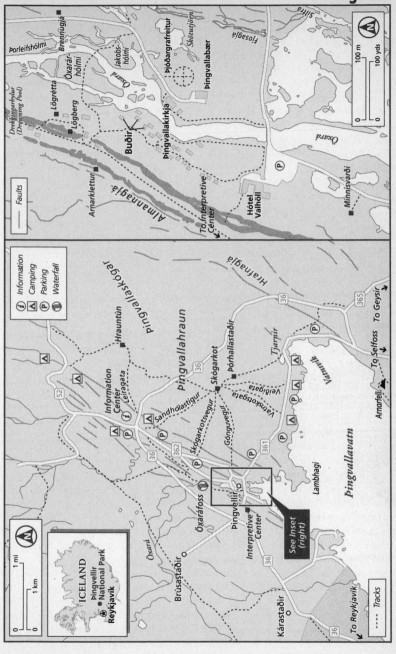

Faults

Þorleifshólmi
Brennugjá
Drekkingarhylur
(Drowning Pool)
Lögrétta
Lögberg
Öxarár-hólmi
Jakobs-hólmi
Þjóðargrafreitur
Þingvallabær
Þingvallakirkja
Búðir
Arnarklettur
Almannagjá
Skötutjörn
Flosagjá
Silfra
Öxará
To Interpretive Center
Hótel Valhöll
Minnisvarði

100 m
100 yds

Information
Camping
Parking
Waterfall

Hrauntún
Þingvallaskógar
Hrafnagjá
Þingvallahraun
Skógarkot
Þórhallsstaðir
Tjarnir
To Geysir
To Selfoss
365
36
Vatnsvík
Information Center
Leiragata
Sandhólastígur
Skógarkotsvegur
Vatnskotsgata
Veiðigata
Arnarfell
361
52
36
362
Göngugvegur
Öxaráfoss
Öxará
Þingvellir
Interpretive Center
See Inset (right)
Lambhagi
Þingvallavatn
Brúsastaðir
36
To Reykjavik
Kárastaðir
36
Tracks

1 mi
1 km

ICELAND
Þingvellir National Park
Reykjavík

Why Does Þingvellir Church Have Two Altarpieces?

Inside the church are two altarpieces. One depicts the Last Supper, and was painted on driftwood by local farmer and craftsman Ófeigur Jónsson in 1834. The other, "Christ Healing the Blind Man," from 1896, is by Danish painter Niels Anker Lund (1840–1922). Ófeigur's painting was the original altarpiece, but it was deemed too primitive and amateurish by church authorities and replaced by Lund's painting at great expense. Ófeigur's painting was bought for a pittance by a Victorian heiress named Mary Disney Leith (1840–1926). Leith, who had a lifelong fascination with Iceland, journeyed there 18 times, wrote travel memoirs, and translated some sagas. The piece ended up in the collection of St. Peter's Church, Shorwell, on the Isle of Wight, near Leith's estate. When Þingvellir church was renovated in 1970, Magnus Magnusson—the prolific author, saga translator, and long-time "Quizmaster" on BBC1's *Mastermind*—tracked it down with the help of Mrs. Leith's granddaughter. The congregation in Shorwell Church returned it in exchange for a replica made at Iceland's National Museum.

was.) The **Lögsögumaður (Law Speaker)**, the only salaried official at the Alþing, recited the laws from this podium by memory. Christianity was proclaimed the national religion at the Law Rock in the year 1000. (All Icelanders had to get baptized, but they were allowed to wait and find a warm geothermal spring on their way home.) Facing toward the south and the river, you can see bulges of earth and stone, the remains of temporary encampments called **búðir (booths)**. The fault of **Flosagjá** forms the eastern border of the assembly. Northeast of the Law Rock, across the river, are the **Neðrivellir (Low Fields)**, thought to be the meeting place for the **Lögretta (Law Council)**.

The **Óxará (Axe River)**—so named when someone accidentally dropped an axe into it, never to find it again—was probably diverted from its original course to provide drinking water for the assembly. A bit north along the river is the **Drekkingarhylur (Drowning Pool)**, where at least 18 women convicted of incest, infanticide, witchcraft, or adultery were tied in sacks and held under water. An informational panel marks the supposed spot. In the Christian millennial celebrations of 2000, a wreath was placed here in atonement for the executions. (Capital punishment was never widely practiced in Iceland, and was phased out entirely by the mid-19th century. Even in the sagas, murderers are simply banished from Iceland for 3 years without imprisonment.) A short walk farther north is a pretty waterfall, **Óxaráfoss.**

Walking east from the Law Rock, you'll cross an islet in the river where duels were fought in the first decades of the Alþing. Dueling came to be known as *hólmganga,* which means "island-going." Duels drew big crowds, but were outlawed in 1008.

Across the river is the simple and charming **Þingvallakirkja (Þingvellir Church)** (Jun–Aug 9am–7pm), which seats about 35. The first church at the site was built around 1016, with a bell and timbers sent by King Olaf of Norway. The current church was consecrated in 1859 and restored in 1970 to something close to its original condition, with the notable exception of the new copper roof.

Next to the church is the unremarkable farmhouse **Þingvellabær,** a summer residence for the Prime Minister—no security fence necessary. It was built in 1930 to commemorate the millennium of the first Alþing, and is not open to the public. Behind the church is **Þjóðargrafreitur,** a raised circular **graveyard.** The honor of burial at this spot has been bestowed to only two men, Jónas Hallgrímsson (1807–1845) and Einar Benediktsson (1864–1940), both poets and key figures in Iceland's nationalist revival.

By the nearest parking lot is a bridge overlooking the **Peningagjá (Money Fault).** Inside the fault is a clear, glistening pool that makes every kid fantasize about diving down to collect all the coins. Visitors have started throwing coins in pools all over the park, so the wardens plan to put up signs prohibiting this practice.

OUTDOOR ACTIVITIES

HIKING   Shoddy trail maps are available for 300kr ($4.80/£2.40) from the visitor centers, but trails are well-marked and you can probably just memorize or jot down your route from signboards. For longer hikes, serious maps should be available at the information center.

Apart from the historical sites, and the north–south trails connecting the sites to the information center, all trails extend east into the **Þingvallahraun** lava field. All the field's lava flowed about 9,000 years ago from **Skjaldbreiður (Shield Volcano),** a perfectly rounded, squat cone visible to the north once you're out in the field. Named for its shape, Skjaldbreiður then lent its name (in translation) to all other shield volcanoes, just as Geysir lent its name to all geysers.

As is clear from the map, virtually all the trails leaving from the western edge of the park converge halfway across the valley at the ruins of **Skógarkot,** a sheep farm abandoned since the 1930s. Each trail takes about 30 to 40 minutes. Skógarkot is now just a pleasant, grassy spot on a high point in the field, with a few stone foundations. Further east lies **Þórhallastaðir,** another farm ruin, but Skógarkot is more picturesque and enough to satisfy most day walkers. It's also an ideal picnic spot, with a great view over the lake to Hengill (p. 161) and the Nesjavellir geothermal power plant (below).

A **recommended loop itinerary** starts and ends at the information center. If you have 3 hours, head south along the fault to the historical sites, then take the trail east from the church to Skógarkot, cutting directly back to the information center. With only two hours to spare, park near the historical sites and squeeze in a hike to Skógarkot and back. If you have just 1 hour, stick to the historical sites and venture north along the fault. Remember that you can time your trip to take advantage of the **free 1-hour guided tours** of the historical sites, leaving from **Þingvallakirkja (Þingvellir Church)** at 10am and 3pm weekdays, June through August. Serious hikers can follow a trail all the way to the eastern edge of the rift—near to where Route 36 climbs the eastern rift wall at Hrafnagjá—but it's too long for a return trip in 1 day, so you'd want to arrange a ride one way.

Forty percent of all Icelandic flora can be found in Þingvellir, but nothing is taller than a dwarf birch. It's especially pretty in fall. As you walk through the valley, be careful not to step into the many fissures along the trail, and keep a close eye on children.

SCUBA DIVING   **Diving** in Þingvallavatn has taken off recently. Dives focus on dramatic fissures on the lake bottom, up to 40m (131 ft.) below the surface. Þingvallavatn is not recommended for beginners, given the cold temperatures and currents inside the fissures. Dives must be reserved in advanced; see p. 69 for more information.

SOUTH OF ÞINGVELLIR

Near the southwest shore of lake Þingvallavatn are the Nesjavellir power plant and the Hengill hiking area (p. 161), which is also accessible from Hveragerði to the south. The brochure *Hiking Trails in the Hengill Area* can be found at Nesjavellir.

Nesjavellir Geothermal Power Plant   Iceland's renewable energy sources, hydropower and geothermal power, are the envy of fossil fuel–guzzling nations around the world. Nesjavellir, which produces municipal hot water and electricity from geothermal hot springs, was built in 1987 and attracts 20,000 visitors a year. Exhibits are informative, and the glassed-in observation platform affords a good view of the plant's gleaming pipery, but visitors expecting something out of a sci-fi movie may be disappointed. **Reykjavík Excursions** (℃ 562-1011; www.re.is) and **Iceland Excursions** (℃ 540-1313; www.icelandexcursions.is) include Nesjavellir in day-long bus tours, often combined with Þingvellir (above) and the geothermal greenhouses of Hveragerði (p. 160).

Off Rte. 360, around 12km (7½ miles) south of the Rte. 36/Rte. 360 junction. ℃ 480-2408. Free admission (admission fees may come soon). Jun–Aug Mon–Sat 9am–5pm, Sun 1–6pm; Sept–May no regular hours; call to inquire about group tours.

GEYSIR ✶

The word "geyser" derives from this fascinating geothermal area full of hot springs, steaming creeks, mud marbled in mineral colors, turquoise pools encrusted with silica, and one reliable geyser. Access is always open.

Geysir (GAY-seer), discovered and named in 1294, refers to both this general area and a specific geyser, which once spouted as high as 80m (262 ft.), but is now just a calm, steamy vent with occasional hisses and gurgles. Rocks and soap were often dumped into Geysir to make it erupt on demand, only accelerating its demise. Recent research has shown that if the water level were lowered 2m (6½ ft.), Geysir would again erupt every 30 to 60 minutes to a height of 8 to 10m (26–33 ft.). Thankfully **Strokkur (The Churn),** another geyser a few meters (about 10 ft.) from Geysir, spouts reliably every 5 minutes or so. Each spout varies in size, so wait to see at least two or three.

The geyser mechanism is not completely understood, but scientists agree that the eruptions are basically caused by a pressure buildup formed when hot water and gas is trapped beneath a cooler layer of water. Strokkur's eruptions reach as high as 35m (115 ft.). (Americans can be seen affecting nonchalance, since Old Faithful reaches 25–55m/82–180 ft., and Steamboat reaches 90–120m/295–394 ft.) The spouting water is around 257°F (125°C), so be careful not to stand downwind. Geysir is no doubt a natural wonder, but leaving Strokkur aside, there are several other Icelandic geothermal fields of equal or greater interest. Some may even find it anticlimactic, as if they had traveled to Sandwich just to eat a sandwich.

Geysir Museum (Geysisstofa)   This mediocre, catch-all museum is not worth your money. A dark hall has lighted panel displays on geysers, geothermal energy, hydro power, and earthquakes; a video screen shows stock volcano footage; and the upper floor is full of random taxidermy and folk artifacts without context.

Rte. 35, across from Geysir. ℃ 480-6800. www.geysircenter.com. Admission 500kr ($8/£4) adults, 250kr ($4/£2) seniors, 200kr ($3.20/£1.60) children 6–12. For opening hours, see Geysir Center, above.

GULLFOSS ✶✶

Along the Hvitá river, just 7km (4 miles) from Geysir, Gullfoss is Iceland's most iconic and visited waterfall, as elegant as it is massive. Gullfoss means "Golden Falls," the probable source of "Golden Circle." The waterfall is a 5-minute walk from the parking area, and you'll hear it well before you see it. Two smaller falls at the top lead to an L-shaped curtain cascade dropping another 21m (69 ft.) into a 2.5km-long (1½-mile) gorge. The viewing angle doesn't quite let you see where the water hits bottom, but the spray (bring a raincoat) would conceal it anyway. When it's sunny, you can always expect a rainbow; in winter the falls are filigreed in beautiful ice formations.

Near the falls is a **monument to Sigríður Tómasdóttir,** who probably saved Gullfoss from being submerged by a hydroelectric dam in the 1920s. The daughter of the farmer who owned the property, Sigríður threatened to throw herself over the falls if the project went through. The courts ruled against her, but the hydroelectric company gave in to public pressure, and the contract simply expired in 1928.

The **visitor center** (Mon–Fri 9am–6pm; Sat–Sun 9–7pm) is right next to a **cafe and gift shop** (Oct–Apr daily 8am–6pm; May–Sept 8am to as late as 10pm).

NEAR THE GOLDEN CIRCLE

The sights below are listed in the order you would encounter them in a return trip from Gullfoss to Reykjavík. Kerið Crater and Skálholt are also included in some organized Golden Circle tours. With your own car, you might also consider a side trip to the Þjórsárdalur Valley (p. 286) or Hveragerði (p. 160).

SKÁLHOLT

Skálholt, about 40km (25 miles) from the town of Selfoss, is off Route 31, a short detour south from Route 35, which connects Gullfoss and Selfoss. Though few visible remnants exist today, Skálholt was once the most wealthy, populated, and influential settlement in Iceland. In 1056 it became the seat of Iceland's first Catholic bishop. A church built at Skálholt in the mid-12th century from two shiploads of Norwegian timber was the largest wooden structure in medieval Scandinavia (and twice the length of the current church). The clerical class got rich from land tenants, but was also an important force in democratizing education: laypersons of both sexes were enrolled, and classes were conducted in Icelandic as well as Latin. By the early 13th century Skálholt was Iceland's largest settlement, with 200 people; just before the Reformation it owned 10% of all land holdings in the country.

In 1550 Jón Arason, Iceland's last Catholic bishop—in fact, the last Catholic bishop of any Nordic country—was beheaded here along with his sons, after leading a rebellion against the Danish king's order to Lutheranize the country. They were buried without coffins in back of the church, and by the following year, the monarchy had appropriated all church lands. Eighty meters (262 ft.) from the current church lies a crude relief on two slabs of stone, **a monument to Jón Arason,** to whom most Icelanders today can trace their ancestry.

The current **neo-Romanesque church** was inaugurated in 1956. The altarpiece, by prominent Icelandic artist Nína Tryggvadóttir (1913–1968), is an enormous mosaic of Christ with arms outstretched. The pulpit, which long predates the church, has a panel featuring the old Icelandic coat of arms: a filet of cod.

As you enter the church, a door to your left leads to a **museum** (© **486-8872; admission 100kr ($1.60/80p); children under 12 free; mid-May to Aug daily 9am–7pm; Sept to mid-May; ask for key from the office building during working hours) in an underground passage that once connected the medieval church with its school buildings. Skálholt's history is well annotated here, but the centerpieces are the bishops' tombstones and the sarcophagus of Bishop Páll Jónsson (1196–1211), carved from a solid block of sandstone. The sarcophagus was discovered in a 1956 excavation, and the lid was raised in a formal ceremony. Páll's head lay on a stone pillow, his crosier (staff) still on his shoulder, but his Episcopal ring had been stolen by grave robbers.

Skálholt Summer Concerts Festival ⭑   Thirty-three years in the running, this free classical music festival features both contemporary music and early Icelandic music (mostly Baroque) with period instruments. The festival, which is held in the church, begins the first week of July and continues for 5 weeks.

℃ **562-1028.** www.sumartonleikar.is. Free admission. Concerts are usually Sat and Sun at 3 and 5pm, plus a few weekday nights. The Sun 5pm performance is part of a church service.

KERIÐ CRATER

Passersby on Route 35 (15km/9¼ miles northeast of Selfoss) should hop out to see this small but shapely scoria crater, formed 6,500 years ago by a collapsing magma chamber at the end of a volcanic eruption. Kerið is 55m (180 ft.) deep, including the stagnant water at the bottom, and the sides are nicely streaked in red, black, and ochre. Björk once did a concert from a raft in the middle, but the acoustics weren't ideal. A path runs around the rim, but watch your footing.

OUTDOOR ACTIVITIES

RIVER RAFTING   The Hvitá is Iceland's most popular river for white water rafting, with fabulous scenery and easy to medium-difficulty rapids that don't require previous experience. Every afternoon from June through August, the recommended tour operator **Arctic Adventures** (Laugavegur 11; ℃ **562-7000;** www.adventures.is), sets out from its Drumbó base camp, signposted from Rte. 35 about 10 minutes' drive south of Geysir. The three-hour tour—with timeouts for cocoa and cliff jumping—runs 6,590kr ($105/£53) per person, or 9,590kr ($153/£77) with pickup/dropoff in Reykjavík (minimum age 12). For 7,990kr ($128/£64) per person, or 9,990kr ($158/£79) from Reykjavík, more daring paddlers can tackle the river in two-person inflatable canoes.

WHERE TO STAY ALONG THE GOLDEN CIRCLE

ÞINGVELLIR & NEARBY

Fosshótel Nesbúð   This modest bungalow-style hotel is convenient for the Hengill hiking area (see www.fosshotel.is for hiking and biking packages), but it is not everyone's idea of a nature retreat: Right next door is the Nesjavellir Geothermal Power Plant, and, depending on the wind, the eggy smell of sulfur ("eggy" being the polite term) could waft through your window. Rooms are utilitarian but hospitable.

℃ **562-4000** or 482-3415. Fax 482-3414. www.fosshotel.is. 50 units, 30 w/private bathroom. June–Aug 13,900kr ($222/£111) double w/private bathroom; 9,900kr ($158/£79) double w/shared bathroom; from 4,400kr ($70/£32) sleeping-bag accommodation. Rates around 22% lower Mar–May and Sept–Dec; children under 12 stay free in parent's room. Special offers available online. Rates include breakfast. AE, DC, MC, V. **Amenities:** Restaurant; bar; hot tubs; activities desk. *In room:* Free Wi-Fi, no phone. From the Rte. 36/Rte. 360 junction, take Rte. 360 for 12km (7½ miles) and exit at Nesjavellir.

Hótel Valhöll ⭑   The Valhöll has it easy. It's the only non-camping accommodation in Þingvellir National Park and is ideally situated close to the river, the lake, all the historical sights, and in summer, the Prime Minister. Prices reflect their monopoly, but could seem worth it once all the tour buses have disappeared. Standard doubles are a bit small, but all rooms have cozy, plush beds.

℃ **480-7100.** Fax 480-7101. www.hotelvalholl.is. 29 units. Mid-June to mid-Sept 21,000kr–25,000kr ($336–$400/£168–£200) double. Rates around 20% lower in winter. AE, DC, MC, V. **Amenities:** Restaurant; lounge; free Wi-Fi in lounge. *In room:* TV, no phone. From the Þingvellir information center on Rte. 36, turn onto Rte. 362 and follow signs.

GEYSIR

Geysir Guesthouse/Haukadalur III Renovated in 2007, this simple, clean, and dependable guesthouse tends to fill up, so book early. Dinner is served on request, and the hot tub is a great spot for winding down.

Rte. 35, just east of the Geysir Center. © 486-8733 or 893-8733. Fax 872-1537. agustath@visir.is. 12 units w/shared bathroom. May–Sept 9,500kr ($152/£76) double. Discounts available Oct–Apr. Breakfast available for 850kr ($14/£7). MC, V. **Amenities:** Guest kitchen; hot tub.

Hótel Geysir This unremarkable but comfortable hotel is right across the road from the geothermal field, but not even the wedding suite has a view of the erupting geyser. Luxury doubles have king-size beds and Jacuzzis, and apartments and cabins are also available.

At the Geysir Center. © 480-6800. Fax 480-6801. www.geysircenter.is. May–Sept 11,200kr–15,900kr ($179–$254/£90–£127) double. Discounts for children under 13. Rates around 10% lower Oct–Apr. Breakfast available for 1,150kr ($18/£9). **Amenities:** Restaurant; outdoor pool and hot tub; activities desk; horse rental. *In room:* TV, pay Wi-Fi, coffee/tea, no phone.

GULLFOSS

Hótel Gullfoss This recently built hotel is slightly more tasteful than others in the area, with medium-size rooms and an outdoor Jacuzzi. With its strategic position at the northeast corner of the Golden Circle area, Hótel Gullfoss is popular among guests who are heading into the interior.

On Brattholt farm, Rte. 35 between Geysir and Gullfoss. © 486-8979. www.hotelgullfoss.is. 16 units. May 15–Sept 30 16,000kr ($256/£128) double; 19,500kr ($312/£156) triple. Rates around 39% lower Oct–May 14. Rates include breakfast. **Amenities:** Restaurant; bar; outdoor Jacuzzi. *In room:* No phone.

FLÚÐIR

Icelandair Hótel Flúðir ⊀ The pretty town of Flúðir, known for its dairy farms and mushroom greenhouses, is ideal for exploring the Golden Circle and Þjórsárdalur Valley. This not-quite-upscale hotel has the usual single-story pre-fab look, but the medium-size rooms feel unusually relaxing. The village geothermal pool and fitness center are close by, and the restaurant is exceptional (see "Where to Dine," below).

Vesterbrún 1, just off Rte. 30. © 486-6630. Fax 486-6530. www.icehotels.is. 32 units. June–Aug 16,000kr ($256/£128) double. Rates around 21% lower May and Sept; 34% lower Oct–Apr. Breakfast available (1,000kr/$16/£8). AE, MC, V. **Amenities:** Restaurant; bar. *In room:* TV, free Wi-Fi, hair dryer.

REYKHOLT

Guesthouse Húsið This friendly, low-key guesthouse with outdoor hot tub is a good economical option, perfect for exploring the area. Reykholt (not to be confused with the Reykholt in west Iceland) is on Route 35, about 30km (19 miles) northeast of Selfoss.

Bjarkarbraut 26. © 486-8680. husid@best.is. 8 units w/shared bathrooms. June–Sept 15 6,400kr ($102/£51) double. Rates around 15% lower mid-Sept to May. Sleeping-bag accommodation 2,500kr ($40/£20) per person. Breakfast available for 900kr ($14/£7.20). No credit cards. **Amenities:** Guest kitchen; Internet access; Wi-Fi. *In room:* No phone.

WHERE TO DINE

Þingvellir's information center has a basic **cafe** (© 482-2660; Apr–Oct daily 8:30am–8pm; Nov–Mar Sat–Sun 9am–5pm). At Geysir, the Geysir Center has a workable **cafeteria** (© 480-6800; June–Aug daily 9am–10pm, May–Sept daily 9am–8pm, Oct–Apr daily 10am–4pm) and the Hótel Geysir (see above) has a much better **restaurant** (main courses for 2,200kr–3,700kr [£$35–$59/£18–£30]). Gullfoss has **Gullfoss Kaffi** (© 486-6500; Mon–Fri 9am–6pm; Sat–Sun 9am–7pm), suitable for light meals.

Hótel Flúðir ⭐ FRENCH/ICELANDIC   Flúðir's 20-something head chef is a pro-
tégé of Iceland's TV celebrity gourmand, Siggi Hall. The menu is short and sweet,
with just five main courses to maximize the freshness of ingredients, many of which
are locally grown and organic. The five mains could include a fine baked cod with
potato mousse, shallot and carrot comfit and beurre noisette (hazelnut butter).

In Hótel Flúðir (see above). ℭ **486-6630.** Reservations recommended. Main courses 3,150kr–3,950kr
($50–$63/£50–£25). Daily 6:30–9pm.

Lindin ⭐ ICELANDIC   This is the only standout restaurant in the Þingvellir to
Gullfoss stretch of the Golden Circle itinerary. (Laugarvatn is a tiny resort town popular with Reykjavíkians, but holds little for tourists beyond sailboat rental in the lake,
a geothermal sauna at the town pool, and basic services.) Look for fresh char from the
lake, and seasonal offerings such as reindeer, goose, and guillemot.

Lindarbraut 2, 1 block from Rte. 37, Laugarvatn. ℭ **486-1262.** Reservations recommended. Main courses
2,190kr–4,190kr ($35–$67/£18–£34). May–Aug Sun–Thurs noon–11:30pm; Fri–Sat noon–1am. Closed Sept–Apr.

5 The Blue Lagoon (Bláa Lónið)

50km (31 miles) SW of Reykjavík.

The **Blue Lagoon** ⭐⭐ (ℭ **420-8800;** www.bluelagoon.is; June–Aug daily
7:30am–9pm; Sept–May daily 10am–8pm) is the most popular tourist attraction in
Iceland, garnering around 360,000 visitors per year—20% more than Iceland's entire
population. The surreal image of bathers in milky blue water, faces smeared with
white mud, backgrounded by a power plant amid an expanse of black lava, may be the
most common photographic emblem of an Iceland vacation. Not everyone sees what
the fuss is about, but all are guaranteed to walk out with that fresh mineral tingle.

WHAT IS THE BLUE LAGOON?   When the neighboring geothermal power plant
was built, deep boreholes were drilled to extract pressurized, blazing-hot, mineral-rich
water from thousands of feet underground. This water produces electricity by driving
steam turbines. The runoff water, still very hot, is too salty to provide central heating
for homes, so it was piped into the lagoon, which was dug out of the lava field. The
water gets its pearly, bluish color from the combination of algae, silica, and other minerals. (In high summer, when the algae is in full bloom, the water is more green than
blue.) One day, an Icelander suffering from psoriasis popped in for a swim. He noticed
an immediate improvement in his skin condition, and the rest is a textbook marketing success story. (The "Blue Lagoon" was named not long after the Brooke Shields
movie.) Recently a bank of lava was added, to shelter swimmers from the wind and to
block views of the power plant. No doubt this was intentional, but some of the sci-fi
ambience is lost.

The spa has drilled its own water boreholes to regulate the temperature and balance
the mineral and salt content. The salinity matches ocean water and reduces the eggy
smell normally associated with geothermal water. Other spas have mimicked the Blue
Lagoon's success, but none can quite duplicate its water formula. Studies have apparently confirmed the water's effectiveness for psoriasis, and the public health system
even covers some visits here. Claims made for curing arthritis, baldness, negative
karma, and the like are less reliable. The two most common ailments treated by the
Blue Lagoon are jetlag and hangovers.

GETTING THERE

BY CAR   The Blue Lagoon is less than an hour from Reykjavík, and just 15 minutes from Keflavík International Airport. From Route 41, which connects Reykjavík and Keflavík, turn south on Route 43. After about 8km (5 miles), turn right on Route 426 and follow the signs.

BY BUS   A **public bus** goes to the Blue Lagoon from BSÍ terminal (p. 85) in Reykjavík, but **organized bus tours** (see below) include the entrance fee and work out to almost the same price, plus they'll pick you up at your hotel. A free shuttle operated by **Bláa Línan (Blue Line)** connects the Blue Lagoon to the airport and the town of Keflavík, including most hotels, with seven departures daily in summer only. Three rounds also extend to Grindavík. For a schedule, call ℂ **420-6000** or visit www.blue lagoon.com and click "Blue Lagoon Spa."

ORGANIZED TOURS   "Tours" to the Blue Lagoon do not include a guide and are really just shepherding. **Þingvallaleið** (ℂ **511-2600;** www.bustravel.is) has the best deal: 3,500kr ($56/£28) includes Reykjavík hotel pickup and dropoff plus admission to the Lagoon. There are six round-trips daily between 9:30am and 6pm, plus three trips from the Lagoon to the airport. **Reykjavík Excursions** (ℂ **562-1011;** www. re.is) has the same offer for 3,800kr ($61/£30); children 11 to 15 are half-price, under 11 free. They also have an evening tour that leaves Reykjavík at 6pm and gets you back at 10pm—order dinner from the restaurant before you jump in.

THE LAGOON EXPERIENCE

No orientation lecture here—basically you're just handed a locker key and sent off to shower and jump in a hot lake. (Make sure to remove your jewelry; the water damages precious metals, especially silver.) White silica mud, which conditions and exfoliates the skin, is scraped from the bottom and left in buckets for guests to smear all over themselves. The water is around 100°F (36°–39°C), but the temperature can change abruptly as you move around. Watch out for the rectangular wood structures, where hot water is introduced. One billows steam just for effect. The water is completely replaced by natural flow every 40 hours.

Minerals in the lagoon water will coarsen and harden your hair. No real harm is done, but conditioner—provided free in the showers—should be left in while you soak, and long hair should be tied up. If growing dreadlocks, reverse these instructions.

It's a very mixed scene: Icelanders are interspersed among visitors—some of whom aren't sure they want to share a bath with so many strangers. (Be reassured: the water is completely replaced by natural flow every 40 hours.) Private locker rooms will soon be added for those who don't like showering en masse.

Any time of year is great for a visit. Winter nights may be best of all, since you can watch the northern lights in complete comfort with icicles forming in your hair.

Basic admission, for 1,800kr ($29/£14) adults; 1,200kr ($19/£9.60) seniors; 900kr ($14/£7.20) children 12–15, and 11 and under for free, includes entrance to the lagoon, sauna rooms, and a pummeling waterfall. BYOT, otherwise towel rental is 350kr ($5.60/£2.80), and suit rental is 400kr ($6.40/£3.20).

Once you've had an **in-water massage,** you might never go back to on-land ones. You lie floating on your back in womblike weightlessness, with a blanket over you, while the masseuse's hands slide between your back and the floating mat. A 30-minute massage for 4,500kr ($72/£36) is ideal; the shortest is 10 minutes for 1,600kr ($26/£13). Call or check the website for a full menu of fabulous **spa treatments.** Book well in advance.

WHERE TO STAY & DINE

The Blue Lagoon is building a luxury hotel, which should be ready around 2010. Until then, your dining and accommodation options are the nearby Northern Light Inn (below) and several places in Grindavík (6km/3¾ miles away) and Keflavík (20km/12 miles away; see below). The Blue Lagoon's 15-room "Clinic" is quite the undiscovered gem and has anything but an antiseptic hospital atmosphere. It is intended primarily for psoriasis patients, but accepts other guests when space is available. The luxurious rooms all have verandas, and guests enjoy a private section of the lagoon. Rates are 17,000kr ($272/£136) for a double in high season.

The Blue Lagoon has an expedient push-your-tray **cafeteria** and the sit-down **Lava Restaurant,** which is surprisingly good and fairly priced, given the captive clientele. The broad menu has an international range, and several main courses are under 2,000kr ($32/£16). Reservations are recommended for dinner.

Borg B&B   This clean and convivial guesthouse in central Grindavík (p. 159) is 5 minutes from the Blue Lagoon and won't break the bank. Rooms are snug and homey, and breakfast is a predictable array of cereal and cold cuts.

Borgarhraun 2 (by Víkarbraut). ℂ **895-8686.** Fax 462-8696. bjorksv@simnet.is. 7 units w/shared bathroom. May 15–Sept 15 8,400kr ($134/£67) double. Rates around 25% lower off season. Rates include breakfast. MC, V. **Amenities:** Internet terminal; guest kitchen; washing machine.

Northern Light Inn ✿   This hotel's prices somewhat reflect its perceived monopoly, but it's an appealing and welcoming place nonetheless, with woolens handknit by the proprietor for sale in the lobby. The glass-walled dining room and sun porch are great for gazing at the lava field. Rooms are simple and sizeable. The **restaurant,** open daily from 7am to 9pm, delivers what it calls "hearty Nordic soul food," but it has a more healthy and refined touch than the label implies (main courses: 2,000kr–4,000kr [$32–$64/£16–£32]).

Rte. 426, just east of Blue Lagoon. ℂ **426-8650.** Fax 426-8651. www.nli.is. 20 units. June–Aug 15,500kr ($248/£124) double; 19,200 ($307/£154) triple. Rates around 10% lower May and Sept, 25% lower Oct–Apr. Rates include breakfast. MC, V. **Amenities:** Restaurant; free airport transfers. *In room:* TV, free Wi-Fi, fridge.

6 Keflavík

47km (29 miles) SW of Reykjavík.

For many visitors, one look down from their descending plane onto Keflavík's sprawling Lego housing is all they need to know. But **Keflavík** ✿ is an underrated town, and you could do much worse than spend your first or last night here. It's also a good base for all of Reykjanes Peninsula. In early September, the sea cliffs are dramatically lit up for the "Night of Lights," with live music, family entertainment, and a fireworks show.

After WWII, Keflavík prospered from providing services for the neighboring NATO base. The base was abandoned in 2006 (p. 154), but Keflavík maintains a strong fishing economy—established centuries before the Americans arrived. To avoid confusion, be aware that Keflavík has merged with Njarðvík, its less interesting neighbor to the east, to form a single municipal entity called Reykjanesbær. Their joint population is over 10,000—by far the largest settlement on the peninsula.

ESSENTIALS

GETTING THERE   Route 41 connects Reykjavík to Keflavík. **SBK** (ℂ **420-6000;** www.sbk.is) links Reykjavík and Keflavík with five to seven scheduled buses each

Keflavík

ATTRACTIONS ●
Duus Hús **2**
Suðsuðvestur **4**

ACCOMMODATIONS ■
B&B Guesthouse **9**
FIT Hostel **13**
Guesthouse Thverholt **10**
Hótel Keflavik **12**
Hótel Keilir **5**
Icelandair Flughótel **11**
Motel Alex **8**

DINING ◆
Kaffi Duus **1**
Paddy's Irish Pub **6**
Ráin **3**
Thai Keflavik **7**

weekday, and three on weekends for 1,020kr ($16/£8); ages 4–11 half-price. The bus leaves from BSÍ terminal in Reykjavík, stopping at Kringlan Mall, and makes several stops in Keflavík. **Bláa Línan (Blue Line)** also offers service (p. 151).

VISITOR INFORMATION   The Reykjanes Peninsula **tourist office,** Hafnargata 57, Keflavík (✆ **421-5155;** www.reykjanes.is; Mon–Fri 10am–8pm, Sat 10am–4pm) is in Keflavík's library, in a small shopping arcade behind the Flughótel.

EXPLORING KEFLAVÍK

If it's your last day in Iceland, and you'd like one last stroll to commune with the ocean, proceed north from the Duus Hús on the well-worn **path along the clifftop.** On a clear day you can see Reykjavík or even Snæfellsnes Peninsula.

For contemporary art incorporating sound and space, **Suðsuðvestur,** Hafnargata 22 (✆ **421-2225;** www.sudsudvestur.is), right on the main strip, is among Iceland's best exhibition venues. Admission is free, and the space is open daily (2–5:30pm).

Duus Hús ☞   This cultural center inside a large warehouse contains an art museum and cultural exhibit—both very competently curated—but is best known for its collection of almost 100 ship models, all built by local skipper Grímur Karlsson. Since his 1984 retirement, Grímur has constructed over 200 .6m to 1.5m (2–5 ft.) models of actual, midsize Icelandic fishing vessels. (He says he's through model-building, but

The U.S. Pull-Out

September 30, 2006, marked the end of an era at Keflavík's NATO military base. In an understated ceremony, the U.S. flag was lowered, and the Icelandic flag was raised in its place. Iceland now has no armed forces on its territory.

In 1940 the British occupied Iceland to prevent a German takeover. The Americans moved in the following year and have guaranteed Iceland's defense ever since. U.S. forces left after the war, but re-established a large base at Keflavík on behalf of NATO soon after the U.S.–Iceland Defense Agreement of 1951. Iceland was crucial in monitoring Soviet submarines and controlling North Atlantic air space: More Soviet aircraft were intercepted from Keflavík than from any other U.S. base. The base consistently aroused some vocal domestic opposition, but commanded governmental and majority support: In 1974, a parliamentary motion to terminate the 1951 agreement was defeated by a petition signed by over half the country.

Before its closing, the Keflavík base hosted 1,200 U.S. servicemen, 100 Defense Department civilian employees, several fighter jets, and a rescue helicopter squad, at a cost of around $260 million a year to the U.S. government. In March 2006, news of the American pull-out was delivered ham-handedly to the Icelandic government by a State Department underling.

The U.S. is still obliged by treaty to defend Iceland, which could one day regain strategic importance from its proximity to prodigious oil tanker traffic. In the meantime, Iceland has considered starting its own military, but plans for the abandoned base site are still uncertain.

no one believes him.) The models are meticulously detailed but not perfectionistic: a good balance to arouse the model-builder in all of us.

A small concert space hosts everything from piano recitals to juggling performances (call for schedule). You can wander in anytime to see an original work by Iceland's best known painter, Jóhannes Kjarval, on the side wall.

Duusgata 2–10. ✆ **421-3796**. Free admission. Daily 1–5:30pm.

WHALE-WATCHING   For whale-watching, Keflavík has two advantages over Reykjavík. First, the prime sighting spots are a little closer. Second, **Dolphin & Whalespotting** (✆ **421-7777**; www.dolphin.is) is the only tour operator in Iceland that conducts scientific research during its trips. Ongoing studies can be read at www.dolphinresearch.dk, the website of chief guide Marianne Rasmussen. The 3-hour trips aboard the *Moby Dick* promise a 98% success rate, though as with all whale-watching, "success" is sometimes a brief glimpse of a minke whale's back.

Tickets cost 3,400kr ($54/£27) adults, 1,800kr ($29/£14) children ages 7 to 12, and are free for children 6 and under. Departures are daily at 10am in April; daily at 9am May, June, and September 1 to 15; 9am and 1pm July through August. Reservations are recommended.

WHERE TO STAY
As the closest town to the airport, Keflavík has many lodging options, most of which offer free airport transfers.

EXPENSIVE

Hótel Keflavík ✪   Compared to the Flughótel below, this hotel is frumpier but more characterful, with a similar wealth of amenities. Make sure to ask for an ocean view. Standard rooms are not a great value; deluxe rooms are significantly more spacious, with desks and bathtubs, and suites have Jacuzzis. Booking online is key, because you'll probably get at least 20% off published rates. Two good **restaurants** are on the premises: Jia Jia for Chinese and the Sunset for traditional Icelandic. The hotel also maintains a six-room **guesthouse** across the street. The rooms are perfectly acceptable, and you get the same access to hotel facilities for half the room price.

Vatnsnesvegur 12–14. ✆ 420-7000. Fax 420-7002. www.kef.is. Hotel: 68 units. 22,800kr–24,800kr ($365–$397/£182–£198) double; 26,800kr ($429/£214) family room; 28,800kr–29,800kr ($461–$477/£230–£238) suite. Guesthouse: 6 units w/shared bathroom. 9,800kr ($157/£78) double. Rates include breakfast. MC, V. **Amenities:** Restaurants; bar; health club; sauna; solarium; free airport transfer; room service. *In room:* Hotel: TV/DVD, DVDs on request, free Wi-Fi, CD player, minibar, hair dryer, trouser press, safe. Guesthouse: TV, no phone.

Icelandair Flughótel ✪   Right next door to the Hótel Keflavík, this modern business-class hotel meets the usual smart and efficient Icelandair standard. A new wing was recently added, and rooms there have better soundproofing. Deluxe rooms are not much larger and probably not worth the extra money.

Hafnargata 57. ✆ 421-5222. Fax 421-5223. www.icehotels.is. 62 units. 19,200kr–23,200kr ($307–$371/£154–£186) double; 24,100kr ($386/£193) junior suite. Rates around 25% lower Apr–May and mid-Sept to Oct, and around 40% lower Nov–Mar (except for junior suites). Rates include breakfast. AE, MC, V. **Amenities:** Restaurant; spa; free airport transfer; same-day laundry/dry cleaning service. *In room:* TV, free Wi-Fi, minibar, hair dryer, iron.

MODERATE

Hótel Keilir   This new downtown hotel undercuts the nearby competition and offers good, personalized service. Rooms could not have a more basic, minimal, modern Blandinavian look, and bathrooms are large by Icelandic standards. Half the rooms have good ocean views from cement balconies; the other half overlook the main drag. Check online for discounts.

Hafnargata 37. ✆ 420-9800. Fax 422-7941. http://eng.hotelkeilir.is. 40 units. May 15–Sept 15 13,900kr ($222/£111) double; 18,900kr ($302/£151) deluxe double/family room. Rates around 40% lower Sept 16–May 14. Rates include breakfast. MC, V. **Amenities:** Restaurant; bar. *In room:* TV, free Wi-Fi, minibar.

INEXPENSIVE

If you need inexpensive options, **B&B Guesthouse,** Hringbraut 92 (✆ **421-8989;** www.bbguesthouse.is), a short walk from Keflavík's main drag, has 10 comfortable and clean (if not cheery) doubles with shared bathroom for 7,500kr ($120/£60) including breakfast. Amenities include a guest kitchen and free airport transfer. **Guesthouse Thverholt,** Thverholt 5 (✆ **863-9280;** www.bigmap.is/thverholt), a 15-minute walk from town, has doable doubles for 9,000kr ($144/£72). Your cheapest option is **FIT Hostel,** Fitjabraut 6a (✆ **421-8889;** www.hostel.is), in neighboring Njarðvík, where clean, basic doubles start at 4,500kr ($72/£36), and dorm beds are 1,750kr ($28/£14). Amenities include Internet access and a hot tub.

Motel Alex   On the outskirts of town, and just 2 minutes from the airport, this functional and spotless choice has sleeping-bag accommodation in a 10-bed dorm, guesthouse doubles, and 19 self-contained mini-huts with kitchenette, fridge, coffeemaker, and a tiny bathroom all squeezed in . . . and there's a hot tub.

Aðalgata 60. ✆ 421-2800. Fax 421-4285. www.alex.is. 26 units, 7 w/shared bathroom. June 15–Aug 8,900kr ($142/£71) double in guesthouse w/shared bathroom; 9,900kr ($158/£79) hut for 2 persons w/private bathroom; 1,750kr ($28/£14) sleeping-bag accommodation. Children 9 and under free. Guesthouse/hut rates include breakfast.

AE, MC, V. **Amenities:** Hot tub; car rental; bike rental; free airport transfer for guesthouse/hut guests, otherwise 250kr ($4/£2); guest kitchen; free Internet.

WHERE TO DINE/NIGHTLIFE

Keflavík's best down-to-earth local bar, **Paddy's Irish Pub,** Hafnargata 38 (© 421-8900; Sun–Thurs 5pm–1am; Fri–Sat 5pm–5am), has live music Friday and Saturday with no cover—and, of course, Guinness by the pint.

Kaffi Duus CAFE/SEAFOOD This charmer tucked away on the north end of town has nice harbor views, outdoor seating, and fishing paraphernalia adorning the walls. By day it's a casual cafe, by night it's fine dining, and after dinner it's an energetic bar with occasional live music. Fish specials are reliably exceptional.

Duusgata 10. © 421-7080. Reservations required for dinner. Main courses 1,250kr–3,500kr ($20–$56/£10–£28), lunch 1,200kr–1,800kr ($19–$29/£9.60–£14). Daily 10am–10pm; bar open late Fri–Sat.

Ráin ICELANDIC The huge dining area, with great ocean views, arcs around a dance floor and stage, where live bands cover oldies but goodies on weekend nights. LPs lining the walls of the bar harken back to the '50s and '60s, when Keflavík was at the vanguard of the rock 'n' roll revolution, thanks to radio broadcasts from the U.S. military base. The whole place is very appealingly unhip—karaoke machine and all—and the food is easily recommended.

Hafnargata 19. © 478-1945. Reservations recommended. Main courses 2,600kr–4,000kr ($42–$64/£21–£32). Sun–Thurs 11:30am–3pm and 6pm–1am; Fri–Sat 6pm–3am.

Thai Keflavík THAI Food here lacks the extra fine touch, but it's tasty and hearty, with big portions and good prices. Spiciness levels are moderate, and the curries and pad thai go down well.

Hafnargata 39. © 421-8666. Main courses 1,090kr–1,490kr ($17–$24/£8.70–£12). Mon–Fri 10am–11pm.

7 Reykjanes Peninsula

47km (29 miles) NE of Reykjavík.

From Keflavík airport, this southwestern extremity of Iceland appears to be a bleak and uniform expanse of lava rock. But however barren and austere, Reykjanes is a wondrous and geologically varied landscape. The north coast is indeed flat and contains most of the peninsula's population. The western, southern, and interior regions, on the other hand, contain striking volcanic ranges, geothermal hotspots, and sea cliffs full of nesting birds. Some parts are so remote that only a few local farmers in search of stray sheep have ever set foot in them. A trail system is well developed, but hiking routes are often unmarked, and it can be difficult to find drinking water or a soft place to pitch a tent.

ESSENTIALS

GETTING AROUND Reykjanes is really only accessible by car or organized tour. Regular bus routes do extend to Garður and Sandgerði in the northeast and Grindavík on the south coast, but departures are few and far between. **SBK** (© 420-6000; www.sbk.is) connects Garður and Sandgerði to Keflavík and Reykjavík twice a day. **Reykjavík Excursions** (© 562-1011; www.re.is) connects Reykjavík and Grindavík three times a day, stopping at the Blue Lagoon. The **Bláa Línan (Blue Line;** p. 151) shuttle runs to Grindavík three times a day.

ORGANIZED TOURS Iceland Excursions (℗ 540-1313; www.iceland excursions.is) has a half-day Super Jeep tour of the wilds of Reykjanes Peninsula for 12,000kr ($192/£96), and a bus tour around the coast, with optional dropoff at the Blue Lagoon, for 4,200kr ($67/£34).

VISITOR INFORMATION Keflavík's **information center,** Hafnargata 57 (℗ 421-5155; www.reykjanes.is; Mon–Fri 10am–8pm, Sat 10am–4pm) and Grindavík's **Saltfish Museum** (p. 159) are the best bets.

The Myndkort **map,** *Reykjanes,* assembled from aerial satellite photographs, is an essential resource for identifying walking and hiking routes.

EXPLORING REYKJANES

The sights listed below follow a counterclockwise loop around the peninsula, but you can also follow the route in reverse.

GARÐUR & GARÐSKAGI

Garður, 15 minutes' drive northwest from Keflavík, is the northernmost town on the peninsula. Its main tourist draw is **Garðskagi,** a rocky point with two lighthouses and a quirky folk museum. To reach Garðskagi, drive through Garður and follow the coast toward the lighthouse in the distance. (As you leave town, consider stopping at **Útskálakirkja,** the lovely church visible from the road on your right.) The larger lighthouse, **Garðskagaviti,** is the tallest in Iceland; the outmoded 1897 lighthouse still stands close by. Built in 1944, Garðskagaviti was a gift from American servicemen grateful for being rescued from a sinking U.S. Coast Guard vessel. Visitors can climb all the way to the 360-degree lookout platform at the top. (If it's locked, ask for a key in the museum.) The last stretch of the climb involves steep, narrow steps and a trap door. Garðskagi offers a broad, flat ocean vista, bird sightings, and lots of wind.

Garður Peninsula Historical Museum (Byggðasafn Garðskaga) 𝕖 This small-town folk museum next to the lighthouse has no exceptional treasures and specializes in mid-century boat engines. Not too enticing, it would seem, but admission is free, and the back rooms—full of old radios, sewing machines, and antiquated domestic knickknacks—sweetly conjure another era. Also look for the homemade organ. The upstairs **cafeteria** (℗ 422-7214) is open from 1pm to midnight daily from April through October.

By Garðskagi lighthouse. ℗ 422-7220. Free admission. Apr–Oct daily 1–5pm.

SANDGERÐI

Sandgerði is a busy fishing village 5km (3 miles) south of Garður on Route 45. The Nature Center, below, is on the north end of town, in a cluster that also includes two art galleries, the Mamma Mía pizzeria, and the Vitinn restaurant.

Hallgrímur Pétursson, Iceland's most revered clergyman, had his first parish at **Hvalsneskirkja** 𝕖, 5km (3 miles) south of Sandgerði. Hallgrímur's only child, Steinunn Hallgrímsdóttir, died here in 1649, profoundly affecting his religious mission. Her gravestone was found in 1964 when the church's stone walkway was built. It now sits near the altar of the beautifully restored church, its crude lettering remarkably intact. Someone should be around to let you in during the summer from 8am to 4pm, but if not, you can borrow a key from the Nature Center, below. The area around the church has only one full-time resident, now in his late 80s.

Fræðasetrið Nature Center   Iceland is rife with local natural history museums that amount to little more than taxidermy displays. This museum adds some unusual specimens—barnacles, shark eggs, and a walrus, for instance—and also hosts actual research on marine invertebrates. Kids can go to the beach, gather seawater and bugs, and examine them under microscopes. A new permanent exhibit on Jean-Baptiste Charcot (1867–1936) a French explorer who reached the South Pole in 1910 and died near Sandgerði in a 1936 shipwreck, does not yet have English translations.

Garðvegur 1, off Rte. 45, Sandgerði. (☎) **423-7551.** www.sandgerdi.is. Admission 400kr ($6.40/£3.20) adults; 300kr ($4.80/£2.40) children ages 6–12; ages 5 and under free. Mon–Fri 9am–5pm; Sat–Sun 1–5pm.

THE WESTERN COAST

2km (1¼ miles) south of Hvalsneskirkja is a junction. The road bearing right dead ends at a bright yellow lighthouse. The new road bearing left continues along the coast until it joins Route 44 near Hafnir. Until 2006, when the nearby NATO base was abandoned (p. 154), this connecting road could not be built because of security concerns.

Hafnir is a sleepy town without much to see. Proceeding south along Route 425, the landscape is suddenly dominated by harsh black lava with little vegetation. This was one of three areas in Iceland used by the Apollo flight crew to practice moonwalking. About 5km (3 miles) south of Hafnir is a parking area on the right, with a small sign indicating the trailhead for **Hafnaberg Cliffs,** a prime nesting site for guillemots, kittiwakes, fulmars, and razorbills. The 1½-hour round-trip hike is recommended for birders, but you'll find more visually dramatic seacliffs at Reykjanes, below. If you do walk to Hafnaberg, keep an eye out for whales.

Another 2km (1¼ miles) farther south is a well-marked turnoff for the **Bridge Between Two Continents,** which is a pointless waste of time. A 15m (49-ft.) footbridge spans an ordinary rift in the rock, claimed to be the dividing line between the North American and Eurasian tectonic plates. Scientifically, this is nonsense; the rifts are all over the Reykjanes Peninsula, in anything but a straight line. Admission is free, but the plan is to sell "I spanned two continents" certificates to the unwary.

REYKJANES

"Reykjanes" means "Smoky Point." The name originally referred only to this southwest corner of the peninsula, with its steamy geothermal hotspots. The highlight is **Valahnúkur** (★★), a magical stretch of coastline where you can clamber up grassy banks and peer over the indented cliffsides at crashing waves, while thousands of birds bob around in the wind currents. To get to Valahnúkur, turn right off Route 425 just before the power plant, and make your way past the lighthouse on the unsurfaced roads. The area can be fully explored in an hour or so. Be very careful at the cliff edges: winds can be extremely gusty, and some grass-tufted patches of earth may not support your weight. The striking, near-cylindrical island **Eldey,** a bird preserve 15km (9¼ miles) offshore, is part of the same volcanic rift line that formed Valahnúkur.

You can return to Route 425 by a different dirt road, which runs south of the power plant and its runoff lake. Once you've passed the lighthouse, just head for the steam rising from a small hill. This is **Gunnuhver,** a typical geothermal field swathed with mineral colors and thick, eggy vapors. Gunnuhver is named for Gunna, a woman who, according to legend, was accused of murder and thrown into the boiling hot spring. *Warning:* Tread carefully: Trail guidance is sparse, and one false step could melt the rubber right off your soles.

GRINDAVÍK

The 17km (11 miles) stretch on Route 425 east from Reykjanes is practically deserted, so it's arresting to suddenly encounter Grindavík's clustered mass of prefab houses and difficult-to-navigate harbor. With its technologically advanced fish-processing plant, the town gives off an industrious and forward-looking air. Reykjanes has little arable land, so local economies are especially dependent on fishing. A helpful **visitor information desk** is inside the Saltfish Museum, below.

Arctic Horses (Arctic Hestar), Hestabrekka 2, Grindavík (© **696-1919;** www.arctichorses.com), leads 90-minute rides around the scenic peninsula southeast of Grindavík for 4,800kr ($77/£38) per person.

The Icelandic Saltfish Museum (Saltfisksetur Íslands)
In his novel *Salka Valka,* Halldór Laxness famously wrote with deadpan irony, "When all is said and done, life is first and foremost salt fish." The motto "Life is saltfish" was adopted by this museum, which attempts to re-create the taste and feel of a fishing village in the 1930s, the heyday of the salt cod industry. No doubt Iceland was built on saltfish, and every effort is made here to convey that history through text, costumed dummies, sound effects, photos, and an affecting film of Icelanders on fish-processing assembly lines.

Hafnargata 12a (between Ránargata and Mánagata). © **420-1190.** www.saltfisksetur.is. Admission 500kr ($8/£4) adults; 250kr ($4/£2) children ages 8–16. Daily 11am–6pm.

SELATANGAR

Route 427 proceeds east from Grindavík to Krýsuvík, fairly close to the south coast. This road will soon be paved, but if you continue directly back to Reykjavik, the route can be a bit rough. This has discouraged tourism to this eastern region of Reykjanes Peninsula, which feels wonderfully remote.

Twelve kilometers (7 miles) east of Grindavík, a small brown sign on the right points to **Selatangar** ⸎, a fishing settlement abandoned since 1880. The gravel road proceeds 1.7km (1 mile) to a small parking area near the shore. From there it's a 10-minute walk east, mostly on black sand, to an assortment of crude stone foundations for huts and storehouses. The setting is stark, poignant, and a little spooky. (Residents claimed they were chased out by a ghost named "Tumi.") Looking east, you can see this was the first decent place to land a boat for quite a stretch.

ROUTE 428

Returning to Route 427 and continuing east, the junction with Route 428 is 3km (2 miles) ahead. **Route 428** ⸎⸎, a spectacularly scenic drive across an interior highland plateau, can be tackled in a conventional car in summer, but only by proceeding slowly and carefully. You'll need at least an hour to get to the Route 42 junction north of Kleifarvatn Lake. Along the way are several opportunities for short hikes to viewpoints on the ridges east of the road. The Myndkort photomap (see "Visitor Information," p. 133) is particularly useful for tracking a route.

KRÝSUVÍK

If instead of turning onto Route 428, you continue straight on Route 427, you'll reach **Krýsuvík Church (Krýsuvíkurkirkja)** in 9km (5½ miles). This tiny, brown, 1857 wood church once served the surrounding farm, which is now abandoned. A priest from Hafnarfjörður, who visits twice a year to conduct services, calls it "the most modest church in Iceland." Leave a note in the guestbook; he likes to read it aloud to congregants. The church is always open, even in the off season. The altarpiece, mounted in summer only, is an abstract work in broad swaths of primary colors by **Sveinn Björnsson** (1925–1997). Sveinn, a sailor inspired by Picasso, primitivism, and the local scenery, lived in the blue house with the red roof visible to the north along Route 42. This house, crammed with Sveinn's paintings, turns into a **museum** (www.sveinssafn.is) on the first Sunday of each summer month (noon–5pm).

Across Route 427, opposite the church, is **Arnarfell,** a large, distinct hill with a rocky crest. Clint Eastwood, in his WWII movie *Flags of Our Fathers,* used Arnarholl to film the climactic scene, which reenacts the famous photograph of U.S. Marines raising the flag at Iwo Jima.

Just east of the church, Route 427 ends at Route 42. Turning right leads you on another beautiful drive to Þorlákshöfn and Hveragerði. Turning left takes you north toward Reykjavík through the Reykjanesfólkvangur wilderness reserve.

REYKJANESFÓLKVANGUR

Only 40km (25 miles) from Reykjavík, **Reykjanesfólkvangur** ⟨★ was designated a nature reserve in 1975 to protect the region's lava formations around ridge volcanoes. Heading north from Krýsuvík on Route 42, the first notable landmark is **Grænavatn,** an oddly tinted green lake inside an explosion crater. A parking area is on the right, and it's worth popping out for a quick look. Another kilometer (¾ mile) farther north is the **Seltún geothermic field** ⟨★. A short loop trail proceeds through the chemical odors and bubbling mud cauldrons.

Slightly farther north is **Kleifarvatn** ⟨★, a large, deep, and starkly beautiful lake with black sand beaches. Intake and outflow of water is very limited, and in 2000, water levels dropped considerably after earthquakes opened fissures on the lake bottom. The scenery is well enjoyed from the spit of **Lambatangi,** a short walk from the road on the southern end of the lake. Watch out for Kleifarvatn's resident monster, which is shaped like a worm but large as a whale.

WHERE TO STAY & DINE

For nearby accommodations, consult the Keflavík and Blue Lagoon sections earlier in this chapter.

Garður's folk museum has a **cafeteria,** and Sandgerði has two **restaurants.** In Grindavík, **Cactus,** Hafnargata 6, where it dead-ends past Ægisgata (ⓒ **426-9999;** Sun–Thurs 6pm–1am; Fri–Sat 6pm–3am), also known as Lukku Láki, is an eclectically designed restaurant and sports bar with main courses in the 750kr to 2,000kr ($12–$32/£6–£16) range. **Salthúsið,** Stamphólsvegur 2 (ⓒ **426-9700;** Mon–Fri 5–9pm; Sat–Sun 11:30am–9pm), is a bit more upscale and specializes in *bacalao,* the Spanish take on salted cod.

---

8 Hveragerði, Selfoss & Nearby

Hveragerði is 45km (28 miles) SE of Reykjavík; Selfoss is 57km (35 miles) SE of Reykjavík.

Unless you're planning a hiking expedition into Hengill, this region is usually more of an operational base or stopover than a destination in itself. Nonetheless, don't pass through on the Ring Road without considering a hike into the geothermally active valley **Reykjadalur,** an exploration of the cave **Raufarhólshellir,** or a gluttonous lobster dinner at **Fjöruborðið** in Stokkseyri (all below).

ESSENTIALS

GETTING THERE Hveragerði and Selfoss are both along Route 1. Frequent buses run daily from BSÍ terminal in Reykjavík to both towns, which are routine stops in many southern itineraries. A ticket to Selfoss is around 1,300kr ($21/£11). **Þingvallaleið** (© 511-2600; www.bustravel.is) has one daily bus to and from Eyrarbakki and Stokkseyri via Þorlákshöfn, and one daily runs connects Selfoss to Eyrarbakki and Stokkseyri.

VISITOR INFORMATION The **regional tourist office** (© 483-4601; www.southiceland.is; Mon–Fri 9am–4:30pm, Sat 10am–2pm) for all of south Iceland is in Hveragerði, at Sunnumörk 2–4. For Selfoss, Eyrarbakki, and Stokkseyri, tourist information is inside the **Selfoss library** (Rte. 1, just east of the roundabout; © 482-2422; http://tourinfo.arborg.is; Mon–Fri 10am–7pm, Sat 11am–2pm).

EXPLORING THE AREA
HVERAGERÐI

Hveragerði is at the southern end of an active geothermal region that extends north through Hengill to Lake Þingvallavatn. (One Hveragerði family recently discovered that a hot spring had erupted into their living room.) Since the 1920s, the town has harnessed this energy to grow fruits and vegetables in **geothermal greenhouses.** At night the greenhouses lend the town an orangey glow.

The horse farm **Eldhestar** (© 480-4800; www.eldhestar.is), on Route 1, about 2km (1¼ miles) east of Hveragerði, is highly recommended for short local rides or longer trips on horseback into the Hengill hiking area. Beginners are welcome.

Eden This geothermal greenhouse is worked into several bus tour itineraries. The plants include bananas, papayas and other unlikely specimens, but the novelty wears off rather quickly. Eden mostly exists to sell troll figurines and puffin snow-domes.

Austurmörk 2. © 483-4900. Mid-June to Aug daily 9am–11pm; Sept to mid-June daily 9am–7pm. Free admission.

NLFÍ Rehabilitation and Health Clinic Those who take their spa treatments very seriously should book a deep heat mud bath—or even an extended stay—at this well-regarded clinic. NLFÍ developed innovative treatments for arthritis and other medical conditions using natural materials, and recently branched into the general spa market.

Frænmörk 10. © 483-0300. www.hnlfi.is.

HENGILL HIKING AREA 🐎🐎

Hengill is not Iceland's most dramatic or well-known hiking and camping region, but the mountain's august slopes and steaming geothermal valleys have a quiet authority and devoted following. The most common access points are Hveragerði to the south and Nesjavellir (p. 146) at lake Þingvallavatn to the north. Hengill itself is an 803m (2,634-ft.) active volcano, though its last eruption was about 2,000 years ago. Trail information is well mapped at all access points, and trails are well pegged in varied colors. Guided hiking and biking tours leave from the Fosshotel Nesbúð (p. 148), next to Nesjavellir.

RAUFARHÓLSHELLIR 🐎🐎

Of all the lava tube caves in Iceland, this one perhaps best combines accessibility and mystique. Raufarhólshellir is essentially an empty riverbed of lava, formed about 3,700 years ago. At 1,350m (4,429 ft.), it's Iceland's second-longest cave, with over 1km (¾ mile) of complete blackness. The cave ceiling reaches as high as 10m (33 ft.)

A Day Hike in Hengill

A hike to **Reykjadalur** ⚞⚟, or "Smoky Valley," is a great way to experience the Hengill area's best scenery—capped off with a swim in a natural hot spring—in as little as 2½ hours. Don't forget your bathing suit.

From Hveragerði, head north on the main street, Breiðamörk, ascending to a level expanse surrounded by mountains. At a division in the road, bear left onto the gravel road marked "Reykjadalur." The road ends at a parking area at the base of the mountains, next to the Varmá River. Across the bridge is a signboard with a trail map of the area. The trail you're looking for is called Rjúpnabrekkur (Ptarmigan Slopes). It proceeds directly from the signboard and is marked with stakes painted like matchsticks.

After an initial ascent, a lesser descent leads into the Reykjadalur valley. The trail then crosses the stream and passes several gurgling mud pools. In just over an hour, you'll reach the head of the valley, with Ökelduhnúkur mountain straight ahead of you. A hot, steaming stream leads uphill to the left (west) along the Klambragil Valley. A cold stream leads uphill to the right (east), where a camping hut is visible. Where the waters merge is the place to swim. If it's too hot, head back downstream to find a suitable temperature.

An enjoyable hour-long trail circumnavigates Ökelduhnúkur. Several trails branch off from this loop trail, but if you stick with the inside route, you'll end up back at the swimming spot. The circuit is spoiled a bit by power lines but has several more geothermal hotspots. Ambitious hikers could continue all the way to Þingvallavatn in a day (after arranging transport on both ends).

and averages 12m (39 ft.) in thickness. The ground is strewn with boulders and ice, making some passages difficult to traverse. The most spectacular lava contortions are at the very end, but fascinating ice formations can be seen throughout the route year-round. Entering the cave should not be attempted without a strong flashlight, warm clothing, and good shoes. A helmet and knee pads would be ideal. Exploring the full length of the cave should take around 2 hours. The unmarked parking area is just off Route 39, about 2km (1¼ mile) west of the Route 39/Route 38 intersection, between Hveragerði and Þorlákshöfn.

SELFOSS

With over 6,000 residents, Selfoss is an important trade center and the largest city in south Iceland, though it doesn't really compel a travelers' attention. Selfoss sprang into existence in 1891, when a bridge was built over the river Öfulsá, replacing ferry transport across the river farther south. The most noteworthy feature is the town's **geothermal pool,** it has a waterslide designed to look like a wedge of Swiss cheese.

EYRARBAKKI

From Selfoss, the coastal towns of Eyrarbakki and Stokkseyri can be reached in about 10 minutes by car. The route proceeds across the Flói marshland, an important breeding ground for birds. Both towns were once prominent fishing and trading centers, but neither had a natural harbor, so they were eclipsed by the bridge at Selfoss and a new harbor at Þorlákshöfn to the west.

Eyrarbakki was once the largest community in southwestern Iceland, and has an unusual concentration of turn-of-the-last-century houses. As you enter town, the dominant white building is the **Litla-Hraun jail,** Iceland's largest. The country's total prison population is under 200, so there should be more than enough room.

Kayakaferðir Stokkseyri, Heiðarbrún 24 (© **896-5716;** www.kajak.is; closed Nov–Mar), runs 1- to 2-hour kayak tours in nearby coastal lagoons and marshland canals full of birdlife.

Museums of Eyrarbakki   This complex of buildings on the western edge of town makes the usual heroic effort to document and preserve local history. The main feature is **Húsið** (The House), a restored 1765 home ordered from a Scandinavian catalog, and the town's only wooden structure at that time. Period-themed rooms have hit-or-miss artifacts—spoons carved from whale teeth, an old loom, products from a defunct drugstore. (The oddest juxtaposition is a club for battering baby seals next to a photo of Brigitte Bardot cuddling one.) The small **Egg House** in back has a nice collection of bird eggs and taxidermy. The **Maritime Museum,** included in the admission price, is 100m (328 ft.) away across a field; look for the flagpole. Items on display include leather seaman outfits softened with fish oil, shark hooks and porpoise harpoons, and a 1915 fishing boat for 16 sailors.

Eyrargata. © **483-1504.** www.husid.com. Admission 500kr ($8/£4) adults; ages 12 and under free. Jun–Aug daily 11am–6pm; Apr–May and Sept–Oct Sat–Sun 2–5pm.

STOKKSEYRI
Stokkseyri has a bizarre mix of tourist attractions, though most visitors are here for the excellent lobster restaurant (see "Where to Dine," below).

The Ghost Center   Visitors here don headphones, and for 40 expensive minutes proceed from one creepy installation to the next listening to traditional Icelandic ghost stories. The props are decent, if low-budget. (The smoke machine produces an eggy sulfur smell, which somehow ruins the illusion.) Not all the stories will resonate with non-Icelanders, and you'll spend lots of time standing in place; but the tour may still produce a few goose bumps. The Ghost Center is not recommended for children ages 12 and under.

Hafnargata 9. © **483-1202.** www.draugasetrid.is. Admission 1,500kr ($24/£12) adults; 990kr ($16/£7.90) seniors and children ages 12–16. June–Aug daily 1–6pm; Sept–May Sat–Sun 1pm–6pm.

Hunting Museum   This shrine to trophy hunting is on the right as you enter town. The museum has an enormous private collection of stuffed victims shot by a man-and-woman team; it includes a polar bear, lion, zebra, and hyena. Exhibits even include racks of hunting handguns and framed displays of specialized bullets.

Eyrarbraut 49. © **483-1558.** www.hunting.is. Admission 1,000kr ($16/£8) adults; 500kr ($8/£4) children ages 6–12. Mar–Oct daily 11am–6pm; Nov and Feb Sat–Sun 11am–6pm; closed Dec–Jan.

Icelandic Wonders   This rather pathetic, overpriced, catch-all museum—also known as "Elves, Trolls, and Northern Lights"—has tried to capitalize on the success of the Ghost Center next door. In a typical installation, elf actors sit around a dinner table; if you're not with a group tour, they'll probably just use the elf mannequins. Younger children might be briefly pacified.

Hafnargata 9. © **483-1202.** www.icelandicwonders.com. Admission 1,500kr ($24/£12) adults; 1,000kr ($16/£8) seniors and children ages 7–16; ages 6 and under free. Sat–Sun 1–8:30pm.

WHERE TO STAY

HVERAGERÐI

The South Iceland tourist office in Hveragerði (see "Visitor Information," above) can help you book regional accommodations for a 300kr ($4.80/£2.40) fee.

Guesthouse Frost and Fire ★ *(Finds*   This is one of the surprisingly few Icelandic guesthouses that are well landscaped into a riverbend. Views over the Varmá river can be enjoyed from guest rooms, the two hot tubs, and the light-filled dining room, where organic breakfasts are served. Each room is named for the artist whose work boldly lines the walls. (You can preview each artist through the "Art Gallery" link at the website; we'd go for the Arnar Herbertsson.)

Hverhamar (just off Breiðamörk, at the northern end of town). © 483-4959. Fax 483-4914. www.frostandfire.is. 14 units. May–Sept 14,300kr ($229/£114) double. Rates around 18% lower Oct–Apr. Rates include breakfast. **Amenities:** Small outdoor pool and hot tubs; sauna. *In room:* TV, Wi-Fi.

Guesthouse Frumskógar *(Value*   This is a cheap and functional option that will not arouse any complaints about comfort or cleanliness. The family-friendly studio apartments sleep two to four and have kitchenettes, fridge, coffeemaker, and Wi-Fi.

Frumskógar 3 (off Heiðmörk, 2 blocks west of Breiðamörk). © 896-2780. www.frumskogar.is. 10 units. 6,100kr ($98/£49) double w/shared bathroom; 11,000kr ($176/£88) studio apartment w/private bathroom. Apt. rates 18% lower Mar–May and Sept–Oct, 27% lower Nov–Feb. Discounts on longer stays. Breakfast available for 800kr ($13/£6.50). **Amenities:** Hot tub. *In room:* TV, no phone. Studios have TV/DVD, CD player, Wi-Fi, fridge, coffeemaker.

Hótel Eldhestar   You don't have to be an equestrian to stay at this smart country hotel on one of Iceland's best horse farms. Rooms have a slightly softer and more personal touch than the Icelandic standard, and the hotel has been approved by the eco-certification organization Nordic Swan for its environmentally sound practices.

On Rte. 1, about 2km (1¼ miles) east of Hveragerði. © 480-4800. Fax 480-4801. www.hoteleldhestar.is. 26 units. June–Aug 15,600kr ($250/£125) double; 3,000kr ($48/£24) per person sleeping-bag accommodation. Rates around 30% lower Apr–May and Sept–Oct, and 45% lower Nov–Mar, except for sleeping-bag accommodation. Rates include breakfast. **Amenities:** Bar; hot tub. *In room:* TV, Wi-Fi.

Hótel Örk   Rooms all have bathtubs, but otherwise arouse little excitement. The main draw here is the wealth of facilities, including tennis courts, golf course, Ping-Pong table, sauna, and swimming pool area, with hot tubs, kiddie pool, and waterslide. Superior doubles give you lots of extra space and a bigger TV.

Breiðamörk 1. © 483-4700. Fax 483-4775. www.hotel-ork.is. 85 units. May–Sept 17,600kr–24,150kr ($282–£286/£141–£193) double; 19,650kr ($314/£157) triple. Rates around 37% lower Oct–Apr. Rates include breakfast. MC, V. **Amenities:** Restaurant; outdoor pool; golf course; tennis courts; sauna; hot tubs; room service. *In room:* TV, Wi-Fi, fridge, hair dryer.

SELFOSS

Hótel Selfoss   This upmarket hotel is clearly the place to make an important business deal followed by a wind-down in the sauna and "rainwater shower" at the brand-new in-house Northern Light Spa. But the only way to lend character to the bland (if comfortable) rooms is to get one facing the river.

Eyrarvegur 2. © 480-2500. www.hotelselfoss.is. 99 units. 17,900kr–20,900kr ($286–$334/£143–£167) double. Rates around 28% lower Jan–Apr, 23% lower Oct–Dec. Rates include breakfast. **Amenities:** Spa; Wi-Fi. *In room:* TV, Internet connection, minibar, hair dryer, safe.

Menam Guesthouse   Perched above a mediocre Thai restaurant of the same name, these well-priced rooms are clean and well-maintained, albeit with a bit of traffic noise. The common TV lounge, which is musty and worn, still manages to be both homey and welcoming.

Eyrarvegur (Rte. 34), just off the central roundabout. © 482-4099. www.menam.is. 5 units w/shared bathrooms. 6,200kr ($99/£50) double; 7,300kr ($117/£58) triple. MC, V. *In room:* No phone.

WHERE TO DINE

Hveragerði's greenhouse products can be sampled at town markets; try the *hverabrauð*, a dark, cakey rye bread cooked in a geothermal oven. **Eden** (see above) has a basic cafeteria-style restaurant. Other options in Hveragerði include **Kjöt & Kúnst,** Breiðamörk 21 (© **483-5010;** Mon–Fri 10am–8pm), a good deli with a stool counter for eating in—or you can take out a picnic—and **Cafe Kidda Rót,** Sunnumörk 2 (© **552-8002;** Sun–Thurs 11am–10pm, Fri–Sat 11am–11:30pm), a popular pizza and burger hangout with some fish and Chinese dishes thrown in for variety.

Fjöruborðið ☆☆ SEAFOOD   Many Reykjavíkians trek all the way to this famed lobster house just for dinner. Beef, lamb, fish, and vegetarian dishes are on hand, but most guests end their meal slurping their garlic- and butter-drenched fingers over a huge pile of exoskeletons. An Icelandic lobster, more accurately termed a *langoustine,* is hardly larger than a jumbo shrimp, and extracting the meat doesn't require the usual heroics with tiny forks or shell-cracking implements.

Eyrarbraut 3a, Stokkseyri. © **483-1550.** www.fjorubordid.is. Reservations recommended. Main courses 1,700kr–3,800kr ($27–$61/£14–£30). Jun–Aug daily noon–10pm; May and Sept Mon–Fri 5–9pm, Sat–Sun noon–9pm; Oct–Apr Wed–Fri 5–9pm, Sat–Sun noon–9pm.

Hótel Örk ICELANDIC   This is your best option in town for finer dining. The menu is small and focused and seasonal, adding a fine touch to standard Icelandic preparations of lamb, beef, and especially seafood: a bacalao with basil and artichokes, perhaps.

Breiðamörk 1, Hveragerði's. © **483-4700.** Main courses 2,650kr–4,100kr ($42–$66/£21–£33). MC, V. Daily 10am–10pm.

Kaffi Krús ☆ CAFE/BISTRO   The town's most appealing hangout has excellent cakes and satisfying light meals. You won't go wrong with the tandoori chicken breast or the bagels and lox. Some nights the cafe features live music, which is usually on the mellow, acoustic side.

Austurvegur 7 (Rte. 1, opposite the library), Selfoss. © **482-1672.** Main courses 1,500kr–2,200kr ($24–$35/£12–18). MC, V. Sun–Thurs 10am–midnight; Fri–Sat 10am–2am; kitchen closes at 9pm.

Rauða Húsið ☆ ICELANDIC   Settle in for a leisurely, classy dinner at "The Red House," a respected Eyrarbakki institution with local history lessons on the menu. The house special fish soup—creamy yet delicate with plenty of vegetables—can be ordered as a main course, but you'll probably want to vary your meal and make it an appetizer. For a main course, try a "fish duet" or beef tenderloin with Madeira glaze. Dessert should not be missed. Afterward, retire to the cellar pub decorated with wooden casks.

Búðarstíg 4 (coastal Rd., at Bakarísstígur), Eyrarbakki. © **483-3330.** www.raudahusid.is. Main courses 1,990kr–5,400kr ($32–$86/£16–£43). Sun–Thurs 11:30am–9pm; Fri–Sat 11:30am–10pm.

7

West Iceland

Snæfellsnes peninsula and the West-fjords—the most compelling scenery of Iceland's west coast—are unjustly neglected by travelers reluctant to make committed detours from the Ring Road. Snæfellsnes is closer to Reykjavík and sees a fair number of visitors, even on day trips from the capital. The Westfjords, on the other hand, receive only 3% of Iceland's tourist traffic. Surely this is the country's highest ratio of beauty to beauty-seekers.

Snæfellsnes, a 70km-long (43 miles) finger of land pointing westward, is closely identified with Snæfellsjökull, the glacier near its tip. Views and ascents of the glacier are unforgettable, but the peninsula has plenty more to offer and can easily sustain 2 or even 3 days of exploring. Circling the periphery is one of Iceland's most enjoyable road trips, especially if outdoor activities are tacked on. Possibilities include some splendid coastal walks; whale-watching from Ólafsvík; horseback riding along beaches on the south coast; and kayak or boat tours among the low-lying islands and mudflats of Breiðafjörður, a thriving habitat for birds and seals.

The Westfjords form a wildly convoluted claw-shape on the map, enticement enough for many would-be explorers. The area comprises a tenth of Iceland's landmass but a third of its coastline, and round every bend is some new variation on how mountains can tumble to the sea. The Westfjords have some of Iceland's grandest bird cliffs, loveliest sand beaches, and loneliest upland moors. Winters are relatively long and harsh, and the population is only 7,500—or less than one inhabitant per square kilometer. The image of the Westfjords as inaccessible, however, is exaggerated. Much of its road network is bumpy and decrepit, but daily flights to Ísafjörður, a likable and sophisticated town, take just 40 minutes from Reykjavík. The next morning you could board a boat for Hornstrandir Nature Reserve, one of Iceland's most ruggedly beautiful and pristine hiking areas. By afternoon you might be staring down an arctic fox, or peering over a dizzying bird cliff at the crashing surf, with civilization left completely behind.

1 Borgarnes, Reykholt & Farther Inland

Overland routes from Reykjavík to all points in west Iceland pass through this region, which draws many historically-minded travelers. Borgarnes has an engaging new museum on the twin themes of the first settlers in Iceland and *Egils Saga*, a classic of medieval European literature. Saga enthusiasts also make pilgrimages to Reykholt, once the residence of Snorri Sturluson, the most prominent historical figure of Iceland's saga-writing age. Farther inland are two of Iceland's most extensive lava caves, Surtshellir and Víðgelmir. From here, an alternate route south to Þingvellir passes between glacier-capped mountains for a taste of Iceland's starkly beautiful interior.

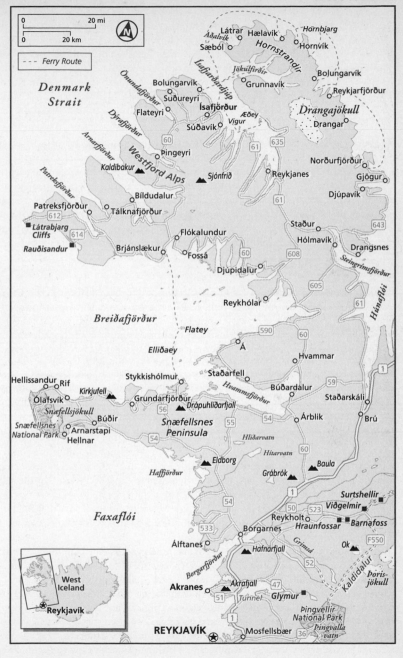

0 ____ 20 mi

0 ____ 20 km

--- Ferry Route

Denmark Strait

Látrar Hælavík *Hornbjarg*
Aðalvík *Hornstrandir* Hornvík
Sæból

Jökulfirðir

Bolungarvík Grunnavík Bolungarvík

Suðureyri Reykjarfjörður

Flateyri **Ísafjörður** Æðey

Súðavík Vigur *Drangajökull*

Þingeyri Drangar

Kaldibakur *Westfjord Alps* Sjónfríð Norðurfjörður

Bíldudalur Reykjanes Gjögur

Patreksfjörður Djúpavík

Tálknafjörður Staður

Látrabjarg Cliffs Flókalundur Hólmavík Drangsnes

Rauðisandur Brjánslækur Fossá Djúpidalur

Reykhólar

Breiðafjörður Flatey

Elliðaey Á Hvammar

Hellissandur Rif Staðarfell Búðardalur

Ólafsvík Kirkjufell Stykkishólmur Staðarskáli

Snæfellsjökull Grundarfjörður Drápuhlíðarfjall Árblik Brú

Snæfellsnes National Park Búðir *Snæfellsnes Peninsula*

Arnarstapi *Hliðarvatn*

Hellnar *Hítarvatn*

Hafffjörður Eldborg Baula

Grábrók

Faxaflói Surtshellir

Viðgelmir

Reykholt *Hraunfossar* Barnafoss

Borgarnes Ok

Álftanes Hafnarfjall *Þóris-jökull*

Borgarfjörður *Grímsá*

Akrafjall *Kaldidalur*

Akranes Glymur *Þingvellir National Park*

Tunnel *Þingvalla-vatn*

REYKJAVÍK Mosfellsbær

West Iceland

Reykjavík

ESSENTIALS

GETTING THERE   Borgarnes is on the Ring Road, 73km (45 miles) north of Reykjavík. Reykholt is on Route 518, about 40km (25 miles) inland from Borgarnes.

Trex buses (© 587-6000; www.trex.is) connect Reykjavík and **Borgarnes** two to four times daily year-round. The trip is 70 minutes and costs 1,700kr ($27/£14) one-way, with a stop at Akranes. Buses from Reykjavík to **Reykholt** leave Fridays and Sundays year-round at 5pm, returning at 7:10pm, with a one-way fare of 2,500kr ($40/£20). The bus stops at Borgarnes and makes several local stops between Borgarnes and Reykholt. See also "Bus Tours," p. 170.

VISITOR INFORMATION   Regional **tourist information** for west Iceland (excluding the Westfjords) is in Borgarnes at the **Hyrnan service center,** Brúartorg 1 (© 437-2214; www.west.is; June–Aug Mon–Fri 9am–6pm, Sat–Sun 10am–3pm; Sept–May Mon–Fri 9am–4pm), which is also the town's main bus stop. The website is hard to navigate, but basic listings are all there. A useful commercial website, with more selective listings for services, is **www.westiceland.is**. The reception office at **Snorrastofa** (© 433-8008; gestastofa@snorrastofa.is; May–Sept daily 10am–6pm; Oct–Apr Mon–Fri 10am–5pm) is well informed on Reykholt and nearby areas.

EXPLORING THE AREA
BORGARNES

Visitors tracing the footsteps of Egil Skallagrímsson, the warrior-poet hero of *Egils Saga,* should pick up the free "Saga Trail" brochure at the Settlement Center museum; the contents are also posted on www.landnam.is. The museum leads guided tours for groups by arrangement, and individuals can sometimes sign on by calling ahead.

The focal point of **Skallagrímsgarður Park,** a public garden on Skallagrímsgata downtown, is a burial mound thought to contain the remains of Egil's father and son. Facing the mound is a relief sculpture of Egil on horseback, his face twisted by grief, as he carries his dead 17-year-old son to the burial site. This affecting work is by Danish sculptor Anne Marie Brodersen (1863–1945), the wife of composer Carl Nielsen, and was presented to Iceland by her children in 1963.

The Settlement Center Visitors to this expensive but worthwhile museum, founded in 2006, strap on headphones for two 30-minute audio exhibits, one on the first sixty years of Icelandic settlement and the other on *Egils Saga.* The settlement exhibit is a basic primer and may feel a bit remedial to those well-versed in the subject. Interactive and multimedia features, such as a video of a re-created Viking ship, make the educational process painless. The exhibit's only serious flaw is that folkloric narratives handed down over the centuries are often presented as established fact, blurring the line between history and fable.

Egils Saga is among the five most celebrated literary achievements of medieval Iceland. Egil is a volatile and ambiguous character, capable of masterful poetry and merciless barbarity. While *Njáls Saga* has more passages illustrative of everyday life in 10th-century Iceland, *Egils Saga* has every dramatic hallmark, from pagan sorcery to bitter love triangles to gory battle scenes featuring outlaws and berserkers. The exhibit ably conveys the strangeness, humor, and versification of the story. Be warned, however, that the installations revel in horror and may traumatize young children. The life-size witch queen of Norway, rocking and murmuring over a fire, with a decomposed beast's head impaled on a pole, could give even grownups nightmares.

Brákarbraut 13-15. (℃ 437-1600. www.landnam.is. Admission 900kr ($14/£7.20) for 1 exhibit; 1,400kr ($22/£11) for both. 700kr ($11/£5.60) seniors/children under 14 for one exhibit; 1,000kr ($16/£8) for both. June–Sept daily 10am–7pm; Oct–May daily 11am–5pm.

REYKHOLT

The historic settlement of Reykholt, less than an hour inland from Borgarnes, sits within the fertile, well-forested, and geothermally active Reykholtsdalur valley. As the former home of chieftain, politician, scholar, and author Snorri Sturluson (1178–1241), Reykholt holds deep cultural resonance for Icelanders. Today the settlement is a cluster of buildings anchored by Snorrastofa, a research institute and museum specializing in medieval Iceland and Snorri's literary works. An 1887 church is charmingly restored, though a 1996 church has taken over its functions, including a classical concert series on and around the last weekend of July (visit www.snorrastofa.is for a schedule).

During the 1986 Reagan-Gorbachev summit in Reykjavík, a step toward ending the Cold War, Icelandic Prime Minister Steingrímur Hermannsson spoke to international reporters while relaxing in a hot tub at his local pool. Likewise, in the early 13th century, Snorri apparently held political powwows at Reykholt in an outdoor bath with crude taps for regulating hot and cold water flow. The exact site of the original **Snorralaug (Snorri's Pool)** is unknown, but in 1959 the National Museum settled on the current spot and built a reconstruction, 4m (13 ft.) in diameter, with hewn blocks of silica stone and stone piping found during excavations. Next to the pool is an underground passageway, perhaps leading to the basement where Snorri was murdered. Snorralaug is well-marked on maps posted around Reykholt.

Snorrastofa 🐾   The permanent exhibit, "Snorri Sturluson and His Time," covers Snorri's life and oeuvre while examining specific facets of 13th-century Icelandic society, from education, language, religion, and music to the use of geothermal heat. Snorri was the likely author of *Egils Saga,* and his own life story, packed with political intrigue and concluding in murder, is of saga-esque proportions. Snorri's other works include the *Prose Edda,* also known as *Snorri's Edda* or *Snorra Edda,* a kind of handbook for poets writing in the traditional skaldic style inherited from Iceland's pre-Christian past. This book provided a systematic account of Norse mythology, much of which might otherwise have been lost to history. The *Snorra Edda* is the focus of an upcoming temporary exhibit, which will replace the current exhibit on the role of women in medieval Icelandic society and literature. The oldest calfskin copies of Snorri's works are held at Culture House in Reykjavík (p. 112), but the Snorrastofa exhibit mounts several photographic enlargements with English translations.

Rte. 518, 5km (3 miles) from the junction with Rte. 50. (℃ 433-8008. www.snorrastofa.is. Admission 500kr ($8/£4). May–Sept daily 10am–6pm; Oct–Apr Mon–Fri 10am–5pm.

FARTHER INLAND

Hraunfossar (Lava Falls) is a kilometer-long succession of small waterfalls that drape over the lava rock on the north bank of the Hvitá River. The falls originate from cold springs and gush out from beneath trees, creating the impression of a giant water sculpture. From Hraunfossar, a short path leads upstream to **Barnafoss** (Children's Falls), a raging ravine named for two children swept to their deaths there. Hraunfossar is marked from the southern branch of Route 518, about 18km (11 miles) east of Reykholt.

Plunging into the monstrous **Surtshellir** 🎖 lava tube cave is an exhilarating adventure but should not be attempted without good shoes, warm clothes, and a strong flashlight; helmets and gloves are also recommended. Proceed with extreme caution: The cave floor can be slippery or strewn with loose boulders, and the complete darkness can throw off your sense of balance or cause panic. The main tube extends nearly 2km (1 mile), but narrow side passageways are the most fun to explore. To reach Surtshellir, take Route F578 for about 8km (5 miles) from the easternmost point of Route 518. Regular cars should have no trouble reaching the marked parking area, which is a five-minute walk from the cave entrance.

Víðgelmir 🎖, a lava cave close to Surtshellir, has particularly dramatic rock, ice, and mineral formations, but can only be accessed on guided tours led by Fljótstunga Farm (© **435-1198;** www.fljotstunga.is). Tours leave May through September, or possibly on weekends off season. The basic 1-hour tour is 1,200kr ($19/£9.60) per person, with a minimum of four people or 4,800kr ($77/£38); 3- to 4-hour excursions can also be arranged. In 1993, Viking-era artifacts were found inside Víðgelmir, including a fireplace, animal bones (leftovers from an ancient meal), and jewelry now on display at the National Museum in Reykjavík.

From Route 518, east of Reykholt and close to Surtshellir and Víðgelmir, Route 550 cuts southwest through **Kaldidalur valley,** passing between the glaciers of Ok, Þórisjökull, and Langjökull before joining Route 52, which continues south to Þingvellir. Regular cars proceeding slowly and carefully usually will not encounter problems between mid-June and mid-September. (The road is sometimes mistakenly identified as mountain road "F550," and "F" usually signifies "4WD only.") However, all drivers should beware of sandstorms in high winds. Kaldidalur is recommended to those who will not otherwise experience Iceland's gritty and desolate interior highlands. The road's highest point, at 727m (2,385 ft.) above sea level, is marked by a huge cairn and has a marvelous view of a rhyolite peak to the east.

TOURS & ACTIVITIES

BUS TOURS   Reykjavík Excursions (© **562-1011;** www.re.is) offers a guided "Saga Circle" tour from Reykjavík on Sundays year-round, and Tuesdays from May 15 through August. The tour visits Borgarnes and the Settlement Centre, Reykholt and Snorrastofa, Hraunfossar and Barnafoss, and Hvalfjörður. Tours last 8 to 9 hours and cost 11,500kr ($184/£92), including lunch and entrance to museums.

CAVING   See "Surtshellir" and "Víðgelmir," above.

GLACIER TOURS   From April to August, **The Activity Group** (© **580-9901;** www.activity.is) has a full-day "Langjökull Glacier Tour" for 23,000kr ($368/£180), including Jeep transport from Reykjavík to Þingvellir, Kaldidalur, and Hraunfossar, and an hour-long snowmobile ride on Langjökull, Iceland's second-largest glacier.

GOLF   Borgarnes has an excellent 18-hole course, **Hamarsvöllur,** run by Golfklúbbur Borgarness (© **437-1663;** gbgolf@simnet.is). The course fee is 4,000kr ($64/£32).

JEEP TOURS   Mountain Taxi (© **544-5252;** www.arcticsafari.is) has a year-round "Iceland in a Nutshell" tour for 19,900kr ($318/£159), which includes Þingvellir, Kaldidalur, Langjökull Glacier, Surtshellir, Hraunfossar, and Reykholt. The "Silver Circle" tour with **Eskimos** (© **414-1500;** www.eskimos.is) is nearly identical, but does not visit caves and costs 18,000kr ($288/£144).

WHERE TO STAY

Both located between Borgarnes and Reykholt, two recommended guesthouse alternatives to the Fosshótel are **Brennistaðir** (Rte. 515; © **435-1193;** brennist@islandia.is; 6,000kr [$96/£48] double) and **Guesthouse Milli Vina** (Rte. 514; © **435-1530;** www. millivina.is; 8,000kr/$128/£64 double, including breakfast), which is sometimes identified by its farm name, Hvítárbakki.

EXPENSIVE

Fosshótel Reykholt   With the Snorrastofa research institute next door, this hotel adopts the themes of medieval Icelandic literature and Norse mythology, and labors to signify deep thought at every turn. (The justification for the "Lord of the Rings lounge" is that J. R. R. Tolkien was inspired by the *Snorra Edda*.) Rooms are spacious, and 24 have been partially renovated; one way to get one is to request a bathtub. The extensive well-being facilities range from the tried-and-true (massage chair, hot tubs with water jets) to the dubious (lavender aromatherapy room, "relaxarium"). The reliable **restaurant** combines health food with the usual sauce-heavy Icelandic staples.

Rte. 518, Reykholt. © **435-1260.** www.fosshotel.is. 53 units. June–Aug 19,000kr ($304/£152) double. Rates around 30% lower Sept–May. Rates include breakfast. AE, DC, MC, V. **Amenities:** Restaurant, bar; spa; hot tubs; bike rental. *In room:* TV, Wi-Fi.

Hótel Hamar 🐟🐟   This Icelandair hotel is adjacent to Hamarsvöllur golf course (though guests get no special access or discount). The decent-size rooms are in modern, minimalist Scandinavian style, with neutral colors, plush bedding, firm mattresses, and floor heating. Half the rooms have glacier views, but all have decks with outdoor seating.

Rte. 1, 3km (2 miles) north of Borgarnes. © **433-6600.** Fax 433-6601. www.icehotels.is. 30 units. June–Aug 17,000kr ($272/£136) double. Rates 25% lower May and Sept; around 35% lower Oct–Apr. Rates include breakfast. AE, DC, MC, V. Closed Dec 17–Jan 7. **Amenities:** Restaurant; hot tubs; laundry/dry cleaning service. *In room:* TV, Wi-Fi, hair dryer.

MODERATE

Ensku Húsin 🐟 *(Finds)*   Meaning "English Lodge," this guesthouse by the Langá River, 6km (3¾ miles) outside Borgarnes, was built in 1884 by English fishermen and restored in 2007. With its nostalgic photos and quirky old furniture, Ensku Húsin has a worn-in charm lacking in most of Iceland's country accommodations. It's certainly not one of those exclusive fishing lodges with its own sauna, masseuse, and macrobiotic chef, but it makes up for it in character. The **restaurant** (p. 172) has a set three-course menu, usually reasonably priced and consisting of meat soup, fish, and dessert.

Rte. 533 (just off Rte. 54, 6km/3¾ miles from Rte. 1), Borgarnes. © **437-1725.** Fax 437-1734. www.enskuhusin.is. 11 units, 5 w/bathroom. May–Sept 14 12,900kr ($206/£103) double; 9,900kr ($19/£9.60) double without bathroom. Rates around 10% lower Sept 15–Dec. Breakfast available: 1,000kr ($16/£8). MC, V. Closed Jan–Apr. **Amenities:** Restaurant. *In room:* Wi-Fi, no phone.

Hotel Borgarnes   Boasting a convenient downtown location, this hotel is rather worn, bland, and taste-challenged, but it meets the basic comfort standards of a business-class hotel. Some doubles are big enough to bring in an extra bed, and children under 12 stay free.

Egilsgata 14-16, Borgarnes. © **437-1119.** Fax 437-1443. www.hotelborgarnes.is. 75 units. June–Aug 13,900kr ($222/£111) double. Rates around 28% lower May and Sept–Oct. Rates include breakfast. AE, DC, MC, V. Closed Nov–Apr. **Amenities:** Restaurant; Internet terminal. *In room:* TV, minibar, hair dryer.

INEXPENSIVE

Bjarg   Guest rooms are basic but cozy, tasteful, and spotless at this farm accommodation just outside of town and overlooking the fjord. The setting is surprisingly rustic and pretty for an accommodation right on the edge of town.

Off Rte. 1, about 1km (¾ miles) northeast of Borgarnes. ℂ/fax **437-1925** or 864-1325. bjarg@simnet.is. 3 units, none w/bathroom, 1 apt. May 15–Sept 14 6,800kr ($109/£54) double; 4,800kr ($77/£38) double w/sleeping bag; 9,000kr ($144/£72) triple; 7,200kr ($115/£58) triple w/sleeping bag; 12,000kr ($192/£96) quadruple; 9,600kr ($154/£77) quadruple w/sleeping bag; 16,000kr ($256/£128) apt for 4 persons. Breakfast available: 900kr ($14/£7.20). Rates around 25% lower Sept 15–May 14. AE, DC, MC, V. **Amenities:** Guest kitchen. *In room:* TV, no phone.

Mótel Venus   With scenic placement on the Ring Road across the fjord from Borgarnes, Venus has well-priced, functional rooms, eight of which overlook the fjord. Despite the name, logo, and passable **pizza restaurant,** no American 1950s retro theme is at play.

Rte. 1, 4km (2½ miles) south of Borgarnes. ℂ **437-2345.** Fax 437-2344. motel@emax.is. 17 units, 8 w/bathroom. June–Aug 9,300kr ($149/£74) double; 6,800kr ($109/£54) double without bathroom; 5,000kr ($80/£40) double w/sleeping bag. Rates around 37% lower Sept–May. Breakfast available: 750kr ($12/£6). AE, DC, MC, V. **Amenities:** Restaurant. *In room:* No phone.

WHERE TO DINE

Hótel Hamar ⟨⟨ (above) has bragging rights to the area's best restaurant (main courses: 2,800kr–5,500kr [$45–$88/£22–£44]; AE, DC, MC, V; daily 11:30am–9pm; reservations recommended in summer), with a menu specializing in fish, lamb, and local produce. Grilled salmon and Italian-style *bacalao* are standbys, and the course of the day—steamed mussels in a white wine and tomato sauce, perhaps—at 2,900kr ($46/£23), is a relative bargain.

Other places to consider are **Ensku Húsin** (ℂ **437-1725;** daily menu: 3,300kr [$53/£26]; June–Aug 7–9pm) for a home-cooked set menu, or **Mótel Venus** (ℂ **437-2345;** main courses: 1,200kr–2,500kr [$19–$40/£10–£20]; June–Aug daily noon–10pm, Sept–May 5–9:30pm) for a casual meal of pizza, fish, or lamb. See "Where to Stay" for locations.

Búðarklettur ⟨ ICELANDIC   Adjoined to the Settlement Center museum, Búðarklettur is the best option in central Borgarnes, with an upbeat, contemporary setting and an array of fish, lamb, and pasta dishes plus cafe-style light meals, such as Parma ham with parmesan and melon.

Brákarbraut 13, Borgarnes. ℂ **437-1600.** Reservations recommended for dinner in summer. Main courses 2,600kr–3,200kr ($42–$51/£21–£26). AE, DC, MC, V. June–Aug daily 10am–9pm; Sept–May Mon–Thurs 11am–5pm, Fri–Sun 11am–9pm.

Matstofan FILIPINO   This casual hangout with soccer on TV serves well-priced stir-fry, rice, and noodle dishes in huge portions. The food is hearty and satisfying if not the most delicate on the system. *Adobo,* a traditional Filipino curry with chicken or pork, is not on the menu, but they're happy to make it on request.

Brákarbraut 3, Borgarnes. ℂ **437-2017.** Main courses 500kr–1,950kr ($8–$31/£4–£16). AE, DC, MC, V. Sun–Thurs 6pm–midnight, Fri–Sat 6pm–3am.

2 Snæfellsnes

With its glistening white cone visible from Reykjavík on a clear day, Snæfellsjökull is the most potent and enduring symbol of **Snæfellsnes** ⟨⟨. If the glacier weren't there, however, the manifold wonders of Snæfellsnes would stand out just the same. With its

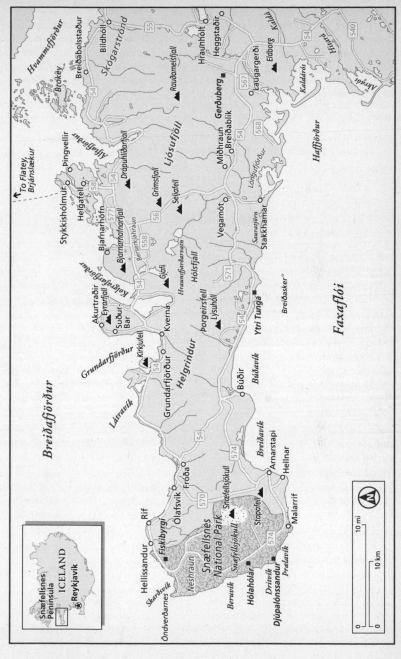

mountainous and glacier-carved spine, black and golden sand beaches, and lava fields blanketed in luminescent moss, Snæfellsnes is almost an Iceland unto itself. An outdoor activity tour is an ideal complement to a Snæfellsnes road trip, so before setting out, consider signing up for whale-watching, horseback riding, or an expedition on the glacier. Another possibility is a boat tour of Breiðafjörður, leaving from Stykkishólmur, the largest town on Snæfellsnes. (Stykkishólmur and Breiðafjörður are covered in section three of this chapter, p. 184.)

The five municipalities of Snæfellsnes have jointly earned a Green Globe certification for their commitment to environmentally responsible tourism, sustainable development, and cultural preservation. No other extended community in the Northern Hemisphere has received this honor.

ESSENTIALS

GETTING THERE & AROUND   Snæfellsnes could be done in a day trip from Reykjavík, but staying 2 days or longer is more agreeable and less hectic. The peninsula has relatively good roads, and—with so many widely dispersed attractions—coming **by car** really pays off. (See p. 38 for more on renting a car in Reykjavík.)

Bus service is more extensive than usual. **Trex** (℡ **587-6000;** www.trex.is) has a daily route year-round between Reykjavík and Hellissandur (3–3¼ hr.; 4,600kr [$74/£37] one-way) stopping at Akranes, Borgarnes, Vegamót (the southern junction of Rte. 54 and Rte. 56), Vatnaleið (where other Trex buses connect to and from Stykkishólmur), Grundarfjörður, and Ólafsvík. From June 15 through August, the bus from Reykjavík leaves daily at 8am (with a later departure every day but Sat) and connects to the **Snæfellsjökull Circle & National Park bus,** which makes a clockwise run around the glacier. This bus leaves Hellissandur at 11:20am and makes half-hour stops at Arnarstapi, Hellnar, and Djúpalónssandur, returning to Hellissandur at 4pm, for a total cost of 3,000kr ($48/£24). (This is too hit-and-run to pass as a "tour," though it can be used that way; there's just enough time for the Arnarstapi-Hellnar trail, p. 177.) Another connecting bus continues back to Reykjavík.

With more time to spare, Trex offers an economical "Snæfellsnes peninsula and National Park" **bus passport** for 11,300kr ($181/£90), valid from June 15 through August 31, with unlimited travel on the Reykjavík-Hellissandur, Stykkishólmur-Hellissandur, and "Snæfellsjökull Circle & National Park" routes.

VISITOR INFORMATION   Information centers for Snæfellsnes are dispersed. On the north coast, local information centers are in **Ólafsvík,** at Pakkhúsið, Route 574 (℡ **436-1543;** May–Sept daily 9am–6pm) and **Grundarfjörður,** at Eyrbyggja Heritage Center, Grundargata 35 (℡ **438-1881;** daily 10am–6pm). For **Snæfellsjökull National Park,** which includes the entire western tip of the peninsula, the visitor center is in **Hellnar** (℡ **436-6888;** www.ust.is; May 20–Sept 20 daily 10am–6pm) on the main road through the village. A good resource outside Snæfellsnes is in **Borgarnes,** Brúartorg 1 (℡ **437-2214;** www.west.is; June–Aug Mon–Fri 9am–6pm, Sat–Sun 10am–3pm; Sept–May Mon–Fri 9am–4pm).

The free brochure map *Snæfellsnes: Magical Iceland* is well-detailed and widely available. A better map, *Snæfellsnes,* published by Mal og Menning, is easy to buy from bookstores, gas stations, and tourist information centers. Online, **www.snaefellsnes. com** has thorough service listings.

EXPLORING THE AREA

The peninsula's southern coast has the most level land between mountains and sea, the best beaches for horseback riding and seal-spotting, and the most rain. The western tip is dominated by Snæfellsjökull and the lava that spouted from the volcano beneath it. The indented northern coastline has the best harbors, and thus the vast majority of the population. The following sights are laid out in a clockwise pattern around the peninsula, but travel can, of course, commence in any direction.

BUS TOURS   Reykjavík Excursions (© **562-1011;** www.re.is) offers a guided, 10-hour "Wonders of Snæfellsjökull" tour, which, despite the name, does not venture onto the glacier. Stops include Arnarstapi, Djúpalónssandur, and Ólafsvík. The tour costs 11,200kr ($179/£90), not including lunch, and leaves Reykjavík four times per week from May 15 to September 15. **Iceland Excursions** (© **540-1313;** www. icelandexcursions.is) has an almost identical tour for 10,900kr ($174/£87), departing 3 days per week from June through August.

SOUTHERN SNÆFELLSNES

Eldborg, a 200m-long (656 ft.) crater at the southeast base of the peninsula, has an elegantly symmetrical, oblong shape rising from the lava field it spawned some 5,000 to 8,000 years ago. More dramatic scoria craters are found elsewhere in Iceland—Hverfell at Lake Mývatn, for example—but for travelers sticking close to Reykjavík, Eldborg is a fairly interesting 2-hour round-trip hike. The best approach is from Snorrastaðir farm (see box below); the turnoff from Route 54 is 35km (22 miles) from Borgarnes.

Gerðuberg, an escarpment of hexagonal basalt columns, is strikingly broad and rectilinear. Gerðuberg is a 1km (¾ miles) detour from Route 54; the turnoff is about 46km (29 miles) from Borgarnes, on a dirt road almost directly opposite Route 567 to Hótel Eldborg.

Proceeding west, Route 54 passes Route 571 about 80km (50 miles) from Borgarnes, and then moves close to the shoreline. About 7km (4¼ miles) after the Route 571 junction is a turnoff for **Ytri-Tunga Farm** on the left, and past the farmhouse is a beach with a seal colony. The farm is private property that recently changed hands, so be respectful of any signs, and do not disturb or try to feed the seals.

Iceland specializes in converting hot springs to swimming pools, however unlikely the location. The **Lýsuhóll geothermal pool** (© **433-9917;** mid-June to Aug 10am–10pm; admission: 250kr [$4/£2]) is so natural that you may find clumps of algae bobbing on the surface. To Icelanders, this is all the more healthful. The turnoff is on the north side of Route 54, about 8km (5 miles) west of Ytri-Tunga.

Just west of Lýsuhóll, Route 54 passes **Búðavík,** a bay with lovely, broad sandbanks, backgrounded by the glacier. After Búðavík, Route 54 cuts overland to the north coast, while Route 574 continues along the south coast. Off Route 574, less than a kilometer from the Route 54 junction, a turnoff leads to Búðir, once a thriving fishing village and now just an 1848 church and a fabulous country hotel (see "Hótel Búðir," p. 182). West of Búðir along the coast is the **Búðahraun lava field,** a protected nature reserve. Route 574 passes north of Búðahraun to **Breiðavík,** another idyllic bay for strolling beachcombers. The free brochure *Snæfellsnes: Magical Iceland* lays out walking routes in these areas.

Horseback Riding on the Southern Coast

The south coast of Snæfellsnes, with its sand beaches, lava fields, and sightings of birds and seals, is a marvelous setting for riders of all levels.

Snorrastaðir Farm (© 435-6628; www.snorrastadir.is), at the base of the peninsula, leads rides on the picturesque sands of Löngufjörður at an hourly rate of around 2,300kr ($37/£18). Accommodations, if needed, are in functional up-to-six-person private cabins at 11,000kr ($176/£88) or on floor mattresses in a large shared farmhouse for 2,500kr ($40/£20) per person with sleeping bag. The turnoff from Route 54 is 35km (22 miles) from Borgarnes, and the farm is 2km (1¼ miles) farther ahead.

Hótel Eldborg (© 435-6602; www.hoteleldborg.is) has a 19,900kr ($318/£159) package that includes a 4-hour ride on Löngufjörður, a night's lodging (before or after the ride), dinner, and breakfast. The hotel is in a school building and operates only from June 5 to August 20; rooms are simple, with shared facilities. To get there, exit Route 54 onto Route 567, about 46km (29 miles) from Borgarnes, and proceed 4km (2½ miles).

Lýsuhóll Farm (© 435-6716; www.lysuholl.is), the leading horse tour operator on the south coast, is based farther west, about 9km (5½ miles) east of the southern junction of Route 54 and Route 574 (next to the Lýsuhóll geothermal swimming pool). Tours range from 90-minute rides for 3,500kr ($56/£26) or day trips for 10,000kr ($160/£80) to 7-day explorations of Snæfellsnes for 113,750kr–122,500kr ($1,820–$1,960/£910–£980) with full room and board. Lýsuhóll is near Búðir and Búðavík, recommended destinations for a few-hour jaunt.

For centuries **Búðir** was the most active trading center on the south coast of Snæfellsnes. 100 people lived here in 1703, the year Iceland's first census was taken. The **church** is well restored and worth a look; ask for the key in the hotel lobby. Búðir is the best starting point for walks over the Búðahraun. A 2km (1¼ miles) trail heads southwest along the coast to **Frambúðir,** an anchorage dating back to the Settlement Age. Ruins of fishermen's huts, fish-drying sheds, and trading booths are still visible, and whales are often spotted offshore. From Frambúðir, a trail cuts inland across the lava field to **Búðaklettur,** a volcanic crater 88 (289 ft.) deep. The surrounding lava flowed from here 5,000 to 8,000 years ago, and has since revegetated with mosses, wildflowers, heather, birch, and eleven varieties of fern. Unusual color variations are found in the rock. To reach Búðaklettur from the hotel, allow 3 hours round-trip.

Just a small cluster of houses on the western end of Breiðavík, **Arnarstapi** is near a small, rocky cove. The village's coastline is popular with birdwatchers, though they could face attacks by arctic terns, especially during the May-June nesting season. **Snjófell** (p. 178), the leading tour operator for glacier expeditions, is based here. The clunky **stone sculpture** set back from the sea cliffs represents Bárður Snæfellsás, a half-human, half-giant saga hero and local guardian spirit. Just outside Arnarstapi, Route 574 skirts the base of **Stapafell,** a mountain long thought to be an elf domicile. A doorway has been painted on the rocks.

The 2.5km (1½ miles) **Arnarstapi-Hellnar trail** 🌟🌟between Arnarstapi and Hellnar, the next village to the west, falls within a protected nature reserve and is understandably the most popular seaside hiking route on Snæfellsnes. Of all the unusual forms of lava erosion seen from the clifftop trail, the most striking is **Gatklettur,** a natural arch extending into the sea. The trail is not well-marked and can be confusing, so allow an hour each way.

Situated on a blissful stretch of rocky coast, the tiny fishing village of **Hellnar** (year-round population: 9) is a perfect rest stop, even for those not hiking the Arnarstapi-Hellnar trail. The Fjöruhúsið Café (see "Where to Dine," p. 184) has an outdoor deck overlooking the **Baðstofa (Bathhouse),** a sea cave resounding with bird cacophony.

SNÆFELLSJÖKULL NATIONAL PARK

Snæfellsjökull glacier lies atop a 1,446m-high (4,744-ft.) volcano that last erupted around the year 250. The national park, inaugurated in 2001, extends down from the glacier and volcano to cover the entire western tip of Snæfellsnes peninsula.

The **National Park Visitor Center (Þjóðgarðurinn Snæfellsjökull)** (© **436-6888** or 855-4260; www.ust.is; June–Aug daily 10am–6pm) is in Hellnar, on the main road leading into the village. A second visitor center will soon be in Hellissandur, on the north coast. Park information is also found in Ólafsvík, at the **Pakkhúsið** on Route 574 (© **436-1543;** May–Sept daily 9am–6pm). All these information centers carry a good topographical hiking map of the park.

When seen from Reykjavík, 120km (75 miles) away, **Snæfellsjökull** glitters by day and glows red at dusk; sometimes the sun sets directly behind it. With its near-symmetrical white cone and iconic stature, Snæfellsjökull could be compared to another

"Hidden People" Lesson #2: Elves

Of all the species of Iceland's hidden people, elves are by far the most numerous and prominent. In fact, many 19th-century folk tales use "elves" and "hidden people" interchangeably. Elves also look the most human, and are frequently mistaken for humans, though some are too small to cause confusion. (A few are tiny enough to live in flower blossoms.) Generally elves are good-looking, and dress in rustic styles prevalent in the early-20th century, sometimes with pointy hats. Male elves are skilled craftsmen and often work as farmers and smiths.

Elves are fiercely protective of their homes, which are usually inside rocks, hills, and cliffs, or occasionally an underground well or spring. People have been lured into elf homes, never to return from the hidden world. Though elves are quite dangerous, especially if their homes are disturbed, they often propose exchanging favors and are true to their word. Elf women have suddenly materialized to help human women with a difficult childbirth. On the other hand, elves have also been known to steal human babies in the night, replacing them with one of their own. To prevent this, Icelandic mothers would make a sign of the cross both above and below their babies after laying them in the cradle.

dormant volcano: Japan's Mt. Fuji. Both mountains have exerted an unusual grip on artists, writers, and spiritualists. Jules Verne, in his 1864 sci-fi novel *Journey to the Center of the Earth,* made Snæfellsjökull the entry portal for a scientific expedition to the earth's core. In the Halldór Laxness novel *Under the Glacier,* Snæfellsjökull inspires an almost hallucinatory religious transformation in a small Snæfellsnes community. New Agers make pilgrimages to the glacier, believing it to be one of the earth's primary "energy points." Snæfellsjökull was exceptional even to the Vikings, who thought trolls lived inside it. (Trolls normally prefer rock dwellings.) Sadly, Snæfellsjökull—already one of Iceland's smallest glaciers—is shrinking rapidly. Since 1996, the icecap has dwindled from 14 sq. km to 11 sq. km (5¼ sq. miles–4¼ sq. miles), and more and more rocks poke through.

ACTIVITIES ON THE GLACIER   Glacier conditions vary, and the visitor center should be consulted before you do any **climbing.** Generally the best access is from Route 570, which skirts the eastern side of the glacier and connects with Route 574 on the south and north coasts, near Arnarstapi and Ólafsvík. Regular cars can usually traverse Route 570 in summer. (Snjófell, the tour operator listed below, can take you from Arnarstapi to the glacier's edge for 1,300kr [$21/£10] round-trip.)

Hiking routes from Route 570 to the summit are inconsistent from year to year. The usual advice is to walk on tracks formed by snowmobiles and snow tractors, lessening the chances of falling into a hidden crevasse. *Warning:* Conditions are worsening as the glacier melts, and as a rule no one should climb Snæfellsjökull on foot before mid-February or after late July. The best time for an ascent is from March to May. Always be prepared for a sudden onslaught of rough weather. No technical equipment is necessary, except at the spire of rock at the final summit, which is sometimes coated in ice, necessitating an ice axe and crampons. The crater, about 1km (¾ miles) in diameter, is filled in with ice, and two lesser summits are along the ring.

Snowmobile and "snow cat" tours up Snæfellsjökull are organized by **Snjófell** (© 435-6783; www.snjofell.is), based in Arnarstapi. Scheduled trips run throughout the day from mid-February to mid-August, with additional 9pm and 11pm departures in summer to enjoy the midnight sun. Snow cats are tractor-like behemoths with bench space for up to 20 passengers. A snowmobile tour is 6,500kr ($104/£52) per person, or 7,500kr ($120/£60) if you ride solo, and snow cat tours are 4,500kr ($72/£37). Prices include snow suit, gloves, and helmet.

THE WESTERN COAST

The park map, available at all nearby tourist information centers, details many excellent alternatives to ascending Snæfellsjökull. The wild-looking peaks northwest of the glacier are particularly intriguing, with nowhere near the tourist traffic.

At the peninsula's southwest end, **Malarrif** ❧ (Pebble Reef) is the starting point for a rewarding 40-minute round-trip walk east along the shore to Lóndrangar, a pair of beautiful sea pillars from a long-extinct volcano. The turnoff from Route 574 is 8km (5 miles) west of Arnarstapi, and the parking area is next to a lighthouse that looks like a rocket.

About 4km (2½ miles) northwest from Malarrif, Route 572 branches off from Route 574 and leads 2km (1¼ miles) to **Djúpalónssandur** ❧, a black-sand beach set amid strangely eroded clumps of lava. The partial remains of a British fishing trawler shipwrecked in 1948 lie scattered on the beach, with an informational sign. The wreckage looks simply like litter, but may resonate as a symbol of Iceland's historic struggles with the British over territorial fishing waters. From Djúpalónssandur, a 15-minute trail leads to **Dritvík** ⚔, an equally scenic cove to the north. Remarkably, Dritvík was the largest seasonal fishing station in all of Iceland from the mid-16th to the mid-19th centuries, with as many as 600 men camped out there during spring and summer. Some remains of stone walls can still be seen.

Hólahólar, a crater cluster that is clearly visible from Route 574, can be reached by a marked turnoff 3km (2 miles) north of the Route 572 junction. The road proceeds right into the largest crater, Berudalur, which forms a natural amphitheater. A wonderful, easy seaside trail proceeds from Hólahólar 4km (2½ miles) north to Beruvík.

The northwest corner of Snæfellsnes is accessed via Route 579, a bumpy road extending 7km (4¼ miles) from Route 574. Within 2km (1¼ miles) the road passes Skarðsvík, an alluring golden-sand beach with a sign marking the Viking grave site discovered there. One kilometer (½ mile) farther is a parking area on the left, with trails heading through the **Neshraun** lava field to Vatnsborg—a small crater with vertical walls descending to a captivating fern-filled hollow—and Grashólshellir, a small cave. Vatnsborg is 2km (1¼ miles) one-way, and the Grashólshellir is a kilometer (½ mile) farther, but neither should be prioritized if time is limited. **Öndverðarnes** is the small peninsula at the very northwest tip, a scene of multiple shipwrecks and bleak cliffs known as **Svörtuloft (The Black Skies).** The lighthouse here is disappointingly stubby, and the sad ruins of a well lie 200m (656 ft.) away.

At **Fiskbyrgi,** the ruins of fish-drying sheds, simple structures of lava rock, are up to six hundred years old and have taken on an eerie stateliness over the centuries. The 5-minute trail to the site starts at a parking area on the south side of Route 574, about 1km (½ mile) east of the Route 579 junction and just west of a 420m-high (1,378 ft.) radio transmitter once used by the U.S. Navy to position ships and aircraft.

THE NORTH COAST

One of Iceland's oldest fishing villages, **Hellissandur** is home to **Sjómannagarður** (© 436-6784; June–Aug Tues–Sun 9:30am–noon and 1–6pm), a humble maritime museum with a re-creation of a typical, turf-roofed fisherman's hut from the early 1900s. The requested donation is 100kr ($1.60/80p), or free for children under 12. Iceland has far better maritime museums, but they usually cost 500kr ($8/£4) a head. Sjómannagarður is on Route 574, across the road from and just west of the N1 gas station.

Ólafsvík is one of Iceland's oldest trade centers, and today nets the most fish of any village in Snæfellsnes. The **Snæfellsbæjar Regional Museum (Byggðasafn Snæfells-bæjar;** Route 574 (© 436-1543; admission 300kr [$4.80/£2.40] adults, free for seniors and children under 12; May–Sept 9am–6pm), is inside an 1841 warehouse that also houses the tourist information office on the ground floor. The exhibits are mostly just antiquated household items and farm implements. The **Sjavarsafnið Ólafsvík** (© 436-6961; admission 300kr [$4.80/£2.40] adults, free for children 15 and under; June–Aug daily noon–5pm), a maritime museum by the harbor, has been closed recently but is slated to reopen (by summer 2009) with water tanks full of marine specimens.

Grundarfjörður is the most picturesque town on the north coast. Kirkjufell, its oblong signature mountain, pokes up from a promontory west of town, while good trails lead south from town into the peninsula's mountainous spine. The **Eyrbyggja Heritage Centre,** Route 54 at Hrannarstígur (© 438-1881; admission 500kr [$8/£4];

Whale-Watching & Horseback Riding on the North Coast

Ólafsvík is one of Iceland's best launch points for whale-watching, with a success rate around 97%. The most common sightings, however, are minke whales, which are 7m to 8m (23–26 ft.) long and only flash their backs for a few quick breaths. Dolphins turn up on two out of three occasions and put on a better show. Lucky passengers see orcas (aka killer whales), sperm whales, or blue whales. Travelers headed to the north coast are advised to wait and take their chances in Húsavík (p. 259), close to a migratory route for the histrionic humpback whale.

Seatours (Sæferðir) (© 433-2254; www.seatours.is) is the only whale-watching tour operator on Snæfellsnes, offering 3½-hour trips from Ólafsvík. Daily departures are at 11am and 3pm from June 10 through August, and 3pm only from September 1 to September 15. The cost is a little higher than elsewhere: 4,900kr ($78/£39) for adults, and 2,450kr ($39/£20) for children 12 to 15 (free for children 11 and under). Boats are 120-passenger catamarans with onboard cafes. Advance booking is advised. **Reykjavík Excursions** (© 562-1011; www.re.is) offers a 15,700kr ($251/£126) day package from Reykjavík to Ólafsvík, including a whale-watching tour and a visit to the shark-curing operation at Bjarnarhöfn Farm—but whale-watching from Reykjavík is almost as good, so the high cost may be hard to justify.

The best **horseback riding** outfit on the north coast is **Kverná** (© 438-6813; www.simnet.is/kverna), a farm 1km (½ mile) east of Grundarfjörður. Tours vary from 1 hour to 14 days and can range all over Snæfellsnes. A compelling nearby destination for a shorter ride is Kirkjufell Mountain for 7,500kr ($120/£60); 2 hours.

June–Aug daily 10am–6pm), which doubles as the tourist information center, has permanent exhibits on "Radical Changes in Rural Iceland 1900–1960" and "French Fisherman in Iceland"—though what's most likely to justify the admission price are the nonstop screenings of Icelandic documentaries and feature films with English subtitles. Films are on a set schedule, but it's not yet posted online.

Meaning "Berserkers Lava Field," the gloriously weird **Berserkjahraun** 𝒦𝒦 lies halfway between Grundarfjörður and Stykkishólmur. The lava flowed some 3,000 to 4,000 years ago and is young enough to retain all kinds of convoluted shapes, with fascinating color and textural contrasts in the rock and thick mosses.

The berserkers, from whom "gone berserk" originates, were a faction of Norse mercenaries known for their savage battle frenzy. In Old Icelandic, *berserkr* meant "bear-shirted," so they may have worn bear pelts; but *berr* also meant "bare," so the name may have only signified fighting without armor. Berserkers disappeared by the 1100s, leaving a wake of mystery for future scholars. Some maintain they were merely symbolic archetypes to be invoked in wartime and as literary figures in the sagas.

The Berserkjahraun was named after a famous incident in the *Eyrbyggja Saga*. In the late 10th century, Vermundur the Slender of Bjarnarhöfn—a farm located just beyond the northwest boundary of the lava field—returned from Norway with two berserkers.

They were difficult to handle, so Vermundur gave them to his brother Víga-Styrr (Killer-Styrr) at Hraun, now Hraunháls farm, at the northeast end of the lava field. One of the berserkers fell in love with Víga-Styrr's daughter Ásdís and demanded her hand. Víga-Styrr agreed, on the condition that the suitor clear a path through the lava field from Hraun to Bjarnarhöfn. The berserkers quickly finished this Herculean task, but Víga-Styrr reneged on the deal and killed them instead (by locking them inside a scalding hot sauna and spearing them as they tried to escape). In the saga, the berserkers are laid to rest in a hollow along the path.

The story could indeed have some basis in truth. A path through the lava field can still be found, and in a late-19th-century excavation alongside it, researchers uncovered the skeletons of two men—both of average height but powerfully built. To reach this path, exit Route 54 at its western junction with Route 577, marked "Bjarnarhöfn." After about 2km (1¼ miles), the road to Bjarnarhöfn branches off to the left. Stay on Route 577, and a sign for the "Berserkjargata" trail is shortly ahead. The trail extends about 1km (½ mile) through the lava field, and halfway along is the hollow, now marked only by a stone cairn and a blank, weather-beaten sign.

The best Berserkjahraun scenery, however, is south of Route 54, where the lava looks like a stormy sea frozen in time. Three access points lead from Route 54; the westernmost and easternmost are marked as Route 558, and the one in the middle is unmarked. The roads are heavily rutted but passable in regular cars. Walking trails appear here and there, but the lava can be difficult to traverse.

The same farm that figures into *Eyrbyggja Saga* (above), **Bjarnarhöfn,** off Route 577, near the western junction of Route 577 and Route 54. (② **438-1581**), now produces Iceland's most indelicate delicacy: cured and putrefied Greenlandic shark, or *hákarl* (p. 101). Visitors see a shark exhibit, tour the facilities, and sample the goods if they dare. **Hákarlsafn** has been featured on several TV cooking shows in the "revolting foreign custom" segment. Admission is 500kr ($8/£4) adults, free for children under 14 (June to mid-Sept daily 9am–6pm or call ahead).

WHERE TO STAY

The listings below—all excellent bases for exploring the entire peninsula—follow a clockwise pattern around the periphery. Accommodations for Stykkishólmur, the largest town on Snæfellsnes, are listed in section three (p. 184) of this chapter.

SOUTH COAST

Guesthouse Hof   Families and self-caterers are particularly well-served by these apartment-style lodgings inside a long log cabin, with views of Snæfellsjökull glacier 30km (19 miles) away. The interior is modern and unfancy; but it has plenty of communal space and feels more like a real home than just a unit to sleep in.

Off Rte. 54, east of Búðavík Bay and just west of Ytri-Tunga Farm. ② **435-6802** or 846-3897. Fax 435-6701. www.gistihof.is. 6 units. May–Sept 9,000kr ($144/£72) double; 7,000kr ($112/£56) double w/sleeping bag. Rates about 40% lower Oct–Apr. Breakfast available: 1,000kr ($16/£8). MC, V. **Amenities:** Hot tubs. *In room:* TV, kitchenette, fridge, no phone.

Guesthouse Langaholt   Rooms here have a simple, tasteful transparency that lets the nearby beach, mountains, and glacier speak for themselves. Guests are entitled to discounted play of the 9-hole golf course on the premises. The website is in Icelandic and German only, but icons help you navigate to at least view some photos.

Rte. 54, at Garðar Farm, east of Búðavík Bay. ② **435-6789.** Fax 435-6889. www.langaholt.is. 12 units. 11,500kr ($184/£92) double. Rates include breakfast. MC, V. **Amenities:** Restaurant, golf course. *In room:* No phone.

Lýsuhóll   Located on the eastern end of Búðavík Bay, next to the Lýsuhóll geothermal pool (p. 175), this horse farm has three adorably rustic cabins that sleep up to four, each has two or three single beds, a pullout couch in the living room, and a glacier view. Sheets and towels are an extra 1,000kr ($16/£8) per person, unless you bring your own. Set **dinner menus** are served on request for 2,400kr ($38/£19).

Off Rte. 54, about 9km (5½ miles) east of the southern junction of Rte. 54 and Rte. 574. ☎ **435-6716**. Fax: 435-6816. www.lysuholl.is. 3 cottages. June–Aug 9,500kr ($152/£76) cottage. Breakfast available: 900kr ($14/£7.20). MC, V. Closed Sept–May. *In room:* Kitchenette, fridge, no phone.

Hótel Búðir 🅐🅐   Just 2 hours from Reykjavík, Hótel Búðir may be the most hyped "romantic getaway" lodging in Iceland, creating expectations that are not always fair to visitors or the hotel. Some rooms have a less ideal view, or perhaps a zebra-striped chair not to everyone's taste, and the hotel can be pervaded by loud office parties from Reykjavík. All that aside, Búðir's hip country elegance is unsurpassed outside the capital. Rooms are individually designed, so ask to look around before choosing. The least expensive room, in the loft, is small but recommended for snugness and great views. The spacious deluxe rooms are a good insurance policy if everything needs to be perfect. No one is disappointed by the spectacular, isolated setting.

At Búðir, off Rte. 574, near the southern junction of Rte. 574 and Rte. 54. ☎ **435-6700**. Fax 435-6701. www.budir.is. 28 units. May–Sept 19,500kr–26,900kr ($312–$430/£156–£215) double; 38,500kr ($616/£308) suite. Rates around 25% lower Oct–Apr. Rates include breakfast. AE, DC, MC, V. Nov–Feb open weekends only. **Amenities:** Restaurant; bar. *In room:* TV/DVD, Wi-Fi, hair dryer.

Snjófell 🄥🄰🄻🅄🄴   Run by the company leading snowmobile and snow cat tours on Snæfellsjökull (p. 177), this guesthouse is a good option for travelers who just need a comfortable, well-maintained room and can suppress their desire for views until reemerging outdoors.

Arnarstapi, along the main road into the village. ☎ **435-6783**. Fax 435-6795. 15 units, none w/bathroom. www. snjofell.is. 6,350kr ($102/£51) double; 5,200kr ($83/£42) double w/sleeping bag. Breakfast available: 890kr ($14/£7). MC, V. **Amenities:** Restaurant; guest kitchen. *In room:* No phone.

Hótel Hellnar 🅐   Practically next door to the Snæfellsjökull visitor center, Hótel Hellnar is a Green Globe–certified eco-hotel serving organic food, buying fair trade, and washing up with green detergents. Rooms are spare but dignified, and walls are a bit thin. All that distinguishes the more expensive doubles is the ocean view. The cottages have kitchens and sleep four to six.

Hellnar, off Rte. 574. ☎ **435-6820**. www.hellnar.is. 20 units. June–Aug 16,500kr–17,950kr ($264–$287/£132–£144) double; 18,500kr ($296/£148) cottage. Rates around 10% lower May and Sept. Rates include breakfast except cottages. MC, V. Closed Oct–Apr. **Amenities:** Restaurant; bar. *In room:* TV, no phone.

NORTH COAST

An agreeable and eco-conscious hostel in a cute, old, red house, **Grundarfjörður Hostel,** Hlíðarvegur 15, Grundarfjörður (☎ **562-6533** or 691-1769; fax 438-6433; www.hostel.is; 7 units, none w/bathroom; May–Sept 5,400kr [$86/£43] double; 4,600kr [$74/£37] double w/sleeping bag; 2,100kr [$34/£17] per person sleeping-bag accommodation in 4–6 person room; rates around 10% lower Oct–Dec 15 and Jan 15–Apr; AE, DC, MC, V; closed Dec 16–Jan 14), has 34 beds but only one single and one double, so most guests stay in four- to six-person rooms. Bike rental is available for exploring the town environs, and the village geothermal pool is just down the block.

Hótel Hellissandur   Service is thorough and rooms are smart if smallish and non-descript at this well-run hotel. Bathrooms have nice large sinks, a rarity in Iceland. Rooms facing south have mountain views, and three rooms glimpse the glacier. Prices include free admission to the geothermal pool in Ólafsvík, 10km (6¼ miles) away.

Klettsbúð 7, Hellissandur. ℂ 430-8600. www.hotelhellissandur.is. 20 units. June–Aug 12,900kr ($206/£103) double; Sept–Dec and Apr–May 15 9,900kr double; Jan–Mar 8,800kr double. Breakfast available: 900kr ($14/£7.20). MC, V. **Amenities:** Restaurant; bar. *In room:* TV.

Hótel Ólafsvík   Located right in the village center, Hótel Ólafsvík has reasonably sized, peach-hued rooms and the basic comforts expected of a mid-scale hotel. The 19 studios each have a sleeping sofa, fridge, microwave, and private bathroom but cost the same as the en suite doubles.

Ólafsbraut 19–20 (Rte. 574), Ólafsvík. ℂ 436-1650. Fax 436-1651. www.hotelolafsvik.is. 29 units, 18 w/bathroom, 19 studio apts. May–Sept 14,800 ($237/£118) double/studio apt; 8,400kr ($134/£67) double without bathroom. Rates around 20% lower Mar–Apr. Rates include breakfast. MC, V. Closed Oct–Feb. **Amenities:** Restaurant; bar; Wi-Fi in bar. *In room:* TV.

Hótel Framnes 🛧   Extensive 2007 renovations by the new owners—Gisli, a former seaman, and Shelagh, a craniosacral therapist from South Africa—have breathed fresh life into this former fishermen's hostel in Grundarfjörður. Not only are the showers powerful, but there's a mechanical massage chair for guests on the first floor. Most rooms have excellent mountain views.

Nesvegur 8, Grundarfjörður. ℂ 438-6893. www.hotelframnes.is. 27 units. June–Aug 13,900kr ($222/£111) double; 18,100kr ($290/£145) triple; 21,500kr ($344/£172) quadruple. Rates around 15% lower May and Sept; around 30% lower Oct–Apr. Rates include breakfast. AE, DC, MC, V. **Amenities:** Restaurant. *In room:* TV, Wi-Fi, coffee/tea.

Kverná   This idyllically located horse farm just east of Grundarfjörður offers no-nonsense accommodation in three guesthouse rooms, plus three cabins for groups of four to six. The smaller cottage, with roof lines mimicking a Viking longhouse, is snazzier and more expensive. **Dinner** is available on request.

Rte. 54, 1km (½ mile) east of Grundarfjörður. ℂ 438-6813. Fax 438-6514. www.simnet.is/kverna. 3 units, none w/bathroom, and 3 cottages for up to 6 persons. 7,000kr ($112/£56) double; 15,000kr–20,000kr ($240–$320/£120–£160) cottages. Rates include breakfast except for cottages. MC, V. *In room:* No phone.

Suður-Bár   Situated on a promontory 7km (4¼ miles) from Grundarfjörður, this homey guesthouse has a glassed-in dining room to take in the stunning scenery. A golf course is just outside, and horseback riding can be arranged.

Rte. 576, 4km (2½ miles) north of Rte. 54. ℂ 438-6815. www.sudurbar.sveit.is. 6 units, 1 w/bathroom. June–Sept 15 10,200kr ($163/£82) double; 9,800kr ($157/£78) double without bathroom; 13,500kr ($216/£108) triple. Rates include breakfast. AE, MC, V. *In room:* No phone.

WHERE TO DINE
SOUTH COAST

Choices are limited in this sparsely populated region, and many travelers stock up on groceries in Borgarnes. The **Vegamót service station** (ℂ 435-6690; daily to 9pm), at the southern junction of Route 54 and Route 56, is a common fast-food pit-stop. Between Vegamót and Búðir, the best dinner option is the buffet at **Guesthouse Langaholt,** Route 54, at Garðar Farm, east of Búðavík Bay (ℂ 435-6789; 3,000kr–3,500kr [$48–$56/£24–£28]; MC, V; May–Sept 7–9pm), with a selection of fish dishes; make sure to call ahead, especially in May or September, so they know to expect you.

The most gourmet option by far is **Hótel Búðir** *(𝔄𝔄*, off Route 574, near the southern junction of Route 574 and Route 54 (© **435-6700;** reservations recommended; main courses 3,200kr–4,200kr [$51–$67/£26–£34]; AE, DC, MC, V; Mar–Oct daily 6–10pm, Nov–Feb Fri–Sun 6–10pm), with a pared-down, seasonal menu emphasizing fresh, local ingredients. On the main road into Arnarstapi, **Arnarbær** (© **435-6783;** main courses 1,190kr–2,490kr [$19–$40/£9.50–£20]; MC, V; daily 10am–10pm) is a reliable and unpretentious choice, with lamb and seafood specials as well as the usual burger regimen. In Hellnar, **Hotel Hellnar** *(𝔄* (© **435-6820;** reservations recommended; main courses 2,690kr–3,590kr [$43–$57/£22–£29]; MC, V; Sept–May daily 7–9pm) tries to use all organic ingredients, but dishes are fairly traditional—perhaps a simple choice between lamb, cod, and hashed fish with brown bread. **Fjöruhúsið** (© **435-6844;** light fare 400kr–1,300kr [$6.40–$21/£3.20–£10]; MC, V; May 15–Sept 15 daily 10am–10pm) is a tiny seaside cafe with limited indoor and outdoor seating, but the atmosphere is sublime; they serve light fare only, including pastries, cakes, and locally famed fish soup.

NORTH COAST

The north coast has a greater array of dining options to choose from, but nothing worth planning your trip around—just the usual array of hotel restaurants (good quality, but predictable and unatmospheric), the village restaurant-bar (burgers and pizzas, with a couple of fish and lamb plates), and fast food at the gas station.

In Hellissandur, the **Hótel Hellissandur,** Klettsbúð 7 (© **430-8600;** reservations recommended; main courses 1,500kr–2,500kr [$24–$40/£12–£20]; MC, V; mid-May to mid-Sept daily 7:30am–9pm), has better-than-expected Icelandic mainstays, a vegetarian option, and reasonable prices, with light fare available all day.

In Ólafsvík, **Hótel Ólafsvík,** Ólafsbraut 19–20 (Rte. 574) (© **436-1650;** reservations recommended; main courses 2,200kr–3,600kr [$35–$58/£18–£29]; MC, V; daily noon–10pm), has a stately ambience and emphasizes fresh catches from the port next door, with burgers and pizzas as a fallback. The new casual restaurant in town is **Gilið,** Grundarbraut 2, at Route 574 (© **436-1501;** main courses 970kr–2,100kr [$16–$34/£17–£17]; AE, DC, MC, V; daily 11am–9pm), with a welcoming air and a serviceable menu of burgers, pizzas, sandwiches, soups, pan-fried cod, lamb, and lasagna.

In Grundarfjörður, **Hótel Framnes** *(𝔄*, Nesvegur 8 (© **438-6893;** main courses 2,300kr–3,100kr [$37–$50/£18–£25]; AE, DC, MC, V; mid-May to Sept daily 7–10pm), is the preferred choice, with a small focused menu; call in advance, especially in May or September. The characterful restaurant-bar **Krákan** *(𝔄*, Sæból 13 (© **438-6999;** main courses 1,200kr–3,000kr [$19–$48/£9.60–£24]; AE, MC, V. Sun–Thurs 11am–midnight, Fri–Sat 11am–3am, kitchen closes at 10pm), with scrumptious seafood dishes, comes in a very close second. **Kaffi 59,** Route 54 (© **438-6446;** main courses 950kr–2,500kr [$15–$40/£7.60–£20]; AE, DC, MC, V; Mon–Thurs 9am–10pm, Fri 9am–1am, Sat 11am–1am, Sun 11am–10pm), offering lamb and *bacalao* as well as burgers and pizza, is not far behind.

3 Stykkishólmur & Breiðafjörður

As the largest town on Snæfellsnes peninsula—and with a ferry link to the Westfjords—Stykkishólmur is often the presumed base or transit hub for any trip in west Iceland. Actually, anyplace on Snæfellsnes is a good base if you have a rental car, and most travelers headed to the Westfjords drive or fly, bypassing Stykkishólmur altogether. Yet Stykkishólmur is an attractive place in its own right, situated at the tip of a peninsula amid the mirage-like islands scattered in Breiðafjörður. Despite its name, Breiðafjörður is more bay than fjord, and its extensive shallows, mudflats, and rocky coastlines sustain one of the most flourishing and diverse ecosystems in Iceland. Breiðafjörður has around 2,500 islands, but its pronounced tidal fluctuations make the final tally unknown. Most of Breiðafjörður falls within a strictly regulated nature reserve, and tours from Stykkishólmur provide opportunities for kayaking, fishing, birding, seal-spotting, and shellfish-slurping. The car ferry *Baldur* links Stykkishólmur to the south coast of the Westfjords, docking along the way at Flatey Island, an historic settlement that is still the only populated island in Breiðafjörður.

ESSENTIALS

GETTING THERE & AROUND   Stykkishólmur is 172km (107 miles) from Reykjavík, with good roads the entire way. **Trex buses** (© **587-6000;** www.trex.is) connect Reykjavík and Stykkishólmur (2½ hours; 3,700kr [$59/£30] one-way), with one or two departures daily in each direction year-round. Another route—also with one or two departures daily—covers the north coast of Snæfellsnes from Stykkishólmur to Hellissandur (65 min.; 1,700kr [$27/£14] one-way), with stops at Vatnaleið (the northern junction of Rte. 54 and Rte. 56), Grundarfjörður, and Ólafsvík.

The car ferry *Baldur* (© **433-2254;** www.seatours.is/ferrybaldur) makes a scenic crossing of Breiðafjörður, linking Stykkishólmur to Brjánslækur in the Westfjords, with a stop at Flatey Island. For detailed information, see p. 186.

VISITOR INFORMATION   Stykkishólmur's **travel information center,** Borgarbraut 4 (© **438-1750;** www.stykkisholmur.is; June–Aug Mon–Fri 7am–10pm, Sat–Sun 10am–7pm), marked from the main road into town, is in the sports/swimming center. The office of the tour operator **Seatours,** Smiðjustígur 3 (© **433-2254;** June–Aug 8am–8pm, Sep–May 8am–5pm) is also helpful with planning.

EXPLORING THE AREA
STYKKISHÓLMUR

The **downtown harbor** is worth a stroll, as Stykkishólmur has admirably preserved and maintained its older buildings. Those interested in architectural history should pick up the free brochure *Old Stykkishólmur* at the travel information center. To continue the walk, head past the ferry landing along a narrow causeway to **Súgandisey Island,** which protects the harbor and has wonderful views of Stykkishólmur's brightly painted buildings and the islands of Breiðafjörður.

Four kilometers (2½ miles) due south of Stykkishólmur is **Helgafell,** a conspicuous, knobby hill of columnar basalt, 73 meters (240 feet) high. Helgafell was held so sacred by early pagan settlers—who believed they would enter it upon death—that a decree forbade anyone to gaze upon it unwashed. Meaning "Holy Mountain," Helgafell figures prominently in two of Iceland's best-known sagas, *Eyrbyggja Saga* and *Laxdæla Saga.* A steep, 10 minute trail leads to the top, which affords great views of Breiðafjörður and surrounding mountains. At the summit are remains of a small stone structure, which may have been a chapel. According to tradition, you are granted three wishes for climbing Helgafell, but only by adhering strictly to these four rules: 1) Don't talk or look back during the climb; 2) Face east while making the wishes; 3) Don't tell anyone what you wished for; and 4) Make your wishes with a true heart. The 1903 church near Helgafell's base is also worth a peek. The turnoff to Helgafell is marked from Rte. 58.

Norwegian House (Norska Húsið)   A prosperous trader imported Norwegian timber for this 1832 building, a palace in its time, and now the folk museum for the Stykkishólmur area. Exhibits recount town history, assemble artifacts from saddles to sewing machines, and re-create the domestic sphere of the original owner—all nicely presented but perhaps too specialized for most visitors.

Hafnargata 5. (C) **438-1640.** Admission 500kr ($8/£4) adults; 300kr ($4.80/£2.40) seniors and children 6–16. June–Aug daily 11am–5pm.

Vatnasafn (Library of Water)   In 2007, New York–based artist Roni Horn—who has traveled widely in Iceland for more than 30 years—unveiled this permanent architectural installation inside a former library on a hill overlooking Breiðafjörður. The space has 24 floor-to-ceiling transparent columns, each filled with water from a different Icelandic glacier or glacial river. English and Icelandic adjectives associated with weather are inscribed on the vulcanized rubber floor. With Iceland's glaciers rapidly shrinking, Vatnasafn has an implicit environmental message but is hardly a polemic. Vatnasafn is also a community center for local reading groups and chess players; check the website for concerts, film screenings, or other events.

Bókhlöðustígur 17. www.libraryofwater.is. Free admission. May 5–Aug daily 11am–5pm.

FLATEY ISLAND

For most of Icelandic history, Flatey—measuring a mere 1 x 2 kilometers—was the commercial hub of Breiðafjörður, peaking in the mid-19th century. Today the island has around 25 colorfully painted homes but only five year-round residents, who like to feel time has passed them by (though it's nice to have cell-phone coverage, too). Visitors simply take in views of Snæfellsnes and the Westfjords, stroll along the low bird cliffs, and keep the world at a manageable distance. The 1926 church is adorned with frescoes painted in the 1960s by Kristjana and Baltasar Samper; the side walls depict scenes from island life, complete with ducks and puffins, while the altarpiece portrays Jesus in a white Icelandic sweater standing over two sheep farmers. The yellow building behind the church, from 1864, is Iceland's oldest, smallest, and cutest library. Visitors in early summer should remain on the lookout for divebomb attacks by arctic terns defending their nesting grounds.

The ferry *Baldur* ((C) **433-2254;** www.seatours.is/ferrybaldur), which connects Stykkishólmur to Brjánslækur on the southern coast of the Westfjords, docks at Flatey four times per day (twice in each direction) from June 10 to August 20. A traveler could, for instance, board the 9am ferry from Stykkishólmur, arriving at Flatey at 10:30am, and return to Stykkishólmur at 1:15pm or 7:30pm. Departures are more limited outside of summer, but continue year-round. The one-way fare to Flatey is 1,720kr ($28/£14). Passengers taking the full route between Stykkishólmur and Brjánslækur may disembark at Flatey and re-embark later that day—or the next day—at no extra cost, even with a car. The ferry has an acceptable restaurant on board.

Flatey's two accommodations are **Hótel Flatey** ((C)/fax **422-7610;** www.hotel flatey.is; June–Aug 16,500kr [$264/£132] double including breakfast; MC, V; closed Sept–May), with snug, old-fashioned en suite rooms inside restored warehouses, and the guesthouse run by **Ólína Jónsdóttir** ((C) **438-1476;** 7,000kr [$112/£56] house for up to eight persons; 2,700kr [$43/£22] per person made-up bed; 1,600kr [$26/£13] per person sleeping-bag accommodation; no credit cards; closed Oct–Apr), which has a guest kitchen and breakfast on request. The only **restaurant** (June–Aug Sun–Thurs

8:30am–10pm; Fri–Sat 8:30am–midnight), serving fresh catch, local puffin, and lighter fare, is at Hótel Flatey.

TOURS & ACTIVITIES

The dominant tour operator in Stykkishólmur is **Seatours,** Smiðjustígur 3 (© 433-2254; www.seatours.is), and their most deservedly popular offering is a 2-hour cruise called the **Unique Adventure Tour** (departures daily May 15–Sept 15; 4,650kr [74/£37]. Breiðafjörður's endless islands, abundant birds and seals, and unusually strong tides are encountered aboard a 120-passenger catamaran with a serviceable restaurant. Nets are dropped overboard so that passengers can slurp the celebrated local scallops straight from the shell. For travelers based in Reykjavík, **Reykjavík Excursions** (© 562-1011; www.re.is) and **Iceland Excursions** (© 540-1313; www.icelandexcursions.is) incorporate the Unique Adventure Tour into bus tours of Snæfellsnes, while **Eagle Air** (© 562-4200; www.eagleair.is) combines the tour with aerial sightseeing.

BIRD-WATCHING Breiðafjörður has 65% of Iceland's rocky shores and 40% of its mudflats, attracting a rich concentration of seabirds, waders, geese, and—the most coveted sighting of all—white-tailed eagles. The free, informative brochure *Birdlife in Breiðafjörður* is easily found in Stykkishólmur. Flatey Island and Seatours' "Unique Adventure Tour," both detailed above, are sure to please bird-lovers. Seatours also schedules 4-day nature cruises of Breiðafjörður, departing from Reykjavík, with three overnights on Flatey.

SEA ANGLING Seatours (© 433-2254; www.seatours.is) leads 2-hour fishing trips for 4,400kr ($70/£35), with daily departures from May 15 to September 15. Seatours also rents fishing equipment for casting from the pier.

KAYAKING Breiðafjörður's countless islands and shallow waters are kayak heaven. **Seakayak Iceland** (© 690-3877; www.seakayakiceland.com) leads various excursions from Stykkishólmur; a half-day excursion is 6,000kr ($96/£48).

WHALE-WATCHING Whale-watching tours depart from Ólafsvík; see p. 180.

WHERE TO STAY

Rooms are no-nonsense at **Sjónarhóll Youth Hostel,** Höfðagata 1 (© 438-1417 or 861-2517. Fax 438-1417 www.hostel.is. 11 units, none w/bathroom; May–Oct 5,100kr [$82/£41] double; 2,200kr [$35/£18] per person; 700kr [$11/£5.60] bed linen for whole stay; AE, DC, MC, V; closed Nov–Apr), located inside one of Stykkishólmur's oldest buildings. Try to book far in advance, especially if trying to secure one of the three doubles. The owner arranges fishing excursions, followed by a grill-up on the patio. Reception is open from 11am–1pm and 5:30–10pm.

Heimagisting Maríu This inexpensive guesthouse has simple attic rooms, a central location, a satisfying breakfast, and a bay view from the veranda. The proprietor is very friendly but speaks little English and doesn't do e-mail, so the easiest way to book is by fax.

Höfðagata 11. © 438-1258. Fax 438-1245. 4 units, none w/bathroom. 8,400kr ($134/£67) double; 9,900kr ($158/£79) triple. Rates include breakfast. MC, V. **Amenities:** Guest kitchen. *In room:* No phone.

Hótel Breiðafjörður Hotel Stykkishólmur may have better views, but this smaller hotel is more intimate and has a more central location, near the restaurants and the harbor. Rooms are rather ordinary but more than adequate for the price. Not to be outdone by Hotel Stykkishólmur, guests have free access to the local golf course.

Aðalgata 8. © 433-2200. Fax 433-2201. www.hotelbreidafjordur.is. 11 units. June–Aug 12,500kr ($200/£100) double; 15,100kr ($242/£121) triple; 17,700kr ($283/£142) family room. Rates 20%–25% lower Sept–May. Rates include breakfast. MC, V. **Amenities:** Cafe; Internet terminal. *In room:* No phone.

Hótel Stykkishólmur ⟨⟨ With its faded concrete exterior and chain hotel ambience, Hótel Stykkishólmur seems easy to snub. Yet, rooms are more spacious than the norm, with plenty of light and great views. The 45 rooms added in 2005 cost the same but have more space and panache, particularly on the third floor, while the old rooms are most likely to have primo views. Guests do not have to pay course fees at the 9-hole golf course next door.

Borgarbraut 8. © 430-2100. Fax 430-2101. www.hotelstykkisholmur.is. 78 units. June–Sept 15,900kr ($254/£127) double; 19,900kr ($318/£159) triple. Rates include breakfast. Rates around 25% lower Oct–May. AE, DC, MC, V. **Amenities:** Restaurant; bar; Internet terminal; Wi-Fi (lobby only); room service; laundry service. *In room:* TV, hair dryer.

WHERE TO DINE

Hótel Stykkishólmur's **Perspectives Ocean View Restaurant,** Borgarbraut 8 (© 430-2100; reservations recommended; main courses 2,400kr–3,400kr [$38–$54/ £19–£27]; AE, DC, MC, V; daily 6–10pm), thoroughly remodeled in 2008, is a fine addition to the following downtown options, serving Icelandic cuisine.

Fimm Fiskar ICELANDIC Meaning "Five Fish"—a reference to the variety of species in the house soup—this respectable backup to Narfeyrarstofa (below) specializes in homemade pasta dishes, guillemot, and puffin as well as fish. The Icelandic catfish, identified here as wolffish and complemented with honey and Dijon; is especially tender and clean-tasting.

Frúarstígur 1. © 436-1600. Reservations recommended. Main courses 1,500kr–3,600kr ($24–$58/£12–£29). MC, V. May 15–Sept 15 daily noon–9pm; Sept 16–May 14 daily 11:30am–1:30pm and 6–8:30pm.

Narfeyrarstofa ⟨⟨ ICELANDIC With its enticing menu and knack for atmosphere, this lively restaurant is popular with tourists—reservations are a necessity in summer. Fish soup and smoked guillemot with port wine sauce are the perennial house starters, and main courses include Breiðafjörður's famous scallops, grilled with garlic and lemon oil. Upstairs seating is more subdued, with an improved harbor view.

Aðalgata 3. © 438-1119. Reservations recommended. Main courses 1,550kr–4,450kr ($25–$71/£12–£36). MC, V. Sun–Thurs 11:30am–10pm; Fri–Sat 11:30am–1am.

4 Westfjords: The Southwest Coast

The Westfjords region feels almost like an island unto itself—which would be the case, if not for a 7km (4¼ miles) bridge of land at its base. The Ring Road bypasses the area altogether, though Westfjorders like to say they have a ring road of their own (comprised of Rtes. 60 and 61). To other Icelanders, the Westfjords conjure historic images of fugitives, shipwrecks, and remote villages hemmed in by pack ice through long winters. More recent associations, unhappily, include depopulation, abandoned farms, and local fishermen losing work because of free-market reforms to the distribution of fishing quotas. Westfjorders are sometimes stereotyped as country bumpkins; as resilient, hard-nosed survivors; as eccentrics; and—having contributed a disproportionate share of Iceland's prominent statesmen—as natural-born leaders.

To set priorities for travelers, this book bypasses the west coast of Iceland between Stykkishólmur (on Snæfellsnes) and Látrabjarg Peninsula (at the southwest corner of the Westfjords). The entire drive is lovely, though rough patches in the roads can be wearying. For help with accommodations en route, see "Where to Stay," p. 193.

Látrabjarg proper, at the southwestern tip of Látrabjarg Peninsula, is Iceland's largest sea cliff, stretching 14km (8¾ miles) and peaking at a height of 441m (1,447 ft.). Many visitors walk along the rim for an hour or two and zoom off again, but the entire peninsula, with its wonderful beaches and trails, handsomely rewards those who linger. May is optimal for birdwatchers since access to Látrabjarg is unrestricted during nesting season, and few other tourists are around. Most birds are gone by September, but fall visitors can bask in the solitude and ponder the Aurora Borealis.

For drivers continuing northeast from Látrabjarg Peninsula, this section also covers the next three coastal villages—Patreksfjörður, Tálknafjörður, and Bíldudalur—and their enviable surroundings.

ESSENTIALS
GETTING THERE & AROUND

Many travelers tour the Westfjords by flying to Ísafjörður and renting a car from there.

BY CAR   A drawback to traveling in this part of the Westfjords is the potholed condition of many roads. With forbearance and caution, however, drivers in regular cars can get around as much as elsewhere. Drivers coming from north Iceland have a choice of shortcuts from the Ring Road over to Route 60, which follows the south coast of the Westfjords. Currently the best link is Route 59, but paving has begun on Route 605, which will become the preferred route (via Rte. 61).

BY FERRY   The car ferry *Baldur* (© 433-2254; www.seatours.is/ferrybaldur) links Stykkishólmur (on Snæfellsnes peninsula) to Brjánslækur (on the south coast of the Westfjords) in a 2½-hour trip with a stop at Flatey island (p. 186); a restaurant is on board. Drivers headed from Reykjavík straight to the Westfjords do not save time by taking the ferry, but can enjoy the Breiðafjörður views and bypass some bumpy roads. Drivers coming from Snæfellsnes may save a short amount of time. From June 10 to August 20, the ferry departs Stykkishólmur daily at 9am and 3:30pm, returning from Brjánslækur at noon and 6pm. For the rest of the year, the ferry departs Stykkishólmur at 3pm weekdays and 11am weekends, returning from Brjánslækur 3 hours later. One-way tickets are 2,400kr ($38/£19) adults, 1,900kr ($30/£15) seniors, 1,200kr ($19/£9.60) children 12 to 15, and free for children under 12, plus 2,400kr ($38/£19) per car. Passengers with cars are advised to reserve in advance.

BY BUS   Trex (© 587-6000; www.trex.is) connects Reykjavík and Króksfjarðarnes (2½ hr.; 4,200kr [$67/£34]), at the base of the Westfjords, 5 days per week, extending another 50 minutes to Reykhólar on Tuesdays and Sundays. This route is a dead-end in terms of public transportation, however.

From June through August, on Mondays, Wednesdays, and Saturdays, **Stjörnubílar** (© 456-5518; www.stjornubilar.is) runs a bus from Ísafjörður to the **Látrabjarg cliffs** and back, with stops at Flókalundur (junction of Rte. 60 and Rte. 62), Brjánslækur (ferry terminal), Patreksfjörður, and Örlygshöfn (Látrabjarg Peninsula). The bus continues to Látrabjarg only if passengers book in advance; otherwise, it turns back at Patreksfjörður. The full route, which is 4½ to 5 hours each way, can be taken as a round-trip day tour from Ísafjörður for 10,000kr ($160/£80), with 90 minutes to walk along the clifftop and a lunch at Guesthouse Breiðavík included. The bus stops at Brjánslækur at 11:30am (on the way to Látrabjarg) and 6pm (on the way back) for ferry connections. Guesthouse Breiðavík (p. 192) can supply van transport all around Látrabjarg Peninsula for overnight guests.

Torfi Elís Andrésson (© 456-2636 or 893-2636) runs a short "flybus" route between Patreksfjörður and **Bíldudalur airport** to meet Eagle Air flights (below), with stops at Patreksfjörður, Tálknafjörður, and Bíldudalur in both directions.

Trex's **Full Circle and Westfjords Bus Passport,** valid from June through August, costs 35,300kr ($565/£282) and includes a complete circuit of Iceland, including the ferry across Breiðafjörður and the Stjörnubílar bus to Látrabjarg Peninsula.

BY PLANE   Eagle Air (© 562-2640; www.eagleair.is) flies between Reykjavík and Bíldudalur, a village on the southwest coast of the Westfjords, every day but Saturday. Flights take 40 minutes and one-way fares start at 7,180kr ($115/£57). Since these flights are slightly cheaper than flights to Ísafjörður, and Bíldudalur is closer to Látrabjarg, flying to Bíldudalur in conjunction with the Torfi Elís Andrésson and Stjörnubílar buses (above) could save time and money while allowing for a visit to Látrabjarg en route to Ísafjörður. This requires careful plotting, however.

VISITOR INFORMATION

The tourist information office in Ísafjörður (p. 200) can provide help for any destination in the Westfjords. On **Látrabjarg Peninsula,** information is provided at the **Egils Ólafsson Folk Museum** (© 456-1511; June–Sept 10 daily 10am–6pm). The **local pools** in **Patreksfjörður** (© 456-1301) and **Tálknafjörður** (© 456-2639; mid-June to Aug Mon–Fri 9am–9pm, Sat–Sun 10am–6pm; Sept to mid-June Mon–Fri 5–9pm, Sat–Sun noon–6pm) double as tourist information centers.

EXPLORING THE AREA
LÁTRABJARG PENINSULA

Entering the peninsula along Route 612, the landscape's allure is soon apparent. Three kilometers (2 miles) from the Route 62 junction is a picnic table, where the fjord view opens up, extending past a stranded ship, a lovely waterfall, and a mountain alley to the ocean.

From Route 612, Route 614 works its way south over the spine of the peninsula to **Rauðisandur** ★, a tiny and spellbindingly beautiful settlement, named for its broad, red-tinted sandbanks sheltering a large lagoon. Once Route 614 winds down from the mountains, an unnumbered road branches to the right and leads west along the coast for a few kilometers. At the end, past Saurbær church, is **Kaffihús Rauðasandi,** Iceland's most absurdly remote cafe, serving coffee, cake, and waffles (late June/early July–Aug 10 daily 1–6pm). The cafe has no telephone, so the only way to confirm it's open is to contact the folk museum, below. Rauðisandur is situated just beyond the eastern boundary of the Látrabjarg cliffs, and makes a great starting point for a coastal hike; see "Hiking Routes," below.

Local history is admirably and painstakingly preserved at **Egils Ólafsson Folk Museum,** Route 612, at Hnjótur Farm, by Örlygshöfn Harbor on the north coast (© **456-1511;** June–Sept 10 daily 10am–6pm), but admission is costly 600kr ($6.80/£4.80) adults; 400kr ($6.40/£3.20) seniors; free for children under 16. Old saw blades, drill bits, and other trifles overwhelm the more deserving artifacts; and English translations are minimal. The most unusual holding is a Russian plane that was stranded in Iceland in 1993.

Each summer, **Látrabjarg** ★★, the largest if not the tallest sea cliff in Iceland, hosts about four nesting birds for every living Icelander. Every major Icelandic cliff-nesting species is found here. Puffins, sure to be the avian stars of your vacation photos, start arriving at the end of April and disappear en masse in mid-August. Látrabjarg is the world's largest nesting area for razor-billed auks, identified by their black head and back, white breast, raven-like beak, and long tail. In May and June, locals rappel down the cliffsides to collect eggs, a skill that came in handy for the *Dhoon* rescue of 1947 (see the "Cliff-Scaling Icelanders to the Rescue" box, p. 192).

The usual way to see Látrabjarg is to park at the end of Route 612, by the lighthouse, and walk east on the well-established trail along the clifftop. The highest point of the cliffs is reached in about an hour. Beware of overhanging grass tufts that may not support your weight. To hike the full length of Látrabjarg, see "Hiking Routes," below.

HIKING ROUTES The south coast of the peninsula from Látrabjarg cliffs to Rauðisandur makes for a memorable **one-way hike** over 1 or 2 days. The shorter route starts along the un-numbered road to Keflavík, a small bay at the eastern edge of the cliffs, and leads 10km (6 miles) west to the lighthouse at the end of Route 612.

Cliff-Scaling Icelanders to the Rescue

As you gaze over Látrabjarg, think of December 12, 1947, when the British fishing trawler *Dhoon* ran aground 500m (1,640 ft.) from the base of the cliff, prompting the most famous and dramatic rescue of shipwrecked sailors in Iceland's history. No roads reached Látrabjarg in 1947, and it took the first rescuers several hours to walk to the cliff's edge in the dark with one pack horse. (In Dec, the Westfjords region has only 4 hr. of daylight.) When the sky lightened on the following day, twelve men descended the 120m (394 ft.) cliff by rope, while three remained on top to hold the rope fast. A rescue line was fired over to the boat, and all twelve British sailors were brought to land suspended on a flotation buoy. When darkness and the tide set in, only seven sailors and one rescuer had been hoisted up the cliff. The rest spent the night huddled together on a small outcrop. It took all the next day, in heavy winds and rain, to hoist up the remaining men, who then had to spend the night in tents near the clifftop. The next morning, they turned down the horses that were brought over to transport them—after the 75-hour ordeal, they were too cold not to walk.

The road to Keflavík branches off from Route 612 a short ways south of Breiðavík, and should be negotiable in a regular car up to the trailhead. The equally enticing **2-day route** begins in Rauðisandur, with an overnight in the Keflavík mountain hut, which sleeps nine on a first-come, first-served basis; there is no way to reserve.

Guesthouse Breiðavík (p. 194), with advance notice, can arrange transportation at one or both ends of the journey, and can also drop off or pick up supplies at Keflavík. The cost is usually around 5,000kr ($80/£40) per trip, regardless of the number of passengers. The hut almost never fills up, but having Guesthouse Breiðavík deliver supplies could be a good insurance measure. The hut has no formal price, only instructions on how to make a voluntary contribution later. For other worthwhile hiking routes on the peninsula, consult Guesthouse Breiðavík and the *Vestfirðir & Dalir* hiking map. A new first-rate hiking map, the fourth in the *Vestfirðir & Dalir* series, covers all Látrabjarg. The map is widely available on the peninsula, and can be ordered in advance from www.galdrasyning.is (click "Magi-craft online store").

PATREKSFJÖRÐUR TO BÍLDUDALUR

The coastal route north from Látrabjarg Peninsula soon passes through or near the villages of Patreksfjörður, Tálknafjörður, and Bíldudalur. All three are stunningly situated and have restaurants, accommodations, and other basic services (including free Wi-Fi within village limits). Patreksfjörður is the third-largest village in the Westfjords, with about 700 residents.

Tálknafjörður has a standard geothermal village pool, 25m (82 ft.) long, with hot tubs, but **Pollurinn**—a little spring-fed beauty overlooking the fjord—is outside of town, completely unmarked, unadvertised, and disguised from the road. To get there, take Route 617 northwest from the village for 2 or 3km (1–2 miles); a driveway on the right leads to the pool, just uphill round the bend. The tiny facilities include showers, changing rooms, a shallow tub shaped like a recliner, and a deeper tub, often too hot for all but the most intrepid soakers. Admission is free anytime year-round.

Jóns Kr. Ólafssonar, a middle-aged Icelandic pop singer with a long performing career, runs **Tónlistarsafn,** Tjarnarbraut 5, Bíldudalur (© **456-2186;** admission 500kr [$8/£4]; mid-June to Sept Mon–Fri 2–6pm), an informal museum of music memorabilia out of his Bíldudalur home. Jóns' tastes are proudly fossilized in the 1950s and 1960s, and his own singing is reminiscent of Engelbert Humperdinck. The mounted LP covers and stage outfits vividly evoke the Icelandic tangent of pop music history, but the collection is poorly organized, with no English guidance and nowhere to sample recordings. You can ask Jóns to put on his favorite records—just don't request anything by Björk.

From Bíldudalur, Route 619 extends 25km (16 miles) northwest along a wondrous stretch of coast to Selárdalur, a remote settlement with one remaining farm, a church, and **Listasafn Samúels,** a museum devoted to the painter, sculptor, and former resident Samúel Jónsson (1884–1969). Since the church didn't need a new altarpiece, Samúel built his own makeshift church to display his work. Outside are several crude concrete sculptures, including a statue of Leifur Eiríksson and a replica of the Alhambra palace in Granada, Spain. While his works could be dismissed as amateurish, his life sets a compelling example of how to reconcile artistic pursuits with poverty and seclusion. Samúel's church is left open from mid-June to August, with a sign requesting a 300kr ($4.80/£2.40) donation into a sealed box.

WHERE TO STAY

The tourist office in Ísafjörður (p. 200) can help locate accommodations and provides comprehensive listings at the website.

THE SOUTH COAST OF THE WESTFJORDS

The few hotels scattered along this barely populated stretch of coast sometimes come in handy for those en route to Látrabjarg.

Hótel Bjarkalundur, Route 60, about 100km/62 miles from Route 1 (© **434-7762;** www.bjarkalundur.is; 7,500kr [$120/£60] double without bathroom, including breakfast; 5,000kr [$80/£40] double with sleeping bag; MC, V; closed Oct–Apr), has eleven presentable, well-priced rooms with sinks, and is part of an all-around pitstop with a restaurant, bar, gas station, and small store.

Proceeding west, the next option is **Djúpidalur,** Route 60, about 122km (76 miles) from Route 1 (© **434-7853;** 6,200kr [$99/£50] double without bathroom; no credit cards), in a geothermal valley popular among trout and salmon fishermen. Lodgings are straightforward, with a guest kitchen and free use of the indoor geothermal swimming pool; the only room with a private bathroom is in the pool building.

The next accommodation on Route 60—located 100km (62 miles) west of Djúpidalur, near the Route 62 junction, and 6km (4 miles) from the Brjánslækur ferry terminal—is **Hótel Flókalundur** (© **456-2011;** www.flokalundur.is; 11,500kr [$184/£92] double, including breakfast; AE, DC, MC, V; closed mid-Sept to mid-May), with fifteen somewhat-cramped en suite rooms and a serviceable restaurant. Five minutes' walk from the hotel is a fabulous outdoor geothermal pool, lined with natural stones and overlooking the fjord. **Rauðsdalur** (© **456-2041;** raudsdal@vortex.is; 5,400kr [$86/£43] double without bathroom; 4,200kr [$67/£34] double with sleeping bag; MC, V), 8km (5 miles) southwest of the Brjánslækur ferry terminal on Route 62, has acceptable rooms, a guest kitchen, and a beautiful beach across the road.

LÁTRABJARG PENINSULA

Guesthouse Breiðavík ⭐⭐   Location is paramount here. Breiðavík, near the westernmost tip of Iceland, is a wonderfully serene and lovely bay, with a vast golden beach and a broad, sheltering arc of mountains—with the Látrabjarg cliffs just a short drive away. Guesthouse rooms are rustic and homey, while en suite rooms are in a prefab row of identical units, cozier inside than anticipated. The owners know the territory inside and out, and run a transportation service; see "Hiking routes," p. 191.

Rte. 612. 🕻 **456-1575**. www.breidavik.net. 32 units, 14 w/bathroom. May 15–Sept 15 12,000kr ($192/£96) double; 8,000kr ($128/£64) double without bathroom; 1,900kr ($30/£15) sleeping-bag accommodation. Rates include breakfast (except for sleeping-bag accommodation). MC, V. Closed Sept 16–May 14. **Amenities:** Restaurant, bar. *In room:* Wi-Fi, no phone.

Hótel Látrabjarg ⭐   This hotel on the peninsula's north coast is in a former school and so can't really be blamed for its drab exterior and poor placement for ocean views. The broader setting is idyllic nonetheless, and vigorous 2006 renovations have really warmed up the rooms. Fishing trips can be arranged, and horses are on call for rides along a picturesque nearby beach. **Dinner** is served on request in advance.

Rte. 615, 3km (2 miles) from the Rte. 612 intersection. 🕻 **825-0025**. www.latrabjarg.com. 10 units, 4 w/bathroom. May–Aug 13,500kr ($218/£108) double; 10,500kr ($168/£84) double without bathroom; 17,500kr ($280/£140) triple; 14,500kr ($232/£116) triple without bathroom; 19,500kr ($312/£156) family room. Rates include breakfast. AE, DC, MC, V. Closed Sept–Apr. *In room:* No phone.

PATREKSFJÖRÐUR & TÁLKNAFJÖRÐUR

Patreksfjörður has three choices, all inexpensive and equipped with guest kitchens. **Guesthouse Erla,** Urðargata 2 (🕻 **456-1227**; 6,000kr [$96/£48] double without bathroom including breakfast; no credit cards), has agreeable rooms, though Erla's English is severely limited. **Guesthouse Eyrar,** Aðalstræti 8 (🕻 **456-4565**; handrad inn@simnet.is; 7,000kr [$112/£56] double with bathroom; MC, V), which shares a building with the local cafe and bakery, is a great value for private facilities. **Stekkaból,** Stekkur 19 (🕻 **456-1675**; stekkabol@snerpa.is; 6,400kr [$102/£51] double without bathroom; 2,000kr [$32/£16] per person sleeping-bag accommodation; MC, V), is a standard guesthouse spread over three buildings.

In **Tálknafjörður,** the cheery, welcoming **Skrúðhamrar Guesthouse,** Strandgata 20 (🕻 **456-0200**; skrudhamar@visir.is; 6,000kr [$96/£48] double without bathroom; MC, V), has TVs and Wi-Fi in each room. The backup is **Guesthouse Bjarmaland,** Túngata 42 (🕻 **891-8038**; bjarmaland06@simnet.is; 6,000kr [$96/£48] double without bathroom; MC, V), with a guest kitchen and one en suite room out of eleven; speak up if you want a TV. *Note:* There are currently no accommodations in **Bíldudalur.**

WHERE TO DINE
LÁTRABJARG PENINSULA

The restaurant at **Guesthouse Breiðavík** is open daily in summer, with soup and bread starting at noon, cakes and waffles at tea time, and, from 7 to 9pm, a tasty, down-home set dinner menu for around 3,000kr ($48/£24); reservations are advised. **Hótel Látrabjarg** also serves dinner by advance request. **Egils Ólafsson Folk Museum** (p. 191) has a cafe, and the cafe **Völlurinn** (no telephone; hours vary) is at the small airfield along Route 612, about 10km (6 miles) from Route 62. See also **Kaffihús Rauðasandi** in Rauðisandur (p. 191).

PATREKSFJÖRÐUR TO BÍLDUDALUR

In Patreksfjörður, **Söluturninn Albína,** Aðalstræti 89 (© **456-1667**), has snacks and fast food, while **Eyrar,** Aðalstræti 8 (© **456-4565;** Mon–Fri 9am–6pm), is the resident cafe and bakery. Patreksfjörður and Tálknafjörður each have a restaurant on the standard small-town Icelandic model: burgers, pizzas, sandwiches, plus a handful of fish, lamb, and pasta plates. The nod goes to the well-priced **Þorpið,** Aðalstræti 73, Patreksfjörður (© **456-1295;** main courses 750kr–1,950kr [$12–$31/£6–£16]; MC, V; June–Sept 15 Mon–Fri 11am–9pm, Sat–Sun 12:30–9pm; Sept 16–May 31 daily 11am–2pm and 6–9pm), followed by **Hópið,** Hrafnadalsvegur in Tálknafjörður (© **456-2777;** main courses 1,000kr–3,500kr [$16–$56/£8–£28]; MC, V; Mon–Wed noon–10pm, Thurs–Sun noon–11pm). **Vegamót/Siggi Ben,** Route 619 in Bíldudalur (© **456-2144;** MC, V; mid-June to Aug Mon–Fri 9am–10pm, Sat–Sun 10am–10pm; Sept to mid-June daily 11am–8pm), serves lighter fare; the most expensive item on the menu is an overloaded pizza for 1,730kr ($28/£14).

5 Central Westfjords

The Westfjords are Iceland's oldest landmass, with no active volcanoes for the last 10 million years. Glaciation created more than half of Iceland's fjords but little lowland suitable for agriculture. The central coastal region of the Westfjords—boundaried by Arnarfjörður to the south and Ísafjarðardjúp to the north—is particularly mountainous and , and in winter, roads to neighboring towns can be cut off for days at a time. Highlights of this area include Dynjandi, the largest and most resplendent waterfall in the Westfjords; the "Westfjords Alps," a prime hiking area; and the village of Suðureyri, where locals invite visitors to experience the fishing life.

ESSENTIALS

GETTING THERE & AROUND   Route 60 is the main artery of the central Westfjords. The distance from Bíldudalur to Ísafjörður, the Westfjords capital, is 145km (90 miles), and the 96km (60 miles) stretch between Bíldudalur and Þingeyri is unpaved. Thanks to a long, three-pronged tunnel built in 1996, Ísafjörður is only 25 minutes from Suðureyri, 20 minutes from Flateyri, and 45 minutes from Þingeyri.

Two **airports** with scheduled flights from Reykjavík are just outside the central Westfjords; to the south is Bíldudalur (p. 190), and to the north is Ísafjörður (p. 199).

From June through August, on Mondays, Wednesdays, and Saturdays, **Stjörnubílar** (© **456-5518;** www.stjornubilar.is) runs a **bus** from Ísafjörður to Látrabjarg peninsula and back, with **ferry connections** to Snæfellsnes peninsula at Brjánslækur; the bus has no scheduled stops in the central Westfjords region, but cuts right through it, and a pickup or dropoff along Route 60 can usually be arranged informally.

F&S Hópferðabílar (© **893-1058** or 847-0285) operates the municipal buses that connect Ísafjörður to **Suðureyri, Flateyri,** and **Þingeyri** on weekdays year-round. The schedule is posted at www.isafjordur.is/ferdamadurinn/samgongur in Icelandic only, but you shouldn't have trouble figuring it out. One-way fares are only 250kr ($4/£2), and buses leave Ísafjörður from the N1 gas station on Pollgata, behind Hótel Ísafjörður.

VISITOR INFORMATION   The tourist information office in **Ísafjörður** (p. 200) covers the entire Westfjords. In **Þingeyri** an information center is at Hafnarstræti 6 (© **456-8304;** umthingeyri@snerpa.is; June–Aug Mon–Fri 10am–6pm, Sat–Sun

11am–6pm; Sept–May Thurs 3–6pm). **Suðureyri** has no tourist office, but all visitor activities are outlined at www.sudureyri.is/online.html.

EXPLORING THE CENTRAL WESTFJORDS

Also known as Fjallfoss, **Dynjandi** ⊛ is an astonishing 100m (328-ft.) waterfall whose name means "resounding" or "thunderous." Dynjandi—which drapes its way down ever-broadening cascades in the shape of a tiered wedding cake—is clearly marked from Route 60, near the head of Dynjandisvogur, an inlet of Arnarfjörður. A short scenic trail leads from the parking area to the base of the waterfall. Remarkably, the view toward Arnarfjörður could soon be marred by an oil refinery, which would be the first large-scale industrial venture in the history of the Westfjords.

A settlement on the north shore of Arnarfjörður, **Hrafnseyri** was the childhood home of nationalist hero Jón Sigurðsson (1811–1879). **Byggðasafnið Hrafnseyri** (© 456-8260; www.hrafnseyri.is; admission 400kr [$6.40/£3.20]; June–Aug 25 daily 1–8pm), the local museum devoted to Jón, is not very compelling but has a nice cafe for a rest stop.

In aerial photos, the Westfjords region is often identified by successions of table-topped mountains, formed by eruptions beneath the crushing weight of thick icecaps. The **Westfjords Alps** ⊛⊛, on the peninsula between Arnarfjörður and Dýrafjörður, were so named by breaking this pattern: Not only are these "Alps" particularly tall—Kaldbakur, at 998m (3,274 ft.), is the highest peak in the Westfjords—but they're topped with razorback ridges that delight photographers and entice every hiker's inner tightrope walker.

The best **hiking routes** in the Alps are outlined at www.thingeyri.is (look for the "English" link), but the trail descriptions are no substitute for a map. The inexpensive *Vestfirðir: Hiking Trails in the Westfjord Alps* is sufficient, but a new map in the *Vestfirðir & Dalir* series—still forthcoming at press time—should be far superior. Given the vertiginous ridges, loose scree, and exposure to the weather, it's a good idea to review and register your route with the tourist information office in Þingeyri or Ísafjörður. **Kaldbakur** is the most challenging and rewarding climb, with stunning panoramic views extending to Snæfellsnes peninsula. Trails approach the peak from both the north and south. At the summit is a 2m (6½ ft.) cairn—with a guestbook inside—artificially raising Kaldbakur's height to four digits.

In 1995 an avalanche crashed into this small fishing village of **Flateyri** on Önundarfjörður, killing 20 people and damaging or destroying 30 homes. As a result, the slope behind Flateyri now has a colossal, A-shaped barricade—1.5km long, 15 to 20m high and 45 to 60m thick (1 mile x 49–66 ft. x 148–197 ft.)—designed to deflect tumbling boulders and snow into the fjord. The barricade is now being cultivated with vegetation.

From 1889 to 1901, Flateyri was the largest whaling station in the North Atlantic, with most trade controlled by Norwegians. The old Flateyri bookstore, **Gamla Bóka-búðin**, Hafnarstræti 3–5 (daily 1–6pm) has a small exhibit on village history, and the local handicraft workshop **Handverkshúsið Purka**, Hafnarstræti 11 (© 456-7710; daily 1–6pm), contains a curious collection of dolls from around the world.

When the fisherman of **Suðureyri** ⊛ began taking steps to ensure an environmentally sustainable future, they were hardly scheming to lure tourists. Later came the realization that tourism revenue, together with carrying the banner of environmental responsibility, could form a virtuous circle.

> **Tips** **Iceland's Only Castles**
>
> All are welcome to participate in an annual **sandcastle competition** held the first Saturday of August at a beach on Önundarfjörður (from Rte. 60, head just over a kilometer northwest on Rte. 625). A pair of Brits won in 2006, proving that the hometown judges aren't biased.

The fishermen make short, fuel-efficient trips in fiberglass boats. All fish are caught by hook and bait, a method far less harmful to marine ecosystems than the practice of dragging weighted nets across the ocean floor. No fish parts are wasted; bones are powdered for animal food, and heads are dried and shipped to Nigeria to be ground into meal. All Suðureyri homes are heated by underground hot springs piped through radiators, and all power comes from a hydroelectric facility.

Fish factory tours run from 9 to 10am and cost 1,000kr ($16/£8), including protective clothing. For 12,000kr ($192/£96), two guests can accompany and assist two fishermen for their entire daily routine, starting with baiting the lines at 7am (be prepared to spend a few hours in a 7.5-m-long/25 ft. boat in open seas); later the catch can be served up at Talisman (p. 198). Many sport fishermen come to Suðureyri to rent boats and set out on their own. You can also arrange for transport to **Galtarviti,** one of Iceland's most magically remote lighthouses, for an overnight stay. For bookings or further information (online only), visit www.sudureyri.is/online.html.

The Route 65 causeway entering the village created a lagoon, now full of cod accustomed to being fed by humans. Fish food is sold at the N1 gas station. You can even pet the cod if you like—just don't let them bite you.

WHERE TO STAY

The welcoming and idyllic **Korpudalur Kirkjuból Hostel** (© 456-7808; fax 556-3620; www.korpudalur.is; 6 units, none w/bathroom; June–Aug 6,600kr [$106/£53] double; 5,800kr [$93/£46] double w/sleeping bag; breakfast available for 950kr [$15/£7.60]; MC, V; closed Sept–May) is in a 1912 farmhouse at the head of Önundarfjörður (on Rte. 627, 5km/3 miles southeast of Rte. 60). Ísafjörður is only 17km (11 miles) away, and airport pickup can be arranged. The hostel is also an excellent resource for arranging kayaking, sailing, and sea-angling trips.

Alviðra This Farm Holidays–affiliated accommodation, beautifully situated on the north shore of Dýrafjörður, offers modest rooms with or without bathroom, a self-catering apartment, and two cottages, with **dinner** served on request.

Rte. 624, 8km (5 miles) from Rte. 60. © 456-8229. Fax 456-8429. alvidra@snerpa.is. May 15–Sept 15 9,000kr ($144/£72) double; 8,000kr ($128/£64) double without bathroom; 11,000kr ($176/£88) triple without bathroom; 2,200kr ($35/£18) per person sleeping-bag accommodation; 9,000kr ($144/£72) 4-person cottage; 10,000kr ($160/£80) 6-person cottage. Rates include breakfast, except cottages. MC, V. Closed Oct–Apr. **Amenities:** Guest kitchen. In room: No phone.

Kirkjuból With a fabulous mountain backdrop, this hospitable farmstay offers well-maintained, mid-sized rooms with a modern look a touch more warm than the standard. **Dinner** is served on request. Kirkjuból is right on Route 60, in Bjarnadalur Valley just south of Önundarfjörður.

Rte. 60. © **456-7679.** www.kirkjubol.is. 5 units, 1 w/bathroom. June 8–Aug 20 9,000kr ($144/£72) double; 6,000kr–6,500kr ($96–$104/£48–£52) double without bathroom; 7,500kr ($120/£60) triple without bathroom. Breakfast available: 900kr ($14/£7.20). MC, V. Closed Aug 21–June 7. **Amenities:** Guest kitchen; Internet terminal. *In room:* No phone.

VEG-Gisting　The owners of this sparkling-clean and comfortable modern hotel are also behind Talisman (see "Where to Dine," below) and Suðureyri's program to give visitors a window on the fishing life (p. 197). The staff is extremely welcoming, and rooms have a spare yet cheerful Scandinavian look with simple furnishings.

Aðalgata 14, Suðureyri. © **456-6666.** www.sudureyri.is/gistiheimili. 15 units, 13 w/bathroom. 9,700kr ($155/£78) double; 7,600kr ($122/£61) double without bathroom. Rates include breakfast. MC, V. **Amenities:** Restaurant; guest kitchen. *In room:* TV, Wi-Fi, hair dryer.

Við Fjörðinn　No one's socks will be charmed off by the neutral rooms here, but Við Fjörðinn—like most Icelandic guesthouses—assumes you came for the outdoor scenery and just attends to basic comforts. The two apartments, with bathrooms, kitchens, TVs, and private entrances, are homier. **Dinner** and **packed lunches** are available on request.

Aðalstræti 26, Þingeyri. © **456-8172.** Fax 456-8172. www.vidfjordinn.is. 8 units, none w/bathroom; 2 apts. 6,600kr ($106/£53) double; 2,500kr ($40/£20) sleeping-bag accommodation; 11,000kr ($176/£88) apts for 3–4 persons. Breakfast available: 950kr ($15/£7.60). MC, V. **Amenities:** Guest kitchen. *In room:* No phone.

WHERE TO DINE

The only food between Þingeyri and Bíldudalur (in the southwest Westfjords) or Flókalundur (on the south coast) is at the **Byggðasafnið Hrafnseyri cafe** (p. 196). Þingeyri is just 45 minutes from Ísafjörður, so many drivers headed north aim to reach the Westfjords capital by dinnertime. The N1 gas stations in **Þingeyri** and **Flateyri** have fast food grills to tide you over. The regular restaurant in Flateyri has just closed, while Þingeyri has a low-key eatery **Sandafell,** Hafnarstræti 7 (© **456-1600;** June–Aug daily 10am–10pm; closed Sept–May) with soups, sandwiches, cakes, and a dish of the day.

Talisman ⋆ ICELANDIC　In Suðureyri, just 25 minutes from Ísafjörður, Talisman is the only restaurant independently worth seeking out in the central Westfjords. The ambience is unexpectedly classy, with fishskin mats on tables. Starters include bacalao carpaccio with roasted pine nuts and cucumber, and main courses depend on the fishermen's daily haul. Plenty of non-fish choices are available, and portions are generous.

Aðalgata 14, Suðureyri. © **456-6666.** Main courses 1,990kr–2,190kr ($32–$35/£16–£18). MC, V. Daily 6–10pm.

6　Ísafjörður & Ísafjarðardjúp

Icelandic towns present a compelling contrast of isolation and worldliness, with no better exemplar than **Ísafjörður** ⋆, the economic, administrative, and cultural capital of the Westfjords. In such a remote and unlikely setting, even the most ordinary tokens of urbanity—nice restaurants, trendy shops, cafes full of laptop users—take on a charmed aura.

Built on a gravel spit in a fjord within a fjord, Ísafjörður possesses an ideal natural harbor and has been one of Iceland's busiest trading centers since the late-18th century. In the late-19th century, it was the same civilizational oasis it is today, with two hotels, several gaming clubs, and a drama club. The current population is around 4,100, more than half the Westfjords total. Its steep mountainous backdrop and conscientiously preserved architecture encourage relaxing strolls around town.

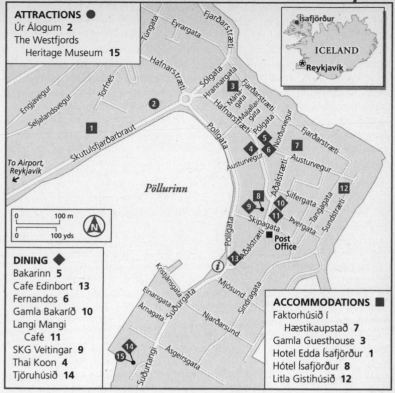

ATTRACTIONS ●
Úr Álogum **2**
The Westfjords
    Heritage Museum **15**

DINING ◆
Bakarinn **5**
Cafe Edinbort **13**
Fernandos **6**
Gamla Bakaríð **10**
Langi Mangi
    Café **11**
SKG Veitingar **9**
Thai Koon **4**
Tjöruhúsið **14**

ACCOMMODATIONS ■
Faktorhúsið í
    Hæstikaupstað **7**
Gamla Guesthouse **3**
Hotel Edda Ísafjörður **1**
Hótel Ísafjörður **8**
Litla Gistihúsið **12**

Boats leaving Ísafjörður soon enter **Ísafjarðardjúp** (p. 201), the enormous fjord that nearly cleaves the Westfjords in half; the lovely, winding drive along its southern shore is also the fastest route to Reykjavík.

ESSENTIALS
GETTING THERE & AROUND

BY PLANE   **Air Iceland** (🕿 570-3030; www.airiceland.is) connects Reykjavík and Ísafjörður two or three times daily year-round. The flight is 40 minutes, and ticket prices average 8,600kr ($138/£69). (Sitting on the left side of the plane grants views of Snæfellsjökull and the most picturesque Westfjords coastline.) All flights from Akureyri to Ísafjörður connect through Reykjavík.

An **airport shuttle** operated by **Valdimar Lúðvík Gíslason** (🕿 456-7195 or 852-1417; 500kr [$8/£4]) starts from Bolungarvík and stops at Hótel Ísafjörður approximately 45 minutes before flight departure times. The shuttle also picks up arriving passengers and stops at the hotel on the way back to Bolungarvík. The driver will stop at other accommodations in Ísafjörður's town center on request.

BY CAR   Drivers traveling from Reykjavík to Ísafjörður have three main options. The fastest route (440km/273 miles; 6½ hr.) follows this road sequence: Ring Road (Rte. 1)—Route 60—Route 608—Route 61. Paving is near complete for the entire route, which is about to be further streamlined by a new bridge over Mjóifjörður. Another route (456km/283 miles; 7½ hr.) follows Route 60 from the Ring Road all the way to Ísafjörður. This route is more scenic and provides access to the southwest and central Westfjords. About a third of the route is unpaved, however, and the rutted sections can be nerve-wracking. The third option is to take the *Baldur* car ferry (p. 186) from Stykkishólmur (on Snæfellsnes peninsula) to Brjánslaekur (in the Westfjords), and then continue to Ísafjörður on Route 62 and Route 60. The total travel time is around 8 hours, with 68km (42 miles) of unpaved road, but the driving distance is cut to 294km (183 miles). Drivers headed to Ísafjörður from north Iceland should simply take Route 61 from the Ring Road.

Ísafjörður has two **rental** agencies, **National/Bílaleiga Akureyrar** (© 461-6000; www.holdur.is) and **Hertz** (© 522-4490; www.hertz.is). Both are airport-based, but deliver cars anywhere in town for no charge.

BY BUS   Bus travel is usually not a convenient or cost-efficient means of getting to Ísafjörður from outside the Westfjords, though if you're coming from Reykjavík or Snæfellsnes, combining the bus with the car ferry has some sightseeing advantages.

Three connecting buses lead from Reykjavík or Akureyri to Ísafjörður. The first leg, with **Trex** (© 587-6000; www.trex.is) leads to Brú, on the Ring Road. Morning buses approach Brú both from the south, starting in Reykjavík, and from the north, starting in Akureyri. The next leg, also with Trex, goes from Brú to Hólmavík. The final leg from Hólmavík to Ísafjörður—which runs only from June to August on Tuesdays, Fridays, and Sundays—is serviced by **Stjörnubílar** (© 456-1575; www.stjornubilar.is). With layovers, the total travel time from Reykjavík to Ísafjörður is 9¾ hours, or 12½ hours coming back, at a total cost of 10,250kr ($164/£82) one-way.

For the bus–ferry route from Reykjavík, the first leg is the morning **Trex** bus from Reykjavík to Stykkishólmur, arriving at 11:10am from June 1 to 15, or 10:35am from June 15 through August. The ferry then goes from Stykkishólmur to Brjánslaekur in the Westfjords. The ferry does not leave Stykkishólmur until 3:30pm, so you'll have some time to kill there; from June 15 through August you might throw in the 11am "Unique Adventure Tour" (p. 187). The connecting bus from Brjánslaekur to Ísafjörður—with service only from June to August on Mondays, Wednesdays, and Saturdays—is handled by Stjörnubílar (see p. 190 for other connections to the southwest Westfjords). The total travel time is 12 hours from Reykjavík to Ísafjörður, or 7¾ hours on the way back (except from June 1–June 15, when travelers need to overnight in Stykkishólmur). The total cost is 8,550kr ($137/£68) one-way.

Trex's **Full Circle and Westfjords Bus Passport** (p. 190), valid from June through August, includes a complete circuit of Iceland, including the ferry *Baldur*.

For buses connecting Ísafjörður to the southwest Westfjords, see above. For municipal buses connecting Ísafjörður to Suðureyri, Flateyri, and Þingeyri, see p. 195.

The main bus stop in Ísafjörður is the N1 gas station on Pollgata.

BY TAXI   **Leigubílar Ísafirði** (© 456-3518) is on call 24/7.

BY BIKE   **West Tours,** Aðalstræti 7 (© 456-5111; www.westtours.is) rents good mountain bikes for 1,500kr ($24/£12) per day and extra-rugged bikes for 2,500kr ($40/£20).

VISITOR INFORMATION

Ísafjörður's **tourist information center,** Aðalstræti 7 (© 450-8060; www.westfjords.is and www.isafjordur.is; June 13–Aug Mon–Fri 9am–7pm, Sat–Sun 10am–5pm;

Sept–June 12 Mon–Fri 11am–4pm) is very efficient and provides information and hotel assistance for the Westfjords.

EXPLORING ÍSAFJÖRÐUR

Ísafjörður is laid out on a coastal spit shaped like the number "7" in a small fjord called Skutulsfjörður. The northernmost part of town—from the mainland to the elbow of the "7"—is known as *Hæstikaupstaður*, which loosely translates to "Uptown." Hæstikaupstaður has most of Ísafjörður's historic homes, built by fishing merchants in the 19th and early-20th centuries. Before walking around town, pick up the *Ísafjörður History* map at the tourist center, or visit the Heritage Museum (below), which has an accessible exhibit on town history. **West Tours** (below) offers a 2- to 3-hour town walking tour on request for 3,300kr ($53/£26), including admission to Heritage Museum; minimum two people, which smartly combines historical sights with introductions to local characters—including Ísafjörður's accordion-playing barber.

Miðkaupstaður (Midtown), boundaried by Silfurgata to the north and Mjósund to the south, is Ísafjörður's commercial center. The main drags are Hafnarstræti and Aðalstræti, which converge at Silfurtorg, the town square. The information center is on Aðalstræti, at Miðkaupstaður's south end. The Heritage Museum, the main harbor, and most of the warehouses and industrial buildings are in *Neðsdikaupstaður* (Downtown), the southernmost section of Ísafjörður.

Set back from the rotary where Ísafjörður meets the mainland, **Úr Álögum (Breaking the Spell II)** is a provocative and intricate rendering of St. George and the dragon, by Iceland's foremost sculptor Einar Jónsson (p. 115). The naked woman curled on George's arm is the Libyan princess he spared from being sacrificed to the dragon. A shriveled female figure, a symbol of the dragon's curse, is morphed into a cloak that the princess casts off as the dragon's head is pierced by George's sword.

WHAT TO SEE & DO

While Iceland Airwaves (p. 18) in Reykjavík is the country's reigning alternative/indie music festival, Ísafjörður's **Aldrei fór ég suður** (www.aldrei.is), on the Friday and Saturday before Easter, is the fresh upstart. Its name, which means "I never went south," is an expression used by locals who have resisted the steady migration of population to the capital. Like Airwaves, international acts are included; but, unlike Airwaves, every performance is free. Flight and accommodation packages are sold by **West Tours** (below).

Other events during Easter Week include art exhibitions and **Ski Week (Skíðavikan),** featuring trail competitions, snowboarding jumps, and a family day. Check with the Ísafjörður information center for details.

Ísafjörður's annual **Act Alone Theater Festival** (www.actalone.net), held over 4 days in late June, is devoted to solo performances by Icelandic and international "monodramatists." Admission is free.

Swamp soccer, a sport recently invented in Finland, is basically what it sounds like: soccer on a muddy field, with some rule modifications. Ísafjörður is a swamp soccer hotbed, with a tournament held the first weekend of August; for more information, visit www.myrarbolti.com.

The Westfjords Heritage Museum (Byggðasafn Vestfjarða)   Housed in a 1784

warehouse near Ísafjörður's southern tip, this engaging if esoteric folk museum features an intelligently laid out maritime exhibit of fishing and nautical paraphernalia, plus an informative primer on Westfjords regional history. An engaging documentary on open rowboat fishing is screened continuously, with English subtitles. As is often the case in Icelandic folk museums, the staff doesn't appear solicitous, but a friendly guided tour could be yours for the asking. Film screenings and other events are held from mid-June to mid-August on Mondays and Thursdays at 8:30pm; no schedule is posted online, but you can call or check with tourist information.

Suðurgata, near southern tip of Ísafjörður (look for flagpoles). © 456-3291. Admission 500kr ($8/£4) adults; 300kr ($4.80/£2.40) seniors; free for children 15 and under. June Mon–Fri 10am–5pm, Sat–Sun 1–5; July–Aug daily 10am–5pm.

TOURS & ACTIVITIES

West Tours, Aðalstræti 7 (© **456-5111;** www.westtours.is), the dominant tour operator in the Westfjords, is highly recommended and has an imaginative range of offerings, from bird watching and sea kayaking to fox-spotting and berry picking. A particularly exciting **day tour** is the 12-hour boat and hiking excursion to Hornvík in Hornstrandir Nature Reserve. (For tours to Hornstrandir, see p. 211.) West Tours rents **mountain bikes** and can suggest fantastic routes, such as the coastal road around the peninsula between Arnarfjörður and Dýrafjörður. Some tours are for groups only, but it's worth asking about any scheduled group tours you could sign on with.

In winter, options are abundant, particularly for cross-country or backcountry skiers. For more on the **Westfjords in winter,** see p. 211.

HIKING   The trail map *Walks in Ísafjörður Area,* sold for 300kr ($4.80/£2.40) at the tourist information center, thoroughly outlines local trails, including distances and difficulty ratings. A new hiking map in the *Vestfirðir & Dalir* series is on the verge of publication and should vastly outclass its predecessors. A pleasant short hike (about an hour round-trip) starts from Route 61, directly across the fjord from the southern tip of Ísafjörður and ascends 220m (722 ft.) along a creek to **Naustahvilft,** a bowl-like indentation in the mountainside (Icelanders call such formations "troll seats"). A recommended **all-day hike** (20km/12 miles; 8 hr.) starts from Ísafjörður's northern suburb Hnífsdalur, ascending Hnífsdalur valley before descending through Seljalandsdalur valley and back into town. On *Walks in Ísafjörður Area,* this route is marked as trail #1 to #1b. A municipal bus (schedule at www.isafjordur.is/ferdamadurinn/samgongur) goes to Hnífsdalur several times daily. An equally recommended and somewhat less grueling hike (16km/10 miles; 6½ hr.) starts by a bridge at the base of Skutulsfjörður and ascends through **Engidalur** valley along the Langá river past a hydroelectric power station, with a detour to Fossavatn lake (trails #6, #7, and #8 on the map).

WHERE TO STAY IN ÍSAFJÖRÐUR

For accommodations in Suðureyri and Önundarfjörður (all within a 25-minute drive of Ísafjörður), see p. 197.

EXPENSIVE

Faktorshúsið í Hæstikaupstað *(★★ (Finds*   This 1788 house, among the oldest in Iceland, has undergone the most tasteful and authentic restoration we've seen in any Icelandic accommodation: from the fastidiously retouched ceiling moldings to the ornate antique Norwegian stoves. Book early, as there's only one guest apartment, with two double beds and a child's bed in a single bedroom, plus a small kitchen and bathroom with tub.

Aðalstræti 7. 🕿 **456-3868** or 899-0742. Fax 456-4075. gistias@snerpa.is. 1 unit. 16,900kr ($270/£135) double. Breakfast available: 1,100kr ($18/£8.80). MC, V. *In room:* Wi-Fi, kitchen, no phone.

Hótel Ísafjörður ⚓ Visitors looking for a spacious, comfortable, modern, en-suite hotel room in the town center need look no further. Most rooms have nice views over the water. The only deluxe double, #508, has a CD player, bathtub, minibar, and a bigger TV. Sleeping-bag accommodation is available October through April for 6,500kr ($104/£52 double).

Silfurtorg 2. 🕿 **456-4111.** Fax 456-4767. www.hotelisafjordur.is. 36 units. June–Aug 17,500kr–25,000kr ($280–$400/ £140–£200) double. Rates 30%–40% lower Sept–May. Rates include breakfast, except sleeping-bag accommodation. Internet specials available. AE, DC, MC, V. **Amenities:** Restaurant; bar; laundry/dry cleaning service. *In room:* TV, Wi-Fi, fridge, coffee/tea, hair dryer.

MODERATE/INEXPENSIVE
Gamla Guesthouse This 1896 ex-nursing-home on a historic residential block has nine decent-size, simple, and serene rooms. Corridors are lined with old photos, and the breakfast room is bright and inviting. Sleeping-bag accommodation (the other five rooms) is in a separate house, 100m (328 ft.) down the street, with a cozy TV lounge and large guest kitchen.

Mánagata 5. 🕿 **456-4146.** Fax: 456-4446. www.gistihus.ls. 14 units, none w/bathroom. May–Sept 8,600kr ($138/ £69) double; 6,000kr ($96/£48) double w/sleeping bag; 11,200kr ($179/£90) triple; 2,100kr ($34/£17) sleeping-bag accommodation in room for 4–6 persons. Rates around 20% lower Oct–Apr. Rates include breakfast, except sleeping-bag accommodation (900kr/$14/£7.20). MC, V. **Amenities:** Guest kitchen; Internet terminal. *In room:* TV, Wi-Fi.

Hótel Edda Ísafjörður A dormitory during the school year, this practical and rather generic summer lodging offers both sleeping-bag accommodation—the super-cheap beds are in the classrooms—and 10 renovated doubles with modern fittings and private facilities. The town center is a 15-minute walk away.

Off Skutulsfjarðarbraut (Rte. 61). 🕿 **444-4960.** Fax 456-4767. www.hotelisafjordur.is. 42 units, 10 w/bathroom. Early June–Aug 20 9,400kr ($150/£75) double; 7,600kr ($122/£61) double without bathroom; 1,200kr–2,300kr ($19–$37/£9.60–£18) sleeping-bag accommodation. Breakfast available: 900kr ($14/£7.20). AE, DC, MC, V. Closed Aug 21–early June. *In room:* No phone.

Litla Gistihúsið Leaving aside the stairway mural of exotic animals, this guesthouse has an appealing vintage look and a relaxing living room with fireplace. Rooms are hospitable if not at all luxurious. The two ground floor rooms have small private bathrooms at no extra cost, but the two upstairs rooms have more space and character. Another two rooms in a neighboring house are more neutral and functional.

Sundstræti 43. 🕿 **474-1455.** reginasc@simnet.is. 6 units, 2 w/bathroom. 7,000kr ($112/£56) double. MC, V. **Amenities:** Guest kitchen. *In room:* TV, no phone.

WHERE TO DINE IN ÍSAFJÖRÐUR
EXPENSIVE
SKG Veitingar ICELANDIC Hótel Ísafjörður has the town's only upscale restaurant, which is proficient and reliable—but preparations lack finish, and the whole dining experience is more memorable at Tjöruhúsið (p. 204). Specialties include salted cod au gratin with garlic flavored potatoes, minke whale carpaccio, and pan-fried puffin from Vigur Island with bleu cheese sauce.

In Hótel Ísafjörður, Silfurtorg 2. 🕿 **456-3360.** Main courses 2,250kr–3,500kr ($36–$56/£18–£28). AE, DC, MC, V. Sun–Thurs 7:30am–10pm, Fri–Sat 7:30am–10:30pm.

MODERATE

Fernandos (★ ITALIAN   Fernandos' wide array of Italian dishes are a bit overburdened with creamy sauces but surprisingly authentic, and no restaurant outside Reykjavík has such delicate and delicious thin-crusted pizzas. (To appease Icelanders they offer "classic," doughy crusts as well.) The weekday lunch buffet, a steal at 1,390kr ($22/£11), lets you pile your plate with pizza, pasta, wings, and other meats.

Hafnarstræti 12. (Ⓒ 456-5001. Main courses 1,200kr–2,600kr ($19–$42/£9.60–£21). AE, DC, MC, V. Sun–Thurs 11am–9pm; Fri–Sat 11am–10pm; lunch buffet Mon–Fri noon–1:30pm.

Tjöruhúsið ★★ (Value SEAFOOD   Nestled inside a 1781 fish warehouse next to the Heritage Museum, with bench seating and long wooden tables, this fabulous seafood restaurant would earn three stars if wine and dessert were available to cap things off. The waiter simply points to a sheet of fish illustrations to indicate which species are freshly available that day. The fish arrives still sizzling in the pan and seasoned to perfection, with potatoes, tomatoes, lettuce, grapes, and lemon slices. Single portions are usually enough to satisfy two.

Suðurgata. (Ⓒ 456-4419 or 897-6733. Reservations recommended. Main courses 2,000kr–4,000kr ($32–$64/ £16–£32). AE, DC, MC, V. June to mid-Sept daily noon–2:30pm and 6–10pm.

INEXPENSIVE

Thai Koon (★ (Value THAI   This casual, cafeteria-style eatery in Ísafjörður's downtown shopping arcade is a welcome break from the interchangeability of most provincial Icelandic restaurants—and the food is genuinely good and not too greasy. Combo plates are generous, with 8 or 10 dishes to choose among.

Neisti Shopping Center, Hafnarstræti 9–11. (Ⓒ 456-0123. Main courses 690kr–1,090kr ($11–$17/£5.50–£8.70). DC, MC, V. Mon–Sat 11:30am–9pm; Sun 5–9pm.

CAFES & BAKERIES

Bakarinn   This local staple has an honest, workaday ambience and offers good crepes, pizza, and other light fare as well as the usual baked goodies.

Hafnarstræti 14. (Ⓒ 456-4771. Pastries and light dishes 70kr–680kr ($1.10–$11/55p–£5.45). AE, DC, MC, V. Mon–Fri 7:30–6pm; Sun 9am–4:30pm.

Cafe Edinborg   Located next to the information center, this coffeehouse has pleasant outdoor seating and rotating art exhibits. Unfortunately, food is limited to cakes, plus a snack or two on a good day.

Aðalstræti 7. (Ⓒ 456-4400. Cakes 500kr ($8/£4). AE, DC, MC, V. Sun–Thurs 11am–1am; Fri–Sat 11am–3am.

Gamla Bakaríð   A perfect spot for a rainy afternoon, this cozy, atmospheric patisserie with an embossed tin ceiling has seating space and soft atmospheric lighting.

Aðalstræti 24. (Ⓒ 456-3226. Pastries 100kr–670kr ($1.60–$11/80p–£5.35). AE, DC, MC, V. Daily 7am–6pm.

Langi Mangi Cafe   Ísafjörður's coolest after-hours hangout offers panini and other light fare—all perfectly digestible, but, for a real lunch, head elsewhere.

Aðalstræti 22. (Ⓒ 456-3022. www.langimangi.is. Sandwiches 750kr–850kr ($12–$14/£6–£6.80). MC, V. Mon–Wed 11am–11pm; Thurs 11am–1am; Fri 11am–3am; Sat noon–3am; Sun 1–11pm.

SHOPPING/NIGHTLIFE

Ísafjörður's boutique stores and souvenir shops are all arrayed along Aðalstræti and Hafnarstræti. The best **bookstore and newsstand** is **Bókhlaðan Penninn,** Hafnarstræti 2 (Ⓒ **456-3123;** Mon–Fri 9am–6pm; Sat 10am–1pm), right off Silfurtorg square. For **outdoor gear,** head downtown to **Hafnarbúðin,** Suðurgata (℃ **456-3245;** Mon–Fri 9am–6pm, Sat 10am–2pm), near the Heritage Museum.

The only dance club in town is **Krúsin** (no phone; Fri–Sat nights only). **Langi Mangi Café,** Aðalstræti 22 (℃ **456-3022**), is the ever-reliable hangout and bar, but the newer **Cafe Edinborg,** Aðalstræti 7 (℃ **456-4400**), is larger and often has live music.

ÍSAFJARÐARDJÚP
BOLUNGARVÍK

14km (9 miles) northwest of Ísafjörður, Bolungarvík—the second-largest town in the Westfjords—braves exposure to raw weather conditions to lie close to fertile fishing grounds. The only eateries are the **gas station grill** and **Kjallarinn Krá,** Hafnargata 41 (℃ **456-7901;** main courses 1,900kr–3,000kr [$32–$48/£15–£24]; June–Aug daily 11am–11pm, Sept–May Fri–Sat 6–11pm), a decent restaurant specializing in fresh catch from the harbor. Bolungarvík's **information center,** Vitastígur 1 (℃ **450-7010;** bolungarvik@bolungarvik.is; June–Aug Mon–Fri 9am–4:30pm; Sat 2–5pm) is next to a crafts shop and the Natural History Museum.

Natural History Museum (Náttúrugripasafn Bolungarvíkur)   Displays of taxidermied animals, bird eggs, and minerals are found all over Iceland. While this one is more professional and extensive than usual, not enough context is posted in English. The most poignant specimens came to Iceland by accident: a polar bear, shot 64km (40 miles) offshore after drifting from Greenland on pack ice, and a poor lost flamingo.

Vitastígur 3. ℃ **456-7005.** Admission 500kr ($8/£4) adults; children under 16 free. Mon–Fri 9–11:45am and 1–4:45pm; June 15–Aug 15 also Sat–Sun 1–4:45pm.

Ósvör Museum   Visitors to this re-creation of a seasonal fishing station from a century ago are greeted by the resident fisherman, who remains in character, hang-drying and salting cod in a sheepskin outfit. (Growing a long beard also seems to be in the job description.) The primitive encampment includes a turf-insulated stone hut, an authentically odorous salting shed, and a restored rowboat with a capstan for hauling it ashore. It's an expensive few minutes, but touchingly earnest nonetheless.

Rte. 61, 1km (½ mile) east of Bolungarvík. ℃ **892-1616.** Admission 500kr ($8/£4) adults; 350kr ($5.60/£2.80) seniors; children under 16 free. May–June Mon–Fri 10am–5pm, Sat–Sun 1–5pm; July–Aug daily 10am–6pm.

VIGUR ISLAND

Owned and occupied by the same family for four generations, Vigur is not the most scenically compelling island in Iceland, but most visitors are pleased enough gazing at birds—especially puffins—and vicariously experiencing the solitary island life (which in this case, we notice, has satellite TV). The family has 25 sheep and also earns money from puffin hunting and harvesting down feathers from eider-duck nests.

Every afternoon from mid-June through late August, **West Tours** (p. 211) offers a 3-hour tour of Vigur for 4,700kr ($75/£38), starting with a 35-minute boat ride from Ísafjörður. The walking is very leisurely, as photographers loiter to inch their way closer to puffins on the low cliff ledges. (Be aware that puffins fly south en masse in mid-Aug, and on sunny days they often go off fishing for sand eels.) Other notable sights include seals and an 1830 windmill, the only one left standing in Iceland. Tours end with coffee and cake at the farmhouse.

HEYDALUR ☞

This picturesque valley near the head of Mjóifjörður, about 135km (84 miles) southeast of Ísafjörður, provides a wonderful interlude in any journey along the Ísafjarðardjúp coast on Route 61. Tours organized by the **Heydalur Country Hotel** (ⓒ **456-4824;** www.heydalur.is) include horseback riding (90 min. for 4,000kr [$64/£32]); sea kayaking in Mjóifjörður, usually accompanied by curious seals (3 hr. for 5,000kr [$80/£40]); and an hour's hike up the valley to a trout fishing lake for 2,000kr [$32/£16] rod rental). All activities wind down with a soak in a fabulous outdoor geothermal pool. Heydalur is also a good spot for mingling with locals, as there are plenty of Icelandic clientele.

The hotel has nine simple, pleasant en suite **guest rooms** for 9,800kr ($157/£78) double, 4,200kr ($67/£34) double with sleeping bag, AE, DC, MC, V; and an atmospheric **restaurant** inside a restored barn with main courses for 1,500kr–3,000kr ($24–$48/£12–£24), open June to August, daily 11am to 10pm. (A parrot named Kobbi lives in the corner, but he only speaks Icelandic.) If you're just passing through in the evening, order the home-caught salmon with pesto, then bathe in the pool while it's cooking.

7 The Strandir Coast

Flanking Húnaflói bay, at the northeast edge of the Westfjords, the Strandir coast has a mysterious allure that's difficult to account for. In many ways, the region accentuates what is already exceptional about the Westfjords. Winters are unusually harsh, and pack ice often remains into late spring. Lowland is scarce, and inhabitants are especially dependent on the sea; even the sheep have been known to taste like seaweed, their backup diet. Strandir's topography is more varied than most of the Westfjords, and the abundance of driftwood lends an enchanting and melancholic cast to the shoreline. Historically Strandir's villages have been among the most isolated in the country, and outlaws have sought refuge on its austerely beautiful upland moors. Whatever the cause, visitors often describe the Strandir coast in quasi-mystical terms, as if they've escaped time or recovered some lost part of themselves.

One day is not enough time for Strandir to work its way into your system; 2 to 4 nights are better, ideally followed by an excursion farther north to Hornstrandir Nature Reserve. Those not keen on roughing it in Hornstrandir—or without the time to spare—can still reach the astonishing sea cliffs at Hornbjarg on day tours from Norðurfjörður twice a week in summer (p. 210).

ESSENTIALS

GETTING THERE   No public buses venture up the Strandir coast past Hólmavík and Drangsnes, so a rental car is almost indispensable. Car rental is not available in Hólmavík or Gjögur, Strandir's only airport, so drivers usually arrive from Reykjavík, Ísafjörður, or Akureyri. Hólmavík, a village at the base of Strandir, is along Route 61, 224km (139 miles) from Ísafjörður and 274km (170 miles) from Reykjavík. A few kilometers north of Hólmavík, Route 643 branches off from Route 61 and heads up the coast, ending 96km (60 miles) later at Norðurfjörður.

Eagle Air (ⓒ **562-2640;** www.eagleair.is) flies twice a week from Reykjavík to Gjögur, 16km (10 miles) southeast of Norðurfjörður for 7,180kr ($115/£57) and up; 40 min.

Buses connecting Ísafjörður to towns outside the Westfjords stop at Hólmavík; see p. 200. On Fridays, the **Trex** (*C* **587-6000;** www.trex.is) bus from Brú (on the Ring Road) to Hólmavík extends a bit farther up Strandir to Drangsnes.

For information on the **ferry** connecting Norðurfjörður to Hornstrandir, see p. 208.

VISITOR INFORMATION   The visitor center for all of Strandir is in **Hólmavík,** Norðurtún 1 (*C* **451-3111;** www.holmavik.is/info; June 10–Aug daily 8am–5pm), at the community center. Off season, rely on the tourist office in Ísafjörður (p. 200).

EXPLORING THE STRANDIR COAST

The coastal route from Hólmavík to Norðurfjörður on Route 643 is among the most scenic, rugged, and mesmerizing drives in all of Iceland. Norðurfjörður has a general store with basic groceries, a gas pump (operable 24 hr. by credit card), and a bank (open weekdays 1–4pm, but no ATM; stock up in Hólmavík accordingly). Also make sure to pick up a hiking map at the Hólmavík information center (above).

HÓLMAVÍK

Museum of Icelandic Sorcery and Witchcraft (Galdrasýning á Ströndum)

Mass hysteria about witches and sorcerers never really took hold in Iceland, at least relative to the rest of Europe. But from 1625 to 1685, around 120 alleged sorcerers were tried across the country, with 25 burned at the stake (23 of them men) and many more flogged. The Strandir coast had more than its share of trials—and more than its share of expert sorcerers, according to this gleefully morbid museum.

Admission includes a 30-minute audio tour through several installations relating the sorcerer's craft. The exhibit is genuinely educational, but doesn't take pains to separate history from folklore. (No historian really knows, for instance, whether Icelandic sorcerers ever skinned a human corpse from the waist down to make "necropants.") Most convicted sorcerers were too poor to leave any historical record, and the only real artifact here is an ancient "blood stone" used for animal sacrifices. In any case, you'll learn plenty of useful formulas, including which symbols to carve on a hunk of cheese before it's eaten by the object of your affection.

An accompanying exhibit called "The Sorcerer's Cottage" is in Bjarnarfjörður, 20 minutes' north on Route 643, but it's very dispensable—basically all you see is a turf hut filled with dummy figures casting spells, without explanations in English.

Höfðagata 8-10. *C* 451-3525. (Sorcerer's Cottage *C* 451-3524.) www.galdrasyning.is. Admission 500kr ($8/£4) adults; children under 12 free. June–Sept 15 daily 10am–6pm; rest of year by request.

DJÚPAVÍK *★★*

The soulful hotel at Djúpavík, a stunningly beautiful inlet of Reykjarfjörður, is the ideal base for exploring Strandir. Activities organized by the hotel (see "Where to Stay," below) include sea angling and sea kayaking—no experience necessary—and touring the ruins of a herring factory next door.

Djúpavík's first houses went up in 1917, soon after herring were discovered in Reykjarfjörður. The factory, finished in 1935, was an engineering marvel and the largest concrete structure in Europe. The herring trade was so lucrative that the factory paid for itself in a single five-month season. During peak summers, 200 workers—mostly teenage girls—worked the machinery round the clock. In the early 1950s the herring simply failed to show up, and in 1971 Reykjarfjörður was completely abandoned. Today the only winter residents are the couple who have run the hotel since 1985—and their adorable Icelandic sheepdog Tína.

Guided 45-minute tours of the factory ruins start at 2pm daily from mid-June through August; the 750kr ($12/£6) cost includes an informative photo-and-text exhibit in an anteroom. The factory is certainly atmospheric, but interest will vary; for some it's just crumbling concrete and rusting metal, while for others it's equal to the Roman Coliseum. Exploring on your own is prohibited for safety reasons.

For further information on Djúpavík, and an extensive online photo gallery of the Strandir coast, visit the hotel's website www.djupavik.com.

GJÖGUR, TRÉKYLLISVÍK & NORÐURFJÖRÐUR

Gjögur, near the tip of the peninsula north of Reykjarfjörður, has a cluster of summer homes. A crude road winds past Gjögur's minuscule airport to **Gjögurstrond**⋆, an evocative stretch of beach and rocky coastline, with steam drifting from underground hot springs.

The next bay to the north is **Trékyllisvík,** and on its south shore is the 19th-century church at **Árnes.** In February 1991, during a severe windstorm, the church was lifted off its foundation and deposited a few feet over, but nothing inside was damaged. Next to the church is the small museum **Minja-og Handverkshúsið Kört** (© 451-4025; arnes2@simnet.is; admission 300kr [$4.80/£2.40]; June–Aug daily 10am–7pm), with a haphazard, regional collection of textiles, dolls, and various fishing and farming artifacts. Without paying admission you could still visit the **handicrafts shop,** which has locally knit woolens plus bowls, vases, and candleholders sculpted from driftwood and whale bone.

Norðurfjörður, a tiny village at the north end of Trékyllisvík, has the only market and gas station beyond Hólmavík. From late June to mid-August, a boat departs from here three times a week for Hornstrandir Nature Reserve (p. 210). Route 643 ends at Norðurfjörður, but a coastal road continues another 4km (2½ miles) to Krossnes farm. Shortly after passing the farm, a driveway on the right leads downhill to **Krossneslaug**⋆, one of Iceland's most sublime geothermal pools. A gorgeous stone beach is just a few feet away, and some intrepid souls brave the freezing ocean water before scrambling back to the heated pool. (Do not attempt this without shoes for traversing the rocks.) The pool is large enough to swim laps, and the temperature is perfect—though the water is a tad over-chlorinated. The admission fee of 250kr ($4/£2) per person is slipped into a secure metal box in the changing rooms. The pool is open anytime, but twilight is especially idyllic.

OUTDOOR ACTIVITIES

HIKING   The inexpensive hiking map *Strandasýsla,* available at the Hólmavík information center, effectively details Strandir's most worthwhile hikes, with thorough directions, distances, and difficulty ratings. (Look for a new *Vestfirðir and Dalir* map shortly.) The hikes recommended below are of moderate difficulty.

A 5km (3 miles) **loop hike** from Hótel Djúpavík heads up a steep cleft behind the hotel, then east along a plateau with fabulous fjord views before descending to meet Route 643; allow 3 hours to stop and smell the mosses.

Starting from Naustvík on the north shore of Reykjarfjörður, an ancient footpath heads through a scenic mountain pass to **Árnes** on Trékyllisvík Bay; the route is 3.5km (2 miles) and about 90 minutes each way.

Just north of Gjögur is **Reykjaneshyrna,** a small mountain and sea cliff rising conspicuously between the road and the ocean. *Strandasýsla* suggests approaching from the Gjögur airfield, but you can park much closer—at a blue sign for Reykjaneshyrna along Route 643—to make the 90-minute round-trip climb. The top has marvelous views in all directions.

Another excellent hike not indicated on *Strandasýsla* is a 4- to 5-hour clockwise loop starting from **Krossneslaug.** Walk back to Norðurfjörður, then turn right on Route 647, which heads overland to Munaðarnes Farm, on the coast of Ingólfsfjörður. Then continue around the peninsular coastline—first on an unmarked trail, then along a road—back to Krossnes for a triumphal dip in the pool.

WHERE TO STAY

Djúpavík and Norðurfjörður, on the northern stretch of the Strandir coast, are the most memorable places to stay. If you need lodging in Hólmavík, or anywhere else in Strandir's southern portion, contact the Hólmavík information center (p. 207) or visit www.westfjords.is.

Hótel Djúpavík ⓐ   Built in 1938, this former boarding house for herring workers is indisputably the most characterful and beautifully situated accommodation on the Strandir coast. Rooms aren't big, beds aren't wide, and sheets and towels aren't plush; but in such an inviting refuge none of that seems to matter. (If you feel cramped, think of the herring days, when eight girls shared each room.) Ever-mindful of local history, the proprietors include herring in the breakfast spread.

© 451-4037. Fax. 451-4035. www.djupavik.com. 14 units, none w/bathroom. 7,400kr ($118/£59) double; 10,600kr ($170/£85) family room. Breakfast available (980kr/$16/£7.85). MC, V. **Amenities:** Restaurant. *In room:* No phone.

NORÐURFJÖRÐUR

Gistiheimili Norðurfjarðar (© **554-4089;** gulledda@simnet.is; 3,000kr [$48/£24] per person made-up bed, 2,000kr [$32/£16] per person sleeping-bag accommodation; no credit cards), in the same building as the general store, has three very straightforward rooms: two doubles and a triple. Very close by is the village's only other guesthouse, **Gistiheimilið Bergistanga** (© **451-4003;** arneshreppur@simnet.is; 2,000kr [$32/£16] sleeping-bag accommodation; no credit cards), with equally serviceable rooms but sleeping-bag accommodation only. Both lodgings have guest kitchens, but only Bergistanga serves breakfast, and only on request for 900kr ($14/£7.20). A 10-minute walk from the general store is **Valgeirsstaðir mountain hut** (© **451-4017;** 3,000kr [$48/£24] per person sleeping-bag accommodation; closed Sept–June), with a well-equipped kitchen, a hot shower, and eight rooms, each accommodating up to six people in sleeping bags. Booking must be done online through the hiking organization **Ferðafélag Íslands** (© **568-2533;** www.fi.is; MC, V); they mail you a voucher, which you bring along to show the warden. If you show up and space is available, you won't be turned away. Note, however, that sleeping-bag accommodation is cheaper in the guesthouses, where you can have a private room.

WHERE TO DINE

Hólmavík has a large **supermarket** for stocking up on supplies; Norðurfjörður has a far more rudimentary one. Hólmavík's only other dining option besides Cafe Riis (below) is fast food at the **gas station.** No restaurants are north of Hótel Djúpavík.

Cafe Riis ICELANDIC   Housed inside Hólmavík's oldest building, with driftwood floorboards and a welcoming air, Cafe Riis has above-average food at reasonable prices. Burritos, mussels, and puffin with blueberry sauce supplement the usual pizza, fish, and lamb regimen.

Hafnarbraut 39, Hólmavík. ☏ **451-3567.** Main courses 1,250kr–2,200kr ($20–$35/£10–£18). Sun–Thurs 11:30am–11:30pm; Fri–Sat 11:30am–3am; kitchen closes daily 10pm.

Hótel Djúpavík ICELANDIC   In summer the hotel's restaurant stays open all day, but lunch is restricted to light meals—say, fish soup, a sandwich, and cake—and dinner is a simple choice between lamb and fish. The food says "home cooking" more than "fine dining;" but out in Strandir, it hits the spot. In August you're likely to get a fabulous dessert of freshly picked berries with skyr and cream. Call ahead so they know you're coming.

Rte. 643, Djúpavík. ☏ **451-4037.** Dinner menu 3,500kr ($56/£28) per person. MC, V. Mid-June to Aug daily 8am–9:30pm, with dinner starting at 7:30pm; other times of year call ahead.

8 Hornstrandir Nature Reserve

Among Iceland's coastal areas, **Hornstrandir** ✦✦✦—the spiky peninsula at the northern tip of the Westfjords—is the truest wilderness. Because of its harsh climate, few Icelanders ever settled here, and the last full-time residents left in 1952. There are no roads, no airstrips, no powerful rivers for hydroelectricity, and just one hot spring for geothermal heat. Hornstrandir was designated a nature reserve in 1975; since grazing by horses and sheep is forbidden, the vegetation—from mossy tundra to meadows full of wildflowers—now resembles when the Vikings first arrived. Arctic foxes, seen scurrying by day and heard cackling at night, are also protected. The coast is lined with idyllic sandy bays, spooky abandoned homes, and rugged sea cliffs teeming with birdlife. Other travelers are few and far between.

Visiting Hornstrandir can require careful planning, but the logistics are not as difficult as they're often made out to be. The best time to come is from late June to mid-August; but, to minimize weather risks, most visitors arrive the second half of July or the first week of August.

ESSENTIALS

VISITOR INFORMATION   The best source is the information center in Ísafjörður (p. 200). The Environment and Food Agency website **www.ust.is** (click "Protected Areas," then "Hornstrandir") has a basic profile of the nature reserve.

GETTING THERE & AROUND   For those not taking an organized tour, the general procedure is to sketch out an itinerary in sync with ferry schedules. Most travelers take **ferries** to Hornstrandir from Ísafjörður or Bolungarvík, the village 14km (9 miles) northwest of Ísafjörður. The other ferry connection is from Norðurfjörður (p. 208), on the Strandir coast. You could start in Ísafjörður and end up in Norðurfjörður, or vice-versa, but Norðurfjörður is a tiny settlement with no scheduled buses or car rentals. A few travelers **walk** the 16km (10 miles) between Norðurfjörður and the tiny Gjögur airport (p. 206), which has twice-weekly **flights** to and from Reykjavík. Hardcore hikers sometimes walk into Hornstrandir over several days, starting from Unaðsdalur, at the end of Route 635 on the north shore of Ísafjarðardjúp.

Contrary to what many have heard, camping is not necessary in Hornstrandir (see "Where to Stay," below). If you like to camp but don't enjoy lugging your tent and gear around in a heavy backpack, the ferry system allows you to set up base camps from which to explore. **West Tours** (below) acts as an agent for all ferries below, and can even arrange for packages to be sent in. Schedules (except for Freydís) are mapped out at their website.

Tips **Don't Stand Up the Ferry Man**

If you're traveling independently in the Nature Reserve, your ferry operator will ask when and where you expect to be picked up. If your plans change, relay a message to the boat operator through a guesthouse or another traveler. Otherwise an expensive search and rescue mission will probably be launched.

Sjóferðir (© 456-3879; www.sjoferdir.is), based in Ísafjörður, has weekly ferry service to Grunnavík for 3,500kr ($56/£28), Hesteyri for 4,000kr ($64/£32), Aðalvík for 4,200kr ($67/£34), Veiðileysufjörður for 4,800kr ($77/£38), Hrafnfjörður for 4,800kr ($77/£38), and Hornvík for 6,800kr ($109/£54) from late June to late August (all prices one-way). The schedule at the website is misleading, because many listed departures are only for organized tours with West Tours (below).

The ferry run by **Ferðaþjónustan Grunnavík** (© 456-4664; www.grunnavik.is) leaves from Bolungarvík and has twice-weekly service to Grunnavík for 3,000kr ($48/£24), Hesteyri for 3,500kr ($56/£28), and Aðalvík for 3,500kr ($56/£28) from mid-June through August (all prices one-way).

Freydís (© 893-6926 or 852-9367; www.freydis.is) operates the ferry from Norðurfjörður twice per week from late June to mid-August, stopping at guesthouses in Reykjarfjörður (not to be confused with the fjord of the same name south of Norðurfjörður) for 5,000kr ($80/£40); Bolungavík (not to be confused with Bolungarvík near Ísafjörður) for 5,500kr ($88/£44); and Látravík (aka Hornbjargsviti) for 6,000kr ($96/£48) en route to Hornvík for 6,500kr ($104/£52) and Hælavík (aka Hlöðuvík) for 6,500kr ($104/£52) and back to Norðurfjörður (all prices one-way). Taking the round-trip route as a sightseeing day trip is 8,000kr ($128/£64). A third weekly trip extends only from Norðurfjörður to Reykjarfjörður.

ORGANIZED TOURS

If you'd like a private guide instead of a group tour, contact the Ísafjörður information center, which keeps a list of licensed guides.

West Tours, Aðalstræti 7, Ísafjörður (© 456-5111; www.westtours.is), the most reputable tour operator in the Westfjords, offers scheduled day tours to Hesteyri (4–5 hr.; 4,900kr [$78/£39]) and Hornvík (12 hr.; 16,300kr [$261/£130]), guided day hikes from Sæból (in Aðalvík) to Hesteyri (12 hr.; 11,300kr [$181/£90]), and spectacular 4-day, 3-night camping expeditions to Hornvík for 60,000kr ($960/£480).

Iceland's premier hiking organization, **Ferðafélag Íslands,** Mörkin 6, Reykjavík (© 568-2533; www.fi.is), leads a variety of Hornstrandir trips even into October.

Borea Adventures, Hlíðarvegur 38, Ísafjörður (© 899-3817; www.boreaadventures. com), offers marvelous 5- to 6-day Hornstrandir trips aboard its 18m (60-ft.) racing yacht. Participants alight from the yacht for kayaking, observing wildlife, or, in winter, backcountry skiing. Prices range from 144,375kr to 157,500kr ($2,310–$2,520/ £1,155–£1,260), including food and equipment.

HIKING HORNSTRANDIR

Currently the best Hornstrandir map, published by Landmælingar Íslands, is sold online at www.nordicstore.net. (Soon forthcoming is an even more practical and detailed map in the *Vestfirðir and Dalir* series, sold online at www.galdrasyning.is.)

The maps indicate which trails are passable only at low tide, and the Ísafjörður information office can supply tide tables. Also make sure to bring a compass, shoes for fording streams, and plenty of warm clothing. Most clear running water is safe to drink, unless it passed through bird nesting areas. Hiking alone is not a good idea.

When sketching out an itinerary, always allow extra time to get from one place to another. Harsh weather or thick fog could roll in, and even the few marked trails can be difficult to follow. (It never gets completely dark, so you can always take your time.) Trails at higher altitudes may have deep snow even in July. Take note of nearby emergency huts, which have radios, heaters, and food. Check weather reports and review the challenges of your route with the Ísafjörður information center.

No one itinerary stands out in Hornstrandir, but one sight is decidedly worth prioritizing. **Hornbjarg** ★★★, a sea cliff on Hornstrandir's north coast, just east of Hornvík bay, is the most spectacular landmark on Iceland's coastline. From its narrow summit, the inland slope descends in a surreal parabolic curve. Gazing down at the birds and surf from the 534m (1,752-ft.) ledge—which is also the highest point on Hornstrandir—is exhilarating and unforgettable. Campers stationed in **Hornvík** ★★, the bay just west of Hornbjarg, should venture to the sea cliff **Hælavíkurbjarg** ★★, the canyon river **Gljúfurá** ★, and the **Látravík lighthouse** ★, also known as Hornbjargsviti. The guesthouse connected to the lighthouse is almost as convenient a base as Hornvík.

On the south side of Hornstrandir, which is more accessible from Ísafjörður, the ghost town of **Hesteyri** ★ is another excellent base camp for hikes. Hesteyri's population peaked at 80 in the 1930s, when the herring trade was in full swing, and a forlorn long-abandoned whaling station lies close by. Hornstrandir's other main settlement was at **Aðalvík** ★★, a 6-hour hike overland from Hesteyri. Some hikers continue from Aðalvík to Straumnes lighthouse, the Rekavíkurvatn lagoon, Fljótsvatn lake, and back to Hesteyri in a memorable, 3-day clockwise loop. The hike between Hesteyri and Hornvík is somewhat demanding and takes 2 days, with an overnight in Hælavík.

This brief overview hardly exhausts the endless hiking and camping possibilities in Hornstrandir, not to mention the equally pristine wilderness south of the nature reserve, including Snæfjallaströnd peninsula and the uplands surrounding Drangajökull.

Campers are trusted to respect the land and pick up after themselves. The truly responsible even pack out their toilet paper. Fires are prohibited. Make sure to keep food inside your tent at night so the foxes don't steal it.

WHERE TO STAY

No guesthouses in Hornstrandir offer made-up beds; you must bring your own sleeping bag. All have guest kitchens and are open from around mid-June to late August. If any guesthouse proves difficult to reach, **West Tours** (p. 211) can act as a booking agent. *Note:* No Hornstrandir guesthouses accept credit cards.

Within the nature reserve, the most accessible guesthouse from Ísafjörður is **Læknishúsið** (© 456-7183 or 853-6953; 1,700kr [$27/£14] per person); this former doctor's house is in Hesteyri, an abandoned village on Hornstrandir's south coast. On the north coast, a few kilometers east of Hornvík, **Óvissuferðir** (© 566-6752 or 892-5219; www.ovissuferdir.net; 2,200kr [$35/£18] per person) sleeps 45 in a building adjoined to the Látravík lighthouse (aka Hornbjarg lighthouse or Hornbjargsviti).

Two rudimentary guesthouses—neither of which have private doubles—lie on the east coast of Hornstrandir, along the Freydís ferry route (p. 211) from Norðurfjörður to Hælavík. The first is **Reykjarfjörður** (© **456-7215** or 853-1615; reykjarfjordur@ simnet.is; 2,500kr [$40/£20] per person), in the fjord of the same name, just outside the nature reserve. Reykjarfjörður's best asset is a large, outdoor geothermal pool. The second guesthouse is **Ferðaþjónustan Mávaberg,** (© **852-8267;** mavaberg@ freydis.is) in Bolungarvík, three fjords west of Reykjarfjörður.

Grunnavík, at the tip of the Snæfjallaströnd Peninsula south of Hornstrandir, is included in some ferry routes and has the guesthouse **Ferðaþjónustan Grunnavík** (© **456-4664** or 852-4819; www.grunnavik.is; 3,000kr [$48/£24] per person).

Wild camping in the nature reserve is free. All accommodations above have tent sites for around 1,000kr ($16/£8) per person, including use of facilities.

8

North Iceland

The north of Iceland is tucked just beneath the Arctic Circle and Greenland Sea, but enjoys relatively hospitable weather and forgiving land. Northerners gloat about their climate, which is sunnier and drier than the southwest in summer. The multiform northern coast bears little resemblance to the south coast, which is dominated by glaciers and worked over by the flow of glacial sediments. The north has the highest population of any region outside the southwest corner; even cod are migrating to the north coast as the oceans warm.

Most visitors cluster in the near northeast region comprising Akureyri, Iceland's thriving northern capital; Mývatn, a wonderland of lava forms, color-stained geothermal fields, and birdlife; Húsavík, Iceland's whale-watching mecca; and Jökulsárgljúfur, a national park along an extensive canyon full of magisterial rock formations and waterfalls. Traveling within this so-called "Diamond Circle"—a bit of marketing one-upsmanship based on the popular "Golden Circle" in the southwest—you may keep recognizing the same tourists, who can access all these sights by day from the same accommodation.

Venture west of Akureyri or east of Jökulsárgljúfur and the tourist sightings quickly diminish. Visitors zoom past Húnaflói on the Ring Road, but would not regret an excursion to a seal colony on its Vatsnses peninsula, or the stone church at Þingeyrar. The Skagafjörður region offers Glaumbær, Iceland's best museum of preserved 19th-century farm buildings; Hólar, seat of Iceland's northern bishopric in the Catholic era; and Siglufjörður, a fjord town as scenically situated as any in the country. The Arctic Circle cuts right through the tiny island of Grímsey, which exerts a mystical pull on those travelers who can't resist remote islands. The northeast corner of Iceland, with its driftwood beaches, sea cliffs, lonely moors, and misty lakes and lagoons, is a wonderful place to forget about hectic, goal-oriented travel.

Online, www.northiceland.is has a good search engine for accommodations and other services throughout the region—though visitor information centers and websites listed in each section below are more thorough.

1 Húnaflói

Húnaflói (Bear Cub Bay) lies between the Westfjords and Skagi Peninsula, and its environs are among the least touristed in the country. Drivers headed from Reykjavík to Akureyri on the Ring Road mostly see undulating agricultural land, but few dramatic landmarks to beckon them off course. Anyone passing through, however, should consider a daytime or overnight detour, particularly for **seal-watching** on Vatsnses peninsula or visiting the **19th-century stone church** at Þingeyrar. For a

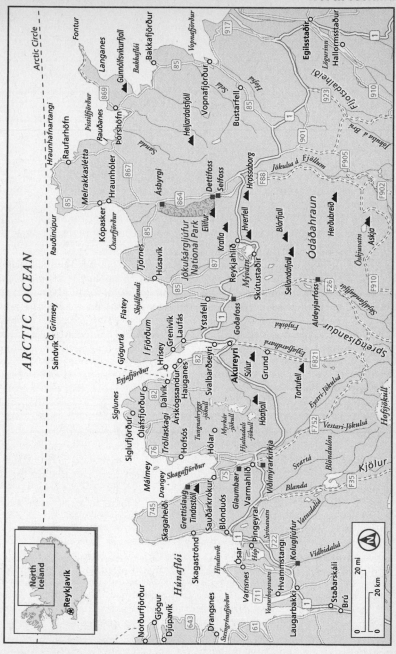

dinner excursion, consider a side trip to Texas courtesy of the **Kántrýbær restaurant,** run by Icelandic country-and-western impresario Hallbjörn Hjartarson (see box, "The Cowboy of Skagaströnd," p. 220). Tune your car radio to FM 96.7, 102.2, or 107.0 to catch Hallbjörn's radio show.

ESSENTIALS

GETTING THERE   The main hubs in Húnaflói are Hvammstangi and Blönduós. Hvammstangi is 6km (3¾ miles) north of the Ring Road on Route 72, 197km (122 miles) north of Reykjavík, and 203km (126 miles) west of Akureyri. Blönduós is along the Ring Road, 243km (151 miles) from Reykjavík and 145km (90 miles) from Akureyri.

Trex (© 587-6000; www.trex.is) runs at least one **bus** daily year-round between Reykjavík and Akureyri, stopping at Hvammstangi and Blönduós. Reykjavík to Hvammstangi is 3 hours and 20 minutes; a ticket costs 4,200kr ($67/£34). Akureyri to Hvammstangi is 3 hours and 3,100kr ($50/£25); Reykjavík to Blönduós is 4 hours and 5,000kr ($80/£40); Akureyri to Blönduós is 2 hours and 10 minutes and 2,300kr ($37/£18). Blönduós has a bus connection to Skagaströnd, but make sure to notify the driver.

VISITOR INFORMATION   The best tourist info for Húnaflói is in **Blönduós** (© 452-4520; www.northwest.is; June 10–Aug 23 daily 8am–9pm), just off the Ring Road on Brautarhvammur; look for the international flagpoles. In **Hvammstangi,** tourist info is at the Icelandic Seal Center (Selasetur Íslands), Brekkugata 2 (© 451-2345; www.selasetur.is; June–Aug daily 9–6pm, Sept 1–15 Mon–Fri 10am–4pm). Off season, rely on the regional tourist office at **Varmahlíð** (© 455-6161; www.visit skagafjordur.is; June 1–14 and Sept daily 9am–5pm; June 15–Aug daily 9am–7pm; Oct–May daily 10am–3pm) in neighboring Skagafjörður.

EXPLORING HÚNAFLÓI
VATNSNES PENINSULA

Húnaflói is home to the majority of **Icelandic harbor seals** (plus a few grey seals), and the best place to spot them is on this nubby peninsula west of Blönduós. The peninsula's only town, **Hvammstangi,** is at its southwestern base. Vatnsnes has a mountainous center, but its shores blend wild coastline with fertile grazing land for horses and sheep. Seals can be viewed any time of year, though they often disappear unpredictably in search of fish. Centuries of hunting have not made the seals any less curious about humans, and they like to shadow your movements from a distance. The harbor seal population is just a third of what it was in 1980, largely because of a viral disease. It is extremely important not to disturb them or try to feed them.

The "World of the Sea People" exhibit at Hvammstangi's **Icelandic Seal Center (Selasetur Íslands),** at Brekkugata 2 (© 451-2345; www.selasetur.is; June–Aug daily 9am–6pm, Sept 1–15 Mon–Fri 10am–4pm) is a good primer on seal biology, seal-human relations, and seal-related folklore, but all you may need there is an update on current seal-viewing locations. Admission is 500kr ($8/£4) adults and 250kr ($4/£2) for children under 14.

From May to September, **Áki Boat Tours** (© 451-2394 or 865-6072; selaskodun@gmail.com) offers 1-hour seal- and bird-watching tours of Vatsnes for 2,700kr ($43/£22) adults; 1,400kr ($22/£11) children 12–16; and 3- to 4-hour sea-angling trips for 5,800kr ($93/£46) adults; 2,900kr ($46/£23) children 12–15; minimum 25,000kr ($400/£200), mainly in search of cod.

From Hvammstangi, Route 711 follows the periphery of Vatnsnes. On clear days, the west side of the peninsula has **great views** of the Strandir coast. Signs are sometimes posted at turnoffs for viewing seal colonies. A particularly accessible **seal colony** is on the peninsula's western shore, about 15km (9 miles) north of Hvammstangi and just north of the Hamarsrétt sheep round-up pen, which is marked from the road.

Hindisvík⟨⚹, a protected area barely west of the peninsula's tip is perfect for a short coastal walk to a seal colony that's also enlivened by ducks and diving birds. The parking area, roughly 6km (3¾ miles) northeast of the Route 711/Route 712 junction, is not well marked from Route 711—look for a sign with the "interesting site" icon, a kind of square with circular corners. Take the stile over the fence and walk past the abandoned farm buildings, following what's left of the dirt road. In 15 minutes the road splits; bear right and follow the coastline for 5 minutes to a rocky promontory.

Ósar⟨⚹ is the most idyllic spot on Vatnsnes for an overnight (see Ósar Youth Hostel, below). **Hvítserkur** ⟨⚹, just off the shoreline near Ósar, is a bizarre, M-shaped, 15m-high (49-ft.) basalt crag with its own bird population. To reach this requisite photo stop, turn off Route 711 a short distance north of Ósar and proceed to the parking area. Scramble down to the black sand beach and, if the tide is low, walk into Hvítserkur's arches. Walk south along the beach for 20 minutes, past the resident ducks, jellyfish, and harbor seals that will probably be seen lounging on the sands across the channel (One or two seals will probably swim over to investigate). From this part of the beach, it's a 10-minute walk uphill to Ósar.

KOLUGLJÚFUR

This picturesque 1km-long (½ mile) gorge on the Viðidalsá river makes for an enjoyable half-hour diversion or picnic spot near the Ring Road. Kolugljúfur plunges 50m (164 ft.) deep and was named for Kola, the troll that dug it out. To reach the gorge, exit the Ring Road onto Route 715 at either junction (Rte. 715 forms a "V," meeting the Ring Road at both ends). From the bottom of the "V," turn off Route 715 and continue south to the sign that reads "Litla-Hlið/Bakki/Kolugljúfur;" turn right and park just before the bridge. Paths head downstream along either side.

ÞINGEYRAR

The distinctive stone **Þingeyrar Church**⟨⚹ (℃ **452-4294;** free admission. June–Aug daily 10am–5pm) lies on pastureland east of Vatsnes peninsula. It was built from 1864 to 1877, and financed entirely by Ásgeir Einarsson, a local farmer and member of parliament. While most Icelandic churches from this time are sided with sheets of corrugated iron made to resemble painted wood, Þingeyrar was constructed at great expense from hewn basalt and limestone. The interior layout varies from the ultra-rectangular Icelandic norm. The apse—the semicircular projection on the eastern end of the church that normally holds just the altar—is deepened and broadened to encircle everything in front of the pews ("apsidal choir" is the technical term). Many Icelandic church ceilings have a few hundred gold stars mounted on square panels; Þingeyrar church has about a thousand gold stars on a smooth, dark-blue ceiling, which is half-domed over the apsidal choir.

The altarpiece, made in the English town of Nottingham in the 15th century, illustrates Biblical scenes with appealingly crude alabaster figures in relief. (A similar altarpiece at Hólar is more compelling; see p. 224). It once had wing panels, lost during a failed attempt to sell the altarpiece abroad. The Baroque-style canopied pulpit and matching baptismal font were made in the Netherlands in the late 17th century. The church's best-known feature is the "Apostles Collection": small, painted oak-wood figurines, placed between the railings of the gallery. The originals were made in Germany in the late 16th century, sold from Þingeyrar in the early 20th century, and then donated to the National Museum. What you see here are expert 1983 replicas.

To reach Þingeyrar Church, exit onto Rte. 721 from the Ring Road, 20km (12 miles) west of Blönduós, and proceed 7km (4¼ miles) to the end.

BLÖNDUÓS

This coastal town and agricultural trading center is the largest settlement in Húnaflói, with nearly 1,000 residents. Visitors have little reason to dawdle for long.

Textile Museum (Heimilisiðnaðarsafnið) ✿   Not everyone will be captivated by century-old crocheted nightgowns and exquisitely embroidered undergarments, but it's hard not to be impressed by the dedication put into this nationwide textile collection. One room is full of mannequins sporting the national costume in several late-19th century variations—the best such display in Iceland. Another section hosts temporary exhibits by contemporary Icelandic textile artists. Guests can weave wool on the loom downstairs, or grab a pair of gloves at reception to fondle specimens at will. Make sure to find the portrait made from lint.

Árbraut 29. ✆ 452-4067. www.simnet.is/textile. Admission 500kr ($8/£4) adults, 350kr ($5.60/£2.80) seniors, free for ages 15 and under. June–Aug daily 10am–5pm. From the Ring Road, turn onto Húnabraut, then bear left on Árbraut, following the northeast side of the river Blanda.

SKAGASTRÖND

Thanks to Icelandic cowboy Hallbjörn Hjartarson (p. 220), this tiny town 23km (14 miles) north of Blönduós is a bastion of country-and-western culture. See "Where to Dine," below.

OUTDOOR ACTIVITIES

HORSEBACK RIDING   Gauksmýri (✆ 451-2927; www.gauksmyri.is), about 50km (31 miles) west of Blönduós, is a reputable horse farm that offers short tours of the Húnaflói area. Rides start at 2,500kr ($40/£20) for 1 hour and can include introductory lessons. Gauksmýri is also an eco-minded guesthouse and restaurant; see "Where to Stay," below.

Arinbjörn Jóhannson at **Brekkulækur Farm** (✆ 451-2938; www.geysir.com/brekkulaekur) has been organizing epic 3- to 15-day riding adventures for three decades. Tour itineraries, outlined on the website, usually include highlands, coastal regions, and some mingling with locals.

WHERE TO STAY
VATNSNES PENINSULA & NEARBY

Gauksmýri   Many guests are here for horseback riding, but non-riders should be equally content. The 18 new en suite rooms are somewhat small and typically featureless, but bright and comfortable nonetheless. Heated towel racks are a welcome perk. Plenty of horse-motifed lounging space is on-hand, and a glassed-in dining room overlooks the farm. **Dinner** is available on request, and meals include homemade bread and vegetables from the farm's own greenhouse.

Rte. 1, about 50km (31 miles) west of Blönduós and 4km (2½ miles) east of the Rte. 1/Rte. 72 junction. ✆ 451-2927. Fax 451-3427. www.gauksmyri.is. 27 units, 18 w/bathroom. June–Sept 11,309kr ($181/£90) double; June–Sept 7,085kr–8,117kr ($113–$130/£130–£65) double without bathroom. Rates around 15% lower Oct–May. Rates include breakfast. MC, V. **Amenities:** Restaurant; bar; Internet terminal. *In room:* Wi-Fi, no phone.

Hanna Sigga Guesthouse (Gistiheimili Hönnu Siggu)   It can take some visitors a while to get used to the custom of staying in other people's houses. This friendly, family-run guesthouse in Hvammstangi makes the transition easy, with bright and spacious rooms, board games in the living room, and a hot tub overlooking the fjord.

Garðarvegur 26, Hvammstangi. ✆ 451-2407. www.simnet.is/gistihs. 4 units, none w/bathroom. May–Dec 6,500kr ($104/£52) double; 2,300kr ($37/£18) sleeping-bag accommodation. Rates around 10% lower Jan–Apr. Breakfast available: 950kr ($15/£7.60). No credit cards. **Amenities:** Guest kitchen; hot tub; washer/dryer access. *In room:* No phone.

Ósar Youth Hostel ⚤   This alluring retreat on Vatnsnes peninsula—25 or 30km (16–19 miles) north of the Ring Road, depending which direction you're coming from—lies close to Hvítserkur (p. 217) and a large seal colony. Though pickup from the Ring Road can be arranged, Ósar is reachable only by car and tends to attract nature lovers who are a tad more sedate than the typical hostel crowd. Guests can stay in the farmhouse or one of three new cabins; the house has more common space and a TV room, while the cabins are a little more private. The nearest market and restaurant is in Hvammstangi, 25 minutes away, but breakfast can be ordered and eaten inside a Mongolian-style yurt. Book well ahead for the summer.

Rte. 711. ✆ 862-2778. www.simnet.is/osar. 10 units without bathroom. 7,200kr ($115/£58) double; 4,900kr–5,600kr ($78–$90/£39–£45) double sleeping-bag accommodation; 10,500kr ($168/£84) triple; 1,750kr–2,100kr ($28–$34/£14–£17) sleeping-bag accommodation in dorm bed; 700kr ($11/£5.60) sheet rental for entire stay. Breakfast available: 950kr ($15/£7.60). AE, DC, MC, V. Closed Dec–Apr. Coming from the west, turn left from the Ring Rd. onto Rte. 711 and proceed about 30km (19 miles). Coming from the east, turn right from the Ring Rd. onto Rte. 716, then turn right again on Rte. 711 and proceed about 19km (12 miles). **Amenities:** Guest kitchen; Internet terminal. *In room:* No phone.

BLÖNDUÓS

Guesthouse Glaðheimar   Run by Hótel Blönduós, this straightforward and efficient guesthouse in a former post office building has a range of rooming options. Superior doubles have more space and TVs but still no private bathroom. Cottages vary from 15 to 58 sq. m (49–190 sq. ft) and sleep two to eight. Most of the large cottages have their own hot tub and sauna.

Blöndubyggð 10. ✆ 452-4205. Fax 452-4208. www.gladheimar.is. 20 units, 8 w/bathroom. May–Sept 7,500kr–10,500kr ($120–$168/£60–£84) double without bathroom; 9,500kr–15,000kr ($152–$240/£76–£120) cottages for 2–8 persons. Rates around 25% lower Oct–Apr. MC, V. **Amenities:** Guest kitchen. *In room:* No phone.

Hótel Blönduós ⚤   The town's top hotel, restaurant, and bar are all under this roof. The homey, welcoming rooms—though unlikely to form any lasting impression—are painted in hot sunset colors and touch on the eccentric. Superior doubles mean extra lounging space. *Note:* Summer weekends book up early.

Aðalgata 6. ✆ 452-4205. Fax 452-4208. www.gladheimar.is. 16 units. May–Sept 15,000kr–17,000kr ($240–$272/£120–£136) double. Rates about 20% lower Oct–Apr. MC, V. **Amenities:** Restaurant; bar. *In room:* TV, Wi-Fi, hair dryer.

WHERE TO DINE

See also **Gauksmýri** in "Where to Stay," above.

HVAMMSTANGI

Café Sirop ICELANDIC   As the resident restaurant-bar for Hvammstangi and environs, Sirop has the expected provincial menu of burgers, pizzas, pastas, fish, and lamb chops. Yet the food—and ambience—have a touch more class and finesse than is strictly necessary to get by.

Norðurbraut 1. © **899-8987.** Main courses 1,000kr–2,400kr ($16–$38/£8–£19). MC, V. Mon–Thurs 11:30am–10pm; Fri–Sat noon–3am; Sun noon–10pm.

BLÖNDUÓS

Potturinn Og Pannan *Kids* ICELANDIC   Eating at this new branch of a chain restaurant is not a memorable experience but is also unlikely to disappoint. The menu has good range within the usual headings of burgers, pizzas, fish, and lamb. All dishes except burgers and pizza include the all-you-can-eat soup and salad bar. Kids get their own AstroTurf hut to watch TV and play games in. The hot chocolate is superb.

Norðurlandsvegur 4. © **453-5060.** Reservations recommended weekends. Main courses 1,750kr–3,290kr ($28–$53/£14–£26), most under 2,400kr ($38/£19). MC, V. Daily 11am–10pm.

Sauðaþjófurinn *Ꙭ* ICELANDIC   This restaurant inside the Hótel Blönduós is the best in town, and the traditional lamb and fish menu has few missteps—or surprises. Tables fill up with locals and visitors alike on summer weekends, but the restaurant may close its close their doors between 2 and 5pm.

Aðalgata 6. © **452-4205.** Reservations recommended. Main courses 2,650kr–3,450kr ($42–$55/£21–£28). MC, V. Late Apr–early Oct daily 11am–10pm; mid-Oct to mid-Apr call in advance.

Við Árbakkann CAFE/LIGHT FARE   This casual roadside cafe with outdoor terrace seating gets a fair amount of Ring Road tourist traffic. Choices include a fine fish soup, salads, sandwiches, bagels, waffles, cakes, and meat and fish dinner specials.

Húnabraut 2. © **452-4678.** Main courses 1,200kr–2,600kr ($19–$42/£9.60–£21); light meals 480kr–1,100kr ($7.70–$18/£3.85–£8.80). AE, MC, V. June–Aug daily 11am–10pm; Sept–May Mon–Thurs 11am–5pm, Fri–Sun 11am–8pm.

SKAGASTRÖND

Kántrýbær TEXAN/ICELANDIC   This saloon-style restaurant in remote Skagaströnd is the inspiration of Hallbjörn Hjartarson (see below), Iceland's avatar of all

---

The Cowboy of Skagaströnd

The youngest of 16 children, Hallbjörn Hjartarson developed his mania for country music in the late 1950s, while working at the American military base in Keflavík. In 1963 he returned home to tiny Skagaströnd, and in 1983, after singing in various bands, founded Kántrýbær (Country Town), his restaurant, bar, radio studio, and all-around country-and-western shrine. (He lives across the street, and is rarely seen without a ten-gallon hat.) He has only visited the U.S. once—in 1988, to record an album in Nashville—but never ventured outside Tennessee. For several years he organized a C&W festival in Skagaströnd, complete with barn dancing, rodeo stunts, and can-shootin' competitions, but unfortunately it's been on hiatus since 2002. Hallbjörn's 24-hour radio show, usually hosted live from 2 to 6pm and 8pm to midnight, airs on FM 96.7, 102.2, and 107.0; it can be heard from as far as Akureyri and the Strandir coast. On air he insists on thanking Johnny Cash, Dwight Yoakam, and other favorites each time their music is played. The request line is © **452-4774.** To listen online, visit www.kantry.is and find the "Hérna getur yú smellt á á Kántrýútvarpið á Netinu" link.

things country-and-western. The menu is more Icelandic with Texan twists than vice-versa, though Tex-Mex burgers, steak sandwiches, chicken fingers, and pecan or apple pie a la mode are hard to come by elsewhere. If you've already eaten, drop in for a beer adorned with Kántrýbær's custom label, and check out Hallbjörn's outlandish exhibit of C&W memorabilia—including his jackets with fringe and rhinestones to spare. The dance floor—country music only, of course!—opens up weekend nights in summer, or twice a month off season.

Hólanesvegur. ⓒ 452-2829. www.kantry.is. Main courses 690kr–1,790kr ($11–$29/£5.50–£14). AE, DC, MC, V. Sun–Thurs 11:30am–10pm; Fri–Sat 11:30am–3am; kitchen closes at 10pm.

2 Skagafjörður

Almost 5,000 people live along this broad fjord or in the fertile valley at its head: Sauðarkrókur, 25km (16 miles) north of the Ring Road, is a likable coastal town with over half of the region's population. Near Sauðarkrókur, Glaumbær Folk Museum is the most engaging of Iceland's many 19th-century turf-roofed farmsteads. Inside the fjord are the strangely-shaped islands of Drangey and Málmey. Hólar, home to Iceland's northern bishop from 1106 to 1798, retains some vestiges of its former glory. Hofsós, halfway up Skagafjörður's eastern shore, was a launch point for Icelandic emigrants to North America, and many of their descendants return there to visit the Emigration Museum and genealogical center. Siglufjörður, the most beautifully situated town in north Iceland, is 55km (35 miles) northeast of Hofsós: the main draws here are the Herring Era museum and the surrounding mountains. Skagafjörður is famous across Iceland for its horse breeding and horsemanship, and for adrenaline-seekers, the Eystri-Jökulsá is one of Iceland's fiercest rivers for white-water rafting.

ESSENTIALS
GETTING THERE
BY CAR The Ring Road passes to the south of Skagafjörður's major sights. Route 75 meets the Ring Road at Varmahlíð—294km (183 miles) from Reykjavík and 94km (58 miles) from Akureyri—and proceeds north to the Glaumbær Folk Museum, Sauðarkrókur, and western Skagafjörður. From the Ring Road 5km (3 miles) east of Varmahlíð, Route 76 leads 97km (60 miles) to Siglufjörður, along the east side of Skagafjörður, past the roads to Hólar and Hofsós.

The only **car rental agency** in Sauðárkrókur is **National/Bílaleiga Akureyrar** (ⓒ **461-6000;** www.nationalcar.is).

BY BUS Trex (ⓒ **587-6000;** www.trex.is) runs at least one bus daily year-round between Reykjavík and Akureyri, stopping at Varmahlíð. Reykjavík to Varmahlíð takes 5 hours and costs 5,800kr ($93/£46); Akureyri to Varmahlíð takes 85 minutes and costs 1,800kr ($29/£14). A bus between Varmahlíð and Sauðárkrókur runs at least twice daily, June through August, and is timed to connect with the Reykjavík–Akureyri bus. Another bus running between Sauðárkrókur and Siglufjörður stops at Hólar and Hofsós. Departures are every day but Saturday, from June through August, and are timed to connect with flights from Reykjavík.

BY PLANE Eagle Air (ⓒ **562-2640;** www.eagleair.is) connects Reykjavík to Sauðarkrókur six times weekly from June through August (twice Tues and Fri, once Thurs and Sun) and five times weekly from September through May (twice Tues, once Thurs, Fri, and Sun). Flights are approximately 40 minutes and 7,180kr ($115/£57) one-way.

VISITOR INFORMATION

Skagafjörður's tourist information office is in **Varmahlíð** (℡ **455-6161;** www.visit skagafjordur.is; June 1–June 14 and Sept daily 9am–5pm, June 15–Aug 9am–7pm, Oct–May daily 10am–3pm), in a turf-roofed building next to the N1 gas station, and has a free Internet terminal. The website **www.northwest.is** has good listings of local services. For Siglufjörður, tourist information is at the Herring Era museum (p. 226).

EXPLORING SKAGAFJÖRÐUR
NEAR VARMAHLÍÐ

Víðimýrarkirkja   This 1834 church with wooden gables, turf roof, and thick sod walls has a simple, elemental quality that charms many visitors. The interior has little architectural detail to speak of, however, beyond some ornamental carving and closed pews up front for prominent families. The 1616 altar painting, probably Danish, is a Last Supper exhibiting the character exaggeration of folk art: Judas holds a moneybag. The pulpit is probably from the 17th century, but the paint has mostly worn off.

Off Rte. 1, 5km (3 miles) west of Varmahlíð. ℡ **453-5095.** Admission 200kr ($3.20/£1.60) adults; free for children under 16. Daily 9am–6pm.

Glaumbær (Skagafjörður Folk Museum) 🌟🌟   Iceland has several museums inside preserved 19th-century turf buildings, and Glaumbær can be a good stand-in for all of them. These farmsteads are reminders of how dramatically Icelandic life has changed within a single lifespan. They are also vital repositories of cultural memory: with no coffeehouses, theaters, or village squares, Icelanders were once homebound on residences such as this through long, dark winters.

Like most of the more prosperous farms of the time, Glaumbær has several buildings, constructed at different times but accessed from a central corridor. Aside from the usual fish-skin shoes and toys made from animal bones, Glaumbær's more unique holdings include driftwood bureaus, primitive brainteasers, and a snuff box made of a

Why Build a House with Turf?

By the mid-12th century, Iceland's climate had cooled considerably, and most of the country had been deforested. Turf housing became the norm and remained so even into the 20th century. Wood was scarce and expensive, and Icelanders roamed the coasts monogramming driftwood to claim it. Roof sod was supported by grids of flat stones and wood rafters. Icelandic grass, which is very thick, with enduring roots, held the turf together. A turf house could last as long as 100 years in areas with moderate rainfall. The roof slope was critical: too flat and it would leak, too steep and the grass would dry out. Glass was costly, too, so windows were often stretched animal skins or abdominal membranes. Turf construction lent itself to small rooms, maze-like interiors, and easy lateral expansion, but required constant repair. Even the best turf house was leaky, damp, dark, cold, and unventilated, with lingering smoke from the burning of peat and dried manure. Sleeping quarters were often directly over the stables, to take advantage of the animals' body heat.

whale tooth. For Icelanders, the most treasured piece is a basket allegedly made by Fjalla-Eyvindur, the beloved 18th-century outlaw. The near-waterproof basket, expertly woven from willow roots, is inside an unmarked glass case at the back of room #5. The church next door is worth a quick look to see the six disassembled panels from a 1685 Danish pulpit.

Áskaffi, in a neighboring 1886 clapboard house, serves hot drinks, cakes, sandwiches, old-fashioned pancakes, and skýr cake in front of a turf-burning fireplace.

Rte. 75, between Varmahlíð and Sauðárkrókur. © 453-6173. www.glaumbaer.is. Admission 500kr ($8/£4) adults, 300kr ($4.80/£2.40) students, free for children 15 and under. June–Sept 20 daily 9am–6pm, other times by appointment.

SAUÐARKRÓKUR ⊛

This town of 2,700 inhabitants is more than a convenient regional base with good dining and accommodations. It's also an agreeable base to come back to at the end of the day and enjoy an after-dinner stroll in the older part of town. Consider unwinding at the **town pool,** which has two large Jacuzzis (ask to have the bubbles turned on).

Minjahús The permanent exhibit features the outmoded workshops of a local blacksmith, watchmaker, carpenter, and several saddlers. Of more interest is the temporary exhibit, which lasts a few years. The current exhibit on regional archaeological digs does a fine job of imparting the thrill of discovery and explaining what can be deduced from artifacts. In 2009, a new exhibit will explore Skagafjörður's musical heritage.

Aðalgata 16b. © 453-6870. Admission 500kr ($8.£4) adults; 300kr ($4.80/£2.40) seniors; free for ages 14 and under. June–Aug daily 1–6pm.

DRANGEY ⊛ & MÁLMEY ⊛

These two uninhabited, bird-rich islands—whose fantastical shapes look like artists' creations—make for an ideal joint tour. Drangey is surrounded by vertical cliffs reaching 180m (591 ft.). From a distance it appears cylindrical, but a closer look reveals strange contortions and indentations in the rock face. It's the ultimate fortress, and in *The Saga of Grettir the Strong* (aka *Grettis Saga*), one of Iceland's best-known legends, the outlaw Grettir spends the last three years of his life here. Sheep once grazed on Drangey's smooth top and had to be hoisted up and down with ropes. From the single landing spot, a steep path ascends to the top with ladders and cable handrails. Málmey is larger, with an elegant S-shaped contour, and reaches 156m (512 ft.) high. A family farm prospered here before burning down in 1950.

Jón Eiríksson, "the Earl of Drangey" (© 453-6503 or 846-8150; fagri@simnet.is), leads tours of both islands on request. Tours can leave from Sauðárkrókur, though he prefers setting off from Fagranes farm or Reykir on Skagafjörður's west coast. The price is 5,000kr ($80/£40) per person, but could be higher if the group numbers fewer than six. If you'd like to include fishing, let him know. Jón's English is limited; if you have trouble, call his son Jón (© 847-9600), who often leads the tours. If a tour with the Jóns doesn't work out, contact visitor information at Varmahlíð and ask them to find a guide in Hofsós.

GRETTISLAUG ⊛

In *Grettis Saga,* Grettir swims from Drangey to the western shore of Skagafjörður, where he bathes in a geothermal spring and then fetches some glowing embers to bring back to the island. 962 years later, in 1992, Jón Eiríksson built **Grettislaug,** a pool in open surroundings at Grettir's legendary bathing spot. An adjacent pool was added in 2006. Both are constructed with natural stones and remain at bathwater temperature. For a memorable swim at Grettislaug, drive north from Sauðárkrókur on Route 748 to the end of the road. The pools do not yet have toilets or changing rooms, and bathers are asked to contribute 200kr ($3.20/£1.60) into a metal box.

Jón's house is close by, and farther uphill is a shed with a fluorescent tube over the door. This is Jón's homemade hydroelectric power station, which utilizes the stream toppling from the mountain 500m (1,640 ft.) away. On a clear day, you could walk farther up the mountain for a view over the fjord.

HÓLAR ⟨⟩

Hólar (𝒞 **455-6300;** free admission; all sites open daily 9am–6pm unless otherwise specified), also known as Hólar Í Hjaltadalur, was the northern seat of power in Iceland's Catholic era. Today's visitors see little direct connection to its bygone prestige, but the present cathedral **Hóladómkirkja** displays perhaps the best artifacts of any church in Iceland.

In 1056, Iceland's first Catholic bishop was installed at Skálholt in the southwest. Northern Icelanders complained he was too far away, and fifty years later a second diocese was added at Hólar. Just before the Reformation, the Hólar bishopric owned a 70-ton ship, invaluable manuscripts, stockpiles of gold and silver, and large holdings of land and livestock—all ripe for confiscation by the Danish king, who, like other European monarchs of the time, realized Protestantism would ease his financial problems. Hólar's last Catholic bishop, Jón Arason (1484–1550) was beheaded at Skálholt, after leading a rebellion against the king. Lutheran bishops remained at Hólar until 1798, when the two bishoprics were consolidated and relocated to Reykjavík. Hólar is now home to about 60 people and Hólaskóli, a small university.

Hólaskóli's main building holds a restaurant, pool, and guesthouse. In the lobby you'll find the free brochure *Hólar History Trail,* which lays out the nearby sights in walking tour format. **Nyibær** is a preserved 19th-century turf farmhouse, but it's empty and hardly worth visiting with Glaumbær (p. 222) so close by. **Auðun's House (Auðunarstofa)** is a reconstruction of a bishop's residence from the early 14th century, built in 2002 with only 14th-century building methods. A 13th-century chalice, vestments, and medieval manuscripts are stored in the basement, which should open as an exhibit around 2010; in the meantime only group tours are let in.

Built in 1763, the current cathedral, though large by Icelandic standards, is the smallest ever built at Hólar. It's also Iceland's oldest stone church, built with local red sandstone and basalt. The detached bell tower was consecrated in 1950; just inside the entrance is a 1957 mosaic of Jón Arason by the well-known contemporary artist Erró, then barely out of art school.

Inside the cathedral, a glass case holds a 1584 Bible, the first printing in Icelandic. A painting of a Hólar bishop, from 1620, is the oldest known portrait of any Icelander. On the side wall is a crucifix from the early 16th century. Its large size and visceral gore are uncharacteristic of Lutheran churches, and it's surprising to learn it was imported in the mid-17th century after the Reformation, probably from southern Europe. The 1674 baptismal font is made of soapstone, which—according to popular lore—drifted to Iceland on an ice floe from Greenland. More likely, it was imported from Norway.

The **altarpiece**☆☆, made around 1500, is an impressive, painted wooden sculpture depicting the Crucifixion story in the center with apostles and saints on the wings. Jón Arason bought the piece in Holland, though it's thought to be German. Both side panels swivel inward, revealing paintings on their back sides; on the right side, Saint Sebastian spurts blood from several arrow wounds, while St. Lucy is indifferent to a sword through her neck. Make sure to ask the attendant to draw out these back panels for you. An even older altarpiece from Nottingham, England, made of alabaster and also in sculpted storybook form, hangs over the side entrance.

An attendant is always on hand for questions, but tours for 300kr ($4.80/£2.40) are only given for groups; so call ahead. A concert series is held in the cathedral from June to August, and the schedule is posted online at www.kirkjan.is/holar, but only in Icelandic. Evening prayers are at 6pm Monday to Saturday, and Sunday services are at 11am. A single Catholic ceremony is held each summer.

HOFSÓS & NEARBY

Hofsós, a trading post dating back to the 16th century, has maintained its throwback feel by preserving some of its 18th-century buildings and replicating others.

Icelandic Emigration Center (Vesturfarasetrið)　　North Americans of Icelandic descent often head straight for this museum and genealogical research center, founded in 1996 and spread across three buildings. The permanent *New Land, New Life* exhibit details Icelandic emigration in the late-19th and early-20th centuries, including the fate of various settlements from Utah to Brazil. (In "New Iceland," a settlement founded in 1875 on Lake Winnipeg, Manitoba, many older people still speak Icelandic as a first language.) By 1914, 15,000 Icelanders—almost 20% of the population—had left for the New World. A temporary exhibit takes on a specific emigration subtheme. Visitors researching their family roots should contact the museum in advance at hofsos@hofsos.is; general enquiries are free, and more intensive archival research can be hired at an hourly rate.

ⓒ 453-7935. www.hofsos.is. Admission 400kr ($6.40/£3.20) adults for each exhibit, or 900kr ($14/£7.20) for all three; free for children under 12; free admission for genealogy room. June–Aug daily 11am–6pm; other times by arrangement.

Skagafjörður Transportation Museum (Samgönguminjasafn)　　Located off Route 76, about 12km (7½ miles) south of Hofsós at Stóragerði Farm, this is basically a vintage car collection, and 75% of visitors are "car guys" asking to peek under the hoods. The range of models is impressive. The owner's favorite is a huge, white 1947 modified Chevy pickup, which he rents out for period movies.

ⓒ 845-7400. Admission 500kr ($8/£4) adults; free for children under 12. Mid-June to Sept daily 1–6pm.

SIGLUFJÖRÐUR ☆☆

The impossibly picturesque town of Siglufjörður is accessible by a single road that winds along a pretty stretch of remote coastline. Visitors experience disbelief that such an established community would be deposited there, inside a short, steep-sided fjord less than 40km (25 miles) from the Arctic Circle.

Siglufjörður, which still runs on fish, was a herring boom town in the early and mid-20th century. During the town's herring heyday, hundreds of ships were docked in the harbor, and hordes of girls came for the summer to gut, salt, and pack the fish in barrels for export. Herring populations plummeted after World War II, thanks to over-fishing aided by sonar equipment, and, in 1969, the herring failed to show up entirely. Since then, thanks to better oversight, herring numbers have largely recovered.

A walk around the docks is a good window on the fishing life. Any pungent odor emanating from the fish factory is what Icelanders call "the smell of money." The town has preserved its older buildings well, and its faded glory is worn gracefully. The population, now around 1400, has slipped slowly but surely each year, but the pattern could reverse when a new tunnel east to Ólafsfjörður is completed in December 2009. Surely Siglufjörður's teenagers are counting the months; the drive to Akureyri will be cut from 3 hours to 1.

Besides strolling around town, or perhaps a round on the **nine-hole golf course,** the main activities for visitors are the Herring Era Museum and the fine hiking nearby. From mid-June to mid-August, you might time your visit for a Saturday, when **herring-salting demonstrations** are presented at 3pm, complete with costumes, song, dance, and accordions. Tickets are 1,000kr ($16/£8) and include museum admission. On the first weekend of August, a celebratory holiday across the country, Siglufjörður draws hundreds of visitors for its nostalgic **"Herring Adventure Festival,"** with musical performances, family entertainment, and yet more fish preparation demos. In early July, a 5-day **folk music festival** (www.siglo.is/festival) includes workshops as well as concerts day and night by Icelandic and international artists.

The Siglufjörður area offers several first-rate **hiking routes.** Avid hikers can sustain themselves for two full day trips, one to the west of the fjord and one to the east. Routes are well annotated at http://siglo.is/en; click the "tourism" link, then "hiking trails." The excellent and widely available new trail map *Gönguleiðir á Tröllaskaga II: Fljót, Siglufjörður, Ólafsfjörður, Svarfaðardalur* has no trail descriptions in English, but you can still deduce estimated walking times and altitudes. A short hike on the fjord's eastern shore leads to the Stadarhólsfjara herring factory, destroyed by an avalanche in 1919. Two routes head east overland to Héðinsfjörður, a wild and beautiful fjord abandoned in 1951; the shorter route is at least 4 hours one-way. A popular hike follows the old road leading west through the 630m (2,067 ft.) Siglufjörðarskarð Pass; this road is usually free of snowdrifts and passable in 4WD vehicles from early July to late August. Instead of taking the full 15km (9 miles) route one-way, and having to arrange transportation back, you could cut north along the ridge and then descend into town in a strenuous but very rewarding 6- to 7-hour loop.

Herring Era Museum (Síldarminjasafnið)

If a museum about herring sounds dull and faintly ridiculous, keep in mind that the herring trade was for Icelanders what the California Gold Rush was for Americans. At various times herring alone accounted for over a quarter of Iceland's export income, and Siglufjörður was the country's largest herring production center. This enormous, ambitious museum is spread across three buildings; one replicates an entire 1930s quayside, complete with herring trawler, and another reconstructs a processing factory for herring meal and oil. Most affecting are the old living quarters for the herring girls; each of those tiny bunkbeds slept two. Not enough information is posted in English, but the staff is responsive to questions.

Snorragata 15. ℂ 467-1604. www.siglo.is/herring. Admission 800kr ($13/£6.40) adults; 400kr ($6.40/£3.20) seniors and children 12–16; free for children under 12. Mid-June to mid-Aug daily 10am–6pm; May 15–June 15 and Aug 15–Sept 15 daily 1–5pm.

Folk Music Center (Þjóðlagasetur)   This museum inside the home of a late 19th-century reverend and folk-music collector features unique Icelandic instruments and videos-on-demand of traditional musical practices, from *rímur* chanting to nursery rhymes. Concerts are held Saturday nights in July and August.

Norðurgata 1. (C) **467-2300**. http://siglo.is/setur. Admission 600kr ($9.60/£4.80) adults; free for children under 14. June 20–Aug 20 daily 10am–6pm, June 1–June 19 and Aug 21–Aug 31 daily 1–5pm.

OUTDOOR ACTIVITIES

HORSEBACK RIDING   The three farms below offer lessons and short rides as well as multi-day adventures for all ability levels. In September, you can participate in round-ups (p. 18), retrieving sheep and horses that have run wild in the highlands all summer; all-night parties follow. Dates are posted at www.northwest.is.

Flugumýri ((C) **453-8814**; www.flugumyri.com), on Route 76, 3km (2 miles) off the Ring Road, presents exhibitions for groups, showing off the talents of the Icelandic horse; call ahead, and, if an exhibition is scheduled, you can sign up for 2,000kr ($32/£16) per person, including coffee and cake.

Hestasport ((C) **453-8383**; www.riding.is), a respected outfit just outside Varmahlíð, has several good route options including the Hólar area, the Kjölur Route (p. 352) through the interior to Gullfoss and Geysir, and local sheep round-ups.

Lýtingsstaðir ((C) **453-8064**; www.lythorse.com), on Route 752, 20km (12 miles) south of Varmahlíð, has a good range of highland tours, including horse and sheep round-ups, and an economical overnight package that includes two meals and a short ride.

RIVER RAFTING   The rivers feeding Skagafjörður provide the best river-rafting in North Iceland. The Eystri-Jökulsá has difficult class III and IV+ rapids, while the Vestari-Jökulsá has easier class II rapids, as well as a cliff-jumping ledge and a hot spring for making cocoa.

Activity Tours ((C) **453-8383**; www.rafting.is), affiliated with the horse tour company Hestasport (above), is the best operator. They also offer super-tame trips on the Blanda River (ages 6 and up), and an exciting 3-day adventure down the Eystri-Jökulsá, starting deep within the desert interior. The Eystri-Jökulsá trip lasts 6 to 7 hours and costs around 8,500kr ($136/£68) all-inclusive, with a minimum age of 18. The Vestari-Jökulsá trip lasts 4 to 5 hours and costs about 5,500kr ($88/£44), minimum age 12. Trips run from May to early October.

WHERE TO STAY

The best backup source for accommodation is Icelandic Farm Holidays ((C) **570-2700**; www.farmholidays.is), which has several member farms in the Skagafjörður Valley south of the Ring Road, and the tourist information office at Varmahlíð.

VARMAHLÍÐ

Flugumýri   This budget-friendly horse farm has three basic, agreeable bedrooms sharing a bathroom, guest kitchen, and TV room; plenty of occupants are non-equestrians.

Rte. 76, 3km (2 miles) off the Ring Road. (C)/fax **453-8814**. www.flugumyri.com. 3 units, none w/bathroom. 8,800kr ($141/£70) double. Rates 10% lower Oct–Apr. Rates include breakfast. MC, V. **Amenities:** Guest kitchen. *In room:* No phone.

Hestasport Cottages   These fetching and spacious wood-paneled cottages are clustered around a stone-lined hot tub. The cottages, which vary in size and may accommodate up to seven, are particularly convenient for families or large parties.

Varmahlíð, just off the Ring Road. ⓒ 453-8383. Fax 453-8384. www.riding.is. 5 cottages. June–Sept 15,000kr ($240/£120) double; 2,800kr each additional person in same cottage. Rates around 40% lower Oct–May. Breakfast available: 1,200kr ($19/£9.60). MC, V. **Amenities:** Hot tub. *In room:* Kitchenette, no phone.

Hótel Varmahlíð   This convenient stopover for travelers passing through on the Ring Road offers spacious, nondescript en suite rooms and a good **restaurant** (see "Where to Dine," below). Anyone actually exploring the area, however, would probably be better served by a stay in Sauðarkrókur.

Rte. 1. ⓒ 453-8170. Fax 453-8870. www.hotelvarmahlid.is. 19 units. May–Sept 16,900kr ($270/£135) double; 23,500kr ($376/£188) family room. Rates around 35% lower May–June 14 and Sept; around 45% lower Oct–Apr. Rates include breakfast. AE, DC, MC, V. **Amenities:** Restaurant. *In room:* TV, Wi-Fi, hair dryer.

SAUÐÁRKRÓKUR

Fosshótel Áning   This large summer-only hotel—it's a dormitory during the school year—resembles a stack of orange Lego blocks, with ample lounge space and a decent restaurant. Rooms are adequate but not a great value. The location is quiet, but removed from the inviting, older part of town.

Sæmundarhlíð. ⓒ 453-6717. Fax 562-4001. www.fosshotel.is. 65 units, 61 w/bathroom. June–Aug 13,900kr ($222/£111) double; 9,900kr ($158/£79) double without bathroom. Rates include breakfast. AE, DC, MC, V. Closed Sept–May. **Amenities:** Restaurant; bar; Internet terminal. *In room:* No phone.

Hótel Tindastóll 🏠🏠   Compared to the rest of Europe, Icelandic accommodations outside Reykjavík are rather antiseptic and featureless, with every furnishing conspicuously mass-produced. Tindastóll, a distinctive, characterful, old-fashioned hotel, gets extra kudos just for breaking the mold. The building is an 1884 Norwegian kit home, with many original beams intact and sea-stone walls lining the atmospheric downstairs bar-lounge. Rooms are dominated by natural wood. Deluxe doubles have a DVD player and more space, with room for extra beds. Bathrobes come standard for the round, natural-stone hot pool in back.

Lindargata 3. ⓒ 453-5002. Fax 453-5388. www.hoteltindastoll.com. 11 units. June–Aug 17,600–19,900kr ($282–$318/£141–£159) double. Rates 10%–30% lower May and Sept; 20%–40% lower Oct–Apr. Rates include breakfast. AE, DC, MC, V. **Amenities:** Bar; hot tub. *In room:* TV, coffee/tea, minibar, hair dryer, trouser press.

Guesthouse Mikligarður   This well-managed guesthouse is ideally located just off the central church square. Walls and floors are thin, and guests in rooms 5, 6, and 7 are woken up by the first breakfasters. The choice rooms are #1 (with bathroom), or #14, without. Sleeping-bag accommodation is available off season.

Kirkjutorg 3. ⓒ 453-6880. www.skagafjordur.com/mikligardur. 14 units, 2 w/bathroom. May 15–Sept 15 11,500kr ($184/£92) double w/bathroom; 8,500kr ($136/£68) double without bathroom; 11,400kr ($182/£91) triple without bathroom. Rates 5%–20% lower Sept 16–May 14. Rates include breakfast (May 15–Sept 15 only). AE, DC, MC, V. **Amenities:** Guest kitchen. *In room:* TV, Wi-Fi (ask for password), no phone.

HOFSÓS

If researching your family tree keeps you in Hofsós overnight, the **Icelandic Emigration Center** (p. 225) can find accommodation for you. **Gistiheimilið Sunnuberg,** Suðurbraut 8 (ⓒ **453-7310;** June–Aug 7,700kr [$123/£62] double; Sept–May 5,500kr [$88/£44] double) has five acceptable rooms with private bathroom. **Lónkot,** 13km (8 miles) north of Hofsós, does not have private bathrooms but is a nicer place to stay, with beds going for 4,900kr ($78/£39) per person; see "Where to Dine," below.

SIGLUFJÖRÐUR

From June to August, the local sports center **Hóll** (© 467-1284), at the end of Langeyrarvegur past the museum, has inexpensive sleeping-bag accommodation in basic rooms for three to six people, with a communal kitchen and a campsite. Hvanneyri, below, is the only other non-camping option; though, if it's full, the Herring Era Museum (p. 226) can probably find someone to put you up.

Hvanneyri Guesthouse This hotel-sized guesthouse is not particularly fashionable or up-to-date, but the rooms are warm and welcoming enough. You may even find the dated lounge furniture and satiny bedspreads endearing.

Aðalgata 10. © 467-1506. Fax 467-1526. www.hvanneyri.com. 19 units, 1 w/bathroom. May 15–Sept 15 9,400kr ($150/£75) double without bathroom; 12,500kr ($200/£100) triple without bathroom; 13,000kr ($208/£104) suite; 3,000kr ($48/£24) per person sleeping-bag accommodation. Rates include breakfast (May 15–June 15 only). AE, DC, MC, V. **Amenities:** Guest kitchen. *In room:* TV, no phone.

WHERE TO DINE
VARMAHLÍÐ

The **N1 gas station** on the Ring Road, open daily to 9pm, is a step up from the usual pit-stop cafeteria, with lamb chops and fish dishes as well as burgers and hot dogs.

Hótel Varmahlíð ✈ ICELANDIC Inside a white hotel easily spotted from the Ring Road, this restaurant is committed to fresh, local, and environmentally friendly ingredients. The manager is married to a farmer, and the lamb comes fresh from their own flock.

Rte. 1. © 453-8170. Main courses 1,550kr–37,900kr ($25–$61/£12–£30). AE, DC, MC, V. June–Aug daily 6:30–9:30pm; May and Sept daily 7–9pm; Oct–Apr (by request in advance).

SAUÐÁRKRÓKUR

Fosshótel Áning, listed above, also has a good restaurant open June through August from 6 to 9pm. The bakery, **Sauðárkróksbakari,** Aðalgata 5 (© 455-5000; June–Aug 7am–6pm, Sept–May 8am–4pm), is perfect for breakfast, a soup and sandwich lunch, or a pastry: try the chocolate cake with coconut sprinkles.

Ólafshús ✈ ICELANDIC This unpretentious, reliable restaurant in the old town center is popular among local families. Main courses include all-you-can-eat at the soup and salad bar. If you can bear it, this is a good time to try foal, which is almost indistinguishable from beef but harder to overcook. It's served here with mushroom sauce, leeks, and grapes. If not, stick with the fish, lamb, pizzas, or BBQ ribs.

Aðalgata 15. © 453-6454. Main courses 770kr–2,770kr ($12–$44/£6.15–£22) AE, DC, MC, V. June–Aug Mon–Fri 11am–2pm and 5:30–10:30pm, Sat–Sun 11am–11pm; Sept–May daily 11am–2pm and 5:30–10pm.

Kaffi Krókur ✈ ICELANDIC This restaurant-bar is in an 1887 house across the street from Ólafshús, and the dishes are a notch more ambitious, pricey, and refined. Starters include pickled goose, or smoked lamb and mozzarella with tomatoes and mustard sauce. For a main, Icelandic lobster is a recommended house specialty. Portions are very generous.

Aðalgata 16b, Sauðárkrókur. © 453-6299. Main courses 2,590kr–3,890kr ($41–$62/£21–£31). AE, DC, MC, V. June–Aug daily 11:30am–11:30pm; Sept–May daily 11:30am–11pm.

HOFSÓS & NEARBY

Within the village, your choices are **Solvík** (℗ 453-7930; May 20–Aug daily 10am–10pm) a pleasant, summer-only restaurant-cafe next to the Emigration Center museum, and **Sigtún,** Suðurbraut 6 (℗ 453-7393; May 20–Aug daily 6–11pm; Sept–May 19 daily 6–9pm), a restaurant-bar with a basic array of burgers, fish, and lamb.

Lónkot ⟨⟨ ICELANDIC   Lónkot is a worthwhile dinner destination from anywhere in Skagafjörður, especially because it's on the fjord north of Hofsós, where you'd never expect to find a gourmet restaurant. If you pass through by day, stop for coffee or snacks in the viewing tower, a converted silo overlooking the fjord. The set dinner menu, usually around 4,500kr ($72/£36), is based on whatever's fresh and available; call ahead to see if it appeals to you. Chef's specialties include puffin, marinated cod, lamb, trout, and ice cream made with wild violets. Lónkot also has a charming **guesthouse** (p. 228), a nine-hole golf course, and an enormous striped tent that holds a local flea market on the third Sunday of each June, July, and August.

Rte. 76, 11km (7 miles) north of Hofsós. ℗ 453-7432 or 895-9852. Reservations recommended for dinner. AE, DC, MC, V. June–Aug 8am–midnight; kitchen closes at 10pm. Closed Sept–May.

SIGLUFJÖRÐUR

The bakery **Aðalbakari,** Aðalgata 36 (℗ 467-1720; MC, V; daily 7am–5pm), serves breakfast and lunch, with sandwiches, pastries, and cakes. **Pizza 67,** Aðalgata 32 (℗ 467-2323; AE, DC, MC, V; daily 5–9pm) is a fun Reykjavík-based chain that also serves salads, burgers, fish, and lasagna. The movie-themed **Bíó Café,** Aðalgata 30 (℗ 467-1111; MC, V. June–Aug daily 11am–9pm; Sept–May noon–2pm and 5–9pm), has well-priced pizza, burgers, fish, and lamb, and is also the best local bar.

BETWEEN SKAGAFJÖRÐUR & AKUREYRI

Halastjarna ⟨⟨ (Finds) ICELANDIC   The Ring Road from Skagafjörður to Akureyri ascends to a 540m (1,772 ft.) pass, with hulking mountains and serrated ridges on both sides. This gem of a restaurant, with just five tables, lies on the descent toward Akureyri. The menu changes opportunistically, but staples include pan-roasted catfish with mint, strawberries, and white-wine stock; lamb filet with house herbs and port sauce; and garlic-roasted lobster. Salads are plucked from the garden outside. For an appetizer, it's definitely worth taking the easy, 2-hour round-trip hike from the restaurant to beautiful Hraunsvatn lake, tucked away in the mountains. Concerts are occasionally hosted in summer.

Háls í Öxnadalur (Rte. 1, about 36km [22 miles] west of Akureyri and 61km [38 miles] east of Varmahlíð). ℗ 461-2200. www.halastjarna.is. Reservations strongly recommended. 5-course menu 6,500kr ($104/£52); 4 courses 5,900kr ($94/£47); 3 courses 4,900kr ($78/£39); main courses around 2,500kr ($40/£20). AE, DC, MC, V. June–Aug daily noon–10pm; Sept–Dec 25 Sat–Sun noon–10pm; Jan–May call ahead.

3 Akureyri

Nestled at the head of Eyjafjörður, Iceland's longest fjord, **Akureyri** ⟨⟨ is north Iceland's largest fishing port, and its cultural, industrial, and trade capital. It's often called Iceland's "second city," but residents don't seem to take this the wrong way. Akureyri has only 17,000 people, so just reaching the status of "city" is an unrivaled achievement outside the Reykjavík metropolitan area. (Technically, Akureyri is Iceland's fourth-largest city, after the Reykjavík suburbs of Kópavogur and Hafnarfjörður.)

Akureyri

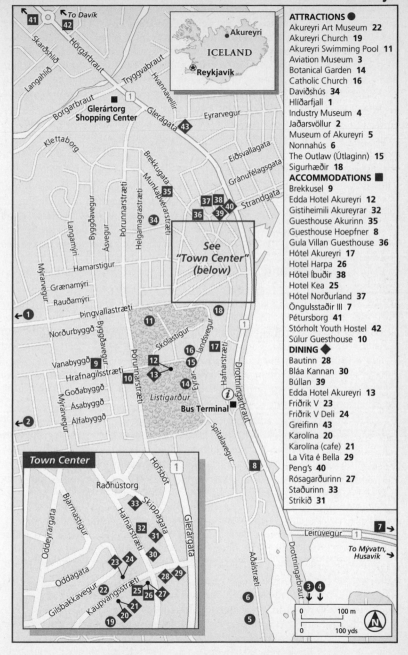

ATTRACTIONS ●
Akureyri Art Museum **22**
Akureyri Church **19**
Akureyri Swimming Pool **11**
Aviation Museum **3**
Botanical Garden **14**
Catholic Church **16**
Davíðshús **34**
Hlíðarfjall **1**
Industry Museum **4**
Jaðarsvöllur **2**
Museum of Akureyri **5**
Nonnahús **6**
The Outlaw (Útlaginn) **15**
Sigurhæðir **18**

ACCOMMODATIONS ■
Brekkusel **9**
Edda Hotel Akureyri **12**
Gistiheimili Akureyrar **32**
Guesthouse Akurinn **35**
Guesthouse Hoepfner **8**
Gula Villan Guesthouse **36**
Hótel Akureyri **17**
Hotel Harpa **26**
Hótel Íbuðir **38**
Hotel Kea **25**
Hótel Norðurland **37**
Öngulsstaðir III **7**
Pétursborg **41**
Stórholt Youth Hostel **42**
Súlur Guesthouse **10**

DINING ◆
Bautinn **28**
Bláa Kannan **30**
Búllan **39**
Edda Hotel Akureyri **13**
Friðrik V **23**
Friðrik V Deli **24**
Greifinn **43**
Karolína **20**
Karolína (cafe) **21**
La Vita é Bella **29**
Peng's **40**
Rósagarðurinn **27**
Staðurinn **33**
Strikið **31**

Akureyri is a sophisticated and thriving town, and Akureyrians boast of their superior weather, warmer and drier than drizzly Reykjavík in summer.

Akureyri's first known settler was Helgi the Lean, who arrived circa 890. By 1602 it was an active trading post, and by 1900 had 1,370 residents. The trade cooperative KEA, formed in 1886, still owns large shares of several Eyjafjörður businesses, and in 1915 Akureyri had the country's first social-democratic government. The University of Akureyri, established in 1987, is the only state-run university outside of Reykjavík.

Akureyri sees about 180,000 visitors a year, and has no shortage of restaurants and museums. The annual Summer Arts Festival, which includes concerts, exhibitions, dance, and theater, lasts from mid-June to late August, with a street party finale.

ESSENTIALS
GETTING THERE & AROUND

Akureyri is on Route 1 (the Ring Road), 388km (241 miles) from Reykjavík and 265km (165 miles) from Egilsstaðir. The downtown, clustered around Hafnarstræti, with Ráðhústorg Square at its northern end, is easily navigable **on foot.** Much of Akureyri is spread along a steep incline, however, so a car is helpful. Akureyri's one bike rental company has closed; check with tourist information to see if it's been replaced.

BSO taxi (© 461-1010) is on call 24 hours and operates a **taxi stand** on Strandgata at Hofsbót, with at least one wheelchair-accessible car.

BY PLANE   Air Iceland (© 470-6000; www.airiceland.is) has eight 45-minute flights daily between Reykjavík and Akureyri. One-way tickets average 9,000kr ($144/£72), but go as high as 13,000kr ($208/£104) and as low as 4,000kr ($64/£32) with early booking online. From Akureyri, direct flights go to Vopnafjörður and Grímsey Island; all other destinations are routed through Reykjavík. From June through August, **Iceland Express** (© 550-0600; www.icelandexpress.com) has two flights a week between Akureyri and Copenhagen. The Akureyri Airport (AEY) is on the Ring Road, 3km (2 miles) south of town.

BY CAR   Rental agencies at the airport are **Alp/Budget** (© 562-6060; www.alp.is), **Avis** (© 461-2428; www.avis.is), **Europcar** (© 565-3800; www.europcar.is), **Hertz** (© 522-4440; www.hertz.is), and **National/Bílaleiga Akureyrar** (© 461-6000; www.nationalcar.is), which has another office at Tryggvabraut 12. All agencies should offer to pick you up anywhere in town. If you rent in Akureyri and leave the car in Reykjavík, the drop-off fee will likely be 5,000kr ($80/£40) to 10,000kr ($160/£80).

The municipal **parking** lots—clustered along Skipagata, one block east of the pedestrian-only stretch of Hafnarstræti—are free, but during working hours you need to dash into an adjacent store or bank and ask for a "parking disc," a windshield sticker with attached clock hands. Signs indicate how long the parking spot is good for, from 15 minutes to 2 hours. Set the clock hands ahead to the time the spot expires. You can park all day if you keep returning to the car to reset the disc.

BY BUS   The tourist information center at Hafnarstræti 82, just south of the town center, doubles as the main bus station and sells tickets.

Trex (© 587-6000; www.trex.is) connects Reykjavík and Akureyri twice daily in summer via the Ring Road (6 hr.; 7,300kr [$117/£58]), and once daily via the Kjölur interior route (10 hr.; 8,600kr [$138/£69]). Trex also has daily summer connections between Akureyri and Dalvík (55 min.; 1,100kr [$18/£8.80]), Húsavik (75 min.; 2,300kr [$37/£18]), and Egilsstaðir (4 hr.; 5,300kr [$85/£42]).

SBA-Norðurleid (© 550-0700; www.sba.is) includes sightseeing stops in its routes, often with guides. One bus connects Reykjavík and Akureyri daily in summer through the Kjölur Route (9 hr.; 8,600kr [$138/£69]), with brief stops at Geysir, Gullfoss, and Hveravellir. Other daily summer routes connect Akureyri to Mývatn, Húsavík, and Jökulsárgljúfur National Park in various combinations. A 3-day trip leads to Askja and Kverkfjöll in the interior (p. 359).

Buses within Akureyri are free—yes, free—with six routes (mysteriously numbered 1, 2, 3, 4, 5, and 7) that run hourly on weekdays from 6:30 or 7:30am to as late as 8:30pm. Buses 3 and 4 also run weekends and holidays, with departures from around noon to 6pm. All routes leave from Ráðhústorg Square, by the shop named Nætursalan. No routes go to the airport. For schedule and route information, pick up a brochure at the tourist information center, call © 462-4929, or visit www.akureyri.is/ferdamenn/samgongur/straetisvagnar.

VISITOR INFORMATION

The very competent tourist information center (© 550-0720; www.akureyri.is or www.nordurland.is; June 1–18 Mon–Fri 7:30am–5pm, Sat–Sun 8am–5pm; June 19–Aug Mon–Fri 7:30am–7pm, Sat–Sun 8am–7pm; May 15–30 and Sept Mon–Fri 8am–5pm, Sat–Sun 9am–1pm; Oct–May 15 Mon–Fri 8am–4pm) is currently at Hafnarstræti 82, 10 minutes' walk south from Ráðhústorg Square, but in 2009 or 2010 it may move to a new cultural center being built by the harbor. The center is useful for all of north Iceland, and the staff can find and book accommodations for a 500kr ($8/£4) fee.

Anyone planning a hiking adventure in north Iceland or the interior can buy maps and get free advice from the local hiking club, Ferðafélag Akureyrar, Strandgata 23 (© 462-2720; www.ffa.is; ffa@li.is; June–Aug Mon–Fri 4–7pm). This is also where to register your itinerary, so that if you don't return, they'll know where to come looking for you.

FAST FACTS: Akureyri

Banks/Currency Exchange Banks are generally open weekdays from 9:15am to 4pm and have commission-free currency exchange and 24-hour ATMs. **Kaupýing Banki (KB)** (© 444-6000) at Glerártorg Mall is open weekdays from 12:30 to 6pm. Hótel KEA exchanges currency but charges an outrageous 10% commission.

Cellphones For thorough information on cellphones in Iceland, see p. 33. Cellphones and calling plans are available at **Síminn**, Hafnarstræti 102 (© 460-6709; Mon–Fri 10am–6pm, Sat 11am–4pm) and **Vodafone**, Glerártorg Mall (© 599-9099; Mon–Fri 10am–6:30pm, Sat 10am–5pm, Sun 1–5pm).

Doctors & Dentists see "Medical Help," below.

Drugstores Apótekarinn (© 461-5800; Mon–Fri 9am–5:30pm) is downtown at Hafnarstræti 95. Drugstores with extended hours are **Apótekið**, Furuvellir 17, Hagkaup Market (© 461-3920; Mon–Fri 10am–7pm, Sat 10am–4pm, Sun noon–4pm) and **Lyf & heilsa**, Glerártorg Mall (© 461-5800; Mon–Fri 10am–6:30pm, Sat 10am–5pm, Sun 1–5pm).

Emergencies Dial © **112** for ambulance, fire, or police. See also "Medical Help," below.

Hospitals See "Medical Help," below.

Internet Access **Akureyri Library** (see "Libraries," below), has multiple terminals, a cafe, and the best price 200kr ($3.20/£1.60) per hour. The **tourist information center** (see "Visitor Information," above) has two terminals for 150kr ($2.40/£1.20) every 15 minutes. Both places, plus several cafes and the Penninn bookstore/cafe (Hafnarstræti 91-93) are **Wi-Fi hot spots.**

Laundry The only self-service laundry machines are at the campsite and youth hostel (p. 237). **Þvottahúsið Höfði,** Hafnarstræti 34 (© **462-2580**; Mon–Fri 8am–noon and 3–5pm), a full-service laundry, charges 900kr ($14/£7.20) for up to 5kg/11 lb.

Libraries **Akureyri Library,** Brekkugata 17 (© **462-4141**; June 16–Sept 19 Mon–Fri 10am–7pm; Sept 20–June 15 Mon–Fri 10am–7pm, Sat 10am–3pm), has cheap Internet access and a decent collection of English-language books and magazines; tourists can borrow books for free.

Lost & Found See "Police," below.

Luggage Storage The **tourist information center** (see "Visitor Information," above) can hold bags for up to one night, but does not have a secure room for this purpose.

Mail See "Post Office," below.

Medical Help For an ambulance, call © **112. Akureyri Hospital** (Spítalavegur, by Eyrarlandsvegur; main number © **463-010**, emergency room © **463-0800**, telephone consultation © **848-2600**; Mon–Fri 5am–9pm, Sat–Sun 7am–noon and 2–4pm) is just south of the botanical garden. **Heilsugæslustöðin Clinic,** Hafnarstrstræti 99 (© **460-4600**; daily 8am–4:45pm), is downtown.

Pharmacies See "Drugstores," above.

Police For emergencies, dial © **112.** The police station (© **464-7700**) is at Þórunnarstræti 138.

Post Office/Mail The **post office** (© **580-1000**; Mon–Fri 9am–4:30pm) is at Skipagata 10, in the city center.

Supermarkets Supermarkets include **Bónus** (Langhólt 1), **Haugkaup** (Furuvellir, near Hjalteyrargata), and **Nettó** (Glerártorg Mall). Supermarkets open late include **10-11** (Þingvallastræti at Mýrarvegur; 24 hr.), **Strax** (Borgarbraut at Hlíðarbraut; 24 hr.) and another **Strax** (Byggðavegur at Hrafnagilsstræti; Mon–Fri 9am–11pm; Sat–Sun 10am–11pm).

Taxis See "Getting There & Around," above.

Telephone Public phones are available at the **tourist information center** (see "Visitor Information," above), **Akureyri Hospital** (see "Medical Help," above), Spítalavegur (by Eyrarlandsvegur), the **city pool** (p. 243), and the **Penninn Eymundsson** bookstore on Hafnarstræti 91-93. See also "Cell Phones," above.

WHERE TO STAY
EXPENSIVE
Hótel Akureyri ⚂   Ideally located a short walk from downtown, and right across from the tourist information center, this hotel isn't aiming for much character distinction; but rooms feel sumptuous, and the staff is obliging. Rooms facing the fjord are booked out first. Breakfast gets extra credit for the waffle iron and whipped cream. Hótel Akureyri also offers six snazzy apartments with kitchens, sleeping five to 10 people. *Note:* The hotel has four floors but no elevator.

Hafnarstræti 67. © 462-5600. Fax 462-5601. www.hotelakureyri.is. 19 units, 6 apts. May–Sep 16,500kr ($264£132) double; 25,000kr ($400/£200) apt. Rates around 25% lower Oct–Apr. Rates include breakfast, except apts. AE, DC, MC, V. *In room:* TV, Wi-Fi, fridge, safe.

Hótel Harpa   The plain but upstanding Hótel Harpa shares management with the adjacent glitzy Hótel Kea, and Harpa's high prices reflect the shared service and amenities. Harpa's rooms are bright and renovated but much less smartly appointed. The one "superior" double has extra space, DVD and CD players, and a bathtub.

Hafnarstræti 83–85. © 460-2000. Fax 460-2060. www.keahotels.is. 25 units. June–Aug 15,900–18,300kr ($254–$293/£127–£146) double; 20,600kr ($330/£165) triple. Rates 20% lower May and Sept; 30% lower Oct–Apr. Rates include breakfast. AE, DC, MC, V. **Amenities:** Restaurant; bar; Wi-Fi in lobby; room service; same-day laundry/dry cleaning service. *In room:* TV, pay Internet (via cable), minibar, coffee/tea, hair dryer.

Hótel Kea ⚂⚂   Built in 1944—and clearly tops in town—this central, four-star hotel presides over the base of the long stairway to Akureyri Church. 2006 renovations added handsome dark-wood furnishings and plush beds but bypassed the small bathrooms. Some fourth-floor rooms open onto a large balcony. "Superior" doubles on the 5th floor have great views, big TVs, and nice bathrooms but not much more size.

Hafnarstræti 87–89. © 460-2000. Fax 460-2060. www.keahotels.is. 73 units. June–Aug 18,600kr–21,400kr ($298–$342/£149–£171) double; 24,100kr ($386/£193) triple. Rates around 20% lower May and Sept, 30% lower Oct–Apr. Rates include breakfast. AE, DC, MC, V. **Amenities:** Restaurant; bar; Wi-Fi in lobby; room service; same-day laundry/dry cleaning service. *In room:* TV, pay Internet (via cable), minibar, coffee/tea, hair dryer.

Hótel Norðurland   Norðurland is in the same chain as the Harpa and Kea, and is equally central. Rooms are well-appointed but a bit dated, spiritless, and small, with tiny TVs. Four rooms have balconies with an unremarkable view over the street. "Superior" doubles on the second floor get you more space.

Geislagata 7. © 462-2600. Fax 462-2601. www.keahotels.is. 34 units. June–Aug 15,900kr–18,300kr ($254–$293/ £127–£146) double; 20,600kr ($330/£165) triple. Rates around 20% lower May and Sept, 30% lower Oct–Apr. Rates include breakfast. AE, DC, MC, V. **Amenities:** Restaurant; bar; same day laundry/dry cleaning service. *In room:* TV, fridge, coffee/tea, hair dryer.

MODERATE
Edda Hótel Akureyri ⚂   Edda hotels are stigmatized for being student dormitories during the school year, but in this case you'll wonder how such nice rooms could be lavished on high-schoolers. The more expensive doubles are in a separate new building, and have spiffier furniture, balconies (with good views on floors 4–6), more space, and a mini-kitchen with sink, microwave, and fridge but no flatware. The location is close to the botanical garden but a steep walk uphill from the town center.

Hrafnagilsstræti, just west of Eyrarlandsvegur. © 444-4000. Fax 444-4901. www.hoteledda.is. 204 units, 190 w/bathroom. Mid-June to late-Aug 11,200kr–12,700 ($179–$203/£90–£102) double; 7,100kr ($114/£57) double without bathroom. Breakfast available: 850kr ($14/£6.80). AE, DC, MC, V. Closed late-Aug to mid-June. **Amenities:** Restaurant; bar; Internet terminal; laundry service. *In room:* TV (rooms w/bathroom only).

Hótel Íbúðir ✿✿ *Value*   Just off Ráðhústorg in the heart of the city, this excellent mid-range choice has attentive staff, a communal kitchen, and classy, understated rooms with marvelous, adjustable "health beds." The lush apartments have balconies, spacious living rooms, and fully equipped kitchens.

Reception and apts at Geislagata 10 (entrance upstairs behind Bónus video store); guesthouse at Brekkugata 13. ℂ 462-3727. Fax 462-3200. www.hotelibudir.is. 6 units, 6 apts. May–Sept 11,900kr ($190/£95) double; 14,900kr ($238/£119) studio double; 16,900kr ($270/£135) 1-bedroom apt; 19,900kr–24,900kr ($318–$398/£159–£199) 2–3 bedroom apts. Rates 15%–25% lower Oct–Apr. AE, MC, V. **Amenities:** Guest kitchen. *In room:* TV, Wi-Fi, hair dryer, no phone.

Öngulsstaðir III   If you have a car and enjoy ending the day in a hot tub overlooking a pastoral scene, consider staying at this hospitable guesthouse 10km (6¼ miles) south of Akureyri. The rooms are short on rustic character, but you'll find nothing dreary about them, either. Dinner is available on request.

Rte. 829, 10km (6¼ miles) south of Akureyri. ℂ 463-1380. www.ongulsstadir.is. 19 units, 17 w/bathroom. June–Aug 10,900kr ($174/£87) double; 8,900kr ($142/£71) double without bathroom; 13,500kr ($216/£108) triple; 15,200kr ($243/£122) family room; 15,000kr ($240/£120) two-bedroom apt. Rates around 10% lower Oct–Apr. Rates include breakfast. AE, DC, MC, V. **Amenities:** Hot tub. *In room:* No phone.

INEXPENSIVE

Brekkusel ✿ *Value*   The location isn't the most central, but for basic value, comfort, and relaxation, this guesthouse is hard to beat. The washing machine is free, the bathroom floor tiles are heated, and with 2 hours' notice they'll fill the hot tub.

Byggðavegur 97. ℂ 461-2660. www.brekkusel.is. 10 units, 2 w/bathroom. 8,700kr ($139/£70) double; 6,800kr ($109/£54) double without bathroom; 10,400kr ($166/£83) triple. **Amenities:** Guest kitchen; hot tub; washer/dryer access. *In room:* Wi-Fi, no phone.

Gistiheimili Akureyrar   All three buildings of this guesthouse are dead central, with not much to choose among them; Hafnarstræti 108 has slightly larger rooms, but the other two have sinks in each room, and Hafnarstræti 104 has desks. Rooms are spare and affectless, with TVs but not even the token framed print on the wall. Ask for an inside room if you're sensitive to noise, especially on weekends. Reception is at Hafnarstræti 104 in July and August, and at Hótel Akureyri from September to June.

Hafnarstræti 104, Hafnarstræti 108, and Skipagata 4. ℂ 462-5588. Fax 462-5601. www.guesthouseakureyri.is. 29 units, 9 w/bathroom. May–Sept 9,900kr ($158/£79) double; 7,300kr ($117/£58) double without bathroom; 9,900kr ($158/£79) triple; 11,900kr ($190/£95) quadruple. Rates around 20% lower Oct–Apr. *In room:* TV.

Guesthouse AkurInn ✿   This sweet old house, a 2-minute walk from the city center, has low-key, tasteful rooms and a charming TV lounge but no guest kitchen. Room 301 is the clear pick, with a private balcony overlooking the city.

Brekkugata 27a. ℂ 461-2500. Fax 461-2502. www.akurinn.is. 7 units, none w/bathroom. May–Sept 7,200kr ($115/£58) double; 8,900kr ($142/£71) triple; 10,800kr ($173/£86) quadruple. Rates about 13% lower Oct–Apr. Breakfast available: 900kr ($14/£7.20). AE, DC, MC, V. *In room:* No phone.

Guesthouse Hoepfner ✿ *Value*   If you like modish furnishings in a house on the historic register, this with-it guesthouse is worth the 15-minute hike to town. Rooms are full of light, and the communal kitchen has free coffee and oranges. The two apartments are even more stylish, with cowskin rugs and Pop Art on the walls.

Hafnarstræti 20. ℂ 463-3360. www.hoepfner.is. 5 units, none w/bathroom; 3 apts. May 20–Aug 20 6,500kr ($104/£52) double; 5,300kr ($85/£42) double with sleeping-bag; 8,500kr ($136/£68) triple; 6,300kr ($101/£50) triple with sleeping bag; 11,900kr ($190/£95) apt. Rates include breakfast, except for sleeping-bag accommodation. MC, V. **Amenities:** Guest kitchen. *In room:* Wi-Fi, no phone.

Gula Villan Guesthouse   This no-complaints guesthouse is about basic habitable rooms and friendly service. In summer a second location opens up at Þingvallastræti 14; the main house is more centrally located, while the Þingvallastræti house is right by Akureyri's fabulous geothermal pool and has Wi-Fi.

Brekkugata 8. 🕻 **896-8464.** Fax 461-3040. www.gulavillan.is. 40 units, none w/bathroom. May 15–Sept 7,200kr ($115/£58) double; 5,600kr ($90/£45) double with sleeping bag; 9,300kr ($149/£74) triple; 7,800kr ($125/£62) triple with sleeping bag; 12,000kr ($192/£96) quadruple; 10,000kr ($160/£80) quadruple with sleeping bag. Rates around 10% lower Sept–May 14. Rates do not include breakfast. MC, V. **Amenities:** Guest kitchen. *In room:* No phone.

Pétursborg 🕿   This is the pick of local farm stays bordering the city. Akureyri is only 5km (3 miles) away, but horses graze across the road, the hot tub is always at the ready, and the house pets—Pookie the cat and Primo the Labrador retriever—are cute and friendly. A short trail leads to the fjord, where you can walk along the shore. Rooms in the two cabins are most inviting, but all are comfortable and unassuming. A three-course dinner is available on request for a very reasonable 2,200kr ($35/£18).

Rte. 817 (1.5km/1 mile off Rte. 1, 5km/3 miles north of Akureyri). 🕻 **461-1811.** Fax 461-1333. www.petursborg. com. 8 units, 3 w/bathroom. June–Aug 8,600kr ($138/£69) double; 6,500kr ($104/£52) double without bathroom; 11,400kr ($182/£91) triple without bathroom; 15,200kr ($243/£122) quadruple without bathroom. Breakfast available (750kr/$12/£6). MC, V. **Amenities:** Guest kitchen, hot tub, washer/dryer access for 300kr ($4.80/£2.40). *In room:* Wi-Fi, no phone.

Stórholt Youth Hostel   If your image of a hostel is a grubby dorm room full of bunk beds and unkempt, snoring backpackers, Stórholt will inspire a drastic revision. Most rooms have two or three beds, plus TVs, and guests include families and travelers of all ages. The location is quiet and residential; the city center is a 15-minute walk, or there's a free hourly bus. Book far in advance if you can. Tour operators for whale-watching and river rafting offer good discounts through the front desk.

Stórholt 1, just east of Rte. 1. 🕻 **894-4299** or 462-3657. Fax: 461-2549. www.akureyrihostel.com. 18 units, 1 w/bathroom. 6,800kr ($109/£54) double; 5,600kr ($90/£45) double with sleeping bag; 8,600kr ($138/£69) triple; 2,300kr ($37/£18) dorm bed. AE, DC, MC, V. **Amenities:** Guest kitchen; washer/dryer access. *In room:* Wi-Fi, no phone.

Súlur Guesthouse 🕿   Not much distinguishes this guesthouse from its competitors, and neither of its two locations are particularly convenient, but both are likable, livable, and good-value. Reception is at the house on Þórunnarstræti, which has Wi-Fi and TVs in every room; the Klettastígur house, with larger rooms, is open in summer only.

Þórunnarstræti 93 and Klettastígur 6. 🕻 **461-1160.** sulur@islandia.is. 20 units, none w/bathroom. May–Sept 7,000kr ($112/£56) double; 9,000kr ($144/£72) triple; 5,400kr ($86/£43) sleeping-bag accommodation. Rates 10% lower Oct–Apr. MC, V. **Amenities:** Guest kitchen, washer/dryer access. *In room:* No phone.

WHERE TO DINE

Reykjavík's restaurants are hard to match, but Akureyri makes a respectable showing and capitalizes on local strengths. The Eyjafjörður valley is a big beef and dairy-producing region, and *skýr*—Iceland's famous whipped whey concoction—was invented here. Delicious blue mussels are cultivated in Eyjafjörður. Perhaps we shouldn't tell you that Eyjafjörður's excellent smoked lamb is smoked "the traditional way"—with dried manure. Iceland's first and only microbrewery, *Kaldi*, is made in the tiny Eyjafjörður village of Árskógssandur, with grains from the Czech Republic. (Beer-flavored ice cream is in the works.) On the workaday side, locals like their burgers with béarnaise sauce and stuffed with french fries. In a stroke of genius, this burger concept has been transferred to the popular *Bókullupizza:* Yes, that would be pizza topped with beef, béarnaise sauce, cheese, and french fries.

For a memorable dinner excursion in the mountains west of Akureyri, see **Halastjarna** (p. 230).

VERY EXPENSIVE

Friðrik V ☽☽ ICELANDIC/FRENCH   Owner and head chef Friðrik Valur is north Iceland's leading food pundit, with frequent newspaper columns, lectures, and TV appearances. Service is attentive and educational, and you'll probably be told how fresh and local the ingredients are and how long the cooks labored before your arrival. (The amazing shellfish broth used in several dishes cooks at a low temperature for 17 hr.) The menu is small and focused, with house specialties marked by a chef's hat icon. The best way to see what Friðrik can do is to shell out 7,980kr ($128/£64) for the five-course chef's menu. The bar, which opens at 5pm and serves tapas and cheese plates, is great for a pre-dinner cocktail.

Kaupvangsstræti 6. ⓒ 461-5775. www.fridrikv.is. Reservations recommended. Main courses 3,070kr–4,980kr ($49/£80). AE, DC, MC, V. Sun–Thurs 6–9pm; Fri–Sat 6–10pm.

EXPENSIVE

If the options below are full, consider the first-rate **Rósagarðurinn** (Rose Garden) at Hotel Kea, with traditional Icelandic main courses around 2,000kr to 3,500kr ($32–$56/£16–£28).

Karolína ☽ INTERNATIONAL   Karolína is a good illustration of current trends in Iceland's high-end restaurant business. First, attention is drawn to the creative mind behind the food: the chef's awards line the wall as you enter, and the kitchen is exposed. Second, the food is European-based but unconcerned with representing any particular cooking tradition. (Asian influences are adept here, as in the arctic char in soy balsamic vinegar.) Third, fresh local ingredients are paramount. Finally, flavorings are balanced and complex but not ascetic: Icelanders like food hearty, saucy, salty, and mouth-melting. This might be the time to try horsemeat, a traditional staple otherwise hard to find in restaurants. Every Thursday in summer, diners get free admission to jazz sets in the adjoining gallery.

Kaupvangsstræti 23. ⓒ 461-2755. www.karolina.is. Main courses 2,750kr–4,450kr ($44–$72/£22–£36). AE, DC, MC, V. Mid-June to Aug daily 6–10pm; Sept to mid-June Sun–Thurs 6–9pm, Fri–Sat 6–10pm.

Strikið ☽ ICELANDIC   Perched on a fifth floor overlooking the harbor, this buzzing restaurant is better than the casual atmosphere suggests. Familiar dishes come with twists: béarnaise sauce on the beef tenderloin tastes of curry and coconut; lobster soup is flavored with cognac; and chocolate mousse comes with sesame crackers. Loopy combinations include monkfish wrapped in Parma ham with basil risotto and lime sauce, and trout with potato cubes and tangerine sorbet. Pizzas are excellent if you like thin crust, sharp tomato sauce, and lots of parm in the cheese mix. Service can be slow, but you can wait outside on the roof patio under a heat lamp.

Skipagata 14. ⓒ 462-7100. www.strikid.is. Reservations recommended. Main courses 1,750kr–4,990kr ($28–$80/£14–£40). AE, DC, MC, V. Sun–Thurs 11am–10pm; Fri–Sat 11am–11pm.

MODERATE

Those staying up the hill should consider the **Edda hotel**'s quality dinner buffet, which costs 3,200kr ($51/£26), with a la carte options available.

Bautinn *(Kids)* ICELANDIC   Right on Akureyri's busiest corner, this crowd-pleaser is reasonably priced and the food is comfortingly predictable. The ambience is more for families than a date, unless your companion enjoys playrooms. All main courses, which come with fried vegetables and potatoes, also include the soup and salad bar.

Hafnarstræti 92. ℂ **462-1818**. www.bautinn.is. Main courses 870kr–2,890kr ($14–$46/£6.95–£23). MC, V. Daily 9am–9pm.

Greifinn *(Kids)* ICELANDIC   This family-oriented restaurant lacks Bautinn's central location, but outdoes it in most other respects: prices are slightly lower, the huge menu branches into Italian and Tex-Mex, and the playroom has video games. Tables have electric buzzers for service; small children find them irresistible and harass the wait-staff. Greifinn was the originator of saltfish pizza, an Eyjafjörður favorite. The 1,390kr ($22/£11) lunch special, weekdays from 11:30am to 2pm, is a steal.

Glerárgata 20 (Rte. 1). ℂ **460-1600**. www.greifinn.is. Main courses 1,240kr–2,760kr ($20–$44/£9.95–£22). AE, DC, MC, V. Daily 11am–11:30pm.

La Vita é Bella ITALIAN   Food here tends to be inauthentic and flooded in creamy sauces, but if you just need a change of pace, you might work around these limitations with a salad or the freshly made pesto. The "Mussolini" pizza, which combines pepperoni, bleu cheese, and bananas, achieves bad taste on multiple levels. Half portions are substantial enough for all but the famished.

Hafnarstræti 92 (behind Bautinn). ℂ **461-5858**. Reservations recommended. Main courses 960kr–2,930kr ($15–$47/£7.70–£23). MC, V. Daily 6–11 pm.

Peng's CHINESE   The food is what you'd expect from the one Chinese restaurant in a place like Akureyri: none of it is particularly authentic or subtle, but most customers get the grease-heavy fix they've come for. The daily 1,250kr ($20/£10) lunch buffet is a great deal. Peng's proclaims itself the world's northernmost Chinese restaurant; sorry, but that would be in Barrow, Alaska.

Strandgata 13. ℂ **466-3800**. Reservations recommended for dinner. Main courses 1,990kr–2,990kr ($32–$48/£16–£24). MC, V. May–Aug daily 10:30am–11pm (until 11:30pm Fri–Sat); Sept–Apr daily 10:30am–2pm and 5–11pm (until 11:30pm Fri–Sat).

Staðurinn *(Kids)* HEALTH FOOD   Akureyri's latest coming of age is this health food restaurant, a welcome antidote to Iceland's heavy diet. Choices are limited to soups, salads, cakes, and a daily special—perhaps a carrot pie, lasagna, or rice noodles. White flour, white sugar, and other dietary evils are taboo. For an Icelandic touch, try the "Skýr boost."

Skipagata 2. ℂ **464-1420**. Main courses 700k–1,350kr ($11–$22/£5.60–£11). June–Sept Mon–Fri 10am–9pm, Sat noon–8pm; Oct–May Mon–Fri 11:30am–8pm, Sat noon–8pm.

INEXPENSIVE

Búllan BURGERS   This low-key joint with American Route 66-style decor serves burgers (including veggie burgers) a notch above standard—and proper milkshakes, too.

Strandgata 11. ℂ **462-1800**. Burgers 400kr–590kr ($6.40–$9.45/£3.20–£4.70). AE, MC, V. Daily 11:45am–9pm.

CAFES & A DELI

Bláa Kannan   This cheerful, roomy hangout, spilling onto Akureyri's main pedestrian street, is ideal for writing postcards over cake and coffee. Real meal options are limited to soups, salads, sandwiches, quiche, spinach pie, and a daily pasta dish.

Hafnarstræti 96. © **461-4600.** Main courses 800kr–1,000kr ($13–$16/£6.40–£8). MC, V. Mon–Sat 9am–10:30pm; Sun 10am–10:30pm.

Friðrik V Deli ⭐   This casual offshoot of Akureyri's best restaurant is perfect for a soup, salad, or sandwich lunch. Check the chalkboard specials: the dish of the day is 1,120kr ($18/£8.95). Seating is in a pleasant, light-filled side room.

Kaupvangsstræti 6. © **461-5775.** Mon–Fri 11am–6pm; Sat 1–5pm.

Karolína   This fashionable cafe-bar, adjoining the upscale restaurant of the same name, serves tasty bagels and sandwiches.

Kaupvangsstræti 23. © **461-2755.** Small dishes 480kr–670kr ($7.70–$11/£3.85–£5.35). AE, DC, MC, V. June–Aug Sun–Thurs 10am–1am, Fri–Sat 10am–4am; Sept–May Sun–Thurs 2pm–1am, Fri–Sat 2pm–4am.

WHAT TO SEE & DO
THE CITY CENTER

Akureyri maintains museums in the former homes of Davíð Stefánsson (1895–1964), a novelist, playwright, and poet laureate, and Matthías Jochumsson (1835–1920), a poet, playwright, and translator. These museums—**Daviðshús** and **Sigurhæðir**—do an admirable job of preserving their legacies, but most information is presented in Icelandic, and neither writer has anything in print in English.

Akureyri Art Museum (Listasafnið á Akureyri) ⭐   The main drag for gallery-trollers is Kaupvangsstræti, which winds uphill from the city center, just north of Akureyri Church. Artists and art enthusiasts, with the city's help, appropriated several disused industrial buildings and converted them to exhibition and performance spaces, an art school, and studios for resident and visiting artists. The overarching arts-sponsoring organization is **Listagil** (© **466-2609;** listagil@listagil.is), and its main showcases are this museum and the **Summer Festival of the Arts,** which lasts from mid-June to late August and utilizes several spaces clustered near the museum. Pick up a *Listasumar* brochure anywhere in town, or check the schedule at www.akureyri.is. Founded in 1993, the well-designed museum has no permanent collection and is devoted mostly to contemporary Icelandic art, with international shows on occasion.

Kaupvangsstræti 12. © **461-2610.** www.listasafn.akureyri.is. Admission 400kr ($6.40/£3.20) adults; free for seniors and children 12 and under; free admission Thurs. Tues–Sun noon–5pm.

Akureyri Church ⭐   A long stairway extends from the city center up to this bravura concrete church, whose Art Deco twin spires have drawn mixed critical responses but rarely fail to make a durable impression. The hilltop location, face-forward design, and beckoning, outstretched spires lend the frontal exterior a Batman-like animal vitality. The church was consecrated in 1940 and designed by Guðjón Samúelsson, the state architect responsible for the even larger Hallgrímskirkja in Reykjavík. However distinctive his bold geometric outlines, Guðjón's signature is just as evident in the fine details, such as the basalt-inspired hexagonal columns above the doorway, and the obsessive tiering in the ceiling, archways, and surrounding lawn. Make sure to inspect the lovely tile work in Iceland spar—a native crystal used to make light prisms—on the pulpit and the illuminated cross hanging from the ceiling. The midsection of the stained glass window directly behind the altar was originally in England's Coventry Cathedral, bombarded in World War II and now a ruined shell.

© **462-7700.** Mon–Fri 8:30am–10pm; until 8:30pm Wed. June–Sept Sun service 11am; Oct–May Sun service 2pm. Prayers Thurs noon.

BOTANICAL GARDENS & NEARBY

The riveting 1901 sculpture **The Outlaw (Útlaginn)** ⟨★—easy to miss amid the greenery in the traffic island formed by Eyrarlandsvegur and Hrafnagilsstræti—established the reputation of Iceland's best-known sculptor, Einar Jónsson. A wild-looking outlaw dressed in skins carries his dead wife over his back, a spade in one hand and his little boy asleep on his other arm. He wants to bury her in consecrated ground, but would be put to death if captured, so he comes secretly at night. This cast metal version conveys tension and detail lacking in the plaster model at the Einar Jónsson Museum in Reykjavík (p. 115).

Catholic Church (Kaþólska Kirkjan)   This inviting church near the botanical garden holds mass in English, Icelandic, and Polish on Saturdays at 6pm and Sundays at 11am. After Sunday mass, attendees are invited downstairs for coffee with Father Patrick Breen, from Ireland, and the Carmelite order of nuns.

Eyrarlandsvegur 26 (at Hrafnagilsstræti). © 462-1119. June–Aug 8am–10pm; Sept–May 8am–8pm. Bus 1, 2, 3, 4, 5.

Botanical Garden (Lystigarður Akureyrar)   This is Iceland's best outdoor botanical garden, with remarkable variety and efflorescence for such a northerly latitude, but for most visitors it's not what they came all this way for.

Eyrarlandsvegur (by Hrafnagilsstræti). Free admission. June–Oct daily 8am–10pm; Nov–May Mon–Fri 8am–10pm. Bus 1, 2, 3, 4, or 5.

SOUTH OF THE CITY CENTER

Museum of Akureyri (Minjasafn Á Akureyri)   This museum is in the oldest section of town, 15 minutes' walk south of the modern city center, and holds a permanent exhibit on the cultural history of Akureyri and environs, plus a temporary exhibit on a subtheme, such as the art of Icelandic headboard carving. Strong points include elaborate woodcarvings and a charming pulpit from Kaupvangur Church, painted with hearts and flowers, but those without a specialized interest in the Eyjafjörður area will get that heavy feeling in their legs.

Aðalstræti 58. © 462-4162. www.akmus.is. Admission 500kr ($8/£4) adults; 250kr ($4/£2) seniors; free for children 15 and under. June–Sept 15 daily 10am–5pm; Sept 16–May Sat 2–4pm. Bus 4 or 7.

Nonnahús (Nonni's House)   This museum is squeezed inside the tiny childhood home of Jón Sveinsson (1857–1944), author of a semi-autobiographical children's book series famous throughout Iceland and Germany. ("Nonni" applies to Jón *and* his fictional boy-hero.) Jón studied abroad and became a Jesuit priest and missionary. The fictional Nonni, along with his younger brother Manni, live on an isolated north Iceland farm and run into all kinds of family drama and adventure, including a brush with polar bears. The books were written in German, but English translations by a deceased nun were recently published, and are sold at reception. The museum, founded in 1957, is full of manuscripts and personal items. Nonnahús and the Museum of Akureyri offer discounted joint admission.

Aðalstræti 54. © 462-3555. www.nonni.is. Admission 350kr ($5.60/£2.80) adults; 300kr ($4.80/£2.40) seniors; children under 17 free. June–Aug daily 10–5. Bus 4 or 7.

Industry Museum (Iðnaðarsafn)   This endearing curiosity honors 72 20th-century companies of the Akureyri area, most of them now defunct. Products on display include everything from clothing to paint cans to canned hot dogs; connoisseurs, take note of the outmoded advertising aesthetics and charming packaging designs.

Krókeyri (off Drottníngarbraut). © 897-0206. www.idnadarsafnid.is. Admission 500kr ($8/£4) adults; 250kr ($4/£2) seniors; free for children under 16. June–Sept 15 daily 1–5pm; Sept 16–May Sat 2–4pm.

Aviation Museum (Flugsafn Íslands) Devoted fans of antique planes will delight in this museum inside an airplane hangar. One display holds the remains of a British war plane that crashed into a glacier in 1941 and was regurgitated at the glacier's edge 58 years later. The funniest contraption—affectionately known as "the stick"—is a homemade, one-man Icelandic plane powered by bike pedals and a small engine.

At south end of Akureyri airport. © 863-2835. www.flugsafn.is. Admission 500kr ($8/£4) adults; 250kr ($4/£2) seniors; free for children 15 and under. June–Aug Thurs–Sun 2–5pm; Sept–May Sat 2–5pm.

OUTDOOR ACTIVITIES

Akureyri's best travel agency for tour bookings is **Nonni Travel,** Brekkugata 5 (© **461-1841;** www.nonnitravel.is; Mon–Fri 9am–5pm). The **tourist information center** (p. 233) can also book many tours.

AERIAL TOURS   Seeing Iceland from an airplane window may seem decadent or extravagant, but few regret this memorable and exhilarating experience. Aerial tour companies that fly from Akureyri are **Eagle Air** (© **562-4200;** www.eagleair.is), **Fjarðaflug** (© **562-6500;** www.fjardaflug.is) and **Mýflug Air** (© **464-4400;** www.myflug.is). Logical destinations include Mývatn, Jökulsárgljúfur National Park, Herðubreið, Askja, and Kverkfjöll; for all these places, however, it's cheaper to take off from Mývatn. Eagle Air and Mýflug flights can be booked through the tourist information office.

SEA ANGLING   Haffari Seatours (© **860-3890;** www.haffari.is; tickets 2,600kr [$42/£21] adults, 1,300kr [$21/£10] children 8–18, free for children 7 and under, minimum charge 10,000kr [$160/£80]; June 28–Aug 31 daily departures at 9am, 1:30pm, and 8:30pm) offers 2-hour fishing and sightseeing tours in 10-passenger boats leaving from Akureyri harbor. More intense anglers could head 44km (27 miles) north to Dalvík, where **Sjóferðir** (© **863-2555;** www.hvalaskodun.is) has 3-hour fishing trips in six-person boats for 3,900kr ($62/£31).

GOLF   Golfklúbbur Akureyrar (© **462-2974;** gagolf@gagolf.is) runs the world-class course **Jaðarsvöllur** (course fee 4,000kr [$64/£32]; club rental 2,000kr [$32/£16]; cart rental 3,500kr [$56/£28]; June–Aug 8am–10pm), which hosts the 36-hole **Arctic Open** (www.arcticopen.is; entry fee 28,125kr [$450/£225]) in late June; contestants tee off into the morning hours under the midnight sun. Tournament slots fill up by February or March. The course is up the hill southwest of the city center, off Eikarlundur.

HIKING   The best local hiking is southwest of Akureyri in and around Glerárdalur Valley, which is surrounded by small glaciers and some of north Iceland's tallest mountains. Most routes are strenuous, and hikers should be aware that harsh weather, even snowstorms, can set in without warning. The place to start is **Ferðafélag Akureyrar** (see "Visitor Information," above), which maintains the **Lambi mountain hut** in Glerárdalur, and publishes the *Glerárdalur* hiking map, also available at the tourist information office.

HORSEBACK RIDING **Pólar Hestar** (© 463-3144; www.polarhestar.is), one of Iceland's most established horse tour companies, is recommended for everything from 1-hour rides for 3,000kr ($48/£24) to multi-day pack trips through the interior. Pickup from Akureyri can be arranged.

SKIING **Hlíðarfjall** (© 462-2280; www.hlidarfjall.is; day pass Mon–Fri 1,300kr [$21/£10], Sat–Sun 1,900kr; early Nov–Apr Mon and Wed–Thurs 1–7pm, Tues and Fri 1–9pm, Sat–Sun 10am–5pm) is the premier ski center in Iceland, with the best conditions usually in February and March. The longest run is 2.5km (1½ miles) with a 500m (1,640 ft.) vertical drop. Hlíðarfjall also offers cross-country trails, a snowboarding course, a ski school, and a restaurant. Courses are floodlit during short winter days. Hlíðarfjall is 7km (4¼ miles) west of town; take Hlíðarbraut or Þingvallastræti to Hlíðarfjallsvegur. No bus serves the mountain, and a taxi costs about 2,000kr ($32/£16) each way.

SWIMMING The **Akureyri swimming pool** (★, Þingvallastræti 21 (© 461-4455; admission 350kr [$5.60/£2.80] adults; 100kr [$1.60/80p] children 6–15; free for children under 6; Mon–Fri 7am–9pm; Sat–Sun 8am–6:30pm), is a water wonderland, with indoor and outdoor pools, a kiddie pool, two waterslides, hot tubs, massaging water jets, a steam bath, fitness equipment, an ice-cream stand, and, for an extra charge, a sauna. Bring a towel to avoid the 300kr ($4.80/£2.40) rental fee.

WHALE-WATCHING Whale-watching in Eyjafjörður is based at Hauganes and Dalvík, north of Akureyri (p. 245). **SBA Norðurleid** (© 550-0700; www.sba.is) offers day tours that include bus transport to Húsavik (p. 259) and a whale-watching trip from there for 6,200kr ($99/£50) in spring or 7,200kr ($115/£58) in summer.

SHOPPING

Most Akureyri shopping can be quickly scanned by perusing Hafnarstræti (especially the northern, pedestrian-only stretch), Skipagata, and Ráðhústorg Square, where the two streets meet. North of the center, along Glerárgata just north of the Glerá River, is **Glerártorg Mall** (© 461-5770; Mon–Fri 10am–6:30pm; Sat 10am–5pm; Sun 1–5pm), with a bank, two restaurants, a supermarket, and 18 stores; the trendy Icelandic outerwear company 66° North is across the street.

Fold-Anna Check here if you're seeking the perfect Icelandic woolens for your next trip to the ski slopes or souvenirs for folks back home. Hafnarstræti 85. © 461-4120. Mon–Fri 9am–7pm; Sat 10am–2pm.

Fruín í Hamborg This second-hand store sells clothing and sundries scouted from old houses in the neighborhood, and there's no shortage of reasonably priced grandma-chic dresses and unintentionally ironic sweaters. Brekkugata 3 (at Ráðhústorg). © 461-5777. Mon–Fri 11am–6pm; Sat 11am–4pm.

Galleri Grúska This small space crammed with clothing, accessories, housewares, and jewelry is the sales outlet of the Akureyri Arts & Crafts society. Strandgata 19. © 461-1823. Mon–Fri 10am–6pm; Sat 10am–2pm.

Galleri Svartfugl og Hvítspói This engrossing gallery-cum-shop is run by two local artists, one specializing in nature-themed prints on paper, the other in textiles—including, of late, clothes made from salmon skin. Brekkugata 3a (behind Nonni Travel). © 461-3449. June to mid-Sept Mon–Fri 10am–6pm, Sat 11am–2pm; mid-Sept to May Mon–Fri 1–5pm.

Penninn Eymundsson   This bright, inviting bookstore on Akureyri's busiest corner has a variety of English-language books, plus maps, souvenirs, Wi-Fi, and a cafe. Hafnarstræti 91-93. © 540-2180. Mon–Fri 9am–10pm; Sat–Sun 10am–10pm.

Sirka   This stylish boutique sells housewares, jewelry, and women's clothing with an intriguing mishmash of nostalgic and modern design. Skipagata 5. © 461-3606. Mon–Fri 11am–6pm; Sat 11am–4pm.

The Viking   This is Iceland's largest souvenir shop, with a good selection of knitwear, crafts, and kitsch. Hafnarstræti 104. © 461-5551. Mid-June to Aug daily 10am–10pm; Sept to mid-June Mon–Fri 11am–6pm, Sat 10am–2pm.

AKUREYRI NIGHTLIFE

Most nights in summer, nighttime activities are not limited to loud bars and night-clubs; the *Listasumar* brochure delineates everything from Thursday night jazz sets to choral concerts and evening "history sailing" in the fjord. Akureyri's bars and night-clubs are within 10 minutes' walk of each other, so do as Icelanders do and roam until you find a scene to your liking. Only live music commands a cover charge, and you'll never be pressured to buy drinks. As elsewhere in Iceland, Akureyri's young people work hard, and work even harder at partying. On Friday and Saturday nights teenagers drive around town at a crawl, dressed as if they're in a Miami convertible, honking and gabbing at each other out the car windows.

The main nightspots are **Café Amour,** Ráðhústorg 9 (© **461-3030**), which has a wine bar downstairs and small DJ room upstairs with holographic bordello wallpaper; **Capone/1929** (aka **Oddvitinn**), Strandgata 53 (© **462-6020**), two clubs in one historic harborside building, with occasional live music; **Græni Hatturinn,** Hafnarstræti 96 (© **461-4646**), a pub inside one of Akureyri's oldest houses, sometimes with live music; **Kaffi Akureyri,** Strandgata 7 (© **461-3999**), whose back room is turned over to DJs on weekends; **Karolína,** Kaupvangsstræti 23 (© **461-2755**), a bar for the knowingly cool and sophisticated; and **Sjallinn,** Geislagata 14 (© **462-2770**), loud, raucous, and packed.

4 Near Akureyri

Akureyri is a great base for excursions fanning out in several directions. Eyjafjörður, with its broad, smoothly sloping bowl shape and rich farmland, seems to welcome human habitation more than other Icelandic fjords. Safnasafnið and Smámunasafn are two of Iceland's most offbeat and inspiring museums. The inhabited islands of Hrísey and Grímsey, both infested with birdlife, are fascinating worlds unto themselves. Farther afield, Goðafoss and Aldeyjarfoss are among Iceland's most exquisite waterfalls. Some sights, notably Safnasafnið and Goðafoss, are on the Ring Road and can fit into trips to Mývatn, Húsavík, and Jökulsárgljúfur National Park.

DALVÍK

This fishing town of just under 2,000 people, on the western shore of Eyjafjörður 44km (27 miles) north of Akureyri, may provide a diversion worth adding to a ferry trip to Hrísey or Grímsey.

ESSENTIALS

By car, take Route 82 from the Ring Road 10km (6¼ miles) north of Akureyri. **Trex** (© **587-6000;** www.trex.is) runs three **buses** between Akureyri and Dalvík on week-days year-round; the ride is 55 minutes and costs 1,100kr ($18/£8.80).

Dalvík's **information center,** Svarfaðarbraut (© **466-3233;** www.dalvik.is; June–Aug Mon–Fri 6:15am–8pm, Sat–Sun 10am–9pm; Sept–May Mon–Fri 6:15am–8pm, Sat–Sun 10am–4:30pm), is at the local swimming pool, and the website has thorough service information in English. **Cafe Sogn,** Goðabraut 3 (© **466-3330**), is the best place to grab a meal.

EXPLORING DALVÍK

Little known among tourists, **"The Great Fish Day" (Fiskidagurinn)** is a huge, outdoor festival that takes place on the first or second weekend of August. Everything is free: food, beverages, live music, folk dancing in traditional costume, short films, and, of course, exhibitions of fish in tubs full of ice. The local fish factory is the main sponsor, and all workers are volunteers. On Saturday from 11am to 5pm, the largest grill in Iceland cooks up cod, haddock, salmon, and about 12,000 fish burgers. The night before, around 70 Dalvík families place two torches outside their doors, a signal that anyone is welcome to stop in for fish soup.

Dalvík Folk Museum (Byggðasafnið Hvoll) This better-than-average local museum displays minerals, taxidermy (including a polar bear), farm artifacts, and a tribute to native son Jóhann Pétursson (1913–1984), who during his lifetime was the world's second-tallest person. Standing at 2.34m (7 ft. 8 in.) in U.S. size 24 (62 European) boots, he appeared in Viking costume as "Jóhann the Giant" in U.S. and European circuses, and made several Hollywood cameos. He was understandably ambivalent about his work and stage name, and returned to Dalvík in his final years. The museum displays his circus costumes and shows a video documentary, mostly in Icelandic but gripping nonetheless.

Karlsrauðatorg. © 466-1497. www.dalvik.is/byggdasafn. Admission 500kr ($8/£4) adults; 200kr ($3.20/£1.60) seniors; 100kr ($1.60/80p) children 6–16. June–Aug daily 11am–6pm; Sept–May Sat 2–5pm.

OUTDOOR ACTIVITIES

Hótel Sóley, Skíðarbraut 18 (© **466-3395;** www.hotel-soley.com), is the best town agent for **bike rental,** guided **hiking tours** on Tröllaskagi Peninsula (including the fabulous 2- to 3-day route from Dalvík west to Hólar), **sea kayaking,** and **horseback riding** in the lovely Svarfaðardalur Valley south of town.

Most vacationers in north Iceland save their **whale-watching** for Húsavík, which has better infrastructure—more scheduled departures, harborside coffee houses, the whale museum—but only a marginal advantage in whale sightings. **Sea Tours (Sjóferðir;** © **863-2555;** www.hvalaskodun.is), based in Dalvík, leads 3-hour whale-watching tours (3,900kr/$62/£31 adults, 1,950kr/$31/£16 children 8–12; June 16–July daily 9am, 1:30pm, 8pm; Aug 1–Aug 20 9am, 1:30pm; Apr–June 15 and Aug 21–Sept 9am), and sea-angling trips by arrangement. **Whale Watching Eyjafjörður** (© **867-0000;** www.niels.is), based in Hauganes, 30km (19 miles)north of Akureyri and 14km (8¾ miles) south of Dalvík, has comparable services.

HRÍSEY ISLAND 𐂷

Heimaey in the Westman Islands is Iceland's largest and most populated offshore island; Hrísey is second on both counts, with about 180 residents. With its paved roads, well-tended homes, and geothermal swimming pool, the village does not feel particularly marginal. Hrísey has been inhabited since the 10th century but sprouted rapidly in the 19th century as a base for processing and exporting herring. The herring vanished at the end of the 1960s, and in 1999 the fish-freezing plant closed, forcing many residents to leave.

Hrísey has a clear view to the northern horizon, and is perfect for witnessing the scooping midnight sun in early summer. Fjord views on the island are heart-stirring if not heart-stopping. In mid-July, Hrísey plays at being a sovereign nation during its "Independence Day" family festival: Guests pass through customs, get their Hrísey passport stamped, then enjoy tractor and fishing trips, dancing, and a children's singing competition.

ESSENTIALS

The main **ferry** to Hrísey, **Sævar** (ℂ 695-5544; round-trip ticket 800kr [$13/£6.40] adults, free for children 11 and under; departures every 1 to 2 hr. daily from 9:30am–11pm), leaves from Árskógssandur, a small village on the western shore of Eyjafjörður, 35km (22 miles) north of Akureyri. The ride lasts 15 minutes.

Hrísey's **information office** is inside the Pearl Gallery (ℂ 466-1762; www.akureyri.is/hrisey/english; mid-June to mid-Aug daily 1–6pm), a crafts store by the ferry landing. The Akureyri tourist office (p. 233) is also helpful.

EXPLORING HRÍSEY ISLAND

In summer, as you disembark the ferry, you'll likely see Ásgeir Halldórsson (ℂ 695-0077) offering **bird-watching tours** in his tractor-pulled trailer, which has seats and a loudspeaker so he can commentate from the driver's seat. Call in advance to make reservations.

Free **trail maps** are available on the ferry. The main trail, color-coded green, ascends to Hrísey's highest point in a 2.3-km (1.4-mile) loop, but the longer trails are best for bird sightings. The far northern section of Hrísey, **Ystabæjarland,** is a private nature reserve accessible only with the owner's permission; consult Ásgeir or the information office if you hope to hike all the way there. Permission is usually not granted until mid-July, to protect birds during nesting season.

Hrísey's **bird populations** chose their residence well. Hunting is prohibited, and no foxes or mink have made it out to the island. Hrísey is a quarantine station for imported pigs and cattle, so Icelandic horses and sheep—which never interbreed with foreigners, at least not in Iceland—are kept off the island to keep them safe from species-hopping diseases. This leaves more vegetation for ground-nesting bird species.

Warning: Arctic terns, which harass and sometimes attack anything that comes near their eggs, are a serious menace and can turn a Hrísey walk into a Hitchcockian nightmare. Terns are very agile—those that spend the winter in Antarctica have the longest annual migration of any known animal—and the attack comes in a quick swoop, with furious flapping and hideous shrieks. (The Icelandic word for tern, *kría,* comes from the shrieking sound.) The worst time is June, when walkers should carry some sort of stick, pole, or umbrella over their heads for protection.

Ptarmigans, on the other hand, haven't the slightest fear of people, and in early September waddle right into village streets and yards seeking protection from falcons. The spindly legged and needle-billed godwits, around from mid-May to mid-August, are another endearing sight.

WHERE TO STAY & DINE

The market **Verslun Hrísey** (ℂ 466-1213; Mon–Fri 11am–6pm; Sat 11am–5pm; Sun noon–5pm), a short walk from the harbor, has seating for snacks such as skýr and hot dogs. The only restaurant and lodgings are at **Brekka** (ℂ 466-1751; brekkahrisey@isl.is; AE, MC, V; restaurant June–Aug daily 11:30am–9pm, Sept–May

Fri–Sat dinner only), a yellow building visible from the harbor. The restaurant is far better than anticipated, with first-rate fish, lobster, and lamb dishes for 2,500kr to 5,400kr ($40–$86/£20–£43) as well as burgers, pizzas, and sandwiches for 850kr to 1,590kr ($14–$25/£6.80–£13). Four basic doubles with shared bathroom and ocean views go for 5,600kr ($90/£45).

GRÍMSEY ISLAND ⍟

Many travelers studying a map of Iceland notice an obscure speck, 41km (25 miles) north of the mainland and bisected by the Arctic Circle, and feel strangely compelled to go there. Grímsey is indeed a worthwhile and exotic destination, with 95 hardy inhabitants, basalt cliffs reaching 105m (344 ft.) tall, and abundant birdlife.

Many visitors come in late June to see the midnight sun "bounce" off the horizon, but this involves a tradeoff. June and early July is also when Arctic terns most aggressively defend their nests, sometimes drawing blood from the scalps of unwitting tourists (see "Exploring Hrisey Island," above).

ESSENTIALS

GETTING THERE   Until 1931, the only way to get to Grímsey was on a mail boat that came twice a year. Today, **Air Iceland** (ⓒ **570-3030;** www.airiceland.is) flies from Akureyri daily at 7:30pm (5pm Saturdays) and returns to Akureyri at 9:15pm. The flight is 25 minutes and costs around 6,800kr ($109/£54) one-way; a connection to or from Reykjavík is around 11,200kr ($179/£90) one-way. From June 10 to August 20, Air Iceland offers an evening tour—round-trip airfare with a 1-hour guided walk, but no dinner—for 14,400kr ($230/£115) from Akureyri or 30,000kr ($480/£240) from Reykjavík (clearly a much better deal from Akureyri). **Mýflug Air** (ⓒ **464-4400;** www.myflug.is;) does the same tour for 15,000kr ($240/£120), but leaves from Mývatn in a smaller plane that does aerial sightseeing along the way.

From May 15 through August, the **Sæfari ferry** (ⓒ **853-2211;** www.land flutningar.is; round-trip from Dalvík 4,820kr [$77/£39] adults; 2,419kr [$39/£19] seniors and children 12–15; free for children 11 and under) sails from Dalvík to Grímsey on Mondays, Wednesdays, and Fridays. A bus leaves Akureyri at 7:50am and connects with the ferry, which leaves at 9am and arrives at 12:30pm. The return trip is at 4:30pm, reaching Dalvík at 7:30pm, where another bus bound for Akureyri awaits. From September through mid-May, the ferry departs for Grímsey at the same times, but heads right back to Dalvík after unloading.

One-way tickets for Air Iceland flights and the ferry are half-price, so it makes sense to mix and match. Taking the ferry there and the flight back, for instance, gives you over 8 hours on Grímsey.

VISITOR INFORMATION   Consult **Akureyri's tourist information office** (p. 233), or either guesthouse listed below.

EXPLORING GRÍMSEY ISLAND

Grímsey is flat-topped and only 5.3 sq. km (3⅓ sq. mile), with the highest cliffs on the east side, and walks are a straightforward matter. The island is home to over 60 **bird species.** The most popular are puffins, which can be observed from May to mid-August.

For the right price, someone is always willing to take you on **sea angling, bird hunting,** or, in May or June, **egg-collecting;** contact either guesthouse listed below.

Gallery Sól, Sólberg (© 467-3190), a gallery and souvenir shop, opens up to greet arriving and departing visitors from the ferry or plane. The community center has a library endowed by Willard Fiske (1831–1904), a wealthy American who never set foot in Grímsey but was touched by how much the locals were dedicated to chess.

WHERE TO STAY & DINE

Most of Grímsey's houses are in the village of Saltvík, which has a small market.

Guesthouse Básar   This simple and warm guesthouse, newly renovated, is right by the airport and just a few steps from the Arctic Circle. Reasonably priced dinners are served by advance request: 1,590kr ($25/£13) for fish and 2,200kr to 3,000kr ($35–$48/£18–£24) for bird or lamb. Some rooms accommodate up to three or four.

© 467-3103. 9 units, none w/bathroom. 5,700kr ($91/£46) double; 2,000kr ($32/£16) per person sleeping-bag accommodation. Breakfast available: 900kr ($14/£7.20). MC, V. **Amenities:** Guest kitchen. *In room:* No phone.

Guesthouse Gullsól   These six elemental guest rooms with a shared TV lounge and guest kitchen are attached to the Gallery Sól handicraft store; the friendly proprietors can help arrange any kind of local activity.

Saltvík. © 467-3190 or 467-3150. grimsey@simnet.is. 6 units, none w/bathroom. 4,800kr ($77/£38) double; 3,600kr ($58/£29) double with sleeping bag. Rates do not include breakfast. AE, DC, MC, V. **Amenities:** Guest kitchen. *In room:* No phone.

Restaurant Kría   Grímsey's hangout by default, Kría serves up burgers, sandwiches, crepes, fish, lamb, and puffin. No pizza, surprisingly; locals with pizza cravings have to get it delivered from Akureyri on the evening flight.

Saltvík. © 467-3112. Main courses 800kr–3,000kr ($13–$48/£6.40–£24). MC, V. May–early Sept daily noon–9pm; bar open late Fri–Sat. Early Sept–Apr usually closed, but call ahead.

UPPER EYJAFJÖRÐUR

Icelanders tolerate and even nurture their single-minded eccentrics, as evidenced by the three sights below. All are on Route 821, which heads directly south from Akureyri.

Christmas House (Jólagarðurinn) *(Kids)*   Iceland's resident year-round Christmas fanatic is responsible for this mock-up gingerbread house, with fake frosting on the roof and endless Christmas kitsch on sale inside. Grýla the troll (p. 304) lives downstairs, and elves have their own turf house. In back is an enormous advent calendar inside a faux medieval turret.

Rte. 821, 10km (6¼ miles) south of Akureyri. © 463-1433. Free admission. June–Aug daily 10am–10pm; Sept–Dec 2–10pm (until 6pm on Christmas); Jan–May daily 2–6pm.

Grund Church   In the late-19th and early-20th centuries, most new Icelandic churches were simple structures with square belfries, sometimes elongated, and topped by a kind of narrow-brimmed hat. This curious 1905 church, atypically aligned north to south, has several Romanesque spires, an onion dome, and a balconied interior reminiscent of an opera house. It's also the largest Icelandic church financed by an individual. If the door is locked, knock at the grey house, not at the closest house.

Rte. 821, 18km (11 miles) south of Akureyri.

Museum of Small Exhibits (Smámunasafn) *(★ (Finds)*   With its long and dark winters, Iceland has bred many compulsive hoarders. This oddball museum is essentially a junk collection meticulously sorted and arranged by master carpenter Sverrir

Hermannsson (b. 1928). Exhibits include mounted arrays of nails, cocktail napkins, colored tacks, fake teeth, hair elastics, waffle irons, and pencil shavings in unbroken spirals. Responses to the museum's holdings will vary greatly. Some will feel Sverrir has transformed unwanted, everyday objects into a fascinating art of pattern and repetition. Others will see only the neurotic obsessions of a pack rat. A café is on-hand, and up the hill is **Saurbæjarkirkja,** a typical turf church from 1858.

Rte. 821, 26km (16 miles) south of Akureyri. © 463-1261. www.smamunasafnid.is. Admission 500kr ($8/£4) adults; 250kr ($4/£2) seniors; free for children 15 and under. May 15–Sept 15 daily 1–6pm.

NORTHEAST OF AKUREYRI

Safnasafnið ★★ *Finds*   The admirable concept behind this enjoyable and penetrating museum is to erase boundaries between folk art, "outsider" art, and contemporary art—and the results here are highly successful. Established artists are included, but curators also scour the country in search of compelling work by anyone, including those with no formal training. Safnasafnið expanded in 2007 and puts on 14 exhibitions a year, in any conceivable artistic genre. The two constants are a rotating exhibit from the Icelandic Doll Museum, and a hands-on toy exhibit inspired by optical illusions. Wondering about that blue-and-yellow cube on the wall? Stare at it for a minute, then focus on the white wall and its inverse image appears. The museum has a wonderful reading room and a birch grove outside with picnic tables.

Rte. 1, 11km (7 miles) northeast of Akureyri. © 461-4066. www.safnasafnid.is. Admission 500kr ($8/£4) adults, 400kr ($6.40/£3.20) seniors; free for children under 14. Early May to mid-Aug daily 10am–6pm; Apr–Oct by appointment.

Laufás   Of the many 19th-century turf-covered farms that are now museums, Laufás—a parsonage built in the 1860s, in a meadow overlooking Eyjafjörður—was the most prosperous. Twenty to thirty people lived in the labyrinthine interior, with rooms designated for weaving, cleaning birds, and dressing brides. The damp and claustrophobic rooms have only thin shafts of light from high windows, but contemporaries would have envied the wood floors and crafting of the walls, with their alternating layers of stone and tweed-patterned sod. The scene would be complete with some peat smoke wafting toward an open chimney, the smell of oil lamps, and household members spinning yarn and churning butter. Unfortunately the museum has no guided tours and little information in English.

Laufás earned money harvesting eider down, which explains a gable carving of a lady's head crowned by a duck. The 1865 church is well-restored and typical of its time; the most endearing feature is the 1698 pulpit, with unschooled but talented carvings of five saints grinning like dolls. An old-fashioned cafe next door serves flatbread with smoked trout, rhubarb pie, and bread with moss baked inside (originally eaten to keep Icelanders from dying of scurvy). On a Sunday in mid-July, Laufás hosts a historical event with staff in period costume carving wood, cooking pancakes, and mowing with scythes.

Rte. 83 (about 10km [6¼ miles] from Rte. 1 and 30km [19 miles] from Akureyri). © 463-3196. www.akmus.is. Admission 500kr ($8/£4) adults; free for children 16 and under. May 15–Sept 15 daily 10am–6pm.

BETWEEN AKUREYRI & MÝVATN
GOÐAFOSS ★

Located right off the Ring Road, about 50km (31 miles) east of Akureyri and 53km (33 miles) west of Reykjahlíð, Goðafoss (Waterfall of the Gods) is not very tall or powerful; but admirers point to the separate cascades forming an elegant semicircular arc, the swirling patterns in the blue-green (or sometimes brown) water, and the strange bubbliness of the surrounding lava. According to legend, Goðafoss was named in the year 1000 when the Law Speaker of the Icelandic parliament, after proclaiming Iceland a Christian country, tossed his pagan statuettes into the falls.

Just downstream is the restaurant and guesthouse **Fosshóll** (© **464-3108;** www. nett.is/fossholl; 11,500kr–13,500kr [$184–$216/£92–£108] double; May 15–Sept daily 6–10pm; closed Oct–May 14), which serves local trout on top of the usual road-stop fare. You can park right by the falls, but walking upstream from Fosshóll is a more satisfying approach.

ALDEYJARFOSS ✿✿

This stunning waterfall is worth the substantial detour from the Ring Road. The falls have awesome churning force, and the freakish basalt formations are enough to make spectators wonder what planet they've been transported to. To reach Aldeyjarfoss, turn south on Route 842 from the Ring Road, just west of Goðafoss, and proceed 41km (25 miles) to the marked turnoff. Buses on the Sprengisandur route from Mývatn to Landmannalaugar all make a sightseeing stop.

5 Mývatn & Krafla

Iceland's president Ólafur Ragnar Grímsson wrote, "The Old Testament teaches us that God created the world in 6 days and then rested. This is not altogether true. Iceland was forgotten when He went to rest." The **Mývatn-Krafla region** ✿✿✿—a volcanic smorgasbord of surreal lava fields, boiling and burping mud pools, sulfurous steam vents, explosion craters, and pseudocraters—is Iceland's most varied place to see the earth in mid-formation. Mývatn lake is also a unique ecosystem and the largest migratory bird sanctuary in Europe, with thousands of waterfowl feeding on bugs and algae in the warm shallow waters.

Mývatn is part of the greater Krafla volcanic system, a swath of faults and fissures 4 to 10km (2.5–6 miles) wide and 80km (50 miles) north to south, with Krafla caldera at its center. Krafla's last two eruption periods were 1724–1729 and 1975–1984. Both times, multiple fissures shifted and dilated, with sporadic eruptions and lava fountains, but much of the magma never surfaced, petering out laterally underground. Today the most active geothermal areas are Krafla and Bjarnarflag, each with a geothermal power plant. Two new plants have been proposed for close by, pitting power companies and some locals against conservationists and the increasingly influential tourist industry. The Krafla region is ideal for plants harnessing geothermal energy, because eruptions are infrequent and foreshadowed by a year of tectonic grumbling.

Mývatn-Krafla is well-touristed, and accommodations fill up quickly in summer, so the May or September shoulder season is advantageous. In high season, it may be a good idea to visit here early in your itinerary, before you've been spoiled by solitude elsewhere. On June weekends there may be choral concerts in the church or at Dimmuborgir; contact tourist information (below) for details. Mývatn-Krafla is also a compelling winter destination; see "Iceland in the Off Season," p. 19. Despite the multitude of sights, 2 days here are enough for the vast majority of visitors.

Mývatn sounds much less inviting in translation: "Midge Lake." Most of these pests don't bite, but they're attracted to carbon dioxide and may fly right into your nose and mouth. Head nets and insect repellent are available in the market at the N1 gas station. A head net may look ridiculous, but on warm, calm days you'll be glad to have one.

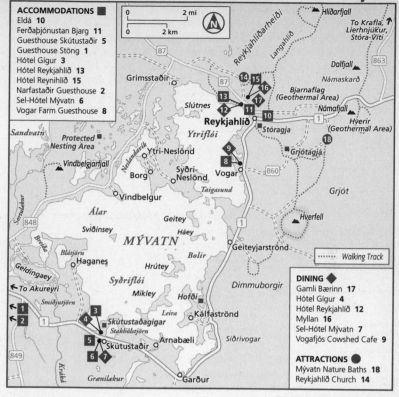

Map legend:

ACCOMMODATIONS ■
Eldá **10**
Ferðaþjónustan Bjarg **11**
Guesthouse Skútustaðir **5**
Guesthouse Stöng **1**
Hótel Gígur **3**
Hótel Reykjahlíð **13**
Hótel Reynihlíð **15**
Narfastaðir Guesthouse **2**
Sel-Hótel Mývatn **6**
Vogar Farm Guesthouse **8**

DINING ◆
Gamli Bærinn **17**
Hótel Gígur **4**
Hótel Reykjahlíð **12**
Myllan **16**
Sel-Hótel Mývatn **7**
Vogafjós Cowshed Cafe **9**

ATTRACTIONS ●
Mývatn Nature Baths **18**
Reykjahlíð Church **14**

ESSENTIALS

GETTING THERE & AROUND

The only village in the area is **Reykjahlíð**, on the northeast shore of Mývatn. **Skútustaðir**, on the south side of the lake, has a small cluster of tourist services.

BY CAR   Reykjahlíð, along Rte. 87 just off the Ring Road, is 103km (64 miles) east of Akureyri and 166km (103 miles) west of Egilsstaðir. The only place to arrange **car rental** is **Hótel Reynihlíð** (© 464-4170; www.myvatnhotel.is).

BY BUS   The **Trex bus** (© 587-6000; www.trex.is) connecting Akureyri and Egilsstaðir stops at Skútustaðir and Reykjahlíð. It runs daily from June through August. The cost is 2,300kr ($37/£18) from Akureyri or 3,000kr ($48/£24) from Egilsstaðir. **SBA Norðurleið** (© 550-0700; www.sba.is) has Mývatn-Krafla **sightseeing day tours** departing from Akureyri and Mývatn; they are detailed in the widely available brochure *Iceland On Your Own*. The tour from Akureyri for 8,100kr ($140/£65); 9 hr. hits Goðafoss (p. 249), Skútustaðagígar, Stóra-Víti, Hverir, Grjótagjá, and Dimmuborgir. From Reykjahlíð, the main daily tour for 4,100kr ($66/£33); 3¼ hr. hits Dimmuborgir, Grjótagjá, Stóra-Víti, Hverir, and the Mývatn Nature Baths. Unforgivably, neither tour goes to Leirhnjúkur (p. 254). All Trex and SBA buses leaving Reykjahlíð board at the N1 gas station.

Unfortunately there's no "hop-on hop-off" bus circling the lake on a regular basis, and SBA Norðurleið's tours generally decline to take passengers on short rides.

BY BIKE   Bike rental is available from **Hótel Reynihlíð** (© **464-4170;** www. myvatnhotel.is), **Ferðaþjónustan Bjarg** (© **464-3800;** ferdabjarg@simnet.is), and **Hlíð campsite** (© **464-4103;** hlid@isholf.is). Bicycles are not permitted anywhere cars are not permitted.

**ON FOOT   **Touring the sights by foot is possible, but most travelers find bus tours, car rental, or bike rental more practical. All hotels, restaurants, and services in Reykjahlíð are within walking distance of each other.

VISITOR INFORMATION

Mývatn's **tourist information office** is at Hraunvegur 8 (© **464-4390;** www.myv.is; June–Aug daily 9am–7pm; May and Sept Mon–Fri 9am–5pm, Sat–Sun 10am–4pm; Oct–Apr Mon–Fri 9am–5pm), next to the N1 gas station in Reykjahlíð. The staff can also help you find accommodation.

EXPLORING THE AREA
AROUND MÝVATN

The following sights form a clockwise route around the lake, starting in Reykjahlíð. The distance around the lake is 36km (22 miles) by car.

In 1729, at the height of the Krafla eruption, a lava stream gobbled up two farmhouses and was headed straight for **Reykjahlíð Church.** At the last moment, the stream split and flowed into the lake. The church site is slightly elevated, but prayer was credited for averting disaster. The current church dates from 1962, and the vivid pulpit carving depicts the old church with the eruption in the background and "27 August, 1729" written in psychedelic font. All that remains of the old church is a foundation wall in the graveyard, and menacing heaves of lava are still clearly visible just beyond the graveyard wall.

The road to the church (and campsite and airfield) leads uphill from Hótel Reynihlíð. Near the end of the road, a pleasant trail leads west over the Eldhraun lava field, before crossing Route 87 and heading back to town along the north shore of the lake; allow 2½ to 3 hours round trip.

Storagjá, Grjótagjá, Hverfell, and **Dimmuborgir** (below) are connected by a recommended and well-marked trail, 7km (4.3 miles) or 2½ to 3 hours in each direction. The **trail** begins from the Ring Road near Reykjahlíð, a few meters east of the Route 87 junction. Between Grjótagjá and Hverfell, the trail has two marked junctures—one coinciding with the Hverfell parking area—where you can detour to **Mývatn Nature Baths** (p. 255).

The **Storagjá fissure** is not directly on the trail, but it's only a short detour, right from the trailhead. Partway along Storagjá is a staircase into the narrow fissure, descending about 5m (16 ft.) to a grassy floor. From there, assisted by a chain and rope, you can peer through a crack at a limpid, turquoise geothermal pool. The pool has recently cooled, attracting too much bacteria for safe swimming.

The steamy **Grjótagjá fissure** 𝒦 is set amid a geothermal valley of red and black gravel. Grjótagjá is 2km (1¼ miles) from the Storagjá-Dimmuborgir trailhead, and also reachable by car on Route 860, which connects with the Ring Road at two points. (Approaching from the west requires opening a sheep gate.) Near the parking area, two portals in the heaving lava lead to an enticing hot spring and pool. You can climb down and sit by the water, but it's too hot for swimming and fogs up camera lenses.

Hverfell *☞☞*—the monolithic, striated black mountain shaped like a dog-bowl—is unmistakable from anywhere in the vicinity. Hverfell—which is often incorrectly identified as "Hverfjall"—is a rare (and particularly enormous) example of a tephra explosion crater. It was formed 2,500 to 2,900 years ago, when rising magma met with groundwater, forcing a massive explosion of steam, ash, and rock. The rim is 1km (½ mile) in diameter, and the crater is 140m (459 ft.) deep, with a round nub at the center.

Hverfell's solemn, elemental grandeur cannot be fully appreciated without walking up to the crater rim. It's a 3km (1.9-mile) walk south from Grjótagjá, but you can also drive from the Ring Road to a parking area on Hverfell's north side. From there it's a 25-minute ascent. The trail loops completely around the rim, and the descent of the southern slope toward Dimmuborgir is steep and more challenging.

Meaning "Dark Castles," **Dimmuborgir** is a surreal lava field 1km (½ mile) in diameter. Its most distinctive features are the contorted crags and pillars reaching 20m (66 ft.) in height; nothing quite like them exists elsewhere, except on the ocean floor. Dimmuborgir was formed around 2,200 years ago, when molten lava formed a temporary "lava lake" on the site. Eventually the lava found an outlet and drained into Mývatn, but hardened pillars had formed around steam vents (lava finds steam chilling) and were left behind. The surface of the lava lake had half-congealed, and left all kinds of crusty "watermarks" on its way out.

Dimmuborgir is a 2km (1-mile) walk from the southern face of Hverfell, and can also be reached by car off the Ring Road. Plan on walking for an hour or two among the well-marked loop trails. The recommended **Kirkjuvegur trail** leads to **Kirkjan** (Church), a lava chute forming an archway. The more hazardous **Krókastígur trail** cuts through the middle of the site, past some of the most bizarre formations. Take care not to step into a fissure, and keep a close eye on children.

Höfði, a lakeside park on a small promontory, makes for a nice hour-long stroll along its peaceful forested pathways. The fragrant spruce and other trees were planted by Höfði's former owner. After entering the park, the trail branching off to the right leads to another juncture where you can detour uphill to a fantastic viewpoint. If instead you bear left after the park entrance and circle the promontory clockwise, you'll pass a clearing that overlooks Kalfarströnd. (The walk at Kalfarströnd farm, below, gives you a far better view.) Near Höfði's center is a rectangular lawn with benches—a good picnic spot, if the midges aren't too bothersome.

The name **Kalfarströnd** *☞* refers to a farm on a grassy peninsula extending into Mývatn, and also to a series of lava columns (*klasar*) rising like strange mushrooms in a cove between the peninsula and Höfði Park. The turnoff from the Ring Road is 1km (½ mile) south of Höfði. After parking, pass through the farm gate, and the 30-minute, staked loop trail past the klasar is shortly ahead on the right. Kalfarströnd is sublime on a calm, soft-lit evening, with the klasar looming, the sky reflected in the aquamarine shallows, Höfði's evergreens in the background, and Mývatn's trim green islands etched in the distance. Bring your head net.

If Mývatn had a visual trademark, it would be **Skútustaðagígar,** the cluster of pseudocraters surrounding Stakhólstjörn pond, at the southwest shore of the lake. Pseudocraters, found primarily in Iceland and on Mars, are so named because they were never conduits for emerging lava. They're formed when lava flowing above ground heats subsurface water, causing explosions from steam and gas buildup. The Skútustaðagígar pseudocraters, each around 20m (66 ft.) deep, are quite striking from the road (or from Vindbelgjarfjall, below); but when viewed from the rims, they're simply grassy bowls. The walk around Stakhólstjörn takes an hour, or a 30-minute circuit begins opposite the Skútustaðir gas station or from Hótel Gígur (p. 256).

The best all-around vista of Mývatn is from the top of **Vindbelgjarfjall mountain** ⚘, near the northwest shore. The 2-hour round-trip hike to the summit leaves from Vagnbrekka farm, off Route 848, 4km (2½ miles) from the junction with the Ring Road. From the farm to the base of the mountain, the trail traverses a protected nesting area for waterfowl. The protected area is off limits from May 15 to July 20, but does not extend to the trail. The ascent is all scree and a bit slippery, but manageable.

BJARNARFLAG & THE KRAFLA CALDERA

The Krafla caldera is the broad crater formed following eruptions of the volcano of the same name. The caldera ring is difficult to discern from the ground because its shape is broken and irregular, and its overall diameter is as large as that of Mývatn. "Krafla" can refer to the volcano cone, the geothermal area within the caldera, or the power plant exploiting that geothermal area. Leirhnjúkur and Stóra-Víti fall within the caldera, while Mývatn Nature Baths, Hverir, and Námafjall Ridge are parts of Bjarnarflag, the geothermal area south of the caldera.

Hverir ⚘, a large geothermal field, full of bubbling mud cauldrons and hissing steam vents, is 7km (4¼ miles) east of Reykjahlíð and easy to spot from the Ring Road. Walking through Hverir feels unreal, as minerals and chemicals in the earth form an exotic color spectrum unlike anything normally associated with nature. Some patches of ground are hot enough to cause severe burns, so stick to the paths. From Hverir, an hour-long trail ascends Námafjall, then cuts north to a parking area off the Ring Road at Námaskarð pass, and then loops back to Hverir. Views are fabulous; but, again, be cautious, stay on the trail, and look out for scalding-hot patches of light-colored earth. The walk can be seriously gloppy after a rain.

Just east of Hverir, Route 863 branches off the Ring Road and leads north into the Krafla caldera. After about 8km (5 miles), the road passes under a pipeline arch at **Krafla Geothermal Power Station (Kröflustöð)**, built in the 1970s. The **visitor center** (© 515-9000; www.landsvirkjun.is; Mon–Fri 12:30–3:30pm; Sat–Sun 1–5pm) has an informative free exhibit for those interested in the process of converting geothermal heat to electricity.

Gritty as burnt toast, **Leirhnjúkur lava field** ⚘⚘⚘ is the best place to witness remnants of the 1975 to 1984 eruptions, and may be the most surreal landscape you will ever see. The parking area is clearly marked from Route 863, and from there it's a 15-minute walk to a geothermal field at the edge. Some visitors make the drastic mistake of looking at the boiling grey mud pots and color-streaked earth, and then heading back to their cars. Allow at least another hour for circling the trails, peering at the subtle range of color, texture, and moss inside each steamy rift. A good way to start is by proceeding from the geothermal field toward a bowl-shaped pseudocrater visible to the north. A recommended trail known as the **Krafla Route** leads straight from here to Reykjahlíð, and takes 3 to 4 hours one-way. *Remember:* Stick to the paths, watch your step, and beware of light-colored earth.

Route 863 dead-ends at a parking area by the rim of **Stóra-Víti,** a steep-sided explosion crater, formed in 1724, with a blue-green lake at the bottom. A trail circles the rim and descends on the far side to an interesting hot spring area. The route, which is worthwhile but not essential, takes about an hour round-trip and is not advised during muddy conditions.

Mývatn Nature Baths (Jarðböðin Við Mývatn) ⚡ It's tempting to tout this nature bath as the undiscovered alternative to the crowded and touristy Blue Lagoon, but it has some catching up to do. Both spas make extravagant claims about the health benefits of their water and sell a full line of beauty products. (We are testing each line in the Frommer's lab, and will report the results in our next edition.) The waters at each bath are a unique solution of minerals, silicates, and microorganisms; only the Blue Lagoon includes seawater. Yet, while the Blue Lagoon blocks views of its surrounding lava field, bathers at Mývatn commune with the colorful, steaming hills. Though it may seem like a lot of money for a swim, it's the best way to unwind after a strenuous day of touristing, and saunas are included in the admission price. The water remains at a comfortable bath temperature, between 36°C and 39°C (96.8°F–102.2°F). Remove any copper or silver jewelry, which will be damaged by sulfur in the water. Bring your own towel and swimsuit—rental for each is 350kr ($5.60/£2.80).

Ásta Price offers 30-minute massages for 3,800kr ($61/£30); to make an appointment, call ✆ **464-4411.** Otherwise the baths offer no spa menu, and locker rooms are like those at any village pool. Ásta also operates out of the Reykjahlíð pool off Hlíðavegur, and runs the holistic health center **Magma Essentials,** Birkihraun 11 (✆ **464-3740** or 898-9964; www.magmaessentials.com), out of her home in Reykjahlíð, offering everything from 90-minute therapeutic massages to yoga instruction and aromatherapy.

Rte. 1, 3km (2 miles) east of Reykjahlíð; turn right at blue sign for "Jarðböðin við Mývatn." ✆ 464-4411. www. jardbodin.is. Admission 1,400kr ($22/£11) adults; 1,100kr ($18/£8.80) seniors/students; 700kr ($11/£5.60) children 12–15. June–Aug daily 9am–midnight, no entry after 11:30pm; Sept–May daily noon–10pm, no entry after 9:30pm.

OUTDOOR ACTIVITIES

Mývatn is a common launch point for tours of the interior, especially to Askja Caldera and Kverkfjöll. The bus that takes the Sprengisandur route across the interior highlands to Landmannalaugar also leaves from Mývatn. Askja, Kverkfjöll, and Sprengisandur are covered in chapter 11.

AERIAL TOURS   Mýflug Air (✆ **464-4400;** www.myflug.is), based at the small airfield just outside Reykjahlíð, runs sightseeing tours of Mývatn-Krafla, Jökulsárgljúfur, Askja, Kverkfjöll, Vatnajökull, Grímsey, and other natural spectacles with a fleet of two six-seaters and a ten-seater. Tours range from 20 minutes and 5,000kr ($80/£40) to 2 hours and 15,000kr to 20,000kr ($240–$320/£120–£160) with a minimum of two passengers, or three for Grímsey. Flights are weather-dependent, and departure times are by agreement.

CAVING   Hótel Reykjahlíð (✆ **464-4142;** www.reykjahlid.is) organizes 5-hour guided tours of **Lofthellir,** a lava cave bedizened with lustrous and ghostly ice formations. The cost is 8,200kr ($131/£66) adults or 5,500kr ($88/£44) children 6 to 12, with a four-person or 32,800kr ($525/£262) minimum. Gloves, helmets, flashlights, and studded boots are provided. Tours run June through September, but after August 15 groups of four can be difficult to assemble. Dress warmly.

HORSEBACK RIDING   Sel-Hótel Mývatn (✆ **464-4164;** www.myvatn.is) arranges 1-hour tours with a choice of destinations for 3,900kr ($62/£31) per person; ask about longer excursions. **Saltvík** (© 847-9515; www.skarpur.is/saltvik), based 5km (3 miles) outside Húsavík, leads unforgettable multi-day tours devoted mostly to the Mývatn-Krafla area.

JEEP TOURS   **Hótel Reykjahlíð** (© 464-4142; www.reykjahlid.is) offers a 6- to 7-hour excursion covering Krafla and Jökulsárgljúfur National Park for 9,900kr [$158/£79] adults, 6,700kr [$107/£54] children 6–12. The tour includes **Gjástykki,** a starkly beautiful volcanic area north of Krafla caldera and inaccessible to regular cars. Gjástykki is under consideration for a new geothermal power plant, so enjoy the scenery while you can. Departures, by reservation only, are from June 15 through September at 8am, with a four-person minimum. From September through May, **Sel-Hótel Mývatn** (© 464-4164; www.myvatn.is) runs a jeep tour of Mývatn for 9,500kr ($152/£76) per person, and a more-off-road tour for 13,500kr ($216/£108).

WHERE TO STAY

All accommodations below are around Mývatn, mostly in Reykjahlíð, the village on the northeast corner of the lake, and Skútustaðir, a small settlement on the south side. On short notice, the information office can tell you which accommodations have vacancies, but in July and early August, every single room could well be occupied. Two guesthouses west of Mývatn are good, relatively inexpensive backups: **Guesthouse Stöng** (© 464-4252; www.stong.is) and **Narfastaðir Guesthouse** (© 464-3102; www.farmhotel.is).

VERY EXPENSIVE

Hótel Reynihlíð ⊛   The standard doubles here—identified as "deluxe"—are decent-sized but not as smart as expected from an upscale hotel. The "superior" doubles, often corner rooms, are worth the upgrade, with more space, swankier furnishings, and bathrooms with short bathtubs. Ask for a lake view. Service is exceptional, and the front desk is helpful with travel arrangements.

Rte. 87, Reykjahlíð. © 464-4170. Fax 464-4371. www.reynihlid.is. 41 units. June–Aug 21,950kr–23,950kr ($351–$383/£176–£192) double. Rates around 30% lower Sept–May. Rates include breakfast. AE, DC, MC, V. **Amenities:** Restaurant; car rental; room service; same-day laundry/dry cleaning service. *In room:* TV, Wi-Fi, coffee/tea, hair dryer.

EXPENSIVE

Hótel Gígur ⊛   Rooms at this summer-only hotel are a bit faded and small, but the dining area, overlooking the lake and the Skútustaðagígar pseudocraters, is the perfect spot for morning coffee. Rooms with lake views are scarce and book quickly.

Rte. 1 at Skútustaðir. © 464-4455. Fax 464-4279. www.keahotels.is. 37 units. May 15–Aug 17,700kr ($283/£142) double; 23,300kr ($373/£186) triple. Rates include breakfast. AE, DC, MC, V. Closed Sept–May 14. **Amenities:** Restaurant; bar; Internet terminal; laundry service. *In room:* TV.

Hótel Reykjahlíð ⊛⊛   This small lakeside hotel is one of Iceland's most appealing country accommodations. The nine rooms are tasteful and pleasant if not purring with luxury. In 2007 new beds were imported and bathrooms were renovated to include tubs. All rooms have lake views except for #5, which has the biggest bathroom. Top-floor rooms—including #11 and #14, the picks of the litter—are slightly larger. The hotel's small size keeps service personal and attentive; the downside is that the entire summer is booked out by April.

Rte. 87, Reykjahlíð, on lake side of road. ✆ **464-4142.** Fax 464-4336. www.reykjahlid.is. 9 units. Jul–Aug 20 18,900kr ($302/£151) double; 28,800kr ($461/£230) triple. Rates around 5% lower June and Aug 21–31; 35% lower May, Sept, and Dec 15–Jan 15; and 40% lower Jan 16–Apr and Oct–Dec 14. Rates include breakfast. MC, V. **Amenities:** Restaurant. *In room:* Wi-Fi, coffee/tea, hair dryer, no phone.

Sel-Hótel Mývatn 🕿

Rooms in this mid-grade hotel, located across the road from the Skútustaðagígar pseudocraters, have just enough of an antiqued look to set them apart from the cold impersonal standard. The hot tub and sauna operate all winter, but in high season *might* be turned on by advance request. In winter Sel-Hótel has outrageous discounts and organizes a panoply of enticing tours.

Rte. 1, Skútustaðir. ✆ **464-4164.** Fax 464-4364. www.myvatn.is. 35 units. June–Aug 17,800kr ($285/£142) double. Rates around 37% lower May and Sept; 50% lower Oct–Apr. Rates include breakfast. AE, MC, V. **Amenities:** Restaurants; bar; hot tub; sauna; same-day laundry service. *In room:* TV, Wi-Fi, hair dryer.

MODERATE

Eldá

This guesthouse operates in four different houses in Reykjahlíð. All have extremely basic and functional rooms, though the house at Birkihraun 11 has a more personal touch. The breakfast buffet is bounteous no matter where you stay and includes freshly baked bread. All guests check in at Helluhraun 15.

Helluhraun 15, Reykjahlíð. ✆ **464-4220.** Fax 464-4321. www.elda.ls. 35 units, none w/bathroom. June 26–Aug 25 9,300kr ($149/£74) double, 13,200kr ($211/£106) triple. Rates 10%–20% lower off season. Rates include breakfast in summer. Just north of the N1 gas station, turn on Hlíðarvegur, then make first right on Helluhraun. At the T junction, turn right; Eldá is shortly ahead on the left. **Amenities:** Guest kitchen. MC, V. *In room:* No phone.

Guesthouse Skútustaðir

This friendly and dependable accommodation in the Farm Holidays network has six spacious but otherwise standard guesthouse rooms, and a nice lake view from the breakfast area. The five en suite rooms are in a pre-fab block that looks like a row of lockers, but from the inside you shouldn't be disappointed.

Rte. 1, Skútustaðir, next to Sel-Hótel Mývatn. ✆ **464-4212.** Fax 464-4322. 11 units, 5 w/bathroom. June–Aug 20 12,000kr ($192/£96) double w/bathroom; 9,200kr ($147/£74) double without bathroom. May and August 21–31 10,500kr ($168/£84) double w/bathroom; 8,500kr ($136/£68) double without bathroom. Rates include breakfast. MC, V. Closed Oct–Apr. **Amenities:** Guest kitchen. *In room:* No phone.

Vogar Farm Guesthouse

These efficient, identical, wood-paneled rooms are not the best value, but if you get to breakfast at 7:30am you can look through a glass partition at cows being milked (see "Vogafjós Cowshed Cafe," below). The location is 3km (2 miles) south of Reykjahlíð, far from any bus stop. Reception is at the cafe.

Rte. 1, 3km (2 miles) south of Reykjahlíð. ✆ **464-4303.** Fax 464-4341. www.vogarholidays.is. 20 units. June–Aug 15,000kr ($240/£120) double. Rates up to 50% lower Sept–May. Rates include breakfast. **Amenities:** Cafe. *In room:* No phone.

INEXPENSIVE

Ferðaþjónustan Bjarg

This campground with good facilities also has two utilitarian guest rooms with fair views. The soft-spoken proprietor knows everything there is to know about the area and is also a one-man travel agency.

Reykjahlíð; exit Rte. 1 onto Rte. 87 and take first left turn. ✆ **464-3800.** Fax 464-4341. ferdabjarg@simnet.is. 2 units without bathroom. May–Oct 8,200kr ($131/£66) double; 6,000kr ($96/£48) double with sleeping bag. AE, DC, MC, V. Closed Nov–Apr. **Amenities:** Guest kitchen; Internet terminal; washer/dryer access. *In room:* No phone.

WHERE TO DINE

Fast food can be found at the **N1 gas station** in Reykjahlíð and at the **cafeteria** adjoining the restaurant at the Sel-Hótel Mývatn in Skútustaðir (below).

EXPENSIVE

Hótel Gígur 🦋 ICELANDIC   This snazzy restaurant is perfectly attuned to its surroundings, with floor-to-ceiling windows overlooking the lake and Skútustaðagígar pseudocraters, and clear vases of lava rock and moss at each table. The menu reaches beyond the usual fish and lamb—pear, bleu cheese, and pine nut salad with arugula and pesto, for example—but quality is hard to predict, due to frequent chef turnover.

Rte. 1 at Skútustaðir. ⓒ 464-4455. Reservations recommended. Main courses 2,600kr–3,700kr ($42–$59/ £21–£30). AE, DC, MC, V. May 15–Aug daily 6–10pm.

Hótel Reykjahlíð 🦋🦋 ICELANDIC   This is the region's best restaurant, both for cooking and ambience, especially if you're seated near a window. Outside, horses graze, ducks paddle, and waves lap the shore. The menu ranges from traditional to daring, with a vegetarian option, but always relies on lamb, salmon, and artic char. The skýr dessert with fresh fruit and cream is utter perfection. Reserve at least a day in advance.

Rte. 87, Reykjahlíð, on lake side of road. ⓒ 464-4142. Reservations recommended. Main courses 2,100kr–3,200kr ($34–$51/£17–£26). MC, V. June–Aug 7:30am–10pm; May and Sept daily 7–10pm; Oct–Apr on request in advance.

Myllan ICELANDIC   This restaurant at the up-market Hótel Reynihlíð is serviceable but hardly a standout. An ambitious starter includes mashed salt cod, at room temperature, wrapped in a roasted bell pepper *and* smoked lamb rolled in a thin pancake—but neither quite work. Stay with the lamb or trout, or perhaps the breast of duck with mango chutney.

Rte. 87, Reykjahlíð. ⓒ 464-4170. Reservations recommended. Main courses 2,400kr–3,600kr ($38–$58/£19–£29). AE, DC, MC, V. Daily 11am–midnight.

Sel-Hótel Mývatn ICELANDIC   Big eaters can take advantage of the lunch and dinner buffets at this plainly decorated, traditional Icelandic restaurant—even if they have to work around Icelandic "specialties" such as putrefied shark, blood pudding, and sheep's head jelly. The a la carte menu also has plenty of palatable alternatives.

Rte. 1, Skútustaðir. ⓒ 464-4164. Reservations recommended. Main courses 2,500kr–4,500kr ($40–$20/£20–£36); lunch buffet 1,550kr ($25/£13), dinner buffet 3,500kr ($56/£28). June–Aug daily 11am–2pm and 7–9pm; Sept–May 7–9pm.

MODERATE

Gamli Bærinn ICELANDIC   As the only casual, non-fast-food restaurant in Reykjahlíð, Gamli Bærinn is overrun in summer. Prepare to be overlooked for a while by the harried teenage waitstaff. Lamb and trout entrees supplement a long roster of sandwiches, burgers, and vegetarian plates. The food is not quite as good as the with-it tavern atmosphere seems to promise. Musicians might just take the stage—and then exit just as unceremoniously. Make sure to reserve a table.

Rte. 87, next to Hótel Reynihlíð. ⓒ 464-4170. Reservations recommended. Main courses 990kr–2,100kr ($16–$34/£7.95–£17). AE, DC, MC, V. Daily 10am–midnight.

Vogafjós Cowshed Cafe 🦋 *Kids* CAFE   Bedrooms in old Icelandic turf farms were often placed directly over the cow stables for sharing body heat. Cow intimacy carries on at this cafe, which looks directly into a milking shed. (Thankfully the barn smell doesn't seep through the glass partition.) Milking times are 7:30am and 5:30 or 6pm, and warm milk is passed around; otherwise the cows are usually outside the shed. The cafe-style menu has sandwiches, crepes, and dishes featuring homemade products such as mozzarella, feta, smoked lamb, and very creamy ice cream.

Rte. 1, 3km (2 miles) south of Reykjahlíð; look for cow-shaped sign. © 464-4303. Reservations required for dinner. Breakfast 1,000kr ($16/£8); main courses 480kr–3,500kr ($7.70–$56/£3.85–£28). MC, V. May 15–Sept daily 7:30am–11:30pm; other times call ahead.

6 Húsavík & Nearby

Húsavík, once a busy whale-hunting port, is now Exhibit A in making the case that whale-watching tours are a better source of income. Packaging itself as the "European Capital of Whale-Watching," this pretty fishing town of 2,700 complements the tours with pleasant harborside eateries and a compelling whale museum. Húsavík's regional folk museum is also a standout, but far more visitors choose to gain a deeper scientific understanding of penises at the Icelandic Phallological Museum, a collection of 235 mammalian male members.

Húsavík is usually just a 1-day wonder in travel itineraries that dwell longer in Akureyri, Mývatn, and Jökulsárgljúfur National Park. Scan the sights and activities below, however, to see if a second day would be worth your time.

ESSENTIALS
GETTING THERE   Húsavík is on Route 85, 92km (57 miles) from Akureyri, 54km (34 miles) from Mývatn, and 65km (40 miles) from Ásbyrgi in Jökulsárgljúfur National Park. The only **car rental agency** in town is **Húsavík Car Rental,** Garðarsbraut 66 (© **464-2500;** b.h@simnet.is).

Trex (© **587-6000;** www.trex.is) connects Akureyri and Húsavík by bus year-round. From June to August three buses depart each weekday, and two each Saturday and Sunday. For the rest of the year, Trex runs four buses each week day, one Saturday, and two Sunday. The trip is 75 minutes and costs 2,300kr ($37/£18). Another bus connects Húsavik to Þórshöfn on weekdays year-round, via Ásbyrgi, Kópasker, and Raufarhöfn (p. 273).

SBA Norðurleið (© **550-0700;** www.sba.is) has a bus from Akureyri to Dettifoss and back daily from mid-June through August, stopping at Húsavík and Ásbyrgi; the cost is 5,400kr ($86/£43) one way. From Dettifoss a connecting bus goes on to Mývatn for 2,100kr ($34/£17), and another bus connects Mývatn and Húsavík twice daily 1,800kr ($29/£14).

SBA also provides **day tours of Húsavík** from Akureyri and Mývatn, including a whale-watching tour. The day trip from Akureyri costs 7,200kr ($115/£58) in high season, 1,000kr ($16/£8) less than buying bus tickets and a whale-watching tour independently. Another tour from Akureyri crams Mývatn and a Húsavík whale-watching tour into one 9-hour trip for 8,500kr ($136/£68).

VISITOR INFORMATION   Húsavík's **tourist office,** Garðarsbraut 5 (© **464-4300;** www.markthing.is; June–Sept Mon–Sat 9am–7pm, Sun 10am–6pm), is on the main street in the center of town and can assist with finding accommodations.

EXPLORING THE AREA
BETWEEN AKUREYRI & HÚSAVÍK
Transportation Museum at Ystafell (Samgönguminjasafnið Ystafelli)   Vintage car junkies should enjoy this collection of 100 vehicles, all veterans of Icelandic

Húsavík

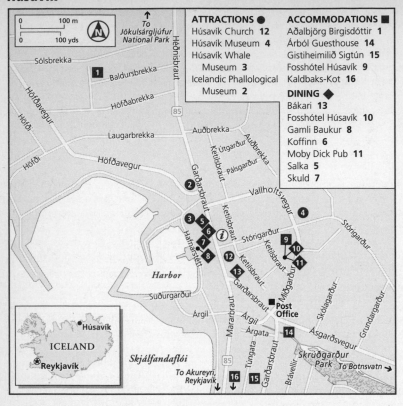

↑
To
Jökulsárgljúfur
National Park

ATTRACTIONS ●
Húsavík Church **12**
Húsavík Museum **4**
Húsavík Whale
  Museum **3**
Icelandic Phallological
  Museum **2**

ACCOMMODATIONS ■
Aðalbjörg Birgisdóttir **1**
Árból Guesthouse **14**
Gistiheimilið Sigtún **15**
Fosshótel Húsavík **9**
Kaldbaks-Kot **16**

DINING ◆
Bákari **13**
Fosshótel Húsavík **10**
Gamli Baukur **8**
Koffinn **6**
Moby Dick Pub **11**
Salka **5**
Skuld **7**

roads. Curator Sverrir Ingólfsson, who restored the magnificent 1969 Ford Mustang with crimson velvet upholstery and window tassels, can lift hoods for inspection. Endearingly, a 1957 Chevrolet Bel Air could be parked next to a 1978 Ford Fiesta.

Rte. 85, 9km (5½ miles) north of Rte. 1 and 37km (23 miles) south of Húsavík. ℰ 464-3133. www.ystafell.is. Admission 500kr ($8/£4) adults; free for children 12 and under. May 15–Sept daily 10am–8pm; Oct–May 14 call ahead.

HÚSAVÍK

Most tourist activity—including the whale-watching ticket booths, four eateries, a bookstore, a market, a handknit woolens store, the Whale Museum, and the Phallological Museum—are clustered on two parallel streets: Hafnarstétt, which runs right along the harbor, and Garðarsbraut, just uphill.

The German- and Swiss-inspired design of **Húsavík Church (Húsavíkurkirkja)**—located along Garðarsbraut—stands out in Iceland, as do the 1907 church's cruciform shape and absence of a pulpit. The lovely patterns painted on the interior walls are from 1924 and feature the Lutheran symbol of a cross within a heart. The 1931 altarpiece depicts Jesus raising Lazarus from the dead, as an onlooker faints. The painter Sveinn Þórarinsson was raised nearby, and the mountains in the background look suspiciously Icelandic.

Húsavík Museum (Safnahúsið) ⊛   Icelandic museums based on regional histories are often too esoteric, but Safnahúsið has an unusually broad range of interesting artifacts. On the first floor is a folksy altar painting of the Last Supper, rejected by the bishop for its naïveté; Judas bites his fingers and an anachronistic crucifix sits behind the table. The natural history collection includes a stuffed polar bear shot at Grímsey Island in 1969, and a rare albino eider duckling, normally stomped to death by its mother to protect its siblings from predators. The maritime exhibit screens old-time fishing documentaries, and just outside is an authentically stinky baiting shack and the skull and chin bone of a blue whale. Among the folk arts on the third floor, don't miss the whale-bone carvings or the display case, marked "Hárfínt Handbragð," full of necklaces and collars made from ladies' hair. Signage in English is limited, but the staff is responsive to questions.

Stórigarður 17. ⓒ **464-1860.** www.husmus.is. Admission 400kr ($6.40/£3.20) adults; 100kr ($1.60/80p) children 7–15; free for children under 7. June–Aug daily 10am–6pm; Sept–May Mon–Fri 9am–noon and 1–4pm.

Húsavík Whale Museum (Hvalasafnið á Húsavík) (Kids ⊛   This engaging and informative museum examines all things whale: whale biology, whale sociology, whale hunting, whale-watching. Full skeletons of 10 species hang from the ceiling. Screens show gripping footage of whales underwater, whales being hunted and processed, and Icelanders gathering to push stranded whales back into the ocean. The museum is sponsored by environmental organizations, but wisely avoids any preachiness, letting the facts on whaling speak for themselves.

Garðarsbraut. ⓒ **464-2520.** www.icewhale.is. Admission 700kr ($11/£5.60) adults; 500kr ($8/£4) seniors/students; 250kr ($4/£2) children 6–16. June–Aug daily 9am–7pm; May and Sept 10am–5pm.

Was Iceland's First Settler Not a Viking?

Húsavík's beginnings pose a vital challenge to the way Icelandic history is told. In the 860s, a few years before the Norse settlement of Reykjavík, a Swede named Garðar Svavarsson spent a winter at Húsavík. According to later accounts, one of Garðar's men, Nattfari, escaped with two slaves—a man and a woman—and stayed behind, settling across the bay and then farther inland. Nattfari's identity, motives, and ultimate fate remain a mystery. He may have been a slave himself. His name isn't Norse, and probably means "Night Traveler," but his origins are unknown. Still, Nattfari may well have been Iceland's first permanent settler—not Ingólfur Arnarson, who is traditionally assigned this role.

Why was Nattfari left out of the picture? The introduction to the *Book of Settlements,* a key Icelandic text from the 13th century, suggests a motive: " . . . we think we can better meet the criticism of foreigners when they accuse us of being descended from slaves or scoundrels if we know for certain the truth about our ancestors." Ingólfur was Norse, with superior class status, and his emigration to Iceland seemed more deliberate and heroic. In 1974, Iceland held its official 1,100-year celebration of Icelandic settlement. Four years before, the people of Húsavík held their own ceremony for Nattfari and his two companions.

The Saga of Icelandic Whaling

Icelanders can be touchy about whaling. Mere mention of the subject could provoke an impassioned speech about how Iceland is unjustly demonized by a sanctimonious and hypocritical outside world.

In 1986, the International Whaling Commission (IWC)—an organization formed in 1946 to promote cooperation among whaling nations—placed a moratorium on commercial whaling. The moratorium had no legal authority, but Iceland withdrew its IWC membership in protest. Iceland rejoined in 2002, but two years later resumed whaling under the pretense of scientific research. This meant that studies were conducted on the whales' stomach contents—and the resulting implications for fish stocks—before the meat was sold off. In 2006 Iceland dispensed with the scientific cover and set a commercial whaling quota in open defiance of the moratorium.

Whaling supporters point out that minke whales, which comprise the vast majority of victims, have a worldwide population of 900,000 and are not an endangered species. Evidence does suggest that minke whales reduce fish stocks, particularly cod, which alone account for as much as 20% of Iceland's export income.

Icelanders have hunted whales for over 300 years, and consider it part of their cultural heritage. From the time of settlement, beached whales were such a precious resource that the Icelandic word for beached whale, *hvalreki,* also means "windfall" or "godsend." Icelanders also feel they have fought too long and hard for control of their territorial waters to let foreigners once again meddle.

Opponents highlight the gruesome details of whale hunting; from the first harpoon strike, these noble and intelligent creatures can take a full hour to die. Whales may compete with fishermen for cod, but whaling provides only a few seasonal jobs, and demand for whalemeat is low. Tourists have shown some interest, but most Icelanders rarely eat whale. Whalemeat costs less than chicken in Icelandic supermarkets, and often ends up as animal food. The main foreign buyer, Japan, is increasingly wary of toxins found in the meat of North Atlantic whales

Since Iceland resumed whaling, Greenpeace has led a tourist boycott. Within Iceland, however, most anti-whaling activists would prefer tourists to come and spend money on whale-watching tours. Decades ago, tourist buses took a 1-hour trip from Reykjavík to Hvalfjörður to watch whales being sliced up and processed. Now nearly 100,000 tourists a year watch Icelandic whales that are very much alive.

In August, 2007, Iceland's fisheries minister announced a halt to commercial whaling unless market conditions improve. The future of Iceland's "scientific" whaling program remains unclear.

Icelandic Phallological Museum   Sigurður Hjartarson began collecting dismembered mammal penises in the 1970s and began this exhibit in Reykjavík while working as a high-school teacher. The inventory, mostly ghost-white and jarred in formaldehyde, includes penises from 52 whales, 30 seals and walruses, 110 land mammals, and a polar bear. The largest, at five feet two inches, belonged to a sperm whale. A magnifying glass is provided for the smallest, which belonged to a hamster. No human specimen is on display, but four men have provided for the museum in their wills. (Two of the men sent plaster casts, so we can see what we have to look forward to.) Recently the museum added testicles and a sperm tube which were surgically removed from an anonymous 50-year-old Icelander. Also on hand are smoked horse penises, originally intended for eating, and lamps made from scrotal sacs of bulls and rams. Visitors are sure to find the scientific education they've come for, learning for instance about all of nature's mechanisms for producing erections.

Héðinsbraut 3a (on main road, just north of the harbor). © **561-6663**. www.phallus.is. Admission 500kr ($8/£4). May 20–Sept 10 daily noon–6pm.

BOTNSVATN *

This isolated, peaceful lake in the hills behind Húsavík is the perfect destination for an easy, after-dinner walk as the sun sets over the bay. Two routes lead to the lake, both starting along the Búðará stream at the eastern edge of town. On the north side of the stream, Ásgarðsvegur becomes a dirt road and leads directly to the lake, but walkers will prefer the path that follows the stream most of the way. Paths on both sides of the stream converge on the north side, and from there it's a 25-minute walk to a pebbly beach and picnic table on the lake's western side. Another path circles the lake.

TJÖRNES

Northeast from Húsavík, Route 85 follows the periphery of this stubby peninsula. Fossil devotees should stop for a look at the **Ytritunga Fossils:** millions of sea shells—deposited when sea levels and water temperatures were far higher—in steep banks where the Hallbjarnarstaðaá stream meets the ocean. The turnoff from Route 85 is about 12km (7½ miles) northeast of Húsavík, just past Ytritunga Farm, and marked by a sign with "fossils" in small lettering. Be careful on the road's final descent to the ocean; if it's washed out, you may never get back up. At the end of the road, walk ahead to the stream and turn the corner.

Mánárbakka Museum   This quirky home museum would be much more fun as an antique store. The collection spans everything from vintage matchboxes to a hand-operated washing machine to a teacup designed to keep moustaches dry. Their most treasured piece, inside a glass case upstairs, is a pearl that supposedly originated in Turkestan and was brought from Norway by the Vikings.

Rte. 85, 23km (14 miles) northeast of Húsavík. © **464-1957**. Admission 400kr ($6.40/£3.20) adults; free for ages 12 and under. June–Aug daily 9am–6pm.

OUTDOOR ACTIVITIES
HORSEBACK RIDING   Saltvík (© **847-9515;** www.skarpur.is/saltvik), 5km (3 miles) outside Húsavík, offers a popular 2-hour strut along the seashore for 3,900kr ($62/£31) per person.

SAILING/BIRD-WATCHING   North Sailing (© 464-2350; www.northsailing. is) offers the memorable 3½-hour tour "Whales, Puffins, and Sails" on a two-masted schooner, combining whale-watching with a visit to **Lundey,** an island bristling with puffins. Passengers can help set sails or even take the helm. Tickets are 5,300kr ($85/£42) for adults, or half-price for children under 15, with one or two departures daily from early May to late August. (After Aug 15, you're unlikely to see puffins.)

SEA ANGLING   Húsavík's two whale-watching companies, **Gentle Giants** and **North Sailing** (see below) both offer fishing trips in pursuit of cod and haddock. Expect to pay around 6,000kr ($96/£48) for a 2- to 3-hour tour, with all equipment provided and arrangements made for grilling the catch. Gentle Giants schedules regular departures at 6pm in summer, but requires a four-person minimum.

WHALE-WATCHING   Húsavík lies close to whale migratory lanes, and whale-watching prospects are somewhat better than elsewhere in Iceland; but visitors should keep expectations in check. Tour companies boast a 98% success rate, but "success" could be a fleeting glimpse of a minke (MINK-ee) whale, which is relatively small and doesn't put on much of a show. The most acrobatic performer is the humpback whale, whose feeding technique involves blowing a vertical spiral of bubbles—immobilizing the fish within—and then launching itself open-mouthed up through the spiral and into the air. Humpbacks appear two times out of three. Odds of seeing a white-beaked dolphin are one in three; a harbor porpoise, one in five. The very lucky see the world's largest creature, the blue whale, whose heart is the size of a VW beetle. The very, very lucky encounter a whale so accustomed to people that it allows itself to be patted; though, tour announcers do their best to pretend everyone has been lucky.

Húsavík has two whale-watching tour operators, **Gentle Giants** (© 464-1500; www.gentlegiants.is) and **North Sailing** (© 464-2350; www.northsailing.is). Despite the intense and sometimes silly advertising competition between the two companies—North Sailing is "The Original," while Gentle Giants is "The Truly Original"—differences are negligible. Gentle Giants charges 3,800kr ($61/£30), North Sailing 3,900kr ($62/£31). Gentle Giants is free for children under 16, while North Sailing is free for children under 15 and half price for children 15 or 16. Those who have difficulty making decisions might consider that Gentle Giants has snazzier two-color jumpsuits and gives away twisted donuts called *kleina,* while North Sailing hands out cinnamon rolls. Each has a ticket kiosk easily spotted from the main road.

The season runs from late April through October, when whales start returning south to breed. From June to August, several tours depart daily from 8am to 5pm. In late April, May, and September, three tours depart daily, the latest at 1:30pm. In October, Gentle Giants has morning tours on Friday, Saturday, and Sunday only. The standard tour lasts 3 hours.

Tours are sometimes cancelled in rough weather, so anyone coming from out of town should call ahead. Seasick pills are a good idea, even if conditions seem calm in the harbor. *Insider tip:* Take the insulated jumpsuits that are supplied to all passengers; we thought we could do without one, and learned otherwise.

WHERE TO STAY

For those who don't like changing accommodations every night, Húsavik can be a base for exploring Jökulsárgljúfur National Park and the Mývatn area. Húsavík's tourist information office (p. 259) can assist in finding vacancies.

The Aðaldalur Valley between Akureyri, Húsavík, and Mývatn is often overlooked, but also makes for good operational headquarters. **Icelandic Farm Holidays** (⟨Ⓣ⟩ 570-2700; www.farmholidays.is) lists several accommodations in and around Aðaldalur; among the most peaceful and welcoming are **Hagi 1** (Rte. 853, off Rte. 845; Ⓣ 464-3526; www.hagi-1.com; 8,000kr [$128/£64] double without bathroom, including breakfast) and **Þinghúsið Hraunbær** (Rte. 845, 3km/2 miles south of Rte. 85 junction; Ⓣ 464-3695; 8,800kr [$141/£70] double without bathroom, including breakfast), both on the river Laxá, 20 minutes from Húsavík. The nicest hotel in Aðaldalur is **Hótel Rauðaskriða** (Rte. 85, around 18km/11 miles from Rte. 1; Ⓣ 464-3504; www.hotelraudaskrida.is; 17,400kr [$278/£139] double including breakfast), with a restaurant, a bar, and hot tubs.

EXPENSIVE

Fosshotel Húsavík Standard doubles at this overpriced, whale-themed hotel are bland, while the 26 new and more expensive rooms have extra space, white-suede chairs, elegant bathrooms with tubs, and photographic imaging of a pebble beach on the flooring. Rooms with ocean views also fall into the higher price bracket, but they don't seem quite worth it.

Ketilsbraut 22. Ⓣ 464-1220. Fax 464-2161. www.fosshotel.is. 70 units. June–Aug 19,000kr–21,500kr ($304–$344/£152–£172) double. Rates around 30% lower Sept–May. Rates include breakfast. AE, DC, MC, V. Amenities: Restaurant; bar; Internet terminal. *In room:* TV, hair dryer.

MODERATE

Kaldbaks-Kot ⟨★⟩ ⟨*Value*⟩ Freestanding mini-cabins are not everyone's idea of a proper hotel room, but in Iceland they're a common and convenient option, especially for self-caterers. These well-equipped cabins aren't the roomiest but have a double bed, bathroom, living area with pullout sofa, kitchenette, and outstanding views across the bay. Two cabins add sleeping lofts. Unless you bring sheets and towels, they cost 800kr ($13/£6) for the entire stay, and guests are expected to clean up after themselves or pay a 1,688kr ($27/£53) cleaning fee.

Rte. 85 just south of Húsavík. Ⓣ 464-1504. Fax: 464-1503. www.cottages.is. 12 units. July to mid-Aug 9,900kr ($158/£79) double cabin; 12,900kr ($206/£103) cabin w/sleeping loft. Rates 10% lower June and late Aug; 30% lower Sept and May; 40% lower Oct–Apr. Stay four nights and the fifth is free. MC, V. *In room:* TV, kitchenette, fridge, no phone.

INEXPENSIVE

Aðalbjörg Birgisdóttir ⟨*Value*⟩ Guests at this small, friendly, and very inexpensive guesthouse feel quite aware of staying in someone's home. Not that the owners, a retired Hungarian fisherman and his Icelandic wife, disrespect anyone's privacy—in fact, their English is very limited. The feeling comes from the homey decorations, and from finding yourself gazing at framed photos of kids and grandkids in the hallway.

Baldursbrekka 20 (at Háhöfði). Ⓣ 464-1005. 4 units, none w/bathroom. June–Aug 5,000kr ($80/£40) double; 2,500kr ($40/£20) sleeping-bag accommodation per person. Breakfast available: 1,000kr ($16/£8). No credit cards. Closed Sept–May. *In room:* No phone.

Árból Guesthouse Situated close to a pleasant stream and park, this former residence of the district governor is the nicest guesthouse in town. The best rooms are in the attic—#8 is particularly prized for its ocean view—if you don't mind showering downstairs. Brand new owners have ambitious renovation plans for the next few years.

Ásgarðsvegur 2. Ⓣ 464-2220. Fax 464-1463. www.simnet.is/arbol. 8 units, none w/bathroom. 8,000kr ($128/£64) double. Breakfast available: 900kr ($14/£7.20). Rates 20% lower Oct–Apr. DC, MC, V. *In room:* No phone.

Gistiheimilið Sigtún   Rooms here are matter-of-fact but comfortable, and guests have free use of a kitchen, Internet terminal, and washing machine. The owner has trouble with English, so e-mail (gsigtun@gsigtun.is) is probably the best way to make arrangements.

Túngata 13. ℭ **464-1674.** Fax: 464-1671. www.gsigtun.is. 5 units, none w/bathroom. 7,000kr–8,700kr ($112–$139/£56–£70) double; 14,000kr ($224/£112) quadruple. Rates include breakfast. MC, V. **Amenities:** Guest kitchen; Internet terminal; washer/dryer access. *In room:* No phone.

WHERE TO DINE

If other places are full, **Fosshótel Húsavík** (see "Where to Stay," above) has both a standard-issue **restaurant** and the more atmospheric **Moby Dick Pub** (ℭ **464-1003**), which serves burgers, pizzas, and pastas. **Bákari** (Garðarsbraut, off Mararbraut; ℭ **464-2901;** June–Aug Mon–Fri 8am–6pm, Sat 10am–4pm; Sept–May Mon–Fri 8am–6pm, Sat 10am–2pm), indeed a bakery, has sandwiches as well as baked goods and could pass for lunch.

Gamli Baukur ICELANDIC   This harborside restaurant provides good maritime ambience for its heavily tourist clientele—the best ocean view is from upstairs—and the food is slightly above expectation. The shellfish soup is predictably overloaded with butter and cream. The herring is prepared in-house, and served in pickled and spiced form, but it's an acquired taste. Grilled lamb is an excellent standby.

Hafnarstétt (by stairs to Garðarsbraut). ℭ **464-2442.** Reservations recommended. Main courses 800kr–2,750kr ($13–$44/£6.40–£22). MC, V. Sun–Thurs 11:30am–10pm; Fri–Sat 11:30am–midnight; kitchen closes at 10pm.

Koffinn LIGHT FARE   Right next to the whale-watching ticket booths, this food kiosk with outdoor seating whips up sandwiches, waffles, hot dogs (in creative variations), and a dish of the day—which can be anything from garlic-fried shrimp to cured reindeer.

Garðarsbraut. ℭ **868-9677.** Small dishes 400kr–1,800kr ($6.40–$29/£3.20–£14). AE, DC, MC, V. June–Aug daily 9am–8pm; often closed in bad weather.

Salka ICELANDIC   Compared to its competitor Gamli Baukur, Salka has more of a parlor feel, but neither has any real edge in food, prices, or atmosphere. The smoked puffin and pickled lamb appetizers vary the palate, and the grilled lamb or the cod with herb crust and tarragon sauce will do for a main course. The reliable pizzas have a deep-dish option and can be delivered to your accommodation.

Garðarsbraut. ℭ **464-2551.** Main courses 1,050kr–2,750kr ($17–$44/£8.40–£22). MC, V. Daily Sun–Thurs 11:30am–9pm; Fri–Sat 11:30am–10pm.

Skuld CAFE   With indoor and outdoor seating overlooking the harbor, this tiny coffeehouse is a prime locale for whiling away some time over light bites like pastries and sandwiches.

Garðarsbraut, downstairs from North Sailing ticket booth. ℭ **860-2901.** Snacks 100kr–750kr ($1.60–$12/80p–£6). AE, DC, MC, V. Mon–Wed 8am–10pm; Thurs–Fri 8am–11pm; Sat–Sun 9am–6pm.

7 Jökulsárgljúfur National Park

Jökulsárgljúfur National Park 𝕲𝕲𝕲 encompasses Iceland's most celebrated canyon of the same name, which channels Iceland's second-longest river, the Jökulsá á Fjöllum. The river's opaque, gray water carries sediments from Iceland's largest glacier, Vatnajökull. A comparison to America's Grand Canyon and the Colorado River is

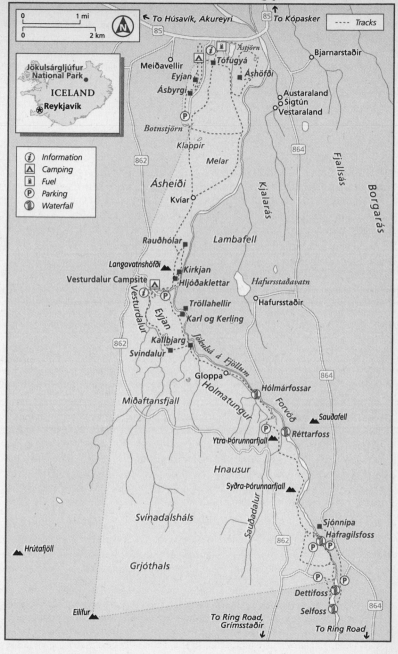

tempting, but Jökulsárgljúfur does not register on such an instantly overwhelming scale. Rather, its treasures—including an extraordinary range of basalt formations, waterfalls, and plant life—unfold at each turn.

The ideal way to experience Jökulsárgljúfur is by taking a 2-day hike from bottom to top, but day hikes suffice for most. The busiest season is mid-June to mid-August, so if you crave solitude—and wish to avoid rowdy revelers at campsites—aim for late May to early June or late August through September.

Jökulsárgljúfur and Skaftafell parks are in the process of merging to form Vatnajökull National Park, the largest in Europe. New parkland will be added—including the entirety of Vatnajökull Glacier—to make the new park contiguous.

ESSENTIALS
GETTING THERE & AROUND

BY CAR Jökulsárgljúfur—a mouthful which simply means "Glacial River Canyon"—is aligned north to south. Roads run along the east and west sides, connecting Route 85 in the north to the Ring Road in the south. In general, regular cars have more access to park sites from the north. On the west side of the canyon, you can navigate Route 862 from Route 85 as far south as the Vesturdalur campsite, near Hljóðaklettar—though potholes can be treacherous, especially in late summer. You might even get as far as the Hólmatungur parking area, but check with your car-rental company, as this could void your insurance. On the east side of the canyon, regular cars can take Route 864 between Route 85 and Dettifoss—and usually all the way to the Ring Road, depending on conditions. Those with 4WD vehicles can probably get from the Ring Road to Route 85 on either side of the canyon, but Route 864 on the east side is far easier.

BY BUS Trex (© 587-6000; www.trex.is) has a bus from Akureyri to Ásbyrgi (at the north end of the park) on weekday mornings year-round, with a bus change at Húsavík, for 3,400kr ($54/£27). The return trip from Ásbyrgi leaves in the afternoon.

From mid-June through August, **SBA Norðurleið** (© 550-0700; www.sba.is) has a daily morning bus from Akureyri to Dettifoss (on the west side of the canyon), stopping at Húsavík, Ásbyrgi, and the Vesturdalur campsite. A one-way trip is 4,500kr ($72/£36). The bus returns to Akureyri in the afternoon. Another bus, also daily from mid-June through August, starts at Mývatn and reaches Dettifoss from the opposite direction—that is, by taking Route 862 north from the Ring Road. These two buses connect with each other, so travelers can loop in either direction. SBA also has a marathon 13-hour "Jewels of the North" tour from Akureyri, covering both the Mývatn-Krafla region and Jökulsárgljúfur for 9,100kr ($146/£73).

ON FOOT Park trails are well-marked and well-tended, with maps posted at trailheads, but it's still a good idea to secure maps and trail brochures at the information office before setting out. Visitors are asked not to venture off the trails, as sub-Arctic vegetation is fragile and slow to recover from trampling.

Hiking the full length of the park over two days can proceed in either direction, but almost everyone heads downstream, from south to north, starting at the parking area for Dettifoss (on the west side of the river) and ending at Ásbyrgi. The only legal campsite along the 34km (21-mile) route is at Vesturdalur. The warden at Vesturdalur is happy to store bags during the day, so clever strategizing can lighten your load. Travelers with cars could drop supplies at Vesturdalur, then park back at Ásbyrgi and take the daily SBA bus (which starts in Akureyri) from Ásbyrgi to Dettifoss, arriving around 1:20pm. (Make sure you can reach Vesturdalur before dark.) Those without cars can still jump off the bus at Vesturdalur and leave things with the warden before continuing on to Dettifoss. The hike has challenging segments and route variations, so make sure to review your plans with the park information office (above).

VISITOR INFORMATION

The Jökulsárgljúfur **information office** ((C) **465-2195;** www.ust.is; mid-June to mid-Aug daily 9am–10pm; mid-May to mid-June and mid-Aug to mid-Sept daily 9am–7pm) is on Route 861; exit Route 85 at the N1 gas station, and it's shortly ahead on the left. The staff is accessible and helpful, and a free exhibit chronicles local geology, flora, and fauna.

EXPLORING JÖKULSÁRGLJÚFUR

Our favorite three walking areas are: Ásbyrgi, the wooded horseshoe canyon at the park's northern end; Hljóðaklettar and Rauðhólar, in the park center; and on the south end of the park, a triumvirate of waterfalls: Hafragilsfoss, Dettifoss, and Selfoss. All three areas could be crammed into one day, but two days or even three are preferable. Another prime walking area is **Hólmatungur** ♦♦, with its luxuriant cascades and vegetation, but access is more limited (see "Getting There & Around," above).

ÁSBYRGI ♦

This broad canyon, near Route 85 and west of the Jökulsá á Fjöllum River, forms a "U" shape about 3.5km (2 miles) north-to-south and 1km (½ mile) across, with a forested plain on the bottom and a rock "island" called Eyjan in the middle. Geologists believe Ásbyrgi was gouged out by catastrophic flooding from Vatnajökull somewhere between eight and 10,000 years ago, and again around 3,000 years ago. Apparently these flood bursts had 2,000 times the force of the Jökulsá á Fjöllum today. The river then shifted east to its current location, leaving Ásbyrgi dry. The Vikings had their own explanation for Ásbyrgi: clearly the god Óðinn's horse, Sleipnir, had left an enormous hoof print with one of his eight legs.

Walks in Ásbyrgi can start from the information office or from a parking area at the southern end of the "U," near the base of the cliffs. Route 861, which splits off from Route 85 at the N1 gas station, passes the information office and ends at the parking area. No favorite asserts itself among the walking routes; so, if you have a car, it makes sense to drive to the parking area and scan the many options from there. Beautiful ferns and orange lichen inhabit the cliff walls, along with 1,200 pairs of nesting fulmars. If you decide to see Ásbyrgi from the rim above, backtrack to the information center and find the trail leading to Tófugjá, where you can ascend the rim with the aid of ropes.

HLJÓÐAKLETTAR & RAUÐHÓLAR

Hljóðaklettar (Echo Rocks) ♦♦ and **Rauðhólar (Red Hills)** ♦♦ form an ideal 2-hour loop hike, starting from a parking area shortly past the Vesturdalur campsite on the west side of the canyon. The trail has tricky footing in spots, but is not otherwise difficult. Leaflets describing the route should be available right at the trailhead. The trail weaves through some of Iceland's most intriguing basalt configurations, often eroded from below to form honeycomb patterns. The human-sized trees along the trail feel oddly companionable, and the woolly willow is easily recognized by its light-green, fuzzy leaves. Hljóðaklettar earned its name from certain locations where the sound of the river echoes and seems to come from the wrong direction. The best spot to witness this phenomenon is right by the marked turnoff for Kirkjan (Church), a fabulous cave once sought out by sheep during storms. Rauðhólar, a crater row tinted with red gravel, marks the northern end of the loop and has great panoramic views. Some trekkers take the bus to Vesturdalur and continue all the way to Ásbyrgi.

HAFRAGILSFOSS, DETTIFOSS & SELFOSS

Moving progressively upstream along the Jökulsá á Fjöllum River, the magnificent waterfalls **Hafragilsfoss, Dettifoss** *ᎡᎡ*, and **Selfoss** *Ꭱ* are a kind of appetizer, main course, and dessert. Hafragilsfoss, at 27m (89 ft.) high and 91m (299 ft.) across, is captivating and monstrously powerful. The best view is from the Sjónnípa lookout point, a 1km (½-mile) hike north from the parking area. Hafragilsfoss is overshadowed, however, by Dettifoss, Europe's mightiest waterfall. On average, the milky-gray glacial water cascades over the 44m (144-ft.) drop at a rate of 200 cubic meters (656 sq. ft.) per second. Selfoss is only 11m (36 ft.) high, but its unusual breadth and parabolic shape are well worth seeking out.

Most travelers see the waterfalls from the east side of the river, since the parking areas on the west side are not accessible to regular cars. Those in 4WD vehicles often approach Dettifoss from the west side, where the view is somewhat better. The SBA buses (p. 268) also stop on the west side. On the east side, however, views of Selfoss are slightly improved and Hafragilsfoss is much more accessible. The drive to the waterfalls from Ásbyrgi—on Route 864, down the eastern side of the canyon—takes about 40 minutes. Selfoss is reached by walking 1.5km (1 mile) south from the Dettifoss parking areas on either side of the river.

WHERE TO STAY

PARK CAMPGROUNDS   Camping within the park is restricted to three campgrounds on the west side of the river: Ásbyrgi, on the park's north end; Vesturdalur, in the middle; and Dettifoss, on the south end. Ásbyrgi and Vesturdalur are supervised from June through September 15 and accessible to regular cars. Ásbyrgi has showers, a shop and snack bar, laundry machines, and facilities for trailers and camper vans. Vesturdalur is for tents only and has no showers, so the party crowd gravitates to Ásbyrgi. Ásbyrgi can be a zoo late at night, especially on summer weekends, despite the quiet policy after 11pm. The Dettifoss campground has minimal facilities—basically just outhouses and a water tap—and is only meant for hikers who traverse the park north to south and then continue on toward Mývatn. The campsites rarely if ever run out of tent space, but it's still a good idea to register in advance through the information office (above).

Camping is 750kr ($12/£6) per person per night, or free for children under 16. Showers at Ásbyrgi are 200kr ($3.20/£1.60), and require four 50-kronur coins. Tents can be rented from the information office for 1,500kr ($24/£12) per night.

OUTSIDE THE PARK   Accommodations below are all on Route 85, near Ásbyrgi.

Hóll *Ꭱ*   This snug farmhouse accommodation has down-home charm, but may not appeal to travelers who dislike the feeling of being a houseguest. Rooms are simple, warm, and endearingly decorated with old books and pastoral prints. A **two-course dinner** is available on request for 2,500kr ($40/£20).

Rte. 85, 9km west of Ásbyrgi. ℂ 465-2270 or 465-2353. Fax 465-2353. hrunda@simnet.is. 4 units, none w/bathroom. 6,000kr ($96/£48) double. Breakfast available: 800kr ($13/£6.50). MC, V. *In room:* No phone.

Hótel Lundur *Kids* This hotel is an elementary school off season, with a run-down playground, stashes of toys and board games, kiddie art displays, and the Icelandic touch: a heated pool and hot tub. Rooms are institutional but perfectly okay. Sleeping-bag accommodation is in classrooms and may revive memories of kindergarten nap time.

Rte. 865, just off Rte. 85, 9km (5½ miles) northeast of Ásbyrgi. © 465-2247. Fax 465-2311. lundur@dettifoss.is. 8 units, none w/bathroom. June–Aug 7,000kr ($112/£56) double; 2,200kr–3,000kr ($35–$48/£18–£24) sleeping-bag accommodation. Closed Sept–May. **Amenities:** Restaurant; heated pool; hot tub. *In room:* No phone.

Keldunes The six rooms in the main house are satisfactory, if sometimes small, while the two cabins outside have their own bathrooms, TVs, and kitchenettes, and can squeeze in a third or fourth person. Prices are higher than nearby competitors, justified only by free use of the washing machine and the hot tub, for which bathrobes are provided in each room. **Dinner** is available by arrangement for 2,500kr ($40/£20).

Rte. 85, 12km (7½ miles) west of Ásbyrgi. © 465-2275. www.keldunes.is. 8 units, 2 w/bathroom. 9,900kr ($158/£79) double/cabin; 2,500kr ($40/£20) sleeping-bag accommodation. Rates 15% lower Oct–Apr. Breakfast available: 1,000kr ($16/£8). MC, V. **Amenities:** Guest kitchen; hot tub; washer/dryer access. *In room:* Wi-Fi, no phone.

Skúlagarður Inn The rooms in this former boarding school are thoroughly ordinary, but the building, with its **restaurant,** bar, dance hall, and theater, has some appealing community spirit.

Rte. 85, 14km (9 miles) west of Ásbyrgi. © 465-2280. Fax 465-2279. skulagardur@simnet.is. 21 units, none w/bathroom. May 15–Aug 8,000kr ($128/£64) double; 10,500kr ($168/£84) triple; 2,000kr ($32/£16) per person sleeping-bag accommodation. Rates around 30% lower Sept–May 14. Rates include breakfast, except sleeping-bag accommodation. MC, V. **Amenities:** Restaurant; bar; guest kitchen. *In room:* No phone.

WHERE TO DINE

Besides the accommodations listed above, and the **snack bar** at the Ásbyrgi campsite, the only dining option near Ásbyrgi is the **N1 gas station** on Route 85, and in high season the few tables are often full. Some kind of fish plate is added to the usual burger and sandwich offerings. Hours are 9am to 10pm from mid-June through August, with earlier closing times in the off season. A small **market** is here, but you're better off bringing groceries from Húsavík or another town.

8 The Northeast Corner

"Land of Fire and Ice," the number-one cliché of Iceland's travel industry, has little bearing on Iceland's peaceful and remote northeast corner, which has no fearsome volcanoes, no mighty glaciers, no one-of-a-kind geological marvels. No romantic villages are nestled in majestic fjords. Not a single restaurant, hotel, museum, church, or saga site exerts any significant pull. And yet travelers come here time and again, just to gaze at birds on misty moors and walk to lonely lighthouses. It may have no star attractions, but the northeast corner is an ideal meeting of pristine beauty and blessed solitude.

ESSENTIALS
GETTING THERE & AROUND
BY CAR The northeast corner is literally out of the loop, as the Ring Road cuts inland from Mývatn to Egilsstaðir. Route 85 circles the coastline instead; the distance from Húsavík to Vopnafjörður is around 300km (186 miles), mostly unpaved.

Route 867 is a tempting shortcut across the Melrakkaslétta Peninsula; but road conditions are poor, and drivers in regular cars are advised to stick with Route 85. A new road across Melrakkaslétta may be completed by 2010.

In Vopnafjörður, the only car-rental agency is **National/Bílaleiga Akureyrar** (✆ **461-6000;** www.holdur.is). In Þórshöfn, the only company is **Avis** (✆ **591-4000;** local ✆ 660-0609; www.avis.is).

BY BUS Trex (✆ **587-6000;** www.trex.is) operates one bus on weekdays year-round from Akureyri to Þórshöfn, with a bus change at Húsavík and stops at Ásbyrgi, Kópasker, and Raufarhöfn. The bus departs Akureyri at 8:30am and reaches Þórshöfn at 12:45pm; the return trip is from 1:30pm to 6:16pm. A one-way ticket from Akureyri to Þórshöfn is 6,100kr ($98/£49). No buses go to Vopnafjörður.

BY PLANE Every weekday, **Air Iceland** (✆ **570-3030;** www.airiceland.is) connects Akureyri to Þórshöfn and Vopnafjörður; service may increase to two flights per weekday in summer. All flights from Reykjavík to Þórshöfn or Vopnafjörður connect through Akureyri. Typical airfares to Þórshöfn or Vopnafjörður are 14,000kr ($224/£112) from Reykjavík or 8,000kr ($128/£64) from Akureyri.

VISITOR INFORMATION

The tourist information office in Akureyri (p. 233) can offer general help. In **Raufarhöfn** the most knowledgeable figure is Erlingur Þoroddsen, proprietor of **Hotel Norðurljós** (✆ **465-1233;** hotel@raufarhofn.is), and basic service information is listed at www.raufarhofn.is. In **Þórshöfn,** tourist information is at the local swimming pool, Langanesvegur (✆ **468-1515;** www.thorshofn.is; mid-June to Aug Mon–Fri 8am–8pm, Sat–Sun 11am–5pm; Sept to mid-June Mon–Thurs 4–8pm, Fri 3–7pm, Sat 11am–2pm). In **Vopnafjörður,** tourist information is next to the fish factory at Hafnarbyggð 4 (✆ **473-1331;** June–Aug 10am–5pm).

EXPLORING THE NORTHEAST

For outdoor activities in this region, arrangements can be made informally. Someone is always willing to take you hiking, bird-watching, fishing, canoeing, or horseback riding, but no specific tours are advertised on websites or brochures. Birdwatchers should pick up the widely available brochure *Birds in the Coastal Areas of Thingeyjarsysla*. To download it, visit **http://norce.org** and click the links for "Wildlife" and then "Thingeyjarsysla."

The following sites form a clockwise route around the northeast corner.

MELRAKKASLÉTTA

Melrakkaslétta, which means "Arctic Fox Plains," is the only general name for the broad peninsula extending to the northernmost point of the Icelandic mainland. Shingle beaches full of driftwood and wading birds are seen along the mostly low-lying coastline, while small lakes, moors, boggy tundra, and eroded hills characterize the interior. Most farms on the peninsula have been abandoned.

An excellent new **hiking map** for Melrakkaslétta, the fifth in the *Útivist & Afþreying* series, is widely available in the region.

Rauðinúpur ⍟, the headland at the northwest tip of the peninsula has a lighthouse, sea stacks, bird cliffs tinted with red slag, and that end-of-the-earth allure. The turnoff from Route 85 is roughly 22km (14 miles) north of the village of Kópasker (and 3.5km/2 miles *after* a turnoff which heads along the coast to Grjótnes). In 8km

(5 miles) the road ends at Núpskatla crater, and Rauðinúpur is visible to the left. Walk along the rocky shore, which can be slow going, then past the lighthouse to the sea cliffs. Beware of attacks by arctic terns, especially in early summer, and have a stick handy to raise over your head in defense. Puffins are seen in large numbers, and one of the sea stacks hosts a gannet colony. Allow 2 hours round-trip.

Hraunhafnartangi is a promontory at the peninsula's northeast corner, less than 3km (2 miles) from the Arctic Circle. (Hraunhafnartangi was once thought to be the northernmost point of the mainland, but Rifstangi, a few kilometers to the west, wins that title by a hair.) The solitary lighthouse is visible from the road, and a 1.7km (1-mile) 4WD track leads directly there along the shore (going toward the lighthouse, the ocean will be on your left). The harbor by the lighthouse was active in the saga age, and a large cairn marks the gravesite of hero Þorgeir Havarsson. As with Rauðinúpur, be on the lookout for attacks from nesting birds.

The eastern region of Melrakkaslétta is dotted with endless **lakes** and ponds, treasured by a small coterie of fishermen and birdwatchers. A lovely, peaceful trail leads 5km (3 miles) from the village of Raufarhöfn to Ólafsvatn Lake; from Hótel Norðurljós, walk up to the power line and follow the staked route from there. A canoeing trail for fishermen is in the works. For further information on the lakes, or to plan a fishing trip, contact Erlingur at Hotel Norðurljós.

RAUFARHÖFN

Raufarhöfn, the **northernmost village on the mainland,** was a major processing center for herring into the 1960s but now numbers less than 250 inhabitants. Erlingur at Hótel Norðurljós is Raufarhöfn's one-man **tourist bureau,** and the best resource for any outdoor activities in Melrakkaslétta. He's also behind a scheme called **Arctic Henge** (www.arctichenge.com), a Stonehenge-inspired sundial structure, 54m (177 ft.) in diameter, on a hill just north of town. It's still under construction and awaiting further investment, but the government has promised matching grants.

If you're staying in Raufarhöfn, consider a walk along the Raufarhafnarhöfði headland, a pleasing locale for observing birds on sea cliffs and watching boats come in and out of the harbor. A 2km (1.2-mile) loop trail starts from the church.

RAUÐANES

The 7km (4-mile) circuit of this small cape halfway between Raufarhöfn and Þórshöfn is one of the best walks in the northeast corner. The route follows the bluffs, with views of sea pillars and archways, and one opportunity to clamber down to a beach. The turnoff from Route 85 is about 35km (22 miles) south of Raufarhöfn, and leads to a farm called Vellir. The trailhead is about 2km (1.2 miles) from the turnoff, on the right side of the road. After circling the periphery of Rauðanes counter-clockwise, the trail ends up farther down the road.

ÞÓRSHÖFN & LANGANES

Anyone with a taste for truly out-of-the-way places should look into **Langanes** ⭐, a 45km-long (28-mile) peninsula shaped like a duck's head. Much of the landscape is moorland full of lakes and ponds, with a few mountains reaching 719m (2,359 ft.) on the east side, some bird cliffs, and a good range of vegetation and wildflowers. The near-total solitude, abandoned farms, driftwood beaches, persistently foggy climate, and remote lighthouse at the narrow tip of the peninsula all give Langanes its own forlorn enchantment.

The village of **Þórshöfn** is the launch point for excursions into Langanes. A regular car can proceed a short ways beyond Þórshöfn on Route 869, and a 4WD road extends along the northwest coast of the peninsula all the way to the lighthouse at Fontur, with side routes branching off to the southeast. Worthwhile destinations include the ruins of Skálar, a village abandoned since 1954; the bird cliffs of Skálabjarg, just southwest of Skálar; the staked trail at Hrollaugsstaðir, where Hrollaugsstaðafjall mountain meets the sea; and the Fontur lighthouse, which has a guestbook to sign. All the hiking and 4WD routes are detailed in English on an essential new hiking map, the seventh in the *Útivist & Afþreying* series.

To plan a trip to Langanes, start with tourist information at Þórshöfn (see above). The **Sauðaneshúsið museum** (© **468-1430;** June 15–Aug 15 Mon–Fri 10am–5pm), 6km (3¾ miles) north of Þórshöfn on Route 869, is devoted to relics of Langanes, and the caretaker is very knowledgeable about the region. The farm hostel **Ytra-Lón** (© **468-1242** or 854-3797; www.simnet.is/ytralon) is located even farther into Langanes, and the website lists several great options for fishing, horseback riding, and participating in farm life. From May 15 to June 10, the **egg-collecting club of Þórshöfn** leads expeditions into Langanes where visitors can rappel down cliffsides snatching bird eggs. (Be prepared to feel like a wimp if you refuse to eat one raw.) The club leader is Halldór Halldórsson (© **862-2905** or 468-1192; fontur@isl.is); his English is limited, so e-mailing is best. Finally, the friendly staff at the **Ytra-Áland farm accommodation** (© **468-1290** or 854-7390; ytra-aland@simnet.is) can arrange 4WD expeditions to Langanes or take you on day tours.

VOPNAFJÖRÐUR & BUSTARFELL

Vopnafjörður is the largest town in the region, with around 725 people, an airport, and one police officer (she covers the nearby village of Bakkafjörður, too). Drivers continuing south along the coast on Route 917 toward Egilsstaðir are treated to incredible views on the steep descent into Fljótsdalshérað valley. Anyone headed west from Vopnafjörður to Mývatn should be sure to fill up the gas tank. The two sights listed below are some distance outside of town.

Vopnafjörður Pool Vopnafjörður is the rare Icelandic settlement without a geothermally heated pool inside the village proper. Many residents, however, feel privileged to have this idyllic alternative next to the Selá, an elite salmon-fishing river patronized by Prince Charles and George H. W. Bush. The simple facility has two hot tubs and changing rooms. The turnoff from Route 85, about 9km (5½ miles) north of Vopnafjörður, is marked by an icon of a head and shoulders bobbing above waves. The pool is 3km (2 miles) from the turnoff.

© 473-1499. Admission 300kr ($4.80/£2.40) adults; 150kr ($2.40/£1.20) children; 7am–11pm daily.

Bustarfell Museum 🖈 Not all that much distinguishes this preserved 19th-century turf farmhouse museum from others of its kind, but it does have a good range of artifacts and an unusually distinct identity from having remained in the same family for 400 years. Bustarfell's more unique holdings include hand-carved chess pieces, snuff boxes made from animal bones, a driftwood shoulder harness with sheep-horn hooks, granddad's winning dark-green bridegroom suit, and a pair of baby booties knitted from human hair. English signage is limited, and it's difficult to get the full import of the exhibit without asking questions of the staff. (Many visitors, for instance, see the short beds and assume Icelanders have become much taller—when in fact they slept partially upright to aid digestion of their low-fiber diets.) A guided tour could well be yours for the asking. For 1 day in early July, usually the second Sunday, staff in period costume demonstrates traditional farming chores. The museum's **Croft Cafe** is open during museum hours to serve old-fashioned cakes and cookies.

Rte. 85, about 20km (12 miles) southwest of Vopnafjörður. ℂ 437-1466. Admission 500kr ($8/£4) adults; 100kr ($1.50/80p) children 9–13. June 10–Sept 10 daily 10am–6pm.

WHERE TO STAY & DINE
RAUFARHÖFN
Hótel Norðurljós This is the only game in town, though proprietor Erlingur Þoroddsen—the northeast corner's leading travel authority—can find guesthouse accommodation when the hotel is full. Rooms do the job, and a pleasant terrace overlooks the harbor. Some rooms don't have TVs, so specify whether you'd like one.

Aðalbraut 2. ℂ 465-1233. Fax 465-1383. www.arctichenge.com. 15 units. 10,000kr ($160/£80) double. Breakfast available: 900kr ($14/£7). MC, V. **Amenities:** Restaurant; bar. *In room:* No phone.

ÞÓRSHÖFN & NEARBY
Guesthouse Lyngholt Rooms here are modern and clean-cut, with cheerful floral-patterned duvets. The common areas, with cozy furniture and lots of natural light, are especially relaxing and inviting.

Langanesvegur 12. ℂ 897-5064. www.lyngholt.is. 5 units, none w/bathroom 7,900kr ($126/£63) double. Rates include breakfast. AE, DC, MC, V. **Amenities:** Guest kitchen. *In room:* TV, no phone.

Hótel Jórvík Despite the "hotel" in the name, this is actually a small guesthouse in a cute private home. The luckiest guests get to sleep in the room with the frilly, satiny, flaming-pink floral bedspread. The breakfast table and some rooms have ocean views.

Langanesvegur 31. ℂ 468-1400. Fax: 468-1399. www.jorvik.vefur.com. 7 units, none w/bathroom. 7,500kr ($120/£60) double. Breakfast available: 850kr ($14/£6.80). MC, V. *In room:* No phone.

Ytra-Áland ⟨⟩ This cozy farm accommodation just west of Þórshöfn is run by an exceptionally nice family that can also arrange hiking, horseback riding, and 4WD excursions throughout the northeast corner. **Dinner** is served on request.

Off Rte. 85, 18km (11 miles) west of Þórshöfn. ℂ 468-1290 or 854-7390. Fax: 468-1390. www.ytra-aland.is. 6 units, 2 w/bathroom. 11,000kr ($176/£88) double; 8,200kr ($131/£66) double without bathroom; 2,200kr ($35/£18) sleeping-bag accommodation per person; 9,000kr ($144/£72) cottage for 3–8 persons. Rates include breakfast, except for cottage. MC, V. **Amenities:** Guest kitchen. *In room:* No phone.

VOPNAFJÖRÐUR
Hótel Tangi Rooms at this functional hotel meet modern standards but fail to make any further impression. En suite rooms also have a TV and a fridge, and rooms without private bathrooms compensate only with sinks.

Hafnarbyggð 17. ℂ 473-1840. Fax 473-1841. hoteltangi@simnet.is. 17 units, 4 w/bathroom. 11,900kr ($190/£95) double; 6,700kr ($107/£54) double without bathroom. Breakfast available: 1,000kr ($16/£8). AE, DC, MC, V. **Amenities:** Restaurant; bar; laundry service. *In room:* Wi-Fi.

Mávahlíð Guesthouse This well-priced guesthouse, opened in 2007, has crisply white, utilitarian rooms, and co-manager Guðni can arrange fishing trips on his boat.

Hafnarbyggð 26. ℂ 695-2952. www.123.is/mavahlid. 6 units, none w/bathroom. May–Sept 6,000kr ($96/£48) double; 2,500kr ($40/£20) sleeping-bag accommodation. Breakfast available: 1,000kr ($16/£8). No credit cards. Closed Oct–Apr. **Amenities:** Guest kitchen; washer/dryer access. *In room:* No phone.

WHERE TO DINE

The villages of Raufarhöfn, Þórshöfn, and Vopnafjörður each have one restaurant and an **N1 gas station** grill.

Hótel Norðurljós ICELANDIC   The hotel's reliable restaurant overlooking the harbor is a friendly respite in this remote corner of the world; you'll feel welcomed and rewarded just for coming this far. Stick with the lamb or a fresh catch.

Aðalbraut 2, Raufarhöfn. © 465-1233. Main courses 450kr–3,000kr ($7.20–$48/£3.60–£24). MC, V. Daily 7–10am and noon–10pm.

Eyrin ICELANDIC   This restaurant-cum-bar by the harbor is the one-and-only hangout for Þórshöfn's 388 residents. The menu is the standard array of burgers, pizzas, fish, and lamb, plus local clam chowder. A large-screen TV and a pool table sweeten the pot.

Eyrarvegur 3, Þórshöfn. © 468-1250. www.eyrin.is. Main courses 1,290kr–3,490kr ($21–$56/£10–£28). MC, V. Mon–Thurs 11am–10pm; Fri–Sat 11am–3am; Sun noon–10pm.

Hótel Tangi ICELANDIC   Tangi admirably upholds its role as Vopnafjörður's gathering place, with a big screen for soccer games and a dependable menu of burgers, pizza, fish, and meats. The bar is open later on weekends.

Hafnarbyggð 17, Vopnafjörður. © 473-1840. Main courses 1,700kr–3,750kr ($27–$60/£14–£30). AE, DC, MC, V. June–Aug daily 11:30am–9pm; Sept–May daily noon–2pm and 6–9pm.

9

South Iceland

The infinite wonders of south Iceland can't be reduced to any single frame, but all visitors remember the experience of driving along the Ring Road (Rte. 1). To the south is the country's most inhospitable coastline, which—east of Vík—expands into vast deserts of black sand. To the north are Iceland's tallest mountains. Enormous glacial tongues droop down the mountainsides, suggesting an unimaginable mass of ice beyond the line of vision. The farms seem harmoniously poised between these poles, and most have their own waterfall. From the main road you can alight upon the country's best folk museum at Skógar; the beautiful black sand beaches around Vík; or Jökulsárlón, an otherworldly lake full of floating icebergs. The south is an ideal road trip: not just a succession of spectacular sights, but an unforgettable progression from one to the next.

In Njáls Saga country around Hella and Hvolsvöllur, every rock, knoll, and crag seems to have a story. The 4-day trek connecting Landmannalaugar and Þórsmörk—each an unbeatable hiking area in its own right—is the most celebrated trail in Iceland. Active tour opportunities abound, from horseback riding to dog sledding. On the enchanting Westman Islands, you can explore dramatic bird cliffs by boat, or by sidling close to puffins on the ledges. No wonder the south is the most trafficked region for tourism outside the Reykjavík orbit.

The south was the last stretch of coastline to be fully claimed by settlers. Most early Norse arrivals took stock of the sand deserts, glaciers, and heavy surf, then moved on to better harbors and more forgiving habitats. Even today, the largest town in southern Iceland is Heimaey, on the Westman Islands, with a population of 4,416; no town on the mainland has even 1,000 residents.

Most of the south is well-served by buses in summer, and the Ring Road bus extends at least to Höfn year-round. But if you're connecting a lot of dots, a rental car is the ideal transport.

For visitor information online, consult the **South Iceland Travel Guide** (**www.southiceland.com**), based in Hveragerði, or **South Iceland** (**www.south.is**), based in Hella.

1 Westman Islands (Vestmannaeyjar)

In traditional annals, Norse settler Hjörleifur Hródmarsson was killed by his Irish slaves on Iceland's south coast, around the year 870. The slaves fled to the islands they could see offshore, but were later hunted down and killed by Ingólfur Arnarson, Reykjavík's first settler and Hjörleifur's brother-in-law. The Norse referred to Irishmen as "west men," and the islands have since been known as the **Westman Islands (Vestmannaeyjar)** ✦✦✦. Herjólfur Bárðarson was thought to be the first Norse inhabitant of the Westmans around 900, but archaeological evidence points to a Norse settlement as early as the 7th century.

The Westmans became world famous in 1963, when a new island, **Surtsey,** was created by a series of volcanic eruptions 120m (394 ft.) beneath the ocean surface. As the magma fought its way out of the sea, huge clouds of steam and ash sailed into the stratosphere. New land was being cooked up right on television. Surtsey was 1.7 sq. km (1 sq. mile) when the eruptions subsided, but has since eroded to half that area. It's now a nature reserve accessible only to scientists, who are studying how life takes root on barren foundations. (See "Tours & Activities," p. 284 for trips that circumnavigate Surtsey.)

Of the fifteen Westman Islands, only the largest, **Heimaey,** is inhabited. Westman Islanders have a strong local identity; a common joke refers to the mainland as "the sixteenth island." A few even dreamed of independence from Iceland, especially because the Westmans are relatively wealthy and contribute more in taxes than they receive in services. But their dependence on the Icelandic state became all too clear, when, on January 23, 1973, a volcano right next to Heimaey town erupted after 5,000 years of dormancy. When the molten rock finally stopped flowing on July 3, 30% of the town was buried in lava and ash, and 400 buildings were destroyed. Heimaey had also grown by 2.5 sq. km (⁹⁄₁₀ sq. miles).

One night in the Westmans will probably not feel like enough; 2 nights are ideal. The first weekend of August is a huge party scene in Heimaey, as Islanders join thousands of visitors on the campgrounds for live music, fireworks, and bonfires through the night. The ferry can sell out, and it's very difficult to find accommodations.

ESSENTIALS
GETTING THERE
BY FERRY   Herjólfur, Þorlákshöfn harbor (© **481-2800;** www.herjolfur.is), makes two round-trips daily in summer between Þorlákshöfn and Heimaey, but only one trip on Saturdays and holidays. One-way tickets are 2,000kr ($32/£16) adults, 1,000kr ($16/£8) seniors and children 12 to 15, and free for children 11 and under. The journey takes 3 hours. The boat leaves Þorlákshöfn at noon and 7:30pm (noon only on Sat), and Heimaey at 8:15am and 4pm (8:15am only on Sat). For fall and winter schedules, call or check the website. Weather cancellations occur only two or three times a year, and almost never in summer. The ferry sometimes sells out for cars, but never for passengers, except possibly the first weekend of August. Buses from Reykjavík and Selfoss to Þorlákshöfn on **Þingvallaleið** (© **511-2600;** www.bustravel.is), are aligned with the ferry schedule and depart from the **BSÍ bus terminal** at Vatnsmýrarvegur 10. One-way bus fare from Reykjavík is 1,050kr ($17/£8.40) for adults, and 600kr ($9.60/£4.80) for children under 12.

It may seem indulgent to take a car, but it's not a bad idea. Transporting the car costs exactly the same as a passenger ticket, and Heimaey has a good road system. If you do bring a car, make sure to reserve in advance. Even if car reservations are full, you have a decent chance of getting on standby; register your name at the ticket office, which opens an hour before departure.

BY AIR   Flying to Heimaey is an exciting and sometimes terrifying experience, as planes are often buffeted in the wind. Flights are regularly cancelled because of weather conditions, so if your itinerary is tight, take the ferry. Both airlines listed below offer day packages, which might include a bus tour of Heimaey or a round of golf. A taxi ride into town costs around 1,100kr ($18/£9), or you could walk there in about 20 minutes. Taxis often wait for Air Iceland flights, but if not, call **Eyjataxi** (© **698-2038**) from the airport.

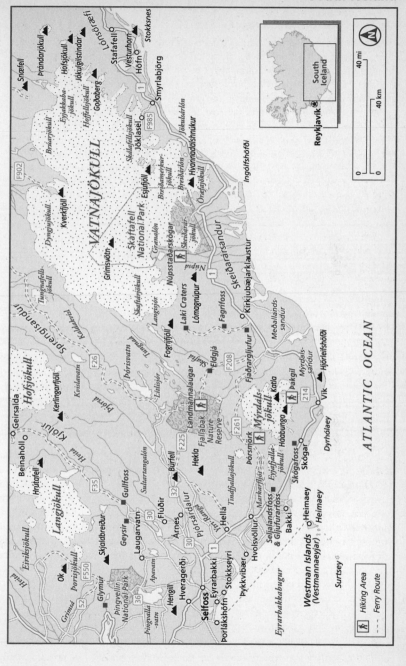

> ## *Tips* Beat the Barf Bag
>
> The ferry to the Westman Islands travels through open sea that can get rough. Most locals **rent a bunk** below deck, where there's less motion and you can sleep off the journey. The scenery isn't much to miss, though occasionally leaping dolphins accompany the ferry. Just make sure to wake up in time for the dramatic approach into Heimaey harbor. A bed with pillow and blanket adds 480kr ($7.70/£3.85) to the ticket cost. Each windowless room contains eight bunks, stacked two at a time, with curtains and private lights. Bring a sleeping bag if you have one. For more privacy, and sheets, two-person cabins cost 2,000kr ($32/£16), and four-person cabins cost 4,000kr ($64/£32). Beds can be booked in advance through **Herjólfur** (p. 278) or at the harbor ticket office before departure. Specific room assignments are given at the snack counter aboard the ferry. **Pills to prevent motion sickness** should be taken an hour before departure.

Air Iceland (© 570-3030; www.airiceland.is) flies from Reykjavík to Heimaey two or three times daily. The flight takes 25 minutes, and a typical one-way fare is 5,750kr ($92/£46) if you book online.

Flugfélag Vestmannaeyja (© 481-3255; www.eyjaflug.is) has inexpensive 20-minute charter flights 4,900kr/($78/£39) one-way, in summer from Selfoss, and can throw in some extra aerial sightseeing en route. The charter flight from Bakki is only 6 minutes and costs 2,900kr ($46/£23) per person each way, with a two-person minimum.

VISITOR INFORMATION

The **tourist information center** (© 481-3555; www.vestmannaeyjar.is: Click on the "i" at the bottom) is located in City Hall *(Ráðhús)*. **Visit Westman Islands** (www.visit westmanislands.com) is also useful. Make sure to pick up the free **walking map** from the tourist office, open May 15 to Sept 15 (Mon–Fri 10am–6pm, Sat–Sun 11am–5pm), and Sept 16 to May 14 (Mon–Sat 11am–5pm).

WHAT TO SEE & DO
HEIMAEY TOWN

Heimaey is the most profitable fishing port in Iceland, bringing in 12 to 13% of the country's annual catch, or about 200,000 tons of fish. During the 1973 eruption lava threatened to cut the harbor off entirely, so Iceland's geologists proposed a novel and successful strategy: pumping seawater onto the molten rock, to create a hard outer layer and retard the flow. Ironically, the harbor ended up more sheltered than before. (The lava also took care of Heimaey's landfill shortage).

On a cliff facing the innermost harbor is a rope hanging from a cliff. This is where local kids are trained in **spranga,** the "national sport" of the Westmans. The sport originated with egg-collecting and involves all sorts of daredevil cliff-scaling maneuvers. Egg-collecting season is in May and June, and it's fun to watch. If you're interested in learning, ask the tourist information office; they might be able to reach an instructor for you.

A **discounted joint pass** costing 700kr ($11/£5.60) for the Folk Museum, Aquarium, and Maternity Museum (see below) is available at all three museums; an upgraded pass for 900kr ($14/£7.20) includes access to the local pool, Brimhólabraut (© **481-1045**), which contains geothermally heated seawater.

Aquarium & Natural History Museum (Fiska og Náttúrugripasafnið) ⚓

The taxidermic display of birds here is above average, but what sets this natural history museum apart are the water tanks full of unusual sea creatures donated by local fishermen. Unfortunately, no supplementary information is provided.

Heiðarvegur 12. © **481-1997**. www.vestmannaeyjar.is/safnahus. Admission 400kr ($6.40/£3.20) adults; 200kr ($3.20/£1.60) children 6–12; children under 12 free. May 15–Sept 15 daily 11am–5pm; Sept 16–May 14 Sat–Sun 3–5pm.

Folk Museum (Byggðasafn Vestmannaeyja)

Located above the library and tourist information center, this large exhibit contains every local folk artifact you do and do not need to see. All annotations are in Icelandic.

Ráðhúströð (toward Skólavegur). © **481-1194**. Admission 400kr ($6.40/£3.20) adults; 200kr ($3.20/£1.80) children 6–12; under 12 free. May 15–Sept 15 11am–5pm; Sept 16–May 14 Sat–Sun 3–5pm.

Volcanic Film Show

This recommended hour-long film includes footage of the creation of Surtsey, the 1973 eruption, puffins, and egg-collecting. In July and August, the 8:30pm show tacks on a 30-minute documentary about the annual rescue of the pufflings (see "The Great Puffling Rescue," p. 283).

Eyjamyndir Félagsheimilinu (cinema), Heiðarvegur (at Vestmannabraut). © **481-1045**. Admission 600kr ($10/£5) adults; 500kr ($8/£4) seniors; 300kr ($4.80/£2.40) children under 12. Admission July–Aug 8:30pm show 800kr ($9/£4) adults; 500kr children under 12. Screenings in English May 15–June 1 and Sept 1–15 11am and 3:30pm; June 11am, 2pm, 3pm and 9pm; July–Aug 11am, 2pm, 3pm and 8:30pm.

SKANSINN

Skansinn is on the east side of town, where the lava meets the harbor. A partially crushed water tank at the lava's edge is a vivid illustration of the volcano's destructive power. The English built a fortification here in the 15th century, when they were Iceland's biggest trading partners. This defense post was of little use in 1627, when Algerian pirates landed on Heimaey's southeast coast. Of the island's 500 inhabitants, about half were taken to Algiers and sold into slavery. Many others were rounded into a storehouse and burned alive. The few remaining islanders survived by hiding in caves or rappelling down cliffs. 39 of the captives were eventually ransomed and returned to Copenhagen.

Maternity Museum (Landlyst)

In 1874 Heimaey built Iceland's first maternity clinic to combat infant mortality. This re-creation would be more interesting if the ominous-looking medical implements—what's that hacksaw for?—and other artifacts were explained in English.

Skansinn. © **481-1194**. Admission 400kr ($6.40/£3.20) adults; 200kr ($3.20/£6.40) children 6–12. May 15–Sept 15 daily 11am–5pm.

The Stave Church (Stafkirkjan)

The Norwegian government presented this building to Heimaey in 2000 to commemorate the millennium of Iceland's official adoption of Christianity. In the year 999 or 1000, the king of Norway sent emissaries to the annual Icelandic assembly *(Alþing)* to lobby against heathenism. According to saga accounts, their instructions were to build a church wherever they first set foot on land, which turned out to be Heimaey. The location of the original site is under dispute, and the new church is based on medieval Norwegian models. In keeping with the saga, the church was built in 2 days. The building process and architectural details are well-documented in a book on display in the Maternity Museum next door. Skansinn. Free admission. May 15–Sept 15 daily 11am–5pm.

AROUND THE ISLAND
ELDFELL & THE "NEW LAVA" Locals refer to the red volcanic cone created in 1973 as **Eldfell** (Fire Mountain), and the surrounding lava as **"the new lava,"** or *nýjahraun,* to distinguish it from the "old lava" *(eldhraun)* around Helgafell on the south side of town. Take a rambling drive or walk through the new lava to witness how islanders are improvising on and shaping their new landscape. Some have built lava gardens, or sculptures, or memorials for homes that are buried directly underneath.

The 5m (16-ft.) wooden cross at the base of Eldfell is a good starting point for an ascent. The cone is still steaming slightly, and the ground is still warm if you scratch beneath the surface. Just southeast of the cone is **Páskahellir,** a lava tube that should not be entered without a strong flashlight; the easiest trail access is near the airport. See also "Tours & Activities," (p. 284) for tips on hiking the new lava.

The Great Puffling Rescue

With their orange beaks and feet, tuxedoed 18cm (7-in.) tall bodies, and sad clown eyes, puffins are by common consent among the world's cutest creatures. Their air speed can reach 80kmph (50 mph), yet they flap awkwardly and frantically, like animals in cartoons who suspend themselves momentarily before crashing to earth. For centuries, Icelanders have hunted puffins by waving a kind of giant butterfly net over cliff ledges to catch them in mid-air. Most puffins breed in Iceland, and the Westman Islands boast Iceland's largest puffin colony. Though, in 2007, puffin numbers declined alarmingly; speculation is that warmer ocean waters have pushed their main food source, sand eels, farther north.

Puffins are usually monogamous for life, and—unless they end up on a dinner plate—have an average lifespan of 25 years. They usually return to the same breeding area, if not the same clifftop nesting burrow, and the females lay two eggs per year, but only one at a time. The pufflings hatch in around 42 days, and both parents gather fish for them. In mid-August the parents abandon the nest, and the pufflings are left to fend for themselves.

In late August, hundreds of hungry pufflings are attracted and disoriented by Heimaey's lights and end up crashing into yards and streets. Locals lock their cats inside, but let their children stay up late to gather the pufflings in cardboard boxes lined with soft fabric. The pufflings stay in the families' homes overnight. The next morning, the children take the pufflings to the sea and free them by tossing them high into the air. Visiting families are most welcome to participate.

A live internet **"puffin cam"** stationed on Heimaey's northeast corner can be viewed all summer at http://puffin.eyjar.is.

Pompei of the North (www.pompeiofthenorth.com) is a work-in-progress: A street with 10 homes covered in ash will be completely excavated to become a kind of time-capsule museum. Only one original occupant objected to the project; his house will stay buried. Others have already been able to pop into their upper-story windows for the first time in over 30 years. Visitors can inspect the site anytime.

OTHER WALKS   A trip to the Westmans is not complete without a good walk. A thrilling, vertiginous, and somewhat dangerous **hiking trail** starts on a 4WD road behind the N1 gas station by the harbor; it continues along Heimaey's northeastern cliffsides, eventually connecting with equally harrowing trails that ascend from Herjólfsdalur, near the golf course. Ropes and chains guide you up and down the steep sections. A gentler trail along **Ofanleitishamar** on the west coast is great for puffin close-ups. The lighthouse at **Stófjörði,** on the southern tip of the island, is officially the windiest spot in Iceland. In the southeast, the sea cliffs of **Litlihöfði** are another picturesque spot for puffin-watching.

TOURS & ACTIVITIES

Boat tours ᘒᘒ led by avian experts offer an entirely different viewpoint on coastal caves and bird cliffs around Heimaey. You might also see seals, dolphins, or even orcas, which populate the sea around the Westmans.

Viking Tours (⌀ **488-4884;** www.boattours.is), headquartered at Cafe KRÓ near the ferry landing, offers a 90-minute circle tour of the island; the captain will likely enter a sea cave and demonstrate the acoustics by playing saxophone for an audience of thousands of nonplussed birds. Tickets are 2,900kr ($46/£23) for adults, 1,900kr ($30/£15) for children ages 9 to 14, and free for children ages 9 and under. Other options include bus tours (with plenty of walking), whale-watching, and dinner sailings. Viking also offers a tour of Surtsey, though the boat is not permitted to land.

Westman Islands Tours (⌀ **481-1045;** http://tourist.eyjar.is) offers horseback riding, bus tours (Skansinn, Eldfell, a lava garden, Pompei of the North, and a puffin colony), and an inexpensive 3-hour "new lava" hiking tour, which includes exploring the lava cave Páskahellir and baking bread in the still-smoldering ash. **Eydís Boat Tours** (⌀ **481-1045;** www.saesport.is), run by the same good people, offers boat tours, whale-watching, sea angling, and evening cruises. Tours for both companies gather at the Guesthouse Hreiðrið on Faxastígur 33 at Heiðarvegur.

Vestmannaeyjavöllur (⌀ **481-2363;** www.eyjar.is/golf) is the only Icelandic golf course situated inside a volcano crater. It may also be Iceland's most scenic course, though you never know where the wind will take the ball. Course fees are 3,000kr ($48/£24), with inexpensive club rental, and tournaments take place most weekends in summer.

WHERE TO STAY

If the recommended accommodations below are full, a complete list of options is available at **www.vestmannaeyjar.is** via the tourist information link. Another option is **Sunnuhóll,** Vestmannabraut 28 (⌀ **481-2900;** fax 481-2900; www.hotelvestmannaeyjar.is; 7 units without bathroom; May–Sept 4,600kr [$74/£37] double; AE, MC, V), the spotless homey hostel owned by Hótel Þórshamar; it is generally indistinguishable from a rudimentary guesthouse—except for the fact that you rent the sheets for 700kr ($11/£5.60) for the entire stay. Though, with money as no object, you may prefer the swanky suites at **Hotel Þórshamar** (below).

EXPENSIVE

Hótel Þórshamar ℱ   The doubles in this three-star hotel are ordinary and a little small. What stands out are the amenities—billiards lounge, Jacuzzis, sauna, the excellent Fjólan restaurant—and the three snazzy suites, each a different size.

Vestmannabraut 28. ℂ **481-2900.** Fax 481-1696. hotel.eyjar.is. 21 units. May–Sept 14,800kr ($237/£118) double; 17,900kr ($286/£143) triple; 19,800kr–25,000kr ($317–$400/£158–£200) suites. Discounts for children under 13. Rates around 10% lower Oct–Apr. Rates include breakfast. AE, MC, V. **Amenities:** Restaurant; Jacuzzis; sauna. *In room:* TV, Wi-Fi, minibar, hair dryer.

MODERATE

Hótel Eyjar ℱ *Value*   Eyjar's straightforward and well-maintained doubles—our personal favorite in town—are more like small apartments with private bathrooms and well-equipped kitchens. The suites have even more space and nicer furnishings.

Bárustígur 2 (at Strandvegur). ℂ **481-3636.** Fax 481-3638. www.hoteleyjar.eyjar.is. 11 units. June–Aug 9,400kr ($150/£75) double; 15,000kr ($240/£120) suite for 2–4 people. Rates around 10% lower Sept–May (except suites). Breakfast available: 800kr ($13/£6.50) adults, 400kr (6.40/£3.20) children under 13. AE, MC, V. **Amenities:** Same-day laundry/dry cleaning. *In room:* TV, Wi-Fi, kitchenette, fridge, coffeemaker.

INEXPENSIVE

Guesthouse Hótel Mamma ℱ   This cheerful, well-appointed guesthouse with sizeable rooms is run by the Hótel Þórshamar across the street. Both floors have a full kitchen, and only the family room has a double bed instead of twins. A slim, harrowing staircase—not for bulky suitcases—leads to a cozy attic double.

Vestmannabraut 25. ℂ **481-2900.** Fax 481-1696. www.hotelvestmannaeyjar.is. 7 units, without bathroom. May–Sept 7,800kr ($125/£62) double; 9,900kr ($158/£79) triple; 12,800kr ($205/£102) family room. Discounts for children under 13. Rates around 15% lower Sept–Apr. AE, MC, V. **Amenities:** 2 guest kitchens; washer/dryer. *In room:* TV/VCR, no phone.

Guesthouse Hreiðrið ℱ *Value*   The couple running this guesthouse also manage the Volcanic Film Show, Westman Island Tours, and Eydís Boat Tours; needless to say, they're very helpful. Rooms are not luxurious, but where else will you find an orca mural, puffin stenciling, and an outdoor grill inside a gazebo?

Faxastígur 33. ℂ **481-1045** or 699-8945. Fax 481-1414. http://tourist.eyjar.is. 10 units without bathroom. May–Aug 5,900kr ($94/£47) double; 7,500kr ($120/£60) triple; 8,800kr ($141/£70) family room; 2,000kr ($32/£16) sleeping-bag accommodation. Rates around 10% lower Sept–Apr. Breakfast available: 800kr ($13/£6.50). **Amenities:** Guest kitchen; tour desk; bike rental; washer/dryer. *In room:* no phone.

Guesthouse Hvíld   This guesthouse is not so centrally located, but it just added **scooter rental** at 2,000kr ($32/£16) for an hour; 4,500kr ($72/£36) per day, a fun way to explore the island. All rooms meet basic comfort standards—but not all have TVs, so you may want to request one that does.

Höfðavegur 16. ℂ **481-1230** or 862-8299. www.simnet.is/hvild. 5 units without bathroom. May 16–Sept 6,000kr ($96/£48) double; 8,000kr ($128/£64) triple; 10,000kr ($160/£80) room for 4 persons; 1,800kr–2,000kr ($29–$32/£14–£16) sleeping-bag accommodation. Rates around 25% lower Oct–May 15. MC, V. **Amenities:** Guest kitchen; scooter rental. *In room:* No phone.

WHERE TO DINE

At press time, a new upscale restaurant **Vestmenn** was slated to open at Bárustígur 11.

Café Maria ℱ ICELANDIC   Fish, pizza, and especially puffin—served rare, with an aromatic sauce that includes Icelandic malt—are the house specialties at this welcoming restaurant with upstairs bar.

Skólavegur 1 (by Vestmannabraut). © **481-3160.** Reservations recommended for dinner. Main courses 1,300kr–3,500kr ($21–$56/£10–£28). AE, DC, MC, V. Daily 11:30am–11pm; bar open to 3am Fri–Sat.

Fjólan ⭑ ICELANDIC   The atmosphere is nothing memorable, but, for the time being, this is Heimaey's best all-around restaurant, especially for seafood dishes. The catch of the day is usually excellent (not to mention a bargain), and you won't regret the mixed seafood plate either. Service is friendly and scrupulous.

At Hótel Þórshamar, Vestmannabraut 28. © **481-2900.** Reservations recommended. Main courses 2,500kr–4,000kr ($40–$64/£20–£32). AE, MC, V. Daily 11:30am–9pm.

Kökuhús BAKERY/CAFE   This popular cafe is great for a casual soup-and-sandwich lunch, typical of the usual British or American offering.

Bárustígur 7. © **481-2664.** Small dishes 750kr–2,000kr ($12–$32/£6–£16). Mon–Fri 7:30am–5:30pm; Sat 8:30am–4pm; Sun 10am–4pm.

Pizza 67 PIZZA   This Icelandic chain with an amusing 1967 theme has reliably satisfying pizza, with toppings ranging from the familiar to the psychedelic (smoked salmon, bananas, and the like). Ask about student discounts.

Heiðarvegur 5. © **481-1567.** Main courses 870kr–3,520kr ($14–$56/£6.95–£28). AE, DC, MC, V. Daily 11am–10pm.

2 Þjórsárdalur & Hekla

The Þjórsá is Iceland's longest and mightiest river, and its valley—Þjórsárdalur—holds what is believed to be the world's most voluminous lava flow since the end of the last Ice Age. The flow is about 8,000 years old, and covers around 805 sq. km (499 sq. miles). In the river's lower reaches, the lava has yielded to fertile grazing land. The upper reaches near Hekla remain bleak, thanks to ash fallout from Hekla's periodic eruptions.

ESSENTIALS

GETTING THERE   Fifteen kilometers (9 miles) east of Selfoss, Route 30 branches off from Route 1 and follows the northwest side of the Þjórsá. At Árnes (your last chance for a hot dog), turn onto Route 32 to continue along the river. Eventually Route 32 bridges the Þjórsá and dead-ends at Route 26. To the left are Hrauneyjar and the Sprengisandur route to the north (p. 356). A right turn leads back to Route 1 on the opposite side of the river, passing near the base of Hekla.

VISITOR INFORMATION   The best resource is the regional tourist office at **Hveragerði** (p. 161). Þjórsárdalur's website is www.sveidir.is, but English translations are still in the works.

EXPLORING THE AREA

This region makes for an ideal day trip from Reykjavík or anywhere within reach. The highlights listed below follow a circular route up the northwest side of the Þjórsá on Route 32, and back down the southeast side on Route 26. No bus tours cover the area, so you'll need a car. Come prepared for a long stretch without food or facilities. If you're planning a hike in the Stöng/Gjáin/Háifoss area, bring a map. *Uppsveitir Árnessýlu,* a brochure widely available in the Hveragerði-Selfoss area, is crude but adequate. Connoisseurs of unlikely bathing spots will want a suit and towel.

ALONG ROUTE 32

Þjórsárdalslaug (© 898-3763; admission 500kr [$8/£4]; discounts for children; June–Aug Wed–Fri 11am–7pm; Sat–Sun 10am–7pm; confirming the hours is advised; closed Sept–May), a geothermally heated public swimming pool, is at a wonderfully random spot in an expanse of nothingness. To reach the pool, turn left off Route 32 onto a gravel road roughly 25km (16 miles) past Árnes; the only signs are a swimmer icon and the name of the abandoned farm, Reykholt. The pool is 6km (3¾ miles) ahead.

Returning to Route 32 and continuing east for approximately 2km (1¼ miles), you'll see a marked turnoff for **Hjálparfoss,** a picturesque waterfall on the right. It's certainly worth the about 1km (½ mile) detour. Clamber up to the vantage point above the cascade.

Return to Route 32 from Hjálparfoss, turn right, and immediately cross a bridge. Within another 1km (½ mile) you'll come to a gravel road (Rte. 327) on the left. It's marked with a small sign for Stöng, which is 7km (4⅓ miles) down the gravel road. The road is very rough, but usually passable—if only just—in a conventional car. From the parking area, look for the red-roofed building that houses the ruins. All that remains of **Stöng** are the simple stone foundations of a 12th-century Viking long-house, but it's probably the most intact Saga Age building yet excavated. The ruins were preserved by ash from the first recorded Mt. Hekla eruption in 1104. As many as 20 farms once occupied this area, which is hard to believe from the bleak vistas seen today. Informative panels map the layout of the women's' quarters, central fireplace, barn, smithy, and church, which has been reconstructed with driftwood.

The lush, peaceful gorge of **Gjáin** ☞☞, in the Rauðá (Red River), full of wildflowers and curious rock formations, is only a 10-minute walk from Stöng; the well-worn trail leaves right from the ruins. Gjáin (pronounced GYOW-in) is so lovely that several people are rumored to have had their ashes spread there.

A very short distance past the turnoff to Stöng and reached by a marked right turn off Route 32, **Þjóðveldisbærinn** (© 488-7713; www.thjodveldisbaer.is; admission 500kr [$8/£4] adults, free for seniors and children under 13; June–early Sept 10am–noon and 1–6pm) is an ambitious reconstruction of a Viking-era homestead—the only such project in Iceland. The longhall design is mostly based on the excavated ruins at Stöng, but is meant to represent all similar settlements from the 11th and 12th centuries. (Consider visiting Þjóðveldisbærinn before Stöng, to better visualize what Stöng once looked like.) It's striking to compare the Vikings' commodious interiors to the damp, claustrophobic living quarters in 19th-century turf farmhouses preserved all over Iceland. Settlers had more access to wood for construction and were not as concerned with insulation since Iceland was warmer before the mid-12th century. The builders of Þjóðveldisbærinn restricted themselves to the same technology available to the Vikings 900 years ago. The exhibit also explains Viking home economics, like how many kilometers a woman had to walk in circles to spin a length of cloth.

Háifoss ☞, a slender and beautiful waterfall, the second tallest in Iceland at 122 meters (400 ft.), is reached by a very rough gravel road. The turnoff, marked "Háifoss" and "Hólaskógur," is on the left side of Route 32, roughly 10km (6 miles) past the turnoff for Þjóðveldisbærinn. (Soon after exiting for Háifoss, another road branches off to the left toward Gjáin and Stöng; this road should not be attempted without four-wheel drive.) Hólaskógur is a mountain hut 2km (1¼ miles) from Route

32, and Háifoss is roughly 6km (3¾ miles) farther. The last stretch of the road may be too rough for a regular car; stop at Hólaskógur and ask about road conditions. In any case, Háifoss is a memorable sight and worth the hike (less than 8km/5 miles) even all the way from Route 32.

HEKLA & ENVIRONS

Shortly after the turnoff for Háifoss, Route 32 crosses the Þjórsá and dead-ends at Route 26. A right turn leads you back to the Ring Road, passing close to the base of **Hekla,** Iceland's most notorious volcano. After a few kilometers (about 2 miles), you'll pass the 4WD road F225 to Landmannalaugar on the left. About 4km (5 miles) later, look out to the right until you see **Tröllkonuhlaup,** a short but broad and command-ing waterfall with an island in the middle; the turnoff is unmarked, but you can eas-ily find your way to the stepladder that climbs over the fence.

At this point you're as close as the road will come to **Hekla,** the majestic, oblong, snow-crested peak rising distinctly from the plains. Hekla is the second most active volcano in Iceland, and its white collar masks its molten heart: *Hekla* means "hood," a name derived from the clouds that usually surround and obscure the peak.

For most nationalities, natural disasters are just periodic intervals in their collective memory. In Iceland's national story, Hekla and its ilk are vital players. A 1585 map of Iceland pictures Hekla in mid-eruption, with the caption: "Hekla, cursed with eternal fires and snow, vomits rocks with a hideous sound." Hekla's first recorded eruption in 1104 blanketed every farm and village within a 50km (31-mile) radius. Since then it's erupted over 100 times. Since the 1970s, Hekla has erupted about once per decade, with the last occurrence in 2000. An enormous reforestation project, covering 1% of Iceland's entire land surface, aims to surround Hekla with trees. The trees should survive the acrid precipitation better than low-lying vegetation, and can even absorb the flow of lava.

Hekla Center (Hekluhof) ⊛ This small but informative exhibit helps bring Hekla volcanically to life. Video screens display eruption footage, a seismometer keeps track of current grumblings, and a screen saver–like software program artistically renders the seismometer. At the end, Hekla itself is framed on the wall—through a window. To reach the exhibit, continue southwest on Route 26; it's at the Leirubakki farm and service center, opposite an N1 gas station.

ⓒ 487-8700. www.leirubakki.is. Admission 600kr ($9.60/£4.80) adults; 300kr ($4.80/£2.40) children 7–11; 6 and under free. Daily 10am–10pm.

WHERE TO STAY & DINE

For other options in the vicinity, see "Hella, Hvolsvöllur & Markarfljót Valley," later in this chapter. **Rjúpnavellir** (ⓒ **892-0409;** rjupnavellir@simnet.is) offers basic sleep-ing-bag accommodation in huts near the base of Hekla.

Hotel Freyja ⊛ This endearing country hotel with lovingly decorated rooms is wedged in an idyllic spot between Þjórsárdalur and Golden Circle. The owner has made 213 quilts to adorn the beds and walls in seasonal alternations. The **restaurant** is open from 7 to 10am, noon to 2pm, and 7 to 9pm, but for dinner they request advance notice. Dinner is usually a simple choice between fish and lamb; a single entree is 2,800kr, and a set three-course meal is 4,800kr ($77/£38). The lamb, cream, eggs, bread, and jam all come right from the premises.

Rte. 329 (on Minni-Mástunga Farm, near Árnes). ⓒ 486-6174. www.hotelfreyja.is. 12 units. 15,900kr ($254/£127) double; 19,500kr ($312/£156) triple. Rates include breakfast. MC, V. Take Rte. 325 north from Árnes and follow signs for hotel. **Amenities:** Restaurant; bar; hot tub. *In room:* TV, coffee/tea, hair dryer.

Ascending Hekla

Hekla remained unclimbed until 1750—perhaps because in popular mythology, it was the gateway to hell. (The rumblings heard for months after each eruption were tormented souls.) Climbing Hekla is no piece of cake: A round-trip hike to the 1,488m (4,751-ft.) summit takes at least 8 hours. A trail on the north side is well-marked, but don't attempt it without a good map and expert advice on current conditions. One good source is the **Hekla information center** (© 487-8700) at Leirubakki Farm on Route 26, near the mountain. Another is **Ferðafélag Íslands** (© 568-2533; www.fi.is), Iceland's premier hiking organization, which leads an **annual overnight climb** to celebrate the summer solstice. Hekla is usually capped in snow, but the summit crater formed in 2000 is still hot.

Toppferðir, at Gistiheimilið Brenna in Hella (© 864-5530; www.mmedia.is/toppbrenna), ascends Hekla by snow tractor from December to mid-June for around 10,000kr ($160/£80) per person. **Hekla Tours (Hekluferðir)** (© 487-6611 or 854-4911; hekluferdir@simnet.is), also based in Hella, can shorten the hike by driving you to the base of the mountain in a 4WD vehicle. **Mountain Taxi** (© 544-5252; www.arcticsafari.is), based in Reykjavík, leads a 10- to 12-hour circuit of Hekla in Super Jeeps, with a stop for a dip in the Landmannalaugar hot spring.

Leirubakki ⊛   This farm and all-around service center in the shadow of Hekla hosts a volcano exhibit (p. 288), a hotel, and respectable Icelandic restaurant. The hotel rooms are plain and functional, but don't feel depressing or cheap. A "Viking Pool" is cut right into the lava, or you can stick with the plastic hot tubs. Horseback riding is also available. The **dining room,** open from 10am to 10pm, has a splendid view of Hekla. Main courses range from 1,400kr to 3,500kr ($22–$56/£11–£28), and reservations are requested for dinner.

Rte. 26. © 487-8700. Fax 487-6692. www.leirubakki.is. 19 units, 15 w/bathroom. May–Sept 14 15,700kr ($251/£126) double w/bathroom; 11,100kr ($178/£89)double without bathroom; 14,100kr ($226/£113) triple without bathroom; 17,100kr ($274/£137) 4-person room without bathroom; 19,200kr ($307/£154) family room without bathroom; 2,700kr sleeping-bag accommodation. Rates around 16% lower Sept 15–Apr. Rates include breakfast. MC, V. **Amenities:** Restaurant; heated outdoor pool; hot tub; sauna. In room: No phone.

3 Landmannalaugar, Fjallabak & Surroundings

Naming Iceland's best hiking area is a pointless exercise, but if the proverbial gun were put to our heads, **Landmannalaugar** ⊛⊛⊛ would edge out the competition. In photographs, this area is usually represented in two ways: by the rhyolite mountains, with their astonishing mineral spectra, and by deeply contented bathers in the natural hot spring by the main camp. But Landmannalaugar is a much wider world unto itself—with glacial valleys, marshes, canyons, moss-covered lava fields, tephra desert, plentiful geothermal hotspots—and can sustain several days' worth of exploring. The ideal follow-up is the Laugavegurinn (p. 292), the world-famous 4-day trek to Þórsmörk.

Landmannalaugar & Rhyolite

Landmannalaugar holds Iceland's largest concentration of rhyolite. Rhyolite is one of over 700 types of igneous rock, which is formed by cooled magma. Rhyolite comes from relatively low-temperature magma that has erupted explosively and cooled rapidly. It looks somewhat glassy, and its components include quartz and mica. Obsidian, an even glassier black mineral found in the vicinity of Landmannalaugar, is a rhyolite that cooled especially quickly. Rhyolite mountains are not inherently colorful, but Landmannalaugar's geothermal chemistry has cooked the rocks into subtle and infinite variations. What's more, these variations can completely change character from close-up and receded perspectives; use every megapixel at your disposal.

Landmannalaugar proper is a flat, gravelly area 600m (1,969 ft.) above sea level, set between a glacial river and a lava flow dating from the 15th century. But the name Landmannalaugar is commonly applied to its surrounding area as well, all part of the **Fjallabak Nature Reserve.** Landmannalaugar is reached from the west by two mountain roads: F225 from Hekla, and F208 from the Hrauneyjar area. F208 continues east (on what is known as "the Fjallabak Route") past the volcanic rift Eldgjá and eventually joins the Ring Road west of Kirkjubæjarklaustur.

ESSENTIALS

GETTING THERE   From June 15 to around Sep 10, daily buses from **Reykjavík Excursions** (© 562-1011; www.re.is) connect Reykjavík and Skaftafell National Park in both directions via Landmannalaugar and the Fjallabak route. Each bus leaves at 8:30am. From June 1 to June 14, the bus from Reykjavík ends at Landmannalaugar and returns to Reykjavík the same day. Buses from Reykjavík—with stops at Hvera gerði, Selfoss, Hella, and Leirubakki—arrive at Landmannalaugar at 12:30pm, and leave 2 hours later. A one-way ticket between Reykjavík and Landmannalaugar is 4,900kr ($78/£39) for adults and 2,400kr ($38/£19) for children under 12.

From July 1 to August 24, another Reykjavík Excursions bus connects Landmannalaugar to Mývatn in the north, via the **Sprengisandur Route** through the interior (p. 356). The bus departs at 8:30am three times per week in each direction, and takes 10 hours, with some sightseeing stops.

It's possible to reach Landmannalaugar by **driving** a conventional car, but only from Hrauneyjar via Route F208, which opens up around the end of June. Insurance for rental cars is usually voided on "F" roads, however, so it's probably not worth the risk. The bus to Landmannalaugar uses Route F225 for scenic reasons, but even drivers with 4WD vehicles should check with the Landmannalaugar hut about road conditions before attempting this route; a particularly hazardous ford is close to Landmannalaugar. Coming from the east, a car could take Route 208/F208 from the Ring Road as far as Eldgjá, but the same insurance problem applies. *Note:* Gas stations are nonexistent between Hrauneyjar and Kirkjubæjarklaustur.

WHERE TO STAY & DINE

Landmannalaugar has just one accommodation, a two-story mountain hut (© 854-1192) open June through early October and run by **Ferðafélag Íslands** (© 568-2533; www.fi.is). Reservations must be made online, with advance payment. Vouchers are sent to you by mail and must be shown to the wardens. If you show up without a reservation and they have room, you can pay with cash, MasterCard, or Visa. The hut is perhaps the most overburdened in Iceland, and reservations should be made months in advance if possible, especially for July and August.

The basic wooden structure has 110 sardine-style beds in four bedrooms, with kitchen, toilets, and showers, though showers cost a small fee. Beds are 3,000kr ($48/£24)for adults, 1,500kr ($24/£12)for ages 7 to 18, and free for ages 6 and under, but you must bring your own sleeping bag. Camping costs 800kr ($13/£6.50) per person, and gives you access to the toilets and showers, but not the kitchen. Some visitors assume they'd prefer sleeping indoors, but the hut can get hot, and it's easy to be kept awake by a room full of rustlers, snorers, and chatterboxes.

From late June through the end of August, **Cafe Fjallafang,** housed inside a green bus, serves coffee, tea, beer, cake, candy, and basic sandwich materials from 11:30am to 8pm daily. Otherwise, all food must be brought in.

EXPLORING THE AREA

Landmannalaugar can be enjoyed in day tours, afternoon visits, and 2-hour bus layovers, but 2 to 4 nights is ideal. Arriving by bus one afternoon and leaving the next just doesn't allow time for hikes that take the better part of a day. **Fjallabak** is often drizzly, so it's smart to include an extra day for weather insurance. A surefire itinerary is to spend 3 nights in Landmannalaugar, 3 nights on the 4-day Laugavegurinn (see box, p. 292), and a final night or two in Þórsmörk (p. 298).

Available at the hut for 1,000kr ($16/£8), **maps** of the Landmannalaugar area lay out the trails in detail. Wardens and other travelers are happy to detail routes of any length or difficulty. Recommended destinations include Brandsgil Canyon, Frostastaðavatn Lake, the summits of Bláhnúkur and Brennisteinsalda, and the unjustly named Ljótipollur (Ugly Puddle), a red crater with a lake full of brown trout. Almost all visitors complete the day with a dip in the famous hot spring near the hut.

East of Landmannalaugar, the roughest stretch of Route F208 leads to **Eldgjá** ☆, or the "Fire Canyon." This 30km-long (19-mile) volcanic fissure reaches a depth of 270m (886 ft.) and width of 600m (1,969 ft.), revealing reddish rockslides and a pretty waterfall named Ófærufoss. The bus heading east stops at Eldgjá for 45 minutes, and the westbound bus stops for an hour and 45 minutes. Eldgjá is also included in some organized tours.

ORGANIZED TOURS & ACTIVITIES

Many tour companies in Reykjavík offer day trips to Landmannalaugar by Jeep, combined with some sightseeing around Þjórsárdalur and Mt. Hekla, but you'll probably feel cheated by having so little time. Also, Jeeps are prohibited from venturing off-road, and do not offer the freedom of access you might anticipate. **Ísafold Travel** (© 544-8866; www.isafoldtravel.is) allows at least some time for a hike at Landmannalaugar, and takes you to Gjáin and Stöng (p. 287) on the way home. For more operators, see "Jeep Tours" (p. 66) in chapter 3.

Enlisting in a **Laugavegurinn hiking tour** has several advantages. All tours include transportation to and from Reykjavík, accommodations and showers in the huts, a guide, and plenty of companionship, usually including Icelanders. Best of all, your bags are delivered from hut to hut.

From July into early September, **Ferðafélag Íslands (Icelandic Touring Association)** (© 568-2533; www.fi.is) leads a few Laugavegurinn tours, with two exclusively

The Laugavegurinn ⭐⭐⭐

This 55km (34 miles) route between Landmannalaugar and Þórsmörk is Iceland's best-known trek, and for good reason. The scenery is breathtaking, endlessly varied—from ice caves and geothermal fields to glacial valleys and woodlands—and perfectly choreographed through each leg of the journey. Sleeping-bag huts with kitchens, toilets, and usually showers are spaced at roughly 14km (9 miles) intervals. Some energetic hikers sprint the entire route in 2 days, but four or even 5 days is ideal for fully digesting your surroundings. The trail opens up anytime from late June to mid-July, and remains passable through some point in September. The season could be extended a little on either end by bringing an ice axe and crampons for the steep, icy sections of the trail.

Either bring a tent or book accommodations well in advance. **Ferðafélag Íslands** (ⓒ **568-2533**; www.fi.is) runs the hut at Landmannalaugar, all three huts along the route, and one of the three huts at Þórsmörk (p. 298). The costs and payment procedures are the same as for the Landmannalaugar hut (p. 290). It's a great luxury to have your bags carried from hut to hut by 4WD; see "Organized Tours," below. You must pack in all of your own food, unless provisions are part of your organized tour.

You'll also want good hiking shoes, a full weatherproof outfit, extra footwear for fording rivers (supportive rubber sandals are best), and a map and compass, even though the trail is heavily trafficked and well-marked. The Landmannalaugar hut sells a standard hiking map of the route, as well as a small book (*The Laugavegurinn Hiking Trail*, by Leifur Þorsteinsson) with good detail on sights along the trail as well as potential side trips.

The route can be done in either direction, but most trekkers head from Landmannalaugar to Þórsmörk. This route evens out the strenuousness of each day, and has a slight net loss of altitude. Many hikers continue from Þórsmörk on the 2-day trek to Skógar (p. 302).

for women. The cost is 41,000kr ($656/£328) per person, which includes a final meal at Þórsmörk. Children under 18 pay half price.

Útivist (ⓒ **562-1000;** www.utivist.is), an equally recommended organization, has even more Laugavegurinn departures for a better price: 34,400kr ($550/£275) per person, and half price for children under 18. As with Ferðafélag Íslands, a meal at Þórsmörk is included. Útivist also offers a choice between more strenuous 4-day trips and less strenuous 5-day trips. Cross-country skiing trips to Landmannalaugar leave in spring, and a Jeep tour of the Fjallabak reserve leaves in late August. Útivist also leads a few 4-day trips to **Sveinstindur-Skælingar** ⭐⭐⭐ in July and August for 32,100kr ($514/£257) (children under 18 half price). This remote and otherworldly landscape northeast of Eldgjá is far less known than Landmannalaugar and Þórsmörk. The medium-difficulty trip features a mountain climb and long traverse of a lovely, river-braided glacial valley. The guides carry the bags.

Icelandic Mountain Guides (© 587-9999; www.mountainguide.is) hosts a Laugavegurinn tour for groups of 6 to 14 at 77,900kr ($1,246/£623) per person. All meals are included and cooked for you, which accounts for the much higher price.

Dick Phillips Specialty Icelandic Travel Service (Whitehall House, Nenthead, Alston, Cumbria, CA9 3PS, England; from the U.K. © 0143/438-1440; outside the U.K. © 44/1434-381440; www.icelandic-travel.com) leads unforgettable, multi-day, off-the-beaten-track hiking trips through Fjallabak and surrounding areas. Trips are launched from the **Fljótsdalur Youth Hostel** (p. 296). Be prepared to carry a heavy backpack.

HORSEBACK RIDING

Riding in this area is spectacular, but may not be suitable for beginners. **Hraun Hestar** (© 566-6693; www.hnakkur.com) offers riding tours from Landmannalaugar, lasting anywhere from 1 hour to all day. **Hekluhestar** (© 487-6598; www.hekluhestar.is) specializes in 6- and 8-day riding trips around Hekla, Landmannalaugar, and the Fjalla bak reserve. The 6-day Hekla–Landmannalaugar pack trip, including horses, equipment, guide, and full board, costs 104,125kr ($1,666/£833) per person.

4 Hella, Hvolsvöllur & Markarfljót Valley

Proceeding east from the capital along the southern coast, this area represents the last broad expanse of agricultural land before mountains and glaciers press more tightly to the coast. The villages of Hella and Hvolsvöllur are right along the Ring Road; east of Hvolsvöllur, the broad Markarfljót river valley leads inland toward Þórsmörk. (For the lower route through the Markarfljót valley to Þórsmörk, see p. 298.)

The area is particularly famous for raising horses and hosts the country's major horse festival, the **Landsmót** (© 514-4030; www.landsmot.is), for a week in late June or early July on even-numbered years. The atmosphere is lively, with about 12,000 attendees, mostly Icelanders. You won't see lots of high-speed racing or hurdling fences—Icelandic horses are bred more for balancing on lava rock and swimming across freezing rivers—but they do show off their unique "tölting" gait. For more on horseback riding and the Icelandic horse, see p. 176.

ESSENTIALS

GETTING THERE   All buses headed from Reykjavík to Þórsmörk, Vík, and Höfn stop at Hella and Hvolsvöllur en route, with plenty of daily options; contact Þingvallaleið (© 511-2600; www.bustravel.is) for schedules.

VISITOR INFORMATION   In **Hella,** the tourist information center (© 487-5165; www.south.is) is along the Ring Road at the corner of Þrúðvangur, just across the bridge as you enter from the west. Hours are Monday to Friday from 10am to 5pm. In **Hvolsvöllur,** tourist information (© 487-8043) is inside the Saga Center, on Route 261 just off the Ring Road. The center is open May 15 to September 15 daily from 9am to 6pm. The free and widely available brochure/map *Power and Purity* has very detailed information for the region.

EXPLORING THE AREA
HELLA

If you want to try out the manageable and good-tempered Icelandic horse in Iceland's premier horse-farming area, consider combining a ride with a **farm stay.** Some farms offer packages for anything from overnights to week-long pack trips.

Hekluhestar, on Austvaðsholt Farm, Route 272, 9km (5½ miles) northeast of Hella (© **487-6598;** www.hekluhestar.is), is mentioned above for its 6- and 8-day trips around Mt. Hekla and the Fjallabak reserve. Like many of the horse farms, they'll negotiate just about any trip in the vicinity. Hekluhestar welcomes you to take part in farm life, which could be especially delightful during lambing season in late April/early May, foaling season in late May, and the sheep roundup in September.

Herríðarhóll, on Route 284, about 5km (3 miles) north of Route 1, and 15km (9⅓ miles) from Hella (© **487-5252** or 899-1759; www.herridarholl.is), offers anything from local beginners' tours to multi-day expeditions through the highlands. Destinations include Þjórsárdalur, Mt. Hekla, Dýrholaey, Skógar, Geysir, and Gullfoss. Look into package deals, for example lodging, dinner and breakfast, a day of riding, and a picnic for only $200. The farmhouse has five guest rooms and its own hot spring nearby.

Hestheimar, on Route 281, just off Route 26, 7km (4⅓ miles) northwest of Hella (© **487-6666;** www.hestheimar.is), is an appealing guesthouse that offers horse rides and locally renowned home cooking. The guesthouse has four rooms, two with private bathroom, and a loft that sleeps ten to twelve on floor mattresses; amenities include a guest kitchen and hot tub.

HVOLSVÖLLUR

The Saga Center   Despite the sword embedded in a boulder outside the entrance, this is not a hokey theme park, but a serious (almost too serious) educational exhibit— It's like walking through the pages of a well-written textbook. Extensive information panels, illustrations, and props cogently explain the historical context and literary significance of the sagas, with a long synopsis of Njáls Saga (see box, "Njál's Saga & Its Sites," below). The 50-minute audio tour mostly just reads off the panels. A CD of the audio tour is being produced; you could just buy that and listen in the car.

Rte. 261 (just off Rte. 1). © **487-8781.** www.njala.is. Admission 700kr ($11/£5.60) adults; 600kr ($9.60/£4.80) seniors and students. Free for ages 15 and under. Audio tour included w/admission price. May 15–Aug daily 9am–7pm; off season, call in advance.

MARKARFLJÓT VALLEY

Before the Markarfljót river was diked and bridged in the 1930s, it would swell with meltoff from Mýrdalsjökull and Eyjafjallajökull and change course, creating havoc downstream for farmers and travelers. From Hvolsvöllur, Route 261 proceeds east along the northern side of the Markarfljót valley for 27km (17 miles) to the Fljótsdalur Youth Hostel (see "Where to Stay," below), where it turns into mountain road F261. The valley becomes progressively narrower, and Þórsmörk seems very close by, but the river is uncrossable unless you have a 4WD vehicle.

If you can't get to Þórsmörk, a day hike up **Þórólfsfell** 👁👁 is a very worthy substitute. The 3-hour round-trip walk from the Fljótsdalur hostel isn't too strenuous, and wandering around the flat-topped peak yields fabulous views. With no single route or marked trail up Þórólfsfell, the best approach is from its northwest side, not from F261 to the south, which is much steeper. In good weather your destination is clearly visible, but if fog rolls in it's best to have a map and compass. From the top you could descend the east side of the mountain and walk back to the hostel along F261.

The most ambitious hikers tackle the 9-hour round-trip from Fljótsdalur to the **Tindfjallajökull ice cap** 👁👁; ask at the youth hostel about trail conditions. The hostel is also used as a base for extensive treks run by Dick Phillips tours (p. 293).

Njáls Saga & Its Sites

Of Iceland's medieval sagas, Njáls Saga is by critical consensus the most lasting literary achievement, and the only one set in south Iceland. It has also been an invaluable historical resource, providing, for example, the most thorough account of Iceland's conversion to Christianity in 1000. The book was written around 1280 by an anonymous author, and purports to recount events almost 300 years earlier. The well-crafted story revolves around Njál Þorgeirsson and his friend Gunnar Hámundarson, both actual historic figures.

Sites associated with Njáls Saga are heavily featured in tourist literature and roadside informational panels: just look for the "S" icon. The history recounted in Njáls Saga has left almost no human trace on the landscape, but the vividly described natural settings are much the same as they were in Njál's time. Local farmers can usually recount any saga event that took place on their property as if it happened yesterday.

For a **horseback riding tour** of the Njáls Saga sites, try **Njála Tours** (© **487-8133** or 865-4655), which operates out of Miðhús farm on Route 262, 2km (1¼ miles) north of Hvolsvöllur.

For an oddball re-creation of a 19th-century turf house, see **Kaffi Langbrók** in "Where to Dine," below.

THE NJÁLS SAGA TRAIL

ÞINGSKÁLAR   In Njál's time this was the annual spring assembly site for the Rangá river district, and the scarce remains of about fifty temporary encampments have been found. Several scenes are set here, including one in which Ámundi the Blind regains his eyesight just long enough to kill Lýtingur á Sámsstöðum.

From the Ring Road, 2km (1¼ miles) east of Hella, exit onto Rte. 264 heading north. In about 7km (4⅓ miles), turn left on Rte. 268 and proceed another 8km (5 miles); Þingskálar is on the left.

KELDUR   This home of Ingjald Höskuldsson, uncle of Njál's illegitimate son, is now a modern dairy farm with over 20 preserved buildings from the 19th century. The most notable survival is a 15th-century hall with stave construction and a hidden underground passageway.

Keldur is at the easternmost point of Rte. 264, about 20km (12 miles) east of Hella. © 487-8452.

GUNNARSSTEINN   In a savage battle scene, Gunnar Hámundarson and his allies are ambushed at this rock, which can be reached on foot from Keldur. Excavations turned up a skeleton and a bracelet engraved with two hearts. This bracelet might have come from Gunnar's brother Hjört (Heart), who in the saga was slain at Gunnarssteinn.

At Keldur, ask to be directed to the Gunnarssteinn trail, which leads 3km (2 miles) to the Rangá river, crosses a bridge, and follows the river south for 1km (½ mile).

HLÍÐARENDI   Once Gunnar's home, this pretty spot overlooking the Markarfljót valley now holds a few farm buildings and a nicely restored country church. After

Gunnar was killed here, he turned over in his grave and spoke cheerfully to his sons in verse. Ruins only amount to simple mounds in the earth. Bergþórshvoll (below) is barely discernible in the distance.

A sign for Hlíðarendi is marked on the left side of Rte. 261, about 17km (11 miles) from Hvolsvöllur.

BERGÞÓRSHVOLL   Once Njál's home, Bergþórshvoll is now just a low hill amid marshy land 3km (2 miles) from the ocean. In the saga account, Njál's family is burned alive inside the house in the year 1011. Excavations from 1927–28 and 1951–52 proved conclusively that there was indeed a fire around this time.

Exit the Ring Road onto Rte. 255, 4km (2½ miles) south of Hvolsvöllur. When 255 ends, turn left on Rte. 252. Bergþórshvoll is 5km (3 miles) ahead on the left.

WHERE TO STAY

On Rte. 261, 27km (17 miles) east of Hvolsvöllur in Markarfljót valley, the remote **Fljótsdalur Youth Hostel** (© 487-8498 or 487-8497; www.hostel.is; 2 units without bathroom; Apr 12–Oct 15 1,700kr [$27/£14] bunk; 250kr [$4/£2] sheet rental; AE, DC, MC, V; Closed Oct 16–Apr 11) is practically a mountain hut. Yet, with its turf roof, beautifully tended garden, library full of yellowing travelogues, and incredible views toward Þórsmörk, it could hardly offer more ramshackle appeal. Book well in advance, and remember that all food must be brought in.

Fosshótel Mosfell   This privately owned guesthouse is leased to the Fosshótel chain in summer, which could explain why the rooms are a bit more old-fashioned (and a lot more *green*) than Fosshótel's bland standard. *Price break:* Twin rooms with shared bathrooms are half the price, but they're tiny and beds may be stacked end to end. Sleeping-bag accommodation is even cheaper.

Þrúðvangur 6 (behind the gas station), Hella. © 487-5828. Fax 562-4001. www.fosshotel.is. 53 units, 35 w/bathroom. June–Aug 19,000kr ($304/£152) double w/bathroom; 9,900kr ($158/£79) double without bathroom; 6,800kr ($109/£54) double sleeping-bag accommodation. Rates around 30% lower Sept–May. Rates include breakfast. AE, DC, MC, V. **Amenities:** Restaurant, lounge; internet terminal. *In room:* No phone.

Hellishólar   A compound with scattered cottages, a golf course, and an adjoining campground full of camper wagons is not everyone's idea of an idyllic farm stay, but this recently renovated guesthouse is unpretentious, comfortable, and popular among Icelanders. Cottages, which come in different sizes, are economical for families or groups. All have kitchenettes, but bathrooms in the smallest cottages don't include showers, which are by the campsite. Horseback riding can be arranged with a neighboring farm.

Rt. 261, 11km (7 miles) east of Hvolsvöllur, in Markarfljót Valley. (© 487-8360. Fax 487-8364. www.hellisholar.is. 40 units. 10,500kr ($168/£84) cottages for 3–5 persons; 11,800kr ($189/£94) cottages for 4–6 persons; 16,000kr ($256/£128) cottages for 6–8 persons. Rates around 38% lower off season. MC, V. **Amenities:** Restaurant; bar; hot tubs. *In room:* Kitchenette, no phone.

Hótel Hvolsvöllur   Don't expect country ambience or any view to speak of at this rather generic hotel; but rooms are large, the restaurant is excellent, the bar is inviting, and prices are reasonable considering this is Hvolsvöllur's only top-tier option. Sleeping-bag accommodation is also rare in this bracket. Ask for a room in the brand-new wing.

Hlíðarvegur 7 (Rte. 261, just off Rte. 1), Hvolsvöllur. © 487-8050. Fax 487-8058. www.hotelhvolsvollur.is. 27 units. May 15–Sept 15 and Christmas season 15,300kr ($245/£122) double w/bathroom; 8,500kr ($136/£68) double without bathroom; 3,500kr ($56/£28) per person sleeping-bag accommodation. Rates around 33% lower Sept 16–May

14 (except Christmas season). Rates include breakfast, except for sleeping-bag accommodation. AE, DC, MC, V. **Amenities:** Restaurant; bar; hot tubs; laundry service. *In room:* TV, Wi-Fi, hair dryer.

Hotel Rangá 🦌🦌 Salmon fishing in Iceland's choicest rivers costs upwards of 93,750kr ($1,500/£750) *a day*, so some of the classiest accommodations are private fishing lodges patronized by the likes of Prince Charles and Eric Clapton. This four-star hotel on the banks of the Rangá, a prime salmon river, mainstreams the luxury lodge model—including the showy taxidermy and cigar bar. A new expansion ups the ante with suites, fitness rooms, a rooftop pool, and a spa with massage rooms, hot tubs, and sauna. The apportionment of Jacuzzis and balconies is very inconsistent within room classes, so make your wishes known. Also decide if you'd rather face the river or a distant Hekla.

Off Rte. 1, 7km (4½ miles) east of Hella. ⓒ **487 5700.** Fax 487-5701. www.allseasonhotels.is. 35 units. June–Aug 21,100kr–24,600kr ($338–$394/£169–£197) double. Rates around 23% lower Apr–May and Sept–Oct; 33–40% lower Jan 5–Feb and Nov–Dec 23. Rates include breakfast. AE, DC, MC, V. Closed Dec 23–Jan 6. **Amenities:** Restaurant; lounge; bar; spa; in-room massage; tour desk; room service; same-day laundry/dry cleaning service. *In room:* TV, Wi-Fi, minibar, hair dryer.

Smáratún Country Hotel 🦌 This sweet, peaceful, down-home affair has a range of options, including camping, "chalets" (small cottages),"cottages" (cabins), rooms in the farmhouse, and a new wing of hotel rooms, one side of which has views of the horse ring. Chalets sleep four with two bunks, a double bed, bathroom, TV, and kitchenette. "Cottages" sleep 6 to 10, and all except one have a private hot tub. A shared hot tub and sauna is accessible to all guests. For chalets and cottages, bed linens must be rented for 1,000kr ($16/£8) per stay. Horse-riding tours and lake-fishing permits are available.

Rte. 261, 13km (8 mile) east of Hvolsvöllur, in Markarfljót Valley. ⓒ **487-8471.** Fax 487-8373. www.smaratun.is. 26 units, 22 w/bathroom. 6,000kr ($96/£48) guesthouse double without bathroom; 2,000kr ($32/£16) sleeping-bag accommodation; 8,000kr ($128/£64) chalet; 11,000kr ($176/£88) cottage; 13,900kr ($222/£111) double in hotel wing. Rates 15% lower off season. Rates include breakfast (hotel guests only). MC, V. **Amenities:** Restaurant; hot tub; sauna; guest kitchen. *In-room:* TV (new wing and chalets only), no phone.

WHERE TO DINE

Café Eldstó CAFE This excellent road stop serves good cakes and light meals, such as quiche, salads, and traditional Icelandic soups with homemade bread. Local pottery made with volcanic glazes is for sale.

Rte. 1, across from the N1 gas station, Hvolsvöllur. ⓒ **482-1011.** Main courses 1,200kr–1,390kr ($19–$22/ £9.60–£11). MC, V. Daily noon–7pm, or later in summer.

Gallery Pizza PIZZA This popular hangout with snug dining booths and local artwork on the wall serves mainly pizza, but also subs, burgers, and fried fish. The pizzas are fluffy in the crust and heavy on the cheese. Each pizza on the menu is named after a famous painting—"The Scream" comes with pepperoni, pineapple, Tabasco, jalapeño, black pepper, and cayenne pepper—but thankfully you can design your own.

Hvolsvegur 29, Hvolsvöllur. ⓒ **487-8440.** Reservations recommended. Pizzas 750kr–2,400kr ($12–$38/£6–£19). MC, V. Sun–Tues noon–9pm; Fri–Sat noon–10pm.

Hótel Hvolsvöllur 🦌 ICELANDIC The food doesn't quite match what you get in Reykjavík for the price, but it's clearly the best option in town; and presentation and service are more than up to par. Dishes are seafood and lamb staples with extra points for effort: say, lightly fried scallops with creamy yogurt sauce and a thin crisp of fried parmesan, followed by lamb filet in red wine sauce with gratinéed potatoes and a vegetable mélange.

Hlíðarvegur 7 (Rte. 261, just off Rte. 1), Hvolsvöllur. ⓒ 487-8050. Reservations recommended. Main courses 2,300kr–3,800kr ($37–$61/£18–£30). AE, DC, MC, V. Daily 6pm–9:30pm.

Hótel Rangá ✦ SCANDINAVIAN/MEDITERRANEAN   The hotel is styled as an elite hunting and fishing lodge, and the restaurant follows suit with a virtuosic menu of seasonal fish and game, plus a token vegetarian dish. A single appetizer could include smoked guillemot, smoked duck, goat pastrami, and marinated reindeer with fig marmalade and sugar-dashed blackberries—but the simple marinated salmon is sublime. Make sure to save room for the chocolate and skýr cake. Portions are small by Icelandic standards, so the four-course chef's menu won't wipe you out.

Off Rte. 1, 7km (3⅓ miles) east of Hella. ⓒ 487-5700. Reservations required. Main courses 2,800kr–4,600kr ($45–$74/£22–£37); four-course chef's menu 6,400kr ($102/£51) per person. AE, DC, MC, V. June–Aug 7–11pm; Sept–Dec 23 and Jan 6–May 7pm–10pm.

Kaffi Langbrók ✦ *Finds* CAFE   The menu in this cozy cabin cafe—with a campground right outside—is limited to coffee, cakes, waffles, and perhaps soup. But a short distance away, co-owner Jón Ólafsson has constructed his own quirky take on a traditional turf farmhouse, and he might give you a tour if you ask nicely: note the unique hingeless door; the 200-year-old whale vertebra fashioned into the wall; the saga-inspired escape hatch; and the basalt-stone xylophone, dampened by an old pair of long underwear. A sundial and steam bath are in the works. Jón also belongs to a guitar-and-vocals quartet that often makes impromptu cafe appearances.

Rt. 261 (about 12km/7½ miles from Rte. 1), in the Markarfljót Valley. ⓒ 863-4662. Daily noon–11:30pm.

Kanslarinn ICELANDIC   This non-touristy local joint has soccer on TV, occasional live music, and the only public pool table in south Iceland (or so they claim; the Westman Islands has another one). Lamb, fish, and lasagna supplement the usual varieties of pizza and burgers. The food is a notch above expectation.

Rte. 1, in the center of Hella. ⓒ 487-5100. Reservations recommended for dinner in summer. Main courses 1,350kr–2,950kr ($22–$47/£11–£24). MC, V. Daily 11am–10pm; bar open late Fri–Sat.

5 Þórsmörk

Thór, the thunderbolt-wielding Norse god of farmers and seafarers and pioneers, has always been especially revered by Icelanders, who see in him an idealization of the persevering Icelandic character. **Þórsmörk** ✦✦✦ (Thor's Wood) has an aura of enchantment in the minds of Icelanders, as its honorary name suggests. Surrounded by broad, silt-covered river valleys and three towering glaciers, Þórsmörk is a kind of alpine oasis; ask any sheep who has sought shelter there. Scenic surprises lie around every corner, from waterfalls, twisted gorges, and dripping, moss-covered caves to wildflowers, mountain grasses, and birch trees.

Come prepared: only basic food supplies are available, and temperatures are colder than in coastal regions. Þórsmörk can be visited on day tours, but staying 1 to 3 nights is recommended.

ESSENTIALS

GETTING THERE   Þórsmörk is accessed via Route 249/F249, which proceeds 30km (19 miles) east from the Ring Road along the southern edge of the Markarfljót valley. Only 4WD vehicles with good clearance can reach one of Þórsmörk's three accommodations (Básar), and possibly another (Skagfjörðsskáli), though it's often safer to park and walk the final kilometer by crossing a pedestrian footbridge a short ways downstream. Even 4WD vehicles should not drive directly to the third accommodation, Húsadalur; drive to Skagfjörðsskáli (or the pedestrian bridge) and walk the 30 to 45 minutes to Húsadalur from there.

From June 1 through September 10, **Reykjavík Excursions** (𝕔 **562-1011;** www. re.is) has a daily bus that leaves Reykjavík at 8:30am and arrives at Húsadalur at noon, with stops in Hveragerði, Selfoss, Hella, and Hvolsvöllur. (The bus is cancelled only two or three times a year in response to surges of glacial meltwater.) At 1pm the bus leaves for Básar, arriving at 1:30pm and then continuing to Skagfjörðsskáli (called "Langidalur" on the schedule). The bus returns to Húsadalur at 2:30pm, and leaves for Reykjavík at 3:30pm. From June 15 through August, every day except Sunday, a second excursion bus leaves Reykjavík at 5pm and arrives at Húsadalur at 8:15pm, returning to Reykjavík at 8:30am the following morning without stopping at the other lodgings. A one-way adult ticket from Reykjavík to Þórsmörk is 3,900kr ($62/£31).

VISITOR INFORMATION   For general information, contact the organizations running the accommodations (see "Where to Stay," below). An excellent **hiking map,** *Þórsmörk og Goðaland,* is for sale at all the huts. An only slightly less detailed map can be downloaded free from **www.thorsmork.is**.

WHERE TO STAY
All three accommodations have tent sites, guest kitchens, and showers. Unless you are staying at Húsadalur, you must bring a sleeping bag. To beat the summer rush, make sure to book at least a few weeks in advance.

Básar (𝕔 **854-2910**), run by and booked through Útivist (𝕔 **562-1000;** www. utivist.is), comprises a small hut (sleeps 23) and a large hut (sleeps 60). Both huts are open May through October, and a warden is on-hand. From November through April the smaller hut remains open, but you need to get a key in advance. Básar is notorious for late-night partying on summer weekends because it's most easily accessible to 4WD vehicles. Sleeping-bag accommodation is 2,000kr ($32/£16) per night.

Húsadalur (𝕔 **580-5404;** www.thorsmork.is), maintained by Reykjavik Excursions (see above), is open from June 1 to September 9. It has the best facilities of the three accommodations, with an extensive compound of huts, cabins, a cafe lounge, and a geothermal pool and sauna. The cafe, open until 9pm, sells drinks, skýr, candy, soup, and basic sandwich supplies. Unlike the other two accommodations, some sleeping quarters have private doubles and made-up beds. Sleeping-bag accommodation in a twin room is 2,300kr ($37/£18) per person per night, and cottages sleeping 1 to 5 people are 7,500kr ($120/£60). Sheets and towels are available for rent. The pool is included, but a sauna and shower is 500kr ($8/£4). Of the three huts, Húsadalur has the least picturesque location, but the best hiking areas are within easy reach. Húsadalur is also the most peaceful after hours, since quiet time is more strictly enforced.

Skagfjörðsskáli (𝕔 **893-1191**), also known as "Langidalur" or simply "Þórsmörk Hut," is run by and booked through **Ferðafélag Íslands** (𝕔 **568-2533;** www.fi.is). The hut, open from mid-May through September, sleeps 75 people in three well-packed rooms. Sleeping-bag accommodation, at 3,000kr ($48/£24), is more expensive than the competition. A tiny store sells chocolate, cookies, soap, and a few other necessities. The Krossá River is just outside the hut.

The Fimmvörðuháls Trek ★★★

This spectacular 20km (12 miles) hike connecting Þórsmörk and Skógar near the south coast traverses the 1,093m (3,586-ft.) Fimmvörðuháls Pass between Eyjafjallajökull and Mýrdalsjökull. A few sections are steep and vertiginous, but no special equipment is usually required between early July and early September. The entire route could be done in 1 exhausting day, but most trekkers spend the night in the **Fimmvörðuskáli hut,** a short detour west of the trail near the top of the pass. The hut sleeps 23 in snug double-bed sleeping bag bunks, and must be reserved in advance through **Útivist** (© **562-1000;** www.utivist.is), at a cost of 2,000kr ($32/£16) per person. Facilities include a kitchen but no showers. No camping is allowed outside the hut or anywhere along the trail. Always check weather forecasts before setting out.

The trek can be done in either direction. Hikers going north to south (Þórsmörk to Skógar) have often started on the Laugavegurinn (p. 292), forming a continuous 6-day journey from Landmannalaugar to Skógar. The north-to-south route has the advantage of a net loss of altitude, but the south-to-north route affords a dramatic descent into Þórsmörk.

Organized tours all go from south to north, to give travelers the option of spending another 1 to 3 nights at the huts in Þórsmörk. The best tour leader is **Útivist** (© **562-1000;** www.utivist.is), which offers Fimmvörðuháls treks every few days in summer. The very reasonable 14,000kr ($224/£112) cost includes transportation from Reykjavík to Skógar and Þórsmörk to Reykjavík, a group guide, and accommodation at the Fimmvörðuskáli hut, but no food. For 15,900kr ($254/£127) you also get a night at the Básar huts in Þórsmörk.

EXPLORING ÞÓRSMÖRK

Reykjavík Excursions (© **580-5461;** www.thorsmork.is) sells reduced-rate bus and accommodation packages for 1 to 4 nights at Húsadalur. They also run 10-hour day tours of Þórsmörk from Reykjavík for 10,300kr ($165/£82), which includes hotel pickup/dropoff, bus fare, and a guide. For a little more zip (and lunch), you could pay 19,900kr ($318/£159) per person for a Super Jeep tour with **Mountain Taxi** (© **544-5252;** www.mountaintaxi.is), but the Jeeps can't go anywhere the buses can't.

See p. 291 for organized tours of the Laugavegurinn trail between Þórsmörk and Landmannalaugar.

THE ROUTE TO ÞÓRSMÖRK Route 249/F249 to Þórsmörk from the Ring Road is fabulously scenic, with the Markarfljót Valley on one side, and waterfalls and glacial tongues on the other.

Seljalandsfoss waterfall, just a short distance up Route 249, is easily spotted from the Ring Road by drivers heading east, and is accessible to regular cars. Buses to Þórsmörk often discharge passengers here for a few minutes to walk behind the falls, where spray fills the air and the roaring sound is dramatically magnified.

A short distance farther along Route 249, **Gljúfurárfoss** ✦ is lesser-known but more mysterious and alluring, as the water falls into an enclosed cavern. Park at the farm with the neat lawn and the turf-roofed houses. From there, it's a precarious 3-minute clamber, aided by a chain and ladder, to a good viewpoint. *Warning:* Once you've climbed the final stretch of rock, it can be very difficult to get back down. A safer alternative is to wade up the stream into the cavern.

Close to Þórsmörk, the bus usually makes a photo stop at the small azure lake **Lónið,** with floating icebergs calved from the glacial tongue **Gígjökull.**

HIKING   The hiking map *Þórsmörk og Goðaland,* available at the huts, sorts out the dense tangle of trails and is essential for exploring the area. The map is less helpful for calculating the length of your hike, so get an estimate from the wardens.

Technically, only the area north of the Krossá River is Þórsmörk. The area south of the Krossá is called Goðaland (Land of the Gods), and the hiking there is generally harder and steeper. Þórsmörk and Goðaland are connected by a pedestrian bridge near the base of Valahnúkur, a short distance west of the Skagfjörðsskáli hut in Langidalur Valley. Climbing Valahnúkur is a good introduction to the area: reaching the summit takes less than an hour from Húsadalur or Langidalur. Most hikers stay north of the Krossá and fashion a loop trail to the east, starting and ending at Langidalur. A 6-hour loop will take you as far east as Búðarhamar and around the peak Tindfjöll. An ambitious and rewarding 8-hour round-trip hike leads through Goðaland to the Tungnakvíslarjökull glacial tongue.

Iceland's most famous trail, the Laugavegurinn, connects Þórsmörk and Landmannalaugar in a 4-day hike (see box, p. 292).

6 Skógar, Vík & Mýrdalsjökull

Here marks the opening stretch of the southern coast's most dramatic scenery. Tall mountains press against the Ring Road, and a long succession of waterfalls originates from the glaciers looming above. This region also boasts Iceland's best folk museum at Skógar, south Iceland's best coastal walks at Vík, and some lesser-known inland detours toward Mýrdalsjökull Glacier. If you are passing this way, add at least 2 nights to your itinerary to take in Vík's environs, including the Þakgil camp.

ESSENTIALS

GETTING THERE   All sights in this section are arrayed on or near Route 1 and can be reached by regular car. Skógar is 155km (96 miles) from Reykjavík, and Vík is 31km (19 miles) farther. In summer five daily buses connect Reykjavík and Skógar for 3,200kr ($51/£26), and four daily buses connect Reykjavík and Vík for 3,800kr ($61/£30). Service continues through the winter, with departures at least three times per week. For tickets contact **BSÍ** (© **562-1011;** www.bsi.is) or **Þingvallaleið** (© **511-2600;** www.thingvallaleid.is).

VISITOR INFORMATION   The regional tourist office at **Hveragerði** (p.161) covers this area. In **Skógar,** limited tourist information can be found at the **folk museum** (p. 302), and at the **Fossbúð market** en route to Skógafoss. In **Vík,** the information center is in the **Brydebúð Museum,** Víkurbraut 28 (© **487-1395;** http://brydebud.vik.is), open June 15 to September 15 from 10am to 1:30pm and 2:30 to 5pm. The free and widely available **map** *Power and Purity* is detailed and useful.

WHAT TO SEE & DO

WEST OF SKÓGAR

Seljavallalaug ⚲   In this "only in Iceland" geothermal swimming pool, built in 1923, one wall is actually a mountainside from which the natural hot water trickles in.

ⓒ 487-8810; May–Sept. From the western junction of Rte. 1 and Rte. 242, take Rte. 242 for 1km (½ mile), and then continue straight as Rte. 242 curves off to the right. Seljavellir is about 2km (1¼ miles) ahead. Park at the farm's newer pool (now closed) and walk 15 min. to Seljavallalaug.

SKÓGAR

Skógar feels more like an outpost than a village, but it's been continuously settled since the 12th century. It is best known for its waterfall and folk museum, and as a launching point for the 2-day Fimmvörðuháls trek to Þórsmörk (p. 298).

For a wonderful day hike—especially if you like continuous and varied waterfalls—walk north from Skógafoss waterfall along the **Fimmvörðuháls trail** ⚲⚲ for about 2 hours, then head back along the same route.

Clearly visible from the Ring Road, the powerful, 62m (203-ft.) **Skógafoss** ⚲ waterfall looks ordinary from a distance but rewards closer inspection. Walk as close as you can on the gravel riverbed to be enveloped in the sound and spray and refracted light. A metal staircase leads to the top, where you can look down at nesting fulmars.

The prolific and affecting **Skógar Folk Museum (Skógasafn)** ⚲⚲⚲ (ⓒ 487-8845; www.skogasafn.is) is all the work of Þórður Tómasson, who has been gathering artifacts from local farms for almost 70 years. Since Þórður started the museum in 1949, countless imitations have sprung up all over Iceland, but none match the inspiration of the original. A pair of ice skates with blades made from sharpened bones. A dog bowl made from a whale vertebra. A barometer made from a cow's bladder, which shrivels at the approach of bad weather. Most displays are annotated in English, but guided tours are free with admission. Þórður prowls around the museum most days and may sing for you while accompanying himself on an old harmonium or dulcimer.

Admission to Skógasafn is 750kr ($12/£6) adults, 500kr ($8/£4) seniors and students, and free for ages 15 and under (June–Aug daily 9am–6:30pm; May and Sept daily 10am–5pm; Oct–Apr 11am–4pm). From Rte. 1, on the eastern side of Skógar, follow signs for "Byggðasafnið í Skógum."

MÝRDALSJÖKULL

A short distance east of Skógar, Rtes. 221 and 222 provide the easiest Ring Road access to **Mýrdalsjökull,** the country's fourth-largest glacier. **Sólheimajökull,** a projectile of Mýrdalsjökull, just 5km (3 miles) from the Ring Road via Route 221, is a worthwhile diversion if you are not bound for greater glories farther east at Skaftafell and Jökulsárlón. Sólheimajökull is retreating up to 100m (328 ft.) every year, a vivid demonstration of the effects of global warming. Some visitors walk atop the glacier, but taking a tour is much safer. Watch out for quicksand at the glacier's edge.

Icelandic Mountain Guides, Vagnhöfði 7b, 110 Reykjavík (ⓒ **587-9999;** www.mountainguide.is), leads daily tours of Sólheimajökull in summer, with explorations of crevasses and an introduction to basic climbing techniques. A 90-minute tour is 3,900kr ($62/£31) per person, and a 3-hour tour is 6,900kr ($55/£30), not including transportation from Reykjavík or elsewhere.

Arcanum Adventure Tours (© 487-1500; www.snow.is) is based at the Sól-heimaskáli hut, 10km (6 miles) from the Ring Road on Route 222, and offers snow-mobile, ice-climbing, and Super Jeep tours of Mýrdalsjökull. A snowmobile for two costs around 10,900kr ($174/£87) for an hour. Road conditions on Route 222 vary, so ask if you'll need a ride from the Ytri-Sólheimar lodge at the base of the road.

Dog Steam Tours (© 487-7747; www.dogsledding.is), also based at Sólheimaskáli and Ytri-Sólheimar, leads 50-minute dogsled tours on Mýrdalsjökull from December through early September with their adorable husky-type Greenland dogs. The cost is 10,900kr ($174/£87) for adults and 5,450kr ($87/£44) for children under 12.

Perhaps the most beautiful southern hiking routes to Mýrdalsjökull are from the **Þakgil campsite** (p. 304) east of Vík.

DYRHÓLAEY ᘓᘓ

This coastal bird sanctuary, whose name means "doorway hill island," derives its moniker from a massive sea archway that photographers—and daredevil pilots—find irresistible. Dyrhólaey is not an island but a promontory, with a shallow inland lagoon full of wading birds, clifftops rife with puffins, and grassy slopes full of ground-nesting avian species. It's ideal walking territory, with some eye-catching sea stacks off-shore. Dyrhólaey is closed during nesting season, from May 1 to June 25, though you can still take a guided tour with Dyrhólaeyjarferðir (see below).

Route 218 leads to Dyrhólaey from the Ring Road, crossing a narrow isthmus and rounding the sanctuary. Consider parking at the far end of the isthmus and walking clockwise around the perimeter to the lighthouse, then cutting through the middle back to the shallows. This circuit takes about 3 hours and has fabulous views in all directions. Those who want to cut to the chase can proceed directly to the famous doorway arch on the south side of the sanctuary.

Dyrhólaeyjarferðir (© 487-8500; www.dyrholaey.com) offers a choice of 75-minute land or sea tours in amphibious vehicles. Only the sea trip passes through the arch, but the land trip—the only option in rough weather—includes refreshments. Tours cost 3,500kr ($56/£28) for adults and 2,500kr ($40/£20) for ages 7 to 13.

EXPLORING VÍK & ENVIRONS ᘓᘓ

Almost at the southern tip of the mainland, the town of Vík (also known as Vík í Mýrdal) is quaintly poised between mountains, sea cliffs, and a long, beautiful black-sand beach. Vík's visual trademark is **Reynisdrangar,** a row of spiky basalt sea stacks that looks like a submerged stegosaurus and has long served as a navigational point for sailors. Lore has it that Reynisdrangar was formed when two trolls were unable to land their three-masted ship before dawn and turned to stone—as will happen when trolls are caught in sunlight. The pillars reach up to 66m (217 ft.) in height and have their own bird populations. In good weather, the coastal walk along the Reynisfjall cliffs west of the town is spectacular.

Brydebúð The tourist information center, Halldórs Cafe, and a local museum are concentrated in this 1831 timber house, which was actually transported to Vík from the Westman Islands in 1895. The museum has an art gallery and paltry exhibitions on town history and shipwrecks: most visitors will want to save their money for the folk museum at Skógar (p. 302).

Víkurbraut 28. © 487-1395. http://brydebud.vik.is. Museum admission 500kr ($8/£4) adults; free for children under 16. June 15–Sept 15 10am–1:30pm and 2:30–5pm.

"Hidden People" Lesson #3: Troll Tales

Trolls arrived in Iceland as stowaways on Viking ships and took to the local landscape, making their homes in caves and cliffs. Their boats are made of stone, and they can fish without line or bait. Most trolls never appear in sunlight, lest they turn into stone themselves.

To Icelanders, trolls are tough, menacing, ugly, and often lonesome—anything but *cute*. It's best not to cross them, though they'll keep their word if you reach an agreement. Trolls who live in bird cliffs are often a great danger to egg collectors. In an emergency, Christianity can help drive trolls off.

Trolls have not survived in the modern age nearly as well as elves. In fact, many people believe them to be extinct. Electricity hasn't been good for hidden people: electric light makes the outer dark darker, diminishing the half-dark in which hidden people take form.

REYNISFJALL

On a clear day or summer evening, the cliffs along **Reynisfjall mountain** west of Vík make for the most beautiful walk on Iceland's southern coastline. The most common approach is from Vík, where the ascent must be made inland along the 4WD road that winds its way up. If you have a 4WD vehicle and want to drive up, the road junctions with the Ring Road at the village's western border. In a regular car you can shorten the trip a bit by driving to a parking area at the base of the ascent; turn off the Ring Road right next to the "Velkomin Til Vikur" sign.

To make the most of your trek, allow 3 hours in total so you can round the cliffs far enough to take in the views north toward the mountains and glaciers and west toward Reynisfjara Beach, Dyrhólaey, and the Westman Islands. The vibrant bird life includes a good many puffins. Reynisfjall can also be climbed from its western side, by driving south on Route 215 and following the trail that leads up from the Reyniskirkja church, near the power lines. You could also use this route to *descend* from Reynisfjall and extend your walk from Vík all the way to Reynisfjara.

REYNISFJARA

The black-pebble beach of **Reynisfjara** at the southern end of Route 215 forms a 2.5km (1½ miles) spit, extending from Reynisfjall almost to Dýrholaey (p. 303), that divides the ocean from Dyrhólaós Lagoon. Reynisfjara is even more beautifully situated than the beach at Vík, but less frequented. On the eastern edge of the Reynisfjara, at the base of Reynisfjall, is the phenomenal basalt sea cave **Hálsanefshellir**. It's inaccessible at high tide, so time your visit accordingly. For tidal schedules, ask around, call the **Icelandic Hydrographic Service** (© 545-2000), or use the "Marine Reports" link at www.myforecast.com.

ÞAKGIL & MÆLIFELL

Four kilometers (2½ miles) east of Vík, Route 214 extends 15km (9⅓ miles) north from the Ring Road to the Þakgil campground, situated in a sheltered enclave amid dramatic mountain scenery near Mýrdalsjökull glacier. Route 214 itself is a fantastic drive, rough but passable in a regular car. At a high point halfway to Þakgil, the road passes some primitive wood shelters built for the movie set of *Beowulf and Grendel* (critics loved the scenery). A crude but serviceable **hiking map** is available at the campground or online at www.thakgil.is. One great hike follows a rough 4WD track, built for rounding up sheep in September, to the base of Mýrdalsjökull in a 4-hour round-trip. Another recommended 4-hour loop includes the viewpoint at **Mælifell** ☆☆. Two long but rewarding trails—about seven hours apiece—lead to Þakgil all the way from Vík; the one farther east, through Fagridalur and Bárðarfell, is slightly more picturesque. **Útivist** (© 562-1000; www.utivist.is) leads a Jeep tour from Þakgil in July; call for other organized tour possibilities, including trips onto Mýrdalsjökull.

MÝRDALSSANDUR & HJÖRLEIFSHÖFÐI
Shortly east of Vík is **Mýrdalssandur** ☆, a vast expanse of black-sand desert. As you enter Mýrdalssandur, a 221m (725-ft.) mountain, just south of the Ring Road, rises eerily from the surrounding wasteland. This is Hjörleifshöfði, named for Hjörleifur Hródmarsson, who wintered here around the year 870 before being murdered by his Irish slaves.

Hjörleifshöfði makes for a memorable short climb. A rough gravel road leads south from the Ring Road along its western edge to an indentation where the trail ascends. The cliffs, which host a fulmar colony, show evidence of shoreline erosion. A farm was on Hjörleifshöfði until 1937, but all that remains are the farmers' gravestones.

WHERE TO STAY
The stretch of coast from Markarfljót to Vík is teeming with idyllic farm accommodations, so **Icelandic Farm Holidays** (© 570-2700; www.farmholidays.is) is a good backup resource to our recommendations below.

WEST OF SKÓGAR
Country Hotel Anna ☆☆ The interiors of Iceland's "country" accommodations usually lack the kind of rustic character visitors hope for, but this three-star hotel full of old furniture and embroidered bedspreads is a charmer. It's also certified by Green

---

Katla: The Next Big One?

The notorious Katla volcano, just 25km (16 miles) north of Vík and submerged beneath Mýrdalsjökull, is showing signs of unrest. Since 1721, it has erupted five times at 34- to 78-year intervals, but there hasn't been an eruption since 1918. Subglacial volcanoes are often the most dangerous. The weight of the ice creates a pressure cooker, and the eventual burst launches a mushroom cloud of steam and rock. The steam plumes can be a conductor for near-continuous bolts of lightning; the 1918 eruption killed hundreds of heads of livestock by electrocution. But the greatest dangers are *jokuhlaups:* sudden flood bursts of melted glacial ice mixed with ash, mud, ice, and toxic chemicals.

Iceland's volcano monitoring systems may be the most sensitive and fine-tuned in the world. Plans have been drawn up for a full evacuation of the Vík area within 2 to 4 hours of an eruption.

Tips   Reading the Weather Signs

Lighted road signs all over Iceland—including one just east of Vík—indicate wind conditions and temperature (in Celsius, of course) farther down the road. North, south, east, and west winds are indicated by N, S, A, and V respectively, and the number following the letter is the wind speed in meters per second. Anything above 20 is very severe, and flying sand could tear the paint right off your car. Thankfully this rarely happens in summer.

Globe for responsible environmental practices. Of the five rooms, the two on the upper floor are best, particularly #4.

Moldnúpur (easternmost farm on Rte. 246). ⓒ 487-8950. Fax 487-8955. www.hotelanna.is. 5 units. June–Sept 15 15,200kr ($243/£122) double. Rates around 38% lower Sept 16–May. Rates include breakfast. MC, V. **Amenities:** Restaurant; hot tub; sauna. *In room:* TV, Wi-Fi, minibar, coffee/tea.

Drangshlíð   This Farm Holidays accommodation near the base of a bird cliff has ample, comfortable en-suite rooms in three separate modern buildings. Nine brand-new family rooms sleep up to four. The restaurant gets high marks as well.

Drangshlíð farm (Rte. 1, 4km [2½] miles west of Skógar). ⓒ 487-8868. www.drangshlid.is. Fax 487-8869. 34 units. June–Sept 15 13,900kr ($222/£111) double; 18,000kr ($288/£144) family room. Rates 50% lower Sept 16–May. Rates include breakfast. *In-room:* No phone.

Guesthouse Edinborg   Rooms at this Farm Holidays accommodation are welcoming if not commodious. Eyjafjallajökull is within view, and the Seljavallalaug thermal swimming pool (p. 302) is just up the road. The two cottages sleep four to six and have kitchenettes.

Lambafell farm (on Rte. 242, close to western junction of Rte. 242 and Rte. 1). ⓒ 487-8011. www.islandia.is/thorn. 6 units and 2 cottages. May–Sept 11,000kr ($176/£88) double; 7,000kr ($112/£56) per person cottage, minimum two persons. Breakfast available: 1,500kr ($24/£12). MC, V. *In room:* No phone.

SKÓGAR

Hótel Skógar   The drab exterior masks a touch of class and a fine restaurant inside. Rooms are warmly and tastefully decorated, even if they look right out of a catalog. Let them know if you'd like one of the rooms with a bathtub, otherwise you get a shower. Despite the location near Skógafoss, only the suite has a partial view.

Close to Skógafoss waterfall. ⓒ 487-4880. Fax 487-5436. www.allseasonhotels.is. 12 units. June–Sept 16,400kr–18,400kr ($262–$294/£131–£147)double. Rates include breakfast. AE, MC, V. Closed Oct–Apr. **Amenities:** Restaurant; hot tub; sauna; Internet terminal. *In-room:* TV, Wi-Fi.

Hótel Edda Skógar   This two-star hotel next to the folk museum has simple and serviceable, if antiseptic, rooms, padded out with an indoor pool, outdoor hot tub, and good dinner buffet. Sleeping-bag accommodation is inside a gym on floor mattresses.

ⓒ 444-4830. Fax 487-8855. www.hoteledda.is. 34 units without bathroom. June–Sept 15 7,600kr ($122/£61) double; 1,200kr–2,300kr ($19–$9.60/£9.60–£18) sleeping-bag accommodation. Breakfast available: 900kr ($14/£7). AE, DC, MC, V. Closed Sept 16–May. **Amenities:** Restaurant; indoor pool; outdoor hot tub. *In room:* No phone.

BETWEEN SKÓGAR & VÍK

Hótel Dyrhólaey   The Farm Holidays network rates this as "Category IV," meaning all rooms have private bathrooms and meet basic hotel standards. The rooms are too "hotelly," in fact, but are sizeable, and more importantly, Dyrhólaey and Reynis-fjara are close by. Ask for a coastal view.

Brekkur Farm (Off Rte. 1, 2.5km/1½ miles) east of the Rte. 1/Rte. 218 junction). © 487-1333. Fax 487-1507. www.dyrholaey.is. 54 units. June–Sept 15 13,125kr ($210/£8) double. Rates around 20% lower Sept 16–May. Rates include breakfast. AE, DC, MC, V. **Amenities:** Restaurant. In room: TV, Wi-Fi (250kr/$4/£2) in some rooms.

VÍK & ENVIRONS

On a slope with great views overlooking the town, the **Norður-Vík Youth Hostel,** Suðurvíkurvegur (© **487-1106** or 867-2389; fax 487-1303; www.hostel.is; 10 units, none w/bathroom; Mar 15–Nov 15 4,900kr [$78/£39] double; breakfast available for 800kr [$13/£6.50]; MC, V; closed Nov 16–Mar 14), is a low-budget option that has more in common with a guesthouse than a flophouse.

Hótel Edda Vík   This hotel meets the modern, comfortable, and functional standard of the Edda chain, but it's in their "PLUS" category, meaning three-star accommodation, not the usual student-style housing. For personality, look elsewhere.

Klettsvegur. © 444-4840. Fax 487-1418. www.hoteledda.is. 21 units. May–Sept 13,500kr ($216/£108) double; 1,200kr–2,300kr ($19–$37/£9.60–£18) sleeping-bag accommodation. Breakfast available: 900kr ($14/£7). AE, DC, MC, V. Closed Oct–Apr. **Amenities:** Restaurant; Internet terminal. In room: TV.

Hótel Höfðabrekka ☞   Well-advertised by a billboard of Icelandic wenches holding food platters, this friendly Farm Holidays accommodation 5km (3 miles) east of Vík is a scene unto itself, with four separate lodges, four outdoor hot tubs, a good restaurant, and a nearby cave and trout fishing lake. The homey, wood-paneled rooms are spacious except for the bathrooms.

Höfðabrekka farm (Off Rte. 1, just east of Rte. 214). © 487-1208. Fax 487-1218. www.hofdabrekka.is. 65 units, 62 w/bathroom. June–Aug 15,500kr ($248/£124) double. May and Sept 13,000kr ($208/£104) double. Rates include breakfast. AE, MC, V. Closed Oct–Apr. **Amenities:** Restaurant; hot tubs; guest kitchen. In room: No phone; rooms w/bathroom have TV, hair dryer.

Hótel Lundi ☞   This hotel in the village center has a nicely worn-in feel and reasonable prices. Sleeping bag accommodation is in the adjoining **Guesthouse Puffin,** which is thin-walled but cozy, with good cooking facilities.

Víkurbraut 26 and 24a. © 487-1212. Fax 487-1404. www.hotelpuffin.is. 17 units, 12 w/bathroom. 12,400kr ($198/£99) double; 15,600kr ($250/£125)triple; 2,600kr ($42/£21) sleeping-bag accommodation. Rates include breakfast, except for sleeping-bag accommodation. AE, MC, V. **Amenities:** Restaurant, bar. In room: Hair dryer.

Þakgil   This wonderfully situated campsite 15km (9⅓ miles) from the Ring Road has just added ten new cabins, each with kitchenette, toilet, and two double beds in bunks—but no hot water, so you'll need to venture outside to the shower stalls. Accommodation is sleeping bag only, and no sheets are available for rent. Enjoy candle-lit dining—inside a natural cave—and bring charcoal for the grill.

© 893-4889, 853-4889, and 487-1246. www.thakgil.is. June–Sept 15 10,000kr ($160/£80) cabin; 700kr ($11/£5.60) camping. MC, V. Closed Sept 16–May. 4km (2½ miles) east of Vík, take Rte. 214 from the Ring Road for 15km (9⅓ miles). In room: Cabins have kitchenettes, fridge, no phone.

WHERE TO DINE

Several accommodations listed above have recommendable restaurants. **Country Hotel Anna,** west of Skógar, is open for dinner from mid-June through August, from 7 to 8:30pm; main courses are in the 2,100kr to 2,900kr ($34–$46/£17–£23) range and include fish, lamb, and schnitzel. **Hotel Höfðabrekka,** east of Vík, has a dinner buffet from 7 to 9pm for 3,500kr ($56/£28); selections usually include lamb, smoked and steam-boiled salmon, and whale. No advance reservation is necessary for either spot.

In Skógar, the **cafeteria** at the folk museum (p. 302) is open daily mid-May through September from 10am to 5pm. Next to the folk museum, the **Edda Hótel** (© **444-4830**) serves lunch from noon to 2pm and a serviceable buffet from 7 to 9pm for 3,400kr ($54/£27). Near the waterfall, **Fossbúð** (© **487-8843**) serves soup, pasta, pizza, and burgers. The restaurant at **Hótel Skógar** (above) is the choicest option, with a small menu of fish and lamb courses averaging 3,500kr ($56/£18). It's open from 8am to 10pm, and reservations are recommended for dinner.

Hótel Lundi ICELANDIC   This restaurant is the best in town, though the food is often ordinary. The menu is slanted toward pasta and chicken dishes, neither of which tend to turn out well in Iceland. Stick with the marinated lamb or the local trout.

Víkurbraut 26, Vík. © **487-1212.** Reservations recommended. Main courses 1,400kr–2,400kr ($22–$38/£11–£19). AE, MC, V. Daily 11am–4pm and 6–9pm.

Halldórskaffi CAFE   This appealing hangout adjoins the local museum and visitor information center. Unlike most Icelandic cafes, it has a full range of coffee and espresso beverages. Food choices include burgers, sandwiches, pizzas, a fish or lamb special, and a tempting display of cakes and muffins.

Víkurbraut 28, Vík. © **487-1395.** Reservations recommended for dinner. Main courses 1,650kr–3,300kr ($26–$53/£13–£26). MC, V. Sun–Thurs 11am–11pm; Fri–Sat 11am–2am. Kitchen closes at 10pm.

Víkurskáli ICELANDIC   Located inside the N1 station on the Ring Road, this restaurant is a small step up from a typical Icelandic gas station grill, both in seating and selection, which includes fish and lamb.

Rte. 1, Vík. © **487-1230.** Main courses 630kr–1,475kr ($10–$24/£5.05–£12). MC, V. Mon–Fri 9am–9pm; Sat 10am–9pm; Sun 11am–9pm.

7 Kirkjubæjarklaustur & Laki Craters

The 272km (169 miles) between Vík and Höfn—the most austerely beautiful stretch of the Ring Road—contain just one small village, Kirkjubæjarklaustur. (You can just call it "Klaustur," as locals do.) Klaustur means "cloister" and refers to a Benedictine convent located here from 1186 until the Reformation. Today the village is not much more than a few houses and a pit stop, but it also serves as a crossroads for the interior route to Landmannalaugar and the Fjallabak reserve (p. 290). Another road leads to the Laki Craters, one of Iceland's most awe-inspiring volcanic formations.

ESSENTIALS
GETTING THERE   Kirkjubæjarklaustur lies along Route 1, 73km (45 miles) northeast of Vík and 259km (161 miles) from Reykjavík. In summer two **buses** per day connect Reykjavík and Höfn via the Ring Road, stopping at Kirkjubæjarklaustur. The direct route is maintained by **Þingvallaleið** (© **511-2600;** www.bustravel.is), and the route with sightseeing stops is handled by **Reykjavík Excursions** (© **562-1011;** www.re.is). From mid-June to early September, Reykjavík Excursions also connects Reykjavík to Kirkjubæjarklaustur and Skaftafell daily through the interior Landmannalaugar/Fjallabak route.

VISITOR INFORMATION   Kirkjubæjarklaustur's **tourist information office** (© **487-4620**) is in the N1 gas station near the main roundabout on the Ring Road.

Opening times are June to August on Monday to Saturday from 9am to 9pm and Sun 10am to 9pm.

EXPLORING THE AREA

A single road leads through town. It turns to gravel at **Systrafoss,** a pretty waterfall. At the top of Systrafoss is **Systravatn,** a pleasant lake surrounded by pasture. If you don't have a car to reach Fjaðrárgljúfur and just need a satisfying walk, a path ascends to Systravatn from the far side of the falls. Alternatively, the road continues past Systrafoss and soon ends at a parking area, where a path continues along the Skaftá River. Within 15 minutes' walk is the **Systrastapa,** a freestanding crag that looks like a giant molar. According to local folklore, two nuns were buried on top of Systrastapa after being burned at the stake—thus the name, which means "Sisters' Crag." A steel cable and chain descend from opposite sides of the crag, but footing is dangerous.

Kirkjugólf (Church Floor), a designated national monument near Route 203 north of the central roundabout, is a kind of natural stone terrace formed by a cross section of hexagonal basalt columns.

FJAÐRÁRGLJÚFUR

For a short hike or picnic spot along this stretch of the Ring Road, look no further than **Fjaðrárgljúfur** ᏯᏯ, a 100m-deep (328-ft.) gorge formed during the Ice Age two million years ago. Its proportions aren't mind-boggling, but it wins high aesthetic marks for its indented cliffsides full of spikes, arches, and scary ledges. The walk along the eastern ledge is not challenging, and the most compelling views can be seen in a 1-hour round-trip.

To reach Fjaðrárgljúfur, turn onto Rte. 206 from the Ring Road, 6km (3¾ miles) west of Kirkjubæjarklaustur. In 2km (1¼ miles) or so, Rte. F206 branches off to the right; continue straight and the parking area is shortly ahead.

LAKI CRATERS (LAKAGÍGAR)

Those with an eye for beauty within bleakness should particularly admire the **Laki crater row** ᏯᏯᏯ, formed during the largest lava eruption ever witnessed. Starting in 1783, and continuing for 8 months, an estimated 14.7 cubic km (3½ cubic miles) of lava emerged from over 100 craters along a 25km-long (16-mile) fissure, flowing as far as 60km (37 miles). The eruption could be seen all over Iceland and was followed by several earthquakes. The sun-obscuring haze lowered temperatures for the entire Northern Hemisphere by about 3°F (1°C–2°C), and reached as far as Asia and North Africa. Within 3 years 70% of Iceland's livestock had died, mostly from fluorine poisoning. Most water and food was not contaminated, but cold weather and famine, combined with an outbreak of smallpox, killed 22% of the Icelandic population in the same time frame. Today, Lakagígar's splattered, scabby landscape has a forlorn grandeur, and the volcanic craters are carpeted in grey mosses that turn bright green after a rainfall. In 2004, the Laki Craters were added to Skaftafell National Park's roster.

The crater row could be explored for days, but all visitors should at least climb Mt. Laki, the tallest of the craters, for astounding 360-degree views of the boundless lava flows and distant glaciers. The climb is not difficult, and takes about 45 minutes one-way from the parking area. Bring a strong flashlight, in case you run into any lava tubes to explore.

Reykjavík Excursions (℃ 562-1011; www.re.is) has one daily bus in July and August from Skaftafell National Park to the Laki Craters and back, with a stop at Kirkjubæjarklaustur and 3½ hours to explore the crater row on foot. From Kirkjubæjarklaustur the price is 5,700kr ($91/£46). **Útivist** (℃ 562-1000; www.utivist.is) and **Icelandic Mountain Guides** (℃ 587-9999; www.mountainguide.is) both lead recommended trekking tours of the Lakagígar area.

En route to Lakagígar, make sure to have a look at the aptly named **Fagrifoss** ⭐ (Beautiful Waterfall). The turnoff is marked from Route F206, roughly 22km (14 miles) from the Ring Road.

The Laki Craters are reached via Rte. 206/F206, which joins the Ring Road 6km (3¾ miles) west of Kirkjubæjarklaustur. This route has difficult river crossings, and should only be attempted in 4WD vehicles with high clearance; always check road conditions in advance.

WHERE TO STAY

Hótel Klaustur ⭐   As with most Icelandair hotels, everything is very professional, and once inside their modern rooms you'd hardly know whether you were at the airport or inside a volcano crater. "Superior" doubles have marginally more space, Nescafé packets, the option of a bathtub, and (drumroll) a hair dryer.

Klausturvegur 6. ℃ 487-4900. Fax 478-4900. www.icehotels.is. 57 units. June–Aug 17,000kr–19,500kr ($272–$312/£136–£156) double; 21,200kr ($339/£170) junior suite. Rates about 18% lower Apr–May and Sept–Oct; about 33% lower Nov to mid-Dec and Feb. Rates include breakfast. AE, DC, MC, V. Closed mid-Dec–Jan. **Amenities:** Restaurant; same-day laundry service. *In room:* TV.

Hótel Laki Efri-Vík ⭐   This ranch-like spread is quite a world unto itself, with a wide range of accommodations plus restaurant, spa, sauna, fishing lake, and nine-hole golf course. The 17 economical cottages have kitchenettes and grills and sleep four to eight. The spa requires advance bookings, especially if you need the services of the local psychic. The restaurant has a nice dinner buffet from 7 to 9pm, usually including lamb, beef, and local trout dishes for 3,500kr ($56/£28).

Efri-Vík 5km (3 miles) south of Kirkjubæjarklaustur on Rte. 204). ℃ 487-4694. Fax 487-4894. www.efrivik.is. 59 units. June–Aug 13,500kr ($216/£108) hotel double; 11,200kr ($179/£90) guesthouse double; 2,600kr ($42/£21) sleeping-bag accommodation; 6,900kr ($110/£55) and up for cottage. Rates include breakfast, except for sleeping-bag accommodation. MC, V. **Amenities:** Restaurant; 9-hole golf course; spa; sauna. *In room:* TV.

Hörgsland ⭐   This friendly compound is sprouted with 13 identical cottages, each with kitchen, porch, two bedrooms, and a sleeping loft with two beds. Each bedroom has a double bed with a single bed bunked above it, so eight guests can squeeze into each cottage. If you're only two, rates are 7,350kr ($118/£59) in sleeping bags and 9,050kr ($156/£72) in made-up beds, and you'll have the cottage to yourself. Dinner is available on request for 2,900kr ($46/£23). Hörgsland also sells fishing permits and organizes Jeep tours extending as far as the Laki Craters.

Rte. 1, 7km (4⅓ miles) east of Kirkjubæjarklaustur. ℃ 487-6655. www.horgsland.is. 13 units. 7,350kr–19,800kr ($118–$317/£59–£158) cottages. Breakfast available (950kr/$15/£7.50). AE, DC, MC, V. **Amenities:** Cafe; hot tubs. *In room:* TV, CD player, no phone.

WHERE TO DINE

Hótel Klaustur ⭐ ICELANDIC   The hotel restaurant maintains very high standards for such a remote location; try the delicate local trout, or the tender lamb with demi-glace and herbed potatoes.

Klausturvegur 6. ℂ 487-4900. Reservations recommended. Main courses 2,600kr–4,000kr ($42–$64/£21–£32). AE, DC, MC, V. May–Sept daily 7:30–10am, noon–2pm, 7–10pm; Oct–Apr daily 8–10am, noon–2pm, 7–9pm.

Systrakaffi ✦ ICELANDIC BISTRO   This cozy cafe-bar has little competition in this lonely territory, but takes this responsibility to heart with a morale-boosting ambience and surprisingly good bistro-style food. Choices include soups and salads, pizzas and, burgers, smoked lamb and pan-fried trout, and a tasty bagel plate with smoked trout.

Klausturvegur 13. ℂ 487-4848. Main courses 950kr–3,000kr ($15–$48/£7.60–£24). MC, V. May 15–Oct Sun–Thurs 11am–11pm, Fri–Sat 11am–midnight; Oct–Dec and Mar–May 14 Sat–Sun 11am–11pm; closed Jan–Feb. Kitchen closes at 10pm.

8 Vatnajökull, Skeiðarársandur & Skaftafell National Park

East of Kirkjubæjarklaustur, the Ring Road enters a long, townless stretch in the shadow of **Vatnajökull,** the largest icecap between the Arctic and Antarctic circles. South of Vatnajökull is a stupendously bleak glacial flood plain called **Skeiðarársandur,** or just "The Sandur." The main regional attraction is **Skaftafell National Park** ✦✦, a popular hiking area bordering Vatnajökull. Most of Skaftafell's day hikes are on scrubby grassland, amid a panoramic theater of spiky mountains and glistening ice.

ESSENTIALS

GETTING THERE   Skaftafell National Park is along the Ring Road, 327km (203 miles) east of Reykjavík. In summer two buses per day connect Reykjavík and Skaftafell via the Ring Road, stopping at the park. The direct route is handled by Þingvallaleið (ℂ 511-2600; www.bustravel.is); Reykjavík to Skaftafell takes 6 hours, and the route continues to Höfn. The route with sightseeing stops is handled by **Reykjavík Excursions** (ℂ 562-1011; www.re.is) and takes almost 9 hours, ending at Skaftafell. From mid-June to early September, Reykjavík Excursions also connects Reykjavík and Skaftafell daily through the interior Landmannalaugar/Fjallabak route, which is more bumpy, expensive, scenic, and time-consuming. From mid-September through May, three weekly Þingvallaleið buses connect Reykjavík and Höfn, stopping at the Freysnes gas station opposite Hótel Skaftafell (p. 314), 5km (3 miles) east of the park entrance.

VISITOR INFORMATION   The **Skaftafell visitor center** (ℂ 478-1627; www. ust.is) is well marked from the Ring Road. Basic **trail maps** are available there for 150kr ($2.40/£1.20), and can also be printed from the website. The center is open daily from 9am to 7pm June 16 to August; daily from 9am to 6pm June 1 to 15 and September; and daily from 10am to 3pm October to April.

EXPLORING THE AREA

Located halfway between Kirkjubæjarklaustur and Skaftafell National Park, on the western edge of the Skeiðarársandur, **Núpsstaður**—a tiny, turf-roofed 1850 chapel and collection of century-old farm buildings—is under the care of the National Museum. Access is free at all hours, so consider a stop to contemplate this remote settlement between a waterfall, the table mountain Lómagnúpur, and the lifeless sands.

   Núpsstaðarskógar ✦✦, near the western edge of Skeiðarárjökull along the Núpsá river, is a scrubland area rife with beautiful gorges, waterfalls, and glacier views; yet it remains one of Iceland's better-kept hiking secrets. The day-tour operator for Núpsstaðarskógar resigned in 2007. Until he is replaced, the only way to get there is

The Glacier Mystique

Those who have never seen a *jökull* (glacier) can find it hard to understand why these huge, dirty sheets of ice arouse so much interest. Part of the appeal is sheer magnitude, but the destructive power of glaciers also inspires respect. Only 10% of Iceland's land mass is covered in glaciers, but 60% of its volcanic eruptions occur beneath them, often causing catastrophic floods. In Icelandic folklore, someone traveling over a glacier might plunge into a hidden crevasse, only to be heard singing hymns from the same spot for decades. But size and might are only part of the glacier mystique. Like an organism, its bodily matter replaces itself over time. Vatnajökull's oldest ice was formed around 1200, but rock, sediment, and human victims also churn through its messy digestive system. Stray airplane parts or ski poles from decades or centuries past often pop out from the glacier's edge. Glaciers also provide endless aesthetic variety. The same glacier can appear pink or white at a distance, brown- and black-streaked on nearer inspection, and a more translucent blue up close. Evidence suggests that glaciers aren't losing their hold on the Icelandic imagination: over 150 living Icelandic men are named Jökull.

via the very difficult 4WD road, by hiking in yourself, or—as we would advise—by signing up for a tour with **Icelandic Mountain Guides** (© 587-9999; www.mountain guide.is). This recommended organization leads 5-day hikes between Núpsstaðar-skógar and the Laki Craters (p. 309), and a 4-day hike through Núpsstaðarskógar to Skaftafell, traversing the Skeiðarárjökull. Participants carry their own camping gear. Also check with **Útivist** (© 562-1000; www.utivist.is), which schedules one yearly trip through the area.

A sandur is not just any desert. *Sandur* is the English as well as Icelandic term for a flood plain full of sand and sediment deposited by subglacial volcanoes. **Skeiðarár-sandur,** formed by flood bursts from Vatnajökull, is the largest sandur in the world. This flat, interminable expanse, braided in meltwater streams and drained of life and color, was impassable until the Ring Road was completed in 1974.

In 1996, after a volcanic eruption at Grímsvötn, underneath Vatnajökull, a huge floodburst was anticipated for several days. Shortly after the film crews from the foreign media got bored of waiting and went home, a torrent of water and sediment rivaling the Amazon in size and force crashed down into the Skeiðarársandur, with house-sized icebergs bobbing along like corks. Once the sediment had settled, Iceland was 7 sq. km (2¾ sq. miles) larger. No one was killed or injured, and no communities were destroyed.

Approaching Skaftafell from the west, the Ring Road crosses three bridges. The first, Núpsvötn, was undamaged by the 1996 floodburst, even though water cascaded right over the roadway. The second bridge, Gígjukvísi, was pounded by icebergs and completely washed away. The third and longest bridge, Skeiðará, was partially demolished. A temporary road was ready in 3 weeks, and replacement bridges were completed in 9 months. A **monument** to the 1996 eruption, constructed from twisted hunks of the demolished bridges, lies between the new bridges and the Skaftafell park entrance.

SKAFTAFELL NATIONAL PARK ⊛⊛

Skaftafell National Park was designated in 1967, and the variety of vegetation, wild-flowers, and butterflies shows what can happen when grazing sheep are kept out for 40 years. The park's hiking trails are mostly on the **Skaftafellsheiði,** a scrubby green oasis wedged between Iceland's largest glacier and its flood plains. The glacier next door makes the weather milder and more hospitable to plant life. Most visitors, however, are not leafing through their field guides but gazing at the astonishing vistas, comprising some of Iceland's most imposing and picturesque mountainscapes, as well as the glacier and the vast black desert to the south.

In 2004, park rezoning tripled its size: it now includes most of Vatnajökull as well as the Laki crater row (p. 309). It is already the biggest park in Europe, but will soon expand farther north to absorb Jökulsárgljúfur National Park (p. 266).

GETTING THERE   Visitors can park either next to the tourist information center or farther into the park, near the Bölti Guesthouse. The second parking area is a few minutes closer to most walking destinations, but you miss three nice waterfalls on the way there (Þjófafoss, Hundafoss, and Magnúsarfoss). In any case, the visitor center is essential if you don't have a trail map. It also has an exhibit on local flora and fauna, and continuous screenings of thrilling footage from the 1996 Grímsvötn eruption.

HIKING   Skaftafell is most rewarding for those who penetrate farthest into the park. The easiest trail leads from the visitor center to the glacial tongue **Skafta-fellsjökull,** and takes about 30 minutes each way. The glacier has retreated for several years, as witnessed by moraines marking its old borders, and you can observe how vegetation reasserts itself in the glacier's wake. Some visitors poke around on the glacier itself, but they're taking a significant risk. This walk is perfectly nice but rather misses the point of the park, since you can drive right up to several equally interesting glacial tongues east of here. **Svinafellsjökull** ⊛, a stranger, spikier, less touristed version of Skaftafellsjökull, is reached by leaving the park and turning left on a signposted gravel road, just east of the entrance. You can park 300m (984 ft.) away and walk right up to it, though climbing on it is unsafe. See also **Kvíárjökull,** p. 316.

An ideal 2- to 3-hour hike takes in the magnificent Svartifoss waterfall, the Sjónarsker viewpoint, and the turf-roofed Sel farmhouse, built in 1912. **Svartifoss** ⊛⊛ (Black Waterfall) was named for its striking formation of black basalt columns eroded from below, forming an overhang resembling a pipe organ. The **Sjónarsker viewpoint** is about 20 minutes past Svartifoss. The farm site known as **Sel** (which simply means "Hut") was originally 100m (328 ft.) farther downhill, but was relocated in the mid-19th century to escape the encroaching sands.

Skaftafell's three premier hikes are much longer but worth the effort. One ascends through **Skaftafellsheiði** past Skerhóll and Nyrðrihnaukur and loops back along the eastern rim of Skaftafellsheiði, with incredible views throughout. An easier if slightly less recommended hike heads northwest, sloping down off the Skaftafellsheiði into **Morsárdalur** (the Morsá river valley). The trail then crosses a footbridge and leads to the Bæjarstaður, Iceland's tallest stand of birch trees. From there, continue southwest along the edge of Morsárdalur, past streams descending from the Réttargil and Vés-tragil gorges. On the far side of Véstragil, a trail leads uphill to a small, natural **geo-thermal pool** that's not shown on the park map. It's often perfect bathing temperature—and built for two. On the way back to the parking area, take the easier route through Morsárdalur without re-ascending Skaftafellsheiði.

The hike to **Kjós** 🐾🐾 through the Morsárdalur is perhaps best of all, but takes at least 10 hours round-trip. Kjós is a steep-sided river valley surrounded by magisterial, spiky peaks and exotic mineral coloring. **Camping** is permitted at a designated site, but only with a permit from the visitor center. Bring extra footwear for fording streams.

ORGANIZED TOURS   Icelandic Mountain Guides (📞 587-9999; www.mountain guide.is) sets up a base camp at Skaftafell from June to August, and runs several recommended hiking and ice climbing tours on Svinafellsjökull and Vatnajökull. Another trip connects Skaftafell and Núpsstaðarskógar (p. 311).

From Coast To Mountains (📞 894-0894; www.hofsnes.com) offers a range of adventurous glacier excursions on Svinafellsjökull and Vatnajökull, including hikes, ski mountaineering, and ice climbing.

Atlantsflug (📞 486-2406; www.atf.is; June–Sept), based at an airfield right across from the park entrance, leads unforgettable aerial tours of Skaftafell, Núpsstaðarskógar, the Laki Craters, and Landmannalaugar, with prices ranging from 9,000kr to 14,000kr ($144–$224/£72–£112) per person. At press time, their plane held three passengers, though by now they may have an eight-seater. Flights are often cancelled because of weather conditions.

WHERE TO STAY

For information on the **Skaftafell park campground** (where you might be kept up late by partiers and visited by pesky ptarmigans), contact the visitor center (p. 311).

The large **Hvoll Hostel,** Skatárhreppur (📞 487-4785; fax 487-4890; www. hostel.is; 25 units without bathrooms; Mar–Oct 4,750kr [$76/£39] double; 1,700kr–2,200kr [$27–$35/£14–£18] sleeping-bag accommodation; AE, DC, MC, V; closed Nov–Feb), has clean and functional rooms at a pretty riverside location 25km (16 miles) east of Kirkjubæjarklaustur and 45km (28 miles) west of Skaftafell National Park, on an unnumbered road 2.5km (1½ miles) south of the Ring Road; look for the Hvoll sign. If you're traveling by bus, you can arrange for the proprietors to pick you up at the junction, and then ask the bus driver to drop you there.

Bölti Guesthouse   Bölti is sleeping-bag accommodation only, in cramped rooms with six bunks apiece; but it's the only guesthouse in the park and fills up faster than you can say Kirkjubæjarklaustur.

📞 478-1626. Fax 478-2426. 7 units without bathrooms. Mar–Oct 2,500kr sleeping-bag accommodation. Breakfast available: 1,000kr ($16/£8). MC, V. Closed Nov–Feb. **Amenities:** Guest kitchen. *In room:* No phone.

Hótel Skaftafell   This ordinary hotel 5km (3 miles) east of the park entrance knows it has the only decent restaurant and en-suite guest rooms in the vicinity, and it charges accordingly. The staff is very helpful with local travel arrangements.

Freysnes, on Rte. 1 opposite the Shell station. 📞 478-1945. Fax 478-1846. www.hotelskaftafell.is. 63 units. June–Aug 14,900kr ($238/£119) double. Rates around 20% lower May and Sept; around 25% lower Oct–Apr. Rates include breakfast. AE, DC, MC, V. **Amenities:** Restaurant; bar. *In room:* TV, Wi-Fi (500kr/$8/£4).

WHERE TO DINE

The Skaftafell Park visitor center has a small selection of snacks. **Shellskálinn** (📞 482-2242; 9am–9pm Mon–Fri, 10am–9pm Sat, 11am–9pm Sun), at the Shell station 5km (3 miles) east of the park entrance, has a mini-mart plus grill and seating area.

Hótel Skaftafell ICELANDIC   This is your only choice for fine dining in the park vicinity. It's not up to Reykjavík standards, but the chefs make an honest effort, with dishes such as seared arctic char with vegetables, thyme, and wasabi. Hopefully the chocolate cheesecake is still on the menu.

Rte. 1, 5km (3 miles) east of the park entrance. (© 478-1945. Reservations recommended. Main courses 1,700kr–3,150kr ($27–$50/£14–£25). AE, DC, MC, V. June–Aug noon–2pm and 6:30–9:30pm; Sept–May noon–2, 6:30–8:30pm.

9 Between Skaftafell & Höfn

In the 136km (85 miles) stretch from Skaftafell to Höfn, **Vatnajökull** is often visually blocked by mountains and clouds. Much of this area is considered part of the region known as Öræfi (Wasteland). This name was earned after a 1362 eruption under the neighboring Öræfajökull glacier, which explosively splattered ash, dust, and rock over a wide radius. The region's most famous attraction by far is **Jökulsárlón,** a fantastical lake full of icebergs calved from the glacier. **Ingólfshöfði,** a bird sanctuary on the cape, and glacier tours from Jöklasel earn some attention as well.

ESSENTIALS
GETTING THERE   Þingvallaleið (© 511-2600; www.bustravel.is) runs one bus daily between Reykjavík and Höfn in each direction from June 1 to September 15. During the rest of the year, three buses travel in each direction weekly. From mid-June through August, **Reykjavík Excursions** (© 562-1011; www.re.is) has departures twice daily from Skaftafell to Jökulsárlón and back, with 2 to 2½ hours at Jökulsárlón. See p. 42 for air travel to Höfn.

VISITOR INFORMATION   No tourist information offices serve the area between Skaftafell and Höfn. The website **www.oraefi.is** has useful information on tours.

EXPLORING THE AREA
INGÓLFSHÖFÐI ⚑
This flat-topped wedge of coastal land seems to hover above the shimmering flats as you drive east from Skaftafell. Around the year 870, Reykjavík's founder, Ingólfur Arnarson, probably spent his first Iceland winter here—thus the name, which means "Ingólfur's Cape." It then had a sheltered harbor and was surrounded by grasslands and scrub; now it's separated from the mainland by an expanse of black volcanic sand. Ingólfshöfði is a nature reserve protected from everyone except seven local families, who have been hunting and egg collecting the land for centuries. The birds most common to the reserve are puffin and skua, a large ground-nesting species.

The only way to visit Ingólfshöfði is on the bird-watching tour led by **From Coast To Mountains** (© 894-0894; www.hofsnes.com). Tours last 2½ hours and run from late April to early August, departing at noon from Hofsnes Farm, about 22km (14 miles) east of Skaftafell Park along the Ring Road. The cost is 2,000kr ($32/£16) (cash or credit), and reservations are accepted. Bring sunglasses to protect your eyes from sand in high winds, and pack a lunch. If the weather is bad, at least be thankful that the puffins are more likely to be loitering on land.

This is no bus tour—guests are herded into a bare hay-cart and hauled behind a tractor for 30 bumpy minutes in each direction. If the tide is right, you may see the sand flats covered with a thin layer of reflective water. The walking is leisurely on

Ingólfshöfði, which peaks at 76m (249 ft.). The guide walks in front holding a walking pole aloft, in case of attack from a skua protecting its eggs. The tour group usually inspects a nest of these intimidating birds, while the mother squawks nearby.

INGÓLFSHÖFÐI TO JÖKULSÁRLÓN

Kvíárjökull 𝒢 thirty-nine kilometers (24 miles) east of Skaftafell, and its scenic valley make for an easy, charmed hour-long hike sans the Skaftafell crowds. The turnoff from the Ring Road is marked "Kvíárjökulskambar," and a parking area is shortly ahead; Kvíárjökull is clearly visible in the distance. About 10km (6 miles) farther east is a marked turnoff for **Fjallsárlón** 𝒢—a kind of Jökulsárlón for loners. The waters are muddier and less sprinkled with icebergs, but the sight of Fjallsjökull calving into the lake is remarkable. The road to Fjallsárlón divides a few times, but all routes end up in the same place, within a 10-minute walk of the best glacier views. **Breiðárlón** is a similar variation on its neighboring lakes Fjallsárlón and Jökulsárlón. The access road is well tended but unmarked from the Ring Road, about 3km (1½ miles) northeast of the Fjallsárlón turnoff. The number of icebergs can vary greatly, but on a good day you'll be glad you came.

JÖKULSÁRLÓN 𝒢𝒢

Nothing quite prepares you for the carnivalesque spectacle of a lake full of icebergs broken off from a glacier. "Calf ice" from glaciers takes on crazier shapes than "pack ice" in the sea. Calf ice is also marbled with photogenic streaks of sediment. Jökulsárlón's clear water creates a magical play of light and tints the icebergs blue. Glacial ice takes a long time to melt, and the icebergs here can last up to five years. The creaking, groaning, and crashing sounds at the glacier's edge are otherworldly. About 60 seals have established a colony at Jökulsárlón, and they can also be seen from the ocean side of the Ring Road.

Jökulsárlón did not exist 75 years ago, when Breiðamerkurjökull reached almost to the ocean. In the last few years, warming temperatures have accelerated the glacier's retreat and clogged the lake with growing numbers of smaller icebergs—an aesthetic demotion, unfortunately.

Tours (© 487-2222; www.jokulsarlon.is), which run May 15 to 30 (daily 10am–5pm), June to August (daily 9am–7pm), and September 1 to 15 (daily 10am–5pm), set out in amphibious vehicles and last 40 minutes. Tickets are 2,300kr ($37/£18) for adults and 500kr ($8/£4) for children. Walking along the shore is almost as nice, but it's worth the money to float among the icebergs, view the glacier up close, and lick your very own ancient ice cube.

VATNAJÖKULL TOURS FROM JÖKLASEL 𝒢

The vast **Vatnajökull glacier** covers about 8,000 sq. km (3,089 sq. miles), with an average thickness of 400m (1,312 ft.) and a maximum thickness of 950m (3,117 ft.). Being atop Vatnajökull is truly transporting, and returning to sea level feels like reentry from outer space. F985 dramatically ascends 16km (10 miles) to **Jöklasel** (© 478-1703), a base camp at the edge of Vatnajökull, 840m (2,756 ft.) above sea level. Jöklasel is open from June 1 to September 10, from 11:15am to 5pm, and the small cafe there serves a daily lunch buffet from 11:15am to 2pm. Jöklasel can be reached in a good 4WD vehicle, but the road is nerve-racking and often thick with fog.

Most visitors come to Jöklasel for the snowmobile and Super Jeep tours based there. (Some visitors take walks on the glacier from Jöklasel, but they're at risk of falling into a crack or getting lost if fog closes in.) Jöklasel's two tour operators are **Glacier Jeeps** (© 478-1000; www.glacierjeeps.is) and **Vatnajökull Travel** (© 894-1616; www. vatnajokull.is). The most popular tour is the 3-hour snowmobile package, which costs 9,900kr ($158/£80)and includes pickup from the intersection of the Ring Road and Route F985 (about 35km/22 miles east of Jökulsárlón and 42km/26 miles west of Höfn), plus an hour on snowmobiles. Glacier Jeeps has scheduled departures at 9:30am and 2pm from late April to September 10 (reservations required). Vatnajökull Travel (see p. 320, chapter 10) runs a daily scheduled bus from Höfn to Jöklasel to Jökulsárlón and back; some of their tours combine snowmobiling with a boat trip at Jökulsárlón.

Snowmobile riders are outfitted with helmets, jumpsuits, rubber boots, and gloves. Make sure to bring sunglasses, since they don't supply goggles. Tours set out rain or shine and reach a height of 1,220m (4,003 ft.). Your views will depend entirely on the weather: you might see 100km (62 miles) in all directions, or just blankets of cloud. Normally you'll at least rise above the cloudline for clear views of the vicinity. Weather conditions are impossible to predict from sea level, so call ahead. Even snowmobile novices could find the riding too tame; everyone proceeds single file at the speed of the most cautious driver. Both tour companies also lead Super Jeep tours on Vatnajökull, from short joyrides to multi-day excursions.

WHERE TO STAY & DINE

The recommended accommodations below are listed in order of location, from west to east along the Ring Road.

The **cafe at Jökulsárlón** (June–Aug daily 9am–7pm; May 15–30 and Sept 1–15 daily 10am–5pm) has sandwiches, waffles, and decent seafood soup. Two accommodations listed above have good restaurants. **Guesthouse Frost and Fire** serve their set-dinner menu of fish for 2,600kr ($42/£21) or lamb for 2,800kr ($45/£22) to non-guests who reserve in advance. **Smyrlabjörg's** enormous dinner buffet—with lamb, pork, chicken, beef, and no less than nine fish dishes—is open to non-guests from 6 to 9pm, June through mid-September; the cost is 3,950kr ($54/£28) and no reservations are necessary. In the off season Smyrlabjörg serves set dinner menus for 2,600kr ($42/£21), but only with a day's advance notice.

Brunhóll   Brunhóll is beautifully situated near Fláajökull, with a marked 6km (3¾ miles) trail leading to the glacier. Rooms are basic and mostly sizeable, some with views of Fláajökull. The Green Globe certification signifies sound environmental practices. We recommend their dinners, which are available on request.

Rte. 1 (30km [19 miles] west of Höfn). © 478-1029. Fax 478-1079. brunnhol@eldhorn.is. 20 units, 18 w/bathroom. June 11–Aug 25 11,400kr ($157/£80) double without bathroom; 13,600kr ($187/£95) double w/bathroom; 18,500kr ($296/£148) triple w/bathroom; 3,500kr ($48/£24) sleeping-bag accommodation without bathroom; 4,200kr ($67/£34) sleeping-bag accommodation w/bathroom. Rates around 15%–25% lower off season. Rates include breakfast. MC, V. Closed Nov–Mar. **Amenities:** Guest kitchen. *In room:* TV, no phone.

Guesthouse Frost and Fire (Frost og Funi) ⚶   Modern art and boldly striped upholstery and bedspreads set the tone at this chic outpost. Try not to get stuck with one of the tiny rooms. Dinner is available on request; non-guests should call in advance. **Hofskirkja,** a wonderful 1884 turf-roofed church, is right next door.

Hof in Öræfi Farm (on Rte. 1, 18km (11 miles) east of Skaftafell Park). ⓒ **478-2260.** Fax 487-2261. www.frostogfuni.is. 21 units, 1 w/bathroom. May 20–Sept 10 12,100kr ($194/£97) double w/bathroom; 11,000kr ($176/£88) double without bathroom. Rates include breakfast. MC, V. Closed Sept 11–May 19. **Amenities:** Restaurant; hot tub; sauna. *In room:* No phone.

Hólmur *(Value* Backgrounded by the Fláajökull glacier tongue, this new farm stay offers simple and snug accommodation at good prices—and opportunities to interact with the resident horses, sheep, and bunnies. Dinner is available on request.

Rte. 1 (33km/21 miles) west of Höfn). ⓒ **478-2063.** www.eldhorn.is/mg/gisting. 8 units without bathroom. June–Sept 6,600kr ($106/£53) double; 2,500kr ($40/£20) sleeping-bag accommodation. Rates around 14% lower Oct–May. Breakfast available: 900kr ($14/£7). MC, V. **Amenities:** Guest kitchen. *In room:* No phone.

Smyrlabjörg Smyrlabjörg is a working farm with cows, horses, and sheep. Look no further for a comfortable, no-nonsense, en-suite room in a motel block, with friendly service and a bounteous restaurant. The road to Jöklasel is only 2km (1¼ miles) away.

Rte. 1 (2km/1¼ miles) west of Rte. 1/Rte. F985 junction). ⓒ **478-1074.** Fax: 478-2043. www.smyrlabjorg.is. 45 units. May 20–Sept 1 13,100kr ($210/£105) double; 18,000kr ($288/£144) triple. Rates include breakfast. MC, V. **Amenities:** Restaurant; bar. *In room:* TV.

10

East Iceland

With no obvious mega-attraction, the east is Iceland's least visited quadrant—but not for lack of appeal. Since Reykjavík is at the opposite end of the country, the East tends to elude the most popular itineraries. Road trips through the south peter out at Jökulsárlón. Visitors to the north trace a compact loop around Akureyri, Mývatn, Húsavík, and Jökulsárgljúfur National Park. Ferries from Europe arrive in the east, at Seyðisfjörður, but through-routes from there bypass the best coastal scenery.

Yet 1 day's journey through the east encompasses picturesque valleys, geothermal hotspots, barren sandscapes, and sensational mountain roads. The east is at the forefront of reforestation efforts, and Iceland's reindeer herds are concentrated in its highlands. The region's main scenic assets are the Eastfjords, which have a compelling and unique geography. Compared with the Westfjords, the waters here are deeper, the slopes steeper, the waterfalls more toppling, the peaks more slender, the coastal roads more near the water.

Not surprisingly, local economies are dominated by fishing. In the heyday of the herring, cod, and whaling industries, the east's rich fishing grounds attracted many Norwegian and French-speaking fishermen. Today most fjords have their own fish-processing plant, and other fjords lie abandoned or near-abandoned in all their pristine majesty.

Two of Iceland's best hiking districts are in the east: Lónsöræfi, a mountainous private reserve near Vatnajökull, and Borgarfjörður Eystri, the northernmost region of the Eastfjords. Seyðisfjörður is the region's prettiest and most culturally thriving coastal town. Southwest of Egilsstaðir are some of Iceland's most ruggedly beautiful highlands; a dam project there has dominated Iceland's political debate. In summer the east has the country's sunniest and warmest weather—though precipitation is actually higher, and winters are colder.

The main transit hubs for the east are Egilsstaðir and Höfn. From September to May, buses from Reykjavík reach no further than Akureyri and Höfn, but bus routes still connect Egilsstaðir to other eastern towns.

For basic service listings, **www.east.is** is a good regional resource.

1 Höfn

Höfn (often used interchangeably with "Hornafjörður") simply means "harbor." Höfn is a busy fishing port, lying on a narrow neck of land within shallow, protected waters. The town has under 2,000 people, but that qualifies it for regional center of the southeast. For travelers Höfn is simply a stopover, or a base for trips to Vatnajökull, Lónsöræfi, and elsewhere in the area. Höfn gets a major share of Iceland's lobster catch, and has a Lobster Festival (*Humarhátíð*) the first weekend in July, with all sorts of family entertainment.

ESSENTIALS

GETTING THERE & AROUND

BY BUS   Þingvallaleið (℡ 511-2600; www.bustravel.is) connects Höfn to Reykjavík (8 hr.) and Egilsstaðir (3½ hr.). From June 1 through September 15, one bus travels daily between Reykjavík and Höfn in each direction, leaving both places at 8:30am. For the rest of the year, the bus runs four times per week. In June through August, the daily bus between Höfn and Egilsstaðir stops at Stafafell, Djúpivogur, Berunes, and Breiðdalsvík.

In June through August, **Vatnajökull Travel** (℡ 894-1616; www.vatnajokull.is) runs a daily bus from Höfn to Jöklasel (p. 316) and Jökulsárlón (p. 316) and back to Höfn, with sightseeing stops at both; the round-trip cost is 5,800kr ($93/£46) for adults (half price for children).

BY PLANE   Eagle Air (℡ 562-2640; www.eagleair.is) flies to Hornafjörður (Höfn) twice daily on Monday, Wednesday, Thursday, and Friday (once on Sun). The trip lasts roughly an hour and costs around 8,500kr ($136/£68). **Hornafjörður Airport** (℡ 487-1250), is a 10-minute drive northwest of town on Route 982, off the Ring Road. Taxis do not wait at the airport, but can be called at ℡ 865-4354. The fare into town is typically 2,000kr ($32/£16).

BY CAR   Car rental agencies at the airport are **National/Bílaleiga Akureyrar** (℡ 461-6000; www.holdur.is), **Avis** (℡ 478-1340; www.avis.is), and **Hertz** (℡ 522-4470; www.hertz.is).

VISITOR INFORMATION

The **Höfn information center** is at the **Glacier Exhibition (Jöklasýning)** (℡ 478-1500; www.ice-land.is; June–Aug daily 9am–9pm; May and Sept daily 1–6pm; Oct–Apr Mon–Fri 1–4pm) at Hafnarbraut 30.

WHAT TO SEE & DO

For glacier tours on Vatnajökull, see **Vatnajökull Tours from Jöklasel** (p. 316, chapter 9).

Pakkhúsið, Krosseyjarvegur, by the harbor (℡ 478-1540; free admission; June–Aug daily 1–6pm), is more of an arts-and-crafts store than a museum, but an unexceptional—and free—nautical exhibit is hosted downstairs.

Gamlabúð Folk Museum   This is not Iceland's best folk museum, but it's free and represents what you'll find elsewhere: carved spoons, old medicine vials, the national costume, taxidermy, and so on. Of particular interest are the ornamented bridles and saddles. Regular screenings of a 50-minute film from the 1960s are in Icelandic only, with demonstrations of traditional fishing and farming techniques.

Hafnarbraut (near campground). ℡ 478-1833. Free admission. Jul–Aug 10 daily 1–9pm; May 15–June and Aug 11–Sept 15 daily 1–6pm.

Glacier Exhibition (Jöklasýning)   This museum in the tourist information center strays from glaciology to a variety of scientific subjects. The presentation alternates between earnest education (in the form of encyclopedic photo-and-text panels) and pure titillation (in the form of videos of subglacial eruptions and a James Bond chase scene set in Jökulsárlón.) Specimen types on display are centuries-old chunks of ice from Vatnajökull and "glacial mice"—pebbles that blow around on the glacier, growing moss on every surface.

East Iceland

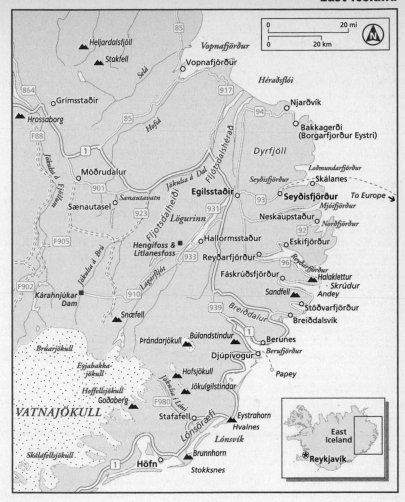

Hafnarbraut 30. ☎ 478-2665. www.ice-land.is. Admission 500kr ($8/£4) adults, 350kr ($5.60/£2.80) seniors; free for children age 11 and under. June–Aug daily 9am–9pm; May and Sept daily 1–6pm; Oct–Apr 1–4pm.

EXPLORING HÖFN

For a view of Vatnajökull Glacier, take a short stroll along the water on the northwest side of town, behind Hótel Höfn (below). For an **easy 2-hour walk** ⊛, head to the Ring Road, drive 16km (10 miles) east, turn right shortly after exiting the tunnel, and proceed 2km (1½ miles) beyond the farm buildings until the road ends. The walk south along the coast is uneventful for the first 30 minutes but eventually reaches a secluded and romantic expanse of sand, surf, and grassy tufts backed by steep mountains. Around the peak of Brunnhorn is another gorgeous beach.

WHERE TO STAY

For backup options, click the "information center" link at **www.ice-land.is**. For farm accommodations between Höfn and Skaftafell Park, see p. 317.

EXPENSIVE

Fosshótel Vatnajökull   Located 10km (6 miles) north of town, near the airport, this no-surprises three-star hotel is not as spiffy as the price would suggest, but has a friendly and helpful staff. Rooms are generally small but adequate, with spacious bathrooms. Some rooms and the dining room have great views of the glacier.

Route 1. © 478-2555. Fax 562-4001. www.fosshotel.is. 26 units. June–Aug 19,000kr ($304/£152) double. Rates around 30% lower May 15–May 31 and Sept 1–Sept 25. Rates include breakfast. AE, DC, MC, V. Closed Sept 26–May 14. **Amenities:** Restaurant; Internet terminal. *In room:* TV, hair dryer.

Hótel Höfn   A few minutes' walk from the town center, this modern hotel doesn't win any style awards, but the rooms are cheerfully decorated and spacious, and the staff and restaurant are professional. Make sure to ask for a glacier view.

Víkurbraut 24. © 478-1240. Fax 478-1996. www.hotelhofn.is. 68 units. June–Aug 17,500–21,100kr ($280–$338/ £140–£169) double; 29,900kr ($478/£232) family room. Rates around 36% lower May and Sept; around 42% lower Oct–Apr. Rates include breakfast. MC, V. **Amenities:** Restaurant. *In room:* TV, Wi-Fi, hair dryer.

MODERATE

Guesthouse Árnanes ✿   Six kilometers (3¾ miles) north of Höfn, this guesthouse spread over a main house and three cottages is a great place to sit on the porch and take in views of the surrounding mountains and Vatnajökull. Sleeping-bag accommodation is in the basement. Dinner, by reservation only, is recommended and reasonably priced.

Route 1. © 478-1550. Fax 478-1819. www.arnanes.is. 16 units, 9 w/bathroom. June–Aug 13,100kr ($210/£105) double w/bathroom; 10,100kr ($162/£82) double without bathroom; 14,900kr ($205/£104) triple without bathroom; 3,950kr ($63/£32) sleeping-bag accommodation. Rates around 15% lower May and Sept; around 25% lower Oct–Apr. Rates include breakfast. AE, DC, MC, V. **Amenities:** Restaurant. *In room:* No phone.

INEXPENSIVE

The **Hostel Höfn,** Hafnarbraut 8 (© **478-1736** or 864-2159; fax 478-1965; www. hostel.is; 10 units, 2 w/bathroom; 5,200kr [$83/£42] double; MC, V), is crowded and a little shabby, but the location is central, and guests have access to kitchen facilities plus a washer/dryer.

Guesthouse Hvammur   Right by the harbor—and sometimes prone to fishy odors—this guesthouse is all about basic rooms and practical facilities. The snazzy two-bedroom suite on the top floor goes for the same price as two doubles. Overflow is sent to their annex on Hvannabraut, on the north side of town.

Ránarslóð 30. © 478-1503. hvammur3@simnet.is. 20 units, none w/bathroom. May–Sept 8,100kr–8,800kr ($130–$141/£65–£70 double; 10,100kr–10,800kr ($162–$173/£91–£86) triple. Rates around 10% lower Oct–Apr. Breakfast available: 950kr ($62/£31). MC, V. **Amenities:** Guest kitchen; Internet terminal; washer/dryer access. *In room:* TV, Wi-Fi, no phone.

Náttaból ✿*Value*   If you're in a group of four to six, you'll find no better value than this mundane campground, with small cabins splayed inartistically about. Only three cabins have bathrooms, and none have showers; you have to use the campground facilities. The facility is on the main road into town, on your left—you can't miss it.

Hafnarbraut 52. © 478-1606. Fax 478-1607. www.simnet.is/camping. 16 units, 3 w/bathroom. May–Sept 6,800kr ($109/£54) cottage for 4–6 persons. Sheet rental 500kr. MC, V. Closed Oct–Apr. **Amenities:** Tour desk; Internet terminal; washer/dryer access. *In room:* Microwave, water heater, no phone.

Höfn

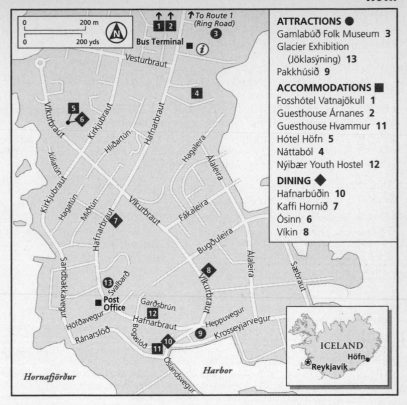

ATTRACTIONS ●
Gamlabúð Folk Museum **3**
Glacier Exhibition
(Jöklasýning) **13**
Pakkhúsið **9**

ACCOMMODATIONS ■
Fosshótel Vatnajökull **1**
Guesthouse Árnanes **2**
Guesthouse Hvammur **11**
Hótel Höfn **5**
Náttaból **4**
Nýibær Youth Hostel **12**

DINING ◆
Hafnarbúðin **10**
Kaffi Hornið **7**
Ósinn **6**
Víkin **8**

WHERE TO DINE

Hafnarbúðin, Ránarslóð 2 (© **478-1095;** main courses 270kr–800kr [$4–$13/ £2–£7]; MC, V; daily 9am–11pm; kitchen closes at 10pm), is an appealing hot-dog, burger, and fish-and-chips shack, right by the harbor, with a handful of tables and a drive-thru window.

Kaffi Hornið ⓡ CAFE   The ambience in this casual, log-cabin restaurant wins you over immediately. Burgers are above average, and the seafood specialties include the popular local lobster. In summer, make reservations as Hornið is often packed and the staff is overworked.

Hafnarbraut 42. © **478-2600.** Main courses 780kr–3,950kr ($12–$63/£6–£32). AE, DC, MC, V. May–Aug daily 10am–11:30pm; Sept–October 15 daily 10am–10pm; October 16–May Mon–Sat 10am–1pm.

Ósinn (Hótel Höfn) ⓡ ICELANDIC   This is Höfn's finest dining, though many visitors prefer Kaffi Hornið's charisma over Ósinn's neutral atmosphere. The menu includes beef, lamb, and duck, but devotes a whole page to Icelandic lobster. Avoid the lobster soup, which is too creamy and starchy. This wouldn't seem like the time to order pizza, but it's awfully good here.

Víkurbraut 24. © **478-1240.** Reservations recommended. Main courses 1,250kr–3,790kr ($20–$61/£10–£31). MC, V. May–Aug daily noon–10pm; Sept–Apr daily 6–9pm.

Víkin PIZZA   Víkin is a stark contrast to Kaffi Hornið—the charmless interior will not set your heart aflutter—but if locals want to hang out over beer and pizza, this is where they usually converge. Prices are reasonable, the food is decent, and the menu also includes soups, salads, burgers, and seafood.

Víkurbraut 2. © 487-2300. Main courses 670kr–3,900kr ($11–$62/£6–£31). MC, V. Sun–Thurs 11am–1am, Fri–Sat 11am–3am; kitchen closes at 10pm July–Aug, at 9pm Sept–May.

2 Lónsöræfi

The next bay east of Höfn—Lónsvík, or "Lagoon Bay"—is dominated by a large lagoon (Lón), fed by the Jökulsá í Lóni (Glacial River of the Lagoon). The mountainous interior region that feeds the Lón is called **Lónsöræfi** 𝕽𝕽𝕽, or "Lagoon Wilderness." This striking and varied landscape, now a 320 sq. km (124 sq. miles) private nature reserve, is easily one of Iceland's best hiking territories.

The best parts of Lónsöræfi are not developed. Glacial streams wind down steep valleys of subtle mineral spectra; yellow rhyolite rocks gleam from streambeds; and reindeer herds are occasionally seen grazing. Only one primitive road leads partly in, and accommodation is limited to basic mountain huts.

ESSENTIALS

GETTING THERE   Forty kilometers (25 miles) east of Höfn, the Ring Road crosses the main branch of the Jökulsá í Lóni River. Northeast of the river valley, just past the main bridge, a road branches off inland and leads a few kilometers into Lónsöræfi, past several summer houses. Some short hikes can kick off from here, but the best routes are accessed by mountain road F980, which meets the Ring Road on the southwest side of the river valley. Route F980 is 25km (16 miles) long and ends at Illikambur, a 1-hour hike from the Múlaskáli mountain hut. The route is technically passable in a 4WD vehicle with good clearance, but definitely not advised, because the river crossings are volatile and dangerous. From mid-June to early September this route is covered daily by **Ragnar** (© 864-4215) and his custom-built bus. From June through August, **Þingvallaleið** (© 511-2600; www.bustravel.is) runs a daily bus between Höfn and Egilsstaðir that stops at Stafafell.

VISITOR INFORMATION   The best source of information and advice is the **Stafafell Youth Hostel** (see below). Basic information can be found at **www.ust.is**; click "Protected Areas" and then "Lónsöræfi." From June to August a **warden** is stationed at Múlaskáli hut, where there is no phone reception. Currently the warden is Helga Davids (© 470-8030 or 822-4036; helgadavids@ust.is). The best **map** of Lónsöræfi is made by Mál og Menning, but a better, small-scale map is in the works.

WHERE TO STAY & DINE

The simple, friendly lodgings at the **Stafafell Youth Hostel** 𝕽 (© 478-1717 or 478-2217; www.eldhorn.is/stafafell; 16 units, 1 w/bathroom; June–Sept 15; 9,500kr [$152/£76] double w/bathroom; 7,000kr [$112/£56] double without bathroom; 2,200kr [$35/£18] sleeping-bag accommodation; rates 33% lower Sept 16–May; breakfast available for 900kr [$14/£7]; AE, DC, MC, V) are either in two-bedroom cottages with kitchens, bathrooms, and living rooms, or in the owner's restored 19th-century farmhouse, which is humble and down-to-earth. Follow Rte. 1 1km (.6 miles) east of the main bridge over Jökulsá í Lóni.

The youth hostel can serve breakfast and dinner on request; otherwise all food must be brought into the area. The nearest **markets** are in Höfn and Djúpivogur. Most of the mountain huts have kitchens.

EXPLORING THE AREA

HIKING   Stafafell Travel Service (© 478-1717 or 478-2217; www.eldhorn.is/stafafell), based at the Stafafell Youth Hostel (above), is the best resource for planning your hiking trip. They can book the F980 bus, arrange transport from Höfn, reserve mountain huts, discuss your route and preparations, sell you a map—and sometimes even arrange to have food sent in.

Útivist (© 562-1000; www.utivist.is), one of our favorite Icelandic tour companies, offers a 6-day guided hiking tour around Lónsöræfi once a year. Mysteriously no other companies offer multi-day guided tours; though, as anywhere in Iceland, you can always find a guide if you ask around.

Several interesting **day hikes** are directly accessible from Stafafell, without taking the bus up Route F980. One particularly nice route leads through Seldalur to **Hvannagilshnúta,** a gorge surrounded by rhyolite rockslides in streaked colors. However, the scenery in these lower reaches of Lónsöræfi pales in comparison to the interior regions.

It's possible to take the F980 bus in and out just for the day—this is even marketed as a "tour"—but you'd be cheating yourself. From mid-June to early September, the bus leaves Stafafell each day at 9am and reaches Illikambur, the end of the road, around 11am. Weather cancellations are rare. A round-trip fare is 5,000kr ($80/£40), or 6,000kr ($96/£48) if you're coming from Höfn. The bus returns from Illikambur at 2pm, reaching Stafafell at 4pm.

An ideal 2-night itinerary would comprise taking the bus to Illikambur, spending the first night at Múlaskáli hut, another night at Egilssel hut, and then walking the 5 to 6 hours back to Illikambur the following morning, in time for the 2pm bus departure. Three nights is even better, and with 4 nights you'd hardly run out of routes to explore: make sure to see the Tröllakrókar (Troll Spires). With another 2 days, you could skip the Illikambur bus and instead hike from Stafafell to Múlaskáli, overnighting at the hut situated halfway.

The Snæfell–Lónsöræfi Trek ☾☾

One of Iceland's better-known treks extends between Lónsöræfi and Snæfell (p. 336), a 1,833m (6,014-ft.) peak northeast of Vatnajökull. The hike takes at least 4 days, and can be extended to 7 days if the start or end point is Stafafell. Mountain huts are spaced along the route at intervals of no greater than 17km (11 miles). The trek's northern half is very different from Lónsöræfi, as it traverses the glacier Eyjabakkajökull and a more desolate, less mountainous landscape. This trek is for experienced outdoorspeople: hikes are fairly strenuous, trails are often poorly marked, and you may need rope, crampons, and an ice axe. The trek can head in either direction, but going from Snæfell to Lónsöræfi gives you a net loss of altitude and saves the most interesting scenery for last. The Stafafell Youth Hostel (p. 324) is your best travel resource; make sure to review trail conditions beforehand. Snæfell is reached via Egilsstaðir by car, so be prepared for a long one-way trip to reconnect with your belongings.

Remember to bring extra shoes for stream crossings; the flow comes mostly from the glacier and is very unpredictable. Keep a map handy as trails can be poorly marked. Also bear in mind that Lónsöræfi has one of the country's highest precipitation rates.

3 Lower Eastfjords: Djúpivogur to Fáskrúðsfjörður

Djúpivogur is at the tip of a peninsula 103km (64 miles) northeast of Höfn. Proceeding further northeast, three more villages lie in this southern third of the Eastfjords, each with its own fjord or bay: Breiðdalsvík, Stöðvarfjörður, and Fáskrúðsfjörður. Tourism slackens off east of Höfn, and, after Djúpivogur, the coast is bypassed by the direct route to Egilsstaðir and the north.

Anyone passing this way, however, should not skip the Eastfjords entirely. On a road trip from the south, the scenery enters yet another glorious phase. The Eastfjords are steeper and less convoluted than the Westfjords, and each fjord has a kind of singular grandeur.

While activities are limited, you can spend a day or two hiking, horseback riding, or sea angling, with perhaps a visit to Papey island or Petra's mineral museum.

ESSENTIALS

GETTING AROUND   Heading from Höfn toward Egilsstaðir, the Ring Road cuts inland at Breiðdalsvík, while coastal road Route 96 continues to Stöðvarfjörður and Fáskrúðsfjörður, then on through a 6km (3¾ miles) tunnel to Reyðarfjörður. However, the most direct route between Höfn and Egilsstaðir uses the Route 939 shortcut. Soon to be upgraded and incorporated into the Ring Road, Route 939 connects with it at the head of Berufjörður, northwest of Djúpivogur, and reconnects with it 43km (27 miles) south of Egilsstaðir. Though it is a rough gravel road, Route 939 is manageable, and the alternative stretch of the Ring Road is not entirely paved either. The Route 939 shortcut bypasses everything in this section except for Djúpivogur, which is also the gateway to Papey island. From Egilsstaðir, the fastest route to Fáskrúðsfjörður and Stöðvarfjörður is via Rtes. 92 and 96, past Reyðarfjörður.

From June through August, Þingvallaleið (© 511-2600; www.bustravel.is) runs a daily bus connecting Höfn and Egilsstaðir via Djúpivogur, Berunes, and Breiðdalsvík. From September through May, no buses connect Höfn and Egilsstaðir. From Egilsstaðir, however, Austfjarðaleid (© 477-1713; www.austfjardaleid.is) has buses year-round on weekdays to Breiðdalsvík, Stöðvarfjörður, and Fáskrúðsfjörður.

VISITOR INFORMATION   The **Djúpivogur information center** (© 478-8220; www.djupivogur.is; June–Aug daily 10am–6pm) is at the Langabúð museum by the harbor. **Breiðdalsvík's information center** (© 475-6660; Mon–Fri 8am–noon and 1–5pm) is at Ásvegur 32; the **Hótel Bláfell**, Sólvellir 14 (© 475-6670; www.blafell.is), is another good source. Tourist information for Stöðvarfjörður is handled at the **Fáskrúðsfjörður Ráðhús (City Hall)**, Hafnargata 2 (© 470-9000; www.fjardabyggd.is). This office also covers the area further north, including Eskifjörður, Reyðarfjörður, Neskaupstaðir, and Mjóifjorður.

EXPLORING THE AREA

HIKING   The trail **map** *Gönguleiðir á Suðurfjörðum Austfjarða*, the fourth in the *Gönguleiðir á Austurlandi* series, covers the coastal region from Berufjörður to Fáskrúðsfjörður, though trail descriptions are in Icelandic only. Two mountain climbs,

Sandfell and Halaklettur, are especially recommended for their breathtaking coastal scenery; don't leave the peaks before signing the guestbook.

Sandfell is a distinctive 743m (2,438 ft.) rhyolite mountain between Stöðvarfjörður and Fáskrúðsfjörður. The best approach is from the south side of Fáskrúðsfjörður. The trail leaves the coastal road between Víkurgerði and Vík farms and proceeds along the Víkurgerðisá river before cutting west for the peak. (On the map, the trail begins as #13 and becomes #14.) The scenery is excellent en route, with views of Fáskrúðsfjörður and Andey and Skrúður islands. Allow 5 hours round-trip.

The 573m (1,880-ft.) peak at the tip of the peninsula between Fáskrúðsfjörður and Reyðarfjörður is **Halaklettur.** Trail #7 starts at the north shore of Fáskrúðsfjörður, just east of the Kolfreyjustaður church. The ascent is less interesting than on Sandfell, but the superior view from the top takes in Fáskrúðsfjörður, Reyðarfjörður, the Vattarnes-tangi lighthouse, and Andey and Skrúður. Allow 4 hours round-trip.

DJÚPIVOGUR ☞

This small, charming fishing village dates from 1589, when merchants from Hamburg were licensed by the Danish king to trade here. After the Danish trade monopoly was imposed in 1602, Djúpivogur became the only commercial port in southeast Iceland. Today most visitors to Djúpivogur are primarily interested in tours to Papey Island.

Those who spend the night should know about the network of trails at the tip of the peninsula. It's a wonderfully peaceful area of shifting black sand dunes, active birdlife, and nice coastal views. For **sea angling,** contact **Papeyjarferðir** (✆ 478-8838; www.djupivogur.is/papey).

Langabúð By the harbor, this long red building, which dates back to 1790, houses the tourist information center, a cafe, and the local folk museum. One wing is devoted to sculptor Ríkarður Jónsson (1888–1977), whose wood carvings and busts display real talent and delicacy. The folk history exhibit in the loft is like a country antique store, with items such as old cash registers and typewriters, a butter churn, and a harmonium.

✆ 478-8220. www.rikardssafn.is. Admission 300kr ($4.80/£2.40) adults; 150kr ($2.40/£1.20) seniors and ages 11 and under. June–Aug daily 10am–6pm.

PAPEY ☞

Papey is not just another set of bird cliffs and a lighthouse; for centuries it was the only inhabited island off Iceland's east coast. Daily 4-hour tours with **Papeyjarferðir** (✆ 478-8838; www.djupivogur.is/papey; tickets 4,000kr [$64/£32] adults, 2,000kr [$32/£16] ages 6–12) leave Djúpivogur harbor every day from June through September 15.

Papey, a Celtic name, means "Friar's Island." Two 12th-century Icelandic sources affirm Irish monks founded a hermitage here, perhaps after being chased off the mainland by the Norse; but excavations have not yet discovered evidence of habitation predating the 10th century. Papey was quite independent of the mainland because of unstable dangerous tidal currents. Settlers lived a mostly self-sufficient life growing potatoes, tending sheep, and eating birds, bird eggs, fish, seals, and sharks. Later generations earned income by harvesting down feathers from eider-duck nests. Papey's population peaked in 1726, at 16. The last full-time resident was a man named Gisli, who bought the island in 1900, lived there 48 years, and lies buried there. The island still belongs to Gisli's family, and his granddaughter, now in her sixties, spends her summers there knitting and collecting eggs.

The best time to visit is June, when Papey is overrun with guillemots, though puffins and other birds stay through July and early August. The seas are often choppy, so ask about conditions before your departure and have seasick pills at the ready. The 1-hour boat trip passes close to a rock shelf frequented by sunbathing or frolicking seals. Before docking at Papey, the boat enters a cove surrounded by low cliffs with chattering birds nesting on every ledge. The tour allows 2 hours for strolling around the island and visiting **Iceland's oldest wooden church,** which dates from 1807.

BREIÐDALSVÍK & BREIÐDALUR

Breiðdalsvík is a traditional coastal town of around 200 people at the base of Breiðdalur (Broad Valley), a fertile enclave that attracts reindeer from the highlands in winter. The Ring Road cuts inland through Breiðdalur, and the surrounding mountains of sloping basalt strata are gorgeous at twilight. Breiðdalur is great for horseback riding, and its waterfalls attract ice climbers in winter. The best **horseback riding** outfit is **Hestaleiga** (© 475-6681), which can be booked through **Hótel Staðarborg** (© 475-6760; www. stadarborg.is). A 2-hour ride costs 2,000kr ($32/£16), and longer trips are possible. Beginners are welcome. Breiðdalsvík hosts an annual strongman competition called **Austfjarðatröllið (Eastfjords Troll)** during the second week of August.

STÖÐVARFJÖRÐUR

This sleepy town 18km (11 miles) from Breiðdalsvík is best-known for a great-grand-mother's rock collection (see below). **Galleri Snæros,** Fjarðarbraut 42 (© 475-8931; daily 2–6pm), is an arts-and-crafts gallery that exhibits and sells paintings, ceramics, jewelry, and textiles by regional artists. You can also arrange for a **cod-fishing trip** with the proprietor of Kirkjubær; see "Where to Stay," below.

Steinasafn Petru ⚐   This collection of rocks and minerals is magnificent, but what brings in 20,000 visitors a year is its personal story. Everything was gathered by Petra Sveinsdóttir, now in her mid-80s and living in a nursing home; the museum is in her house and garden. A gift shop sells rocks with googly eyes stuck on.

Sunnuhulið. © 475-8834. Admission 400kr ($6.40/£3.20) adults; free for ages 14 and under. Daily 9am–6pm; from Apr–Sept call ahead.

FÁSKRÚÐSFJÖRÐUR

Formerly known as Búðir, Fáskrúðsfjörður was settled by French-speaking sailors (mostly Belgian and Breton) in the 1800s as a fishing base for half the year. In the cod boom of 1880 to 1914, about 5,000 French and Belgian fishermen came to east Iceland each season. Cod fishing was one of the world's most dangerous professions; over 4,000 French-speaking fishermen alone died in Icelandic waters between 1825 and 1940. In Fáskrúðsfjörður, they introduced locals to cognac and chocolate, stole eggs and sheep, and built a local chapel and hospital. Street signs are in Icelandic and French, and a cemetery east of town along the shore holds the graves of 49 French and Belgian sailors. For 4 days in late July, Fáskrúðsfjörður celebrates its French heritage with the *Franskir Dagar* (French Days) family festival.

In 2005, a 6km (3¾-mile) tunnel opened up between Fáskrúðsfjörður and Reyðarfjörður, shortening the route by 34km (21 miles). Fáskrúðsfjörður became close enough to Reyðarfjörður's new aluminum smelter to share in its economic revitalization.

Einar Jónsson, Iceland's preeminent sculptor, designed the **Memorial to the Shipwreck of Dr. Charcot,** an intriguing tribute to arctic explorer Jean-Baptiste Charcot (1867–1936), shortly after Charcot's death in a shipwreck off the Icelandic coast. A guardian angel watches over a line of men, who ascend heavenward in a formation evoking a ship's prow. The sculpture is on Buðave, just east of the museum.

For **sea angling,** contact the Hotel Bjarg, below.

Fransmenn á Íslandi   This small museum effectively tells the story of French-speaking fishermen in Iceland, with annotated photos and a smattering of artifacts. If the guestbook is any indication, the exhibit is mostly of interest to the French.

Búðarvegur 8. © 475-1525. www.austurbyggd.is/fransmenn. Admission 480kr ($7.70/£3.85) adults; free for ages 14 and under. June–Aug 10am–5pm.

ANDEY & SKRÚÐUR ISLANDS

These two islands near Fáskrúðsfjörður beckon, yet are not covered by tours. Skrúður is especially intriguing, with a large puffin colony, 160m (525 feet) cliffs, and an enormous cave. Skruður's owner plans to reinstate tours; ask at the Hótel Bjarg (below).

WHERE TO STAY

The friendly, well-managed **Berunes Youth Hostel** 𝕒 (© **478-8988;** fax 478-8902; www.hostel.is for booking; 15 units, none w/bathroom; May–Sept; 4,700kr [$75/£38] double; breakfast available for 1,000kr [$16/£8]; AE, DC, MC, V; closed Oct–Apr) is along the Ring Road 25km (16 miles) south of Breiðdalsvík, with comfortable rooms and great views of Berufjörður, and access to a guest kitchen and washer/dryer. Berunes itself is a very dignified-looking settlement: the house, farm buildings, church, and accommodations all blend harmoniously. The church is always open, and guests are welcome to play the organ.

Guesthouse Café Margrét   Poised on a hillside overlooking the fjord, this log cabin guesthouse and restaurant—run by a German émigré—has four attractive rooms decorated with German antiques and Persian rugs; two rooms have balconies.

Rte. 96, just east of the Ring Road junction, Breiðdalsvík. © 475-6625. cafemargret@simnet.is. 4 units. June–Aug 9,400kr ($128/£65) double. Rates 15% lower Sept–May. Breakfast available: 1,200kr ($19/£9.50). AE, DC, MC, V. **Amenities:** Restaurant. *In room:* TV.

Hótel Bjarg *(Kids*   Guests are lulled to sleep by a tinkling stream that runs directly beneath the hotel. The smallish, recently renovated rooms come in assorted cheerful designs—you could have a painted fan depicting a palm beach over your bed. Kids will appreciate the game room with Ping-Pong, pool, foosball, and video games. Dinner is available on request.

Skólavegur 49, Fáskrúðsfjörður. © 475-1466. www.hotelbjarg.com. 8 units, 4 w/bathroom. 15,000kr ($240/£120) double; 13,000kr ($208/£104) double without bathroom; 25,000kr ($400/£200) suite. Rates around 15% lower in winter. Rates include breakfast. MC, V. **Amenities:** bar; hot tub. *In room:* Wi-Fi, no phone, rooms w/bathroom have fridge.

Hótel Bláfell   This timber hotel in the center of town has a nice fishing lodge feel, with a clientele composed largely of tour groups. The guest rooms are snug and welcoming, and the lounge with open fireplace is a perfect place to wind down.

Sólvellir 14, Breiðdalsvík. © 475-6770. Fax 475-6668. www.blafell.is. 22 units. June–Sept 15 13,200kr ($211/£106) double. Rates 40% lower Sept 16–May. Rates include breakfast in summer only. MC, V. **Amenities:** Restaurant; bar; sauna; solarium. *In room:* TV.

Hótel Framtíð   This cute harborside hotel has a new wing appended to a 1909 house. The new rooms are midsize, with a wood-cabin feel; the harbor-view rooms are booked out first. If you can do without a private bathroom, the rooms in the old house are appealing—especially #9—and far cheaper.

Vogaland 4, Djúpivogur. ⓒ 478-8887. Fax 478-8187. www.simnet.is/framtid. 46 units, 22 w/bathroom. June–Aug 14,000kr ($224/£112) double w/bathroom; 8,500kr ($136/£68) double without bathroom; 5,500kr ($88/£44) double sleeping-bag accommodation. Rates 25% lower Sept–May. AE, DC, MC, V. **Amenities:** Restaurants; bar; sauna; Wi-Fi in lobby. *In room:* TV, only en suite rooms have phones.

Hótel Staðarborg   Opened in 2000, this hotel in a former schoolhouse has comfortable if smallish and nondescript rooms. Guests tend to spend more time fishing, horseback riding, or playing pool in the lounge than relaxing in their rooms anyway.

Rte. 1, 7km (4⅓ miles) west of Breiðdalsvík. ⓒ 475-6760. Fax 475-6761. www.stadarborg.is. 30 units. May–Sept 11,600kr ($186/£93) double; 14,600kr ($234/£117) family room; 2,500kr ($40/£20) sleeping-bag accommodation. Rates 30% lower Jan–Apr. Rates include breakfast, except sleeping-bag accommodation. MC, V. Closed Oct–Dec. **Amenities:** Restaurant; bar; Jacuzzi. *In room:* TV, no phone.

Kirkjubær   This is Iceland's only public accommodation inside a former church. (Not every local was amused.) The church is quite small and dates from 1925. The altar and pulpit are intact, pews are arranged around a dining table, and a kitchen was installed under the loft, which sleeps 10 people rather intimately. The owner can arrange everything from fishing to skiing to goose hunting.

Fjarðarbraut 37a, Stöðvarfjörður. ⓒ 892-3319. www.simnet.is/birgiral. 1 unit. 2,000kr ($32/£16) sleeping-bag accommodation; 3,500kr ($45/£28) made up bed. No credit cards. **Amenities:** Guest kitchen. *In room:* No phone.

WHERE TO DINE

In Djúpivogur, the cafe at the **Langabúð** cultural center serves soup, sandwiches, and cake from 10am to 6pm daily, and **Við Voginn** at the gas station dishes up basic fish plates as well as the usual hot dogs and burgers until 9pm daily. All of your dining options are right by the harbor.

Serving Breiðdalsvík, **Hótel Bláfell** and **Hótel Staðarborg,** listed above, both have restaurants as good as or better than Café Margrét. Bláfell's restaurant is a bit more traditional. Reservations are recommended at both places. **Fast food** is on hand at the N1 gas station.

Fransmenn á Íslandi, above, has a simple cafe serving cakes and quiche in Fáskrúðsfjörður during opening hours. **Hotel Bjarg** serves set dinners on request for 3,000kr to 4,000kr ($48–$64/£24–£32) per person. The Shell station serves **fast food** daily until 9pm.

Berunes Youth Hostel 🍴 ICELANDIC   Youth hostels may not be associated with great home cooking or dining ambience, but this restaurant overlooking Berufjörður has both in abundance. A traditional Icelandic dinner is around 3,000kr ($48/£24), with a simple choice between fish and lamb. Make sure to call ahead.

Rte. 1, 25km (16 miles) south of Breiðdalsvík, in Berufjörður. ⓒ 478-8988 or 896-7227. AE, DC, MC, V. June to late Sept 8–10am and 6:30–10pm.

Brekkan FAST FOOD   This basic burger, soup, and sandwich stop is simply a stomach-filler to get you to your next destination. Stöðvarfjörður has no further options, except for groceries at the small market next door.

Fjarðarbraut 44, Stöðvarfjörður. ⓒ 475-8939. Main courses 300kr–950kr ($4.80–$15/£2.40–£7.60). MC, V. Mon–Fri 9:30am–10pm; Sat 10am–10pm; Sun 11am–9pm.

Café Margrét GERMAN   The decoration and fjord views outdo the food, but a pork schnitzel—or even a jellied pork chop or pickled pork knuckle—can be a nice change of pace. Beware the chicken schnitzel, which contains processed meat.

Rte. 96, just east of the Ring Road junction, Breiðdalsvík. (© **475-6625**. Reservations recommended. Main courses 1,200kr–2,300kr ($19–$37/£9.60–£18). AE, DC, MC, V. June–Aug daily 8am–11pm; Sept–May noon–9pm.

Café Sumarlína ICELANDIC This cafe-restaurant-bar with soccer on TV is clearly the place to be in the evening, with occasional performances by what Icelanders call "troubadours"—that is, singers with guitars, playing as if they were out camping. Crepes with ham, bacon, salad, onion, or rice are a variation on the usual fare, or just stick with the battered salt cod with potatoes and veggies.

Búðavegur 59 (Along Rte. 96, close to the harbor), Fáskrúðsfjörður. (© **475-1575**. Main courses 1,190kr–1,690kr ($19–$27)/£9.50–£14). AE, DC, MC, V. Sun–Thurs 10am–11pm; Fri–Sat 10am–3am.

Hótel Framtíð ✐ ICELANDIC The cooking and presentation are more refined than expected for a provincial hotel restaurant, and the dining room has a nice harbor view. You can't go wrong with the locally caught cod, haddock, and plaice.

Vogaland 4, on the harbor, Djúpivogur. (© **478-8887**. Reservations recommended. Main courses 1,500kr–4,000kr ($24–$64/£12–£32). AE, DC, MC, V. June–Aug noon–2pm and 6:30–9pm; Sept–May noon–1:30pm and 6:30–8:30pm.

4 Middle Eastfjords: Reyðarfjörður, Eskifjörður & Neskaupstaður

In Iceland, Reyðarfjörður is now inescapably associated with Alcoa, the world's largest aluminum company, which recently built a 2km-long (1¼-mile) smelting plant on the outskirts of town. The smelter, powered by new hydroelectric dams in the country's interior, remains a very contentious subject (p. 338). However short-sighted this project may turn out to be, Reyðarfjörður and its satellite towns are bustling with energy after years of economic stagnation and population decline. A housing boom is rushing to meet the needs of hundreds of foreign workers, and locals no longer have to drive to Egilsstaðir to go to the movies or a shopping arcade. Resident opinion runs strongly in favor of the smelter; and the needs of tourists, whose fjord views have been blighted with power lines, factory buildings, and ugly housing developments, were properly left out of the equation. The three towns are the largest in the Eastfjords, and each still has a range of attractions, dining, and accommodations; the latter can be found at **www.fjardabyggd.is**: Click "i" for information, then "Gisting."

ESSENTIALS

Route 92 connects Egilsstaðir to Reyðarfjörður, Eskifjörður, and Neskaupfjörður, a distance of 71km (44 miles). By bus, **Austfjarðaleið** (© **477-1713**; www.austfjardaleid.is) links all four towns (Mon–Sat year-round). **Regional tourist information** is in **Fáskrúðsfjörður's Ráðhús,** Hafnargata 2 (© **470-9000**; www.fjardabyggd.is). The tourist office in Egilsstaðir (p. 333) is also helpful.

EXPLORING THE AREA

Neskaupstaður, the easternmost town in Iceland, is more picturesque and remote than Reyðarfjörður and Eskifjörður, and its surrounding coastline is full of wonderful bird cliffs, sea caves, inlets, and pebble beaches. **Fjarðaferðir Ocean Adventure** (© **864-7410**; www.fjardaferdir.is) offers sightseeing and sea-angling tours, while **Kayakklúb-burinn Kaj** (© **863-9939**; www.123.is/kaj) leads kayak trips.

As with all the Eastfjords, peninsular hiking trails offer great coastal scenery. A good **hiking map** with trail descriptions in English is *Gönguleiðir á Fjarðaslóðum,* number II in the *Gönguleiðir á Austurlandi* series.

If you have a strong flashlight and pass near Eskifjörður, consider poking around **Helgustaðanáma,** an abandoned spar quarry. *Iceland spar,* a type of calcite that can be cut along different planes to make light prisms, has been used in everything from microscopes to machines studying the emission of light from atoms. The shaft is 80m-long (62 ft.), and the calcites shimmer in the light. (Taking anything is illegal.) To get there from Eskifjörður, take the gravel road east of town along the coast. After 9km (5½ miles), a sign for Helgustaðir, and a marked trailhead, park at the informational sign about the quarry and walk 10 minutes uphill.

Icelandic Wartime Museum (Íslenska Stríðsárasafnið)   Reyðarfjörður was a military base for the Allies in World War II, and this museum is housed next to (and inside) some of the original barracks. The museum has plenty of artifacts, but the best way to bring the era alive is to reminisce with the old Icelanders who work there.

Spítalakampi, Reyðarfjörður. ⓒ 470-9063. www.fjardabyggd.is. Admission 400kr adults ($6.40/£3.20); 300kr ($4.80/£2.40) ages 10–15; free for seniors. June–Aug daily 1–6pm.

5 Egilsstaðir

All roads in east Iceland fan out from Egilsstaðir, a service center for all the eastern towns. The regional airport is here, and ferry passengers from Europe pass through after docking at Seyðisfjörður. The town has expanded rapidly in the wake of the Kárahnjúkar hydroelectric project (p. 338). About 3,500 people live in greater Egilsstaðir, but most workers are here temporarily.

Egilsstaðir lies next to Lagarfljót (aka Lögurinn), Iceland's third-largest lake. Most services—supermarket, gas stations, bus depot, bank, camping, tourist info, shops—are clumped together off the Ring Road. The store for **outdoor equipment** is **Verslunin Skógar,** Dynskógar 4 (ⓒ **471-1230**), near Fosshótel Valaskjálf.

ESSENTIALS
GETTING THERE & AROUND

Egilsstaðir is on the Ring Road 1,246km (774 miles) northeast of Höfn and 265km (165 miles) southeast of Akureyri. For the quickest driving route from Höfn to Egilsstaðir, see p. 326. The distance from Egilsstaðir to Reykjavík is 653km (406 miles) by the northern route, or 696km (432 miles) by the southern route—though with the Route 939 shortcut, the difference is negligible.

BY BUS   Bus travel between Reykjavík and Egilsstaðir requires an overnight in Akureyri or Höfn, and costs more than flying unless you have a **bus passport** (p. 42). From June through August, **Trex** (ⓒ **587-6000;** www.trex.is) runs one bus daily between Akureyri and Egilsstaðir, and **Þingvallaleið** (ⓒ **511-2600;** www.bustravel.is) makes one run daily between Höfn and Egilsstaðir. From September through May, no buses connect Egilsstaðir to Akureyri or Höfn.

Austfjarðaleið (ⓒ **477-1713;** www.austfjardaleid.is) connects Egilsstaðir to the surrounding towns of Breiðdalsvík, Stöðvarfjörður, Fáskrúðsfjörður, Reyðarfjörður, Eskifjörður, and Neskaupstaður (identified as "Norðfjörður") year-round on weekdays. **Ferðaþjónusta Austurlands** (ⓒ **472-1515;** www.sfk.is/gamli/ferdamal/fas.htm) connects Egilsstaðir to Seyðisfjörður in summer (p. 340). **Jakob Sigurðsson** (ⓒ **472-9805** or 894-8305) takes passengers by van between Egilsstaðir and Borgarfjörður Eystri on weekdays (p. 346).

Egilsstaðir

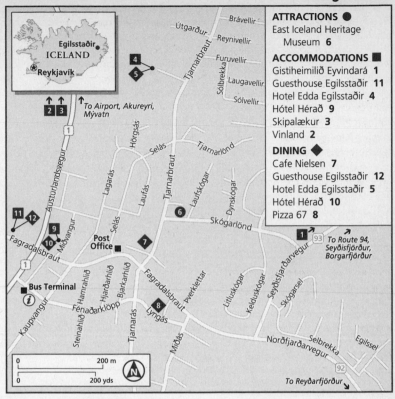

ATTRACTIONS ●
East Iceland Heritage
  Museum **6**

ACCOMMODATIONS ■
Gistiheimilið Eyvindará **1**
Guesthouse Egilsstaðir **11**
Hotel Edda Egilsstaðir **4**
Hótel Hérað **9**
Skipalækur **3**
Vinland **2**

DINING ◆
Cafe Nielsen **7**
Guesthouse Egilsstaðir **12**
Hotel Edda Egilsstaðir **5**
Hótel Hérað **10**
Pizza 67 **8**

BY PLANE Flights from Reykjavík are generally cheaper than bus tickets, and in good weather you get an aerial tour of Vatnajökull. **Air Iceland** (℃ 570-3030; www.airiceland.is) flies from Reykjavík to Egilsstaðir six times daily in each direction. Typical airfare is 10,000kr ($160/£80) one-way. **Taxis** are at the airport.

BY CAR Car rental agencies at the Egilsstaðir airport are **National/Bílaleiga Akureyrar** (℃ 461-6000; www.holdur.is), **Avis** (℃ 660-0623; www.avis.is), and **Hertz** (℃ 522-4450; www.hertz.is).

BY TAXI The two drivers to contact are Jón Björnsson (℃ 898-2625) and Jón Eiður (℃ 892-9247).

VISITOR INFORMATION

Egilsstaðir's excellent **tourist information center,** Kaupvangur 10, at the campsite (℃ 471-2320; www.east.is; June 15–Sept 15 daily 8am–10pm; Jan–May 15 Mon–Fri 9am–5pm; May 15–June 15 Mon–Fri 9am–6pm; Sept 15–Dec Mon–Fri 9am–6pm, Sat–Sun noon–4pm) serves all of east Iceland, and also offers Internet access.

WHERE TO STAY

If you require additional options, contact the information center (above) or check the complete list of accommodations at **www.east.is.**

EXPENSIVE

Hótel Hérað 🕏🕏   This three-star hotel in the Icelandair chain is at the center of a modern town with no real town center, so the setting and views are nothing to speak of. The rooms are up to business-class standards, however, and an excellent restaurant is downstairs. A huge expansion took place in 2004, but the new rooms are barely distinguishable from the old ones.

Miðvangur 5–7. © 471-1500. www.icehotels.is. 60 units. June–Sept 15 18,300kr ($293/£146) double. Rates around 25% lower Apr–May and Sept 16–Oct 31; around 40% lower Nov–Mar. Rates include breakfast. AE, DC, MC, V. Closed Dec 23–Jan 3. **Amenities:** Restaurant, bar; room service; same-day laundry/dry cleaning service. *In room:* TV, hair dryer.

MODERATE

Gistiheimilið Eyvindará   This cozy, unfussy establishment 2km (1¼ miles) outside of Egilsstaðir is in a beautiful wooded area overlooking Lagarfljót, and has a range of options: five guesthouse doubles without bathroom, one family room with bathroom, two cottages for two, one cottage for three, and one cottage for four. Some cottages only have bunk beds.

Rte. 94, 1km (½ mile) north of the Rte. 94/Rte. 93 junction. © 471-1200. Fax 471-2079. www.eyvindara.is. 10 units, 5 w/bathroom. 12,000kr ($192/£96) double; 10,000kr ($160/£80) double without bathroom; 12,000kr–15,000kr ($192–$240/£96–£120) cottages for 2 to 4 persons. Breakfast available (900kr/$14/£7.20). Rates discounted off season. MC, V. *In room:* No phone.

Guesthouse Egilsstaðir 🕏🕏   This country estate along the lake is close to town but takes no part in Egilsstaðir's modern drabness. In fact, the town took its name from this farm, not vice versa. Rooms are warmly and tastefully decorated with antiques, a rarity outside the capital. Doubles vary in size, and those looking out on the lake and tree grove are in high demand.

Rte. 932 (300m [984 ft.] west of Rte. 1/Rte. 92 intersection). © 471-1114. Fax 471-1266. www.egilsstadir.com. 18 units. May–Sept 14,000kr ($224/£112) double; 18,900kr ($302/£151) triple. 50% discount children 2–11. Rates around 28% lower Oct–Apr. Rates include breakfast. AE, MC, V. **Amenities:** Restaurant; bar; Internet terminal. *In room:* TV, coffee/tea, hair dryer.

Hótel Edda Egilsstaðir 🕏*Kids*   This hotel, like most in the Edda chain, utilizes student housing during summer vacation, and the rooms and hallways have a slightly depressing institutional feel. Some rooms have nice lake views. Parents can take advantage of the enormous split-level family rooms and Egilsstaðir's excellent geothermal swimming pool and sauna across the street.

Menntaskólinn (off Tjarnarbraut, across from pool). © 444-4880. Fax 471-2776. www.hoteledda.is. 52 units. June 2–Aug 19 11,900kr ($190/£95) double. AE, DC, MC, V. Closed Aug 20–June 1. **Amenities:** Restaurant; bar. *In room:* No phone.

Skipalækur   Located in Fellabær, 3km (2 miles) northwest of Egilsstaðir, this multi-faceted compound along the lake has camping, sleeping-bag accommodation, cottages with kitchens, and guesthouse rooms with and without bathrooms. The smaller cottage is ideal for parents with two kids. Sleeping-bag accommodation is in double rooms, so it's an especially good deal. Horseback riding and fishing permits are available.

Rte. 931, off the Ring Road, and across the bridge from Egilsstaðir. © 471-1324. Fax 471-2413. 20 units, 16 w/bathroom. 12,000kr ($192/£96) double; 8,400kr ($134/£67) double without bathroom; 8,000kr ($128/£64) cottage for 2–4 persons; 11,000kr ($176/£88) cottage for 5–6 persons; 2,200kr ($35/£18) per person sleeping-bag accommodation. Rates around 10% lower off season. Rates include breakfast, except sleeping-bag accommodation. MC, V. **Amenities:** Guest kitchen. *In room:* No phone.

Vinland ✿ Located across the bridge from Egilsstaðir in the satellite town of Fellabær, this new accommodation somehow makes a pre-fab, metal-sided block of six identical rooms feel endearing on the outside and pleasing within. The pastel-mod rooms are well appointed—with thoughtful extras like heated towel racks—and each has a private entrance.

Signposted off Rte. 1 in Fellabær. ⓒ 895-2079. www.vinland-gisting.net. 6 units. 12,600kr ($202/£101) double. Rates 29% lower Sept–May. *In room:* TV/DVD, Internet cable, fridge, coffee/tea.

WHERE TO DINE
EXPENSIVE

Cafe Nielsen ✿ ICELANDIC With three intimate dining rooms on two floors and arborescent seating outdoors, Nielsen has charming ambience even if the food doesn't quite keep pace. Many dishes over-rely on battering and deep frying, and not every entree is as exquisite as the reindeer in wild game sauce.

Tjarnarbraut 1. ⓒ 471-2626. Reservations recommended. Main courses 2,900kr–4,550kr ($46–$80/£18–£36). MC, V. Mon–Thurs 11:30am–11:30pm; Fri 11:30am–2am; Sat 1pm–2am; Sun 1–11:30pm.

Guesthouse Egilsstaðir ✿✿ ICELANDIC This summer-only restaurant's main competition is the Hótel Hérað (below); while Hérað has the narrow edge in food, many still prefer dining in a room enveloped by a shady grove. The stellar seafood combo appetizer, depending on the season, could include scallops with mango chutney, pan-fried garlic shrimp, and smoked salmon with guacamole. The beef tenderloin is raised on the premises; ours was overcooked, so err on the rare side.

Rte. 932 (300m [984 ft.] west of Rte. 1/Rte. 92 intersection). ⓒ 471-1114. www.egilsstadir.com. Reservations recommended. Main courses 2,290kr–3,990kr ($37–$64/£18–£32). AE, MC, V. Daily 6–9:30pm. Closed mid-Sept to mid-May.

Hótel Hérað ✿✿ ICELANDIC This is perhaps the only restaurant in east Iceland that meets Reykjavík's cooking standards. The menu is grouped into suggested three-course combinations at discounted prices. Items to watch for are the cured salmon appetizer and anything with vegetables, which are exquisitely attended to. The house specialty is reindeer steak in wild berry sauce: reindeer eat the same berries, and the sauce is said to draw out flavors inherent in the meat. The steak is seared for 30 seconds in brown butter and crystal sugar, then oven-roasted for 15 minutes.

Miðvangur 5-7. ⓒ 471-1500. Reservations recommended. Main courses 3,100kr–5,100kr ($50–$82/£25–£41), three-course menus 4,950kr–5,900kr ($79–$94/£40–£47). AE, DC, MC, V. Daily 11:30am–9pm.

MODERATE

Hótel Edda Egilsstaðir ICELANDIC The restaurant on the upper floor of this utilitarian domicile offers a decent a la carte dinner. Expect dependable lamb and fish dishes and prices a notch below the competition.

Menntaskólinn (off Tjarnarbraut, across from pool). ⓒ 444-4880. Main courses 1,800kr–3,400k. ($29–$54/£14–£27) AE, DC, MC, V. June 2–Aug 19 daily 6–9pm. Closed Aug 20–June 1.

INEXPENSIVE

Pizza 67 PIZZA This chain started in Reykjavík with a 1967 theme and spread across Iceland, then to the Faeroes, Denmark, and China. The pizza is hearty and satisfying if not spectacular, with thick crust and lots of gooey cheese. The "Rolling Stones" pizza is all meat. Other choices include salads, burgers, fish, and lasagna.

Lyngás 1 (across from the Shell station on Rte. 92, on the second floor). ⓒ 471-2424. Main courses 870kr–3,520kr ($14–$56/£6.95–£28). AE, DC, MC, V. Sun–Thurs 5–10pm; Fri–Sat 5–11pm.

WHAT TO SEE & DO

For activities around Lake Lagarfljót (aka Lögurinn), see below.

East Iceland Heritage Museum (Minjasafn Austurlands)   This above-average folk museum holds a diverse collection of local artifacts, including a restored turf farmhouse and a few pre-Christian relics. Information in English is limited, but the staff is usually eager to show visitors around. On summer weekends, the museum often holds spinning and weaving demos or offers horse-drawn carriage rides.

Laufskógar 1. (C) 471-1412. www.minjasafn.is. Admission 400kr ($6.40/£3.20) adults; 200kr ($3.20/£1.60) seniors and ages 11 and under; free admission Wed. June–Aug daily 11am–5pm, to 9pm Wed; Sept–May Mon–Fri 1–5pm.

---

6 Inland From Egilsstaðir: Lögurinn, Snæfell & Kárahnjúkar

Southwest of Egilsstaðir, the Lagarfljót River widens into a 38km-long (24-mile), narrow lake known as Lögurinn—or still Lagarfljót, as "fljót" implies a very wide river. A round-the-lake drive is a popular and agreeable day trip, though much of its appeal derives from forestation projects and social campground retreats, both of which usually attract Icelanders more than visitors. Locals are especially fond of their fall foliage, but New Englanders might just take a pass and head for the Eastfjords instead.

Roads from Lögurinn branch off into the interior highlands, where reindeer roam through ruggedly beautiful scenery. Serious hikers are lured by Snæfell, the tallest Icelandic mountain not underneath Vatnajökull. A paved road leads to Kárahnjúkar dam, part of a controversial hydroelectric project (p 338).

ESSENTIALS

GETTING THERE   No scheduled buses head in this direction. Route 931—which meets the Ring Road both 10km (6 miles) south of Egilsstaðir and 3km (1½ miles) north of Egilsstaðir—circumnavigates the lake, crossing a bridge near the southwest end. Route 933 branches off from Route 931 on both sides of that bridge, and forms its own loop via another bridge further southwest. Route 910 branches off from Route 933 (on the lake's northwest side) towards Snæfell, Kárahnjúkar, and elsewhere in the interior. Those headed directly from Egilsstaðir to Route 910 should take the north side of the lake for slightly less distance, or the south side for better roads.

VISITOR INFORMATION   This entire area is covered by the **Egilsstaðir tourist information office** (p. 333). For **Kárahnjúkar,** the **Végarður visitor center** ((C) 471-2044; www.karahnjukar.is; Apr 27–Oct 15 daily 9am–5pm) is not directly en route to the dam: It's on Route 933 *past* the Route 910 turnoff. **Ferðafélag Fljótsdalshéraðs** ((C) 863-5813; ferdafelag@egilsstadir.is), which runs the Snæfell mountain hut, is the best source of information for hiking in the highlands.

EXPLORING THE AREA

The following destinations follow a circular path around Lögurinn.

Hallormsstaðaskógur, located 24km (15 miles) from Egilsstaðir on Lagarfljót's southeastern shore, is Iceland's largest forest—a fact which never fails to draw sniggers from passing tourists. Iceland, which was substantially forested when settlers first arrived, currently leads the world in annual per capita planting of trees. Hallormsstaðaskógur has far more diversity than Iceland's original forests, with larch, red spruce, and other species added to native birch, rowan, and willow. A free **trail map** of Hallormsstaðaskógur is available at the Shell gas station along Route 931. A more formal **arboretum**—the best in Iceland for what it's worth—is on the lake side of the road, marked "Skógrækt Ríkisins/Trjásafn/Arboretum" on a brown wooden sign. A pleasant trail from the parking area leads to the lake.

Atlavík is a lakeshore campground that is extremely popular with Icelandic families and partiers. To reserve a campsite, call ✆ 471-1774 or 849-1461. It is also the departure point for evening cruises on the **Lagarfljótsormurinn** (✆ 471-2900; www. ormur.is). This 110-passenger ship, named for the Loch Ness–style sea monster dwelling in Lagarfljót, takes groups on lake cruises involving cookouts, fishing, or even live music (mid-June to Aug); call to see if an expedition is scheduled.

Gunnar Gunnarsson (1889–1975) wasn't much recognized in his native Iceland until late in his career, but from 1920 to 1946 he was Germany's second best-selling author, after Goethe. Gunnar was best-known for historical fiction—notably *The Black Cliffs (Svartfugl),* based on a double murder case in the Westfjords Along Route 933, 2km (1¼ miles) south of the Route 933/Route 910 junction, Gunnar's distinctive stone house, where he lived from 1935 to 1948, is now the **Gunnarstofnun cultural institute** (✆ 471-2990; www.skriduklaustur.is; admission 500kr [$8/£4] adults; 300kr [$4.80/£2.40] students; 250kr [$4/£2] seniors; free for children 15 and under; May 26–Aug 19 daily 10am–6pm; May 5–25 and Aug 20–Sep 16 daily noon–5pm), which includes a lovingly curated, permanent exhibit on the author (with some of his books for sale), temporary exhibits on local themes, an art gallery, and a first-rate cafe. Outside is an archeological excavation of **Skriðuklaustur,** an Augustinian monastery founded in 1500. Findings are exhibited inside, where bored children can make use of the kids room full of toys and art materials.

Located 3km (2 miles) southwest of Skriðuklaustur, the **Végarður Visitor Center** has free exhibits on the Kárahnjúkar hydroelectric project; see below for details.

A 90-minute round-trip hike with nice views over the lake leads along the Hengifossá river uphill for 2.5km (1½ miles) to two photogenic waterfalls: **Hengifoss** ⍟ **and Litlanesfoss** ⍟. The parking area is clearly marked from Route 933, between the junctions with Route 910 and 931. Hengifoss, at 118m (387 ft.), is Iceland's third highest waterfall and has a distinctive pattern of red clay stripes wedged between thick layers of black basalt. Unless the flow is especially strong, you can climb up to a cave behind the falls. Litlanesfoss, halfway along the trail, is no less beautiful, with fantastical formations of columnar basalt.

SNÆFELL, KÁRAHNJÚKAR & THE INTERIOR

From Lagarfljót, the newly paved Route 910 winds steeply up the hillside and finally levels off in **Fljótsdalsheiði** ⍟, a highland environment utterly distinct from the lake below. Chances are good you'll see a reindeer herd in this austerely beautiful landscape, dominated by rocky tundra, lakes, clumpy moss, lichen, and scrub. Compared to interior deserts such as Sprengisandur, it's positively lush. Route 910 reaches **Kárahnjúkar dam** within an hour's drive, passing close to the northern slopes of the imposing 1,833m (6,014-ft.) peak **Snæfell.**

The Kárahnjúkar project (p. 338) encompasses five dams, of which the Kárahnjúkar dam itself is the largest. Water is tunneled from the new reservoirs to a hydroelectric power station built into a mountainside substation on the northwest bank of the Jökulsá í Fljótsdal River, about 10km (6 miles) southwest of the Route 933/Route 910 junction.

Kárahnjúkar: Iceland's Most Divisive Buzzword

Among Iceland's natural resources, renewable energy—generated from geothermal heat and flowing water—is second only to fish. Aluminum smelting, which requires abundant energy and ready access to ports, seems the perfect fit.

Enter Kárahnjúkar—a $3-billion hydroelectric network of dams, reservoirs, water tunnels, generators, and 52km (32 miles) of monstrous power lines in the eastern interior highlands—all built to power a new aluminum plant at Reyðarfjörður in the Eastfjords. This mile-long behemoth is run by the American company Alcoa, the world's largest producer of aluminum products. Processed alumina powder is shipped in from as far away as Australia, and aluminum is produced in enormous vats cooked to 900°C (1,652°F).

Kárahnjúkar mobilized a worldwide protest campaign. In 2002 about one in six Icelanders petitioned against the project, but the parliament approved it by a large majority. Many foreign activists staged protest actions near the construction sites—a tactic which probably backfired. In 2006, stoppers were stuck in the drains, and huge swaths of tundra disappeared underwater.

Support for Kárahnjúkar runs high in the east, where sagging local economies have already been revitalized. Local fishermen were often idle after being outbid for fishing quotas. Iceland relies on dwindling fish stocks for most of its export income, and needs to diversify its economy. Kárahnjúkar's backers also stress that hydroelectric power is a "green" energy source: If aluminum plants were built elsewhere and powered by fossil fuels, they would produce 10 times the carbon emissions. Alcoa even has a relatively good environmental track record.

Kárahnjúkar's opponents, however, see no reason to sacrifice Iceland's pristine wilderness just to feed the world's energy gluttony and lower the cost of beer cans. On a per capita basis, Iceland is already one of the world's 10 richest countries. The overall unemployment rate is low, and most of Kárahnjúkar's new jobs have been filled by foreign workers. Kárahnjúkar has soaked up capital that could have been invested in more forward-looking sectors, such as universities, scientific research institutions, or software companies.

The dams have drastically altered the most intact and extensive glacier-to-sea ecosystem in Iceland. Some feeding grounds of reindeer and nesting grounds of pink-footed geese and other birds have already disappeared. Sand and clay have washed down from construction sites and devastated local fishing grounds. In the longer term, soil erosion could send storms of dust and sand onto farmland. The dams could prove vulnerable to volcanoes and earthquakes. Vatnajökull glacier, the source of the dammed rivers, is melting rapidly and reservoirs could eventually dry up.

Support for Kárahnjúkar among Icelanders has slipped, but remains high at around 64%. Support for similar, planned projects is waning, however, and in April, 2007, residents of Hafnarfjörður voted to reject a $1.2-billion smelter expansion by the Alcan corporation. When the next Kárahnjúkar comes along, the government will be more cautious.

The substation is currently inaccessible to visitors. To find out if tours of this high-tech wonder have been instituted, contact the **Végarður Visitor Center** (𝒞 471-2044; www.karahnjukar.is; Apr 27–Oct 15 daily 9am–5pm), located on Route 933, about 5km (3 miles) southwest of the Route 933/Route 910 junction. Végarður is run by the Icelandic power company Landsvirkjun, and the video presentation on Kárahnjúkar's engineering marvels is very effective PR. If the screening is in Icelandic, ask for the English version.

Visitors to **Kárahnjúkar** will probably be disappointed by how little there is to see. The paved road ends at a viewpoint overlooking Hálslón Reservoir, which is as large as Lögurinn (Lagarfljót), covering 57 sq. km (22 sq. miles). The more interesting and revealing viewpoint would look downstream from the dam, where the once-raging Dimmugljúfur Gorge has been reduced to a trickle. At press time, walking near the dam is forbidden, though **Tanni Travel** (𝒞 476-1399; www.tannitravel.is), based in the Eastfjords town of Eskifjörður, plans to start tours of Kárahnjúkar.

HIKING & CLIMBING   The *East Iceland Highlands* **map,** produced by Iceland's national power company Landsvirkjun, details several rewarding hiking routes in the Snæfell-Kárahnjúkar area, with trail descriptions and difficulty ratings. (The map is not available online, but you can contact Végarður Visitor Center, above, and ask them to send you one.) Few trails are pegged, however, and some hikes require experience and advance planning.

Route 910 passes within 12km (7½ miles) of the **Snæfell mountain hut** (𝒞 853-9098). A 4WD track leads all the way there, though you may encounter difficult river crossings. The hut is on Snæfell's western side, about 800m (2,625 ft.) above sea level, and sleeps 62, with a kitchen, tent sites, and showers. **Ferðafélag Fljótsdalshéraðs** (𝒞 863-5813; www.fljotsdalsherad.is/ferdafelag; ferdafelag@egilsstadir.is) operates the hut, leads occasional hiking tours, and is the best source for information on regional hiking. The website is in Icelandic only, though you might at least glean tour dates and destinations. **FA Travel,** Kaupvangur 6, Egilsstaðir (𝒞 471-2000; www.fatravel.is) leads less-demanding multi-day tours that include Snæfell and the eastern highlands.

Snæfell presides royally over its surroundings, and its spiky 1,833m (6014-ft.) snow-capped peak tempts many climbers. A pegged trail leads up the western slope to the summit, but the climb requires some experience and equipment (crampons at the very least). Consult with the hut warden beforehand, and allow at least 7 to 9 hours round-trip. Hikes around the periphery of Snæfell are also recommended, and the full circuit is 29km (18 miles); check the *East Iceland Highlands* **map** for details.

For the glorious multi-day trek from **Snæfell to Lónsöræfi,** see p. 325.

WHERE TO DINE

If driving around Lagarfljót, your best lunch option is the **cafe at Skriðuklaustur** 𝒢𝒢 (p. 337), which doesn't require museum admission. A fabulous, homemade, all-you-can-eat lunch buffet is served until 2pm, costing only 1,650kr ($26/£13) for adults, 850kr ($14/£7) for children 6 to 12. A cake buffet from 2pm to museum closing time costs 1,200kr ($19/£10) adults; 600kr ($10/£5) kids. In **Hallormsstaðaskógur,** the **Fosshótel Hallormsstaður** off Route 931 has a summer-only restaurant, and the **Shell gas station** has seating space and serves burgers, pizzas, and sandwiches. **Kárahnjúkar Dam** has a small cafe open from 11am to 8pm daily, but serves only drinks, candy, and packaged sandwiches. For **Snæfell,** all food must be brought in.

7 Seyðisfjörður

Icelandic villages nestled in fjords are likened to pearls in a shell, and none fit this description better than Seyðisfjörður ⚜⚜. The 17km-long (11-mile) fjord is lined with sheltering, snow-capped mountains and tumbling waterfalls. The dizzying descent into the fjord makes drivers feel like swooping gyrfalcons. The village, enlivened by colorful, Norwegian wood kit homes from the 19th and early-20th centuries, is a popular summer retreat for artists and musicians; the ferry from Europe arrives here weekly.

Seyðisfjörður is an ideal harbor, and became a trading center in the early-18th century. In the late-19th century it became a boom town, thanks to the herring trade, largely controlled by Norwegian merchants. In 1906, Seyðisfjörður was chosen as the entry point for Iceland's first undersea telegraph link to the outside world. During World War II Allied forces built a camp on the fjord, and a German air raid sank the *El Grillo* oil tanker, which still lies at the fjord bottom. Seyðisfjörður's economy still relies on fishing, and is prone to the same uncertainties faced by other Eastfjord villages. The fish factory went bankrupt in 2003 but is now back in operation.

ESSENTIALS

GETTING THERE

BY CAR   Seyðisfjörður is at the end of Route 93, only 26km (16 miles) from Egilsstaðir. From the Ring Road, take Route 92 through central Egilsstaðir, then turn left on Route 93.

Route 93 to Seyðisfjörður is often foggy, which could reduce your breathtakingly scenic drive to a blind, harrowing crawl. **Viewing conditions** can be checked on three live webcams run by the Icelandic Road Administration; visit www.nat.is, click "travel guide," navigate to Seyðisfjörður, and click "Web Camera Fjarðarheidi."

About 7km (4⅓ miles) before reaching Seyðisfjörður, a gravel road branches off to the left. This road enabled construction crews to build avalanche barricades, which can be seen from Route 93 further downhill. In 1885, Seyðisfjörður suffered the most deadly avalanche in Icelandic history. Twenty-four people were killed, many more were injured, and several houses were knocked right into the fjord. In 1996 another avalanche leveled a factory, but no one died. A **memorial sculpture** made from the factory's twisted girders stands near the town center, at the intersection of Ránargata and Fjarðargata.

BY BUS   From June through August, **Ferðaþjónusta Austurlands** (☏ 472-1515; www.sfk.is/gamli/ferdamal/fas.htm) connects Seyðisfjörður and Egilsstaðir with three **buses** daily on weekdays, and one bus on Sunday. From June 29 to August 8, they add a Saturday bus and a second Sunday bus. Tickets are 800kr ($13/£6) for adults, 500kr ($8/£4) for seniors, and 400kr ($6/£3) for children.

BY FERRY   In summer, the **Norröna car and passenger ferry** (p. 22) arrives from Europe on Thursday mornings, departing later the same day.

VISITOR INFORMATION

The **tourist information center** (☏ 472-1551; www.sfk.is; mid-May to mid-Sept Mon–Fri 8am–5pm, July–Aug also Sat 1–3pm) is inside the ferry terminal building by the harbor. From mid-September to mid-May, if the ferry is running, the information center should be open on arrival days and possibly the day before. The staff sells bus passes and can help book accommodations.

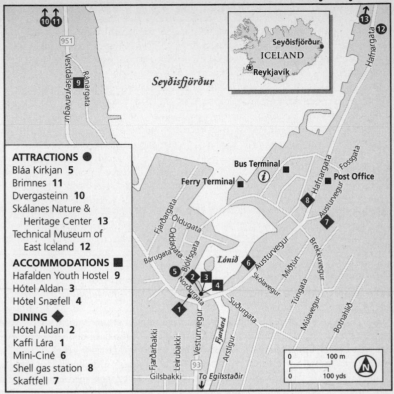

ATTRACTIONS ●
Bláa Kirkjan **5**
Brimnes **11**
Dvergasteinn **10**
Skálanes Nature &
    Heritage Center **13**
Technical Museum of
    East Iceland **12**

ACCOMMODATIONS ■
Hafalden Youth Hostel **9**
Hótel Aldan **3**
Hótel Snæfell **4**

DINING ◆
Hótel Aldan **2**
Kaffi Lára **1**
Mini-Ciné **6**
Shell gas station **8**
Skaftfell **7**

WHAT TO SEE & DO

Among Iceland's smaller towns, Seyðisfjörður has perhaps the best concentration of **historic buildings and homes.** Most compelling are the chalet-style houses inspired by German and Swiss models, and clustered along Bjólfsgata and Norðurgata streets. Well-off merchants imported these houses from Norway—assembly required— roughly between 1890 and 1910. The free brochure *Historic Seyðisfjörður,* which can be found all over town, provides an in-depth history and walking tour of the architectural highlights.

Despite Seyðisfjörður's reputation as a magnet for Iceland's artsy community, the population is under 800, and visitors should not expect to find streets bristling with shops and galleries. Things do liven up the nights before and after the ferry arrival, however. It's also a good idea to check with the information center for **special events.** The various cultural festivities known as **Á seyði** are concentrated in early June but extend through July. The less-known **LungA festival** (*©* **861-5859;** www.lunga.is), in the third week of July, invites young people aged 16 to 25 to join workshops led by artists specializing in everything from visual art to circus performance to fashion design. Non-Icelanders are welcome, and the week culminates with live concerts by prominent Icelandic bands. Classical concerts are presented in **Bláa Kirkjan** (*©* **472-1775**), a blue-painted church in the center of town, on six consecutive Wednesdays in

June and July at 8:30pm. Tickets cost 1,500kr ($24/£12) and go on sale half an hour before the performance.

Besides the **Skaftfell restaurant and cultural center** (listed below in "Where to Dine"), Seyðisfjörður has not had consistent art gallery locations. Exhibitions have been held at **Skálinn,** an old gas station on Bjólfsgata near the church, but the building's future status is unclear.

From mid-May to mid-September, a **crafts market (handverkmarkaður)** is held on Austurvegur at Brekkuvegur from 2 to 4pm weekdays, though it could return to Wednesday and Thursday only; call ⓒ 866-7859 or contact the tourist office for an update. The tax-free shop **Ósk,** Norðurgata 8 (ⓒ 472-1208; Mon–Wed and Fri 2–6pm, Thurs 9am–6pm), sells souvenirs, woolens, and local handicrafts.

Technical Museum of East Iceland (Tækniminjasafn Austurlands) 🔎 Seyðisfjörður was quite the cradle of modern technology, with Iceland's first telegraph station (1906), the first machine shop to run on hydroelectricity (1907), and the first modern electric power station (1913). This museum encompasses the original telegraph station and the machine shop, which has original belt-driven metalworking machines, turbines, a foundry furnace, and a blacksmith's forge. Upstairs from the machine shop is an exhibit recounting Seyðisfjörður's technical triumphs and an old telephone switchboard to play with.

The highlight here is the telegraph station, located 100m (328 ft.) from the machine shop inside a blue-grey house, which was bought from a rich Norwegian merchant in 1905. That same year, a telegraph cable was laid under the ocean to the Faeroe Islands, and then on to Scotland and the rest of Europe. In the summer of 1906, a crew of over 300 Icelanders and Norwegians planted 14,000 telegraph poles in a 614-km (382-mile) course from Seyðisfjörður to Reykjavík.

The devoted staff maintains the original telegraph equipment, which must be seen in action to be truly appreciated. Ask them to demonstrate the transmission of Morse code onto hole-punched rolls of paper, using a machine powered by a spring and hand crank. A customized typewriter then converts the paper to words.

Hafnargata 44. ⓒ 472-1596. www.tekmus.is. Admission 500kr ($8/£4) adults; free for seniors and ages 18 and under. Free admission Fri. June–Sept 15 daily 11am–5pm; Sept 16–May Mon–Fri 1–4pm.

TOURS & ACTIVITIES

From June through September, Hótel Aldan (ⓒ 472-1277; www.hotelaldan.com) leads a 2-hour **cultural walking tour** for 1,000kr ($16/£8).

Local sailor **Hlynur Oddsson** (ⓒ 865-3741; www.iceland-tour.com) offers individually tailored **fishing, cycling, kayaking,** and **sailing tours.** Fishing trips generally pursue cod, haddock, and coalfish. Mountain-bike rental starts at 1,500kr ($24/£12) for a half-day. Guided kayak tours range from 1 hour in the harbor at 1,500kr ($24/£12) to 2-day excursions to Skálanes and back for 17,000kr ($272/£136).

For **bird-watching tours** of Skálanes, 19km (12 miles) from Seyðisfjörður, see below.

VENTURING FROM SEYÐISFJÖRÐUR

The lonely, pristine, and beautiful fjords north and south of Seyðisfjörður make for wonderful adventures off the beaten path. The best **topographical hiking map** of this entire region, including Borgarfjörður Eystri to the north, is titled *Víknaslóðir: Trails of the Deserted Inlets.* To buy this map in advance of your trip, contact Helgi at ⓒ 894-1012 or helgima@mi.is.

A Day Hike in Seyðisfjörður 𝕮𝕮

The 5- to 6-hour hiking route from **Stafdalur to Vestdalur** 𝕮𝕮 is a spectacular traverse through peaceful upland heath, past the mountain-sided lake Vestdalsvatn, and down into Seyðisfjörður along the cascading Vestdalsá River. Other than the steep downhill stretch at the end, the trail isn't too difficult or strenuous. It's a one-way route, and you'll need to arrange transport at either end. Any clear day from late June to early September is suitable, though late June and early July have the best show of wildflowers. The trail is poorly staked, so bring a topographical map. Early in the season, ask about snow conditions and bring sunglasses to protect your eyes from glare.

The trail begins from a ski lift along Route 93, about 8km (5 miles) outside of Seyðisfjörður. The turnoff is indicated by a large sign with the Shell Oil logo and the words "VELKOMIN Á SKÍÐASVÆÐIÐ Í STAFDAL" The trail is marked with yellow-tipped stakes and leads north, away from Route 93, with Stafdalsfell mountain on the left and the boggy Stafdalsá River Valley on the right. In the pass between Stafdalsfell and Bjólfur peaks, the trail crosses the Stafdalsá. At this point you are about halfway to Vestdalsvatn Lake. Make sure to round the lake clockwise; another yellow-staked trail takes the near side of the lake and will lead you astray. At the northeast corner of Vestdalsvatn, you can sign the guestbook in the Vatnsklettur shed. From there it's all downhill, due east, along the Vestdalur Valley, with waterfalls and fabulous fjord views the whole way. Upon reaching the Vestdalsá River, the trail divides and proceeds down both banks; the southern (right-hand) trail is a little easier. Both trails end up on the coastal road, 2km (1¼ miles) north of the village center.

The reverse route uphill from Seyðisfjörður through Vestdalur to Vestdalsvatn, then back the same way, does not require one-way transport and is almost as rewarding. Allow 5 hours round-trip, or six if you start from the village center.

A road leads along the **north shore** of Seyðisfjörður, reaching halfway to the tip of peninsula. Close to the water, about 6km (3¾ miles) from the village and 5 minutes' walk from the road, is **Dvergasteinn** (Dwarf's Rock), a 3m-high (10-ft.) rock that looks like a petrified cross-section of pock-marked foam. At the end of the road, a 4WD track extends another 5.5km (3½ miles) to **Brimnes,** an abandoned farm with a lighthouse, and a good destination for a coastal walk. Campers should definitely consider the hike overland to **Loðmundarfjörður,** which once had several farms but was abandoned in 1973. Loðmundarfjörður is 8 hours' walk from the village, or 6 hours from further up the coastal road. For more information on Loðmundarfjörður and other deserted inlets to the north, see Borgarfjörður Eystri (p. 345). Another wonderful trek leads from the southern shore of Seyðisfjörður overland to **Mjóifjörður**—yet another incredible find for connoisseurs of obscure fjords. Mjóifjörður is particularly long, steep, and narrow, with a beautiful series of waterfalls at its base, abundant crowberries in August, and about 35 inhabitants. **Brekka** (see "Where to

Stay," below) lies right where the trail meets the fjord, and a gravel road (Rte. 953) leads back to Egilsstaðir.

The isolated **Skálanes Nature and Heritage Center** 🅰 (✆ **690-6966** or 861-7008; www.skalanes.com; May–Sept 15), 19km (12 miles) from the village on Seyðisfjörður's south shore, is a great day trip or overnight from Seyðisfjörður, especially for bird-watchers. Skálanes provides very basic, shared accommodation for up to 16 people and leads guided tours of the area, including high cliffs and a beach popular with seals. The lodging lacks privacy, but has made-up beds and showers and serves three meals a day—largely fish, birds, and eggs harvested by the staff. Meals are by reservation only, but traditional Icelandic soup is usually on hand for drop-ins. Regular cars can reach within 6km (3¾ miles) of Skálanes, and 4WD vehicles go all the way. Transportation can be arranged from as far as Seyðisfjörður; other options include biking or kayaking with the help of Hlynur Oddsson (p. 342). The **Hótel Aldan** (below) can also put together a Skálanes package for you.

WHERE TO STAY IN SEYÐISFJÖRÐUR

The ferry from Europe arrives on Thursdays, so it's near impossible to find a room for Wednesday or Thursday nights in summer without booking far in advance. Early June is also difficult, because of the *Á seyði* festival. Many arriving passengers move on to Egilsstaðir, which has more choices and is only 26km (16 miles) away. At press time, a new guesthouse in Seyðisfjörður was under construction; check with the tourist information office, which can help book accommodations anywhere in the region.

The friendly, offbeat **Hafalden Youth Hostel,** Ránargata 9 (✆ **472-1410** or 891-7010; fax 472-1610; www.simnet.is/hafaldan; 7 units, none w/bathroom; 5,600kr [$90/£45] double; 2,400kr [$38/£19] sleeping-bag accommodation in 4-person room; 750kr [$12/£6] sheet rental; MC, V; closed Oct 16–Apr 14) has straightforward bunk-bed rooms, Wi-Fi, and access to a guest kitchen, Internet terminal, and washer/dryer. The common room, with large windows overlooking the fjord, is a perfect spot for writing postcards.

In Mjóifjörður, **Brekka** (✆ **476-0007;** mjoi@simnet.is) offers a few bedrooms, with a guest kitchen, plus two cottages with small private kitchens for 6,800kr ($109/£54) double; 5,200kr ($83/£42) sleeping-bag accommodation; 8,000kr ($128/£64) cottage. A basic **cafe** (11am–5pm daily July 1–Aug 15) serves sandwiches and cakes.

Hótel Aldan 🅰🅰 With its deft arrangements of hand-crafted bedspreads, embroidered rugs, real and fake antiques, this former bank building has the classiest interior decoration of any hotel in east Iceland. The rooms offer no views to choose from, but speak up if you like bathtubs. Iceland's president and his wife stay in one of the top-floor corner triples, where the extra single bed is tucked inside a cute alcove. The entire summer books up well in advance.

Oddagata 6 (reception in the Hótel Aldan restaurant, at Norðurgata 2). ✆ 472-1277. Fax 472-1677. www.hotel aldan.com. 9 units. June–Aug 17,300kr ($277/£138) double; 20,300 ($325/£162) triple/suite. Rates around 13% lower May and Sept; around 27% lower Oct–Apr. Rates include breakfast. MC, V. **Amenities:** Laundry/dry cleaning service for stays of 3 nights or more. *In room:* TV/DVD, Wi-Fi, minibar, hair dryer, no phone.

Hótel Snæfell 🅰 Snæfell is under the same ownership as Hótel Aldan (above), and is basically a simpler and humbler but no less homey version. The two cheaper doubles are very small and—unlike most of the regular doubles—have no fjord view.

Austurvegur 3 (reception in the Hótel Aldan restaurant, at Norðurgata 2). ✆ 472-1277. Fax 472-1677. www.hotel aldan.com. 9 units. June–Aug. 12,800kr–14,800kr ($205–$237/£102–£118) double, 16,800kr ($269/£134) triple.

Rates around 15% lower May–Sept; around 21% lower Oct and Apr. Rates include breakfast. MC, V. Closed approximately mid-Oct to Apr. **Amenities:** Laundry/dry cleaning service for stays of 3 nights or more. *In room:* TV/DVD, hair dryer, no phone.

WHERE TO DINE IN SEYÐISFJÖRÐUR

The **Shell gas station,** Hafnargata 2 (© **472-1700;** daily noon–9pm), serves fish soup or even a main course as well as hot dogs. The **Mini-Ciné** movie theater, listed below, is a funky, casual cafe from 11am to 9pm in summer, serving tea, coffee, smoothies, cakes, and small vegetarian plates.

Brekka (see "Where to Stay," above) serves snacks in its simple eatery in Mjóifjörýur.

Hótel Aldan ☆ ICELANDIC/MEDITERRANEAN   The cooking may be a bit orthodox and unsurprising, but the Aldan compensates with super-fresh, organic ingredients and recipes that ease up on the cream and butter without compromising flavor. The herbal marinated salmon appetizer is perfection. Good main courses include the grilled catfish, roasted lamb prime, and—for nearly twice the money— roasted reindeer with shitake mushroom, forest berries, and wild game sauce. Ask for a table in the small room overlooking the harbor.

Norðurgata 2. © 472-1277. Reservations required. Main courses 2,700kr–5,200kr ($43–$83/£22–£42). MC, V. May–Sept 15 daily 7:30–10am, noon–2pm, and 7:30–9pm. Closed Sept 16–Apr.

Skaftfell ☆☆ CAFE/BISTRO   With its cement floors, homemade benches, and art exhibits lining the walls, Skaftell looks more like a wine-and-quiche gallery cafe than the fine restaurant it recently became. The chefs worked at Hótel Aldan (above) before establishing themselves here with a more focused and creative menu. Small courses include the delicious roast beef and potato salad with horseradish cream, radicchio, and apple. The steamed cod is understated and superb. Free Wi-Fi, an Internet terminal, perusable art books, and a table with paper and colored pencils complete the scene.

Austurvegur 42. © 472-1632. Reservations recommended Wed–Thurs in summer. Main courses 2,100kr–3,300kr ($34–$53/£17–£26); pizzas 800kr–1,600kr ($13–$26/£6.40–£13). MC, V. June–Aug Sun–Mon and Thurs noon–11pm; Tues–Wed 10am–11pm; Fri–Sat noon–2am. Sept–May call ahead to see if open.

8 Borgarfjörður Eystri

Borgarfjörður Eystri ☆☆☆ is one of Iceland's supreme hiking areas, but recognition has been slow in coming. Road access is bumpy and limited; some of the best trails are free of snow for only 2 months, from early July to early September; and the scenery lacks immediate, overwhelming visual impact. It's the second-biggest rhyolite area in Iceland, with mountainsides draped in silky swaths of mineral color, but can't compete with Landmannalaugar. The fjords, inlets, and coastline are lovely but cannot match the majestic grandeur of Seyðisfjörður or the staggering cliffs of Hornstrandir. The flowering plants may be the most beautiful and diverse in all of Iceland, yet the vegetation does not overtake the senses as it does in Þórsmörk. Put all of its assets together, however, and the comparisons fade away. Most hikers here are Icelanders, ahead of the tourist curve.

Borgarfjörður Eystri means "East Borgarfjörður," to distinguish it from Borgarfjörður in the west. The main village in the area, Bakkagerði, is in the fjord Borgarfjörður, and is sometimes itself referred to as Borgarfjörður. Borgarfjörður Eystri can refer to the village, the fjord, the village and the fjord, or the entire municipality, north to Njarðvík and south to Loðmundarfjörður.

Getting the best of Borgarfjörður Eystri requires venturing far from the village of Bakkagerði and ideally spending two or more nights by the abandoned inlets of Breiðavík and Húsavík, which have mountain huts with Jeep access. Trails are well-marked and signposted, and organized tours of the area are excellent.

ESSENTIALS

GETTING THERE   Bakkagerði is 71km (44 miles) from Egilsstaðir. From the Ring Road, take Route 92 through Egilsstaðir, turn left on Route 93, and turn left again 1km (½ mile) later on Route 94, which goes all the way to Bakkagerði. Transportation between Egilsstaðir and Bakkagerði is available in the postal van with **Jakob Sigurðsson** (© 472-9805 or 894-8305; hlid@centrum.is). Tickets are 1,500kr ($24/£12) adults, 1,000kr ($16/£8) seniors, and 500kr ($8/£4) for children 12 and under. Departures are on weekdays only, leaving Bakkagerði at 8am and the Egilsstaðir tourist information office at noon.

VISITOR INFORMATION   Egilsstaðir's tourist information office (p. 333) covers this area and is a good place to buy a map. In Bakkagerði, limited tourist information is available at **Álfasteinn** (p. 347) and the community center **Fjarðarborg** (© 472-9920; bergrunj@mi.is; June–Aug daily 11am–8pm), both of which should stock maps. The best website is **www.borgarfjordureystri.is**. The essential map *Víknaslóðir: Trails of the Deserted Inlets,* with trail descriptions in English, was designed by the guide Helgi Arngrímsson (© 894-1012; helgima@mi.is); contact him to buy the map in advance of your trip.

ORGANIZED & SELF-GUIDED TOURS

You can arrange camping or lodging at the two mountain huts independently, but guided tours have definite advantages. Tour companies have Jeep access all the way south to Loðmundarfjörður and can transport baggage and food. Guides are also well-versed in local history, geology, flora, and fauna, and can lead you to that unique milky waterfall, rare wildflower, or elf church off the main trail routes.

Ferðafélag Fljótsdalshéraðs (© 863-5813; www.fljotsdalsherad.is/ferdafelag; ferdafelag@egilsstadir.is) operates the mountain huts at Breiðavík and Húsavík and occasionally leads tours in the area. The website is Icelandic only but you should be able to glean tour dates.

FA Travel (Ferðaskrifstofa Austurlands), Kaupvangur 6, Egilsstaðir (© 471-2000; www.fatravel.is), offers tours of Borgarfjörður under the unfortunate heading "Walking with Elves." Costs are around 39,375kr ($630/£315) for 3-day tours and 87,500kr ($1400/£700) for 7-day tours, including full board, transportation from Egilsstaðir, luggage transport, and guide. For about 15% more they'll provide bedding and a private room when possible. Seven-day **horseback riding** tours starting at 121,625kr ($1946/£973) bring an entire herd along, so participants can ride two or three horses each day.

Helgi Arngrímsson (© 894-1012; helgima@mi.is), who lives in Bakkagerði, leads customized trips and knows everything about the area. He can also organize **self-guided tours** with food and supplies delivered to the huts. 4WD delivery services are also offered by Fjarðarborg and Guesthouse Borg; see "Where to Stay," below. You can drive these routes yourself in a rugged 4WD vehicle with good clearance.

EXPLORING THE AREA

Route 94 traverses Fljótsdalshérað valley before entering Borgarfjörður Eystri through a dramatic mountain pass. From Fljótsdalshérað, **Mt. Dyrfjöll**—distinctively notched, like the blunt end of a razorblade—is visible on the right. After the mountain pass, the road descends steeply into **Njarðvík,** a tiny settlement northwest of Bakkagerði. Near the bottom of the descent, on the right-hand side of the road, look for a sign for **Innra-Hvannagil** 𝕮, a narrow rhyolite gorge. A 5-minute trail leads from the parking area into the gorge, which has colorful banks of rock shards, a vertical surface of intricately patterned stone, and a stream running over slabs of gleaming yellow rhyolite. Walking further into the gorge is impossible.

After Njarðvík, the road follows a sinuous, knuckle-whitening coastal route along the **Njarðvíkurskriður** (Njarðvík Screes), steep banks of loose rock at the base of the cliffs and mountains. On the ocean side is the **Naddakross,** a wooden cross with the Latin inscription *Effigem Christi qui transit pronus honora. Anno 1306* ("You who pass the sign of Christ, bow your head in reverence. Year 1306"). This marks the legendary spot where, in 1306, a brave farmer named Jón Árnason killed a half-human, cave-dwelling monster named Naddi by wrestling him into the ocean. Naddi had been gnawing loudly on rocks and terrorizing anyone crossing the screes after nightfall. The present cross dates from the 1950s, but is apparently planted on the original site.

BAKKAGERÐI 𝕮 (BORGARFJÖRÐUR)

Njarðvík and Bakkagerði are the only inhabited parts of Borgarfjörður Eystri, with a total population of around 145. Borgarfjörður has a nice seaweedy **beach,** and seals often congregate on the eastern shores. A **submarine mine** from World War II is mounted along the main road. On the south side of the village, the **Álfasteinn** store and cafe, Iðngarðar (© **470-2000;** June–Aug daily noon–8pm; Sept–May 10am–noon and 1–5pm), sells kitschy souvenirs made from rock, including candle holders, clocks, and, of course, trolls. Next to Álfasteinn is a small **fish factory;** you could drop in and ask to look around, if you don't mind some fishy splatter on your clothes.

Borgarfjörður takes its name from **Álfaborg,** the distinct rocky hill behind the village. Álfaborg is home to the elf queen herself—the name translates either to "elf rock" or "elf town." A stroll up the hill is a pleasant way to orient yourself to the valley. At the top is a view disc identifying the surrounding mountains.

Locals are mystified as to why **Bakkagerðiskirkja** 𝕮, their 1901 church, is aligned facing the fjord, rather than east-west, like every other Icelandic church of its day. According to local legend, the town planned to build the church on top of the Álfaborg, but an elf appeared to a town elder in a dream and requested the current site. Bakkagerðiskirkja hosts the town's most treasured possession: an **altarpiece painting** of Christ on the Mount by Jóhannes S. Kjarval. Christ stands on what looks like a miniaturized Álfaborg, with the unmistakable outline of Dyrfjöll in the background. The townspeople commissioned the painting in 1914, when Kjarval was 29 and studying in Copenhagen. Iceland's bishop hated the painting and refused to consecrate it. The church is easy to locate by sight, and is generally open all day.

On the main street is **Lindarbakki,** an oft-photographed, turf-roofed house with reindeer horns over the door. If you knock, the friendly summer resident will probably invite you in to sign the Gestabók. Note the now-framed rat skeleton she found in the wall.

"Hidden People" Lesson #4: Elves & Modern Iceland

In polls, only about 20% of Icelanders rule out the existence of elves. Construction projects can still be thwarted by fears of disturbing elf dwellings. In 1996, as ground was prepared for a graveyard in a Reykjavík suburb, two bulldozers leveling a suspected elf hill mysteriously broke down. Elf arbitrators were called in. "We're going to see whether we can't reach an understanding with the elves," the project supervisor told Iceland's daily newspaper, *Morgunblaðið*.

Many Icelanders are tired of being asked if they really believe in elves, because they can't give a simple yes or no answer. Saying "yes" would not mean they believe, in the most literal sense, that little people emerge from rocks every night and dance around. And saying "no" would not mean they dismiss related supernatural concepts and phenomena.

Icelanders by necessity have always been strongly attuned to their strange and harsh environment. Spend enough time outdoors in Iceland's long twilights—which play strange tricks on the eyes—and Icelanders' unwillingness to rule out hidden people starts to make intuitive sense.

Six kilometers (3¾ miles) northeast of the village, next to a fishing boat harbor, **Hafnarhólmi** ⟡ has two excellent platforms for viewing puffins and cliff-nesting birds. The best time to visit is in the morning or late afternoon, when puffins are least likely to be off fishing. The platforms are closed in May for nesting season, and open from 11am to 7pm in June and July. In August the platforms are open 24 hours, though the puffins disappear by mid-month. The fence atop the cliff is to prevent puffins from digging burrows in the territory of eider ducks, whose nest feathers are harvested once the nests have been abandoned for the winter. The lower platform by the picnic table is ideal for observing the gull-like kittiwakes.

Kjarvalsstofa (the Kjarval Experience) is on Bakkagerði's main road at Fjarðarborg community center, on the second floor. Jóhannes Sveinsson Kjarval (1885–1972), Iceland's most highly regarded painter, grew up in Borgarfjörður. This museum pays tribute to the man more than his art, which is featured at the Kjarvalsstaðir in Reykjavík (p. 116). Even Kjarval's admirers can probably skip the displays of his soiled hat and ties, but the gallery with prints of his portrait drawings of locals is touching. A screening room shows old Super 8 movies and TV news clips of Borgarfjörður Eystri in Icelandic. Kids can play in a room with painting supplies.

Two prints of Kjarval's landscape paintings are posted outdoors, east of town. To find them, take the short trail (marked #18 on the *Víknaslóðir* map) to the Hólar mounds.

Argarður. ☏ 472-9950. Admission 500kr ($8/£4) adults; free for ages 15 and under. June–Aug daily noon–6pm.

HIKING ROUTES

As mentioned above, *Víknaslóðir: Trails of the Deserted Inlets* is essential for exploring the region. Trails are well-marked from the main road, and a map is posted at each trailhead. The best time for hiking is from early July to early September, though many routes are clear of snow by June. In late August you can eat your fill of *krækiber* (black crowberries)—keep an eye out for the rare albino variety. The weather is rainier in September, but you'll have plenty of solitude.

The best trips in Borgarfjörður Eystri last two to 7 days, but if you have just 1 day (and no access to a 4WD vehicle), the two best **day hikes** are to Stórurð and Brúnavík. Both destinations take around five to 6 hours round-trip.

Stórurð ✿✿ is a mystical jumble of oddly shaped boulders around a blue-green stream and pond with grassy banks. Don't come before early July, when the snow lifts. The best trail route (marked #9 on the *Víknaslóðir* map) starts at the 431m (1,414-ft.) Vatnskarð pass on Route 94 west of Njarðvík, and crosses the 634m (2,080 ft.) Geldingafjall peak before descending into Stórurð. This trail has some ankle-twisting stretches of loose gravel and scree. Somewhat easier trails (#8 and #10) reach Stórurð from different parts of the road, but #9 has the best approach to Stórurð, as well as astounding views of Njarðvík, Fljótsdalshérað Valley, and even Snæfell and Vatnajökull. You could return by one of the easier trails, but would have to walk back to your car along the road.

Brúnavík ✿✿, the first cove east of Borgarfjörður, has a lovely beach of rhyolite sand and was inhabited by two families until 1944. Two trails lead to Brúnavík from the coastal road on Borgarfjörður's eastern side. For the optimally dramatic descent into Brúnavík, the best circular route is clockwise, heading to Brúnavík through the 345m (1,132-ft.) Brúnavíkurskarð Pass (the trail marked #19 on the map) and returning through the 321m (1,053-ft.) Hofstrandarskarð Pass (trail #20).

The trails and Jeep tracks—and the best **multi-day trips**—extend all the way south to **Loðmundarfjörður,** or perhaps even to Seyðisfjörður. Loðmundarfjordur had 87 residents at the outset of the 20th century, but the last ones left in 1973, after failing to convince authorities to build a road around the coast from Seyðisfjörður. A partially restored 1891 church is still standing but stays locked up. (Húsavík also has a cute church near the ocean; it dates from the late 1930s and always remains open.)

The scenic highlights of Borgarfjörður Eystri are manifold, but **Hvítserkur** should be singled out, as many consider it the most strangely beautiful mountain in Iceland. The main bulk is pale-rose rhyolite, but glacial erosion has exposed dark basaltic ribbons that look like paint splattered by Jackson Pollock. Hvítserkur's best side faces south, and can be seen from Húsavik and the 4WD road leading there.

WHERE TO STAY

The **mountain huts** at Breiðavík *(Breiðuvíkurskáli)* and Húsavík *(Húsavíkurskáli)* are operated by **Ferðafélag Fljótsdalshéraðs** (✆ 863-5813; ferdafelag@egilsstadir.is). The Breiðavík hut has a warden in the morning and evening. Both huts sleep 33 in bunks (2,300kr [$37/£18] adults; 1,150kr [$18/£9] ages 7–15) and neither has cellphone reception. The same organization plans to build another hut at Loðmundarfjörður soon.

Camping is allowed only at Bakkagerði's campsite and next to the Breiðavík and Húsavík mountain huts. Some people camp at Loðmundarfjörður, but it's illegal.

The **Ásbyrgi Youth Hostel** (✆ 472-9962; fax 472-9961; www.hostel.is; 6 units, none w/bathroom; AE, DC, MC, V) is a cheap place to bed down for the night, but only one room is a double that costs 4,900kr ($78/£39).

Two new accommodations in Bakkagerði are breaking ground at press time; one will have spa facilities. Ask at the tourist center for updates.

Guesthouse Borg   This guesthouse is spread over three houses around town, all with unexciting but serviceable rooms and guest kitchens. The manager Skúli doesn't speak much English, but can transport food and bags to the mountain huts for guests.

(© 472-9870 or 894-4470. Fax 472-9880. www.borgarfjordureystri.is. 12 units, none w/bathroom. 8,400kr ($134/£67) double; 2,300kr–3,300kr ($37–$53/£18–£26) per person sleeping-bag accommodation per person. Breakfast available: 900kr ($14/£7). MC, V. **Amenities:** Guest kitchen; washer/dryer access. *In room:* No phone.

Réttarholt   Until the new hotels are built, this simple but homey guesthouse is the best option in town. Two rooms are doubles, and one has five beds. Owner Helgi also doubles as a tour guide and is your best possible resource for local travel information.

(© 472-9913 or 894-1012. www.borgarfjordureystri.is. 3 units, none w/bathroom. 6,800kr ($109/£54) double; 2,100kr ($34/£17) sleeping-bag accommodation per person. Breakfast available: 900kr ($14/£7). No credit cards. **Amenities:** Guest kitchen. *In room:* No phone.

Skólasel   Fjarðarborg community center operates this basic guesthouse building, with access to the guest kitchen and laundry at the youth hostel. Jóhanna, who runs Fjarðarborg, speaks limited English but also arranges Jeep transport of food, baggage, and passengers to and from the mountain huts for hikers.

(© 472-9920. Fax 472-9961. 12 units, none w/bathroom. Summer 3,600kr ($58/£29) per person; 2,200kr ($35/£18) sleeping-bag accommodation. MC, V. Closed Sept–May. **Amenities:** Restaurant. *In room:* no phone.

WHERE TO DINE

Consider stocking up at Egilsstaðir's **supermarkets** before heading to Borgarfjörður Eystri, since Bakkagerði has few dining options, all accommodations have guest kitchens, and food must be brought in to mountain huts. From June through August, the community center **Fjarðarborg** (above) offers passable burgers, soup, sandwiches, vegetable pitas, lamb chops, and fried fish from 11am to 8pm daily. No main courses exceed 1,650kr ($26/£13). **Álfasteinn** (p. 347) has a limited cafe, serving drinks, snack food, and servings of tasty fish soup with traditional Icelandic brown-rye flatbread for 850kr ($14/£7).

9 Fljótsdalshérað Valley

Fljótsdalshérað is the broad, flat valley that extends from Egilsstaðir northeast to the ocean, providing an outlet for two major rivers, Jökulsá á Brú (aka Jökulsá á Dal) and Lagarfljót. The Jökulsá á Brú has been drastically affected by the new Kárahnjúkar Dam (p. 338), far upstream. The diversion of water and blockage of sediments is disrupting the local ecosystem and could devastate the hundreds of harbor seals who breed in the river delta. Nonetheless, the valley—walled in by mountains, with plenty of pretty farms and bird ponds—is a beautiful place to do some **horseback riding.**

Want to feel totally removed from the world in an adorable rustic farmhouse, cooking your own meals and riding horseback along peaceful ocean beaches, grasslands, and riverbanks in search of birds and seals? If so, **Húsey** ✿, (© **471-3010** or 854-8554; fax 471-3009; www.husey.de; 5 units, none w/bathroom. 4,625kr [$74/£37] double; 3,875kr [$62/£31] double sleeping-bag accommodation; 3,250kr [$52/£26] made-up bunk; 2,438kr [$39/£20] sleeping-bag bunk. May–Sept AE, DC, MC, V; Oct–Apr no credit cards), a picturesque farm at the headwaters of the Jökulsá á Brú, is the place for you. Horse trips are tailored for beginners and experts and range from 2-hour seal-watching jaunts to 7-day excursions to a historic farmstead. Non-riders may be perfectly content walking the trails and reading on the porch all day. Breakfast is available for 1,100kr ($18/£9), but all other food must be brought in and can be prepared in the guest kitchen.

The drive from Egilsstaðir to Húsey is about an hour. Take the Ring Road north for 26km (16 miles), then turn right on Route 925, just before the Jökulsá á Brú bridge (ignore the earlier junction with Rte. 925). At the farm Litlibakki, as Route 925 turns off to the right, go straight on Route 926 and continue to the end. If you need a ride, inquire at the hostel. For up to six people, the round-trip price is 11,375kr ($182/£91) from Egilsstaðir or 56,875kr ($91/£46) from the bridge. A taxi costs far more.

10 Egilsstaðir to Mývatn

The lonely 167km (104 miles) stretch of the Ring Road between Egilsstaðir and Mývatn can be a blur of barren gravelly plains—but it also affords beautiful vistas, especially on a clear day when Mt. Herðubreið is visible to the south. Make sure your gas tank is full before setting out.

Almost halfway from Egilsstaðir to Mývatn and 13km (8 miles) south of the Ring Road, **Sænautasel** ☏ (© 855-5399)—a reconstructed turf farm on a 60km-long (37-mile) heathland called Jökuldalsheiði—is a great detour to break up the trip. Sænautasel was abandoned in 1875 after the Askja eruption fouled the area with ash. In 1992, a descendant of Sænautasel's first settler reconstructed the original farm, which now welcomes visitors daily from June through August 10 (9am–10pm). To reach Sænautasel, exit the Ring Road at its western junction with Route 901, roughly 70km (43 miles) west of Egilsstaðir. A few kilometers later, turn left on Route 907 and continue for another 10 minutes. After desolate expanses of nothingness, the road arrives at a vision from another age: two turf-roofed houses next to a pleasant lake surrounded by vegetation. Pancakes and coffee are served inside the welcome building. Admission to the farmhouse, close to the welcome building, costs 300kr ($4.80/£2.40) for adults, and is free for children ages 11 and under. No information is posted about each room and its function, so if no warden is there, ask to be shown around.

Buses connecting Egilsstaðir and Mývatn stop at **Möðrudalur,** an isolated sheep farming settlement along Route 901, 8km (5 miles) south of Route 901's western junction with the Ring Road. Möðrudalur dates back to the Saga age, and at 469m (1,539 ft.) above sea level is Iceland's highest working farm. The **Fjalladýrð Cafe and Guesthouse** (© 471-1858 or 894-1758; www.fjalladyrd.is) offers pastries, lamb and vegetable soups, sandwiches, and hot dogs. The owners also arrange Jeep trips to Vatnajökull.

11

The Interior

Almost a third of Iceland is consumed by highland plateaus blanketed with volcanic gravel, and punctuated only by glacial rivers, scattered mountains and lakes, smatterings of vegetation, and perhaps a stray boulder. Amid this pristine desert wasteland, travelers often pose for pictures next to directional signs at road junctions. The signs seem to point nowhere, and, in the photo, the traveler invariably grins at the absurdity—and otherworldly beauty—of the scene. The Apollo astronauts came to Iceland's interior to train, and until tourism reaches the moon, this place may be the closest substitute.

The interior is often described as Europe's last great untouched wilderness. This is somewhat misleading, as much of the land was vegetated before settlers and their voracious sheep first arrived. (In efforts to reseed the desert, Icelandic scientists are experimenting with dropping bombs full of fertilizer from a WWII–era DC-3 plane.) Early settlers often traversed the interior for parliamentary meetings at Þingvellir, but many routes were closed off when temperatures cooled in the 13th century. In popular mythology, the interior became a refuge for outlaws and outcasts, much like the Wild West in the American imagination.

The two main south-to-north routes through the interior are Kjölur, in the western half of the country, and Sprengisandur, in the dead center. The Kjölur Route is relatively hospitable, and can be crossed easily in a 4WD vehicle. The Sprengisandur Route passes through Iceland's most fantastically bleak territory, with more hazardous road conditions. Further east is Askja caldera, a dramatic ring of mountains formed largely in the aftermath of a catastrophic 1875 eruption. South of Askja is Kverkfjöll, where intense geothermal activity and Vatnajökull glacier surreally converge. Some interior highland destinations fall elsewhere in this book, notably Landmannalaugar and Þórsmörk in the south (chapter 9), Snæfell in the east (chapter 10), and the Kaldidalur Route in the west (chapter 7).

Traveling season is generally restricted to mid-summer. In July the sparse plant life heroically blooms, but August is generally prettier, since more snow has lifted. River crossings are often more difficult in July, because of higher water levels. July can also be buggier.

High winds and severe temperature fluctuations are endemic to the highlands. Volcanic sands are lightweight and swirl easily in the wind, so eye and face protection can be crucial. Driving in the interior presents serious challenges; see "Getting Around Iceland," in chapter 2 (p. 37), for details.

1 Kjölur Route

Leaving aside the much shorter Kaldidalur Route in the west, Kjölur—which runs from Geysir and Gullfoss in the southwest to Húnaflói and Skagafjörður in the north—is the most accessible, most trafficked, and least barren route through Iceland's

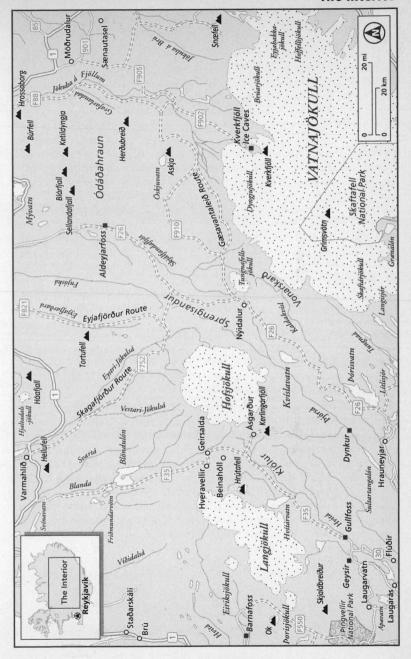

highland interior. The highest point of the road, at 700m (2,297 ft.) above sea level, is in the valley between Langjökull and Hofsjökull, Iceland's second- and third-largest glaciers. Strictly speaking, Kjölur refers only to this valley, but the word commonly applies to the entire 165km (103 miles) course of mountain road F35. Kjölur is often called a "shortcut" to Akureyri, but this only makes sense if you're already near Geysir and Gullfoss—*and* you have a 4WD car. In a regular car Kjölur is usually navigable, and all rivers are bridged, but your insurance will likely be voided.

The government has initiated talks with a private company to build a paved toll road through Kjölur. The new road would cut a straighter path and remain open all year. Supporters speak of increasing access to the interior, but Iceland's Travel Industry Association opposes the project, arguing that visitors entranced by the interior's unspoiled landscape don't want to hear trucks echoing across the plains.

ESSENTIALS

GETTING THERE   The Kjölur Route opens in early- to mid-June, and can remain open even into October. If you're **driving**, note that the only **gas station** (June–Sept 20) is at Hveravellir, 93km (58 miles) from Gullfoss.

From mid-July through August, **Trex buses** (© 587-6000; www.trex.is) connect Reykjavík and Akureyri via Kjölur daily in both directions, leaving Reykjavík at 12:30pm and Akureyri at 8:30am. **SBA Norðurleið** (© 550-0700; www.sba.is) covers the same route daily for more of the year—mid-June through early September—and buses leave at 8am from both Reykjavík and Akureyri. Both companies charge 8,600kr ($137/£69) one-way, and stop at Hveragerði, Selfoss, Geysir, Gullfoss, Hvítárnes, Kerlingarfjöll, Hveravellir, Svartábrú, and Varmahlíð, with short sightseeing breaks at Geysir, Gullfoss, and Hveravellir. The SBA bus takes 9 hours, while the Trex bus takes 10, adding a break at Kerlingarfjöll. The Kjölur Route is also included in two of SBA's bus package deals, the **Highlights Passport** from 28,000kr ($448/£224) and **Highland Circle Passport** from 25,100kr ($402/£201)—both offered by **SBA Norðurleið** (© 550-0700; www.sba.is), an affiliate of Reykjavík Excursions.

VISITOR INFORMATION   The best information sources for Kjölur are the people or organizations who run accommodations along the route. The hiking organization **Ferðafélag Íslands** (© 568-2355; www.fi.is) operates five mountain huts around Kjölur and has the most regional expertise. The folks at **Ásgarður** (© 894-2132; www.kerlingarfjoll.is) know the Kerlingarfjöll area. **Hveravallafélag** (© 452-4200 or 894-1293; www.hveravellir.is) supervises Hveravellir and the website has printable maps of all hiking routes from there. Ample information on Kjölur's geology, flora, and fauna is found at www.ust.is, the website of the **Environment and Food Agency of Iceland** (click "Protected Areas," then "Hveravellir").

OUTDOOR ACTIVITIES

HIKING   Ferðafélag Íslands (© 568-2533; www.fi.is), Iceland's premier hiking organization, leads a couple of multi-day trips around Kjölur each summer.

HORSEBACK RIDING   Two of Iceland's most reputable stables run Kjölur tours on horseback. The **Íshestar** (© 555-7000; www.ishestar.is; 166,250kr [$2,660/£1,330] per person) tour is 9 days, while **Eldhestar** (© 480-4800; www.eldhestar.is; 148,750kr [$2,380/£1,190] per person) tours are 8; both give you 6 days in the saddle. Food, accommodation, and transportation to and from Keflavík airport are included.

The Kjölurvegur Trek

The **Kjölurvegur** 🕏🕏 (aka Kjalvegur) is a rewarding and very manageable 3-day hike along an old horse trail from Hvítárnes to Hveravellir, with mountain huts spaced at 4- to 6-hour (12–14km/7½–9-mile) intervals. The route skirts Langjökull, with interesting but optional detours from Þjófadalir hut east through Kjalhraun lava field or west toward Langjökull. Buses stop at both ends of the Kjölurvegur, though you'll have to walk the 6km (4 miles) from Route F35 to the Hvítárnes hut. (Reserving bus seats in advance is a smart precaution.) Online, www.fi.is has a day-by-day breakdown of the route—under the heading "Hveravellir–Hvítárnes (the Old Kjalvegur Hiking Trail)"—but it takes you from north to south. Hiking south to north lets you end the trek with a valedictory dunk in Hveravellir's geothermal hot tub. To reserve space in the huts, see "Where to Stay & Dine," below.

EXPLORING THE AREA

The **map** *Kjölur: Arnarvatnsheiði–Kerlingarfjöll,* available at tourist offices and online at www.nordicstore.net, has good detail on hiking and driving routes.

HVÍTÁRVATN & HVÍTÁRNES 🕏

Around 45km (28 miles) northeast of Gullfoss, a turnoff from Route F35 leads 6km (4 miles) to Hvítárnes, a well-vegetated, marshy plain overlooking Hvítárvatn, a broad aquamarine lake with floating icebergs calved from Langjökull. The scenery is austere but captivating, and the Hvítárnes mountain hut, built in 1930, is a charming throwback with white gables and turf-insulated side walls. For engaging hikes around Hvítárvatn, ask at the hut or click the "Hiking Tracks" link at www.hveravellir.is.

KERLINGARFJÖLL 🕏🕏

This vast volcanic system near the southwest corner of Hofsjökull is one of the most glorious and underappreciated hiking areas in Iceland. The range of highland scenery is astounding, with peaks ranging in height from 800 to 1,477m (2,625–4,846 ft.); rhyolite mountainsides in spectral shadings of red, yellow, and green; shimmering glaciers; chiseled ravines; and steaming geothermal hotspots, some with swimmable ponds and springs. If Landmannalaugar is not on your itinerary, Kerlingarfjöll is a very worthy alternative, and spending two or 3 nights here is an ideal way to break up the Kjölur Route. The website www.kerlingarfjoll.is has downloadable maps of all the hiking trails.

Kerlingarfjöll is reached via Route F347, which branches off from Route F35 about halfway between Hvítárnes and Hveravellir. The accommodations at Ásgarður (see below) are about 10km (6 miles) down the road. If you're coming by bus, note that the SBA bus can drop you at the crossroads, but only the Trex bus goes right to Ásgarður.

HVERAVELLIR 🕏

About 93km (58 miles) from Gullfoss, Route F735 detours 2km (1¼ miles) from Route F35 to reach Hveravellir (Hot Spring Plains), an intriguing geothermal hot spot and Kjölur's main summer service center, with a gas station, restaurant, bar, small market, and sleeping-bag accommodation in mountain huts. Hveravellir's weather station is staffed year-round, providing one of Iceland's best jobs for loners. The geothermal field is worth a stop, especially to bathe in the waist-deep pool, or to see Öskurhólshver, a white-crusted conical fumarole hissing eggy steam. Stick to the boardwalks to protect both yourself and the land. Hveravellir is also a terminus for the Kjölurvegur trek; see box, above.

WHERE TO STAY & DINE

The only **restaurants** along the Kjölur Route are at Ásgarður (in Kerlingarfjöll) and Hveravellir, which also has a small **market.** Don't expect fine dining.

For mountain huts in **Hvítárnes** and along the **Kjölurvegur Route** (except for Hveravellir), sleeping-bag space must be reserved online through **Ferðafélag Íslands** (✆ **568-2533;** www.fi.is; 3,000kr [$48/£24] per person per night). All huts have kitchens but no utensils. None have showers, and only Hvítárnes has a warden. All food must be brought in, and all garbage must be packed out.

At **Kerlingarfjöll,** from mid-June through September, **Ásgarður** (✆ **894-2132** or 852-5132; www.kerlingarfjoll.is) offers a wide range of lodgings, from sleeping-bag accommodation in a bunk room for 28 people at 2,800kr ($45/£22) to made-up beds in private cottages for 5,000kr–13,000kr ($80–$208/£40–£104) per person. Facilities include guest kitchens, a restaurant, and a bath house with showers and three hot tubs. All cottages have heat and electricity, and the website outlines each rooming option, with photos.

The mountain huts at **Hveravellir** are run by **Hveravallafélag** (✆ **452-4200** or 894-1293; www.hveravellir.is; 2,000kr [$32/£16] sleeping-bag accommodation) and remain open year-round. One hut has three bedrooms and sleeps 35, while the other has one bedroom and sleeps 20. Both have fully-equipped kitchens and hot water.

2 Sprengisandur Route

Sprengisandur, the desert expanse at Iceland's heart, is a true moonscape—so much so, in fact, that conspiracy theorists believe this is where the U.S. government "faked" the moon landing. Such bleak, lifeless scenery is transporting and sublime to some, depressing and monotonous to others. But on a clear day, no one is unimpressed by the grand tableau of mountains and glaciers in all directions. If you've ever doubted the world is round, come here and witness the sky arching overhead.

The Sprengisandur Route has no strict beginning or end, but loosely corresponds to Route F26, which spans 196km (122 miles) from the Hrauneyjar highland area to the Aldeyjarfoss waterfall. However desolate the route, it's hardly featureless, and opportunities for exploration abound.

ESSENTIALS
GETTING THERE

BY CAR   With its rough surfaces and hazardous river fords, Route F26 is only for rugged 4WD vehicles with good clearance. The road's opening date varies, but usually falls at the end of June. The **Public Roads Administration** (✆ **354-1777;** www. vegag.is; May–Oct 8am–4pm; Nov–Apr 8am–5pm) continually monitors road conditions; but for the latest on water levels or other dangers at river crossings, the warden at **Nýidalur** (✆ **854-1194**) is the better source. Traffic on the Sprengisandur

Route has increased greatly, so in high season—as long as you stick to Route F26—driving in convoy is not an absolutely necessary precaution. **Warning:** Gas is not available on Route F26, and the gas stations at Hrauneyjar and Goðafoss are 240km (149 miles) apart. (Unprepared drivers are often seen begging for fuel at Nýidalur.)

From the south, Route F26 is reached via Route 26 or Route 32; for sights en route, see "Þjórsárdalur & Hekla," p. 286.

Three significant interior routes branch off from Route F26. A few kilometers north of Nýidalur, Route F910 links Route F26 to Askja. This road—also known as the **Gæsavantaleið Route**—has incredible scenery but should only be attempted by experienced drivers in convoy; allow 9 hours from Nýidalur to Askja's Drekagil huts. Route F752, also known as the **Skagafjörður Route,** links Route F26 to the town of Varmahlíð and Skagafjörður. Rtes. F881 and F821, jointly known as the **Eyjafjörður Route,** link Route F26 to Akureyri. At its north end, Route F26 connects with Route 842, which leads 41km (25 miles) through the Bjarðardalur valley to the Ring Road near Goðafoss. The northern end of Route F26 is far more dependable than the Skagafjörður and Eyjafjörður routes, which are sometimes closed to traffic altogether.

BY BUS Reykjavík Excursions (© 562-1011; www.re.is) connects Landmannalaugar and lake Mývatn via the Sprengisandur Route from July 1 to August 24. Departures from Mývatn are Monday, Wednesday, and Friday at 8:30am, and departures from Landmannalaugar are Sunday, Tuesday, and Thursday, also at 8:30am. The full one-way trip lasts 10 hours and costs 8,000kr ($128/£64), with stops at Hrauneyjar, Nýidalur, and Skútustaðir, plus sightseeing breaks at the Aldeyjarfoss and Goðafoss waterfalls. Passengers taking the bus from Mývatn to Landmannalaugar must wait until the following day for connections to Reykjavík and elsewhere. The Sprengisandur Route is included in two multi-trip bus package deals—the **Highlights Passport** and **Highland Circle Passport** (p. 42).

VISITOR INFORMATION

No specific tourist information office is assigned to the Sprengisandur Route, but regional offices in Hveragerði, Varmahlíð, Akureyri, and Mývatn can provide help. The **Hrauneyjar Highland Center** (© 487-7782; www.hrauneyjar.is) is a useful resource, and the warden at **Nýidalur** (© 854-1194; July–Aug)—while not responsible for helping non-guests—is usually happy to answer questions.

ORGANIZED TOURS

HIKING **Icelandic Mountain Guides** (© 587-9999; www.mountainguide.is) leads epic, unforgettable treks off the beaten path, including Askja to Nýidalur in 6 days for 65,900kr ($1,054/£527) and Nýidalur to Eldgjá in 7 days for 72,900kr ($1,166/£583). Plan on carrying a heavy pack.

HORSEBACK RIDING **Eldhestar** (© 480-4800; www.eldhestar.is) offers an 8-day Sprengisandur traverse with 6 days spent on horseback for 155,313kr ($2,485/£1,243), while **Íshestar** (© 556-7000; www.ishestar.is), an equally experienced and reputable company, tackles the route in 12 days with 9 in the saddle for 227,500kr ($3,640/£1,820).

EXPLORING THE AREA

At the northern end of Route F26, make sure to stop at the enthralling waterfall Aldeyjarfoss (p. 250).

Hrauneyjar Highland Center, a year-round highland oasis at the southern terminus of the Sprengisandur Route, has two hotels and restaurants (see "Where to Stay & Dine," below), an information desk, and the last gas station for the next 240km (149 miles). A trail map of the surrounding area is available at reception.

As a base, Hrauneyjar is best for travelers with their own 4WD transport. The Highland Center organizes tours only for groups, and the best local destinations—such as Veiðivötn lakes (below), or the lovely **Dynkur** ✦, a waterfall on the Þjórsá river—are inaccessible to regular cars. Hrauneyjar is especially handy for visitors who want to explore Landmannalaugar by day and then retire to a private room with a made-up bed. Landmannalaugar is an hour from Hrauneyjar via Route F208, which opens up in late June. (Regular cars can negotiate the route, but this would void your insurance.)

The Hrauneyjar area has some excellent fishing, and the Highland Center sells licenses and rents rods. Prices are steep, however, with licenses starting around 4,900kr ($78/£39) per rod per day in lakes and 9,900kr ($158/£79) for fly fishing in streams.

VEIÐIVÖTN ✦

Trout fishermen are particularly drawn to this idyllic and peaceful cluster of fifty volcanic crater lakes, located close to Landmannalaugar but accessed through Hrauneyjar on Route F228. Fishing permits cost 2,000kr/day ($32/£16) and sleeping-bag accommodation 2,500kr ($40/£20) per person in four bunk-style cottages are handled by **Landmannahellir** (© 893-8407; www.landmannahellir.is).

NÝIDALUR ✦

An overnight stay at this remote desert outpost, combined with a day hike east to **Vonarskarð pass** ✦✦, makes for a memorable episode along the Sprengisandur Route. Nýidalur is right on Route F26, about 100km (62 miles) from Hrauneyjar and 20km (12 miles) from the northwest corner of Vatnajökull. Vonarskarð forms a dramatic saddle between Vatnajökull and the small glacier Tungnafellsjökull, and the hiking route skirts some restless geothermal fields. Sudden releases of glacial meltwater can make stream crossings difficult, so speak to the warden before setting out. Those just passing through Nýidalur can still take the short easy hike east to a nearby hill with panoramic views.

WHERE TO STAY & DINE

No food is sold anywhere in the 240km (149-mile) stretch between Hrauneyjar and Goðafoss.

Hrauneyjar may be the last outpost at the desert frontier, but for travelers with 4WD vehicles, it's also a centralized base for exploring Þjórsárdalur, Hekla, Landmannalaugar, and Veiðivötn. Hrauneyjar's two hotels, run by the same management, are 1.4km (1 mile) apart, and each has its own restaurant (see below).

The **Nýidalur mountain huts** (© 854-1194; 3,000kr [$48/£24] sleeping-bag accommodation; MC, V; July–Aug), sleep 120 people and are operated by **Ferðafélag Íslands** (© 568-2533; www.fi.is). Advance bookings can be made online, but walk-ins are usually accommodated. Showers cost an additional 300kr ($4.80/£2.40), and the kitchen has pots and pans but no utensils. All food must be brought in. Come prepared to sleep in a packed room with 30 other travelers, or in bunks that look like singles but are meant for two.

Hótel Highland   Walking into this high-end hotel and restaurant is a surreal transition from the wild and remote landscape outside. The Highland was a farm accommodation as recently as 2005, and some rooms are still transitioning design-wise, but you won't suffer for sheets with an insufficient thread count. The fine **restaurant** ✦ is open for dinner only, from 7 to 10pm, with main courses in the 2,800kr to 4,500kr ($45–$72/£22–£36) range. The menu has the expected elegant dishes—surf and turf, game platters, and the like—but we recommend the grilled local trout with white wine sauce and potatoes. As for dessert, you're unlikely to find a better slice of skýr cake.

Rte. 26, Hrauneyjar. ℭ 487-7750. Fax 487-7781. www.allseasonhotels.is. 24 units. May 15–Sept 16,100kr ($258/£129) double; 18,900kr–28,500kr ($302–$456/£151–£228) suites for 2–6 persons; Rates around 25% lower late May and Sept. Rates include breakfast. AE, DC, MC, V. Closed Oct–May 15. **Amenities:** Restaurant; hot tub; sauna; solarium; fitness room. *In room:* TV, Wi-Fi, hair dryer.

Hrauneyjar Highland Center   This hotel is adjoined to Hrauneyjar's gas station and information desk, and the Reykjavík Excursions bus through Sprengisandur stops here. The rooms are spartan but comfortable, and, if you've just come through the desert interior, the whole place is Shangri-La. Confusingly, 17 of the rooms—which share a guest kitchen—and the four apartments are located next to Hótel Highland but classified with the Highland Center. The restaurant, open from 11:30am to 10pm daily, is limited to basic grilled dishes plus salads, sandwiches, wraps, and perhaps a daily special. The burgers are surprisingly delicious. Late at night the staff puts leftovers outside for the foxes, and you can watch them cavorting.

Rte. 26, Hrauneyjar. ℭ 487-7782. Fax 487-7781. www.hrauneyjar.is. 73 units, none w/bathroom. June–Aug 8,700kr ($139/£70) double; 4,500kr ($72/£36) double w/sleeping bag; 12,300kr–21,900kr ($197–$350/£98–£175) apts for 2–6 persons. Rates 15%–25% lower Sept–early June. Rates include breakfast (except sleeping-bag accommodation). AE, DC, MC, V. **Amenities:** Restaurant; bar; hot tub. *In room:* Wi-Fi, no phone.

3 Askja, Kverkfjöll & Eastern Interior Routes

Among the scenic landmarks of Iceland's desert highlands, the vast stratovolcano **Askja** ✦✦ is the most visited—and not just for its stark, elemental beauty and grandeur. If the weather cooperates, you can take a warm unforgettable swim in a crater lake with milky-blue, sulfurous water. Trips to Askja often extend to **Kverkfjöll** ✦✦, a mountain spur protruding from the northern margin of Vatnajökull amid a bleak expanse of rugged hills and gritty lava. The Kverkfjöll region is suffused with geothermal activity, and hot springs sculpt elaborate ice caves as they emerge from the glacier's edge.

These areas can only be accessed in sturdy 4WD vehicles or on organized tours. All accommodations are in mountain huts, and all food must be brought in. Clear skies can switch suddenly to rain, and snowstorms can arise even in midsummer. Askja can be reached on day tours from the Mývatn, but seeing Kverkfjöll requires at least 1 night apart from civilization. Two nights at Kverkfjöll should be the minimum, since the best hikes take the better part of a day.

ESSENTIALS
GETTING THERE   The 4WD roads to Askja and Kverkfjöll generally remain open from mid-June through mid-September or later. No mountain roads (designated by an "F" before the route number) in the region have gas stations. Inexperienced drivers may have trouble negotiating rock shards, potholes, and fords over rivers.

The standard route to **Askja** is Route F88, which branches off from the Ring Road (Rte. 1) 32km (20 miles) east of Mývatn and stretches 95km (59 miles) to the Drekagil mountain hut at Askja's outskirts. From there, it's a bouncy 8km (5 miles) drive on Route F894 to the Vikraborgir parking area, a 2.5km (1½-mile) walk from Víti crater in central Askja.

Drivers headed from Askja to **Kverkfjöll** backtrack from Drekagil on Route F88 and then take Route F910 southeast to Route F902 (confusingly, another branch of Route F910 heads directly from Drekagil west to Nýidalur in Sprengisandur). Those headed straight from the Ring Road to Kverkfjöll usually start on Route F905 (by the Möðrudalur gas station/cafe, 65km/40 miles east of Mývatn), and then take Route F910 to Route F902. The distance from Möðrudalur to the Sigurðarskáli hut at Kverkfjöll is 108km (67 miles).

For **bus travel** to Askja and Kverkfjöll, see "Organized Tours," below.

VISITOR INFORMATION   Offices in Akureyri, Mývatn, and Egilsstaðir can all provide information on the Askja and Kverkfjöll region. For consultation on hikes in the Askja area, contact **Ferðafélag Akureyrar** (p. 363). This organization runs the mountain huts at **Þorsteinsskáli,** Route F88, at Herðubreiðarlindir (© **864-9301**) and **Drekagil,** Route F88, at Drekagil (© **853-2541**), and the hut wardens have current information on road and weather conditions. For hikes in the Kverkfjöll area, the authority is **Ferðafélag Fljótsdalshéraðs** (p. 363), which runs the **Sigurðarskáli hut** (p. 363); again the wardens have the local lowdown. The huts are generally staffed from mid-June through August or mid-September; see "Where to Stay" below.

ORGANIZED TOURS

Most visitors to Askja and Kverkfjöll come on organized tours, which makes sense, given the poor roads and other logistical hassles. However, except for the infrequent hiking trips led by Ferðafélag Akureyrar and Ferðafélag Fljótsdalshéraðs, no tours allow extensive time for exploring either destination. For Askja, Mývatn Tours is usually willing to leave you at the Drekagil hut and pick you up a day or two later. The SBA-Norðurleið tour allows 2 nights and a day at Kverkfjöll, but for more time you'll need your own 4WD vehicle.

Mývatn Tours (© **464-1920;** www.askjatours.is) leads a popular 11- to 12-hour guided tour of Askja, starting from the Mývatn information center, for 11,000kr ($176/£88) adults and 5,500kr ($88/£44) for children 6 to 12. Departures are daily from July 10 to August 20, and three times weekly in late June, early July, and late August. Bring lunch, warm clothes, strong shoes, and a bathing suit and towel. **Hótel Reykjahlíð** in Mývatn (© **464-4142;** www.reykjahlid.is) offers roughly the same tour, but in Super Jeeps instead of a bus. The cost is 14,800kr ($237/£118) for adults and 9,500kr ($152/£76) for children 6 to 12, with a four-person or 59,200kr ($947/£474) minimum. Off-road driving is prohibited, however, so the much higher price is hard to justify. Departures are from June 15 through September by advance request.

From early July to late August, **SBA-Norðurleið** (© **550-0700;** www.sba.is) offers a 3-day trip from Akureyri or Mývatn to Askja and Kverkfjöll, with 2 nights at Kverkfjöll's Sigurðarskáli hut. Departures are Mondays only, and the 21,500kr ($344/£172) price (half-price for children 12–15) includes a guide but no food or accommodation. If you ask, they can at least reserve a bed for you at the hut.

In July, **Ferðafélag Akureyrar** (p. 233), Akureyri's hiking organization, leads an adventurous 7-day backpacking trek for 53,000kr ($848/£424) per person, including accommodation, food and guide from Herðubreið to Askja and onward to Svartárvatn lake, at the southern terminus of Route 843. The website is in Icelandic only; find the "Ferðaáætlun" link, and scan the tour listings for "Öskjuvegur." A 3-day trip to climb Herðubreið should also be listed. **Ferðafélag Fljótsdalshéraðs** (p. 363) occasionally leads hiking trips in the Askja–Kverkfjöll region (click on the "ferðir" link to glean tour listings, or just call instead.). For **aerial tours** of Askja and Kverkfjöll from Mývatn, see p. 242.

EXPLORING THE AREA
ROUTE F88 TO ASKJA

Starting from the Ring Road, the first 60km (37 miles) of Route F88 follow the western side of the Jökulsá á Fjöllum—the same river that forms the canyon in Jökulsárgljúfur National Park further downstream. Just south of the Ring Road and west of Route F88 is **Hrossaborg,** a 10,000-year-old crater formed when rising magma heated groundwater, prompting a massive explosion of steam and rock. Hrossaborg was once used as a pen for rounding up horses—thus the name, which means "Horse Castle." A small road leads from Route F88 right into Hrossaborg's natural amphitheater through a collapsed crater wall.

In roughly 40km (25 miles), Route F88 comes to its first major ford at the **Grafarlandaá river,** known for its pure-tasting water. 20km (12 miles) further south is **Herðubreiðarlindir,** a lovely highland oasis of moss, wildflowers, and springs gushing from beneath the lava rock to converge on the Lindaá River. **Herðubreið** ✿, a majestic table mountain, looms 6km (3¾ miles) to the west. Herðubreiðarlindir has a mountain hut and summer warden, and is also the launch point for the **Öskjuvegurinn** ✿, a memorable 5-day trek through some of Iceland's starkest wastelands. (Most of the route traverses the Ódáðahraun, which translates to "Lava Field of Evil Deeds.") The Öskjuvegurinn skirts Herðubreið, and reaches Askja's Drekagil hut on the second night. For further details on all the huts along the route, contact **Ferðafélag Akureyrar** (p. 233). A 5-minute trail leads from Herðubreiðarlindir to the remains of a tiny underground shelter, where Fjalla-Eyvindur—Iceland's most legendary outlaw—reportedly survived the winter of 1774–75 on a diet of dried horsemeat and angelica roots. The original shelter collapsed and was renovated in 1922. A map available at the hut outlines other short, pleasant hikes in the Herðubreiðarlindir area.

In clear weather, the view of Herðubreið is awe-inspiring. In 2002 a national poll was conducted to determine "Iceland's favorite mountain," and Herðubreið was the overwhelming winner. Its name means "Broad Shoulders," and its flattened top is the result of eruptions beneath the crushing weight of a glacier. With its steep screes and vertical cliff faces, Herðubreið is a very challenging and somewhat dangerous climb. If you do make the attempt, consult the warden at Herðubreiðarlindir first, and allow 12 hours round-trip.

ASKJA ✿✿

In Iceland's recorded history, no cataclysm produced more ash than the 1875 volcanic eruption at Askja, which means "Caldera" in Icelandic. The ash blanketed 10,000 sq. km (3861 sq. miles) of land, killing livestock and forcing hundreds of Icelandic farmers to emigrate to North America. Askja—designated a stratovolcano because of its layers of lava from periodic eruptions—erupted most recently in 1961, but most of the current topography took form in 1875. Askja is also Iceland's most dramatic illustration of a subsidence cauldron, formed when underground passageways of molten rock empty and collapse, leaving an enormous bowl at the center of the volcanic edifice. Askja's collapsed center, dominated by **Öskjuvatn** lake, is 8km (5 miles) wide and still sinking. Öskjuvatn is Iceland's deepest lake, at 220m (722 ft.).

The mountain hut closest to Askja is at **Drekagil gorge,** 35km (22 miles) from Herðubreiðarlindir. From Drekagil, Route F894 extends 8km (5 miles) to **Vikraborgir,** a crater row formed during the 1961 eruption. Tour buses park at Vikraborgir for the easy 35-minute walk south to **Víti** *&*, a lake-filled crater formed in 1875 and separated from Öskjuvatn by a narrow ridge. (*Víti,* by the way, means "Hell.") The Icelanders are usually the least hesitant to scoot down Víti's steep walls and plunge into the warm, opaque, eggy-smelling water, which reaches a depth of 60m (197 ft.). The water temperature ranges from 72°F to 86°F (22°C–30°C)—a bit tepid at times, but it's warmer if you swim out to the middle. You can also dig your toes into the hot mud on the lake floor, but be careful not to get burned. Trails proceeding from Víti around Öskjuvatn are often blocked by signs prohibiting access, so check with the warden at Drekagil before setting out.

A longer, more suspenseful approach to Víti starts at the Drekagil hut and proceeds through Dyngjufjöll, bypassing Vikraborgir. Consult the warden on the status of the trail, and allow 3 hours each way. A stroll up the Drekagil gorge is also worthwhile.

KVERKFJÖLL *&&*

The Kverkfjöll volcanic system—which reaches 1,936m (6,352 ft.) in height and extends 10km (6 miles) on a south-to-north axis—is mostly buried beneath Vatnajökull, but its northern rim protrudes from the glacier's edge. With so much geothermal activity churning beneath Europe's largest mass of ice, Kverkfjöll is usually characterized as a collision of natural extremes. Yet the most lasting impressions are of its austere and solemn beauty: the mesmerizing pattern inside an ice cave, perhaps, or a view over reddish-black wastes with the barest etching of pale grey lichen.

The most common tourist mistakes are to wear jeans, a real encumbrance in the rain, or sneakers, which shred on lava trails and soak through in snow or mud. Also remember to bring a water bottle, as it can be difficult to find drinking water free of silt.

HIKING ROUTES   The wardens at Sigurðarskáli, the only mountain hut in the Kverkfjöll vicinity, sell hiking maps and dispense excellent advice.

From Sigurðarskáli, a well-marked manageable trail leads up **Virkisfell** *&* for fabulous views; allow at least 90 minutes round-trip. From the mountain, the trail continues past several volcanic fissures to **Hveragil** *&*, a river gorge and oasis of vegetation nurtured by hot springs; a marvelous natural bathing pool is fed by a waterfall. Hveragil is 12km (7½ miles) from Sigurðarskáli, and the round-trip hike takes around 7 hours. A rough Jeep track extends to Hveragil from Route F903, but talk to a warden before braving it.

A road extends 4km (2½ miles) from the hut to the edge of the Kverkjökull glacial tongue; a more direct walking trail is only 3km (2 miles). From the end of the road, it's a 10-minute walk west to where a river emerges from a spectacular **ice cave** *(íshellir)* *&&* at the edge of the glacier. The play of light on the sculpted hollows and undulating walls is utterly entrancing. Eerie crashing sounds emanate from deep within the cave, and venturing inside is very dangerous. (Tour guides usually tell you not to go in, and then tactfully look the other way.) The escaping river is warmer in winter, when hot springs are less diluted by glacial meltoff.

Each day in summer, a Sigurðarskáli warden leads a **day hike** 𝕣𝕣 onto Kverkjökull. The maximum group size is 20, and slots often fill up; call the hut and reserve in advance. The price is low—just 1,500kr to 2,500kr ($24–$40/£12–£20), depending how long the hike is—and includes crampons, walking poles, and safety harnesses. In good weather, the hike lasts 8 to 10 hours and extends past the Langafönn slope to **Hveratagl** 𝕣, an expanse of steaming springs, bubbling mud cauldrons, and ice caves along the glacier's margin. The hike may continue further to **Gengissig,** a pretty lagoon next to a small mountain hut. For independent hikers, it's possible to spend the night here and continue to **Skarphéðinstindur,** Kverkfjöll's highest mountain; from the peak, the trail loops more directly back to Sigurðarskáli by a different route. All unguided hikes on the glacier are discouraged, but if you do go, be sure to tell the wardens where you're headed and stick to established trails.

WHERE TO STAY

Mountain huts in the Askja–Kverkfjöll region are generally open from mid-June to mid-September. Expect costs to be around 2,500kr ($40/£20) per person per night, with an extra charge for showers (usually around 350kr [$5.60/£2.80]). The Þórsteinsskáli, Drekagil, and Sigurðarskáli huts all have kitchens with cookware and utensils. No food is sold at the huts, and you must bring your own sleeping bag. As usual, guests are packed into large rooms with minimal privacy. If you bring a tent, expect to pay around 800kr ($13/£6.40) per person for use of the facilities. In July and August advance reservations are strongly advised.

All mountain huts in the Askja area, including **Þórsteinsskáli** and **Drekagil,** are owned and operated by **Ferðafélag Akureyrar** Strandgata 23, Akureyri (℘ **462-2720;** www.ffa.is). The wardens at Þórsteinsskáli (℘ **864-9301**) and Drekagil (℘ **853-2541**) can be reached directly, but reservations are made with Ferðafélag Akureyrar by email (ffa@ffa.is).

The **Sigurðarskáli hut,** Route 902, at Kverkfjöll (℘ **853-6236**) is booked through **Ferðafélag Fljótsdalshéraðs** (℘ **863-5813;** ferdafelag@egilsstadir.is; www. fljotsdalsherad.is/ferdafelag); e-mail contact is preferred. The remote hut at Gengissig—simply known as **Kverkfjöll hut**—has no electricity or running water and sleeps six (or 12, more intimately). For reservations, contact the **Icelandic Glaciological Society** (℘ **893-0742;** skalar@jorfi.is).

Icelandic Pronunciation & Useful Vocabulary

Most Icelanders speak English, often with remarkable fluency—especially among younger and more urban demographics. (In 1999, English replaced Danish as the first foreign language taught in every school.) You can easily get by without learning Icelandic, but it really pays to at least learn the rules of pronunciation. Asking for directions will go far more smoothly, and Icelanders are extremely appreciative when you say their names correctly.

If you do absorb some vocabulary, be aware that Icelandic words are notorious for constantly shifting in form. All nouns are gendered, and adjectives have to match the gender, number, and case of the nouns they modify. Even proper names have multiple forms: a restaurant on a street called Strandgata would give its address as *Strandgötu*, and a guesthouse run by a woman named Hanna Sigga is called *Gistiheimili Hönnu Siggu*.

1 Pronunciation Guide

Icelandic inflections are difficult to get the hang of, but rules of pronunciation are relatively straightforward. Stress usually falls on the first syllable of each word. The Icelandic alphabet has 36 letters, with 12 vowels. Two consonants, the *eth* (ð, Ð) and the *thorn* (þ, Þ), were borrowed from Old English. For the most part, Icelandic letters are pronounced as in English; the most notable exceptions are listed below. For a free online lesson in Icelandic pronunciation, visit www.travlang.com/languages.

VOWELS

á	*ow* as in *plow*
é	*ye* as in *yellow*
i, y	*i* as in *big*
í, ý	*ee* as in *teen*
ó	*o* as in *tone*
ö	*i* as in *whirl*
ú	*oo* as in *pool*
æ	*i* as in *wine*
au	*uh-ee,* as in *hurry* (without the h or rr)

CONSONANTS

ð (Ð)	*th* as in *bathe*
þ (Þ)	*th* as in *thought*
dj	*j* as in *junk*
hv	*kv* as in *kvetch,* but softer
j	*y* as in *yes*
ll	*ddl* as in *cuddle*
r	rolled, as in Spanish

Icelanders: On a First-Name Basis

Iceland is alone among Scandinavian countries in retaining the Old Norse system of patronymics as opposed to surnames. If a man named Einar has a son named Jón, the son's name is Jón Einarsson. If Einar has a daughter named Ásta, her name is Ásta Einarsdóttir. Women do not change names when they marry, so if a married couple has a son and a daughter, every family member has a different last name. Children are often named after their grandparents, further adding to the confusion. The upside is that when you speak to Icelanders, you always know which form of address to use. Icelanders all call each other by first name, no matter what their social relations. Even the country's single, slender phone book is alphabetized by first name.

2 Basic Vocabulary & Phrases

Yes **Já**

No **Nei**

Hello **Hallo** *or* **Góðan daginn**

Goodbye **Bless**

Excuse me **Fyrirgefðu**

Please **Vinsamlegast** *or* **Takk**

Thank you **Takk** *or* **Takk fyrir**

You're welcome **Þú ert velkominn**

Do you speak English? **Talar þú ensku?**

I don't understand **Ég skil ekki**

My name is . . . **Ég heiti . . .**

What is your name? **Hvað heitir þú?**

Nice to meet you **Gaman að kynnast þér**

Cheers! **Skál!**

Where is the . . . ? **Hvar er . . . ?**

Tourist information office **Upplýsingaþjónustu fyrir ferðafólk**

Toilet **Snyrting**

Bank **Banki**

ATM **Hraðbanki**

Restaurant **Veitingahús**

Bus **Strætisvagn** *or* **Rúta**

Airport **Flugvöllur**

Post office **Pósthús**

Police station **Lögureglustöð**

Pharmacy **Apótek**

Hospital **Sjúkrahús**

Doctor **Læknir**

Help **Hjálp**

Left **Vinstri**

Right **Hægri**

North **Norður**

South **Suður**

East **Austur**

West **Vestur**

Map **Kort**

Passport **Vegabréf**

How much is it? **Hvar koster þetta?**

Do you have . . . **Hefur þú . . .**

Do you have any vacancies? **Eru herbergi laus?**

Room **Herbergi**

Reservation **Bókun**

Sleeping bag/sleeping bag accommodation **Svefnpoka/svefnpoka gisting**

Today **Í dag**

Tomorrow **A morgun**

Open **Opið**

Closed **Lókað**

NUMBERS, DAYS & MONTHS

Zero **Núll**

One **Einn**

Two **Tveir**

Three **Þrír**

Four **Fjórir**

Five **Fimm**

Six **Sex**

Seven **Sjö**

Eight **Átta**

Nine **Níu**

Ten **Tíu**

One hundred **Eitt hundrað**

One thousand **Eitt þúsund**

Monday **Mánudagur**

Tuesday **Þriðjudagur**

Wednesday **Miðvikudagur**

Thursday **Fimmtudagur**

Friday **Föstudagur**

Saturday **Laugardagur**

Sunday **Sunnudagur**

January **Janúar**

February **Febrúar**

March **Mars**

April **Apríl**

May **Maí**

June **Júní**

July **Júlí**

August **Ágúst**

September **September**

October **Október**

November **Nóvember**

December **Desember**

3 Glossary of Geographical Terms

Icelandic place names are usually pieced together from local geographical features and other landmarks. The village of *Kirkjubæjarklaustur*, for example, means "Church Farm Cloister," while *Jökulsárgljúfur* is "Glacial River Canyon." Farm names are usually inspired by nearby topography; *Rauðaskriða*, for instance, is surrounded by slopes of red scree (*rauða skriða*). Identifying the components of place names provides a key to local environments, both scenically and historically, as you travel through Iceland.

á   river
alda   ridge of several hills
bær   farm, small settlement
bakki   riverbank
berg   rock, cliff
bjarg   cliff
brekka   slope, scree
brú   bridge
bruni   lava
dalur   valley
djúp   long coastal inlet
eiði   isthmus
ey   island (plural *eyjar*)
eyri   spit of land, point
fell   hill, mountain
fjall   mountain, (plural *fjöll*)
fjörður   broad inlet or fjord
fljót   wide river
flói   large bay
foss   waterfall
gil   gorge
gjá   fissure
gljúfur   canyon
gnúpur   steep mountain, promontory
hæð   hill
háls   ridge
heiði   heath, moor
hlíð   mountainside
höfði   promontory, headland
höfn   harbor
hóll   rounded hill (plural *hólar*)
hólmur   small island

hraun   lava flow
hver   hot spring
jökull   glacier
jökulsá   glacial river
kirkja   church
klauster   cloister
klettur   cliff, crag (plural *klettar*)
laug   hot spring (plural *laugar*)
múli   headland
nes   headland, peninsula, point
ós   estuary, mouth of river
reykur   smoke, steam
sandur   sands, beach
sjór   ocean, sea
skagi   peninsula, cape, headland
skarð   mountain pass
sker   rocky islet, reef, skerry
skógur   woodland, scrubland
skriða   scree, rockslide
staður   place, stead (plural *staðir*)
stapi   crag
tangi   spit of land, point
tindur   peak
tjörn   small lake, pond
tunga   spit of land, point
vað   ford
vatn   lake, water (plural *vötn*)
vegur   path, road, way
vellir   plains (singular *völlur*)
vík   small inlet, bay, cove
vogur   inlet, creek, cove

Index

Accommodations, 43–46, 48
best, 8–9
Act Alone Theater Festival
(Ísafjörður), 201
Active vacations, 56–71
The Activity Group, 56, 60,
61–62, 170
Activity Tours, 227
Aðalstræti (Reykjavík), 110
Aðalvík, 212
Adventures Abroad, 35
Aerial tours, 56–57
Akureyri, 242
Mývatn-Krafla region, 255
Afangar (Stages; Videy*)*, 119
Air travel, 20–22, 42
Akrafjall, 139
Akranes, 138, 139
Akranes Museum Center, 139
Akurey, 121
Akureyri, 5, 230–244
accommodations, 235–237
banks/currency exchange, 233
cellphones, 233
drugstores, 233
excursions near, 244–250
getting to and around,
232–233
Internet access, 234
medical help, 234
nightlife, 244
in the off season, 20
outdoor activities, 242–243
restaurants, 237–240
shopping, 243
sights and attractions,
240–242
supermarkets, 234
visitor information, 233
Akureyri Art Museum
(Listasafníd á Akureyri), 240
Akureyri Church, 240
Akureyri Summer Arts Festival,
17, 240
Akureyri Swimming pool, 243

Álafoss Factory Outlet
(Mosfellsbær), 137
Aldeyjarfoss, 4, 250
Aldrei fór ég sudur (Ísafjörður),
201
Álfaborg, 347
Almannagjá (Everyman's
Gorge), 142
Alþingishús (Parliament House;
Reykjavík), 110–111
Andey, 329
Apartment rentals, 45–46
Aquarium, Reykjavík, 117
Aquarium & Natural History
Museum (Heimaey), 282
Arbæjarlaug (Reykjavík), 121
Arbær Museum (Arbæjarsafn,
or Reykjavík City Museum),
119
Arcanum Adventure Tours, 303
Arctic Adventures, 56, 57, 59,
62, 69, 148
Arctic Henge, 273
Arctic Horses (Arctic Hestar;
Grindavík), 159
Arctic Open, 17
Arinbjörn Jóhannsson, 64, 65,
218
Arnarfell, 160
Arnarhóll (Reykjavík), 111
Arnarstapi, 176
Arnarstapi-Hellnar trail, 177
Arnes, 208
Around Iceland, 13, 46
Ásbyrgi, 269
Á seydi (Seyðisfjörður), 341
Ash Wednesday (Öskudagur), 16
ASI Art Museum (Asmundarsalur;
Reykjavík), 115
Askja, 4, 359–362
Asmundur Sveinsson Sculpture
Museum (Asmundarsafn;
Reykjavík), 117
Astronomy Magazine, 36–37
Atlantsflug, 314
ATMs (automated teller
machines), 23

Audun's House (Audunarstofa;
Hólar), 224
Austurvöllur Square (Reykjavík),
110
Aviation Museum (Akureyri),
242

Bakkagerði (Borgarfjörður),
347
Bakkagerðiskirkja, 347
Bar 11 (Reykjavík), 128
Barinn (Reykjavík), 128
Barnafoss (Children's Falls), 169
Beer Day, 16
Bergmann, Daniel, 67
Bergþórshvoll, 296
Berserkjahraun, 180
B5 (Reykjavík), 128
Biking and mountain biking,
57–58, 202, 252, 342
Bird-watching, 58–59
Dyrhólaey, 303
Grímsey, 247
Hrísey, 246
Húsavík and environs, 264
Ingólfshöfði, 315
Melrakkaslétta, 272, 273
Papey, 328
puffins, 121, 247, 273, 283
Reynisfjall, 304
Seyðisfjörður, 342
southern Snæfellsnes, 176
Stykkishólmur and
Breiðafjörður, 187
Vatnsnes Peninsula, 216
Bjarnarflag, 254–255
Bjarnarhöfn, 181
Bláa Kirkjan (Seydisfjördur),
341–342
Bláa Lónið (Blue Lagoon),
1, 150–152
Bláfjöll, 70
Blönduós, 218–220
Blue Biking, 57
Blue Lagoon (Bláa Lónið),
1, 150–152

Boat travel and cruises, 22–23, 42
Heimaey area, 284
Lögurinn, 337
Bolludagur, 16
Bolungarvík, 205
Book of Settlements, 112, 261
Books, recommended, 50–51
Borea Adventures, 67, 70, 211
Borgarfjörður (Bakkagerði), 347
Borgarfjörður Eystri, 6, 345–350
Borgarnes, 166–172, 174
Borton Overseas, 35
Boston (Reykjavík), 128
Botanical Garden (Lystigarður Akureyrar), 241
Botnsvatn, 263
Breiðafjördur, 185–188, 190
Breiðárlón, 316
Breiðavík, 175
Breiðdalsvík, 328
Brekka, 343–344
Brekkulækur Farm, 64, 65, 218
Bridge Between Two Continents, 158
Brimnes, 343
Brúnavík, 349
Brydebúð Museum (Vík), 301, 303
Búðahraun lava field, 175
Búðaklettur, 176
Búðavík, 175
Búðir, 176
Business hours, 52
Bustarfell Museum (near Vopnafjördur), 274–275
Bus travel, 41–42
Butterfield & Robinson, 36
Byggðasafn Garðskaga (Garður Peninsula Historical Museum), 157
Byggðasafnid Hrafnseyri, 196
Byggðasafnid Hvoll (Dalvík Folk Museum), 245
Byggðasafn Snæfellsbæjar (Snæfellsbæjar Regional Museum), 179
Byggðasafn Vestfjarda (Ísafjörður), 201–202
Byggðasafn Vestmannaeyja (Folk Museum; Heimaey), 282

Cabins, 43
Cafe Amsterdam (Reykjavík), 130
Cafe Oliver (Reykjavík), 128–129
Calendar of events, 15–19

Campers, 39
Camping, 45
Borgarfjörður Eystri, 349
Jökulsárgljúfur, 270
Skaftafell, 314
Canyon Calling, 37
Carpooling, 41
Car rentals, 38–39
Car travel, 37–41
Catholic Church (Kaþólska Kirkjan; Akureyri), 241
Caving, 59
Mývatn-Krafla region, 255
Cellphones (mobile phones), 33–34
Central Westfjords, 195–198
Charcot, Dr., Memorial to the Shipwreck of (Fáskrúðs-fjörður), 328
Christmas House (Jólagarðurinn; near Akureyri), 248
Christmas season, 18
Cintamani (Reykjavík), 126
City Cathedral (Dómkirkjan; Reykjavík), 111
Classical music, Reykjavík, 130–131
Climate, 15
Climbing, 178, 185, 196, 289. *See also* specific mountains and volcanoes.
Codex Regius of the Elder Edda, 112
Cod-fishing, 328
Consulates, 53
Continental Journeys, 36
Couch-swapping, 46
Credit and debit cards, 23–24
Crime, 26
Cross-Culture Journeys, 37
Cruises. *See* Boat travel and cruises.
Culture House (Reykjavík), 112
Currency, 23
Customs regulations, 52–53

Dalvík, 244–245
Dalvík Folk Museum (Bygg-ðasafnid Hvoll), 245
Davidshús (Akureyri), 240
Dettifoss, 4, 270
Dhoon rescue, 191, 192
Dick Phillips Icelandic Travel Service, 64, 293
Dillon (Reykjavík), 129
Dimmuborgir, 252, 253
Disabilities, travelers with, 27–28

Djúpalónssandur, 178–179
Djúpavík, 207–208
Djúpivogur, 326, 327, 329–331
Dog sledding, 59–60, 303
Dog Steam Tours, 303
Dómkirkjan (City Cathedral; Reykjavík), 111
Drangey, 223
Drekagil gorge, 362
Drekkingarhylur (Drowning Pool), 144
Dritvík, 179
Driving laws, 39–40
Driving safety, 40
Duus Hús (Keflavík), 153–154
Dvergasteinn, 343
Dynjandi (Fjallfoss), 196
Dynkur, 358
Dyrhólaey, 303

Easter Sunday, 16
The Eastfjords
lower, 326–331
middle, 331–332
East Iceland, 319–351
East Iceland Heritage Museum (Minjasafn Austurlands; Egilsstaðir), 336
Echo Rocks (Hljóðaklettar), 269–270
Ecotourism, 31
Eden, 161
Educational tours, 36–37
Egg-collecting club of Þórshöfn, 274
Egg House (Eyrarbakki), 163
Egils Olafsson Folk Museum (Örlygshöfn), 191
Egils Saga, 168
Egilsstaðir, 332–336, 351
871±2 Settlement Museum (Reykjavík), 112
Einar Jónsson, 111, 116, 201, 241, 328
Museum (Reykjavík), 7, 115
Eldborg, 175
Elderhostel, 23, 29
Eldey, 158
Eldfell, 283
Eldgjá, 291
Eldhestar, 65, 74, 161, 354, 357
Elli Aár valley, 119
Ellidaár river, 121, 122
ELM (Reykjavík), 124
Elves. *See* Hidden people.
Embassies, 53
Emergency shelters, 26
Engidalur valley, 202

Entry requirements, 13–14
Esja, 138
Eyjafjörður, Upper, 248–249
Eyjafjörður Route, 357
Eyrarbakki, 162–163
Eyrbyggja Heritage Centre
    (Hrannarstígur), 179
Eyrbyggja Saga, 50, 180,
    181, 185

Fagrifoss, 310
Families with children, 29–30,
    114
Farmer's Market (Reykjavík),
    126
Farm stays, 43–44, 293
Fáskrúðsfjörður, 326–331
FA Travel (Ferðaskrifstofa
    Austurlands), 339, 346
Faxaflói Bay, 120
Ferðafélag Akureyrar, 360–361
Ferðafélag Fljótsdalshérads,
    336, 339, 346, 349, 360,
    361, 363
Ferðafélag Islands, 56, 63, 71,
    209, 211, 289–292, 299, 354,
    356, 358
Festival of the Sea, 16
Fimmvörðuháls trail, 300, 302
Fish factory tours, Suðureyri,
    197
Fishing, 60–61
    Akureyri, 242
    Breiðafjörður, 187
    Grímsey, 247
    Húsavík and environs, 264
    Reykjavík, 122
    Seyðisfjörður, 342
Fiska og Náttúrugripasafnið
    (Heimaey), 282
Fiskbyrgi, 179
Fiskidagurinn (The Great Fish
    Day; Dalvík), 245
Five Stars of Scandinavia, 36
Fjaðrárgljúfur, 4, 309
Fjallabak, 291
Fjallabak Nature Reserve, 290
Fjallfoss (Dynjandi), 196
Fjallsárlón, 316
Fjörukráin (Viking Village;
    Hafnarfjörður), 134
Flatey Island, 186–187
Flateyri, 196
Fljótsdalsheiði, 337
Fljótsdalshérað valley, 350–351
Flosagjá, 144
Flúðir, 149, 150

Flugsafn Islands (Aviation
    Museum; Akureyri), 242
Flugumyri, 227
Fold-Anna (Akureyri), 243
Folk Museum (Byggðasafn
    Vestmannaeyja; Heimaey),
    282
Folk Music Center (Þjóðlagase-
    tur; Siglufjörður), 227
Food and Fun, 16
Fótógrafí (Reykjavík), 123
Fræðasetrið Nature Center, 158
Frambúðir, 176
Fransmenn á Islandi
    (Fáskrúðsfjörður), 329
Freaky Friday (Reykjavík), 128
Freewheeling Adventures, 58
From Coast to Mountains, 71,
    314, 315
Frommers.com, 32
Fruín í Hamborg (Akureyri), 243

Galdrasýning á Ströndum
    (Hólmavík), 207
Gallerí Gel (Reykjavík), 128
Gallerí Grúska (Akureyri), 243
Gallerí Svartfugl og Hvítspói
    (Akureyri), 243
Gallery KSK (Reykjavík), 123
Gallery Sól (Grímsey), 248
Galtarviti, 197
Gamlabúð Folk Museum
    (Höfn), 320
Garðskagaviti, 157
Garðskagi, 157
Garður, 157
Garður Peninsula Historical
    Museum (Byggðasafn
    Garðskaga), 157
Gæsavantaleið Route, 357
Gas stations, 41
Gatklettur, 177
Gauksmyri, 218
Gavia Travel, 58
Gay and lesbian travelers, 28,
    129–130
Gay Pride, 17
Gengissig, 363
Geothermal areas, 25
Geothermal pools. See Thermal
    pools.
Gerðuberg, 175
Geysir, 140, 146, 149
Geysir Center, 141
Geysir Museum (Geysísstofa),
    146
The Ghost Center (Stokkseyri),
    163

Gígjökull, 301
Gjáin, 287
Gjástykki, 256
Gjögur, 208
Gjögurstrond, 208
Glacier Exhibition (Jöklasýning;
    Höfn), 320–321
Glaciers, 25–26, 312
Glacier tours, 61–62, 170, 320
Glaumbær (Skagafjörður Folk
    Museum), 7, 222
Glerárdalur Valley, 242
Glerártorg Mall (Akureyri), 243
Glíma (Icelandic wrestling),
    Reykjavík, 122
Gljúfrasteinn (near Mosfells-
    bær), 136–137
Gljúfurá, 212
Gljúfurárfoss, 301
Glymur, 1, 138–139
Goðafoss (Waterfall of the
    Gods), 249–250
Goðaland, 301
Golden Circle, 140–150
Golf, 62
    Akureyri, 242
    Borgarnes, 170
    Reykjavík, 122
    Siglufjörður, 226
Grænavatn, 160
Grafarlandaá river, 361
Grand Rokk (Reykjavík), 130
Great Canadian Travel
    Company, 28, 36
The Great Fish Day (Fiskida-
    gurinn; Dalvík), 245
Greenhouses, geothermal,
    49, 161
Greenland, 21
Grettislaug, 223–224
Grettis Saga (The Saga of
    Grettir the Strong), 223
Grímsey Island, 247–248
Grindavík, 159
Grjótagjá, 252
Grjótagjá fissure, 252
Grundarfjörður, 179
Grund Church (near Akureyri),
    248
Guddmundur Jónasson
    Travel, 35
Guesthouses, 43
Gullfoss, 1, 140, 146–147, 149
Gunnarssteinn, 295
Gunnarstofnun cultural insti-
    tute (near Lögurinn), 337
Gunnuhver, 158

Hælavíkurbjarg, 212
Hæstikaupstaður (Ísafjörður),
    201
Hafn (Old Harbor; Reykjavík),
    113
Hafnaberg Cliffs, 158
Hafnarfjörður, 133–136
Hafnarhólmi, 348
Hafnarhús (Harbor House
    Museum; Reykjavík), 113
Hafnir, 158
Hafragilsfoss, 270
Háifoss, 287–288
Háihnúkur, 139
Hákarlsafn, 181
Halaklettur, 327
Hallbjörn Hjartarson, 216,
    218, 220
Halldór Laxness, 50, 159, 178
    Museum (near Mosfellsbær),
    136–137
Hallgrímskirkja (Hallgríms
    Church; Reykjavík), 115–116
Hallormsstadaskógur, 336–337
Hálsanefshellir, 304
Handball, 122
Handknitting Association of
    Iceland (Handprjónasamband
    Íslands), 127
Harbor House Museum (Haf-
    narhús; Reykjavík), 7, 113
Haunted Iceland (Reykjavík), 86
Health concerns, 25, 26
Health insurance, 24
Heimæy (Home Island; Videy),
    5, 118, 278, 280–286
Heimilisiðnaðarsafnið (Textile
    Museum; Blönduós), 218
Hekla, 286–289
Hekla Center (Hekluhof), 288
Hekluhestar (near Hella),
    293, 294
Helgafell, 185
Helgi Arngrímsson, 346
Helgustaðanáma, 332
Hella, 293–294, 296–298
Hellissandur, 179
Hellnar, 177
Hengifoss, 337
Hengill hiking area, 161, 162
Herðubreið, 361
Herðubreiðarlindir, 361
Herrídarhóll (near Hella), 294
Herring, Siglufjörður, 225–226
Herring Era Museum (Síldarmin-
    jasafnið; Siglufjörður), 226
Hestasport, 65, 227

Hesteyri, 212
Hestheimar (near Hella), 294
Heydalur, 206
Hidden people (elves, dwarves,
    gnomes, trolls), 134, 136,
    177, 304, 348
Hidden Worlds (Hafnarfjörður),
    134, 136
Hiking, 47, 63–64
    Akureyri area, 242
    best hikes, 5–7
    Borgarfjörður Eystri, 345,
        348–349
    Dalvík, 245
    Hekla and Stöng/Gjáin/Háifoss
        area, 286–289
    Hengill area, 161
    Hornstrandir, 211–212
    Ísafjörður area, 202
    Jökulsárgljúfur National Park,
        268–269
    Kjölur, 354, 355
    Kverkfjöll and Kverkjökull,
        362, 363
    Landmannalaugar, 291
    Látrabjarg Peninsula,
        191–192
    Lónsöræfi area, 325–326
    lower Eastfjords, 326–327
    Melrakkaslétta, 272
    middle Eastfjords, 331–332
    Myvatn-Krafla region,
        252–254
    Seyðisfjörður, 342, 343
    Siglufjörður area, 226
    Skaftafell, 313
    Snæfell-Kárahnjúkar area, 339
    southern Snæfellsnes, 177, 178
    Sprengisandur, 357, 358
    the Strandir Coast, 208–209
    suggested itineraries, 81–82
    Þakgil, 305
    Þingvellir, 145
    Þórsmörk, 299–301
    Westfjords Alps, 196
    the Westmans, 284
Hindisvík, 217
Hjálparfoss, 287
Hjörleifshöfði, 305
Hlíðarendi, 295–296
Hlíðarfjall, 243
Hljóðaklettar (Echo Rocks),
    269–270
Höfði, 253
Höfn, 319–324
Hofsós, 225, 228–230
Hóladómkirkja (Hólar), 224
Hólahólar, 179
Hólar, 224–225

Holidays, 53
Hornbjarg, 4, 212
Hornbjargsviti (Látravík
    lighthouse), 212
Hornstrandir Nature Reserve,
    5, 210–213
Hornvík, 212
Horseback riding, 65
    Akureyri area, 243
    Borgarfjörður Eystri, 346
    Breiðdalur, 328
    Fljótsdalshérad Valley, 350
    Húnaflói area, 218
    Húsavík area, 263
    Kjölur, 354
    Landmannalaugar area, 293
    Mosfellsbær, 137
    Mývatn-Krafla region,
        255–256
    Njáls Saga sites, 295
    north Iceland, 227
    Reykjavík, 122
    Snæfellsnes, 180
    southern Snæfellsnes, 176
    Sprengisandur, 357
    Svarfaðardalur valley, 245
Hostels, 44
Hótel Borg (Reykjavík), 111
Hótel Eldborg, 176
House or apartment rentals,
    45–46
House-swapping, 46
Hrafnagjá (Raven Gorge), 142
Hrafnseyri, 196
Hrauneyjar Highland Center,
    358
Hraunfossar, 169
Hraunhafnartangi, 273
Hressingarskálinn (Reykjavík),
    129
Hrísey Island, 245–247
Hrossaborg, 361
Húnaflói, 214–221
Hunting, 66
Hunting Museum (Stokkseyri),
    163
Húsavík, 259–271
Húsavík Church
    (Húsavíkurkirkja), 260
Húsavík Museum (Safnahúsid),
    8, 261
Húsavík Whale Museum
    (Hvalasafnid á Húsavík), 261
Húsið (The House; Eyrarbakki),
    163
Hvalalíf (Reykjavík), 120–122
Hvalfjörður, 138
Hvalsneskirkja, 157
Hvammstangi, 219–220

Hvannagilshnúta, 325
Hverageroi, 140, 160–165
Hveragil, 362
Hveratagl, 363
Hveravellir, 355–356
Hverfell, 4, 252, 253
Hverir, 254
Hvitá River, 148
Hvítárnes, 355, 356
Hvítárvatn, 355
Hvítserkur, 217, 349
Hvolsvöllur, 293, 294

Ice Bar (Reykjavík), 129
Icelandair, 20–21
Iceland Airwaves Festival
  (Reykjavík), 18, 130
Iceland America, 36
Icelander Tours/Highlander
  Adventures, 58–59
Iceland Excursions, 35, 59, 86,
  137, 141, 146, 157, 175, 187
Icelandic Alpine Club, 69, 70
Icelandic Dance Company, 131
Icelandic Emigration Center
  (Vesturfarasetrið; Hofsós),
  225
Icelandic Farm Holidays, 27, 29,
  44, 227, 265, 305
Icelandic Mountainbike Club
  (Reykjavík), 57
Icelandic Mountain Guides, 64,
  71, 293, 302, 310, 312, 314,
  357
The Icelandic Opera (Reykjavík),
  131
Icelandic Phallological Museum
  (Húsavík), 263
The Icelandic Saltfish Museum
  (Saltfisksetur Islands), 159
Icelandic Seal Center (Selasetur
  Islands; Brekkugata), 216
Icelandic Sport Museum
  (Akranes), 139
Icelandic Wartime Museum
  (Íslenska Stríðsárasafnið;
  Reydarfjördur), 332
Icelandic Wonders (Stokkseyri),
  163
Iceland Refund, 123
Iceland Rovers, 59, 62, 67
Iceland Saga Travel, 36
Iceland spar, 332
Iceland Symphony Orchestra,
  131
Iceland Total, 22, 35, 141
Imagine Peace Tower (Videy),
  119

Industry Museum (Iðnaðarsafn;
  Akureyri), 241–242
Ingólfshöfði, 315–316
Ingólfur Arnarson, 110, 116,
  261, 277, 315
  statue of (Reykjavík), 111
Innra-Hvannagil, 347
Insurance, 24, 39
The interior, 352–363
Internet access, 34–35
Irish Days festival (Akranes),
  139
Ísafjörður, 4–5, 198–205
Ísafold Travel, 37, 291
Íshestar, 65, 122, 354, 357
Itineraries, suggested, 72–82

Jarðböðin Við Mývatn
  (Mývatn Nature Baths), 255
Jazz, Reykjavík, 131
Jeep tours, 66–67, 170, 256
Jewelry, Reykjavík, 125
Jöklasel, 316–317
Jöklasýning (Glacier Exhibition;
  Höfn), 320–321
Jökulsárgljúfur National Park,
  5, 266–271
Jökulsárlón, 4, 315, 316
Jólagarðurinn (Christmas
  House; near Akureyri), 248
Jón Arason, monument to
  (Skálholt), 147
Jón Sigurðsson
  grave of (Reykjavík), 114
  statue of (Reykjavík), 110

Kaffibarinn (Reykjavík), 129
Kaffihús Rauðasandi
  (Rauðisandur), 191
Kaffi Reykjavík (Reykjavík), 129
Kaldbakur, 196
Kaldidalur valley, 170
Kalfarströnd, 253
Kaþólska Kirkjan (Akureyri), 241
Kárahnjúkar dam and hydro-
  electric project, 332,
  337–339, 350
Katla, 305
Kayaking, 67
  Breiðafjörður, 187
  Dalvík, 245
  Eyrarbakki area, 163
  Seyðisfjörður, 342
Kayakklúbburinn Kaj, 67, 331
Keflavík, 152–156, 191,
  192, 220

Keflavík International Airport,
  20, 21
Keldur, 295
Kerið crater, 140, 148
Kerlingarfjöll, 6, 355
Kirkjubæjarklaustur, 308, 310
Kirkjugólf, 309
Kirkjuvegur trail, 253
Kirsuberjatréð (Reykjavík), 123
Kisan (Reykjavík), 125
Kjarvalsstaðir (Reykjavík), 116
Kjarvalsstofa (the Kjarval
  Experience), 348
Kjölur Route, 352–356
Kjölurvegur Trek, 355
Kjós, 314
Kleifarvatn, 160
Klifurhúsið, 69
Kolaportið (Reykjavík), 126
Koluglúfur, 217–218
Krafla caldera, 254–255
Krafla Geothermal Power
  Station (Kröflustöð), 254
Krafla Route, 254
Kringlan (Reykjavík), 126
Kringlan Mall (Reykjavík), 126
Krókastígur trail, 253
KronKron (Reykjavík), 124
Krossneslaug, 208, 209
Krýsuvík Church (Krýsu-
  víkurkirkja), 159–160
Kverkfjöll, 7, 359, 360, 362
Kvíárjökull, 316

Lækjargata (Reykjavík), 111
Lækjartorg Square (Reykjavík),
  111
Laki Craters (Lakagígar), 4,
  308–310
Lambatangi, 160
Landlyst (Maternity Museum;
  Heimaey), 282
Landmannalaugar, 5, 289–293
Langabúð (Djúpivogur), 327
Langanes, 273–274
Language, 53
Language courses, 37
Látrabjarg, 1, 4, 191
Látrabjarg Peninsula, 191–192,
  194
Látravík lighthouse (Horn-
  bjargsviti), 212
Laufás (Eyjafjörður), 249
Laugardalshöll (Reykjavík), 130
Laugardalslaug (Reykjavík),
  121
Laugardalsvöllur Stadium
  (Reykjavík), 122

Laugardalur (Reykjavík), 116–117
Laugar Spa (thermal pools), 120
Laugavegur (Reykjavík), 112
Laxnes Horse Farm, 65–66, 122, 137
Leifur (Leif) Eiríksson, statue of (Reykjavík), 116
Leirhnjúkur lava field, 4, 254
Liborius (Cobn), 124
Lindarbakki, 347
Liquor laws, 53
Listasafnið á Akureyri (Akureyri Art Museum), 240
Listasafn Islands (National Gallery of Iceland; Reykjavík), 114
Listasafn Samúels (Selárdalur), 193
Literary Walking Tours (Reykjavík), 86
Litla-Hraun jail (Eyrarbakki), 163
Litlanesfoss, 337
Litlihöfði, 284
Living Art Museum (Nýlistasafnið, or Nýló; Reykjavík), 112
Loðmundarfjörður, 343, 349
Lofthellir, 255
Lögberg (Law Rock), 142, 144
Lögretta (Law Council), 144
Lögsögumaður (Law Speaker), 144
Lögurinn, 336–337
Lónið lake, 301
Lónsöræfi, 6, 324–326
Lost and found, 53
Lost-luggage insurance, 24
Lundey Island, 120, 121, 264
LungA festival (Seyðisfjörður), 341
Lystigarður Akureyrar (Botanical Garden), 241
Lýsuhóll Farm, 176
Lýsuhóll geothermal pool, 175
Lýtingsstaðir (near Varmahlíð), 227

Mælifell, 305
Mail, 53–54
Malarrif, 178
Malls, Reykjavík, 126
Málmey, 223
Mánárbakka Museum (near Húsavík), 263
Maps, 13, 41

Maritime Museum (Eyrarbakki), 163
Markarfljót valley, 294–295
Maternity Museum (Landlyst; Heimaey), 282
Melrakkaslétta, 272–273
Middle Eastfjords, 331–332
Miðkaupstaður (Ísafjörður), 201
Minjahús (Sauð Arkrókur), 223
Minja-og Handverkshúsið Kört (Trékyllisvík), 208
Minjasafn A Akureyri (Museum of Akureyri), 241
Minjasafn Austurlands (East Iceland Heritage Museum; Egilsstaðir), 336
Mjóifjörður, 343
Mobile phones (cellphones), 33–34
Möðrudalur, 351
Money and costs, 23–24
Morsárdalur (Morsá river valley), 313–314
Mosfellsbær, 136–137
Mountaineers of Iceland, 56, 57, 59, 67
Mountain huts, 45
Museum of Akureyri (Minjasafn A Akureyri), 241
Museum of Icelandic Sorcery and Witchcraft (Hólmavík), 207
Museum of Small Exhibits (Smámunasafn), 7, 248–249
Museums, best, 7–8
Museums of Eyrarbakki, 163
Mýrdalsjökull, 301–303, 305
Mýrdalssandur, 305
Mývatn-Krafla region, 250–259, 351
Mývatn Nature Baths (Jarðböðin Við Mývatn), 255
Mývatn Tours, 360

Naddakross, 347
The Naked Ape (Reykjavík), 125
Nasa (Reykjavík), 130
National Day, 16–17
National Gallery of Iceland (Listasafn Íslands; Reykjavík), 114
National Gallery of Photography (Reykjavík), 115
National Museum of Iceland (Reykjavík), 7, 115
National Theater (Reykjavík), 131

Nattfari, 261
Natural History Museum (Náttúrugripasafn Bolungarvíkur; Bolungarvík), 205
Naustahvilft, 202
Nauthólsvík Beach (Reykjavík), 117
Neðrivellir (Low Fields), 144
Neðsdikaupstaður (Ísafjörður), 201
Neshraun, 179
Nesjavellir Geothermal Power Plant, 140, 146
Neskaupstaður, 331
New Year's Day, 15
New Year's Eve, 18–19
Night Circle Tour (Reykjavík), 128
Nightlife Friend (Reykjavík), 128
Njáls Saga, sites associated with, 295–296
Njarðvík, 347
Njarðvíkurskriður, 347
NLFI Rehabilitation and Health Clinic, 161
Nonnahús (Nonni's House; Akureyri), 241
Nonni Travel, 35, 56, 242
Nordic Adventure Travel, 10, 35, 45, 56
NordicaSpa (thermal pools), 120
Nordic Saga Tours, 36
Norðurfjörður, 208
The northeast corner, 271–276
North Iceland, 214–276
Norwegian House (Stykkishólmur), 186
Núpsstaðarskógar, 6, 311–312
Núpsstaður, 311
Nýibær (Hólar), 224
Nýidalur, 358
Nýlistasafnið (Nýló, or Living Art Museum; Reykjavík), 112

Odysseys Unlimited, 36
Ofanleitishamar, 284
Off season, 19–20
  car travel, 41
Olafsson, Sigurjón, Museum (Reykjavík), 117
Olafsvík, 179
The Old Churchyard (Suðurgata or Hólavallagarður Cemetery; Reykjavík), 114
Old Harbor (Hafn; Reykjavík), 113

Öndverðarnes, 179–180
Ono, Yoko, Imagine Peace
  Tower (Videy), 119
Osar, 217
Öskjuhlíð Hill (Reykjavík),
  117–118
Öskjuvatn Lake, 362
Öskjuvegurinn, 361
Osvör Museum (near Bol-
  ungarvík), 205
Outdoor gear, Reykjavík, 126
The Outlaw (Utlaginn;
  Akureyri), 241
Oxará (Axe River), 144
Oxaráfoss, 144

Package tours, 35–36
Packing suggestions, 47
PADI Dive Center (Reykjavík),
  69–70
Pakkhúsið (Höfn), 320
Papey, 327–328
Parliament House (Alþingishús;
  Reykjavík), 110–111
Parliament House Garden
  (Reykjavík), 111
Páskahellir, 283
Passports, 13, 54
Patreksfjörður, 192–195
The Pearl (Perlan; Reykjavík),
  118
Peningagjá (Money Fault), 145
Penninn Eymundsson
  (Akureyri), 244
Photography, 67–68
Photography Museum of
  Reykjavík, 113
Polar Hestar, 66
Police, 54
Pollurinn, 192–193
Pompei of the North, 284
Pools. See Thermal pools.
Puffins, 121, 247, 273, 283

Ráðhús (Reykjavík City Hall),
  114–115
Rauðanes, 273
Rauðhólar (Red Hills), 269, 270
Rauðinúpur, 272–273
Rauðisandur, 191
Raufarhöfn, 273, 275, 276
Raufarhólshellir, 1, 161–162
Regions of Iceland, 12–13
REI Adventures, 64
Restaurants, 9–10, 48–49
Réttir (sheep round-up), 18
Rex (Reykjavík), 129

Reyðarfjörður, 331, 332, 338
Reykholt, 149, 169, 171
Reykjadalur, 160, 162
Reykjahlíð Church (Myvatn), 252
Reykjanes, 158
Reykjanesfólkvangur, 160
Reykjaneshyrna, 208–209
Reykjanes Peninsula, 156–160
Reykjavík, 12, 83–132
  accommodations, 88–98
  arriving in, 83–84
  attractions, 107–119
  drugstores, 86–87
  embassies, 87
  emergencies, 87
  getting around, 84–85
  Internet access, 87
  for kids, 114
  lost and found, 87
  luggage storage, 87
  medical help, 87
  nightlife, 127–132
  in the off season, 19–20
  organized tours, 85–86
  police, 88
  post offices, 88
  restaurants, 98–107
  restrooms, 88
  shopping, 123–127
  supermarkets, 88
  telephones, 88
  visitor information, 84
  websites, 84
Reykjavík Arts Festival, 16
Reykjavík City Hall (Ráðhús),
  114–115
Reykjavík City Museum (Arbær
  Museum or Arbæjarsafn),
  119
Reykjavík City Theatre, 131
Reykjavík Dance Festival,
  17, 131
Reykjavík Excursions, 35, 42,
  85. See also specific
  destinations.
Reykjavík International Film
  Festival, 17
Reykjavík Jazz Festival, 17, 131
Reykjavík Marathon and
  Culture Night, 17
Reykjavík Maritime Museum
  (Víkin; Reykjavík), 113
Reykjavík Tourist Card, 110
Reykjavík Zoo & Family Park,
  117
Reynisdrangar, 303
Reynisfjall, 304
Reynisfjara, 304
Rhyolite, 290

The Ring Road, suggested
  itinerary, 74–77
Rite of Spring Festival, 16
Road maps, 41
Rock climbing, 69
Route 428, 159
Route F88, 361

Sænautasel, 351
Safety, outdoor, 25–26
Safn (Reykjavík), 112
Safnahúsið (Húsavík Museum),
  261
Safnasafnið (near Akureyri),
  8, 249
The Saga Center (Hvolsvöllur),
  294
Saga Museum (Reykjavík), 118
The Saga of Grettir the Strong
  (Grettis Saga), 223
Saltfisksetur Islands (The Ice-
  landic Saltfish Museum), 159
Salurinn (Reykjavík), 131
Samgönguminjasafn (Skaga-
  fjörður Transportation
  Museum; near Hofsós), 225
Samgönguminjasafnið Ystafelli
  (Transportation Museum at
  Ystafell), 259–260
Samtökin '78, 28
Sandcastle competition
  (Önundarfjörður), 197
Sandfell, 327
Sandgerði, 157–158
The Sandur (Skeiðarársandur),
  311, 312
Satellite phones, 34
Sauðaneshúsið museum
  (Þórshöfn), 274
Sauðárkrókur, 221, 223,
  228, 229
SBA-Nordurleid, 360
Scanam World Tours, 36
Scantours, 36, 62
Scuba diving and snorkeling,
  69–70
Scuba diving, Þingvallavatn,
  145
Sea angling. See Fishing.
Seafarer's Day, 16
Seakayak Iceland, 67, 187
Seal-watching, 214, 216, 217,
  263, 316, 350
Search and rescue, 26
Seasons, 14–15, 19–20
Seatours, 180, 185, 187
Sel, 313
Selárdalur, 193

Selasetur Islands (Icelandic Seal Center; Brekkugata), 216
Selatangar, 159
Selfoss, 160–165, 270
accommodations, 164–165
Seljalandsfoss, 300
Seljavallalaug, 302
Seltjarnarneslaug (Reykjavík), 121
Seltún geothermic field, 160
Senior travelers, 28–29
Serra, Richard, *Afangar (Stages;* Videy*)*, 119
The Settlement Center (Borgarnes), 7, 168–169
Seyðisfjörður, 5, 340–345
Sheep round-up (réttir), 18
Siglufjörður, 5, 225–227, 229, 230
Sigríður Tómasdóttir, monument to (near Gullfoss), 147
Sigurhæðir (Akureyri), 240
Sigurjón Olafsson Museum (Reykjavík), 117, 131
Síldarminjasafnið (Herring Era Museum; Siglufjörður), 226
Single travelers, 30
Sirka (Akureyri), 244
Sirkus (Reykjavík), 129
66° North (Reykjavík), 126
Sjálfsbjörg, 27
Sjavarsafnið Olafsvík, 179
Sjómannagarður (Hellissandur), 179
Sjónarsker viewpoint, 313
Skaftafell National Park, 6, 311, 313
Skaftafellsheiði, 313
Skaftafellsjökull, 313
Skagafjörður, 221–230
Skagafjörður Route, 357
Skagafjörður Transportation Museum (Samgönguminjasafn; near Hofsós), 225
Skagaströnd, 218, 220–221
Skálanes Nature and Heritage Center (near Seyðisfjörður), 344
Skálholt, 140, 147–148
Skálholt Summer Concerts Festival, 148
Skallagrímsgarður Park (Borgarnes), 168
Skansinn, 282–283
Skarphéðinstindur, 363
Skeiðarársandur (The Sandur), 311, 312

Skiing and ski touring, 70–71, 243
Ski Week (Skíðavikan; Ísafjörður), 201
Skjaldbreiður (Shield Volcano), 145
Skógafoss, 302
Skógar, 301, 302, 306, 308
Skógar Folk Museum (Skógasafn), 8, 302
Skógarkot, 145
Skriðuklaustur, 337
Skrúður, 329
Skútustaðagígar, 253
Sleeping-bag accommodation, 44
Smáralind (Reykjavík), 126
Smoking, 55
Snæfell, 337, 339
Snæfell-Lónsöræfi trek, 325
Snæfellsbæjar Regional Museum, 179
Snæfellsjökull National Park, 174, 177–178
Snæfellsnes, 172–184
Snorralaug (Snorri's Pool), 169
Snorrastaðir Farm, 176
Snorrastofa (Reykholt), 169
The Snorri Program, 37
Snowmobiling and snowmobile tours, 61–62, 178, 303, 317
Soccer, Reykjavík, 122
Sólheimajökull, 302
Solo travelers, 30
Southern Treks, 64
South Iceland, 277–318
Spaksmannsspjarir (Reykjavík), 125
Spas and spa treatments, 68, 120, 151
Spectator sports, Reykjavík, 122
Sprengidagur, 16
Sprengisandur Route, 356–359
The Square (Reykjavík). *See* Austurvöllur Square.
Stafdalur to Vestdalur, 343
Stapafell, 176
Star-rating system, 46
Start Art (Reykjavík), 127
The Stave Church (Stafkirkjan; Heimaey), 282–283
Steinasafn Petru, 328
Steinunn (Reykjavík), 125
Stöðvarfjörður, 328
Stófjörði, 284
Stokkseyri, 163
Stöng, 287

Storagjá, 252
Storagjá fissure, 252
Stóra-Víti, 254–255
Stórurð, 349
Strabo Tours, 67–68
The Strandir Coast, 206–210
Strokkur (The Churn), 146
Student travelers, 30
Stykkishólmur, 184–190
Suðsuðvestur (Keflavík), 153
Suðureyri, 4, 196–197
Suðurgata (The Old Churchyard; Reykjavík), 114
Súgandisey Island, 185
Summer, 14
First Day of, 16
Summer Solstice, 17
Sundhöllin (Reykjavík), 121
Surtsey, 278
Surtshellir, 170
Sustainable tourism, 31
Svarfaðardalur valley, 245
Svartifoss, 313
Sveinn Björnsson, 160
Sveinstindur-Skælingar, 6, 292
Svinafellsjökull, 313
Svörtuloft (The Black Skies), 179
Swamp soccer (Ísafjörður), 201
Swimming, Akureyri, 243
Systrafoss, 309
Systrastapa, 309
Systravatn, 309

Tálknafjörður, 192, 194, 195
Taxes, 55
Technical Museum of East Iceland (Tækniminjasafn Austurlands; Seyðisfjörður), 342
Telephones, 31–34
Textile Museum (Heimilisidnadarsafnið; Blönduós), 218
Þakgil, 6, 304–305
Thermal pools, 68
Reykjavík, 119–121
Selfoss, 162
Seljavallalaug, 302
southern Snæfellsnes, 175
Þingeyrar Church, 217–218
Þingskálar, 295
Þingvallahraun, 145
Þingvallakirkja (Þingvellir Church), 144–145
Þingvallavatn, 142
Þingvallabær, 145
Þingvellir, 140–142, 144–145

Þjódargrafreitur, 145
Þjóðlagasetur (Folk Music
  Center; Siglufjörður), 227
Þjödmenningarhúsid (Culture
  House; Reykjavík), 112
Þjóðvelðisbærinn, 287
Þjórsárdalslaug, 287
Þjórsárdalur valley, 140,
  286–289
Þórhallastadir, 145
Þórólfsfell, 294
Þorrablót, 15
Þórshöfn, 273–276
Þórsmörk, 6, 289, 292,
  298–301
3 Floors (Reykjavík), 125
Þrettándinn, 15
Time zone, 55
Tindfjallajökull ice cap, 294
Tipping, 55
Tjörnes, 263
Tjörnin (Reykjavík), 114–115
Tónlistarsafn (Bíldudalur), 193
Touris, 39, 56, 67
Tours, organized, 35–37
  for disabled travelers, 27
  for gays and lesbians, 28
  glacier, 61–62
  Hornstrandir, 211
  jeep tours, 66–67
  for women, 37
Transportation, 37–42
  for disabled travelers, 27
Transportation Museum at
  Ystafell (Samgöngumin-
  jasafnið Ystafelli), 259–260
Traveling to Iceland, 20–23
Travel insurance, 24
Travelling Theatre Company,
  131
Travel 333 Chicago, 36
Trékyllisvík, 208
Trilogía (Reykjavík), 125
Trip-cancellation insurance,
  medical insurance, 24
Tröllaskagi Peninsula, 245
Tröllkonuhlaup, 288
Trolls. See Hidden people.
Turf houses, 222

Unknown Official, The
  (Reykjavík), 111
Upper Eyjafjördur, 248–249
Ur Alögum (Ísafjörður), 201

Utilíf (Reykjavík), 126
Utivist, 56, 63, 71, 292, 300,
  305, 310, 312, 325
Utlaginn (The Outlaw;
  Akureyri), 241
Utskálakirkja (Garður), 157

Valahnúkur, 158
Valtours, 59
Varmahlíð, 216, 221, 222,
  227–229
Vatnajökull, 311–317
Vatnasafn (Library of Water;
  Stykkishólmur), 186
Vatnsnes Peninsula, 214,
  216–219
VAT (value-added tax) refunds,
  123
Vegetarian travel, 30
Veiðivötn, 358
Verslunarmannahelgi (August
  Long Weekend or Bank
  Holiday Weekend), 17
Vestdalur Valley, 343
Vestmannaeyjar (Westman
  Islands), 277–286
Véstragil, 313
Vesturbæjarlaug (Reykjavík),
  121
Vesturey (West Island), 118
Vesturfarasetrid (Icelandic
  Emigration Center; Hofsós),
  225
Videy Island, 118–119
Videyjarkirkja (Videy), 119
Videyjarstofa (Videy House),
  118–119
Vídgelmir, 170
Vídimyrarkirkja (near
  Varmahlíð), 222
Vigur Island, 205
Vík, 5, 301, 303, 306–308
Víkin (Reykjavík Maritime
  Museum; Reykjavík), 113
The Viking (Akureyri), 244
Viking Festival, 17
Viking Village (Fjörukráin;
  Hafnarfjörður), 134
Vikraborgir, 362
Vindbelgjarfjall mountain, 254
Virkisfell, 362
Visas, 13–14
Visitor information, 13
Víti, 362

Voice over Internet Protocol
  (VoIP), 34
Volcanic Film Show (Heimaey),
  282
Volcanoes, 25. See also specific
  volcanoes.
Volcano Show (Reykjavík),
  131–132
Volunteer vacations, 37
Vonarskarð pass, 358
Vopnafjörður, 274–276
Vopnafjörður Pool, 274

Water, drinking, 55
Weather, 15
Weather signs, 306
Websites, best, 10–11
Westfjords, 166, 188–198
Westfjords Alps, 196
The Westfjords Heritage
  Museum (Ísafjörður),
  201–202
West Iceland, 166–213
Westman Islands (Vestman-
  naeyjar), 277–286
West Tours, 35, 56, 58, 67,
  200–202, 205, 210–212
Whale-watching, 71
  Akureyri area, 243
  Dalvík, 245
  Húsavík area, 264
  Keflavík, 154
  Reykjavík, 120–121
  Snæfellsnes, 180
Whale Watching Reykjavík,
  120, 122
Whaling, 262
  Museum, Húsavík, 261
  station, Hvalfjörður, 139
White-water rafting, 69,
  148, 227
Wi-Fi access, 34–35
Wilderness Travel, 64
Winter Lights Festival, 16
Woolens, 126–127
Working in Iceland, 14
World Expeditions, 64

Ystabæjarland (Hrísey), 246
Ytri-Tunga Farm, 175
Ytritunga Fossils, 263